GOVERNMENT IN AMERICA

PEOPLE, POLITICS, AND POLICY

Brief Version

Second Edition

Robert L. Lineberry
University of Houston

George C. Edwards III
Texas A & M University

Martin P. Wattenberg
University of California, Irvine

 HarperCollins*CollegePublishers*

To
our Introduction to American Government students

Acquisitions Editor: Leo Wiegman
Development Editor: Michael Kimball
Project Coordination, Text and Cover Design: Interactive Composition Corporation
Cover Photo: F. Sieb/H. Armstrong Roberts
Photo Researcher: Roberta L. Knauf
Electronic Production Manager: Eric Jorgensen
Compositor: Interactive Composition Corporation
Printer and Binder: R. R. Donnelley & Sons Company
Cover Printer: The LeHigh Press, Inc.

Library of Congress Cataloging-in-Publication Data

Lineberry, Robert L.
    Government in America : people, politics, and policy / Robert L.
Lineberry, George C. Edwards III, Martin P. Wattenberg. —Brief
version, 2nd ed.
        p.   cm
    Includes bibliographical references and index.
    ISBN 0-673-99658-1 :
    1. United States—Politics and government. I. Edwards, George C.
II. Wattenberg, Martin P., 1956-   . III. Title
JK274.L573 1994   94-36374
320.473—dc20   CIP

95 96 97 98 9 8 7 6 5 4 3

CONTENTS

Since 1980, *Government in America* has been widely used in courses on American government. This has been very gratifying, and in this brief version we have retained the qualities that have proven themselves in the classroom.

The job of a text is to help the instructor teach well. It should, first, attract the interest of students. Second, it should convey ideas and evidence to support those ideas, in order to provide a basic structure on which a good teacher can base a course of instruction. We, the authors, have over sixty years of experience among us teaching American government, and we have learned to present this complex subject in an engaging and understandable fashion.

A brief edition should include the essential information students require to understand American government and politics, as well as a framework with which to interpret this information. Although *Government in America Brief Version* has abridged the material in the full-length edition, it retains both the crucial information and thematic structure of the original.

This edition of *Government in America* continues to adopt a policy approach to American government. We feel that the principal reason for studying politics is to study the policies governments produce, and our discussion of politics is tied to the central question of "What difference does it make?" This focus engages students' interest and stimulates consideration of the most important aspects of governing. This approach was fairly unusual when introduced in the early editions, but today many other texts follow our lead.

In addition to a policy focus, two important themes run throughout the book: democracy and the scope of government. Each chapter ends with specific sections relating these themes to the topic of the chapter.

The first theme, democracy, deals with the initial great question central to governing—*How should we be governed?* The democracy sections evaluate how well the American system lives up to citizens' expectations of democratic government. As with previous editions, we continue to incorporate theoretical issues in our discussion of different models of American government. We encourage students to think analytically about the theories and to develop independent assessments of the American government's politics and policy.

Our second theme, the size of government, focuses on another great question of governing: *What should government do?* In the sections on scope of government, we discuss alternative views concerning the ideal role and size for American government and the influence that the workings of government and politics have on the size of government. The government's scope is the core question around which politics revolves in contemporary America, and this question pervades many crucial issues, from equality to budgeting.

This edition has thoroughly updated chapters, including 1994 election material. We have also made an important content addition to the second edition of the text. In keeping with our policy orientation, we have added a new chapter 14, "The Budget." This new chapter tackles the perennial questions of where money comes from and where it goes, addressing the fiscal dimensions of government that profoundly shape the debate about public policy. The appendix has been expanded to include Federalist papers No. 10 and No. 51, as well as a glossary of key terms.

Finally, we would like to thank many instructors and colleagues whose thoughtful and detailed reviews helped shape this edition. We hope they find the results pleasing and effective. Our thanks go, especially, to: E. Perry Ballard, Anne Arundel Community College; Joseph Moore, Jr., Fresno City College; Nelson Wickstrom, Virginia Commonwealth University; M. M. Eskandari-Qajar, Santa Barbara City College; Mark C. Ellickson, Southwest Missouri State University; Steven Peterson, Alfred University; Jeanette Fregulia, Hartnell College; Forest Grieves, University of Montana; David H. Ray, University of Oklahoma; Larry D. Vandermolen, Schoolcraft College; Ruth A. Harrison, University of Tennessee-Knoxville; Perri L. Lampe, Maple Woods Community College; James L Renneker, Francis Marion University; Gerald B Money, El Paso Community College; Randy Hagerty, Northeast Missouri State University; Donald T. Jelfo, Cuyahoga Community College; and William Bloomquist, Indiana University-Purdue University.

ABOUT THE AUTHORS

ROBERT L. LINEBERRY

is Professor of Political Science at the University of Houston and has been its Senior Vice President. He served from 1981–1988 as Dean of the College of Liberal Arts and Sciences at the University of Kansas in Lawrence.

A native of Oklahoma City, Oklahoma, he received a B.A. degree from the University of Oklahoma in 1964 and a Ph.D. in political science from the University of North Carolina in 1968. He taught for seven years at Northwestern University in Evanston, Illinois.

Dr. Lineberry has been President of the Policy Studies Section of the American Political Science Association and is currently the editor of *Social Science Quarterly*. He is the author or coauthor of five books in political science. Dr. Lineberry has also authored or coauthored numerous articles in professional journals. In addition, he has taught regularly, including twenty-five years of instruction of first-year American government.

He has been married to Nita Lineberry for thirty years. They have two children, Nikki, who works in Kansas City, and Keith, a student at the University of Texas.

GEORGE C. EDWARDS III

is Distinguished Professor of Political Science at Texas A&M University and Director of the Center for Presidential Studies. From 1985–1988 he was Visiting Professor of Social Sciences at the U.S. Military Academy at West Point. One of the country's leading scholars of the presidency, he has written fifteen books on American politics and policy-making, including *At the Margins: Presidential Leadership of Congress, Presidential Approval, Implementing Public Policy,* and *National Security and the U.S. Constitution.*

Professor Edwards has served as President of the Presidency Research Section of the American Political Science Association and on many editorial boards. In 1988 he went to Brasília to advise those writing the new constitution for Brazil. That same year he was also an issue leader for the National Academy of Public Administration's project on the 1988 Presidential Transition, providing advice to the new president. In 1993 he spent six weeks in China lecturing on democracy, and in 1994 he was a consultant to Russian democratic leaders on building a political party system in that country.

When not writing, speaking, or advising, Professor Edwards prefers to spend his time with his wife Carmella, skiing, sailing, scuba diving, playing tennis, or attending art auctions.

MARTIN P. WATTENBERG

is Professor of Political Science at the University of California, Irvine. His first regular paying job was with the Washington Redskins in 1977, from which he moved on to receive a Ph.D. at the University of Michigan in 1982.

While at Michigan, Professor Wattenberg authored *The Decline of American Political Parties* (Harvard University Press), currently in its fourth edition. Most recently, he has written *The Rise of Candidate-Centered Politics: Presidential Elections of the 1980s,* also published by Harvard. In addition, he has contributed many professional articles to such journals as the *American Political Science Review, American Journal of Political Science, American Politics Quarterly, Public Opinion Quarterly,* and *Public Opinion.*

Professor Wattenberg has also lectured abroad about American politics in Australia, Asia, and Europe. Presently, he is working with a colleague in Canberra on a project comparing American and Australian electoral behavior.

When not writing or lecturing, he can most often be found on the beach at Newport or at the local tennis courts.

CHAPTER 1   *Introduction*

The twenty-first century is fast approaching, bringing with it unimagined challenges. We want to be able to respond to these challenges individually, as citizens, and collectively, as a nation. In your lifetime, for example, the United States has turned from being the world's largest creditor to its largest debtor nation; you have seen the decline and dissolution of what President Reagan called the "Evil Empire" of the Soviet Union; and the United States has gone from the quagmire of Vietnam to the pyrotechnics of the Persian Gulf War. There are inevitably other challenges to come. It is our hope that *Government in America* will help you become a well-informed citizen, a citizen better able to lead our country into the next century.

Chapter 1 begins this process by introducing you to three important concepts: *government*, *politics*, and *public policy*. It also raises two fundamental questions about governing that will serve as themes for this book:

1. *How should we govern?* Americans take great pride in calling their government democratic. Today there is a rush to establish democracy in many countries, but not everyone agrees on what democracy means. This chapter will examine the workings of democratic government. The chapters that follow will evaluate the way American government actually works against the standard of an "ideal" democracy. We will continually ask who holds **power** and who influences the policies adopted by government.

2. *What should government do?* This text will explore the consequences of the way American government works on what the government does. In other words, "Does our government do what we want it to do?"

The second theme is closely linked to the first—the process of government is tied to the substance of public policy. What government should do can be examined in terms of "the scope of government." Debates about the role of government, including its functions, its budget, and the number of its employees, are among the most important in American political life. These debates are at the core of disputes between the major political parties and between liberals and conservatives.

GOVERNMENT, POLITICS, AND PUBLIC POLICY

Government, politics, and public policy are interrelated. Government is important because of what it does for us—and to us. It can protect us, feed us, educate us, send us to war, tax us, and affect us in just about every aspect of our lives. All of these actions involve setting public policies. The way government makes decisions about public policies is through politics. This chapter will first examine government itself to see how it works and how these procedures affect the policies it produces.

Government

The institutions that make public policy for a society are collectively known as **government.** In our national government, these institutions are Congress, the president, the courts, and federal administrative agencies (often called "the bureaucracy"). We also have thousands of state and local governments in the United States, and they make policies that affect us as well. All told, there are roughly 500,000 elected officials in the United States; this means that somewhere, on almost every day of the year, someone is running for office.

Every government has a means of changing its leaders. Some changes, like those in American government, are orderly and peaceful. The 1981 transition between the Carter and Reagan Administrations was more dramatic than usual because of the last-minute negotiations regarding the release of American hostages in Iran. Rejected by the voters, the Carter people had packed their belongings. Bookshelves were bare. White House carpenters were screwing in the appropriate nameplates for the new president and his staff; the guard was changing just as the agreement with Iran was being reached. Some officials had special phones at home, connected directly to the White House. At exactly noon, however, as Ronald Reagan completed his oath of office, their phones went dead.[1]

Not all governments change in such a peaceful and orderly fashion. The twentieth century has been a time of revolutionary upheaval. Iran's revolution, which overthrew the Shah, eventually led to the seizing of American hostages. The Russians in 1917 and the Chinese in 1949 changed their governments through violent revolution in order to adopt communist governments. Sometimes a change in government is less orderly than in America, but less bloody than a revolution. Massive protests disrupted the government of Philippine president Ferdinand Marcos until he left office—and the country—to be replaced by the government of Corazon Aquino. Regardless of how they assumed power, however, all governments have certain functions in common.

What Governments Do.   Big or small, democratic or not, governments in the modern world are similar in the following ways:

1. *Governments maintain national defense.* The United States spends about $250 billion a year on national defense. Some politicians think the United States spends too much on defense; others think this amount provides only minimal defensive capabilities. With the end of the Cold War between the United States and the former Soviet Union, the costs of defense should decline.

2. *Governments provide public goods.* **Public goods** are things that everyone can share. Contrast a loaf of bread, a private good, with clean air, a public good. You can buy a loaf of bread and easily consume it by yourself. Clean air, however, is available to everyone. A public good, unlike a loaf of bread, is indivisible and nonexclusive. A central principle of modern political science and economics is that individuals have little incentive to provide public goods because no one can make a profit from them. For instance, many businesses seem unconcerned with cleaning the air, because they do not make a profit from providing clean air. Thus governments are usually left to provide things like public parks and pollution control.

3. *Governments have police powers to provide order.* Every government has some means of maintaining order. When people protest en masse, governments may resort to extreme measures to restore order. Chinese security forces occupied streets around Tiananmen Square in June of 1989 to crush the student protest. Even in the United States, governments consider the power to maintain order one of their most important jobs. Americans today are generally supportive of an increase in the government's police powers to control high crime rates and drug abuse.

4. *Governments provide public services.* Hospitals and other public services do not build themselves. Governments in our country spend billions of dollars on schools, libraries, weather forecasting, halfway houses, and dozens of other public services.

5. *Governments socialize the young into the political culture.* Most modern governments do not trust education to chance. Almost every one of them runs a school system whose curriculum consists, in part, of courses on the philosophy and practice of their country's government. Also important are symbolic acts in school, such as the daily recitation of the Pledge of Allegiance.

6. *Governments collect taxes.* In 1994, one of every three dollars earned by an American citizen was used to pay national, state, and local taxes. Although Americans often complain about the high cost of government, our tax burden is actually much lower than that of citizens in most other democratic nations.

The tasks of government listed above add up to tremendous responsibilities for our political leaders. Many important and difficult questions must be addressed regarding what government should do. The way we answer such questions is through politics.

Like most governments around the world, the American government uses the public schools to socialize its children. Required civics courses and government approval of curriculum and textbooks help ensure that the young understand and support the American system of government.

Politics

Politics determines whom we select as our governmental leaders and what policies they pursue. Political scientists often cite a famous definition of politics by Harold D. Lasswell: "Who gets what, when, and how."[2] It is one of the briefest and most useful definitions of politics ever penned. Admittedly, this broad definition covers a lot of ground (office politics, sorority politics, and so on) in which political scientists are not interested. They are interested primarily in politics related to governmental decision making.

The media usually focuses on the *who* of politics. At a minimum, this includes voters, candidates, groups, and parties. *How* people play politics is important, too. They get what they want through bargaining, supporting, compromising, lobbying, and so forth. *What* refers to the substance of politics and government—the public policies that come from government. Govern-

Permission granted by the *Detroit News*

ments distribute benefits, such as new roads, and burdens, such as new taxes. In this sense, government and politics involve winners and losers.

Public Policy

More and more, Americans expect government to do something about their problems. The president and members of Congress are expected to keep the economy humming along; voters will penalize them at the polls if they do not. When people confront government officials with problems to be solved, they are trying to influence the government's **policy agenda.** John Kingdon defined a policy agenda as "the list of subjects or problems to which government officials, and people outside of government closely associated with those officials, are paying serious attention at any given time."[3] One of the key elements of democratic government is that officials, if they want to get elected, must pay attention to the problems to which people want them to pay attention. When you vote, you are partly looking at whether a candidate shares your agenda or not.

A government's policy agenda changes regularly. Almost no one thought about flag burning until the Supreme Court ruled in 1989 that the First Amendment protected flag burning as free expression. When jobs are plentiful and inflation is low, economic problems occupy a low position on the government's agenda. Nothing works better than a crisis to elevate an issue on a policy agenda. An oil spill, an airline crash, or a brutal shooting will almost ensure that ecology, air safety, or gun control will rise to near the top of a government's agenda.

Political issues often draw the attention and active participation of entertainment stars. Talk-show host Oprah Winfrey was a prominent spokesperson on behalf of a 1993 law signed by President Clinton that established a nationwide database enabling child care centers to check on prospective employees.

Public policy is a choice that government makes in response to some issue on its agenda (see Table 1.1). It is also worth noting that policymakers can establish a policy by doing nothing as well as by doing something. Doing nothing—or doing nothing different—is a choice. Often a debate about public policy centers on whether government should do something rather than nothing. Reporter Randy Shilts' book about the American government's response to the AIDS crisis tells a sad tale of inaction, even when the AIDS epidemic reached crisis levels.[4] Shilts reveals how governments in Washington and elsewhere long ignored AIDS because it was viewed as a gay person's disease. The issue remained a low priority on the government's policy agenda until infections started to spread to the general population, including celebrities like basketball star Magic Johnson.

THE POLITICAL SYSTEM

A **political system** is a set of institutions and activities that link together government, politics, and public policy.[5] Most systems, political or not, can be diagrammed. We can create simple renderings of how a nuclear power plant

TABLE 1.1 — Types of Public Policies

There are many types of public policies. Every decision that government makes—a law it passes, a budget it establishes, and even a decision not to act on an issue—is public policy. Here are the most important types of public policies:

Type	Definition	Example
Congressional statue	Law passed by Congress	Social Security Act
Presidential action	Decision by president	American troops sent to the Persian Gulf
Court decision	Opinion by Supreme Court or other court	Supreme Court ruling that school segregation is unconstitutional
Budgetary choices	Legislative enactment of taxes and expenditures	The federal budget
Regulation	Agency adoption of regulation	Food and Drug Administration approval of a new drug

or an automobile works. Figure 1.1 is a model of how a political system works. The rest of this book will flesh out this skeletal version of our political system, but for now the model will help you to identify several key elements.

Politics begins, of course, with people, and people do not always agree on the best course of action. A **political issue** arises when people disagree about a problem or about public policy choices made to combat a problem. There is never a shortage of political issues in this country; government, however, will not act upon an issue until it is high on the agenda.

In a democratic society, parties, elections, interest groups, and the media are key **linkage institutions** between the preferences of citizens and the government's policy agenda. Parties and interest groups both exert much effort to get the issues they feel are important to the top of the government's agenda. Elections and the media are two major forums through which potential agenda items receive public attention.

Policymakers stand at the core of the political system. Working within the government's institutions, they scan the issues on the policy agenda, select some for attention, and make policies concerning them. The U.S. Constitution establishes three policy-making institutions: Congress, the presidency, and the courts. Today, the power of the bureaucracy is so great that most political scientists consider it a fourth policy-making institution.

Very few policies are made by a single policy-making institution. (Part Three discusses these institutions separately, but they do not operate independently.) Environmental policy is a good example. Some presidents have used their influence with Congress to urge clean-air and clean-water policies. When Congress responds by passing legislation to clean up the environment, bureaucracies have to implement the new policies. Rules and regulations

FIGURE 1.1 — The Political System

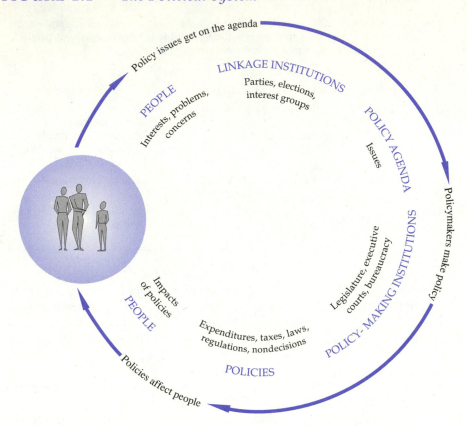

issued by the bureaucratic agencies fill fat volumes. In addition, every law passed and every rule made can be challenged in the courts. Courts make decisions about what the policies mean and whether they conflict with the Constitution. In policy-making, every political institution gets involved.

The political system does not stop when a policy is announced. **Policy impacts** are the effects a policy has on people and society's problems. People who raise a policy issue usually want more than just a new law, a fancy proclamation, a bureaucratic rule, or a court judgment. They want a policy that works. Environmentalists want a policy that not only claims to prevent air pollution, but does so. Consumers want a policy that actually reduces inflation. Minority groups want a policy that not only promises them more equal treatment, but ensures it. Understanding policy impacts carries us full circle back to the people, their concerns and problems. This translation of citizens' private desires into public policy is crucial to the workings of democracy.

DEMOCRATIC GOVERNMENT

In 1848, the intellectual founders of modern communism, Karl Marx and Friedrich Engels, wrote *The Communist Manifesto,* one of the most famous political documents ever written. It began with these words: "A specter is haunting Europe. It is the specter of communism." Today one could write: "A specter is haunting Europe (and everywhere else). It is the specter of democracy."

The nations of Eastern Europe, long under the thumb of the Soviet Union, began throwing off their Communist governments in 1988 and moving toward democratic regimes. This was made possible by Soviet President Mikhail Gorbachev's policies of *glasnost* (openness) and *perestroika* (restructuring). Ultimately, these policies led not only to the breaking away of the Soviet Union's satellites, such as Poland and East Germany, but also to the dissolution of the Soviet Communist Party itself. One after another, the Republics of the Soviet Union declared their independence and held free elections for the first time in their history. By the beginning of 1992, the Soviet state that had threatened Americans for decades had ceased to exist.

A statue of Vladimir Lenin, leader of Russia's Communist revolution, is hauled away in Bucharest, Romania, after the Communist government there was toppled in December 1989. Like Romania's Communist regime, the statue did not go down easily—it took two days of intensive work to remove the 25-foot high likeness of Lenin.

Not just in Eastern Europe were the resounding demands for democracy heard. In 1989, a quarter of a million Chinese students staged one of the world's largest protest demonstrations in Beijing. Under the watchful eye of a gigantic poster of Mao, the students gathered, waited, and talked with hundreds of foreign reporters about the need for democracy in China. The Chinese government, however, sent soldiers and tanks into the square and crushed the protest. Governments around the world condemned the action.

In Argentina, Nicaragua, and other Latin-American countries, one-party or military regimes gave way to competitive party systems and civilian governments. In South Africa, over three centuries of white rule came to an end in 1994 as the result of the first election open to all races. Despite this global move towards democracy, not everyone defines democracy the way Americans do—or think they do.

Defining Democracy

The word *democracy* is overused. It takes its place among terms like *freedom*, *justice*, and *peace* as a word that has, seemingly, only positive connotations. Today, says political scientist Giovanni Sartori, almost any political activity can be justified if done in the name of democracy.[6] Democracy was not always so popular. The writers of the U.S. Constitution had no fondness for democracy. Elbridge Gerry of Massachusetts, a delegate to the Constitutional Convention, said that "the evils we experience flow from the excesses of democracy." Another delegate, Roger Sherman, said that the people "should have as little to do as may be with the government." Only much later did Americans come to cherish democracy.

Today, most Americans would probably say that democracy is "government by the people." This phrase, of course, is part of Abraham Lincoln's famous definition of democracy from his Gettysburg Address: "government of the people, by the people, and for the people." The best that can be said of this definition is that it is brief; it is not, however, very informative. The late E. E. Schattschneider claimed that "we ought to get rid of confusing language such as 'government by the people.' To say that 230 [now 250] million Americans 'govern' does not shed much light on the role of people in the American political system."[7] In our representative form of government, the people do not actually govern themselves, but rather choose the leaders who will make the governing decisions. Thus, **democracy** can be defined as a *means of selecting policymakers and of organizing government so that policy represents and responds to the people's preferences.*

Traditional Democratic Theory

What we call **traditional democratic theory** rests upon several principles. These principles specify how a democratic government makes its decisions.

One contemporary democratic theorist, Robert Dahl, suggests that "an ideal democratic process would satisfy five criteria."[8] Here are his five cornerstones of an ideal democracy:

1. *Equality in voting.*   The principle of one person, one vote is basic to democracy.

2. *Effective participation.*   Political participation need not be universal, but it must be representative. If only the rich vote, a system cannot be very democratic.

3. *Enlightened understanding.*   A democratic society must be a market-place of ideas. A free press and free speech are essential to civic under-standing.

4. *Citizen control of the agenda.*   Citizens should have the collective right to control the government's policy agenda. If wealthy or powerful indi-viduals or groups distort the agenda, citizens cannot make government address the issues they feel are most important.

5. *Inclusion.*   The government must include, and extend rights to, all those subject to its laws.

Only by following these principles can a political system be called "demo-cratic." In addition, democracies must practice **majority rule** and preserve **minority rights.** In a democracy, choosing among alternatives (whether poli-cies or officeholders) means weighing the desires of the majority.

Nothing is more fundamental to democratic theory than majority rule. Alexis de Tocqueville, the great French intellectual who traveled through America in the 1830s, wrote that "the very essence of democratic government consists in the absolute sovereignty of the majority. The power of the majority in America is not only preponderant, but irresistible."[9] Although Americans believe in majority rule, most also feel it is vital to protect minority rights, such as freedom of speech. In a society too large to make its decisions in open meet-ings, a few will have to carry on the affairs of the many. The relationship between the few leaders and the many followers is one of **representation.** The closer the correspondence between representatives and their electoral majority, the closer the approximation to democracy. Three contemporary theories pre-senting different views on how the representation process works are discussed in the following section.

Three Contemporary Theories of American Democracy

Theories of American politics are plentiful. Each focuses on a key element of politics, and each reaches a somewhat different conclusion. Theories of Ameri-can democracy are essentially about who has power and influence. All, in one way or another, ask the question, "Who really governs in our nation?"

Pluralism.   One important theory of American democracy, **pluralist theory,** contends that many centers of influence vie for power and control. Groups compete with one another for control over public policy, with no one group or set of groups dominating. Pluralists' views of American government are thus generally positive. There are, they say, multiple access points to our government. Because power is dispersed among the various branches and levels of government, groups that lose in one arena can take their case to another. According to pluralists, bargaining and compromise are essential ingredients in our democracy. The result is a rough approximation of the public interest in public policy.

Elite and Class Theory.   Critics of pluralism believe that this view paints too rosy a picture of American political life. By arguing that almost every group can get a piece of the pie, they say, pluralists miss the larger question of who owns the pie. **Elite and class theory** contends that our society—like all societies—is divided along class lines, and that an upper-class elite rules. Wealth—the holding of assets such as property, stocks, and bonds—is the basis of this power. Over a third of the nation's wealth is held by just one percent of the U.S. population. Elite and class theorists believe that this one percent of Americans control most policy decisions because they can afford to finance election campaigns and control key institutions, such as large corporations.

Hyperpluralism.   A third theory, **hyperpluralism,** offers a different critique of pluralism. Hyperpluralism is pluralism gone sour. Just as it is said that too many cooks spoil the broth, hyperpluralists claim that too many influential groups cripple government's ability to govern. Hyperpluralism states that many groups—not just the elite ones—are so strong that government is unable to act. These powerful groups divide the government and its authority. Hyperpluralist theory holds that government caves in to every conceivable interest and single-issue group. When policymakers try to placate many powerful groups, the result is muddled and inconsistent policy. Thus, one part of the government can subsidize tobacco farmers while another preaches about the evils of smoking.

Some Key Questions About Democracy

Regardless of whether one accepts pluralism, elitism, or hyperpluralism, there are a number of continuing challenges to democracy. These challenges apply to American democracy as well as to the fledgling democracies around the world.

Throughout *Government in America* you will be asked to assess American democracy. The chapters that follow will acquaint you with the history of American democracy and ask important questions about the current state of democracy in the United States. For example, the next chapter will show that the U.S. Constitution was not originally designed to promote democracy, but has slowly evolved to its current form. Much of America's move toward greater democracy has centered around the extension of civil liberties and civil

One of the most hotly debated issues of the Clinton presidency has been gun control. Here, advocates of restrictions on gun sales show the media a variety of firearms that could be readily purchased.

rights (which Chapter 4 will review). Probably the most important civil right is the right to vote. Upcoming chapters will examine voting behavior and elections and ask the following questions about how people's opinions are formed and to what extent they are expressed via elections:

- Are people knowledgeable about matters of public policy?
- Do they apply what knowledge they have to their voting choices?
- Are American elections designed to facilitate public participation?

These are the sorts of questions you will need to ask about the people's input into government.

Linkage institutions, such as interest groups, political parties, and the media, help translate input from the public into output from the policymakers. When you explore these institutions you will consider the extent to which they either help or hinder democracy.

- Does the interest group system allow for all points of view to be heard, or are there significant biases that advantage particular groups?

- Do political parties provide voters with clear choices, or do they obscure their stands on issues in order to get as many votes as possible?
- If there are choices, does the media help citizens understand them?

It is up to public officials to actually make the policy choices, since American government is a *representative* rather than a pure democracy. For democracy to work well, elected officials should be responsive to public opinion.

- Is the Congress representative of American society, and is it well organized to react to changing times?
- Does the president look after the general welfare, or has the office become too powerful in recent years?

These are some of the crucial questions you will address in discussing the executive and legislative branches of government. In addition, the way our nonelected institutions—the bureaucracy and the courts—function is also crucial to evaluating how well American democracy works. These institutions are designed to implement and interpret the law, but bureaucrats and judges often cannot avoid making public policy as well. When they do so, are they violating democratic principles for policy decisions, as neither institution can be held accountable at the ballot box?

All of these questions concerning democracy in America have more than one answer. A goal of *Government in America* is to familiarize you with the different ways to approach, and answer, these questions. One way to approach all of the preceding questions is to address one of the most important questions facing modern American democracy: Is the scope of government too vast, just about right, or not comprehensive enough?

THE SCOPE OF GOVERNMENT IN AMERICA

Some political leaders and voters think that American government is so intrusive into the affairs of individual citizens and businesses that it does more harm than good. Former Presidents Ronald Reagan and George Bush were staunch opponents of expanding the scope of the federal government's powers. They argued that government should not be telling businesses what to do, except to prevent harm to individuals or society. During their presidential terms, any plan to involve the federal government in ensuring health care to all Americans would surely have drawn a presidential veto. In contrast, President Clinton believes that the federal government should step in and require businesses to provide a basic level of health insurance for their employees.

Those who are inclined toward government intervention in matters such as health care argue that it is the only means of achieving important goals in American society. How else, they ask, can we ensure that everyone has enough to eat, clean air and water, and affordable housing? How else can we ensure that the disadvantaged are given opportunities for education and jobs, and are not discriminated against? Opponents of widening the scope of government agree that these are worthwhile goals, but challenge whether involving the federal government is an effective way to pursue them.

To understand the dimensions of this debate, it is important to get some sense of the current scope of the federal government's activities.

How Active Is American Government?

In terms of dollars spent, government in America is vast. Altogether, our governments—national, state, and local—spend about one out of every three dollars of our *gross domestic product,* the total value of all goods and services produced annually by the United States. In 1994, expenditures for all American governments amounted to about $2.5 trillion. Government not only spends large sums of money, but also employs large numbers of people. About eighteen million Americans work for one of our governments, mostly at the state and local level—teachers to teach America's children, police officers to deal with growing crime problems, university professors to teach college students, and so on.

Consider some facts about the size of our national government:

It spends more than $1.5 trillion annually (printed as a number, this figure is $1,500,000,000,000 a year).

It employs nearly five million people.

It owns one-third of the land in the United States.

It occupies 2.6 billion square feet of office space, more than four times the office space located in the nation's ten largest cities.

It owns and operates 437,000 nonmilitary vehicles.[10]

How does the American national government spend almost $1.5 trillion a year? National defense takes about one-sixth of the federal budget, a much smaller percentage than it did three decades ago. Social Security consumes more than one-fifth of the budget. Medicare is another big-ticket item, requiring over $160 billion a year. State and local governments also get important parts of the federal government's budget. The federal government helps fund highway construction, airport construction, police departments, school districts, and other state and local functions. Americans often complain about the high cost of government, but most Americans approve of what government does with its money. There is little support to cut spending on most specific government programs.

When expenditures grow, tax revenues must grow to pay the additional costs. When taxes do not grow as fast as spending, a budget deficit results. Budget deficits have occurred for decades in the United States. The national government has recently fallen short of paying its bills by as much as $290 billion a year. Each year's deficit is piled onto the previous deficits, and the entire sum equals the national debt, all the money owed by the national government. Today, the national debt is nearing $5 trillion.

Whatever the national problem—pollution, AIDS, earthquake relief, homelessness, hunger, sexism—many people expect Congress to solve the problem with legislation. Thus, American government certainly is large in terms of dollars spent, persons employed, and laws passed. Our concern, however, is less about the absolute size of government and more about whether government activity is what we want it to be.

Liberals and Conservatives. Of all the issues that divide liberals and conservatives, probably the most important is their differing views on the appropriate scope of government. In the United States, liberals support a more active role for government (in most spheres), together with higher spending and more regulation. In general, liberals favor

- More governmental regulation of the economy to promote such goals as health care, consumer protection, and a pollution-free environment.
- More policies to help disadvantaged groups, including policies to ensure and expand opportunities for poor people, minorities, and women.
- More policies to redistribute income, through taxation, from those with more to those with less.

Conservatives, on the other hand, favor

- Fewer governmental regulations and a greater reliance on the market to provide such things as jobs, health care, and pollution control.
- Fewer governmental policies in the name of disadvantaged groups, who conservatives believe will benefit most from a strong economy free from governmental intervention.
- Fewer tax laws that discourage business growth by establishing high rates for capital investment.

Liberals do not always favor governmental action, and conservatives do not always oppose it, however. Conservatives, for example, typically favor using the power of government to restrict or prohibit abortions and to organize prayers in public schools, whereas liberals generally oppose such policies. Conservatives are less likely to support restrictions on individual freedom in the economic sphere, while liberals usually oppose governmental interference with individual freedom in noneconomic matters.

A Comparative Perspective.   A useful way to think about political issues, such as the scope of government, is to compare the United States with other countries, especially other democracies with developed economies. For example, it is possible to compare the percentage of the gross domestic product spent by all levels of government in the United States with similar expenditures in other prosperous nations. We find that compared with most other economically developed nations, the United States devotes a smaller percentage of its resources to government. The tax burden on Americans is also small compared to other democratic nations.

Further, most advanced industrial democracies have a system of national health insurance that provides most health care; the United States does not, though President Clinton hopes to have a system in place that will eventually guarantee health care to all Americans. The airlines in virtually every nation except America are owned by the national government, as are the telephone companies and most television stations. Governments have built much of the housing in most Western nations, compared to only a small fraction of the housing in America. Thus, in terms of the impact on the everyday lives of citizens, the government in the United States actually does less—is small—compared to the governments in similar countries.

Questions About the Scope of Government

Debate over the scope of government is central to contemporary American politics, and it is a theme this text will examine in each chapter that follows. The goal is not to determine for you the proper role of the national government. Instead, you will explore the implications of the way politics, institutions, and policy in America affect the scope of government. By raising questions such as those in the next few paragraphs, you can draw your own conclusions about the appropriate role of government in America.

Chapters 1 through 4 of *Government in America* examine the constitutional foundations of American government. A concern with the proper scope of government leads to a series of questions regarding the constitutional structure of American politics, including

- What role did the Constitution's authors foresee for the federal government?
- Does the Constitution favor big government, or is it neutral on this issue?
- Why did the functions of government increase, and why did they increase most at the national rather than at the state level?
- Has bigger, more active government constrained freedom—as some feared?
- Or, does the increased scope of government serve to protect civil liberties and civil rights?

Chapters 5 through 9 focus on those making demands upon government, including the public, political parties, interest groups, and the media. Here you will seek answers to questions such as

- Does the public favor a large, active government?
- Do competing political parties predispose the government to provide more public services?

- Do elections help control the scope of government, or do they legitimize an increasing role for the public sector?
- Are pressures from interest groups necessarily translated into more governmental regulations, bigger budgets, and the like?
- Has media coverage of government enhanced government's status and growth, or have the media been an instrument for controlling government?

Governmental institutions themselves, obviously, deserve close examination. Chapters 10 through 13 discuss these institutions and ask

- Has the presidency been a driving force behind increasing the scope and power of government (and thus of the president)?
- Can the president control a government the size of ours?
- Is Congress, because it is subject to constant elections, predisposed toward big government?
- Is Congress too responsive to the demands of the public and organized interests?

The nonelected branches of government, which are also discussed in these chapters, are especially interesting when considering the issue of the scope of government. For instance

- Are the federal courts too active in policy-making, intruding on the authority and responsibility of other branches and levels of government?
- Is the bureaucracy too acquisitive, constantly seeking to expand its size, budgets, and authority, or is it simply a reflection of the desires of elected officials?
- Is the bureaucracy too large, and thus a wasteful menace to efficient and fair implementation of public policies, or is it too small to carry out the responsibilities assigned to it?

In sum, the next 12 chapters will search for answers to these and many other questions regarding the scope of government. You will, undoubtedly, add a few questions of your own as you seek to resolve the issue of the proper scope of government involvement.

SUMMARY

This first chapter serves several important purposes. First, it introduces you to the meaning of government itself. Government consists of those institutions that make authoritative public policies for society as a whole. In the United States, there are four key institutions that make policy at the national level: Congress, the president, the courts, and the bureaucracy. Politics is, very simply, who gets what, when, and how. People engage in politics for a variety of reasons, and all their activities in politics are collectively called political participation. The result of government and politics is public policy. Public policy includes all of the decisions and nondecisions by government.

The first question central to governing is "How should we be governed?" Americans are fond of calling their government democratic. Democratic government includes, above all else, a commitment to majority rule and minority rights. This text will help you evaluate the way American government works against the standards of democracy and continually inquire as to who holds power and who influences the policies adopted by government.

The second fundamental question regarding governing is "What should government do?" One of the most important issues about government in America has to do with the scope of government. One recent president, Ronald Reagan, talked often about the evils of an intrusive government. Others see the national government as rather modest in comparison to both what it could do and to the functions governments perform in other democratic nations. *Government in America* will explore the effects of the workings of American government upon what government actually does.

FOR FURTHER READING

Brzezinski, Zbigniew. *The Grand Failure.* New York: Scribner's, 1989. An explanation for the decline of the Soviet empire.

Dahl, Robert A. *Democracy and Its Critics.* New Haven: Yale University Press, 1989. Dahl is one of the world's most articulate thinkers about democracy.

Kettl, Donald F. *Sharing Power: Public Governance and Private Markets.* Washington DC: Brookings Institution, 1993. Explores the problems with contracting out government services to the private sector.

Kingdon, John W. *Agendas, Alternatives, and Public Policies,* 2nd ed. New York: HarperCollins, 1995. One of the first efforts by a political scientist to examine the political agenda.

Savas, E. S. *Privatization: The Key to Better Government.* Chatham, NJ: Chatham House, 1987. His subtitle calls privatization the key to better government; liberals would disagree.

Shilts, Randy. *And the Band Played On: Politics, People, and the AIDS Epidemic.* New York: Penguin Books, 1987. A sad but eye-opening study of the politics surrounding the AIDS epidemic.

Smith, Hedrick. *The Power Game: How Washington Works.* New York: Ballantine, 1988. A good introduction to the political life of our nation's capital.

Stanley, Harold W., and Richard G. Niemi. *Vital Statistics on American Politics,* 4th ed. Washington, DC: Congressional Quarterly, 1994. Useful data on government, politics, and policy in the United States.

NOTES

1. Hedrick Smith, *The Power Game: How Washington Works* (New York: Ballantine, 1988), 395.
2. Harold D. Lasswell, *Politics: Who Gets What, When, and How* (New York: McGraw Hill, 1938).

3. John Kingdon, *Agendas, Alternatives, and Public Policies* (Boston: Little, Brown, 1984), 3.

4. Randy Shilts, *And the Band Played On: Politics, People, and the AIDS Epidemic* (New York: Penguin Books, 1987).

5. All models of political systems are indebted to David Easton, "An Approach to the Analysis of Political Systems," *World Politics 9* (April 1957): 379–389.

6. Giovanni Sartori, *Theory of Democracy Revisited*, vol. 1 (Chatham, NJ: Chatham House, 1987), 3.

7. E. E. Schattschneider, *Two Hundred Million Americans in Search of a Government* (New York: Holt, Rinehart & Winston, 1969), 63.

8. Robert A. Dahl, *Dilemmas of Pluralist Democracy* (New Haven, CT: Yale University Press, 1983), 6.

9. Alexis de Tocqueville, *Democracy in America* (New York: Mentor Books, 1956), 112–113.

10. E. S. Savas, *Privatization: The Key to Better Government* (Chatham, NJ: Chatham House, 1987), 13.

A **constitution** is a nation's basic law. It creates political institutions, assigns or divides powers in government, and often provides certain guarantees to citizens. A constitution is also an unwritten accumulation of traditions and precedents that have established acceptable styles of behavior and policy outcomes.

A constitution sets the rules of the game of politics, allowing certain types of competition among certain players. These rules are never neutral, however. Instead, they give some participants advantages over others in the policy-making process, which is why understanding them is so important to understanding government.

Americans have a special reverence for the **U.S. Constitution**. They view it as the foundation of their freedom and prosperity. Where did the Constitution come from? Why did it take the form it did? What was it designed to accomplish? This chapter will address these questions; it will examine the background of the Constitution and show that its ultimate source was a concern for limited government and self-determination.

THE ORIGINS OF THE CONSTITUTION

In 1776, a small group of men met in Philadelphia and passed a resolution that formally began an armed rebellion against the government of the most powerful nation on earth. The resolution was, of course, the Declaration of Independence, and the armed rebellion was the American Revolution.

The Road to Revolution

Life was not bad for most people in eighteenth-century America (slaves and indentured servants being obvious exceptions). In fact, white American colonists "were freer, more equal, more prosperous, and less burdened with cumbersome feudal and monarchical restraints than any other part of mankind."[1]   Although the colonies were part of the British empire, the King and Parliament generally confined themselves to governing America's foreign policy and trade. Almost everything else was left to the discretion of individual colonial governments.

Britain obtained an enormous new territory in North America after the French and Indian War ended in 1763. But the British needed money to pay for defending this vast realm, and thus decided to levy some taxes on its North American colonies—the beneficiaries, after all, of their own defense. The colonists resisted these taxes, crying "taxation without representation." This resistance culminated in the Boston Tea Party, in which the colonists threw 342 chests of tea into Boston Harbor to protest the newly enacted Tea Tax. Britain reacted by applying economic pressure through a naval blockade of the harbor, further fueling the colonists' anger. The colonists responded by forming the First Continental Congress in September 1774, sending delegates from each colony to Philadelphia in order to discuss the future of relations with Britain.

Declaring Independence

As colonial discontent with the English festered, the Continental Congress was in almost continuous session during 1775 and 1776. On June 7, 1776, Richard Henry Lee of Virginia moved "that these United States are and of rights ought to be free and independent states." A committee composed of Thomas Jefferson, John Adams of Massachusetts, Benjamin Franklin, Roger Sherman of Connecticut, and Robert Livingston of New York was busily drafting a document to justify the inevitable declaration. On July 2, Lee's motion to declare independence from England was formally approved. The famous **Declaration of Independence**, primarily written by Jefferson, was adopted two days later on July 4.

Politically, the Declaration was a polemic, announcing and justifying a revolution. Most of the document lists the ways in which the King had abused the colonies, even blaming him for inciting the "merciless Indian savages" to war on the colonists. The polemical aspects were important because the colonists needed foreign assistance to take on the most powerful nation in the world. France, which was engaged in a war with Britain, was a prime target of the delegates' diplomacy, and eventually provided aid that was critical to the success of the Revolution.

The English Heritage: The Power of Ideas

Philosophically, the Jeffersonian pen put ideas on paper that were by then common knowledge on both sides of the Atlantic, especially among those people who wished to challenge the power of kings.[2] Franklin, Jefferson, Madison, Morris, Hamilton, and other intellectual leaders in the colonies were learned and widely read men, familiar with the works of English, French, and Scottish political philosophers.

John Locke was one of the most influential philosophers read by the colonists. His writings, especially *The Second Treatise of Civil Government* (1689), profoundly influenced American political leaders. The foundation upon which Locke built his powerful philosophy was a belief in **natural rights**—rights inherent in human beings, not dependent on governments. Before governments arise, Locke held, people exist in a state of nature, where they are governed only by the laws of nature. Natural law brings natural rights, including life, liberty, and property. Because natural law is superior to human law, it can even justify a challenge to the rule of a tyrannical king. Government, Locke argued, must be built on the **consent of the governed**; in other words, the people must agree on who their rulers will be. It should also be a **limited government**—there must be clear restrictions on what rulers can do. Indeed, the sole purpose of government, according to Locke, was to protect natural rights.

Two limits on government were particularly important to Locke. First, governments must provide standing laws so that people know in advance whether their acts will be acceptable. Second, and Locke was very forceful on this point, "the supreme power cannot take from any man any part of his property without his consent." To Locke, "the preservation of property was the end of government." This idea of the sanctity of property was one of the few ideas with no direct parallel in Jefferson's draft of the Declaration of Independence. Even though Jefferson borrowed from and even paraphrased Lockean ideas, he altered Locke's phrase "life, liberty, and property" to "life, liberty, and the pursuit of happiness." We will soon see, though, how the Lockean idea of the sanctity of property figured prominently at the Constitutional Convention.

In an extreme case, said Locke, people have a right to revolt against a government that no longer has their consent. Locke anticipated critics' charges that this right would lead to constant civil disturbances. He stressed that people should not revolt until injustices become deeply felt.

Jefferson's Handiwork: The American Creed

There are some remarkable parallels between Locke's thought and Jefferson's language in the Declaration of Independence (see Table 2.1). Jefferson, like Locke, finessed his way past the issue of how the rebels *knew* men had rights. He simply declared that it was "self-evident" that men were equally "endowed by their Creator with certain unalienable rights," including "life, liberty, and the pursuit of happiness." Since the purpose of government was to "secure" these rights, if a government failed to do so, the people could form a new government.[3]

Locke represented only one element of revolutionary thought. There was also a well-established tradition of opposition to the executive power of the Crown and support for recovering the rights of the people based in the English countryside. A native American republicanism, stressing moral virtue,

TABLE 2.1 — *Locke and the Declaration of Independence: Some Parallels*

LOCKE	DECLARATION OF INDEPENDENCE
NATURAL RIGHTS	
"The state of nature has a law to govern it, which obliges everyone."	"Laws of Nature and Nature's God"
"life, liberty, and property"	"life, liberty, and the pursuit of happiness"
PURPOSE OF GOVERNMENT	
"to preserve himself, his liberty, and property"	"to secure these rights"
EQUALITY	
"men being by nature all free, equal and independent"	"all men are created equal"
CONSENT OF THE GOVERNED	
"for when any number of men have, by the consent of every individual, made a community, with a power to act as one body, which is only by the will and determination of the majority"	"Governments are instituted among men, deriving their just powers from the consent of the governed."
LIMITED GOVERNMENT	
"Absolute arbitrary power, or governing without settled laws, can neither of them consist with the ends of society and government."	"The history of the present King of Great Britain is a history of repeated injuries and usurpations."
"As usurpation is the exercise of power which another has a right to, so tyranny is the exercise of power beyond right, which nobody can have a right to."	
RIGHT TO REVOLT	
"The people shall be the judge . . . Oppression raises ferments and makes men struggle to cast off an uneasy and tyrannical yoke."	"Prudence, indeed, will dictate that Governments long established should not be changed for light and transient causes; and accordingly all experience hath shewn, that mankind are most disposed to suffer, while evils are sufferable, than to right themselves by abolishing the forms to which they are accustomed. But when a long train of abuses and usurpations, pursuing invariably the same Object evinces a design to reduce them under absolute Despotism, it is their right, it is their duty, to throw off such Government."

patriotism, relations based on natural merit, and the equality of independent citizens, intensified the radicalism of this "country" ideology and linked it with older currents of European thought stretching back to antiquity.

It was in the American colonies that the powerful ideas of European political thinkers took root and grew into what Seymour Martin Lipset has termed the "first new nation."[4] With these revolutionary ideas in mind, Jefferson claimed in the Declaration of Independence that people should have primacy over governments, that they should rule instead of being ruled. Moreover, each person was important as an individual, "created equal" and endowed with "unalienable rights." Consent of the governed made the exercise of political power legitimate, not divine rights or tradition. No government had ever been based on these principles.

Winning Independence

The pen may be mightier than the sword, but declaring independence did not win the Revolution—it merely announced that it had begun. John Adams wrote his wife Abigail, "You will think me transported with enthusiasm, but I am not. I am well aware of the toil, blood, and treasure that it will cost us to maintain this Declaration, and support and defend these states." Adams was right. The colonials seemed no match for the finest army in the world. In 1775, the British had 8,500 men stationed in the colonies and had hired nearly 30,000 mercenaries. Initially the colonists had only 5,000 men in uniform, and their number waxed and waned as the war went on. How they eventually won is a story best left to history books. How they formed a new government, however, will be explored in the following sections.

The "Conservative" Revolution

Revolutions such as the 1789 French Revolution, the 1917 Russian Revolution, and the 1978–1979 Iranian Revolution produced great societal change—as well as plenty of bloodshed. The American revolution was different. Although many people lost their lives during the Revolutionary War, the Revolution itself was essentially a conservative movement that did not drastically alter the colonists' way of life. Its primary goal was to restore rights the colonists felt were already theirs as British subjects.

American colonists did not feel the need for great social, economic, or political upheavals. They "were not oppressed people; they had no crushing imperial shackles to throw off."[5]

As a result, the revolution did not create class conflicts that would split society for generations to come. The colonial leaders' belief that they needed the consent of the governed blessed the new nation with a crucial element of stability—a stability the nation would need.

The Revolution in Transition: 1776–1787

We sometimes forget that the system of government we enjoy today derives from the second, not the first, constitution of the United States. The first constitution was the Articles of Confederation.[6]

Government Under the Articles.   The Continental Congress, which adopted the Declaration of Independence, was only a voluntary association of the states. In 1776, the Congress adopted a plan for permanent union. That plan was called the **Articles of Confederation**. The Articles established a government dominated by the states. The United States, it said, was a "league of friendship and perpetual union" among thirteen states that were themselves sovereign. The Articles established a national legislature with one house; states could send as many as seven delegates or as few as two, but each state had only one vote. There was no president and no national court, and the powers of the national legislature, the Congress, were strictly limited. Most authority rested with the state legislatures because the new nation's leaders feared a strong central government would become as tyrannical as British rule.

Because unanimous consent of the states was needed to put them into operation, the Articles adopted by Congress in 1777 did not go into effect until 1781, when laggard Maryland finally ratified them. In the meantime, the Continental Congress barely survived, lurching from crisis to crisis.

The Congress had few powers outside of maintaining an army and navy, and little money to do even that. Because it had no power to tax, it had to requisition money from the states. If states refused to send money (which they often did), Congress did without. In desperation, Congress sold off western lands to speculators, issued securities that sold for less than their face value, and used its own presses to print money that was virtually worthless. Congress also had to disband the army, despite continued threats from the British and Spanish, and it lacked the power to regulate commerce, which inhibited foreign trade and the development of a strong national economy. However, the Congress did manage to develop sound policies for the management of the western frontiers, passing the Northwest Ordinance of 1787, which encouraged the development of the Great Lakes region.

In general, the weak and ineffective national government could take little independent action. All the power rested in the states. The national government could not compel the states to do anything, and it had no power to deal directly with individual citizens. The weakness of the national government prevented it from dealing with the hard times that soon faced the new nation. There was one benefit of the Articles, though: when the nation's leaders began to write a new constitution, they could look at the provisions of the Articles of Confederation and know what to avoid.

Changes in the States.   What was happening in the states was more important than what was happening in the Continental Congress. The most important change was a dramatic increase in democracy and liberty, at least for white males. Many states adopted bills of rights to protect freedoms, abolished religious qualifications for holding office, and liberalized requirements for voting. Expanded political participation brought a new middle class to power. With expanded voting privileges, farmers and craftworkers became a decisive majority, and the old elite saw its power shrink.

The structure of government in the states also became more responsive to the people. Because legislators were considered to be closer to the voters than governors or judges, power was concentrated in the legislatures. Governors were often selected by the legislatures and were kept on a short leash, with brief tenures and limited veto and appointment powers. Legislatures overruled court decisions and criticized judges for unpopular decisions.

The idea of equality was driving change everywhere. Although the Revolutionary War itself did not transform American society, it unleashed the republican tendencies in American life. Americans were in the process of becoming "the most liberal, the most democratic, the most commercially minded, and the most modern people in the world."[7] Members of the old colonial elite found this turn of affairs quite troublesome.

Economic Turmoil.   After the Revolution, James Madison observed that "the most common and durable source of faction has been the various and unequal division of property."[8] The postrevolutionary legislatures epitomized Madison's argument that economic inequality played an important role in shaping public policy. At the top of the political agenda were economic issues. A postwar depression had left many small farmers unable to pay their debts and threatened them with mortgage foreclosures. Now under control of people more sympathetic to debtors, the state legislatures listened to the demands of small farmers. A few states, notably Rhode Island, demonstrated their support by passing policies to help debtors, favoring them over creditors. Some printed tons of paper money and passed "force acts" requiring reluctant creditors to accept the almost worthless money.

Shays' Rebellion.   Policies favoring debtors over creditors did not please the economic elite who had once controlled nearly all the state legislatures. They were further shaken when, in 1786, a small band of farmers in western Massachusetts rebelled at losing their land to creditors. Led by Revolutionary War Captain Daniel Shays, this rebellion, called **Shays' Rebellion**, was a series of armed attacks on courthouses to prevent judges from foreclosing on farms. Neither Congress nor the state was able to raise a militia to stop Shays and his followers, and a privately paid force was assembled to do the job—fueling dissatisfaction with the weakness of the Articles of Confederation system.

The Aborted Annapolis Meeting.   In September 1786, a handful of continental leaders assembled at Annapolis, Maryland, to discuss the problems with the Articles of Confederation. It was an abortive attempt at reform—only five states were represented at the meeting. Yet these representatives boldly issued a call for a meeting of the states in Philadelphia the following May. Their move worked, as the Continental Congress called for a meeting of all the states, and in May 1787 what we now call the Constitutional Convention got down to business in Philadelphia.

MAKING A CONSTITUTION: THE PHILADELPHIA CONVENTION

Representatives from twelve states came to Philadelphia for a meeting called "for the sole and express purpose of revising the Articles of Confederation." (Note that they disregarded their instructions.) Only Rhode Island, a stronghold of paper-money interests, refused to send delegates.

Gentlemen in Philadelphia

The fifty-five men who attended the Convention were certainly a select group of economic and political notables. They were mostly wealthy planters, successful (or once-successful) lawyers and merchants, and men of independent wealth. Many were college graduates. Most were coastal residents, rather than residents of the expanding western frontiers, and a significant number were urbanites, rather than part of the primarily rural American population.

Philosophy into Action

Both philosophy and politics were prevalent at the Constitutional Convention. The delegates at Philadelphia were uncommonly well-read and began the Convention with a two-week debate on the philosophy of government. After that, very practical, and very divisive issues sometimes threatened to dissolve the meeting.

Obviously, the fifty-five men did not share the same political philosophy. Democratic Benjamin Franklin held very different views from aristocratic Alexander Hamilton, who hardly hid his disgust for democracy. Yet at the core there was agreement on questions of human nature, the causes of political conflict, and the object and nature of a republican government.

Views of Human Nature. Common to the times, delegates held a cynical view of human nature. People, they thought, were self-interested. Hamilton said, "Men love power." The men at Philadelphia believed that government should play a key role in checking and containing the natural self-interest of people.[9]

Views of Political Conflict. We have already learned that James Madison (and the other founders) believed that the primary source of political conflict was the unequal distribution of wealth (property was the main form of wealth in those days). Other sources of conflict included religion, views of governing, and attachment to various leaders.[10] Arising from these sources of conflict are **factions**, as Madison called them (we might call them parties or interest groups). A majority faction might well be composed of the many who have little or no property, the minority faction of those with property. Each would try to seize the reins of government in its own interest. Factions had to be checked.

Views of the Objects of Government.   To Gouverneur Morris of Pennsylvania, the preservation of property was the "principal object of government." Property-holders themselves, they could not imagine a government that did not make its principal objective an economic one: the preservation of individual rights to acquire and hold wealth.

Views of Government.   Human nature, the delegates believed, is avaricious and self-interested. The principal cause of political conflict is economic inequality. Either a majority or a minority faction will be tyrannical if it has too much power. Property must be protected against the tyrannical tendencies of faction. Given this set of beliefs, what sort of government did the delegates believe would work? The delegates answered in different ways, but the message was always the same. Power should be set against power, so that no one faction would overwhelm the others. The secret of good government is "balanced" government. A limited government would have to contain checks on its own power. So long as no faction could seize the whole of government at once, tyranny could be avoided. A complex network of checks, balances, and separation of powers would be required for a balanced government.

THE AGENDA IN PHILADELPHIA

There was not only a political philosophy on the line in Philadelphia. There were real, practical issues confronting the United States—issues of equality, the economy, and individual rights.

The Equality Issues

The Declaration of Independence states that all men are created equal; the Constitution, though, is silent on equality. Some of the most important issues on the policy agenda at Philadelphia, however, concerned equality.

Equality and Representation of the States.   One crucial policy issue was how the new Congress would be constituted. One scheme put before the delegates by William Paterson of New Jersey is usually called the **New Jersey Plan**. It called for each state to be equally represented in the new Congress. The opposing strategy was suggested by Edmund Randolph of Virginia and is usually called the **Virginia Plan**. It called for giving each state a share of Congress that matched the state's share of the American population.

The delegates resolved this conflict with a compromise. Devised by Roger Sherman and William Johnson of Connecticut, it has been immortalized as the **Connecticut Compromise**. The compromise solution was to create two houses in Congress. One body, the Senate, would have two members from each state, and the second body, the House of Representatives, would have

When the Constitution was written, many Northern and Southern delegates assumed that slavery, being relatively unprofitable, would soon die out. A single invention—Eli Whitney's cotton gin—made it profitable again. Although Congress did act to control the growth of slavery, the slave economy became entrenched in the South.

representation based on population. The United States Congress is still organized in this way. Each state has two senators and its representation in the House is determined by its population.

Whether giving large and small states equal representation in the Senate is "fair" is a matter of debate. What is not open to question is that the delegates to the 1787 convention had to accommodate various interests and viewpoints in order to convince all the states to join an untested union.

Slavery.   The second equality issue was slavery. The contradictions between slavery and the sentiments of the Declaration of Independence are obvious, but slavery was legal in every state except Massachusetts. It was concentrated in the South, however, where slave labor was commonplace in agriculture. Some delegates denounced it. Southerners defended it. The delegates could only agree that Congress could limit future *importing* of slaves (they outlawed it after 1808), but nowhere did they forbid slavery itself. The Constitution, in fact, tilted toward recognizing slavery; it stated that slaves fleeing to free states had to be returned to their owners.

DOONESBURY   Garry Trudeau

Another sticky question about slavery arose. How should slaves be counted in determining representation in Congress? Delegates answered with the famous *three-fifths compromise*. Representation and taxation were to be based upon the "number of free persons," plus three-fifths of the number of "all other persons." Everyone, of course, knew who those "other persons" were.

Political Equality.   The delegates dodged one other issue on equality. A handful of delegates, led by Franklin, suggested that national elections should require universal manhood suffrage (that is, a vote for all free, adult males). This democratic thinking did not appeal to those still smarting from Shays' Rebellion. Many delegates wanted to put property qualifications on the right to vote. Ultimately, as the debate wound down, they decided to leave the issue to the states. People qualified to vote in state elections could also vote in national elections.

The Economic Issues

Economic issues were high on the Constitution writers' policy agenda. People disagreed (in fact, historians still disagree) as to whether the postcolonial economy was in shambles or not. The writers of the Constitution, already committed to a strong national government, charged that the economy was indeed in disarray. Specifically, they claimed that the following problems had to be addressed:

- States put up tariffs against products from other states.
- Paper money was virtually worthless in some states, but many state governments, which were controlled by debtor classes, forced it on creditors anyway.

- The Continental Congress was having trouble raising money as the economy went through a recession.

Understanding something about the delegates and their economic interests gives us insight into their views on political economy. They were, by all accounts, the nation's postcolonial economic elite. Some were budding capitalists. Others were creditors whose loans were being wiped out by cheap paper money. Many were merchants who could not carry on trade with a neighboring state. Virtually all of them thought a strong national government was needed to bring economic stability to the chaotic union of states that existed under the Articles of Confederation.[11]   It is not surprising, then, that the framers of the Constitution would seek to strengthen the economic powers of the new national government. The delegates made sure that the Constitution clearly spelled out the economic powers of Congress (see Table 2.2). Consistent

TABLE 2.2 — Economics in the Constitution

POWERS OF CONGRESS

1. Levy taxes.
2. Pay debts.
3. Borrow money.
4. Coin money and regulate its value.
5. Regulate interstate and foreign commerce.
6. Establish uniform laws of bankruptcy.
7. Punish counterfeiting.
8. Punish piracy.
9. Create standard weights and measures.
10. Establish post offices and post roads.
11. Protect copyrights and patents.

PROHIBITIONS ON THE STATES

1. States cannot pass laws impairing the obligations of contract.
2. States cannot coin money or issue paper money.
3. States cannot require payment of debts in paper money.
4. States cannot tax imports or exports from abroad or other states.
5. States cannot free runaway slaves from other states (*now defunct*).

OTHER KEY PROVISIONS

1. The new government assumes the national debt contracted under the Articles of Confederation.
2. The Constitution guarantees a republican form of government.
3. The states must respect civil court judgments and contracts made in other states.

with the general allocation of power in the Constitution, Congress was to be the chief economic policymaker.

Congress, the new Constitution said, could obtain revenues through taxing and borrowing. These tools, along with the power to appropriate funds, became crucial instruments for influencing the economy. By maintaining sound money and guaranteeing payment for the national debt, Congress was to encourage economic enterprise and investment in the United States. Congress was also given power to build the nation's infrastructure by constructing post offices and roads, and to establish standard weights and measures. To protect property rights, Congress was charged with punishing counterfeiters and pirates, ensuring patents and copyrights, and legislating rules for bankruptcy. Equally important (and now a key congressional power, with a wide range of implications for the economy) was Congress's new ability to regulate interstate and foreign commerce.

In addition, the framers prohibited practices in the states that they viewed as inhibiting economic development, such as printing the hated paper money, placing duties on imports from other states, and interfering with lawfully contracted debts. Moreover, the states were to respect civil judgments and contracts made in other states. To help the states, the national government guaranteed them "a republican form of government" to prevent a recurrence of Shays' Rebellion.

The Individual Rights Issues

There was another major item on the Constitutional Convention agenda; the delegates had to design a system that would preserve individual rights. They felt this would be relatively easy, because they were constructing a limited government that, by design, could not threaten personal freedoms. In addition, they dispersed power among the branches of the national government and between the national and state governments so that each branch or level could constrain the other. Also, most of the delegates believed that the various states were already doing a sufficient job of protecting individual rights.

As a result, the Constitution says little about personal freedoms. The protections it does offer are as follows:

- It prohibits suspension of the **writ of habeas corpus** (except during invasion or rebellion). Such a writ enables persons detained by authorities to secure an immediate inquiry into the causes of their detention, and, if no proper explanation is offered, a judge may order their release. (Article I, Section 9.)
- It prohibits Congress or the states from passing bills of attainder (which punish people without a judicial trial). (Article I, Section 9.)
- It prohibits Congress or the states from passing *ex post facto* laws (which punish people or increase the penalties for acts that were not illegal or not as punishable when committed). (Article I, Section 9.)

- It prohibits the imposition of religious qualifications for holding office in the national government. (Article VI.)
- It narrowly defines and outlines strict rules of evidence for conviction of treason. To be convicted, one must levy war against the United States or adhere to and aid its enemies during war. Conviction requires confession in open court or the testimony of *two* witnesses to the *same* act. The framers of the Constitution would have been executed as traitors if the revolution had failed, and they were therefore sensitive to treason laws. (Article III, Section 3.)
- It upholds the right to trial by jury in criminal cases. (Article III, Section 2.)

The delegates were content with their document. When it came time to obtain ratification of the Constitution, however, there was widespread criticism of the absence of specific protections for individual rights.

THE MADISONIAN MODEL

James Madison was the principal architect of the government's final structure, and his work still shapes our policy-making process.[12] He and his colleagues feared both majority and minority factions, either of which could take control of the government and use it to its own advantage. Factions of the minority, however, were easy to deal with; they could simply be outvoted by the majority. Factions of the majority were harder to handle. If the majority united around some policy issue, such as the redistribution of wealth, it could ride roughshod over the minority, violating their basic rights.[13]

Separation of Powers and Checks and Balances

As Madison would later explain in *The Federalist Papers*, "Ambition must be made to counteract ambition."[14] To prevent the possibility of a tyranny of the majority, Madison proposed the following:

1. Place as much of the government as possible beyond the direct control of the majority.

2. Separate the powers of different institutions.

3. Construct a system of checks and balances.

To thwart tyranny of the majority, it was first essential to keep most of the government beyond their power. Madison's plan placed only one element of government, the House of Representatives, within direct control of the votes of the majority. In contrast, senators were to be elected by the state legislatures and the president by special electors; in other words, they would be elected by a small minority, not by the people themselves. Judges were to be appointed by the president (see Figure 2.1). Even if the majority seized control of the

FIGURE 2.1 — The Constitution and the Electoral Process: The Original Plan

Under Madison's plan, incorporated in the Constitution, voters' electoral influence was limited and mostly indirect. Only the House of Representatives was directly elected. Senators and presidents were indirectly elected, and judges were appointed. Over the years, Madison's original model has been substantially democratized.

The Seventeenth Amendment (1913) made senators directly elected by popular majorities. Today, members of the electoral college are selected by the voters (originally most were selected by state legislatures). As a result, the electoral college has become largely a rubber stamp, voting the way the popular majority in each state votes.

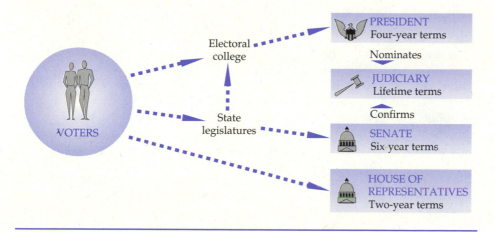

House of Representatives, they still could not enact policies without the concurrence of the Senate and the president. To further insulate governmental officials from public opinion, judges were given lifetime tenure and senators terms of six years, with only one-third elected at a time, as opposed to the two-year terms given to representatives to the House.

The Madisonian scheme also required a **separation of powers**. Each of the three branches of government—executive, legislative, and judicial—would be relatively independent of one another so that neither could control the others. The president, Congress, and the courts were all given independent elements of power. Power was not separated absolutely, however, but rather shared among the three institutions.

Because power was not completely separate, each branch required the consent of the others for many of its actions. This created a system of **checks**

and balances that reflected Madison's goal of setting power against power to constrain government actions. If one institution was seized by a faction, it still could not damage the whole system, he reasoned. The president checks Congress by holding veto power; Congress holds the purse strings of government and must approve presidential appointments.

The courts also figured into the system of checks and balances. Presidents could nominate judges, but they required confirmation by the Senate. The Supreme Court itself, in *Marbury v. Madison* (1803), asserted its power to check the other branches through judicial review: the right to hold actions of the other two branches unconstitutional. This right, not specifically outlined in the Constitution, considerably strengthened the Court's ability to restrain the other branches of government. (For a summary of separation of powers and the checks and balances system, see Figure 2.2.)

The Constitutional Republic

Because the founders did not wish to have the people directly make all decisions (as in a town meeting where everyone has one vote), and because the country was far too large for such a proposal to be feasible, they did not choose to create a direct democracy. Their solution was to establish a **republic**: a system based on the consent of the governed in which power is exercised by *representatives* of the public. This deliberative democracy required and encouraged reflection and refinement of the public's views through an elaborate decision-making process.

The system of checks and balances and separation of powers has a conservative bias that favors the *status quo*. People desiring change must usually have a sizable majority, not just a simple majority of 51 percent. Those opposed to change need only win at one point in the policy-making process, say in obtaining a presidential veto, whereas those who favor change must win every battle along the way. Change usually comes slowly, if at all. As a result, the Madisonian system encourages moderation and compromise. It is difficult for either a minority or a majority to tyrannize, and both property rights and personal freedoms (with occasional lapses) have survived.

The End of the Beginning

On the 109th day of the meetings, in stifling heat (the windows of the Pennsylvania statehouse were closed to ensure secrecy), the final version of the Constitution was read aloud. Then Dr. Franklin rose with a speech he had written, but the enfeebled Franklin had to ask James Wilson to deliver it. In it, Franklin noted that "there are several parts of this Constitution of which I do not at present approve, but I am not sure that I shall never approve them." Some representatives, Edmund Randolph among them, rose to announce that they did not intend to sign. Then, on Franklin's motion, a vote was taken. Ten states voted yes, none voted no, but South Carolina's delegates were divided. The members themselves adjourned to a tavern. It was the end of the beginning.

FIGURE 2.2 — *Separation of Powers and Checks and Balances in the Constitution*

The diagram shows how Madison and his fellow Constitution writers used the doctrine of separation of powers to allow the three institutions of government to check and balance one another. Judicial review, the power of courts to hold executive and congressional policies unconstitutional, was not explicit in the Constitution but was asserted by the Supreme Court under John Marshall in *Marbury v. Madison*.

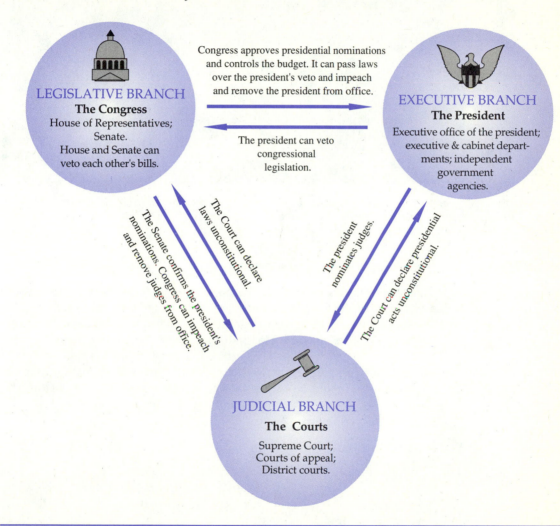

George Washington presided over the signing of the Constitution. "The business being closed," he wrote, "the members adjourned to the City Tavern, dined together and took cordial leave of each other."

RATIFYING THE CONSTITUTION

The Constitution did not automatically go into effect. It had to be ratified by the states. Our awe of the founders sometimes blinds us to the bitter politics of the day. There is no way of gauging the public's feelings about the new document, but as future Chief Justice John Marshall suggests, "it is scarcely to be doubted that *in some of the adopting states, a majority of the people were in opposition.*"[15] The Constitution itself required that only nine of the thirteen states approve the document before it could be implemented, ignoring the requirement that the Articles of Confederation be amended only by unanimous consent.

Federalists and Anti-Federalists

Throughout the states, a fierce battle erupted between the *Federalists*, who supported the Constitution, and the *Anti-federalists*, who opposed it. Newspapers were filled with letters and articles, many written under pseudonyms, praising or condemning the document. In praise of the Constitution, three men—James Madison, Alexander Hamilton, and John Jay—wrote a series of eighty-five articles under the name Publius. These articles, known as **The Federalist Papers**, are second only to the Constitution itself in characterizing the thought of the framers.

Far from being unpatriotic or un-American, the Anti-federalists sincerely believed that the new government was an enemy of freedom, the very freedom they had just fought a war to ensure. Adopting names like Aggrippa, Cornelius, and Monteczuma, the Anti-federalists launched bitter, biting, even brilliant attacks on the Philadelphia document. They frankly questioned the motives of the Constitution writers. One objection was central to the Anti-federalist's attacks: the new Constitution was a class-based document, intended to ensure that a particular economic elite controlled the public policies of the national government. Said one critic, "These lawyers, men of learning, and moneyed men expect to get into Congress themselves so they can get all the power and all the money into their own hands."[16]   These and other equally strong charges of conspiracy and elitism were being hurled at the likes of Washington, Madison, Franklin, and Hamilton.

The Anti-federalists had other fears. Not only would the new government be run by a few, but it would erode fundamental liberties. It was no accident, they thought, that the men at Philadelphia had omitted a Bill of Rights, something included in most state constitutions. To allay fears that the Constitution would restrict personal freedoms, the Federalists promised to add amendments to the document specifically protecting individual liberties. James Madison introduced twelve constitutional amendments during the First Congress in 1789. Ten were ratified by the states and took effect in 1791. These first ten amendments to the Constitution, which restrain the national government from limiting personal freedoms, have come to be known as the **Bill of Rights** (see Table 2.3). Another of Madison's original twelve amendments was ratified 201 years later as the Twenty-seventh Amendment.

Further, opponents said that the Constitution would weaken the power of the states (which it did). Many state political leaders feared that their own power would be diminished as well. Finally, not everyone wanted the economy to be placed on a sounder foundation. Creditors opposed the issuance of paper money because it would produce inflation and make the money they received as payment on their loans decline in value. Debtors favored paper money, however. Their debts (such as the mortgages on their farms) remained constant, but if money became more plentiful, it would be easier for them to pay off their debts.

Ratification

Federalists may not have had the support of the majority, but they made up for it in shrewd politicking. They knew that many members of the legislatures of some states were skeptical of the Constitution, and that state legislatures were populated with political leaders who would lose power under the Constitution. Thus, they specified that the Constitution be ratified by special conventions in each of the states—not by state legislatures.

Delaware was the first to approve, on December 7, 1787. Only six months passed before New Hampshire's approval, the ninth, made the Constitution official. Virginia and New York then voted to join the new union. Two states were holdouts; North Carolina and Rhode Island made the promise of the Bill of Rights their price for joining the other states.

TABLE 2.3 — The Bill of Rights (Arranged by Function)

PROTECTION OF FREE EXPRESSION
Amendment 1: Freedom of speech, press, and assembly
              Freedom to petition government

PROTECTION OF PERSONAL BELIEFS
Amendment 1: No government establishment of religion
              Freedom to exercise religion

PROTECTION OF PRIVACY
Amendment 3: No forced quartering of troops in homes during peacetime
Amendment 4: No unreasonable searches and seizures

PROTECTION OF DEFENDANT'S RIGHTS
Amendment 5: Grand-jury indictment required for prosecution of serious crime
              No second prosecution for the same offense
              No compulsion to testify against oneself
              No loss of life, liberty, or property without due process of law
Amendment 6: Right to a speedy and public trial by a local impartial jury
              Right to be informed of charges against oneself
              Right to legal counsel
              Right to compel the attendance of favorable witnesses, and to cross-
              examine witnesses
Amendment 7: Right to jury trial in civil suit where the value of controversy
              exceeds $20
Amendment 8: No excessive bail or fines
              No cruel and unusual punishments

PROTECTION OF OTHER RIGHTS
Amendment 2: Right to bear arms
Amendment 5: No taking of private property for public use without just compensation
Amendment 9: Unlisted rights are not necessarily denied
Amendment 10: Powers not delegated to the national government or denied to the
              states reserved for the states or the people

With the Constitution ratified, it was time to select officeholders. The framers of the Constitution assumed that George Washington would become the first president of the new government—even giving him the convention's papers for safekeeping—and they were right. The general was the unanimous choice of the electoral college for president. He took office on April 30, 1789, in New York City, the first national capital. New Englander John Adams became "His Superfluous Excellence," as Franklin called the vice president.

CONSTITUTIONAL CHANGE

The U.S. Constitution is frequently referred to as a living document. It is constantly being tested and altered. Generally, constitutional changes are made either by formal amendments or by a number of informal processes. Formal amendments change the letter of the Constitution. There is also an unwritten body of tradition, practice, and procedure that, when altered, may change the spirit of the Constitution. For instance, political parties and national conventions are not part of our written Constitution, but they are important parts of the unwritten constitution. Informal processes, such as political party platforms and current political practice, alter this unwritten constitution and thus have a profound impact on the interpretation of the Constitution.

The Formal Amending Process

The most explicit means of changing the Constitution is through the formal process of amendment. Article V of the Constitution outlines procedures for formal amendment. There are two stages to the amendment process—proposal and ratification—and each stage has two possible avenues (see Figure 2.3). An amendment may be proposed either by a two-thirds vote in each house of Congress or by a national convention called by Congress at the request of two-thirds of the state legislatures. An amendment may be ratified either by the legislatures of three-fourths of the states or by special state conventions called in three-fourths of the states. The president has no formal role in amending the Constitution, although the chief executive may influence the success of proposed amendments.

All but one of the successful amendments to the Constitution have been proposed by Congress and ratified by the state legislatures. The exception was the Twenty-first Amendment, which repealed the short-lived Eighteenth Amendment, the Prohibition Amendment that outlawed the sale and consumption of alcohol. Today, state legislatures rather than Congress are calling for a national convention to amend the Constitution to require a balanced budget every year. Thirty-two of the thirty-four required states have formally requested such an amending convention, but no new state has joined the list in more than a decade.

Unquestionably, formal amendments have made the Constitution more egalitarian and democratic. The emphasis on economic issues in the original document is now balanced by amendments that stress equality and increase the ability of a popular majority to affect government. The amendments are headed by the Bill of Rights (see Table 2.3), which Chapter 4 will discuss in detail. Later amendments, including the Thirteenth Amendment abolishing slavery, have forbidden various political and social inequalities based on race, sex, and age (also discussed in Chapter 4). Other amendments, discussed later in this chapter, have democratized the political system, making it easier for voters to influence the government. Only one existing amendment specifically

FIGURE 2.3 — How the Constitution Can Be Amended

The Constitution sets up two alternative routes for proposing amendments and two for ratifying them. One of the four possible combinations has been used in every case but one, but there are persistent calls for a constitutional convention to propose some new amendment or another. (Amendments to permit school prayers, to make abortion unconstitutional, and to require a balanced national budget are recent examples.)

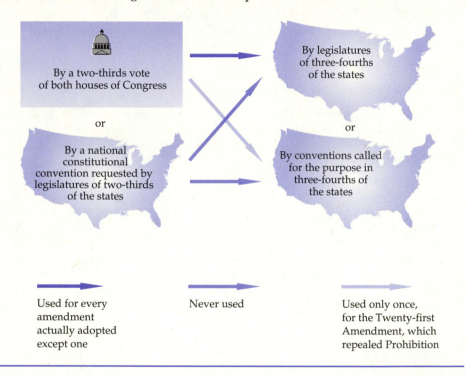

By a two-thirds vote of both houses of Congress

or

By a national constitutional convention requested by legislatures of two-thirds of the states

By legislatures of three-fourths of the states

or

By conventions called for the purpose in three-fourths of the states

Used for every amendment actually adopted except one

Never used

Used only once, for the Twenty-first Amendment, which repealed Prohibition

addresses the economy—the Sixteenth, or "income tax," Amendment. Overall, it is plain that the most important effect of these constitutional amendments has been to expand liberty and equality in America.

Some amendments have been proposed but not ratified. The best-known of these in recent years is the *Equal Rights Amendment,* or ERA. First proposed in 1923 by the nephew of suffragist Susan B. Anthony, the ERA had to wait fifty years—until 1978—before Congress passed it and sent it to the states for ratification. It stated simply that "equality of rights under the law shall not be denied or abridged by the United States or by any State on account of sex."

This seemingly innocuous amendment—who, after all, could truly oppose equal rights for women and men in this day and age?—sailed through Congress and the first few state legislatures. Public opinion polls showed substantial support for the ERA, even among people with traditional views of women's roles.[17]

Winning the right to vote was just the first step in the movement for women's rights; it took several decades before the second feminist wave of reform occurred.

Nevertheless, the ERA was not ratified. It failed in part because of the system of checks and balances. The ERA had to be approved not by a national majority but by three-fourths of the states. Many conservative southern states opposed it, thus exercising their veto power despite approval by a majority of Americans.

The Informal Process of Constitutional Change

Think for a moment of all the changes in American government that have taken place without altering a word or letter of the Constitution; in fact, there is not a word in it that would lead one to suspect any of the following developments:

- The United States has the world's oldest two-party system, whereunto one member of Congress and no president since Washington has failed to say, "I'm a Democrat (or a Republican, or Federalist, or Whig, or whatever)."
- Abortions through the second trimester of pregnancy when the fetus cannot live outside the mother's womb are legal in the United States.
- Members of the electoral college consider themselves honor bound (and in some places even legally bound) to follow the preference of their state's electorate.

- Both the Senate and the House are now on TV; TV has come to set our political agenda and guide our assessments of candidates and issues.
- Government now taxes and spends about a third of our gross domestic product, an amount the Convention delegates might have found gargantuan.

None of these things are "unconstitutional." The parties emerged, television came to prominence in American life, first technology and then the law permitted abortions—all without having to tinker with the founders' handiwork. This is because the Constitution changes *informally* as well as *formally*. There are several ways the Constitution changes informally: through judicial interpretation and political practice, and as a result of changes in technology and in the demands on policymakers.

Judicial Interpretation.   Disputes often arise about the meaning of the Constitution. If it is the "supreme law of the land," someone has to decide how to interpret the Constitution when disputes arise. In 1803, in the famous case of **Marbury v. Madison,** the Supreme Court decided it would be the one to resolve differences of opinion. It claimed for itself the power of **judicial review**. Implied but never explicitly stated in the Constitution, this power gives courts the right to decide whether the actions of the legislative and executive branches of state and national governments are in accord with the Constitution (see "In Focus: John Marshall and the Growth of Judicial Review").

Because the Constitution usually means what the Supreme Court says it means, judicial interpretation can profoundly affect how the Constitution is understood. For example, in 1896 the Supreme Court decided that the Constitution allowed racial discrimination, despite the presence of the Fourteenth Amendment. Sixty years later it overruled itself and concluded that segregation by law violated the Constitution. In 1973, the Supreme Court decided that the Constitution protected a woman's right to an abortion during the first two trimesters of pregnancy when the fetus is not viable outside the womb—an issue the founders never addressed (these cases will be discussed in Chapter 4).

Changing Political Practice.   Current political practices also change the Constitution, stretching it, shaping it, and giving it new meaning. Probably no changes are more important than those related to parties and presidential elections.

Political parties as we know them did not exist when the Constitution was written. In fact, its authors disliked the idea of political parties, which encourage factions. Regardless, by 1800 a party system had developed and it plays a key role in making policy today. American government would be radically different if there were no political parties, even though the Constitution is silent about them.

Changing political practice has also altered the role of the electoral college, which has been reduced to a clerical one in selecting the president. The writers of the Constitution (to avoid giving too much power to the uneducated majority) intended there be no popular vote for the president; instead,

IN FOCUS

John Marshall and the Growth of Judicial Review

Scarcely was the government housed in its new capital when Federalists and Democrats clashed over the courts. In the election of 1800, Democrat Thomas Jefferson had beaten Federalist John Adams. Determined to leave at least the judiciary in trusted hands, Adams tried to fill it with Federalists. He allegedly stayed at his desk until nine o'clock signing commissions on his last night in the White House (March 3, 1801).

In the midst of this flurry, Adams appointed William Marbury to the minor post of justice of the peace in the District of Columbia. In the rush of last-minute business, however, Secretary of State John Marshall failed to deliver commissions to Marbury and sixteen others. He left the commissions to be delivered by the incoming secretary of state, James Madison.

When the omission was discovered, Madison and Jefferson, furious at Adams' actions, refused to deliver the commissions. Marbury and three others in the same situation sued Madison, asking the Supreme Court to issue a writ of mandamus ordering Madison to give them their commissions. They took their case directly to the Supreme Court under the Judiciary Act of 1789, which gave the Court original jurisdiction in such matters.

The new chief justice was none other than Adams' secretary of state and arch-Federalist John Marshall, himself one of Adams' "midnight appointments" (he took his seat on the Court barely three weeks before Adams' term ended). Marshall and his Federalist colleagues were in a spot. Threats of impeachment came from Jeffersonians, who were fearful that the Court would vote for Marbury. Moreover, if the Court ordered Madison to deliver the commissions, he was likely to ignore it, thereby risking ridicule for the nation's highest court over a minor issue. Marshall had no means of compelling Madison to act.

The Court could also deny Marbury's claim. Taking that option, however, would concede the issue to the Jeffersonians and give the appearance of retreat in the face of opposition, thereby reducing the power of the Court.

Marshall devised a shrewd solution to the case *Marbury v. Madison*. In February 1803, he delivered the unanimous opinion of the Court. First, Marshall and his colleagues argued that Madison was wrong to withhold Marbury's commission. The Court also found, however, that the Judiciary Act of 1789, under which Marbury had brought suit, contradicted the plain words of the Constitution about the Court's original jurisdiction. Thus, Marshall dismissed Marbury's claim, saying that the Court, according to the Constitution, had no power to require that the commission be delivered.

Conceding a small battle over Marbury's commission (he did not get it), Marshall won a much larger war, asserting for the courts the power to determine what is and is not constitutional. As Marshall wrote, "An act of the legislature repugnant to the Constitution is void," and "it is emphatically the province of the judicial department to say what the law is." Thus, the chief justice established the power of judicial review, the power of the courts to hold acts of Congress, and by implication the executive, in violation of the Constitution.

Marbury v. Madison was part of a skirmish between the Federalists on the Court and the Democratically controlled Congress. Partly, for example, to rein in the Supreme Court, the Jeffersonian Congress in 1801 abolished the lower federal appeals courts and made the Supreme Court justices return to the unpleasant task of "riding circuit"—serving as lower court justices around the country. Congress even canceled the Court's entire 1802 term. This was a bit of studied harassment of the Court by its enemies. After *Marbury*, angry members of Congress,

Continued

IN FOCUS — John Marshall and the Growth of Judicial Review, *continued*

together with other Jeffersonians, claimed that Marshall was a "usurper of power," setting himself above Congress and the president.

This view, however, was unfair. State courts, before and after the Constitution, had declared acts of their legislatures unconstitutional. In "Federalist #78," Alexander Hamilton had declared the courts had a "duty . . . to declare all acts contrary to the manifest tenor of the Constitution void," and the federal courts had actually done so. *Marbury* was not even the first case of striking down an act of Congress; a lower federal court had done so in 1792, and

the Supreme Court itself had approved a law after a constitutional review in 1796. Marshall was neither inventing nor imagining his right to review laws for their constitutionality.

The case also illustrates that the courts must be politically astute in exercising their power over the other branches. By in effect reducing its own power—the authority to hear cases such as Marbury's under its original jurisdiction—the Court was able to assert the right of judicial review in a fashion that the other branches could not easily rebuke.

---

state legislatures or the voters (depending on the state) would select wise electors who would then choose a "distinguished character of continental reputation" (as *The Federalist Papers* put it) to be president. These electors formed the electoral college. Each state would have the same number of electors to vote for the president as it had senators and representatives in Congress.

In 1796, the first election in which George Washington was not a candidate, electors scattered their votes among thirteen candidates. By the election of 1800, domestic and foreign policy issues had divided the country into two political parties. To avoid dissipating their support, the parties required electors to pledge in advance to vote for the candidate that won their state's popular vote, leaving electors with a largely clerical function.

Although electors are now rubber stamps for the popular vote, nothing in the Constitution prohibits an elector from voting for any candidate. Every so often, electors have decided to cast a vote for their own favorites; some state laws require electors to vote for the candidate chosen by a majority of their state's citizens, but such laws have never been enforced. The idea that the electoral college would exercise wisdom independent of the majority of people is now a constitutional anachronism, changed not by formal amendment but by political practice.

Technology.   The Constitution has also been greatly changed by technology. The mass media now play a role unimaginable in the eighteenth century, questioning governmental policies, supporting candidates, and helping shape citizens' opinions. The bureaucracy has grown in importance as the result of the development of computers, which create new potential for bureaucrats to serve the public (such as writing over 40 million Social Security checks each month) and, at times, create mischief. Electronic communications and the development of atomic weapons have given the president's role as commander in chief added significance, increasing the power of the president in the constitutional system.

Increasing Demands on Policymakers.   The significance of the presidency has also grown as a result of increased demands for new policies. The United States' evolution in the realm of international affairs—from an insignificant country that kept to itself to a superpower with an extraordinary range of international obligations—has located additional power in the hands of the chief executive, who is designated to take the lead in foreign affairs. Similarly, the increased demands of domestic policy have resulted in the president taking a more prominent role in preparing the federal budget and a legislative program.

The Importance of Flexibility.   It is easy to see that the document the framers produced over 200 years ago was not meant to be static, written in stone. Instead, the Constitution's authors created a flexible system of government, one that could adapt to the needs of the times without sacrificing personal freedom. This flexibility has helped ensure the Constitution's—and the nation's—survival. Although the United States is young compared to other Western nations, it has the oldest functioning Constitution. France, which experienced a revolution in 1789, the same year the Constitution was ratified, has had twelve constitutions over the past two centuries. Despite the great diversity of the American population, the enormous size of the country, and the extraordinary changes that have taken place over the nation's history, the Constitution is still going strong.

The Elaboration of the Constitution

The Constitution, even with all twenty-seven amendments, is a very short document, containing fewer than 8,000 words. It does not prescribe the structure and functioning of the national government in detail. Regarding the judiciary, Congress is told simply to create a court system as it sees fit. The Supreme Court is the only court required by the Constitution, and even here the number of justices and their qualifications is left up to Congress. Similarly, many of the governing units we have today—such as the executive departments, the various offices in the White House, the independent regulatory commissions, and the committees of Congress, to name only a few examples—are not mentioned at all in the Constitution. The framers allowed future generations to determine their needs. As muscle grows on the constitutional skeleton, it inevitably gives new shape and purpose to the government.

UNDERSTANDING THE CONSTITUTION

Our theme of the role of government runs throughout this chapter, which focuses, of course, on just what it is that the national government can and cannot do. This section will examine the Constitution in terms of our theme of democracy and also look at the impact of the Constitution on policy-making.

MIKE LUCKOVICH
Courtesy Times-Picayune (New Orleans)

The Constitution and Democracy

Despite the fact that America is often said to be one of the most democratic societies in the world, the Constitution itself is rarely described as democratic. This is hardly surprising, considering the political philosophies of the men who wrote it. Among eighteenth-century upper-class society, democratic government was roundly despised. If democracy was a way of permitting the majority's preference to become policy, the Constitution writers wanted no part of it. The American government was to be a government of the "rich, well-born, and able," as Hamilton said, where John Jay's wish that "the people who own the country ought to govern it" would be a reality. Few people today would consider these thoughts democratic.

The Constitution did not, however, create a monarchy or a feudal aristocracy. It created a republic, a representative form of democracy modeled after the Lockean tradition of limited government. Thus, the undemocratic—even antidemocratic—Constitution established a government that permitted substantial movement toward democracy.

One of the central themes of American history is the gradual democratization of the Constitution. What began as a document characterized by numerous restrictions on direct voter participation has slowly become much more democratic. Today, few people share the founders' fear of democracy.

The Constitution itself offered no guidelines on voter eligibility, leaving it to each state to decide. As a result, only a small percentage of adults could vote; women and slaves were excluded entirely. Five of the 17 constitutional amendments passed since the Bill of Rights have focused on the expansion of the electorate. The Fifteenth Amendment (1870) prohibited discrimination on the basis of race in determining voter eligibility (although it took the Voting Rights Act of 1965, discussed in Chapter 4, to make the amendment effective). The Nineteenth Amendment (1920) gave women the right to vote (some states had already done so). The Twenty-third Amendment (1961) accorded the residents of Washington, DC, the right to vote in presidential elections. Three years later, the Twenty-fourth Amendment prohibited poll taxes (which discriminated against the poor of all races). Finally, the Twenty-sixth Amendment (1971) lowered the voter eligibility age to eighteen.

Not only are more people eligible to vote, but voters also have more officials to elect. The Seventeenth Amendment (1913) provided for direct election of senators. Presidential elections have been fundamentally altered by the development of political parties. By placing the same candidate on the ballot in all the states and requiring members of the electoral college to support the candidate receiving the most votes, parties have increased the probability that the candidate for whom most Americans vote will also receive a majority of the electoral college vote. Although it is possible for the candidate who receives the most popular votes to lose the election, this has not happened since 1888. According to the Constitution, the United States selects its president through an electoral college, but in practice American citizens now directly elect the president. (For more on the electoral college, see Chapter 7.)

Technology has also diminished the separation of the people from those who exercise power. Officeholders communicate directly with the public through television, radio, and targeted mailings. Air travel makes it easy for members of Congress to commute regularly between Washington and their states and districts. Similarly, public opinion polls and the telephone make it possible for officials to track citizens' opinions on important issues. Even though the American population has grown from fewer than 4 million to about 260 million people since the first census was taken in 1790, the national government has never been closer to those it serves.

The Constitution and the Scope of Government

The Constitution created political institutions and the rules of the game of politics and policy-making. Many of these rules limit government action. This is a fundamental purpose of the Bill of Rights and related provisions in the Constitution. No matter how large the majority, for example, it is unconstitutional to establish a state-supported church.

Most of these limitations are designed primarily to protect liberty and to open the system to a broad range of participants. Even so, the potential range of action for the government is actually quite wide. Thus, it is constitutionally permissible, if highly unlikely, for the U.S. government to abolish social security payments to the elderly or adopt socialism.

Yet the system of government created by the Constitution has profound implications for what the government does. On the one hand, individualism is reenforced at every turn. The separation of powers and the checks and balances established by the Constitution allow almost all groups some place in the political system where their demands for public policy can be heard. Because many institutions share power, a group can usually find at least one sympathetic ear. Even if the president opposes the policies a particular group favors, Congress, the courts, or some other institution can help the group achieve its policy goals.

In the early days of the civil rights movement, for example, African Americans found Congress and the president unsympathetic, so they turned to the Supreme Court. Getting their interests on the political agenda would have been much more difficult if the Court had not had important constitutional power.

On the other hand, the Constitution created a purposefully inefficient system of policy-making, making it difficult for the government to act. The separation of powers and the system of checks and balances promote the politics of bargaining, compromise, and playing one institution against another. The system of checks and balances implies that one institution is checking another. *Thwarting, blocking* and *impeding* are synonyms for *checking*. But if I block you, you block someone else, and that person blocks me, none of us is going to accomplish anything.

Some scholars suggest that so much checking was built into the American political system that effective government is almost impossible. If the president, Congress, and the courts all pull in different directions on policy, the result may be either no policy at all or a makeshift and inadequate one. The outcome may be nondecisions when hard decisions are needed. If government cannot respond effectively because its policy-making processes are too fragmented, its performance will be inadequate. Perhaps the Madisonian model has reduced the ability of government to reach policy decisions.

SUMMARY

The year 1787 was crucial in American nation-building. The fifty-five men who met in Philadelphia created a policy-making system that responded to a complex policy agenda. There were critical conflicts over equality, which led to key compromises in the New Jersey and Virginia Plans, the three-fifths compromise on slavery, and the decision to toss the issue of voting rights into the hands of the states. There was more agreement, however, about the economy. These merchants, lawyers, and large landowners felt that the American economy was in a shambles, and they intended to make the national government an economic stabilizer. The specificity of the powers assigned to Congress left no doubt that it was to forge national economic policy. The delegates knew, too, that the global posture of the fledgling nation was pitifully weak. A strong national government would be better able to ensure its own security.

Madison and his colleagues were less clear about the protection of individual rights. They felt that the limited government they had constructed would protect freedom, so they said little about individual rights in the Constitution. However, the ratification struggle revealed that protection of personal freedoms was much on the public's mind, so the Bill of Rights was proposed. These first ten amendments to the Constitution, along with the Thirteenth and Fourteenth Amendments, provide Americans with protection from governmental restraints on individual freedoms.

It is important to remember that 1787 was not the only year of nation-building. The nation's colonial and revolutionary heritage shaped the meetings in Philadelphia. Budding industrialism in a basically agrarian nation put economic issues on the Philadelphia agenda. What Madison was to call an "unequal division of property" made equality an issue, particularly after Shays' Rebellion. The greatest inequality of all, that between slave and free, was so contentious an issue that it was simply evaded at Philadelphia.

Nor did ratification of the Constitution end the nation-building process. Constitutional change—both formal and informal—continues to shape and alter the letter and the spirit of the Madisonian system.

That system includes a separation of powers and many checks and balances. Today, Americans still debate whether the result is a government too fragmented to be controlled by anyone. In Chapter 3 we will look at yet another way that the Constitution divides the government's power: between the national and the state governments.

FOR FURTHER READING

Bailyn, Bernard. *The Ideological Origins of the American Revolution.* Cambridge, MA: Harvard University Press, 1967. A leading work on the ideas that spawned the American Revolution.

Becker, Carl L. *The Declaration of Independence: A Study in the History of Political Ideas.* New York: Random House, 1942. Classic work on the meaning of the Declaration.

Hamilton, Alexander, James Madison, and John Jay. *The Federalist Papers,* 2nd ed. Edited by Roy P. Fairfield. Baltimore: Johns Hopkins University Press, 1981. Key tracts in the campaign for the Constitution and cornerstones of American political thought.

Jensen, Merrill. *The Articles of Confederation.* Madison: University of Wisconsin Press, 1940. Definitive treatment of the Articles.

Jillson, Calvin C. *Constitution Making: Conflict and Consensus in the Federal Convention of 1787.* New York: Agathon, 1988. Sophisticated analysis of the drafting of the Constitution.

Lipset, Seymour Martin. *The First New Nation.* New York: Basic Books, 1963. Political sociologist Lipset sees the early American experience as one of nation-building.

McDonald, Forrest B. *Novus Ordo Seclorum: The Intellectual Origins of the Constitution.* Lawrence: University Press of Kansas, 1986. Discusses the ideas behind the Constitution.

Morris, Richard B. *The Forging of the Union, 1781–1789*. New York: Harper & Row, 1987. Written to coincide with the bicentennial of the Constitution, this is an excellent history of the document's making.

Rossiter, Clinton. *1787: The Great Convention*. New York: Macmillan, 1966. A well-written study of the making of the Constitution.

Storing, Herbert J. *What the Anti-Federalists Were For*. Chicago: University of Chicago Press, 1981. Analysis of the political views of those opposed to the ratification of the Constitution.

Wood, Gordon S. *The Creation of the American Republic, 1776–1787*. Chapel Hill: University of North Carolina Press, 1969. In-depth study of American political thought prior to the Constitutional Convention.

Wood, Gordon S. *The Radicalism of the American Revolution*. New York: Knopf, 1992. Shows how American society and politics were thoroughly transformed in the decades following the Revolution.

NOTES

1. Gordon S. Wood, *The Radicalism of the American Revolution* (New York: Vintage, 1993), 4.
2. Garry Wills, *Inventing America: Jefferson's Declaration of Independence* (New York: Doubleday, 1978).
3. On the Lockean influence on the Declaration of Independence, see Carl L. Becker, *The Declaration of Independence: A Study in the History of Political Ideas* (New York: Random House, 1942).
4. Seymour Martin Lipset, *The First New Nation* (New York: Basic Books, 1963).
5. Gordon S. Wood, *The Creation of the American Republic, 1776–1787* (Chapel Hill: University of North Carolina Press, 1969), 3.
6. On the Articles of Confederation, see Merrill Jensen, *The Articles of Confederation* (Madison: University of Wisconsin Press, 1940).
7. Wood, *The Radicalism of the American Revolution*, 6–7.
8. "Federalist #10," in Alexander Hamilton, James Madison, and John Jay, *The Federalist Papers*, 2nd ed. Roy P. Fairfield, ed. (Baltimore: Johns Hopkins University Press, 1981).
9. See Arthur Lovejoy, *Reflections on Human Nature* (Baltimore: Johns Hopkins University Press, 1961), 57–63.
10. "Federalist #10," in Hamilton, Madison, and Jay, *The Federalist Papers*.
11. Clinton Rossiter, *1787: The Grand Convention* (New York: Macmillan, 1966).
12. A brilliant exposition of the Madisonian model is found in Robert A. Dahl, *A Preface to Democratic Theory* (Chicago: University of Chicago Press, 1956).
13. "Federalist #10," in Hamilton, Madison, and Jay, *The Federalist Papers*.
14. "Federalist #51," in Hamilton, Madison, and Jay, *The Federalist Papers*.
15. Quoted in Charles A. Beard, *An Economic Interpretation of the Constitution of the United States* (New York: Macmillan, 1913), 299. Italics ours.
16. Quoted in Cecelia M. Kenyon, *The Antifederalists* (Indianapolis, IN: Bobbs-Merrill, 1966), 1.
17. Jane J. Mansbridge, *Why We Lost the ERA* (Chicago: University of Chicago Press, 1986).

The relationship between governments at the local, state, and national levels often confuses many Americans. Governmental institutions, it seems, must be able to serve many masters. Neighborhood schools are run by locally elected school boards but also receive state and national funds, and with those funds come state and national rules and regulations. Local airports, sewage systems, pollution control systems, and police departments also receive a mix of local, state, and national funds, and hence operate under a complex web of rules and regulations imposed by each level of government.

This chapter will explore *American federalism*, the complex relationships between different levels of government in the United States. It will show the ways that the federal system has changed over two centuries of American government and why American federalism is at the center of important battles over policy.

WHAT FEDERALISM IS AND WHY IT IS SO IMPORTANT

Federalism is not the typical way nations organize their governments. It is a rather unusual system for governing, with particular consequences for those who live within it. This section explains what a federal system is and what difference it makes to Americans living in such a system.

What Federalism Is

Federalism is a way of organizing a nation so that two or more levels of government have formal authority over the same area and people. It is a system of shared power between units of government. For example, the state of California has formal authority over its inhabitants, but the national government can also pass laws and establish policies that affect Californians.

Most governments in the world today are not federal but **unitary governments**, in which all power resides in the central government. If the British parliament, for instance, wants to redraw the boundaries of local governments or change their forms, it can (and has). However, if the U.S. Congress wants to abolish Alabama or Oregon, it cannot.

American states are unitary governments with respect to their local governments. Local governments get their authority from the states; they can be created or abolished by the states. States also have the power to make rules for their own local governments. They tell them what their speed limits can be, the way in which they should be organized, how they can tax people, what they can spend money on, and so forth. States, however, do not receive their authority from the national government but *directly* from the Constitution.

There is a third form of governmental structure, a *confederation*. The United States began as such, under the Articles of Confederation. In a confederation, the national government is weak and most or all the power is in the hands of its components, for example, the individual states. Today, confederations are rare except in international organizations such as the United Nations.

The workings of the federal system are sometimes called **intergovernmental relations**.[1] This term refers to the entire set of interactions among national, state, and local governments.

Why Federalism Is So Important

The federal system in America *decentralizes our politics*. Senators are elected as representatives of individual states, not the entire nation. Likewise, presidents are elected not by a national election but by statewide elections. It is the states that run primaries to nominate presidential candidates. On election day in November, there are actually fifty-one presidential elections, one for each state plus Washington, DC. It is even possible—as last happened in 1888—that a candidate receiving the most popular votes in the country can lose the election because of the way the electoral votes are distributed by state.

The federal system decentralizes our politics in more fundamental ways. With more layers of government, there are more opportunities for political participation. With more people wielding power, there are more points of access in government and more opportunities for interests to have their demands for public policies satisfied. If you lose in city hall, you can still take your case to the state capital or to Washington. In addition, with most decisions made in the states, there are fewer sources of conflict at the national level.

As we will see, federalism also enhances judicial power. Dividing government power and responsibilities necessitates umpires to resolve disputes between the two levels of government; in the American system, the umpires are judges. Placing prohibitions on the states ensures that issues will arise for the courts to decide.

At a 1983 press conference, Transportation Secretary Elizabeth Dole announced her support of MADD and of congressional legislation which would raise minimum drinking ages. Small groups such as MADD, lacking resources to change policy in fifty states, often attempt to move traditionally local issues onto the national government's policy agenda.

The federal system not only decentralizes our politics, but *decentralizes our policies*, too. The history of the federal system demonstrates the tension between the states and the national government about policy—who controls it and what it should be. In the past, people debated whether the states or the national government should regulate the railroads, pass child labor laws, or adopt minimum wage legislation. Today, people debate whether the states or the national government should regulate abortions, enforce school desegregation, determine speed limits on highways, or tell 18-year-olds they cannot drink. Because of the overlapping powers of the two levels of government, most of our public policy debates are also debates about federalism.

States are responsible for most public policies dealing with social, family, and moral issues. The Constitution does not give the national government the power to pass laws that *directly* regulate drinking ages, marriage and divorce, or speed limits. These policy prerogatives belong to the states. They become national issues, however, when aggrieved or angry groups take their cases to Congress or the federal courts in an attempt to use the power of the national government to *influence* states or to get federal courts to find a state's policy unconstitutional.

Candy Lightner, for example, a New Jersey mother whose child was killed by a teenage drunken driver, formed MADD (Mothers Against Drunk Driving). This group was the seed from which sprouted hundreds of local MADD chapters, as well as offshoots like SADD (Students Against Drunk Driving). Lightner's lobbyists inundated state capitals to get the drinking age raised. Between 1976 and 1983, nineteen states raised their drinking age, typically to age 21. MADD supporters realized, however, that it was much easier to get a national law passed once than to lobby each of fifty state legislatures separately. Therefore, in 1983, Lightner and Secretary of Transportation Elizabeth Dole announced their intentions to support a nationally standard drinking age. They could not pass a bill directly setting the drinking age in the states, so they proposed using federal highway funds as an incentive for the states to pass their own bills.

The American states have always been policy innovators.[2] The states overflow with reforms, new ideas, and new policies. From clean air legislation to welfare reform, the states constitute a national laboratory to develop and test public policies and share the results with other states and the national government. Almost every policy the national government has adopted had its beginnings in the states. One or more states pioneered child labor laws, minimum wage legislation, unemployment compensation, antipollution legislation, civil rights protections, and the income tax. More recently, states have been active in reforming health care, education, and welfare—and the national government is paying close attention to their efforts.

THE CONSTITUTIONAL BASIS OF FEDERALISM

The word *federalism* is absent from the Constitution, and not much was said about it at the Constitutional Convention. Eighteenth-century Americans had little experience in thinking of themselves as Americans first and state citizens second. On the contrary, loyalty to state governments was so strong that the Constitution would have been resoundingly defeated had it tried to abolish them. In addition, a central government, working alone, would have had difficulty trying to govern eighteenth-century Americans.

Thus, there was no other practical choice in 1787 but to create a federal system of government. As Chapter 2 explained, the delegates did, however, ensure that the new national government would be stronger, and the state governments weaker, than under the Articles of Confederation.

The Division of Power

The Constitution's writers carefully defined the powers of state and national governments (see Table 3.1). Although favoring a stronger national government, the framers still made states vital cogs in the machinery of government. The Constitution guaranteed states equal representation in the Senate (and even made this provision unamendable). It also made states responsible for

TABLE 3.1 — The Constitution's Distribution of Powers

SOME POWERS SPECIFICALLY GRANTED BY THE CONSTITUTION

To the National Government	To Both the National and State Governments	To the State Governments
To coin money	To tax	To establish local governments
To conduct foreign relations	To borrow money	To regulate commerce within a state
To regulate commerce with foreign nations and among states	To make and enforce laws	To conduct elections
To provide an army and a navy	To establish courts	To ratify amendments to the federal Constitution
To declare war	To charter banks and corporations	To take measures for public health, safety, and morals
To establish courts inferior to the Supreme Court	To spend money for the general welfare	To exert powers the Constitution does not delegate to the national government or prohibit the states from using
To establish post offices	To take private property for public purposes, with just compensation	
To make laws necessary and proper to carry out the foregoing powers.		

SOME POWERS SPECIFICALLY DENIED BY THE CONSTITUTION

To the National Government	To Both the National and State Governments	To the State Governments
To tax articles exported from one state to another	To grant titles of nobility	To tax imports or exports
To violate the Bill of Rights	To permit slavery (Thirteenth Amendment)	To coin money
To change state boundaries	To deny citizens the right to vote because of race, color, or previous servitude (Fifteenth Amendment)	To enter into treaties
	To deny citizens the right to vote because of sex (Nineteenth Amendment)	To impair obligations of contracts
		To abridge the privileges or immunities of citizens or deny due process and equal protection of the law (Fourteenth Amendment)

both state and national elections—an important power. Further, the Constitution virtually guaranteed the continuation of each state; Congress is forbidden to create new states by chopping up old ones, unless a state's legislature approves—an unlikely event.

The Constitution also created obligations of the national government toward the states. For example, it is to protect states against violence and invasion. At times the states find the national government wanting in meeting its obligations. Several states, including California, Texas, New York, and Florida, have sued the national government for failing to control the country's borders, thus forcing the states to pay for social services and detention for illegal aliens.

In Article VI of the Constitution, the framers dealt with what remains a touchy question: In a dispute between the states and the national government, which prevails? The answer that the delegates provided, often referred to as the **supremacy clause**, seems clear enough. They stated that the following three items comprised the supreme law of the land:

1. The Constitution

2. Laws of the national government (when consistent with the Constitution)

3. Treaties (which can only be made by the national government)

Judges in every state were specifically told to obey the Constitution, even if their state constitutions or state laws directly contradicted the U.S. Constitution. Today all state executives, legislators, and judges are bound by oath to support the Constitution.

The national government, however, can only operate within its appropriate sphere. It cannot usurp the states' powers. The question, then, is over the boundaries of the national government's powers. According to some, the **Tenth Amendment** provides part of the answer. It states that the "powers not delegated to the United States by the Constitution, nor prohibited by it to the states, are reserved to the states respectively, or to the people." To those advocating states' rights, the amendment clearly means that the national government has only those powers specifically assigned by the Constitution. The states or people have supreme power over any activity not mentioned there. Despite this interpretation, in 1941 the Supreme Court (in *United States v. Darby*) called the Tenth Amendment a constitutional truism, a mere assertion that the states have independent powers of their own—not that their powers are supreme to the national government's.

The Court seemed to backtrack on this ruling in favor of national government supremacy in a 1976 case, *National League of Cities v. Usery*, in which it held that extending national minimum-wage and maximum-hours standards to employees of state and local governments was an unconstitutional intrusion of the national government into the domain of the states. In 1985, however, (in *Garcia v. San Antonio Metro*) the Court overturned the *National League of Cities* decision. The Court held that Congress, not the courts, should decide which actions of the states should be regulated by the national government. Once again, the Court ruled that the Tenth Amendment did not give states power superior to that of the national government for activities not mentioned in the Constitution.

Occasionally an issue arises in which states challenge the authority of the national government. South Dakota sued the federal government over its efforts to raise states' drinking-age laws and over its efforts to mandate a 55 mile-per-hour speed limit on highways. The state lost both cases.

Establishing National Supremacy

Why is it that the federal government has gained so much power relative to the states? Three key events have largely settled the issue of how national and state powers are related: the *McCulloch v. Maryland* court case, the Civil War, and the civil rights movement.

McCulloch v. Maryland.   As early as 1819, the issue of state versus national power came before the Supreme Court in the case of **McCulloch v. Maryland.** The new American government moved quickly on many economic policies. In 1791, it created a national bank. It was not a private bank like today's "First National Bank of Such and Such," but a government agency empowered to print money, make loans, and engage in many other banking tasks. A darling of such Federalists as Alexander Hamilton, the bank was hated by those opposed to strengthening the national government's control of the economy. Those opposed—including Thomas Jefferson, farmers, and state legislatures—saw the bank as an instrument of the elite.

Railing against the "Monster Bank," the state of Maryland in 1818 passed a law taxing the national bank's Baltimore branch $15,000 a year. The Baltimore branch refused to pay, whereupon the state of Maryland sued the cashier, James McCulloch, for payment. The next year the case came before the U.S. Supreme Court. Two of the country's ablest lawyers argued the case, Daniel Webster for the bank and Luther Martin, a signer of the Declaration of Independence, for Maryland. Martin maintained that the Constitution was very clear about the powers of Congress and the power to create a national bank was not among them. Webster advocated a broader interpretation of the powers of the national government. The Constitution was not meant to stifle congressional powers, he said, but rather permit Congress to use all means "necessary and proper" to fulfill its responsibilities.

The Chief Justice of the Supreme Court was arch-Federalist John Marshall. He and his colleagues set forth two great constitutional principles in their decision. The first was the *supremacy of the national government* over the states. As long as the national government behaved in accordance with the Constitution, said the Court, its policies took precedence over state policies. Thus, federal laws or regulations, such as many civil rights acts and rules regulating hazardous substances, water quality, and clean air standards, *preempt* state and local laws or regulations, precluding their enforcement.

The Court also held that Congress *was* behaving consistently with the Constitution when it created the national bank. It was true, Marshall admitted, that Congress had certain **enumerated powers**, powers specifically listed in Article I, Section 8 of the Constitution. Congress could coin money, regulate its value, impose taxes, and so forth. Creating a bank was not enumerated. But the Constitution added that Congress has the power to "make all laws necessary and proper for carrying into execution the foregoing powers." That, said Marshall, gave Congress certain **implied powers**. It could make economic policy in a number of ways consistent with the Constitution. The other key principle of *McCulloch*, therefore, was that *the national government has certain implied powers that go beyond its enumerated powers.*

Today the notion of implied powers has become like a rubber band that can be stretched without breaking—the "necessary and proper" clause of the Constitution is often referred to as the **elastic clause**. Especially in the domain of economic policy, hundreds of congressional policies involve powers not specifically mentioned in the Constitution. Federal policies to regulate food and drugs, build interstate highways, protect consumers, try to clean up dirty air and water, and do many other things are all justified as implied powers of Congress.

The Constitution gives Congress the power to regulate interstate and international commerce. American courts have spent many years trying to define commerce. In 1824, the Supreme Court, in deciding the case of *Gibbons v. Ogden*, defined commerce very broadly, encompassing virtually every form of commercial activity. Today commerce covers not only the movement of goods, but also radio signals, electricity, telephone messages, insurance transactions, and much more.

The Supreme Court's decisions establishing the principles of the federal government's implied powers (*McCullouch v. Maryland*) and a broad definition of interstate commerce *(Gibbons v. Ogden)* created a source of national power—as long as Congress employed its power for economic development through subsidies and services for business interests. In the latter part of the nineteenth century, however, Congress sought to use these same powers to regulate the economy rather than promote it. The Court then interpreted the interstate commerce power as giving Congress no constitutional right to regulate local commercial activities such as establishing safe working conditions for laborers or protecting children from working long hours.

Beginning in 1933, the New Deal produced an avalanche of regulatory and social welfare legislation, much of which was voided by the Supreme Court (see Chapter 13). But in 1937 the Court reversed itself and ceased trying to restrict the efforts of the national government to regulate commerce at any level. In 1964, Congress even relied on the interstate commerce power to prohibit racial discrimination in places of public accommodation such as restaurants, hotels, and movie theaters. Thus, regulating commerce is one of the national government's most important sources of power.

Federalism as the Battleground of the Struggle for Equality.   What *McCulloch* pronounced constitutionally, the Civil War (1861–1865) settled militarily. The Civil War is often thought of as primarily a struggle over slavery. It was that, of course, but it was also, and perhaps more importantly, a struggle between states and the national government. In fact, Abraham Lincoln announced in his 1861 inaugural address that he would willingly support a constitutional amendment guaranteeing slavery if it would save the Union. Instead, it took a bloody civil war for the national government to assert its power over the Southern states' claim of sovereignty.

In 1963, Alabama Governor George Wallace made a dramatic stand at the University of Alabama to resist integration of the all-white school. Federal marshalls won this confrontation, and since then the federal government in general has been able to impose national standards of racial equality on the states.

A century later, conflict between the states and the national government again erupted over states' rights and national power. Again the policy issue was equality. In 1954, the Supreme Court held that school segregation was unconstitutional. Southern politicians responded with what they called "massive resistance" to the decision. When a federal judge ordered the admission of two black students to the University of Alabama in 1963, Governor George Wallace literally "stood in the schoolhouse door" to prevent federal marshalls and the students from entering the Admissions Office. Despite Wallace's efforts, the students were admitted, and throughout the 1960s the federal government enacted law after law and policy after policy to end segregation in schools, housing, public accommodations, voting, and jobs. The conflict between states and the national government over equality issues was decided in favor of the national government; national standards of racial equality prevailed.

States' Obligations to Each Other

Federalism involves more than relationships between the national government and state and local governments. The states must deal with each other as well, and the Constitution outlines certain obligations that each state has to every other state.

Full Faith and Credit.   Suppose that, like millions of other Americans, a person divorces and then remarries. For each marriage, this person purchases a marriage license, registering the marriage with a state. On the honeymoon for the second marriage, the person travels across the country. Is this person married in each state passed through, even though the marriage license is with only one state? Can the person be arrested for bigamy because the divorce occurred in only one state?

The answer, of course, is that a marriage license and a divorce, like a driver's license and a birth certificate, are valid in all states. Article IV of the Constitution requires that states give full faith and credit to the public acts, records, and civil judicial proceedings of every other state. This reciprocity is essential to the functioning of society and the economy. Without the **full faith and credit** clause, people could avoid their obligations to, say, make payments on automobile loans simply by crossing a state boundary. In addition, contracts between business firms can be enforced across state boundaries, allowing firms incorporated in one state to do business in another.

Extradition.   What about criminal penalties? Almost all criminal law is state law. If someone robs a store, steals a car, or commits a murder, the chances are that this person is breaking a state, not a federal, law. The Constitution says that states are required to return a person charged with a crime in another state to that state for trial or imprisonment. This practice is called **extradition**. Although there is no way to force states to comply, they usually are happy to do so, not wishing to harbor criminals and hoping that other states will reciprocate. This is why a lawbreaker cannot avoid punishment by simply escaping to another state.

Privileges and Immunities.   The most complicated obligation among the states is the requirement that citizens of each state receive all the **privileges and immunities** of any other state in which they happen to be. The goal of this constitutional provision is to prohibit states from discriminating against citizens of other states. If, for example, a Texan visits California, the Texan will pay the same sales tax and receive the same police protection as residents of California.

The states allow many exceptions to the privileges and immunities clause, however. Many readers of this book attend public universities. If you are such a student, and you also reside in the same state as your university, you usually pay a substantially lower tuition than do your fellow students from out of state. Similarly, only residents of a state can vote in state elections. States often attempt to pass the burdens of financing the state government to those outside the state such as in special taxes on tourists renting hotel rooms.

The Supreme Court has never clarified just which privileges a state must make available to all Americans, and which privileges can be limited to its own citizens. In general, the more fundamental the right—such as owning property or receiving police protection—the less likely it is that a state can discriminate against citizens of another state.

INTERGOVERNMENTAL RELATIONS TODAY

American federalism has changed quite a bit over the past two centuries. This section focuses first on the federal system's gradual change from a dual federalism to a cooperative federalism.[3] It then looks at the cornerstone of the relationship between the national government and state governments: federal grants-in-aid. Later, the chapter will explore the relative growth of the national government and state governments.

From Dual to Cooperative Federalism

One way to understand the changes in American federalism over the past 200 years is to contrast two types of federalism. The first type is called **dual federalism**. In this kind of federalism, states and the national government each remain supreme within their own spheres. The states are responsible for some policies, the national government for others. For example, the national government has exclusive control over foreign and military policy, the postal system, and monetary policy. States are exclusively responsible for schools, law enforcement, and road building. In dual federalism, the powers and policy assignments of the layers of government are distinct, as in a layer cake, and proponents of dual federalism believe that the powers of the national government should be interpreted narrowly.

Most politicians and political scientists today argue that dual federalism is outdated. They are more likely to describe the current American federal system as one of **cooperative federalism**. Instead of a layer cake, they see American federalism as more like a marble cake, with mingled responsibilities and blurred distinctions between the levels of government. In cooperative federalism, powers and policy assignments are shared between states and the national government.[4] Costs may be shared, with the national government and the states each paying a part. Administration may also be shared, with state and local officials working within federal guidelines. Sometimes even blame is shared when programs do not work well. Before the national government began to assert its dominance over state governments, the American federal system leaned toward dual federalism. The American system, however, was never neatly separated into purely state and purely national responsibilities. For example, education was usually thought of as being mainly a state

Cooperative federalism began in earnest during the Great Depression of the 1930s. In this photo, Works Progress Administration workers, paid by the federal government, build a local road in Tennessee. In subsequent decades the entire interstate highway system was constructed with a combination of national and state dollars.

and local responsibility, yet even under the Articles of Confederation, Congress set aside land in the Northwest Territory to be used for schools. During the Civil War, the national government adopted a policy to create land grant colleges. Important American universities like Wisconsin, Texas A & M, Illinois, Ohio State, North Carolina State, and Iowa State owe their origins to this national policy.

In the 1950s and 1960s, the national government began supporting public elementary and secondary education. In 1958, Congress passed the National Defense Education Act, which provided federal grants and loans for college students and financial support for elementary and secondary education in science and foreign language. In 1965, Congress passed the Elementary and Secondary Education Act, which provided federal aid to numerous schools. Although these policies expanded the national government's roll in education, they were not a sharp break with the past.

Today, the federal government's presence is felt in even the tiniest little red schoolhouse. Almost all school districts receive some federal assistance. To do so, they must comply with numerous federal rules and regulations. They must, for example, maintain desegregated and nondiscriminatory programs.

Cooperative federalism today rests on several standard operating procedures. For hundreds of programs, cooperative federalism involves the following:

Shared costs.   Washington foots part of the bill, but states or cities that want to get their share must pay part of a program's costs. Cities and states can get federal money for airport construction, sewage treatment plants, youth programs, and many other programs, but only if they pay some of the costs.

Federal guidelines.   Most federal grants to states and cities come with strings attached. Congress spends billions of dollars to support state highway construction, for example, but to get their share, states must adopt and enforce particular speed limits.

Shared administration.   State and local officials implement federal policies, but they have administrative powers of their own. The U.S. Department of Labor, for example, gives billions of dollars to states for job retraining, but states have considerable latitude in spending the money.

The cooperation between the national government and state government is such an established feature of American federalism that it takes place even when the two levels of government are in conflict on certain matters. For example, in the 1950s and 1960s southern states cooperated well with Washington in building the interstate highway system, while clashing with the national government over racial integration.

In his first inaugural address, Ronald Reagan argued that the states had primary responsibility for governing in most policy areas and promised to "restore the balance between levels of government." Few officials at either the state or national level agreed with him about ending the national government's role in domestic programs. However, Reagan's opposition to the national government's spending on domestic policies and the huge federal deficits of the 1980s forced a reduction in federal funds for state and local governments and shifted some responsibility for policy back to the states. Despite Reagan's move toward a more dual federalism, most Americans adopt a pragmatic view of governmental responsibilities, seeing the national government as more capable of—and thus responsible for—handling some issues, whereas state and local governments are better at managing others.

Fiscal Federalism

The cornerstone of the national government's relations with state and local governments is **fiscal federalism**: the pattern of spending, taxing, and providing grants in the federal system. Subnational governments can influence the national government through local elections for national officials, but the national government has a powerful source of influence over the states—

FIGURE 3.1 — Fiscal Federalism: Federal Grants to State and Local Governments, 1955–1995

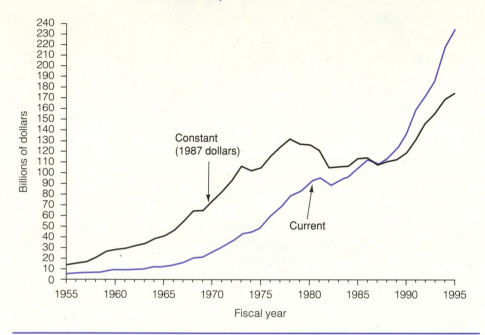

SOURCE: *Budget of the United States, Fiscal Year 1995. Historical Tables* (Washingtion, DC: Government Printing Office, 1994), 178–179.

money. Grants-in-aid are the main instrument the national government uses for both aiding and influencing states and localities.

Despite the efforts of the Reagan administration to whittle away aid to states and cities, state and local aid from Washington (including loan subsidies) still amounts to about $230 billion each year. Figure 3.1 illustrates the growth in the amount of money spent on federal grants. Federal aid, covering a wide range of policy areas (see Figure 3.2), accounts for more than one-fifth of all the funds spent by state and local governments and for about 15 percent of all federal government expenditures.

The Federal Grant System: Distributing the Federal Pie. There are two major types of federal aid for states and localities. **Categorical grants**, accounting for nearly 90 percent of all federal aid to state and local governments, are the main source of federal aid. These grants can be used only for one of 578 specific purposes, or categories, of state and local spending.

Because direct orders from the federal government to the states are rare (an exception is the Equal Opportunity Act of 1982, barring job discrimination by state and local governments), most federal regulation is accomplished in a more indirect manner. Instead of issuing stern edicts that tell citizens or states

FIGURE 3.2 — Functions of Federal Grants

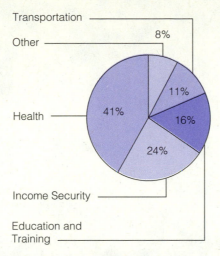

Transportation

Other

8%

11%

16%

Health 41%

24%

Income Security

Education and
Training

SOURCE: *Budget of the United States, Fiscal Year 1995, Analytical Perspectives* (Washington, DC: Government Printing Office, 1994), 169.

what they can and cannot do, Congress attaches conditions to the grants states receive. The federal government has been especially active in appending restrictions to grants since the 1970s.

One string commonly attached to categorical and other federal grants is a nondiscrimination provision, stating that aid may not be used for purposes that discriminate against minorities, women, or any other group. Another string, a favorite of labor unions, is that federal funds may not support construction projects that pay below the local union wage. Other restrictions may require an environmental impact statement for a federally-supported construction project or provisions for community involvement in the planning of the project.

The federal government may also employ *cross-over santions*—using federal dollars in one program to influence state and local policy in another. For example, funds may be withheld for highway construction unless states raise the drinking age to 21, establish highway beautification programs, or lower the speed limit to 55 miles per hour (or 65 in certain rural areas).

Cross-cutting requirements. These occur when a condition on one federal grant is extended to all activities supported by federal funds regardless of their source. The grandfather of these requirements is Title VI of the 1964 Civil Rights Act (see Chapter 4), which bars discrimination in the use of federal funds because of race, color, national origin, sex, or physical disability. For example, if a university discriminates in one program, such as athletics, it may lose the federal aid it receives for *all* its programs. There are also cross-cutting requirements dealing with environmental protection, historic preservation, contract wage

The federal government often uses grants-in-aid as a carrot and stick for the states. For example, aid has been withheld from some cities until police departments have been racially and sexually integrated.

rates, access to government information, the care of experimental animals, the treatment of human subjects in research projects, and numerous other policies.

There are two types of categorical grants. The most common type is a **project grant** (419 of the 578 categorical grants are project grants). A project grant is awarded on the basis of competitive applications. Grants obtained from the National Science Foundation by university professors are examples of project grants.

Formula grants are distributed, as their name implies, according to a formula (there are 159 formula grant programs). These formulas vary from grant to grant and may be computed on the basis of population, per capita income, percentage of rural population, or some other factor. A state or local government does not apply for a formula grant; a grant's formula determines how much money it will receive. As a result, Congress is the site of vigorous political battles over the formulas themselves. The most common formula grants are those for Medicaid, Aid for Families with Dependent Children, child nutrition programs, sewage treatment plant construction, public housing, community development programs, and training and employment programs.

Applications for categorical grants typically arrive in Washington in boxes, not envelopes. Complaints about the cumbersome paperwork and the many strings attached to categorical grants led to the adoption of the other major type of federal aid, **block grants**. These grants are given more or less automatically to states or communities, which have discretion in deciding how to spend the money. Block grants, first adopted in 1966, are used to support broad programs in areas like community development and social service. About 10 percent of all federal aid to state and community governments is in the form of block grants.

The Scramble for Federal Dollars.   With $230 billion at stake in federal grants, most states and many cities have set up full-time staffs in Washington. Their task is to keep track of what money is available and help their state or city get some of it. There are many Washington organizations of governments—the U.S. Conference of Mayors and the National League of Cities, for example—that act like other interest groups in lobbying Congress. Senators and representatives regularly go to the voters with stories of their influence in securing federal funds for their constituencies. They need continued support at the polls, they say, so that they will rise in seniority and get key posts to help "bring home the bacon."

A general rule of federalism is that, the more money at stake, the more people will argue about its distribution. There are some variations in the amount of money that states give to, and get back from, the national government. On the whole, though, federal grant distribution follows the principle of *universalism*—something for everybody. The vigilance of senators and representatives keeps federal aid reasonably well spread among the states. There are not many things in America—not income, access to education, or taxes—more equitably distributed than federal aid to states and cities.

This equality makes good politics, but it also may undermine public policy. Chapter 1 of the 1965 Elementary and Secondary Education Act is the federal government's principal endeavor to assist public schools. The primary intent of Chapter 1 was to give extra help to poor children. Yet the funds are allocated to 95 percent of all the school districts in the country. President Clinton's proposal to concentrate Chapter 1 funds on the poorest students failed when it ran into predictable opposition in Congress.

The Mandate Blues.   States and localities are usually pleased to receive aid from the national government, but there are times when they would just as soon not have it. For example, say Congress decides to extend a program administered by the states and funded, in part, by the national government. It passes a law requiring the states to extend the program if they want to keep receiving aid—which most states do. Congress usually (but not always) appropriates some funds to help pay for the new policy, but either way the states suddenly have to budget more funds for the project just to receive federal grant money.

Medicaid, which provides health care for poor people, is a prime example of a federal grant program that puts states in a difficult situation. Administered by the states, Medicaid receives wide support from both political parties. The national government pays about 55 percent of the bill, and the states pick up the rest. Since 1984, Congress has moved aggressively to expand Medicaid to specific populations, requiring the states to extend coverage to certain children, pregnant women, and elderly poor. Congress also increased its funding for the program a whopping 146 percent in the 1980s. Increased federal spending for Medicaid means increased spending for the states as well. In 1989, troubled by the drain on their states' budgets, forty-nine of the fifty governors called for a two-year moratorium on mandated expansions of Medicaid. In effect, they told Washington to keep its money and leave them alone for awhile.

A related problem arises when Congress passes a law creating financial obligations for the states but provides *no* funds to meet these obligations. For example, in 1990 Congress passed the Americans with Disabilities Act. States were required to make public facilities, such as state colleges and universities, accessible to individuals with disabilities, but were allocated no funds with which to implement the policy. Similarly, the Clean Air Act of 1970 establishes national air quality standards, but leaves implementation and administration of the standards up to the states.

Federal courts also create unfunded mandates for the states. In recent years, federal judges have issued states orders in areas such as prison construction and management, school desegregation, and facilities in mental health hospitals. These court orders often require states to spend funds to meet standards imposed by the judge.

Federal courts can order states to obey the Constitution or federal laws and treaties, but the Eleventh Amendment prohibits individual damage suits against state officials. Recently the Supreme Court has made it easier for citizens to control the behavior of local officials. The Court ruled that a federal law passed in 1871 to protect newly freed slaves also permits individuals to sue local governments for damages or seek injunctions against any local official acting in an official capacity whom they believe has deprived them of *any* right secured by the Constitution or by federal law.[5] Such suits are now common in the federal courts.

A combination of federal regulations and a lack of resources may also put the states in a bind. For example, the national government requires that a local housing authority must build or acquire a new apartment for each one it demolishes. Yet Congress has provided little money for the construction of public housing. As a result, a provision intended to help the poor by ensuring a stable supply of housing actually hurts them, as local governments are financially unable to replace unsafe and inadequate housing.

The federal government may also create financial obligations for the states unintentionally. In 1994, California, New York, Texas, Florida, and several other states sued the federal government for reimbursement for the cost of health care, education, prisons, and other public services that the states provide to illegal residents. The states charged that the federal government's failure to control its borders created huge new demands on their treasuries and that Washington, not the states, should pay for the problem.

In the past quarter century the national government has become more active in attaching conditions to federal grants-in-aid and directly regulating state and local governments through mandates. Thus, federalism continues to evolve and play a crucial role in American government.

UNDERSTANDING FEDERALISM

The federal system is central to politics, government, and policy in America. This book's themes of democracy and the scope of government are especially helpful in understanding federalism. Federalism has a particularly profound effect on democracy.

Federalism and Democracy

The founders established a federal system for several reasons, one of which was to allay the fears of those who believed that a powerful and distant central government would tyrannize the states and limit their voice in government. By decentralizing the political system, federalism was designed to contribute to democracy—or at least to the limited form of democracy supported by the founders. Has it done so?

Advantages for Democracy. Federalism has many implications for democracy. The more levels of government, the more opportunities there are for participation in politics. State governments provide thousands of elected offices for which citizens may vote or run.

Adding additional levels of government also contributes to democracy by increasing access to government. Because different citizens and interest groups will have better access to either state-level governments or the national government, the two levels increase the opportunities for government to be responsive to demands for policies. For example, in the 1950s and 1960s advocates of civil rights found themselves stymied in southern states, so they turned to the national level for help in achieving racial equality. Business interests, on the other hand, have traditionally found state governments to be more responsive to their demands. Organized labor is not well established in some states, but it can usually depend on some sympathetic officials at the national level who will champion its proposals.

Different economic interests are concentrated in different states: oil in Texas, tobacco farming in Virginia, and copper mining in Montana, for example. The federal system ensures that each state can establish a power base to promote its interests. James Madison, among others, valued this pluralism of interests within a large republic.

Because the federal system assigns states important responsibilities for public policies, it is possible for the diversity of opinion within the country to be reflected in different public policies among the states. If the citizens of Texas wish to have a death penalty, for example, they can vote for politicians who support it, whereas those in Wisconsin can vote to abolish the death penalty altogether.

IN FOCUS

The Downside of Diversity: Spending on Public Education

The downside of the public-policy diversity fostered by federalism is that states are largely dependent on their own resources for providing public services; these resources vary widely from state to state. This table shows the wide variation among the states in the money spent on each child in the public schools.

State	Dollars per Pupil				
Alabama	3,675	Florida	5,639	Maine	5,969
Alaska	9,248	Georgia	4,720	Maryland	6,273
Arizona	4,750	Hawaii	5,453	Massachusetts	6,323
Arkansas	3,770	Idaho	3,528	Michigan	5,630
California	4,686	Illinois	5,248	Minnesota	5,510
Colorado	5,259	Indiana	5,429	Mississippi	3,344
Connecticut	8,299	Iowa	4,949	Missouri	4,534
Delaware	6,080	Kansas	5,131	Montana	5,127
District of Columbia	8,116	Kentucky	4,616	Nebraska	4,676
		Louisiana	4,378	Nevada	4,910
				New Hampshire	5,500
				New Jersey	10,219
				New Mexico	4,692
				New York	8,658
				North Carolina	4,857
				North Dakota	4,119

State	Dollars per Pupil
Ohio	5,451
Oklahoma	3,939
Oregon	5,972
Pennsylvania	6,980
Rhode Island	6,834
South Carolina	4,537
South Dakota	4,255
Tennessee	3,736
Texas	4,651
Utah	3,092
Vermont	6,992
Virginia	5,487
Washington	5,331
West Virginia	5,415
Wisconsin	5,972
Wyoming	5,333
1992 Average:	**5,466**

SOURCE: U.S. Department of Commerce, *Statistical Abstract of the United States, 1993* (Washington DC: U.S. Government Printing Office, 1993), 164.

By handling most disputes over policy at the state and local level, federalism also reduces decision making and conflict at the national level. If every issue had to be resolved in Washington, the national government would be overwhelmed.

Disadvantages for Democracy.   On the other hand, relying on the states to supply public services has some drawbacks. States differ in the resources they can devote to services like public education (see "In Focus: The Downside of Diversity"). Thus, the quality of education a child receives is heavily dependent on the state in which the child's parents happen to reside. For instance, in 1992 New Jersey state and local governments spent an average of $10,219 for each child in the public schools; in Utah the figure was only $3,092.

Diversity in policy can also discourage states from providing services that would otherwise be available. Political scientists have found that generous welfare benefits can strain a state's treasury by attracting poor people from states with lower benefits. As a result, states are deterred from providing generous benefits to those in need. A national program with uniform welfare benefits, however, would provide no incentive for welfare recipients to move to

TABLE 3.2 — How Many American Governments Are There?

National government	1
State governments	50
Local governments	86,692
Counties	3,043
Municipalities	19,296
Townships	16,666
School districts	14,556
Special districts	33,131
TOTAL	*86,743*

SOURCE: U.S. Bureau of the Census, *1992 Census of Governments* (Washington DC: U.S. Government Printing Office, 1992).

another state in search of higher benefits.[6] Federalism may also have a negative effect on democracy insofar as local interests are able to thwart national majority support of certain policies. As discussed earlier in this chapter, in the 1960s the states, especially those in the South, became battlegrounds when the national government tried to enforce national civil rights laws and court decisions. Because state and local governments were responsible for public education and voting eligibility, for example, and because they had passed most of the laws supporting racial segregation, federalism itself complicated and delayed efforts to end racial discrimination.

Finally, the sheer number of governments in the United States is, at times, as much a burden as a boon to democracy. Program vendors say at baseball games that "you can't tell the players without a scorecard"; unfortunately, scorecards are not available for local governments, where the players are numerous and sometimes seem to be involved in different games. The U.S. Bureau of the Census counts not only people but also governments. Its latest count revealed an astonishing 86,743 American governments (see Table 3.2).

Certainly nearly 87,000 governments ought to be enough for any country. Are there too many? Americans speak eloquently about their state and local governments as grass-roots governments, close to the people. Yet having so many governments makes it difficult to know which governments are doing what. Exercising democratic control over them is even more difficult; Americans participate in local elections at about half the already low rate in which they participate in presidential elections.

Federalism and the Growing Scope of the National Government

President Ronald Reagan negotiated quotas on imports of Japanese cars in order to give advantages to the American auto industry, raising the price of all automobiles in the process. At the behest of steel companies, President George Bush exercised his authority to continue Reagan's quotas on the amount of steel that could be imported into the country (thereby making steel products more expensive). The first major piece of legislation the Bush administration sent to Congress was a bail-out plan for the savings and loan industry, which had gotten itself into financial trouble through a combination of imprudent loans, incompetence, and corruption. Bill Clinton proposed to have the Pentagon spend nearly $600 million to fund the development of a U.S. industry in "flat-panel displays" used for lap-top computers, video games, and advanced instruments.

In each of these cases and dozens of others, the national government has involved itself (some might say interfered) in the economic marketplace with quotas and subsidies intended to help American businesses. As Chapter 2 explained, the national government took a direct interest in economic affairs from the very founding of the republic. As the United States changed from an agricultural to an industrial nation, new problems arose and, with them, new demands for governmental action. The national government responded with a national banking system, subsidies for railroads and airlines, and a host of other policies that dramatically increased its role in the economy.

The industrialization of the country raised other issues as well. With the formation of large corporations—Cornelius Vanderbilt's New York Central Railroad or John D. Rockefeller's Standard Oil Company, for example—came the potential for such abuses as monopoly pricing. If there is only one railroad in town, it can charge farmers inflated prices to ship their grain to market; if a single company distributes most of the gasoline in the country, it can set the price at which gasoline sells. Thus, many interests asked the national government to restrain monopolies and encourage open competition.

There were additional demands on the national government for new public policies. Farming interests sought services such as agricultural research, rural electrification, and price supports. Labor interests wanted the national government to protect their rights to organize and bargain collectively and help provide safer working conditions, a minimum wage, and pension protection. Along with others, labor unions supported a wide range of social welfare policies, from education to health care. As the country became more urbanized, new problems arose in the areas of housing, welfare, the environment, and transportation. In each case, the relevant interest turned to the national government for help.

Why not turn to the state governments instead? In most cases, the answer is simple: a problem or policy requires the authority and resources of the national government. The Constitution forbids states from having independent defense policies, but even if it did not, would states want to take on a responsibility that represents more than half of the federal work force and about one-sixth of federal expenditures?

It is constitutionally permissible but not sensible for the states to handle a wide range of other issues. It makes little sense for Louisiana to pass strict controls on polluting the Mississippi River if most of the river's pollution occurs

FIGURE 3.3 — Fiscal Federalism: The Public Sector and the Federal System

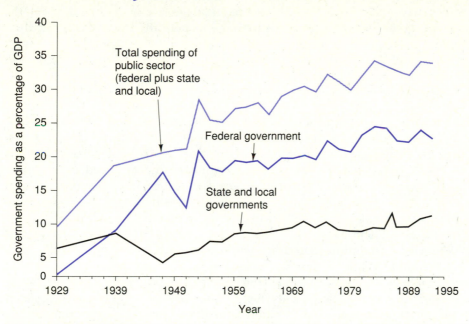

SOURCE: *Budget of the United States, Fiscal Year 1995, Historical Tables* (Washington, DC: Government Printing Office, 1994), 178–179.

upstream, where Louisiana has no jurisdiction. Rhode Island has no incentive to create an energy policy, since there are no energy reserves located in the state. Similarly, how effectively can a state regulate an international conglomerate such as General Motors? How can each state, acting individually, manage the nation's money supply?

Each state could have its own space program, but it is much more efficient if the states combine their efforts in one national program. The largest category of federal expenditures is for economic security, including the Social Security program. Although each state could have its own retirement program, how could state governments determine which state should pay for retirees who move to Florida or Arizona? A national program is the only feasible method of insuring the incomes of the mobile elderly in today's society.

The national government's growth is illustrated in Figure 3.3. The figure shows that the national government's share of American governmental expenditures has grown rapidly since 1929. Then, the national government spent only 2.5 percent of our gross domestic product; today it spends more than a fifth of our GDP. The proportion of our GDP spent by state and local governments has grown less rapidly than the national government's share. States and localities spent 7.4 percent of our GDP in 1929; they spend 12 percent today.

Figure 3.3 demonstrates that the states have not been supplanted by the national government; indeed, they carry out virtually all the functions they always have. Instead, with the support of the American people, new responsibilities have been taken on by the national government. In addition, the national government has added programs to help the states carry out their own responsibilities.

SUMMARY

Federalism is a governmental system in which power is shared between a central government and other governments. Federalism is much less common than the unitary governments typical of most parliamentary democracies. American federalism consists of fifty state governments joined in an "indestructible union," (as the Supreme Court once called it) under one national government. Today, federal power over the states is indisputable; the Supreme Court case *McCulloch v. Maryland* helped determine national supremacy. The federal government has recently used its fiscal leverage to impose speed limits of 55 miles per hour and discourage teenage drinking in the states.

The United States has moved from a system of dual federalism to one of cooperative federalism, in which the national and state governments share responsibility for public policies. Fiscal federalism is of great help to states; even after the Reagan administration reductions, the federal government distributes about $230 billion in federal funds to states and cities each year.

Federalism was instituted largely to enhance democracy in America, and it strengthens democratic government in many ways. At the same time, diverse state policies and the sheer number of local governments cause some problems as well. Demands for new policies and the necessity for national policy on certain issues have contributed to the growth of the national government relative to the state governments, but the state governments can continue to play a central role in the lives of Americans.

Although American federalism is about state power and national power, it is not a concept removed from most Americans' lives. Federalism affects a vast range of social and economic policies. Slavery, school desegregation, abortion, teenage drinking, and even "secular humanism" have all been debated in terms of federalism.

FOR FURTHER READING

Anton, Thomas. *American Federalism and Public Policy*. Philadelphia: Temple University Press, 1989. An overview of how the national, state, and local governments share responsibility for policies.

Browning, Rufus P., Dale Rogers Marshall, and David H. Tabb. *Protest Is Not Enough*. Berkeley, CA: University of California Press, 1984. A study of ten California cities and the role played by federal programs in enhancing minority political power.

Conlan, Timothy J. *New Federalism: Intergovernmental Reform from Nixon to Reagan.* Washington, DC: Brookings Institution, 1988. An analysis of the efforts of Presidents Nixon and Reagan to restructure intergovernmental relations.

Elazar, Daniel J. *American Federalism: A View from the States,* 3rd ed. New York: Harper & Row, 1984. A well-known work surveying federalism from the standpoint of state governments.

Kettl, Donald F. *The Regulation of American Federalism.* Baltimore: Johns Hopkins University Press, 1987. Examines the regulations that national government imposes on state and local governments.

Nathan, Richard P., and Fred C. Doolittle. *Reagan and the States.* Princeton, NJ: Princeton University Press, 1987. A study of the effects of the Reagan administration's budgetary cuts on state governments.

Riker, William. *Federalism.* Boston: Little, Brown, 1964. A highly critical account of American federalism.

Walker, David B. *Toward a Functioning Federalism.* Cambridge, MA: Winthrop, 1981. A concise history of American federalism, with some blueprints for improvement.

Wright, Deil S. *Understanding Intergovernmental Relations,* 3rd ed. Belmont, CA: Brooks/Cole, 1988. A review of the relations between the local, state, and national levels of government.

NOTES

1. One useful introduction to federalism and intergovernmental relations is Deil S. Wright, *Understanding Intergovernmental Relations,* 3rd ed. (Belmont, CA: Brooks/Cole, 1988).
2. On the states as innovators, see Jack L. Walker, "The Diffusion of Innovations in the American States," *American Political Science Review* 63 (September 1969): 880–899; Richard P. Nathan and Fred C. Doolittle, *Reagan and the States* (Princeton, NJ: Princeton University Press, 1987).
3. The transformation from dual to cooperative federalism is described in David B. Walker, *Toward a Functioning Federalism* (Cambridge, MA: Winthrop, 1981), chapter 3.
4. The classic discussion of cooperative federalism is found in Morton Grodzins, *The American System: A New View of Governments in the United States,* ed. Daniel J. Elazar (Chicago: Rand McNally, 1966).
5. *Monroe v. Pape,* 1961; *Monell v. New York City Department of Social Welfare,* 1978; *Owen v. Independence,* 1980; *Maine v. Thiboutot,* 1980; *Oklahoma City v. Tuttle,* 1985; *Dennis v. Higgins,* 1991.
6. Paul E. Peterson and Mark Rom, "American Federalism, Welfare Policy, and Residential Choices," *American Political Science Review* 83 (September 1989): 711–728.

At about 1:00 A.M. on April 26, 1989, in the Rush-Presbyterian Hospital, one of Chicago's largest, Rudy and Tammy Linares went to visit their infant son. He had been in an irreversible coma for more than six months after he choked on a piece of birthday balloon and had become brain damaged. His parents had rushed him to the hospital, where doctors were convinced he would die. On that April night, Mr. Linares hid a .357 Magnum under his coat. Each of the parents held Sammy. Then, after his wife had left the hospital room, Mr. Linares unhooked the respirator from his baby, ordered the nurses out of the room, and held the baby until he died. A grand jury in Cook County, Illinois, refused to indict him for the crime.[1] Mr. Linares' case illustrates one of the murkiest areas of American constitutional law: what to do when two values of society collide, in this case the right of the parents to make decisions about their children and the right of all to life. The case of Mr. Linares illustrates one other important fact: Whatever our values, beliefs, and opinions, we still proceed—we think and hope—by an orderly set of rules governing our behavior.

In fact, the Chicago baby case is an exception in some important ways. The vast majority of cases involving civil liberties and civil rights are pretty much open and shut. The brutal, public murder of Mr. A by Mr. B in the corner tavern does not have many subtleties. Despite the pleas of the defendants, they rarely rise beyond the level of the trial court. And yet constitutional protections extend not only to Mr. Linares, but to the Mr. A who so publicly and visibly murdered Mr. B. When Employer Q announces to Ms. P that "we don't put women into top management jobs around here," this violation of civil rights is just as straightforward. For the most part, the cases involving our civil liberties and civil rights are grim, unpleasant, and yet routine. What makes the constitutional law important, then, is what happens when things are complicated.

This chapter about civil liberties and civil rights is filled with saints and sinners, and ordinary people, too. It will introduce you to some individuals involved in the legal process, caught up in issues that eventually make legal history. You will meet some heroes of the civil rights movements, men and women who sought courageously to extend rights to others. You will also meet some unsavory characters in this chapter. One of the civil liberties most widely known to Americans—at least those who watch cop shows—is the right to be informed of your rights upon arrest. A convicted killer and rapist named Ernesto Miranda gave his name to one of the most famous cases in American legal history, *Miranda v. Arizona.* As a result of the *Miranda* case, police now routinely deliver "Miranda warnings" to arrestees ("You have the right to remain silent. . . ."). In one of those ironic twists of fate, when Ernesto Miranda was murdered, the suspect was promptly read his "Miranda warning."

Broadly, there are twin thrusts to this chapter, joined together like the strands of a double helix. They are civil liberties and civil rights. **Civil liberties** are individual legal and constitutional protections against the government. There are two broad areas of civil liberties protections: the great *political freedoms* (mostly found in the First Amendment), which protect our political liberties; and *protections at the bar of justice,* which protect both political and (more likely these days) criminal defendants. Because the Supreme Court ultimately interprets our Constitution, disputes about where government's power ends, and your liberties begin, are vital constitutional questions. Can you start up a newspaper and print vicious things about African Americans, or Filipinos, or Hispanics? If you do, can representatives of those groups protest in front of your building and block access to your employees or your suppliers? If you are arrested for some offense, can the government keep you in jail without charging you for an hour, a day, a week? Could it search your personal belongings to collect evidence against you?

Civil rights, sometimes confused with civil liberties, are policies that protect persons against arbitrary or discriminatory treatment by government or individuals. In the United States, civil rights policies have focused on extending basic rights to groups historically subject to discrimination, providing equality under the Constitution. Throughout our history, African Americans, other minorities, and women have raised constitutional questions about slavery, segregation, equal rights to vote, equal pay, and a host of other issues. Today, debates about equality typically center on these key types of inequality in America:

- *Racial discrimination.*   Two centuries of discrimination against racial minorities have produced historic Supreme Court and congressional policies that eliminate racial discrimination from the constitutional fabric. Issues such as the appropriate role of affirmative action programs have yet to be resolved, however.

- *Sexual discrimination.* The place of women in society is changing, and women's groups want their rights constitutionally guaranteed.
- *Discrimination based on age, disability, and other factors.* As America has "grayed," older Americans, too, have sought a place under the civil rights umbrella. Disabled Americans are among the newest claimants for a rightful place there. Also seeking constitutional protections against discrimination are groups such as gays, AIDS victims, and the homeless.

Throughout this chapter, you will find special features entitled "You Are the Judge." Each feature describes an actual case brought before the courts and asks you to evaluate the case and render a judgment about it. Although you certainly do not have as much legal background as a judge, your sense of fairness and your ethical standards—very much embedded in our constitutional system—are as reliable as a judge's. Try your hand at deciding these cases. The actual court decisions are collected at the end of the chapter in a feature entitled "The Court Decides" (page 117).

The basis for understanding American civil liberties, and some of the basis for American civil rights, is found in the Bill of Rights.

THE BILL OF RIGHTS—THEN AND NOW

Although the Constitution of 1787 contained no Bill of Rights, all the states had them in their own constitutions; some of these have survived intact to this day. Many states made it clear that a condition of ratification was the adoption of a Bill of Rights by the first Congress, which it promptly did. Thus, we call the first ten Amendments to the Constitution the **Bill of Rights** (see "In Focus: The Bill of Rights"). It assures Americans basic liberties: freedom of speech and religion, freedom from arbitrary searches and seizures, and so forth. As you read it, pay particular attention to the **First Amendment,** the source of our great freedoms of speech, press, religion, and assembly. Political scientists have discovered that Americans are great believers in all of these noble principles, at least up to a point. Generally, Americans are believers in the principle of free speech, for example, but not of the right of someone to teach socialism in the public schools or of the Ku Klux Klan to speak in their neighborhoods.[2]

Rights in Conflict: Hard Cases

Some cases involving civil liberties are easy to decide. Say that a police officer, looking for a burglar, kicks in your door, grabs you, searches you, hauls you to the police station, refuses to let you call your lawyer, and then puts you in a cell for weeks with no prospect for bail or a hearing. You might want to scour the Bill of Rights again to see how many of your rights have just been violated.

IN FOCUS

The Bill of Rights

(These amendments were passed by Congress on September 25, 1789, and ratified by the states on December 15, 1791.)

AMENDMENT I—RELIGION, SPEECH, ASSEMBLY, PETITION

Congress shall make no law respecting an establishment of religion, or prohibiting the free exercise thereof; or abridging the freedom of speech, or of the press; or the right of the people peaceably to assemble, and to petition the Government for a redress of grievances.

AMENDMENT II—RIGHT TO BEAR ARMS

A well regulated militia, being necessary to the security of a free State, the right of the people to keep and bear arms, shall not be infringed.

AMENDMENT III—QUARTERING OF SOLDIERS

No Soldier shall, in time of peace be quartered in any house, without the consent of the owner, nor in time of war, but in a manner to be prescribed by law.

AMENDMENT IV—SEARCHES AND SEIZURES

The right of the people to be secure in their persons, houses, papers, and effects, against unreasonable searches and seizures, shall not be violated, and no warrants shall issue, but upon probable cause, supported by oath or affirmation, and particularly describing the place to be searched, and the persons or things to be seized.

AMENDMENT V—GRAND JURIES, DOUBLE JEOPARDY, SELF-INCRIMINATION, DUE PROCESS, EMINENT DOMAIN

No person shall be held to answer for a capital, or otherwise infamous crime, unless on a presentment or indictment of a Grand Jury, except in cases arising in the land or naval forces, or in the militia, when in actual service in time of war or public danger; nor shall any person be subject for the same offense to be twice put in jeopardy of life or limb; nor shall

be compelled in any criminal case to be a witness against himself, nor be deprived of life, liberty, or property, without due process of law; nor shall private property be taken for public use, without just compensation.

AMENDMENT VI—CRIMINAL COURT PROCEDURES

In all criminal prosecutions, the accused shall enjoy the right to a speedy and public trial, by an impartial jury of the State and district wherein the crime shall have been committed, which district shall have been previously ascertained by law, and to be informed of the nature and cause of the accusation; to be confronted with the witnesses against him; to have compulsory process for obtaining witnesses in his favor, and to have the assistance of counsel for his defense.

AMENDMENT VII—TRIAL BY JURY IN COMMON-LAW CASES

In Suits at common law, where the value in controversy shall exceed twenty dollars, the right of trial by jury shall be preserved, and no fact tried by a jury shall be otherwise reexamined in any Court of the United States, than according to the rules of the common law.

AMENDMENT VIII—BAILS, FINES AND PUNISHMENT

Excessive bail shall not be required, nor excessive fines imposed, nor cruel and unusual punishment inflicted.

AMENDMENT IX—RIGHTS RETAINED BY THE PEOPLE

The enumeration in the Constitution, of certain rights, shall not be construed to deny or disparage others retained by the people.

AMENDMENT X—RIGHTS RESERVED TO THE STATES

The powers not delegated to the United States by the Constitution, nor prohibited by it to the States, are reserved to the States respectively, or to the people.

Even when it seems that one or more of our civil liberties are pummeled and stretched to the breaking point, however, others may disagree. Most Americans were appalled by the videotaped scenes of Rodney King being beaten by a group of Los Angeles police officers after they stopped him following a high-speed chase in the spring of 1991. Yet a California jury failed to convict any of the officers, and that acquittal was followed by large-scale riots in Los Angeles. (A second trial did end in the conviction of some of the officers.)

Even more difficult are those cases in which liberties are in conflict—free press versus a fair trail or free speech versus public order, for example—or where the facts and interpretations are subtle and ambiguous. These are the sorts of cases we address in this chapter.

The Bill of Rights and the States

Note the first words of the First Amendment: "Congress shall make no law...." The Bill of Rights was written to protect against the new, powerful national government. A literal reading would thus permit the *states* to pass laws establishing a religion, prohibiting freedom of speech, and so on. What happens, then, if a state passes a law violating one of the rights protected by the federal Bill of Rights and the state's constitution does not prohibit this abridgement of freedom? In 1833, the answer was simple: nothing. In that year, the Supreme Court, under Chief Justice John Marshall, decided a Maryland case involving a man named Barron, who had claimed that the state had taken his property "without due process of law." The Bill of Rights, said the Court in *Barron v. Baltimore*, restrained only the national government, not states and cities.

Nearly a century later, however, the Court ruled that a state government should respect at least some First Amendment rights. In the 1925 case of *Gitlow v. New York*, the Court first held that the **Fourteenth Amendment** made parts of the Bill of Rights applicable to the states. Ratified in 1868 as one of the three post–Civil War amendments, the Fourteenth Amendment declared the following:

> No state shall make or enforce any law which shall abridge the privileges or immunities of citizens of the United States nor shall any state deprive any person of life, liberty, or property, without due process of law; nor deny to any person within its jurisdiction equal protection of the laws.

The meaning of the Fourteenth Amendment is thus crucial in this interpretation. One way of reading it is that it was meant to take the whole of the Bill of Rights and apply it to the states (but if it meant that, critics said, why didn't it simply say so?). Thus, ever since 1925, the Supreme Court has engaged in what some constitutional scholars have called *selective incorporation*—the piece-by-piece application of the Bill of Rights to the states. Especially during the time of Supreme Court Chief Justice Earl Warren in the

TABLE 4.1 — The Nationalization of the Bill of Rights

Date	Right	Case
1925	Freedom of Speech	Gitlow v. New York
1931	Freedom of the Press	Near v. Minnesota
1932	Right to Counsel in Capital Cases	Powell v. Alabama
1937	Freedom of Assembly	De Jonge v. Oregon
1940	Free Exercise of Religion	Cantwell v. Connecticut
1947	Separation of Church and State	Everson v. Board of Education
1948	Right to Public Trial	In re Oliver
1949	Right Against Unreasonable Searches and Seizures	Wolf v. Colorado
1958	Freedom of Association	NAACP v. Alabama
1961	Exclusionary Rule	Mapp v. Ohio
1962	Right Against Cruel and Unusual Punishment	Robinson v. California
1963	Right to Counsel in Felony Cases	Gideon v. Wainwright
1964	Immunity from Self-incrimination	Mallory v. Hogan
1965	Right of Privacy	Griswold v. Connecticut
1965	Right of Confrontation of Witnesses	Pointer v. Texas
1966	Right to Impartial Jury	Parker v. Gladden
1967	Right to Speedy Trial	Klopfer v. North Carolina
1967	Right to Compulsory Process for Obtaining Witnesses	Washington v. Texas
1968	Right to Jury Trial for Serious Crimes	Duncan v. Louisiana
1969	Immunity from Double Jeopardy	Benton v. Maryland
1972	Right to Counsel for All Crimes Involving Jail Terms	Argersinger v. Hamlin

1950s and 1960s, elements of the Bill of Rights were selectively applied to the states (see Table 4.1).

Today, for all practical purposes, the Bill of Rights guarantees individual freedom against infringement by state and local governments as well as by the national government. Only the Second, Third, and Seventh Amendments and the grand jury requirement of the Fifth Amendment have not been applied specifically to the states.

Now that we have seen that, with few exceptions, the great freedoms and protections at the bar of justice contained in the Bill of Rights apply to both Washington and your local police force, let us look at them in detail.

THE FIRST AMENDMENT FREEDOMS

Freedom of Religion

The First Amendment says not one but two things about religious freedom. These are commonly referred to as the establishment clause and the free exercise clause. The **establishment clause** says that "Congress shall make no law respecting an establishment of religion." The **free exercise clause** prohibits the abridgement of the citizens' freedom to worship, or not to worship, as they please.

The Establishment Clause. Some nations have an established church that is officially supported by the government and recognized as a national institution such as the church of England in Great Britain. A few American colonies had official churches, but the religious persecutions that incited many colonists to move to America discouraged any desire for the first Congress to establish a national church in the United States. Thus, established religion is prohibited by the First Amendment.

It is much less clear, however, what else the first Congress intended to be included in the establishment clause. Some people argued that the clause prevented the government from favoring one religion over another. In contrast, Thomas Jefferson argued that the First Amendment created a "wall of separation" between church and state, forbidding not just favoritism but any support for religion at all. These interpretations continue to provoke argument, especially when religion is mixed with education.

Debate is especially intense over aid to church-related schools and prayers in the public schools. Proponents of *parochiaid* (short for "aid to parochial schools"), which has existed in various forms since the 1960s, argue that government funding does not favor any particular religion. Opponents claim that the Roman Catholic Church has by far the largest religious school system in the country and gets most of the aid. In *Lemon v. Kurtzman* (1971) the Supreme Court declared that aid to church-related schools must have a secular legislative purpose, cannot be used to advance or inhibit religion, and should avoid excessive government "entanglement" with religion.

There is a fine line between federal aid that is permissible and federal aid that is not. For instance, the Court has allowed parochial schools to use federal funds to build buildings, buy textbooks, provide student lunches, transport students to and from school, and subsidize off-campus testing services. Federal funds cannot, however, pay for teachers' salaries, tape recorders, or transportation for students on field trips. The theory underlying these decisions is that it is possible to determine that buildings, textbooks, lunches, school buses, and national tests are not used to support sectarian education, but that it requires complex and constitutionally impermissible regulation of religion to ascertain how teachers handle a subject in class, use equipment, and/or focus a field trip.

Controversy over aid to schools is not limited to Roman Catholic schools. In 1994 (*Kiryas Joel v. Grumet*), the Supreme Court ruled that New York state had gone too far in favoring religion when it created a public school district for the benefit of a village of Hasidic Jews.

At the same time, the Supreme Court has been opening public schools to religious activities. The Court decided that public universities that permit student groups to use their facilities must allow student religious groups on campus to use the facilities for religious worship (*Widmar v. Vincent*, 1981). In the 1984 Equal Access Act, Congress made it unlawful for any public high school receiving federal funds (almost all of which do) to keep student groups from using school facilities for religious worship if the school opens its facilities for other student meetings (the Court upheld this law in *Westside Community Schools v. Mergens*, 1990). Similarly, in *Lamb's Chapel v. Center Moriches Union Free School* (1993), the Court required public schools that rent facilities to organizations to do the same for religious groups.

The threshold of constitutional acceptability becomes higher when public funds may be used more directly to support religious education. Thus, school authorities may not permit religious instructors to enter the public school buildings during the school day to provide religious education (*Illinois ex rel McCollum v. Board of Education*, 1948)—although they may release students from part of the compulsory school day so they can receive religious instruction (*Zorach v. Clauson*, 1952).

School prayer is one issue that remains more controversial than just about any other religious issue. In 1962 and 1963 the Court aroused the wrath of many Americans by ruling that voluntary recitations of prayers or Bible passages, when done as part of classroom exercises in public schools, violated the establishment clause. *Engel v. Vitale* and *School District of Abington Township, Pennsylvania v. Schempp* observed that "the place of religion in our society is an exalted one, but in the relationship between man and religion, the State is firmly committed to a position of neutrality." In 1980 the Court also prohibited the posting of the Ten Commandments on the walls of public classrooms (*Stone v. Graham*).

It is not, however, unconstitutional to pray in public schools. Students may pray silently as much as they wish. What the Constitution forbids is the sponsorship or encouragement of prayer, directly or indirectly, by public school authorities. Thus, in 1992 in *Lee v. Weisman* the Court ruled that a school-sponsored prayer at a public-school graduation violated the constitutional separation of church and state. Three Alabama laws—passed in 1978, 1981, and 1982—authorized schools to hold one-minute periods of silence for "meditation or voluntary prayer," but the Court rejected this approach in *Wallace v. Jaffree* (1985) because the state made it clear that the purpose of the statute was to return prayer to the schools. However, the Court indicated that a less clumsy approach would be acceptable.

Political scientist Kenneth D. Wald observes that the last few years have been marked by great ferment in the relationship between religion and American political life. Religious issues and controversies have assumed much greater importance in political debate than they had commanded previously.[3] Much of this new importance is due to fundamentalist religious groups that have spurred their members to political action. Some religious groups have pushed for a constitutional amendment permitting school prayer, while many school districts have simply ignored the decision and continue to allow prayers in their classrooms. The public remains divided on the issue.

The debate over what information should be taught in the public education system is another source of conflict. Fundamentalist Christian groups have pressed some state legislatures to mandate the teaching of "creation science"—their alternative to Darwinian theories of evolution—in public schools. Louisiana, for example, passed a Balanced Treatment Act requiring schools that taught Darwinian theory to teach creation science, too. Regardless, the Supreme Court ruled in *Edwards v. Aguillard* (1987) that this law violated the establishment clause. The Court also held (in *Epperson v. Arkansas,* 1968) that states cannot prohibit Darwin's theory of evolution from being taught in the public schools.

The Supreme Court, then, has struggled with interpreting the establishment clause. In 1984 the Court found that Pawtucket, Rhode Island, could set up a Christmas nativity scene on public property (*Lynch v. Donelly*). Five years later, in *County of Allegheny v. American Civil Liberties Union* (1989), the Court extended the principle to a Hanukkah menorah. The Court concluded that these displays had a secular purpose and provided little or no benefit to religion.

In *Lynch,* the Court said the Constitution does not require complete separation of church and state; it mandates accommodation of all religions and forbids hostility toward any. At the same time, the Constitution forbids government endorsement of religious beliefs. Drawing the line between neutrality toward religion and promotion of it is not easy, and issues regarding the establishment of religion are likely to endure for some time.

The Free Exercise Clause.   The First Amendment also guarantees the free exercise of religion. This guarantee seems simple enough at first glance. Whether people hold no religious beliefs, go to church or temple, or practice voodoo, they have the right to practice religion as they choose. The matter is, of course, more complicated. Religions sometimes forbid actions that society thinks are necessary; or, conversely, religions require actions that society finds disruptive. For example, what if somebody's religion justifies multiple marriages or using illegal drugs? Muhammad Ali, the boxing champion, refused induction into the armed services during the Vietnam War because, he said, military service would violate his Muslim faith. Amish parents often refuse to send their children to public schools. Jehovah's Witnesses and Christian Scientists may refuse to accept certain kinds of medical treatment for themselves or for their children.

Consistently maintaining that people have an inviolable right to *believe* what they want, the courts have been more cautious about the right to *practice* a belief. What if, the Supreme Court once asked, a person "believed that human sacrifices were a necessary part of religious worship?" In *Employment Division v. Smith* (1990) the Court decided that state laws interfering with religious practices but not specifically aimed at religion are constitutional. Aside from the specific area of denying people unemployment compensation, as long as a law does not single out and ban religious practices because they are engaged in for religious reasons, or only because of the religious belief they display, a general law may be applied to conduct even if it is religiously inspired. In *Smith*, the state of Oregon was allowed to prosecute persons who used the drug peyote as part of their religious rituals.

Even before this decision, the Supreme Court had never permitted religious freedom to be an excuse for any behavior. The court had upheld laws and regulations forbidding polygamy, outlawing business activities on Sunday as applied to Orthodox Jews, denying tax exemptions to religious schools that discriminate on the basis of race, and constructing a road through ground sacred to some Native Americans. You can see what happened in another case involving religious practice in "You Are the Judge: Can the Air Force Make Captain Goldman Remove His Yarmulke?"

The Court did, however, allow Amish parents to take their children out of school after the eighth grade. Reasoning that the Amish community was well established and that its children would not burden the state, *Wisconsin v. Yoder* (1972) held that religious freedom took precedence over compulsory education laws. More broadly, a state can compel parents to send their children to an accredited school, yet parents have a right to choose a religious school rather than public schools for their children's education. Extending this religious freedom further, a state may not require Jehovah's Witnesses or members of other religions to participate in public school flag-saluting ceremonies, and in 1993 the Court overturned a city ordinance that prohibited the use of animal sacrifice in religious ritual.

In the Religious Freedom Restoration Act of 1993, Congress attempted to overturn the principle the Court articulated in *Smith*. This law conferred on all

YOU ARE THE JUDGE

Can the Air Force Make Captain Goldman Remove His Yarmulke?

Captain S. Simcha Goldman was an orthodox Jewish Rabbi and an Air Force captain. He served as a clinical psychologist for the Air Force. Being an orthodox Jew, it was Goldman's custom to wear a yarmulke, a small skullcap traditionally worn by orthodox Jewish males. The Air Force had a problem; an Air Force regulation (A.F.R. 35-10) required that "Air Force members will wear the Air Force uniform while performing their military duties" and stipulated that "headgear [may] not be worn ... [indoors] except by armed security police in the performance of their duties." In 1981 therefore, Captain Goldman's superiors ordered him to cease wearing his yarmulke on duty indoors (even though he had never been ordered to comply with this rule in his years of service prior to 1981). When he refused to comply, he was reprimanded and threatened with discipline. His commanding officer, for example, withdrew a recommendation that Goldman's application for an extension of his Air Force service be approved, and wrote a negative reference instead.

The issue is this: Does the First Amendment, which guarantees the free exercise of religion, prohibit the Air Force from interfering with Captain Goldman's religious practice? For the Court's answer, see The Court Decides on page 117.

persons the right to perform their religious rituals unless the government can show that the law or regulation in question is narrowly tailored and in pursuit of a "compelling interest." Whether Congress has the authority to set aside state laws or regulations as applied to persons who claim a conflict with their religious practices raises interesting questions of federalism and remains to be resolved.

Freedom of Expression

A democracy depends on the free expression of ideas. Totalitarian governments know this, which is why they go to great lengths to suppress free expression. Freedom of conscience in America is absolute; Americans can *believe* whatever they want to believe. The First Amendment plainly forbids the national government from limiting freedom of expression, that is, the right to say or publish what one believes. Is freedom of *expression* then, like freedom of conscience, also *absolute?*

Yes, said the distinguished Supreme Court Justice Hugo Black: "no law means no law," as he was fond of saying. In 1992, the Supreme Court in *R.A.V. v. St. Paul* ruled that legislatures or universities may not single out racial, religious, or sexual insults or threats for prosecution as "hate speech" or "bias crimes." Yet there are plenty of exceptions to the "no law" approach. In 1919, Justice Oliver Wendell Holmes said that "the most stringent protection of free speech would not protect a man in falsely shouting 'fire' in a crowded theater" (*Schenck v. United States*). Where, if anywhere, should we draw the line on freedom of expression?

Prior Restraint. One principle stands out clearly in the complicated history of freedom of speech: time and time again, the Supreme Court has struck down prior restraint on freedom of speech and the press. **Prior restraint** refers to a government's actions that prevent material from being published in the first place; in other words, censorship. One signal case was *Near v. Minnesota* (1931), in which an acerbic newspaper editor called local officials "grafters" and "Jewish gangsters." The state shut him down, but the Supreme Court ordered the paper reopened.[4] Still, the Supreme Court has tolerated some prior restraint, for example, in the case of high school newspapers. Perhaps the most famous recent case of prior restraint is the "Pentagon Papers" case, in which renegade Pentagon officials stole and gave to newspapers damaging Defense Department documents about the Vietnam War. In 1971, the government even took the prestigious *New York Times* to court, but the Supreme Court upheld the paper's right to print the Pentagon papers.

Obscenity. In *The Brethren,* a gossipy portrayal of the Supreme Court, Bob Woodward and Scott Armstrong recount the tale of former Justice Thurgood Marshall lunching with some law clerks at Trader Vic's in Washington. Glancing at his watch at about 1:50, Marshall exclaimed, "My God, I almost forgot. It's movie day. We've got to get back."[5] Movie day at the court was an annual event where movies brought before the Court on obscenity charges were shown in a basement storeroom. Almost nothing has been tougher than the Supreme Court's effort to deal with obscenity. In one famous opinion, which probably haunted him for the rest of his career, former Justice Potter Stewart said that he couldn't define pornography, but "I know it when I see it." (During a particularly racy scene on "movie day," Supreme Court clerks would yell out: "That's it! That's it! I know it when I see it.")

Clearly, the Supreme Court has never intended to include obscenity in its listing of protected forms of expression. In 1957, it held that "obscenity is not within the area of constitutionally protected speech or press" (*Roth v. United States*). But findings of obscenity have varied wildly across the country. "Tarzan" stories have been banned; the acclaimed film *Carnal Knowledge* was banned by the state of Georgia. At least one local cable company has taken MTV off the air—a decision that would sit well with countless parents. In 1973, the Court tried to clarify its definition by spelling out what would and would not be obscene. The case was *Miller v. California.* Chief Justice Warren Burger wrote that materials were obscene if the work—a movie, book, or whatever—taken as a whole appealed to a prurient interest in sex, *and* if it showed "patently offensive sexual conduct"; *and* if it "lacked serious artistic, literary, political, or scientific merit." Decisions should be made by local officials, and not on the basis of national standards.

And yet, the problems persisted. In one notable case, a small town in New Jersey tried to get rid of a nude dancing parlor by using its zoning power to

Although the Supreme Court has ruled in Roth v. United States *that obscenity is not protected by the First Amendment, determining just what is obscene has proved difficult. Both the availability and demand for sexually oriented material is large, as Madonna proved with her book of photos entitled* Sex.

ban all live entertainment. Yet the Supreme Court said in *Schad v. Mount Ephraim* (1981) that the measure was too broad—it would have prevented a clown act—and therefore unlawful. Jacksonville, Florida tried to prevent any drive-in movies from showing "bare buttocks, female bare breasts, or human bare pubic areas," but the Court held that this would have prevented perfectly innocent showings of a naked baby.

Defamation: Libel and Slander.   Another type of utterance not protected by the First Amendment is **libel,** the publication of statements known to be false that are malicious and tend to damage a person's reputation. *Slander* is the spoken version of libel. This is an important protection to people's reputations. Yet, if every time that someone said anything the slightest bit critical of someone else, a massive libel suit was filed—"he called me a 'turkey' and I'm suing for $20 million"—we would certainly chill freedom of speech. For public officials, the chilling effect would be worse. If a senator could haul every editorial writer and cartoonist into court for their criticism, there would not be much left of the freedom of press.

To encourage public debate, the Supreme Court has held, in cases such as **The New York Times v. Sullivan** (1964), that statements about *public officials* are libelous only if they are defamatory falsehoods made with malice and reckless disregard for the truth. This standard makes libel cases very difficult for public officials to win. General William Westmoreland, the commander of American troops during the Vietnam War, sued CBS, claiming that a documentary made it appear that he systematically lied about successes in Vietnam. Ultimately, the power of the press—in this case, a sloppy, arrogant press—prevailed. Destined to lose the case, Westmoreland settled for a mild apology from CBS.[6] Yet, from time to time, a celebrity can wrestle a libel judgment from supermarket tabloids (Carol Burnett and Elizabeth Taylor were both successful). Still, freedom of the press gives the press enormous latitude in this country to express its opinions freely, especially about public figures.

Private individuals have a lower standard to meet for winning lawsuits for libel. They need show only that statements made about them were defamatory falsehoods and that the author of the statements was negligent. Nevertheless, it is unusual for someone to win a libel case—most people do not wish to publicize critical statements about themselves.

Symbolic Speech.   There is a new form of expression not mentioned in the First Amendment, and we call it *symbolic speech.* Traditionally, "speech" meant a literal speech in front of other people. Now there are expressions that are not exactly "speeches" but are equally important. When an Iowa high school student during the middle of the Vietnam War wore a black arm band, and was suspended from school, the Supreme Court ultimately vindicated her for exercising a form of symbolic speech. In one of its most controversial decisions, the Supreme Court held that Gregory Johnson's burning of an American flag in 1984 was protected under the Constitution (*Texas v. Johnson,*

1989), and millions of Americans said that "there ought to be a law" against burning a flag.

Commercial Speech.   Not all forms of communication receive the full protection of the First Amendment. As *commercial speech*, advertising is restricted far more extensively than expressions of opinion on religious, political, or other matters. The Federal Trade Commission (FTC) decides what kinds of goods may be advertised on radio and television and regulates the content of such advertising. These regulations have responded to changes in social mores and priorities. Thirty years ago, for example, tampons could not be advertised on TV, while cigarette commercials were everywhere. Today, the situation is just the reverse.

The FTC also attempts to make sure that advertisers do not make false claims for their products. Unfortunately, "truth" in advertising does not prevent misleading promises; for example, an ad for mouthwash or deodorant may imply that using the product will improve one's love life. This dubious message is perfectly legal.

Nevertheless, regulation of commercial speech on the airwaves can go to lengths impossible in the political or religious realm. For example, the FTC forced makers of Excedrin, the pain reliever, to add the words "on pain other than headache" in its commercials describing tests that supposedly supported the product's claims of superiority. (The test results were based on pain experienced after giving birth.)

Although commercial speech does not receive the same protections as other types of speech, the courts have been broadening its privileges under the Constitution. For years, many states had laws that prohibited advertising for professional services, such as legal and engineering services, and for certain products ranging from eyeglasses and prescription drugs to condoms and abortions. Advocates of these laws claimed that they were designed to protect consumers against misleading claims, while critics charged that the laws prevented price competition. In recent years, the courts have struck down many of these restrictions as violations of freedom of speech. In 1994, the Supreme Court also ruled that cities cannot bar residents from posting signs (commercial or otherwise) on their own property.

The Airwaves: A New Kind of Speech Not Imagined by the Founders.   In addition to symbolic speech, there is yet one more sort of expression not mentioned by the writers of the First Amendment. Electronic means of communication used today (radio and television) are very different from, say, Patrick Henry's making a speech to his fellow Virginians. There is one important difference between the days of Patrick Henry and the days of radio and television: There was an almost unlimited supply of street corners for Patrick Henry, but nature limits the number of television and radio channels available. The Federal Communications Commission regulates the content, nature, and very existence of mass media in this country. Although newspapers do not need licenses, radio and TV do. These are also regulated by federal law. For example, the comedian

Drawing by Mankoff; © 1992 The New Yorker Magazine

"The way I see it, the Constitution cuts both ways. The First Amendment gives you the right to say what you want, but the Second Amendment gives me the right to shoot you for it."

George Carlin had a famous routine called "Seven Words You Can Never Say on Television." A New York radio station tested Carlin's assertion by airing his routine. The ensuing events proved Carlin right. In *FCC v. Pacifica Foundation* (1978), the Supreme Court upheld the Commission's policy of barring these words from radio or television when children might hear them.

Similarly, in 1992 the FCC fined New York disc jockey Howard Stern $600,000 for indecency. What is most interesting about the case, however, is that if Stern's commentaries had been carried by cable or satellite instead of the airwaves, he could have expressed himself with impunity. Technological change has blurred the line between broadcasting and private communications between individuals. With cable television now in about two-thirds of American homes, the Supreme Court will soon be faced with ruling on the application of free speech guidelines to cable broadcasting.

Free Speech and Public Order.   Not surprisingly, government has sometimes been a zealous opponent of speech that opposes its policies. In wartime and peacetime, the biggest conflict between press and government has been about the connection between a free press and the need for public order. Wartime

The limits of free speech are tested in new ways in each generation. Here, rap singer Ice-T announces he will pull the controversial song "Cop Killer" from his "Body Count" album.

often brings censorship. Obviously, sometimes government can and should limit the right of the press (to report troop movements, for example). Critics of the press during the Persian Gulf War complained that press reporting might have helped to pinpoint locations of SCUD missile attacks, knowledge of which could be used to aim future missiles more precisely. Defenders of the freedom of the press complained that never before had the press been as "managed" as in that conflict: reporters could only get to the field in the company of official Pentagon press representatives—and some who tried other ways of getting there were captured by the Iraqis.

These are not new issues. During World War I, Charles T. Schenck, the secretary of the American Socialist Party, distributed thousands of leaflets urging draft resistance. He was charged with resisting the war effort. In 1919, (*Schenck v. United States*) the Court upheld his conviction. In that case, Justice Holmes articulated an important principle of *clear and present danger*. Government could, he said, limit speech only if it posed a "clear and present danger" of substantive evils. It is difficult to say, of course, when speech becomes "dangerous" rather than simply inconvenient for the government.

Fearful of communists in government and everywhere else, in 1940 Congress passed the Smith Act, which forbade the advocacy of violent overthrow of the government of the United States. In *Dennis v. United States* (1951), the

Supreme Court upheld sentences for several major Communist leaders in the United States. Later, the Court came to toughen its standards for inciting civil revolution. Today, you could probably stand on any street corner and call for the overthrow of the government of the United States—and probably no one, even the police, would pay much attention.

When Rights Collide: Free Press versus Fair Trial. The Bill of Rights is an inexhaustible source of conflicts among different types of freedoms. One is the conflict between a freedom of expression—the right of the press to print what it wants—and a freedom at the bar of justice—the right to a fair trial. Journalists, of course, seek the right to cover every trial. The public, they argue, has a right to know. Defense counsel argue that pretrial publicity should not inflame the community—and potential jurors—against their clients. A controversial case in West Palm Beach, Florida, in 1991, led to rancorous conflict between the prosecutors and attorneys for William Kennedy Smith, nephew of Senator Edward Kennedy. Smith was accused of sexual assault, and well before the trial, prosecutors released reams of depositions from other women claiming to have been sexually assaulted by Smith. The judge did not admit these depositions as evidence.

Although reporters always want trials to be open to them, they do not always want to open their own files to the courts. Once in a while, a reporter sits on some critical evidence that either the prosecution or the defense wants in a criminal case. Reporters argue that "protecting their sources" should exempt them from revealing notes from confidential sources. More than one reporter has gone to jail for this principle, arguing that they had no obligation to produce evidence that might bear on the guilt or innocence of a defendant. The Supreme Court has decided that reporters do *not* have a Constitutional right to withhold information from the Courts, but some states have passed *shield laws* to protect reporters' rights to keep sources anonymous. Other states have been equally adamant in insisting that the freedom of the press ends when evidence about guilt or innocence begins.

Freedom of Assembly

The last of the great rights guaranteed by the First Amendment is the freedom to "peaceably assemble." This freedom is often neglected alongside the great freedoms of speech, press, and religion, yet it is the basis for forming interest groups, political parties, and professional associations as well as for picketing and protesting.

Right to Assemble. There are two facets of the freedom of assembly. First is the literal right to assemble, that is, to gather together in order to make a statement. This freedom can conflict with other societal values when it disrupts public order, traffic flow, peace and quiet, or bystanders' freedom to go about their business without interference. Within reasonable limits, called *time, place,* and *manner restrictions,* freedom of assembly includes the rights to parade,

"*Since you have already been convicted by the media, I imagine we can wrap this up pretty quickly.*"

picket, and protest. Whatever a group's cause, it has the right to demonstrate, but no group can simply hold a spontaneous demonstration anytime, anywhere, and anyway it chooses. Usually, a group must apply to the local city government for a permit and post a bond of a few hundred dollars—a little like making a security deposit on an apartment. The governing body must grant a permit as long as the group pledges to hold its demonstration at a time and place that allows the police to prevent major disruptions. There are virtually no limitations on the content of a group's message. In one important case the American Nazi Party applied to the local government to march in the streets of Skokie, Illinois, a Chicago suburb where many survivors of Hitler's death camps lived. You can examine this case in "You Are the Judge: The Case of the Nazis' March in Skokie."

The balance between freedom and order is tested when protest verges on harassment. Protestors lined up outside abortion clinics are now a common

YOU ARE THE JUDGE

The Case of the Nazis' March in Skokie

Hitler's Nazis, it is widely estimated, slaughtered six million Jews in death camps like Bergen-Belsen, Auschwitz, and Dachau. Many of the survivors migrated to the United States, and many settled in Skokie, Illinois. Skokie, with 80,000 people, is a suburb just north of Chicago. In its heavily Jewish population are thousands of survivors of German concentration camps.

The American Nazi party was a ragtag group of perhaps twenty-five to thirty members. Their headquarters was a storefront building on the West Side of Chicago, near an area of expanding black population. Denied a permit to march in a black neighborhood of Chicago, the American Nazis announced their intention to march in Skokie in 1977. Skokie's city government required that they post a $300,000 bond to get a parade permit. The Nazis claimed that the high bond was set in order to prevent their march and that it infringed on their freedoms of speech and assembly. The American Civil Liberties Union (ACLU), despite its loathing of the Nazis, defended the Nazis' claim and their right to march. (The ACLU lost half its Illinois membership because it took this position.)

You be the judge: Do Nazis have the right to parade, preach anti-Jewish propaganda, and perhaps provoke violence in a community peopled with survivors of the Holocaust? What rights or obligations does a community have to maintain order? For the Court's response, see The Court Decides on page 117.

sight. Members of groups like "Operation Rescue" try to shame women into staying away and may harass them if they visit a clinic. Rights are in conflict in such cases: a woman seeking to terminate her pregnancy has the right to go forward with an abortion; the demonstrators have the right to protest the very existence of the clinic. The courts have acted to restrain these protestors, setting limits on how close they may come to the clinics and upholding damage claims of clients against the protestors. In 1994, Congress passed a law enacting broad new penalties against abortion protestors.

Right to Associate.   The second facet of freedom of assembly is the right to associate with people who share a common interest, including an interest in political change. In a famous case at the height of the civil rights movement, Alabama tried to harass the state chapter of the National Association for the Advancement of Colored People by requiring it to turn over its membership list. The Court found this demand an unconstitutional restriction on freedom of association (*NAACP v. Alabama*, 1958).

RIGHTS AT THE BAR OF JUSTICE

The Bill of Rights supplies only forty-four words that guarantee your freedoms of speech, press, religion, and assembly. Most of the rest concern the rights of people accused of crimes. These rights were originally intended to protect the accused in *political* arrests and trials; today they are mostly applied in criminal justice cases. The Bill of Rights protects suspects at every stage of the criminal justice system. These stages in the judicial process may be viewed as a series of funnels decreasing in size. Generally speaking, a *crime* is (sometimes) followed by an *arrest* which is (sometimes) followed by a *prosecution*, which is (sometimes) followed by a *trial*, which (usually) results in a *verdict* of innocence or guilt. The funnels get smaller and smaller, each dripping into the next. Many more crimes occur than are reported; many more crimes are reported than arrests are made (the ratio is about five to one); many more arrests are made than prosecutors prosecute; and many more prosecutions occur than jury trials. In the next few pages you will move through the criminal justice system, pausing at each stage to see how the Constitution protects the rights of the accused (see Table 4.2).

TABLE 4.2 — *The Bill of Rights and the Stages of the Criminal Justice System*

Although our criminal justice system is complex, it can be broken down into stages. The Bill of Rights protects the rights of the accused at every stage. Here are some key constitutional guarantees at various stages of the criminal justice system.

Stage	Protections
1. Evidence gathered	"unreasonable search and seizure" forbidden (Fourth Amendment)
2. Suspicion cast	guarantee that "writ of habeas corpus" will not be suspended, forbidding imprisonment without evidence (Article I, Section 9)
3. Arrest made	self-incrimination forbidden (Fifth Amendment)
	right to have the "assistance of counsel" (Sixth Amendment)
4. Interrogation held	"excessive bail" forbidden (Eighth Amendment)
5. Trial held	"speedy and public trial" by an impartial jury required (Sixth Amendment)
	"double jeopardy" (being tried twice for the same crime) forbidden (Fifth Amendment)
	trial by jury required (Article III, Section 2)
	right to confront witnesses required (Sixth Amendment)
6. Punishment imposed	"cruel and unusual punishment" forbidden (Eighth Amendment)

Searches, Seizures, and Arrests.   Even if a crime is committed, police cannot arrest a suspect arbitrarily. They need what the courts call *probable cause* to make an arrest. Typically, police need to get physical evidence—a car thief's fingerprints, for example—to use in court. How evidence is collected is governed by the Fourth Amendment. It is quite specific in forbidding **unreasonable searches and seizures.** To prevent abuse of police powers, the Constitution requires that no court may issue a search warrant unless probable cause exists to believe that a crime has been committed or is about to occur. Courts may issue a search warrant only when a crime has been committed or when police reasonably believe it is likely to occur. The warrant must specify what the police believe is likely to be found in a search.

One very significant case—and one that involved extending the Bill of Rights to the states—occurred in Cleveland when a woman named Dollree Mapp was under suspicion for having illegal gambling devices. Police broke into her home looking for a fugitive, but found a cache of pornographic materials instead. She was convicted of possessing them, but appealed, claiming that the Fourth Amendment should be applied to state and local governments. In *Mapp v. Ohio* (1961), it was applied. The Supreme Court ruled that the evidence had been seized illegally and reversed Ms. Mapp's conviction. Since then, the Fourth Amendment's provision against unreasonable searches and seizures has been incorporated into the rights that protect citizens against both the states and the federal government.

Ever since 1914, the Supreme Court has used an **exclusionary rule** to weigh evidence in a criminal case. This rule prevents illegally seized evidence from being introduced in court. In recent years, however, the Supreme Court has made some exceptions to the rule. Now, illegally obtained evidence is admissible in court when this evidence led police to a discovery that they eventually would have made without it or if the police who seized it mistakenly thought they were operating under a constitutionally valid warrant (the "good faith" rule). For a bizarre case of search-and-seizure, see "You Are the Judge: The Case of Ms. Montoya."

Self-Incrimination.   One of our most important civil liberties is the protection against self-incrimination. The **Fifth Amendment** states that "no person shall be compelled to be a witness against himself." As everyone who watches police shows knows, this protection begins at arrest. These rights originated from a famous decision—perhaps the most important modern criminal justice case.[7] Ernesto Miranda was convicted in an ugly rape-kidnapping in Arizona. Police questioned him for two hours, telling him neither of his right against self-incrimination nor of his right to a lawyer. The Supreme Court reversed his conviction (***Miranda v. Arizona,*** 1966) and laid down the following guidelines for questioning suspects:

- Suspects must be told that they have a constitutional right to remain silent and may stop answering questions at any time.

YOU ARE THE JUDGE

The Case of Ms. Montoya

On March 5, 1983, Rose Elviro Montoya de Hernandez arrived at the Los Angeles International Airport on Avianca Flight 080 from Bogatá, Colombia. Her first official encounter was with U.S. Customs Inspector Talamantes, who noticed that she spoke no English. Interestingly, Montoya's passport indicated eight recent quick trips from Bogatá to Los Angeles. She had five thousand dollars in bills but no billfold or credit cards.

Talamantes and his fellow customs officers were suspicious. Stationed in Los Angeles, they were hardly unaware of the fact that Colombia was a major drug supplier. They questioned Montoya, who explained that her husband had a store in Bogatá and that she planned to spend the five thousand dollars at Kmart and J.C. Penney, stocking up on items for the store.

The inspector, growing warier and warier, handed Montoya over to female customs inspectors for a search. These agents noticed what the Supreme Court later referred to delicately as a "firm fullness" in Montoya's abdomen. Suspicions, already high, grew higher. The agents applied for a court order to conduct a pregnancy test, X rays, and other examinations, and eventually they found eighty-eight balloons containing 80 percent pure cocaine in Montoya's alimentary canal.

Montoya's lawyer argued that this constituted unreasonable search and seizure and that her arrest and conviction should be set aside. There was, he said, no direct evidence that would have led the officials to suspect cocaine smuggling. The government argued that the arrest had followed a set of odd facts leading to reasonable suspicion that something was amiss.

You be the judge: Was Montoya's arrest based on a search-and-seizure incident that violated the Fourth Amendment? For the Supreme Court's answer, see The Court Decides on page 117.

- They must be warned that what they say can be used against them in a trial.
- They must be told that they have a right to have a lawyer during questioning and that a public defender will be appointed for indigent defendants.

The Right to Counsel.   One of the most important rights in a "Miranda warning" is the right to counsel. Although the *Sixth Amendment* guarantees a right to a lawyer in a federal court, not until 1963 was this right extended to defendants in state courts (where the vast majority of prosecutions take place). A man named Clarence Earl Gideon had been jailed in a Florida state prison for a nickel-and-dime burglary of a pool hall vending machine. He was too poor to hire a lawyer. Using the prison's law books, he wrote a *pauper's petition* to the Supreme Court. The Court read the petition and, in *Gideon v. Wainwright* (1963), ordered him retried. (He was acquitted with the aid of a public defender.) Today, every court is required to appoint an attorney for those who cannot afford one.[8]

Trial By Jury.   Jury trials are dramatic events, the stuff of which great television drama is made. Yet the jury trial is a rare event in the criminal justice system. In fact, 90 percent of all cases begin and end with a guilty plea. Most cases are settled through a process known as **plea bargaining.** This results from an actual bargain struck between defendants' lawyers and prosecutors to the effect that defendants will plead guilty to a lesser crime (or fewer crimes) in exchange for the government's not prosecuting the more serious (or additional) crime. Even so, there are some 300,000 cases annually in the United States that do go to a jury trial.

Critics of the plea-bargaining system believe that it permits many criminals to avoid "facing the music" or as much music as they could face if tried for a more serious offense. The process, however, works to the advantage of both sides; it saves the state the time and money that would otherwise be spent on a trial, and it permits defendants who think they might be convicted of a serious charge to plead guilty to a lesser one.

Cruel and Unusual Punishment.   The *Eighth Amendment* forbids **"cruel and unusual punishment,"** although it does not define the phrase. There has actually been very little debate in American law about the cruelty and unusualness of various punishments. Today, the major issue centers on the death penalty. Some two thousand people are on death row; about one quarter are in two states alone, Florida and Texas. There is little evidence that the death penalty deters crime. States that do not have it have crime rates similar to those that do. Historically, most of the victims of the death penalty have been members of minority groups. Today, about half of those on death row are members of minority groups.

On perhaps no other issue in the criminal justice system has the Supreme Court vacillated so much as on the death penalty. In the early 1970s, the Court seemed to signal that the death penalty might be unconstitutional. Then, in 1976, in *Gregg v. Georgia,* Gregg's attorney made the argument directly that the death penalty was cruel and unusual punishment. The Court disagreed, saying that "Capital punishment is an extreme sanction, suitable to the most extreme of crimes." Even today the death penalty remains a rarity. Legal delays and appeals stave off a death row inmate's execution.

Despite decades of legal debate, the death penalty is still, as Justice Potter Stewart once remarked, freakish in the way lightning is freakish. In 1994, Justice Harry Blackmun declared that "no combination of procedural rules or substantive regulations ever can save the death penalty from its inherent constitutional deficiencies. . . . [The] system fails to deliver . . . fair, consistent and reliable sentences of death . . . " (*Callins v. Collins*). Nevertheless, in response to growing concern about crime in America, more and more offenses are made punishable by death, and the number of inmates on death row continues to grow.

There have been other issues connected with the cruel and unusual punishment clause. The typical case essentially raised the question: How cruel and unusual does a punishment have to be to qualify as unconstitutional? In

1991, the Supreme Court addressed this issue in great detail. In *Harmelin v. Michigan*, the defendant argued that his punishment was cruel and unusual when he was sentenced to life in prison without the possibility of parole for possessing 672 grams of cocaine. The Supreme Court, though, upheld this stiff sentence, observing that the severity of a punishment alone did not make it cruel or unusual.

THE RIGHT TO PRIVACY

The members of the First Congress who drafted the Bill of Rights would have been shocked to discover Americans going to court to argue about wiretapping, surrogate motherhood, abortion, or pornography. New technologies have raised ethical issues unimaginable in the eighteenth century. Today, one of the greatest debates concerning Americans' civil liberties lies in the emerging area of privacy rights.

Is There a Right to Privacy?

Nowhere does the Bill of Rights say that Americans have a **right to privacy.** Clearly, though, rights to freedom of expression imply that one has a right to private beliefs; rights to be protected from unreasonable searches and seizures imply that one has the right to privacy in one's own home. In 1928, Justice Brandeis hailed privacy as "the right to be left alone—the most comprehensive of the rights and the most valued by civilized men."

The Supreme Court first clearly articulated such a right in a 1965 case (*Griswold v. Connecticut*) involving an old Connecticut law forbidding contraceptives. Certainly, the Constitution never mentioned a right to birth control, but seven justices finally decided that various portions of the Bill of Rights contain "penumbras"—unstated liberties on the fringes of the more explicitly stated rights—protecting a right to privacy, including a right to family planning for couples. Critics of the ruling claimed that the Supreme Court was inventing new rights. Abortion, though, not family planning, was the most important—and most controversial—aspect of the right to privacy. In 1973, the Supreme Court unleashed a constitutional firestorm that has not yet abated.

Firestorm over Abortion

In the summer of 1972, Supreme Court Justice Harry Blackmun returned to Minnesota's famed Mayo Clinic, where he had once served as general counsel. The Clinic lent him a tiny desk in the corner of a librarian's office, where he worked quietly for two weeks. His research focused on the medical aspects of abortion. He had been assigned the task of writing the majority opinion in one of the most controversial cases ever to come before the Court. The opinion, in ***Roe v. Wade*** (1973), generated more conflict than any court decision since the school desegregation case in 1954. Roe, the pseudonym of a Texas woman, argued that Texas law allowing for abortion only to save the life of the mother was unconstitutional. Texas argued that the Constitution reserved to the states the power to regulate moral behavior, including abortion. The Court's reasoning followed medical authorities in dividing pregnancy into three trimesters. *Roe* forbade any state regulation of abortion during the first trimester, it permitted states to allow abortion in the second trimester only to protect a mother's health, and it permitted them to forbid abortions in the third. The decision itself unleashed a firestorm of protest. Since the decision, about a million and a half abortions have been performed annually.

The furor has never subsided. During the conservative presidencies of Ronald Reagan and George Bush, Congress passed numerous legislative amendments forbidding the use of federal funds for abortions. Many states passed similar restrictions. Missouri went as far as any other state, forbidding the use of state funds or state employees to perform abortions. A clinic in St. Louis challenged the law as unconstitutional, but in *Webster v. Reproductive Health Services* (1989) the Court upheld the law. It has also upheld laws requiring minors to obtain the permission of one or both parents or a judge before obtaining an abortion.

In 1991, the conservative Court went even further in upholding restrictions on abortions. In *Rust v. Sullivan*, the Court found that a Department of Health and Human Services ruling—specifying that family planning services that received federal funds could not provide women *any* counseling regarding abortion—was constitutional. This decision was greeted by a public outcry that the rule would deny many poor women abortion counseling and limit the First Amendment right of a medical practitioner to counsel a client. On his third day in office, President Clinton lifted the ban on abortion counseling.

In 1992, in *Planned Parenthood v. Casey*, the Court changed its standard for evaluating restrictions on abortion from one of "strict scrutiny" of any restraints on a "fundamental right" to one of "undue burden" that permits considerably more regulation. The Court upheld a 24-hour waiting period, a parental or judicial consent requirement for minors, and a requirement that doctors present women with information on the risks of the operation. (The Court struck down a provision requiring a married woman to tell her husband of her intent to have an abortion.) At the same time, the majority also affirmed their commitment to the basic right of a woman to obtain an abortion.

There is almost no issue of public policy on which Americans are more divided than abortion. Polls can be found indicating strong support for a woman's right to choose, and also strong majorities opposing unlimited abortion. Because passions run so strongly on this issue, advocates on both sides may take extreme action. Recently, for example antiabortion activists have murdered two physicians who performed abortions.

The abortion issue may also force individual rights into conflict, as when the First Amendment right to protest abortion (which involves the rights to speech and assembly) conflicts with the right to obtain an abortion. In 1994, in

Madsen v. Women's Health Center, the Supreme Court consolidated the right to abortion established in *Roe* with protection of a woman's right to enter an abortion clinic. Citing the government's interest in preserving order and maintaining women's access to pregnancy services, the Court upheld a state court's order of a 36-foot buffer zone around a clinic in Melbourne, Florida. In another case, the Court decided that abortion clinics can invoke the federal racketeering law to sue violent antiabortion protest groups for damages. In 1994, Congress passed the Freedom of Access to Clinic Entrances Act, making it a federal crime to intimidate abortion providers or women seeking abortions.

A Time to Live and a Time to Die

Today, even issues of life and death wind up in the courts. At a time when 90 percent of us die either in a state-regulated nursing home or hospital, public policy choices cannot be disconnected from decisions about life, birth, and death. In few areas are ethical issues so closely bound up with public policy. Some of the toughest ethical—and policy—issues involve birth itself.

Courts face questions about the right to die as well as the right to life. Modern medicine can keep people alive, though barely functioning, for

One of the most difficult issues facing our high-tech society is whether there is a right to choose to die. Here, Dr. Jack Kervorkian, popularly known as the "suicide doctor," poses with two terminally-ill individuals shortly before assisting them in ending their lives. Because not everyone approves of assisted suicide, Dr. Kervorkian spends much of his time in court defending his actions.

months, even for years. The most celebrated case concerning the right to die involved a 21-year-old woman in New Jersey named Karen Quinlan, who lapsed into a coma after being injured in an automobile accident. Her parents waged a long court battle with the hospital, which insisted on keeping her connected to life-support systems. Eventually the New Jersey Supreme Court sided with the Quinlans. In fact, when taken off the life support systems, Karen Quinlan continued living for almost a decade.

As medical science increasingly makes possible surrogate motherhood, the use of fetal tissue for research on diseases, and genetic alteration, more issues about the human body will face legislatures and courts. Abe and Mary Ayala, for example, conceived and gave birth to a baby for the sole purpose of providing a life-saving bone marrow transplant for their 14-year-old daughter. Nearly half of all Americans agreed that it is "morally acceptable for parents to conceive a child in order to obtain an organ or tissue to save the life of another one of their children."[9] Critics called this "baby farming," and the issue will likely once again emphasize that matters of public policy are matters of ethics as well as law.

THE STRUGGLE FOR EQUALITY

The struggle for equality in America is the struggle for civil rights. Historically, the issues were first debated with respect to minority groups. Later, the struggle widened, as new groups, particularly women, took up the call for equality. The fight for equality in America today affects everyone. Philosophically, the struggle involves defining the term *equality*. Constitutionally, it involves interpreting the Constitution and laws. Politically, it often involves power.

The Constitution and Equality

Although Thomas Jefferson wrote in the Declaration of Independence that "all men are created equal," he insisted, as did most of his contemporaries, that African Americans were inherently inferior to whites. The word *equality* does not appear in the original Constitution. The privileged delegates to the 1787 convention would have been baffled, if not appalled, by claims of equal rights for African Americans, deaf students, gay soldiers, and female road dispatchers. The delegates came up with a plan for government, not guarantees of individual rights. Not even the Bill of Rights mentions equality. It does, however, have implications for equality, because it does not limit its guarantees to specific groups within society.

The first and only place in which the idea of equality appears in the Constitution is in the **Fourteenth Amendment,** one of the three amendments passed after the Civil War. (The Thirteenth abolished slavery, and the Fifteenth extended the right to vote to African Americans—African-American males over 21, that is.) The amendment forbids the states from denying "equal protection of the laws." These five words represent the only reference to the idea of equality in the entire Constitution, yet within them was enough force to begin assuring equal rights for all Americans. Today, the equal protection clause has few rivals in generating legal business for the Supreme Court.[10]

But what does **equal protection of the laws** mean? The Fourteenth Amendment does not say that "states must treat everyone exactly alike" or that "every state must promote equality among its people." The Court has consistently held that a state may treat classes of citizens differently (unequally) if the classification is *reasonable*. No one could successfully argue, for instance, that denying 10-year-olds the right to drive, or to vote, was unreasonable, even if it was technically unequal. A state, though, would have a tough time arguing that women could not be police officers. Conditions for women and minority groups would be vastly different today if it were not for those five constitutional words. For the first hundred years or so of the American republic, the issues of equality were mostly those of race.

Race, the Constitution, and Public Policy

Three eras delineate African Americans' struggle for equality in America: the era of *slavery,* from the beginning of colonization until the end of the Civil War; the era of *reconstruction and resegregation,* from roughly the end of the Civil War until 1954; and the era of *civil rights,* roughly from 1954 to the present.

The Era of Slavery.   From the beginning of American colonial history, slaves were imported, bought, and sold. Once slavery became economically profitable in the South, the slave system took firm hold of Southern economies. The boldest decision in defense of slavery—and one of the milestones leading to the Civil War—was *Dred Scott v. Sandford* (1857). Chief Justice Taney bluntly announced that a black man, slave or free, had no rights under a white man's government, and that Congress had no power to ban slavery in the western territories that were not yet states. In a sense, it took the Union victory in the Civil War to reverse the *Dred Scott* decision. The ratification of the Thirteenth Amendment formally abolished slavery in the United States.

The Era of Reconstruction and Resegregation.   After the Civil War, the period of Reconstruction followed. Despite the promises of the end of slavery, white Southerners lost little time in reclaiming control of their governments and imposed a code of *Jim Crow,* or segregation, laws on African Americans. ("Jim Crow" was the name of a stereotypical Negro in a nineteenth-century minstrel song.) These laws mandated separate facilities, separate school systems, and even separate rest rooms.

The Supreme Court provided a constitutional justification for segregation in the important 1896 case, *Plessy v. Ferguson.* Although Homer Plessy was seven-eighths white, he was arrested for violating Louisiana law requiring segregated railway cars. *Plessy* enunciated the principle of "separate but equal," but much more attention was subsequently paid to the "separate" than the "equal" part of the decision. Southern states were permitted under the

In the era of segregation, housing, schools, and jobs—as well as such lesser things as drinking fountains and rest rooms—were, in one way or another, classified "white" or "colored."

Plessy doctrine to provide high schools and professional schools for whites, but not for African Americans.

The Era of Civil Rights.   Although the Supreme Court had been chipping away at the constitutional foundations of segregation for decades, legal segregation came to an end in 1954, when, in **Brown v. Board of Education,** it set aside its earlier precedent in *Plessy.* In *Brown,* the Supreme Court held that under the Fourteenth Amendment school segregation in Topeka, Kansas (and several other cities), was inherently unconstitutional. You can read more about this case—perhaps the most important of the twentieth century—in "In Focus: *Brown v. Board of Education.*"

Throughout the South, the reaction to *Brown* was swift and negative. A few counties actually closed their public schools, and enrollment in private (white and segregated) schools soared. Congress, in the Civil Rights Act of 1964, responded by cutting off federal aid to schools that remained segregated. Slowly, desegregation proceeded throughout the South. Some federal judges ordered school busing to achieve racially balanced schools, a practice the Supreme Court upheld in *Swann v. Charlotte-Mecklenberg Board of Education* (1971). Federal courts also ordered desegregation in states that had not had mandatory segregation laws on the books, but subtly encouraged it, for example, by the drawing of attendance boundaries.

Almost coterminous with the *Brown* decision, the *civil rights movement* was born. In 1955, an African-American woman named Rosa Parks refused to give up her bus seat to a white man in Montgomery, Alabama. A local minister named Martin Luther King, Jr., led a bus boycott that ushered in a movement to end all kinds of segregation throughout the South. Sit-ins, protests, and marches were key strategies of the civil rights movement. They were intended not only to appeal to the conscience of America, but to get its public policies changed.

The 1950s and 1960s saw a number of public policies intended to increase racial equality. The **Civil Rights Act of 1964** made racial discrimination illegal in hotels, motels, restaurants, and other places of public accommodations. It also forbade many forms of job discrimination. By the end of the 1970s, there were few forms of segregation that had not been overturned by either Congress or the courts.

The struggle for *suffrage,* the right to vote, was one of the most important elements of the civil rights movement. The *Fifteenth Amendment,* adopted in 1870, had guaranteed that former slaves had the right to vote. In practice, however, states seemed to outdo one another in inventing ways of getting around the mandate of equal suffrage. Most southern states relied on *poll taxes,* which were small taxes levied on the right to vote that often fell due at a time of year when poor sharecroppers had the least cash. The Twenty-fourth Amendment, ratified in 1964, prohibited poll taxes in federal elections, and the Supreme Court prohibited poll taxes in state elections two years later.

One key method of reducing African-American participation in southern elections was the *white primary,* a device that permitted political parties in the heavily Democratic South to exclude African Americans from primary elections on the grounds that they were "private." Anyone could vote in the general elections, where it mattered least. In 1944, the Supreme Court held that white primaries were unconstitutional.

The most important public policy in expanding suffrage was the **Voting Rights Act of 1965** (extended and strengthened by Congress in 1970, 1975, and 1982), which prohibited voting registration procedures (such as literacy tests) that denied the vote based on race or color and sent federal registrars to states and counties with long histories of voting discrimination.

The effects of the Voting Rights Act were swift and certain. Hundreds of thousands of African Americans in the South were added to the voting rolls. When the Act was passed, only seventy African Americans held public office in eleven southern states. By the 1980s, more than 2,500 African Americans held public office in those states. Virginia elected the first African-American governor in modern times, Douglas Wilder.

The Voting Rights Act not only secured the right to vote for African Americans, but also ensured that their votes would not be diluted through racial gerrymandering. Elected officials could no longer "carve up" areas with a high

IN FOCUS

Brown v. Board of Education

After searching carefully for the perfect case to challenge legal school segregation, the National Association for the Advancement of Colored People (NAACP) selected the case of Linda Brown. An African-American student in Topeka, Kansas, Brown was required by Kansas law to attend a segregated school. In Topeka, the visible signs of education—teacher quality, facilities, and so on—were substantially equal between black schools and white ones. Thus the NAACP chose the case in order to test the *Plessy v. Ferguson* doctrine of "separate but equal." The Court would be forced to rule directly on whether school segregation was *inherently* unequal and thereby violated the Fourteenth Amendment's requirement that states guarantee "equal protection of the laws." Decisions in several recent cases (*Sweatt* and *McLaurin*, for example) had hinted that the Supreme Court was ready to overturn the *Plessy* precedent. The NAACP's general counsel, Thurgood Marshall, argued Linda Brown's case before the Supreme Court.

Chief Justice Earl Warren had just been appointed by President Eisenhower. So important was *Brown* that the Court had already heard one round of arguments before Warren joined the Court. The justices, after hearing the oral arguments, met in the Supreme Court's Conference Room. As is traditional, the chief justice summarized the case to his colleagues briefly and then turned to the most senior associate justice to present his views. Each, from the most senior to the newest member of the Court, spoke. Believing that a unanimous decision would have the most impact, the justices agreed that Warren himself should write the opinion.

Shortly before the decision was to be announced, President Eisenhower invited the Warrens to dinner at the White House. Pointedly seating the chief justice near John W. Davis, the lawyer arguing the southern states' case in *Brown*, the president went out of his way to tell Warren what an able man Davis was. Taking Warren by the arm on the way to after-dinner coffee and drinks, Eisenhower put in his word against school integration. After Warren announced the *Brown* decision, he was never again invited to the White House by the man who appointed him. Although Eisenhower objected strongly to the decision, he later sent federal troops to Central High School in Little Rock, Arkansas, in 1957 to enforce its desegregation.

minority population to prevent a geographically-concentrated minority from electing a council member. When Congress amended the Voting Rights Act in 1982, it further insisted that minorities be able to "elect representatives of their choice" when their numbers and configuration permitted. Thus, legislative redistricting was to avoid discriminatory *results* and not just discriminatory *intent*. In 1986, the Supreme Court upheld this principle in *Thornburg v. Gingles*.

Officials in the Justice Department responsible for enforcing the Voting Rights Act and state legislatures that drew new district lines interpreted these actions as a mandate to create minority-majority districts. Consequently, when congressional district boundaries were redrawn following the 1990 census, several states, including Florida, North Carolina, Texas, Illinois, New York, and Louisiana, created odd-shaped districts that were designed to give minority-group voters a numerical majority. Fourteen new U.S. House districts were specifically drawn to help elect African Americans to Congress, and six districts were drawn to elect new Hispanic members (these efforts were successful, as we will see in Chapter 10).

However, in 1993, the Supreme Court heard a challenge to a North Carolina majority-African-American congressional district that cut in places no wider than a superhighway, winding snakelike for 160 miles. In its decision in *Shaw v. Reno*, the Court decried the creation of districts based solely on racial composition, as well as the abandonment of traditional redistricting standards such as compactness and contiguity. Thus, the Court gave legal standing to challenges to any congressional map with an oddly-shaped majority-minority district that may not be defensible on grounds other than race (such as shared community interest or geographical compactness). The next year in *Johnson v. DeGrady*, the Court ruled that a state legislative redistricting plan does not violate the Voting Rights Act if it does not create the greatest possible number of districts in which minority-group votes would make up a majority.

Yet even if a district is created solely on the basis of race, it may still pass constitutional muster if a lower court determines that it is "narrowly tailored to further a compelling governmental interest." Thus, we can expect substantial litigation on the question of district boundaries over the next few years.

African Americans are not the only racial group that has suffered legally imposed disadvantages. Even before the civil rights struggle, native Americans, Asian Americans, and Hispanics learned how powerless they could become in a society dominated by whites. The civil rights laws for which African-American groups like the NAACP fought have benefited members of these groups as well.

Women, the Constitution, and Public Policy

The first women's rights activists were closely connected to the abolitionist movement. Two of these women, Lucretia Mott and Elizabeth Cady Stanton, organized a meeting at Seneca Falls, in upstate New York. On July 19, 1848, one hundred men and women signed the Seneca Falls Declaration of Sentiments and Resolutions. It proclaimed that "the history of mankind is a history of repeated injuries and usurpations on the part of man toward woman, having in direct object the establishment of an absolute tyranny over her." Thus began the movement that would culminate in the ratification of the *Nineteenth Amendment* seventy-two years later, giving women the right to vote.

But winning the right to vote did not automatically give equal rights, equal pay, and equal status to women. In fact, the feminist movement seemed to lose steam after the right to vote was secured. One reason is that the right to vote was the only issue on which virtually all feminists agreed. Many supporters of the right to vote nonetheless still accepted the traditional model of the family: fathers were breadwinners and mothers were bread bakers.

State laws tended to enshrine this view of the family in public policy. Women's opportunities to work outside the home were restricted. In most states, husbands were legally required to support their families even after a divorce. Women were forbidden to enter some lines of work altogether. Alice Paul, the author of the **Equal Rights Amendment,** was one activist who argued that the real result of these public policies was to limit the opportunities of women.

The Equal Rights Amendment read simply: "Equality of rights under the law shall not be denied or abridged by the United States or by any state on account of sex." It was first introduced in Congress as an amendment in the 1920s by a nephew of Susan B. Anthony. However, many people saw it as a threat to the family, and it languished for decades. In fact, women were less likely to vote for the amendment than men were.

In a sense, the feminist movement was reborn in the civil rights movement of the 1950s and 1960s. Women activists joined the civil rights movement and some also became leaders in the movement to oppose the Vietnam War. Books began to appear encouraging women to question traditional assumptions. The National Organization for Women (NOW) and the National Women's Political Caucus were organized in the 1960s and 1970s. The Civil Rights Act of 1964, in a little-noticed portion, even banned sex discrimination in employment. Title IX of the Education Act of 1972 forbade sex discrimination in all federally subsidized education programs, including athletics. The Pregnancy Discrimination Act of 1978 made it illegal for employers to exclude pregnancy and childbirth from their sick-leave and health-benefits plans. The 1991 Civil Rights Act shifted the burden of proof in justifying hiring and promotion practices to employers, who must show that employment practices are related to job performance and that they are consistent with "business necessity" (an ambiguous term, however).

The Equal Rights Amendment was revived in the early 1970s, and states at first seemed to stumble over one another to be the first to ratify it. Yet, in spite of its initial overwhelming support, the ERA was never ratified. Congress even passed an extension of time for the states to ratify, but by 1982 the ERA was still stalled three states short of ratification.[11]

Women also used the same route to the courts that African Americans had taken. In 1971, the Court ruled in *Reed v. Reed,* that any "arbitrary" sex-based classification under state law violated the equal protection clause. Plenty of equality issues remained for public policymakers, however. Two of the most important are those of wage discrimination and the role of women in the military.

The issue of wage discrimination arose in part because of the changing American family structure. At the end of World War II, the vast majority of women stayed at home and raised children. Today, a majority of single women with children work. Once, American men and women debated the wisdom of a woman working outside the home. Today, they debate about the wisdom of having a "mommy track" and a "professional track" in middle-class occupations. Traditionally, of course, women's jobs have paid lower wages than men's jobs. Nurses earned less than physicians, teachers earned less than principals.

Today, women employed full-time earn less than two-thirds of men's wages. This gives rise to the thorny issue of *comparable worth*, the idea that *jobs*, not individual positions, should be equally compensated if equally important. The State of Washington took the lead in this debate, deciding in 1983 that its state government had discriminated against women by not equally paying men and women in positions of comparable worth. The Supreme Court has yet to confront this controversial notion of equality.

Congress, though, has confronted the issue of women in the military. Women comprise 11 percent of the armed forces, and compete directly with men for promotion. Women have done well in the military, including graduating at the head of the class at the Naval Academy in Annapolis, and serving as First Captain of the Corps of Cadets at West Point. Nevertheless, until recently combat positions (and the opportunities for responsibility and advancement that go with them) were closed to women. Times are changing, however. Since 1993, women have been permitted to serve as combat pilots and aboard naval warships.

Whether in the military, on the assembly line, or in the office, women for years voiced concern about *sexual harassment,* which, or course, does not affect only women. In 1986, the Supreme Court articulated the broad principle that when sexual harassment becomes so pervasive as to create a hostile or abusive work environment, it is a form of sexual discrimination, which is forbidden by the 1964 Civil Rights Act. In 1993, in *Harris v. Forklift Systems,* the Court reinforced its decision. No single factor, the Court said, is required to win a sexual harassment case under Title VII of the 1964 Civil Rights Act. The law is violated when the workplace environment "would reasonably be perceived, and is perceived, as hostile or abusive." Thus, workers are not required to prove that the workplace environment is so hostile as to cause them "severe psychological injury" or that they are unable to perform their jobs. The protection of federal law comes into play before the harassing conduct leads to psychological difficulty.

New Groups under the Constitutional Umbrella

Policies to further equality of women and minorities can be applied to other groups, too. The civil rights umbrella is a large one, and many groups have used it to challenge mainstream America.

Civil Rights and the Graying of America. America is aging rapidly. People in their eighties comprise the fastest growing segment of the American population. Many persons, including housewives and veterans who want to return to the workplace, often face age discrimination in their efforts to obtain education and employment. In 1975, Congress passed legislation cutting off federal grants and contracts for any corporation or institution discriminating against men and women over 40 (thus technically making men under 40 the only group in the United States not protected by antidiscrimination legislation). Congress has now phased out the rule that people should be required to retire at the age of 65, or 70, or some other arbitrary age.

Civil Rights and the Disabled.   Disabled Americans comprise about 17 percent of the American population. Many disabled Americans have been kept out of the workforce and isolated without overt discrimination. Throughout American history, public and private buildings have been hostile to the blind, deaf, and mobility-impaired. As one slogan popular with the disabled says: "Once African Americans had to ride at the back of the bus. We can't even get on the bus." The Rehabilitation Act of 1973 added disabled Americans to the list of people protected from discrimination. The *Americans with Disabilities Act of 1990* strengthened these protections, requiring employers and public facilities to make "reasonable accommodations" for the disabled and prohibiting employment discrimination against disabled persons. AIDS (Acquired Immune Deficiency Syndrome) victims and other victims of infectious diseases, too, have fought to ensure their protection under this antidiscrimination umbrella. In 1991, Congress passed a law requiring that all medical personnel with AIDS disclose their illness to their patients. The law did not, however, require the reverse, that AIDS patients inform their medical providers. The issue of extending equal rights to those with contagious diseases is likely to remain with us as long as contagious diseases remain with us.

Gay Rights.   Until the late 1960s, most homosexuals concealed their sexual preference from the outside world. Many Americans still believe that they do not know any gay people, yet the best estimate is that about 10 percent of the American population is homosexual. AIDS has had a devastating effect on male homosexuals in the United States, but gays face other challenges as well. The Supreme Court has upheld making homosexual activity illegal (*Bowers v. Hardwick*, 1986), and homosexuals often face prejudice in hiring, education, access to public accommodations, and housing.

Both gay men and lesbians organized throughout the 1970s and 1980s, learning political skills and forming powerful interest groups. Most colleges and universities now have gay rights organizations on campus, something unheard of twenty-five years ago. Despite setbacks—like *Bowers*, rulings permitting the Armed Forces to exclude homosexuals, and the efforts of some states (such as Colorado) to prohibit homosexuals from receiving protection against discrimination—gay activists have won important victories. Seven states, including California, and more than a hundred communities have passed laws protecting homosexuals against some forms of discrimination. President Clinton established a "don't ask, don't tell" rule for gays serving in the military, under which the armed services are not to inquire about a person's sexual orientation and homosexuals are not to engage in public displays of homosexual activity or openly declare their sexual orientation.

Homophobia—fear and hatred of homosexuals—has many causes; some are very powerful. Some religions, for instance, condemn homosexuality. Such attitudes will probably continue to be characteristic of a large segment of the American public for years to come, as President Clinton discovered when he moved to end the ban on gays serving in the military.

The New Debate About Equality: Affirmative Action

The public policy paths for women and minorities have not been identical. However, they have converged in the debate about affirmative action to overcome the effects of past discrimination. **Affirmative action** involves efforts to bring about increased employment, promotion, or admission for members of such groups. The goal is to move beyond *equal opportunity* (everyone having the same chance of obtaining good jobs, for example) toward *equal results* (the same percentage of success in obtaining those jobs). This goal might be accomplished through special rules in the public and private sectors that recruit or otherwise give special treatment to previously disadvantaged groups. Numerical quotas that ensure a portion of government contracts, or law school admissions, or police department promotions, go to minorities and women are the strongest and most controversial form of affirmative action.

The constitutional status of affirmative action has not, however, been very clear. New state and federal laws have provided for discrimination *in favor* of these previously disadvantaged groups. Some state governments adopted affirmative action programs to increase minority enrollment, job holding, or promotion. Eventually the federal government mandated that all state and local governments, together with each institution receiving aid from or contracting with the federal government, adopt an affirmative action program.

The Court has been more deferential to Congress than to local government in upholding affirmative action programs. While it upheld a federal rule setting aside 10 percent of all federal construction contracts for minority owned firms, it found unconstitutional a Richmond, Virginia, plan that reserved 30 percent of city subcontracts for minority firms. The Court also agreed that Congress may require preferential treatment for minorities to increase their ownership of broadcast licenses, but it rejected an effort by the medical school at the University of California, Davis to set aside a set number of places in the entering class for "disadvantaged groups" (*Regents of the University of California v. Bakke*, 1978).

To confuse matters further, the Court approved a voluntary union-and-management-sponsored program (intended to rectify years of past employment discrimination) to admit more African Americans than whites into a special training program at the Kaiser Aluminum Company. The Court also approved preferential treatment of minorities in promotions and ordered quotas for minority union memberships. (You can examine a case of a public employer using affirmative action promotions to counter underrepresentation of women and minorities in the workplace in "You Are the Judge: The Case of the Santa Clara Dispatcher.")

Not everyone agrees that affirmative action is a wise or fair policy. There is little support from the general public for programs that set aside jobs or employ quotas for members of minority groups. Opposition is especially strong when people view affirmative action as *reverse discrimination* where less-qualified individuals get hired or admitted to educational or training programs because of their minority status.

YOU ARE THE JUDGE

The Case of the Santa Clara Dispatcher

For four years Diane Joyce patched asphalt with a Santa Clara country road crew around San Jose, California, and its suburbs. She applied for a promotion, hoping to work in the less-strenuous and better-paid position of dispatcher. Another applicant for the job was Paul Johnson, a white male who had worked for the agency for thirteen years.

Like Diane, Paul did well on the exam given to all applicants; in fact, the two scored among the top six applicants, Diane with a score of seventy-three, and Paul with seventy-five. Knowing that Paul's score was a shade better and his work experience longer, the supervisor decided to hire him. The county's affirmative action officers overruled the supervisor, however, and Diane got the job. Paul decided to get a lawyer.

Paul's lawyer argued that Diane's promotion violated Title VII of the Civil Rights Act of 1964. This law, originally passed to guarantee minorities' access to jobs and promotions, makes it unlawful for an employer to deprive any individual of employment opportunities because of their race, color, religion, sex, or national origin.

You be the judge: Should Diane Joyce have been promoted? For the Supreme Court's answer, see The Court Decides on page 117.

UNDERSTANDING CIVIL LIBERTIES, CIVIL RIGHTS, AND THE CONSTITUTION

Civil liberties and civil rights lie at the core of governing. They have shaped profoundly both the nature of American democracy and the role of the federal government.

Civil Liberties, Civil Rights, and Democracy

Unquestionably, the extension of both civil liberties and civil rights has expanded our democratic system. The rights ensured by the First Amendment—the freedoms of expression, religion, and assembly—are essential to a democracy. If people are to govern themselves and make intelligent decisions, they must have the right to express themselves and have access to all available information and opinions. Majority rule is also essential for democracy, but the majority does not have the freedom to decide that there are some ideas it would rather not hear or deprive the minority of their rights.

When groups are denied the right to organize, express opinions, or vote on the basis of their opinions, democracy loses. The steady expansion of civil rights—particularly the right to vote—has drawn more groups into the democratic process. The rights under the First and Fourteenth Amendments were essential in helping African Americans, women, and now other groups secure a place in the electoral system.

Civil Liberties, Civil Rights, and the Scope of Government

There is no doubt that civil liberties limit the power of government. Today's government is large, powerful, and utilizes technologies unimaginable by the Founding Fathers. Despite this, Americans' civil liberties have expanded, not contracted, over the two centuries of the American Constitution. We have steadfastly marched away from, not toward, the rigid regimentation of thought, speech, and opinion often found in the rest of the world.

And yet, somewhat paradoxically, we have also expanded the power of government through civil rights policies. These laws and court decisions tell groups and individuals that there are certain things they may and may not do. Employers must accommodate the disabled and make an effort to hire minority workers, whether they want to or not. The founders might have been troubled had they known about the civil rights laws our government would enact. These policies do not conform to the eighteenth-century idea of limited government. Government's power to regulate employers, law school admission committees, and state legislators has increased since the origins of the civil rights movement. And yet there are few Americans who would willingly turn back the clock to the days of *Plessy v. Ferguson,* when U.S. citizens were kept "separate," and therefore unequal.

SUMMARY

This chapter has examined the closely connected issues of *civil liberties* and *civil rights.* Both are critical to understanding the Constitution and our current public policies.

Civil liberties are the protections we enjoy against the government. There are two major elements of civil liberties found in the Bill of Rights, the first ten amendments to the Constitution. One element is central to the First Amendment, and contains the great freedoms of speech, press, religion, and assembly. The other element includes protections at the bar of justice, originally designed to protect political prisoners but now more important in ensuring the rights of the accused. Even though the size of our government has grown, the scope of our civil liberties has grown as well.

Civil rights are policies that protect persons against arbitrary or discriminatory treatment by government or individuals. They are designed to expand opportunities and equality in the American political system. The history of civil rights involves the struggle of African Americans for many decades, whose struggle through slavery, reconstruction and resegregation, and then civil rights, led to numerous policies to promote equality. The struggle for equal rights for women is a newer struggle, and that of older Americans, disabled Americans, and others is newer still. There have been philosophical struggles over the meaning of equal rights and affirmative action, constitutional struggles over the equal protection clause of the Fourteenth Amendment, and, of course, political struggles as well.

THE COURT DECIDES

Captain Goldman's Yarmulke
In a five to four decision, the Supreme Court upheld the right of the Air Force to enforce its dress code even against religiously-based dress choices. The narrow majority reaffirmed the Court's traditional rule that things acceptable for civilians may not be acceptable for the military. However, Congress intervened to permit the wearing of yarmulkes.

The Nazis' March
A federal district court ruled that Skokie's ordinance did restrict freedom of assembly. In October 1978, the Supreme Court let this lower court decision stand. In fact, the Nazis did not subsequently march in Skokie, but had to settle for a few poorly attended demonstrations in Chicago.

Ms. Montoya's Case
The Court concluded that U.S. Customs agents were well within their constitutional authority to search Montoya. Even though collection of evidence took the better part of two days, Chief Justice Rehnquist remarked wryly that "alimentary-canal smuggling cannot be detected in the amount of time in which other illegal activities may be investigated."

The Santa Clara Dispatcher
The Supreme Court held that carefully constructed affirmative action plans, designed to remedy specific past discriminations, could be constitutional. Thus, Diane Joyce got to keep her job. In a stinging dissent, Justice Scalia complained that the Court was "converting [the law] from a guarantee that race or sex will not be a basis for employment determinations, to guarantee that it often will."

FOR FURTHER READING

Adler, Renata. *Reckless Disregard*. New York: Knopf, 1986. The story of two monumental conflicts between free press and individual reputations.

Baer, Judith A. *Equality Under the Constitution: Reclaiming the Fourteenth Amendment*. Ithaca, NY: Cornell University Press, 1983. A liberal interpretation of the amendment.

Baker, Liva. *Miranda: The Crime, the Law, the Politics*. New York: Atheneum, 1983. An excellent book-length treatment of one of the major criminal cases of our time.

Berger, Raoul. *Government by Judiciary: The Transformation of the Fourteenth Amendment*. Cambridge, MA: Harvard University Press, 1977. Berger is not one who favors use of the Fourteenth Amendment to expand equality.

Berry, Mary F. *Why ERA Failed*. Bloomington: Indiana University Press, 1986. An excellent account of public policies for women, with particular attention to the demise of the Equal Rights Amendment.

Kluger, Richard. *Simple Justice*. New York: Knopf, 1976. The story of the *Brown* case.

Levy, Leonard W. *The Emergence of a Free Press*. New York: Oxford University Press, 1985. A major work on the framers' intentions regarding freedom of expression.

Levy, Leonard W. *The Establishment Clause: Religion and the First Amendment*. New York: Macmillan, 1986. The author argues that it is unconstitutional for government to provide aid to any religion.

Lewis, Anthony. *Gideon's Trumpet*. New York: Random House, 1964. The story of how Clarence Gideon won his right-to-counsel case and one of the best case studies of a court case ever written.

Mansbridge, Jane. *Why We Lost the ERA*. Chicago: University of Chicago Press, 1986. The politics of women's rights.

McGlen, Nancy, and Karen O'Connor. *Women's Rights: The Struggle for Equality in the Nineteenth and Twentieth Centuries*. New York: Praeger, 1983. A good account of the struggle for equal rights for women.

Petchesky, Rosalind. *Abortion and Woman's Choice*. New York: Longman, 1983. An insightful treatment of issues regarding reproductive privacy.

Wilkinson, J. Harvie, III. *From Brown to Bakke*. New York: Oxford University Press, 1979. The political and legal history of civil rights policies between *Brown* and *Bakke*.

NOTES

1. This story, together with several significant examples of issues under the Bill of Rights, is told in Ellen Alderman and Caroline Kennedy, *In Our Defense: The Bill of Rights in Action* (New York: William Morrow, 1990), 149–155.
2. One classic study along these lines is James W. Prothro and Charles M. Grigg, "Fundamental Principles of Democracy: Bases of Agreement and Disagreement," *Journal of Politics* 22 (1960): 276–294. A more recent explanation is John L. Sullivan et al., "The Sources of Political Intolerance: A Multivariate Analysis," *American Political Science Review* 75 (1981): 100–115.
3. Kenneth D. Wald, *Religion and Politics in the United States*, 2nd ed. (Chatham, NJ: Chatham House, 1992).
4. See the story in Fred W. Friendly, *Minnesota Rag* (New York: Random House, 1981).
5. Bob Woodward and Scott Armstrong, *The Brethren* (New York: Avon, 1979), 233.
6. See Renata Adler, *Reckless Disregard* (New York: Knopf, 1986).
7. On the *Miranda* case, see Liva Baker, *Miranda: The Crime, the Law, the Politics* (New York: Atheneum, 1983).
8. See Anthony Lewis, *Gideon's Trumpet* (New York: Random House, 1964).
9. *Time*, June 17, 1991, 54f.
10. See Judith A. Baer, *Equality Under the Constitution: Reclaiming the Fourteenth Amendment* (Ithaca, NY: Cornell University Press, 1983). For a less sympathetic view of the use of the equal protection clause, see Raoul Berger, *Government by Judiciary: The Transformation of the Fourteenth Amendment* (Cambridge, MA: Harvard University Press, 1977).
11. One excellent analysis of the ERA is in Jane Mansbridge, *Why We Lost the ERA* (Chicago: University of Chicago Press, 1986).

CHAPTER 5

Public Opinion and Political Action

How many times have you heard politicians or columnists express their personal views in terms of "the American people . . ."? Because American society is so complex, it would be hard to find a statement about the American people—who they are and what they believe—that is either 100 percent right or wrong. The American people are wondrously diverse. There are about 250 million Americans, forming a mosaic of racial, ethnic, and cultural groups. America was founded on the principle of tolerating diversity, and it remains one of the most culturally diverse countries in the world today. Most Americans view this diversity as one of the most appealing aspects of their society.

Such diversity makes the study of American public opinion especially complex, for there are many groups with a great variety of opinions. This is not to say that public opinion would be easy to study even if America were a more homogeneous society; as you will see, the measurement of public opinion involves careful interviewing procedures and question wording. Further complicating the task is the fact that people are often not well-informed about the issues. Those who are least informed are also the least likely to participate in the political process, creating inequalities in who takes part in political action.

For American government to work efficiently and effectively, the diversity of the American public and its opinions must be faithfully channeled through the political process. This chapter reveals just how difficult a task this is.

THE AMERICAN PEOPLE

One way of looking at the American public is through **demography**, the science of human populations. The most valuable tool for understanding demographic changes in America is the **census**. The U.S. Constitution requires that

When the Census Bureau was criticized for failing to take into account the hundreds of thousands of Americans who are without homes, it responded in 1990 by sending out employees to attempt to count the homeless in major cities. Here, census takers are shown counting people sleeping in the park just across the street from the White House.

the government conduct an "actual enumeration" of the population every ten years; the first such census was conducted in 1790, the most recent in 1990. Getting a question included on the census form is a highly competitive enterprise, as groups of all different kinds seek to be counted.[1] Once a group can establish its numbers, it can then ask for federal aid in proportion to its size. In 1990, advocates for the disabled came out as one winner when the census added a question designed to count people who have difficulty taking care of themselves or getting where they need to go. The census also responded to complaints that the homeless were being left out of the count by sending out 15,000 workers one night to count them—the final tally coming to 228,621.

The next few sections will examine the ways the American culture and political system are changing as a result of population changes.

The Immigrant Society

The United States has always been a nation of immigrants. As John F. Kennedy said, America is "not merely a nation but a nation of nations." All Americans, except for American Indians, either are descended from immi-

Just north of San Diego, the problem of illegal immigration from Mexico has taken a dangerous turn. Seeking to make their way around a freeway check-point, immigrants sometimes attempt crossing the busy San Diego Freeway. After a number of people had been hit by cars, authorities posted signs like these to warn motorists to look out for people crossing the freeway.

grants or are immigrants themselves. Today, federal law allows up to 630,000 new immigrants to be legally admitted every year. This is equivalent to adding a city with the population of Washington, D.C., every year. And in recent years the illegal immigrants have outnumbered the legal immigrants.

There have been three great waves of immigration to the United States:

- Before the Civil War, northwestern Europeans (English, Irish, Germans, and Scandinavians) constituted the first wave of immigration.
- After the Civil War, southern and eastern Europeans (Italians, Jews, Poles, Russians, and others) made up the second wave.
- After World War II, Hispanics and Asians made up the third wave. The 1980s saw the second largest number of immigrants of any decade in American history.

Immigrants bring with them their aspirations as well as their own political beliefs. Cubans in Miami, the near-majority of the city's population, typically have fled Castro's Marxist regime and brought their anti-communist sentiments with them. Similarly, the Vietnamese came to America after the United States failed to prevent a communist takeover there. Many Mexican Americans, by contrast, have come to the United States to escape poverty; every day Mexicans cross the Rio Grande in search of economic opportunity. Because the children of these immigrants are often poor and speak little English, many Mexican-American leaders have advocated a system of bilingual education in American public schools. The push for bilingual education is just one of the many examples of how immigration has shifted the policy agenda over the years.

The American Mosaic

With its long history of immigration, the United States has often been called a **melting pot**. This phrase refers to a mixture of cultures, ideas, and peoples. As the third wave of immigration continues, policymakers have come to speak of a new **minority majority**, a clever phrase meaning that America will soon cease to have a white, generally Anglo-Saxon majority. The 1990 census data show an all-time low in the percentage of non-Hispanic white Americans—just over 75 percent of the population. African Americans now number 12 percent of the population, Hispanics 9 percent, Asians 3 percent, and American Indians slightly less than 1 percent of the population. Significantly, minority populations are growing at a much faster rate than the white population, due to their higher birth rates and immigration levels. It is now estimated that all the minority groups combined should pass the 50 percent mark by the year 2060. (Of course, should birth and immigration rates change, so will these estimates.)

Currently, the largest component of the minority majority is the African-American population—one in eight Americans. These are the descendents of reluctant immigrants, namely Africans who were brought to America by force as slaves. As Chapter 4 explained, a legacy of racism and discrimination has left our African-American population economically and politically disadvantaged. Nearly 33 percent of blacks currently live under the poverty line, compared to about 10 percent of whites.

Despite being near the bottom of the economic spectrum, the geographic concentration and cohesive voting behavior of African Americans has enabled them to exercise a good deal of political clout since the implementation of the Voting Rights Act. The number of black elected officials has increased from 1,469 in 1970 to 7,552 in 1992.[2] In 1989, two notable electoral milestones were reached. Douglas Wilder of Virginia became the nation's first elected African-American governor, and David Dinkins became the first African-American mayor of New York City. And in 1992, Carole Mosley-Brown of Illinois became the first African-American woman to be elected to the U.S. Senate.

The familiar problems of African Americans sometimes obscure the problems of other minority groups, such as Hispanics (composed largely of Puerto Ricans, Cubans, Mexicans, and Haitians). By the year 2013, however, the Hispanic population should outnumber the African-American population. Like African Americans, Hispanics are concentrated in cities. They are rapidly gaining power in the Southwest, and cities such as San Antonio and Denver have elected mayors of Hispanic heritage. As of 1990, the state legislatures of New Mexico, Texas, Arizona, Colorado, Florida, and California all had at least 5 percent Hispanic representation.

"Well, it all depends. Where are these huddled masses coming from?"

Drawing by Handelsman; © 1992 The New Yorker Magazine, Inc.

An issue of particular concern to the Hispanic community is what to do about the problem of illegal immigration. A new immigration law, called the **Simpson-Mazzoli Act** after its congressional sponsors, required that as of June 1987 employers document the citizenship of their employees. Whether people are born in Canton, Ohio, or Canton, China, they now have to prove that they are either citizens or legal immigrants in order to work. Civil and criminal penalties can now be assessed against employers who knowingly employ illegal immigrants. This law causes concern among leaders of immigrant groups, who worry that employers might simply decline to hire members of such groups rather than take any chances.

Unlike Hispanics who have come to America to escape poverty, the recent influx of Asians has been driven by a new class of professional workers looking for greater opportunity. As Ronald Takaki documents, Asians who have come to America since the 1965 Immigration Act opened the gate to them make up the most highly skilled immigrant group in American history.[3] Indeed, Asian Americans have often been called the super achievers of the minority majority. This is especially true in the case of educational attainment, with 37 percent of Asian Americans over the age of 25 holding a college degree—almost twice the national average. As a result, their median family income has already surpassed that of non-Hispanic whites.

The emergence of the minority majority is just one of several major demographic changes that have altered the face of American politics. In addition, the population has been moving and aging.

The Regional Shift

For most of American history, the most populous states have been concentrated north of the Mason-Dixon line and east of the Mississippi River. As you can see in Figure 5.1, though, over the last fifty years much of America's popu-

---

FIGURE 5.1 — Shifting Population

These maps paint a population portrait of the United States over the last five decades. The states are drawn to scale based on population. In 1940, the most populous states were concentrated east of the Mississippi River: New York, Pennsylvania, and Illinois stand out. By 1990, the national population picture—and the map—had changed considerably. Today the country's 250 million citizens are scattered more widely, and though large concentrations of population still dominate the East, there has been huge growth on the West Coast, in Texas, and in Florida.

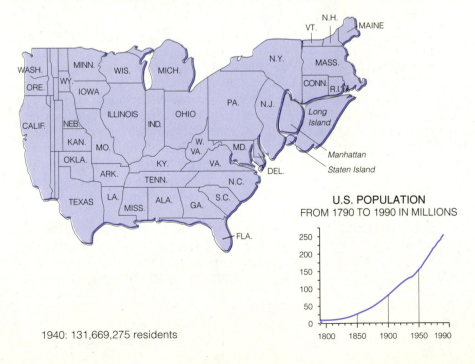

1940: 131,669,275 residents

U.S. POPULATION
FROM 1790 TO 1990 IN MILLIONS

Shifting Population (continued)

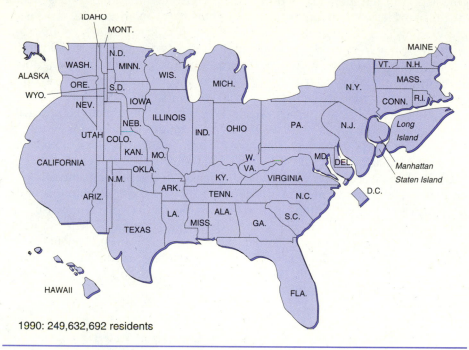

1990: 249,632,692 residents

SOURCE: The 1940 map was the work of the National Opinion Research Center, University of Denver, as printed in John Gunther's 1946 book, *Inside U.S.A.* The 1990 map was designed after that work by Richard Furno of *The Washington Post*, using 1990 census data.

lation growth has been centered in the West and South. In particular, the populations of Florida, Texas, and California have grown rapidly as people moved to the Sunbelt. From 1980 to 1990, the rate of population growth was 33 percent in Florida, 26 percent in California, and 20 percent in Texas. In contrast, there was virtually no population growth at all in so-called "rust belt" states like Pennsylvania, Ohio, and Michigan.

Demographic changes are associated with political changes. Because states gain or lose congressional representation as their populations change, power shifts as well. This process is called **reapportionment**, and it occurs after every census, when the 435 seats in the House of Representatives are reallocated to the states based on population changes. Thus, as California has grown throughout this century its representation in the House has increased from just 7 in 1900 to 52 in 1992. California was again the biggest winner in the 1990 reapportionment, gaining 7 seats. The biggest loser in 1990 was New York (3 seats), which has lost about one-third of its delegation over the last fifty years.

The Graying of America

One aspect of the movement to the Sunbelt has been the migration of senior citizens to Florida and other warm-weather states. Nationwide, the fastest growing age group in America is composed of citizens over sixty-five. Not only are people living longer as a result of medical advances, but the birth rate has dropped substantially. About 60 percent of adult Americans living today grew up in families of four or more children. If the current baby bust continues, this figure will eventually be cut to 30 percent.[4]

By the year 2020, as the post–World War II baby boom generation reaches senior citizen status, there will be just two working Americans for every person over the age of sixty-five. If you think Social Security is being stretched to the limit now, just wait until 2020. The Social Security system, begun under the New Deal, is exceeded only by national defense as America's most costly public policy. The current group of older Americans and those soon to follow can lay claim to nearly $5 trillion guaranteed by Social Security. They also hold title to roughly $1 trillion in public and private pension plans. There is a political message in these numbers: people who have been promised benefits expect to collect them, especially benefits for which they have made monthly contributions. Thus, even Ronald Reagan's budget-cutting policies treated Social Security benefits as sacrosanct.

WHAT AMERICANS LEARN ABOUT POLITICS: POLITICAL SOCIALIZATION

As the most experienced segment of the population, the elderly have undergone the most political socialization. **Political socialization** is "the process through which an individual acquires his or her particular political orientations—his or her knowledge, feelings, and evaluations regarding his or her political world."[5] As people become more socialized with age, their political orientations grow firmer. It should not be surprising that governments largely aim their socialization efforts at the young, not the old.

Only a small portion of Americans' political learning is formal. Some Americans may take civics or government classes in high school or political science classes in college. In such formal settings, citizens learn some of the nuts and bolts of government—how many senators each state has, what presidents do, and so on. But formal socialization is only the tip of the iceberg. Americans do most of their political learning without teachers or classes. In fact, there is little evidence that formal learning about politics is long lasting; although millions of American teenagers are required to take a high school civics course, for the vast majority of white teenagers studied, taking civics made virtually no difference in their political attitudes and beliefs.[6]

Informal learning is really much more important than formal, in-class learning about politics. Most informal socialization is almost accidental. Few parents sit down with their children and say, "Johnny, let us tell you why

These children—the faces of the coming minority majority population—suggest the unique problem of American political socialization: transforming people of diverse cultural backgrounds and beliefs into American citizens.

we're Republicans." Words like *pick up*, *absorb*, and *acquire* perhaps best describe the informal side of socialization. Still, the family's role is central because of its monopoly on two crucial resources in the early years: time and emotional commitment. Most students in an American government class like to think of themselves as independent thinkers, especially when it comes to politics, yet one can predict how the majority of young people will vote simply by knowing the political leanings of their parents. In Table 5.1 you can see how well high school seniors and their parents matched up on party affiliation in a classic 1965 study by M. Kent Jennings and Richard Niemi.

As children approach adult status, though, some degree of adolescent rebellion against parents and their beliefs often takes place. Witnessing the outpouring of youthful rebellion in the 1960s, many people thought a generation gap was opening up. Radical youth supposedly condemned their backward-thinking parents. Though such a gap did exist in a few families, the overall evidence for it was slim. When Jennings and Niemi reinterviewed their sample of young adults and their parents eight years later in 1973, they still found far more agreement than disagreement across the generational divide.

TABLE 5.1 — Parent-Child Agreement on Party Identification

In 1965, Jennings and Niemi selected a sample of high-school seniors throughout the country and interviewed them as well as one of their parents. Below you will find how closely the two generations matched on party affiliation. The numbers represent the percentage of parent-child pairs that fell into each category. (For example, the 32.6 figure indicates how often the parent and the child both said they were Democrats.)

CHILDREN	PARENTS		
	Democrat	Independent	Republican
Democrat	32.6	7.0	3.4
Independent	13.2	12.7	9.7
Republican	3.6	4.1	13.6
	Agreement=58.9%	Disagreement=7.0%	

SOURCE: Adapted from M. Kent Jennings and Richard G. Niemi, *The Political Character of Adolescence* (Princeton, NJ: Princeton University Press, 1973), 39.

Moving out of the family nest and into adulthood did result in the offspring becoming somewhat less like their parents politically, however.[7] Other socialization agents had apparently exerted influence in the intervening years.

The mass media is "the new parent" according to many observers. Average grade-school youngsters spend more time each week watching television than they spend at school. Television now displaces parents as the chief source of information as children get older. Unfortunately, today's generation of young adults is significantly less likely to watch television news than their elders. A recent Times-Mirror study attributed the relative lack of political knowledge of the youth of the 1990s to their media consumption habits (or more appropriately, their lack thereof).[8] In 1965, Gallup found virtually no difference between age categories in frequency of TV-news viewing. By the 1990s, a considerable gap had opened up, though, with older people paying the most attention to the news and young adults the least. If you have ever turned on the TV news and wondered why all the commercials seem to be for Geritol, Ex-lax, or denture cream, now you know why.

Political learning does not, of course, end when one reaches 18, or even when one graduates from college. Politics is a lifelong activity. Because America is an aging society, it is important to consider the effects of growing older on political behavior. Aging does increase one's political participation, as well as one's strength of party attachment. Young people lack experience with politics, as they do with other things. Because political behavior is to some degree learned behavior, they have some learning yet to do. Political participation rises steadily with age until the infirmities of old age make it harder to participate.[9] Like other attachments, such as religion, party identification grows not so much with "age per se, but rather as a function of the length of time that the individual has felt some generalized preference for a particular party and repetitively voted for it."[10]

Politics, like most other things, is thus a learned behavior. Americans learn to vote, to pick a party, and to evaluate political events in the world around them. One of the products of all this learning is what is known as public opinion.

WHAT AMERICANS BELIEVE: PUBLIC OPINION AND POLICY

The public holds opinions about many topics. In the following sections you will explore a particular kind of **public opinion**: the distribution of the population's beliefs about politics and policy issues. Saying that opinions are distributed among the population implies that there is rarely a single public opinion; in other words, so many people, so many opinions. Because there are differences of opinion, not everyone can be represented on every issue. Thus, understanding the content and dynamics of public opinion is crucial to assessing the extent to which citizens actually guide policy-making.

Measuring Public Opinion

Although public opinion polling is a relatively new science, very sophisticated technology is now available for measuring public opinion. Public opinion polling was first developed by a young man named George Gallup, who did some polling for his mother-in-law, a longshot candidate for secretary of state in Iowa in 1932. With the Democratic landslide of that year, Gallup's mother-in-law won a stunning victory, further stimulating his interest in politics. From that little acorn the mighty oak of public opinion polling has grown. The firm that Gallup founded spread throughout the democratic world, and in some languages, a Gallup is actually the word used for an opinion poll.[11]

It would be prohibitively expensive to ask every citizen his or her opinion on a whole range of issues. Instead, polls rely on a **sample** of the population—a relatively small proportion of people who are chosen as representative of the whole. Herbert Asher draws an analogy to a doctor's blood test to illustrate the principle of sampling.[12] Your doctor doesn't need to drain a gallon of blood from you to determine whether you have mononucleosis, AIDS, or any other disease. Rather, a small sample of blood will reveal its properties.

In public opinion polling, a sample of about fifteen hundred to two thousand people can accurately represent the "universe" of potential voters. The key to the accuracy of opinion polls is the technique of **random sampling**, which operates on the principle that everyone should have an equal probability of being selected. Your chance of being asked to be in the poll should therefore be as good as that of anyone else—rich or poor, black or white, young or old, male or female. If the sample is randomly drawn, about 12 percent of those interviewed will be black, slightly over 50 percent female, and so forth, matching the population as a whole.

It should be kept in mind that the science of polling involves estimation; a sample can only represent the population with a certain degree of confidence. The level of confidence is known as the **sampling error**, which depends on the size of the sample. The more people interviewed in a poll, the more confident one can be of the results. A typical poll of about fifteen hundred to two thousand respondents has a sampling error of ± 3 percent. What this means is that 95 percent of the time the poll results are within 3 percent of what the entire population thinks. If 60 percent of the sample say they approve of the job the president is doing, one can be virtually certain that the true figure is between 57 and 63 percent. Still, there is always a certain amount of risk involved. About 5 percent of the time, a sample will produce results far off the mark, but the odds are definitely in favor of the pollsters.

In order to be within the margin of error, researchers must follow proper sampling techniques. In perhaps the most infamous survey ever, a 1936 *Literary Digest* poll underestimated the vote for President Franklin Roosevelt by 19 percent, erroneously predicting a big victory for Republican Alf Landon. The well-established magazine suddenly became a laughingstock and soon went out of business. Although the number of responses the magazine obtained for its poll was a staggering 2,376,000, its methods were badly flawed. Trying to reach as many people as possible, the magazine drew names from the biggest lists it could find—telephone books and motor-vehicle records. In the midst of the Great Depression, the people on these lists were above the average income level (only 40 percent had telephones then; fewer still owned cars), and thus more likely to vote Republican. The moral of the story is this: accurate representation, not the number of responses, is the most important feature of a public opinion survey. Indeed, as techniques have advanced over the last fifty years, typical sample sizes have been getting smaller, not larger.

The newest computer and telephone technology has made surveying less expensive and more commonplace. Until recently, pollsters needed a national network of interviewers to canvass door-to-door in their localities with a clipboard of questions. Now most polling is done on the telephone with samples selected through **random digit dialing**. Calls are placed to phone numbers within randomly chosen exchanges (for example, 512-471-xxxx) around the country. In this manner, both listed and unlisted numbers will be reached at a cost of about one-fifth that of person-to-person interviewing.

From its modest beginning with George Gallup's 1932 polls for his mother-in-law in Iowa, polling has become a big business worldwide. Public opinion polling is one of those American innovations, like soft drinks and fast-food restaurants, that has spread throughout the world. From Manhattan to Moscow, from Tulsa to Tokyo, people apparently want to know what other people think.

The Role of Polls in American Democracy

Polls help political candidates detect public preferences. Supporters of polling insist that it is a tool for democracy. With it, they say, policymakers can keep in touch with changing opinions on the issues. No longer do politicians have to wait until the next election to see if the public approves or disapproves of the government's course. If the poll results suddenly turn, government officials can make corresponding midcourse corrections.

Critics of polling, by contrast, think it makes politicians more concerned with following than leading. Polls might have told the constitutional convention delegates that the Constitution was unpopular, or they might have told Jefferson that people did not want the Louisiana Purchase. Certainly they would have told William Seward not to buy Alaska (known widely at the time as "Seward's Folly"). Polls may thus discourage bold leadership, like that of Winston Churchill, who once said:

> Nothing is more dangerous than to live in the temperamental atmosphere of a Gallup poll, always taking one's pulse and taking one's temperature. . . . There is only one duty, only one safe course, and that is to try to be right and not to fear to do or say what you believe.[13]

Polls can also weaken democracy by distorting the election process. In particular, they play to the media's interest in the horse race, that is, who's hot and who's not. Recent presidential campaigns have seen the issues frequently drowned out by a steady flood of daily poll results.

Probably the most criticized type of poll is the election-day **exit poll**. For this type of poll, voting places are randomly selected from around the country. Workers are then sent to these places and told to ask every tenth person how they voted. The results are accumulated toward the end of the day and enable the television networks to project the results of all but very close races before the polls even close. In the presidential elections of 1980, 1984, and 1988 the networks declared a winner while millions on the West Coast still had hours to vote. Critics have charged that this practice discourages many from voting, and thereby affects the outcome of some state and local races. Although most voters in western states have been outraged by this practice, careful analysis of survey data shows that few voters have been influenced by exit-poll results.[14]

Perhaps the most pervasive criticism of polling is that by altering the wording of a question, pollsters can get pretty much the results they want. Sometimes even subtle changes in question wording can produce dramatic differences. For example, a month before the start of hostilities against Iraq, the ABC/*Washington Post* poll showed 63 percent of the public thought we should go to war, but the CBS/*New York Times* poll recorded only 45 percent for war. The difference was that the former asked whether the United States should go to war "at some point after January 15 or not," while the latter asked if the "United States should start military actions against Iraq, or should the United States wait longer to see if the trade embargo and other economic sanctions work."[15]

"*Glad you brought that up, Jim. The latest research on polls has turned up some interesting variables. It turns out, for example, that people will tell you any old thing that pops into their heads.*"

Because polling sounds scientific with its talk of random samples and margins of error, it is easy to take survey results for solid fact. Being an informed consumer of polls requires more than just a nuts-and-bolts knowledge of how they are conducted; you should think about whether the questions are fair and unbiased before making too much of the results. Good, bad, or indifferent, polls are here to stay.

What Polls Reveal About Americans' Political Information

Abraham Lincoln spoke stirringly of the inherent wisdom of the American people: "It is true that you may fool all of the people some of the time; and you can even fool some of the people all of the time; but you can't fool all of the people all the time." Obviously, Lincoln recognized the complexity of public opinion.

Thomas Jefferson and Alexander Hamilton had very different views about the wisdom of common folk. Jefferson trusted people's good sense and believed that education would enable them to take the tasks of citizenship ever more seriously. Toward that end, he founded the University of Virginia. Hamilton held a contrasting view. His infamous words—"Your people, sir, are a great beast"—do not reflect confidence in people's capacity for self-government.

If there had been polling data in the early days of the American republic, Hamilton would probably have delighted in throwing some of the results in Jefferson's face. If public opinion analysts are agreed about anything, it is that the level of public knowledge about politics is dismally low. For example, in the 1992 National Election Study (conducted by the University of Michigan), a random sample was asked to identify the political office held by some of the most prominent political leaders. The results were as follows:

- 88 percent knew Dan Quayle was Vice President of the United States
- 45 percent knew Boris Yeltsin was President of Russia
- 26 percent knew Tom Foley was Speaker of the House
- 8 percent knew William Rehnquist was chief justice of the Supreme Court

All told, the study found that only 5 percent of the population could identify all four individuals.

No amount of Jeffersonian faith in the wisdom of the common people can erase the fact that Americans are not very well informed about politics. Asking most people to explain their opinion on affirmative action, MX missiles, or fiscal policy often elicits blank looks. When trouble flares in a far-off country, polls regularly find that people have no idea where that country is. For example, in 1981, only 35 percent knew the location of El Salvador, despite the fact that it was constantly in the news. (Many thought it was in the Middle East, a well-known trouble spot.) Surveys show that citizens around the globe lack a basic awareness of the world around them. (See "In Focus: America in Perspective")

As Lance Bennett points out, these findings provide "a source of almost bitter humor in light of what the polls tell us about public information on other subjects."[16] He notes that more people know their astrological sign (76 percent) than know the name of their representative in the House. Slogans from TV commercials are better recognized than famous political figures. (For example, 82 percent of the public could identify the toilet tissue that completes the slogan "Please don't squeeze the . . . ," and 79 percent knew which upset-stomach remedy used the jingle "Plop, plop, fizz, fizz. Oh, what a relief it is.")

The "paradox of mass politics," says Russell Neuman, is that the American political system works as well as it does given the discomforting lack of public knowledge about politics.[17] Part of the reason for this phenomenon is that people may not know the ins and outs of policy questions or the actors on the political stage, but they know what basic values they want upheld.

AMERICA IN PERSPECTIVE

Citizens of the World Show Little Knowledge of Geography

In the spring of 1988, twelve thousand people in ten nations were asked to identify sixteen places on the following world map. The average citizen in the United States could identify barely more than half. Believe it or not, 14 percent of Americans tested could not even find their own country on the map. Despite years of fighting in Vietnam, 68 percent could not locate this Southeast Asian country. Such lack of basic geographic knowledge is quite common throughout the world. Here is the average score for each of the ten countries in which the test was administered.

Country	Average Score
1 Sweden	11.6
6 United States	8.6
2 West Germany	11.2
7 Great Britain	8.5
3 Japan	9.7
8 Italy	7.6
4 France	9.3
9 Mexico	7.4
5 Canada	9.2
10 Soviet Union	7.4

How would you do? To take the test yourself, match the numbers on the map to the places listed.

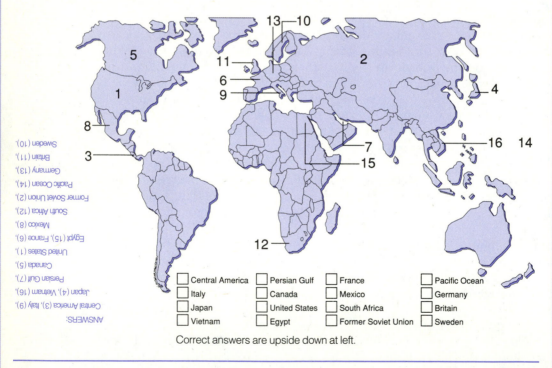

ANSWERS: Central America (3), Italy (9), Japan (4), Vietnam (16), Persian Gulf (7), Canada (5), United States (1), Egypt (15), France (6), Mexico (8), South Africa (12), Former Soviet Union (2), Pacific Ocean (14), Germany (13), Britain (11), Sweden (10).

☐ Central America ☐ Persian Gulf ☐ France ☐ Pacific Ocean
☐ Italy ☐ Canada ☐ Mexico ☐ Germany
☐ Japan ☐ United States ☐ South Africa ☐ Britain
☐ Vietnam ☐ Egypt ☐ Former Soviet Union ☐ Sweden

Correct answers are upside down at left.

SOURCE: Warren E. Leary, "Two Superpowers' Citizens Do Badly in Geography," *New York Times*, November 9, 1989, A6.

When these values are violated, the sleeping giant of public opinion may be stirred to action. Examining these values is thus of great importance.

WHAT AMERICANS VALUE: POLITICAL IDEOLOGIES

A coherent set of values and beliefs about public policy is a **political ideology**. An ideology is much more than a collection of "gut reactions"; it is a set of coherent and consistent policy preferences. Liberal ideology, for example, supports a strong central government that sets policies to promote equality. Conservative ideology, in contrast, supports a small, less activist government that gives freer reign to the private sector (see Table 5.2).

Do People Think in Ideological Terms?

The authors of the classic study *The American Voter* first looked carefully at the ideological sophistication of the American electorate in the 1950s.[18] They divided the public into four groups, according to ideological sophistication.

TABLE 5.2 — *How to Tell a Liberal from a Conservative*

	Liberals	Conservatives
ON FOREIGN POLICY:		
Military spending	Believe we should spend less	Believe we should maintain peace through strength
Use of force	Less willing to commit troops to action, such as in the Persian Gulf War	More likely to support military intervention around the world
ON SOCIAL POLICY:		
Abortion	Support "freedom of choice"	Support "right to life"
School prayer	Are opposed	Are supportive
Affirmative action	Favor	Oppose
ON ECONOMIC POLICY:		
Scope of government	View government as a regulator in the public interest	Favor free-market solutions
Taxes	Want to tax the rich more	Want to keep taxes low
Spending	Want to spend more on the poor	Want to keep spending low
ON CRIME:		
How to cut crime	Believe we should solve the problems that cause crime	Believe we should stop coddling criminals
Defendants' rights	Believe we should guard them carefully	Believe we should stop letting criminals hide behind laws

The Health Security Act that President Clinton proposed in 1993 was the most ambitious presidential proposal to increase the scope of the federal government in the last quarter century. Soon after he presented the plan before a joint session of Congress, Clinton held a televised town meeting in Tampa where he answered questions about the plan from the public.

Their portrait of the American electorate was not a flattering one. Only 12 percent of the people showed evidence of thinking in ideological terms, and thus were classified as ideologues. These people could connect their opinions and beliefs with broad policy positions taken by parties or candidates. They might say, for example, that they liked the Democrats because they were more liberal or the Republicans because they favored a smaller government. Forty-two percent of Americans were called group benefits voters. These people thought of politics mainly by the groups they liked or disliked (for example, "Republicans support small businessmen like me" or "Democrats are the party of the working man"). Twenty-four percent of the population were nature-of-the-times voters. Their handle on politics was limited to whether the times seemed good or bad to them; they might vaguely link the party in power with the country's fortune or misfortune. Finally, 22 percent of the voters were devoid of any ideological or issue content in their political evaluations. They were called the no-issue-content group. Most of them simply voted routinely for a party or judged the candidates solely by their personalities. Overall, at least during the 1950s, Americans seemed to care little about the differences between liberal and conservative politics.

There has been much debate about whether this portrayal accurately characterizes the public today. Nie, Verba, and Petrocik took a look at the changing American voter from 1956 to 1972,[19] and argued that voters were more sophisticated in the 1970s than in the 1950s. Others, though, have concluded that people only seemed more informed and ideological because the wording of the questions had changed.[20] If the exact same methods are used to update the analysis of *The American Voter*, one finds just 6 percent more ideologues in 1988 than in 1956.

This does not mean that the vast majority of the population lacks a political ideology. Rather, for most people the terms *liberal* and *conservative* are just not as important as they are for the political elite such as politicians, activists, and the like. Relatively few people have ideologies that organize their political beliefs as clearly as shown in Table 5.2. Thus, the authors of *The American Voter* concluded that to speak of election results as indicating a movement of the public either left (to more liberal policies) or right (to more conservative policies) is a misnomer, because most voters do not think in such terms. Furthermore, those that do are actually the least likely to shift from one election to the next.

The American Voter argued persuasively that Eisenhower's two election victories did not represent a shift in the conservative direction during the 1950s. In the 1980s, the issue of whether public opinion had undergone a major rightward change was once again raised with the victories of Ronald Reagan—who campaigned vigorously against big government.

Public Attitudes on the Scope of Government

An FDR liberal in the 1930s and 1940s, Reagan led what he proclaimed to be a conservative revolution in the 1980s. Central to his ideology was that the scope of government activities had grown too vast over the years. According to Reagan, government was not the solution to society's problems—it was the problem. He called for the government to "get off the backs of the American people."

Reagan's rhetoric about the bloated size of government was reminiscent of the 1964 presidential campaign rhetoric of Barry Goldwater, who lost to Lyndon Johnson in a landslide. Indeed, Reagan first made his mark in politics by giving a televised speech on behalf of the embattled Goldwater campaign. Although the rhetoric was much the same in 1980, public opinion about the size of government had changed dramatically. In 1964, only 30 percent of the population thought the government was getting too powerful; by 1980 this figure had risen to 50 percent.

For much of the population, however, questions about the serge of government have consistently elicited no opinion at all among many voters. Indeed, the 1992 National Election Study found that two-fifths of the population had not thought about the question. The question of government power is a complex one, but as *Government in America* will continue to stress, it is one of the key controversies in American politics today. Once again it seems that the public is not nearly as concerned with political issues as would be ideal in a democratic society.

Nor do public opinions on different aspects of the same issue hold together well. Thus, although more people today think the government is too big rather than too small, a plurality has consistently called for more spending on programs like education, health care, aid to big cities, protecting the environment, and fighting crime.[21] Many political scientists have looked at these contradictory findings and concluded that Americans are ideological conservatives but operational liberals—meaning that they oppose the idea of big government in principle but favor it in practice.

People Liked Reagan but Not His Policies

There was little inconsistency in the political beliefs of Ronald Reagan, however. During his eight years as president, he pressed ahead with a thoroughly conservative agenda. With Reagan's landslide reelection victory in 1984, some political observers felt that a conservative wildfire had swept the country.

Despite Reagan's victories, a common theme in the press throughout the 1980s was that people liked Reagan but not his policies. Indeed, the 1984 National Election Study revealed that although Reagan had the advantage of high approval ratings, on the major policy questions more people felt closer to the stand of Democratic candidate Walter Mondale. By fairly substantial margins, those with opinions disagreed with Reagan's willingness to commit military help to Central America and his desire to spend more on defense. By somewhat smaller margins, people saw Reagan as wanting to cut government services too deeply, not providing enough aid to minorities and women, and being too tough with the Soviet Union.[22]

With the exception of a rise in support for military spending during the 1980 campaign, public opinion specialists have been unable to document any shift toward conservative attitudes during the 1980s. As Ferguson and Rogers concluded, "If American public opinion drifted anywhere over Reagan's first term, it was toward the left, not the right, just the opposite of the turn in public policy."[23] Asked to assess Reagan's time in office, the 1988 electorate was evenly split on the wisdom of defense increases, and generally unaware and unsupportive of domestic cuts.[24]

If so many people disagreed with Reagan, why was he such a popular president, and why was George Bush able to follow in his footsteps? The answer is simply that many swing voters, those that *The American Voter* classified as nature-of-the-times voters, care more about results than ideology.[25] The 1980 election was more about voting Carter out of office than voting Reagan into it. In 1984 and 1988 the Republicans had years of relative peace and prosperity on their side, and this was the key to their victories. With the economic downturn in 1992, these same swing voters decided that it was time for a change, and propelled Bill Clinton into the White House.

In sum, conservatives may have become more visible participants in the 1980s, but they did not necessarily become more numerous. Just how they— and other Americans—participate in politics is the topic of the next section.

HOW AMERICANS PARTICIPATE IN POLITICS

In politics, like many other aspects of life, the squeaky wheel gets the grease. The way citizens "squeak" in politics is to participate. Americans have many avenues of political participation open to them.

- Mrs. Jones of Iowa City goes to a neighbor's living room to attend her local precinct's presidential caucus.
- Tipper Gore, wife of Vice President Al Gore, testifies before a Senate committee to express her view that warning labels should be put on record albums that contain vulgar language.
- Protestors against the massacre in Tiananmen Square gather outside the Chinese embassy in Washington to condemn the Chinese government.
- Parents in Alabama file a lawsuit to oppose textbooks that, in their opinion, promote "secular humanism."
- Mr. Smith, a Social Security recipient, writes to his senator to express his concern about a possible cut in his cost-of-living benefits.
- One hundred million people vote in the 1992 presidential election.

All of these activities are types of political participation. **Political partici- pation** encompasses the many activities used by citizens to influence the selection of political leaders or the policies they pursue.[26] Participation can be overt or subtle. The mass protests throughout Eastern Europe in the fall of 1989 were an avalanche of political participation, yet quietly writing a letter to your congressperson is also participating. Political participation can be violent or peaceful, organized or individual, casual or consuming.

Generally, the United States has a participatory political culture. Citizens express pride in their nation: 87 percent say they are very proud to be Americans.[27] Nevertheless, just 55 percent of adult Americans voted in the presidential election of 1992 and only 38 percent turned out for the 1994 congressional elections. At the local level the situation is even worse, with elections for city council often drawing less than a quarter of eligible voters and school board elections sometimes less than 10 percent. (For more on voter turnout and why it is so low, see Chapter 7.)

Conventional Participation

Although the line is hard to draw, political scientists generally distinguish between two broad types of participation: conventional and unconventional. Conventional participation includes many widely accepted modes of influencing government: voting, trying to persuade others, ringing doorbells, running

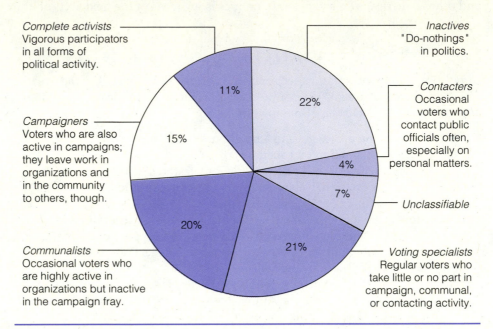

FIGURE 5.2 — *Participators in American Politics: Six Types*

Complete activists
Vigorous participators
in all forms of
political activity.

Inactives
"Do-nothings"
in politics.

Contacters
Occasional
voters who
contact public
officials often,
especially on
personal matters.

Campaigners
Voters who are also
active in campaigns;
they leave work in
organizations and
in the community
to others, though.

Unclassifiable

Communalists
Occasional voters who
are highly active in
organizations but inactive
in the campaign fray.

Voting specialists
Regular voters who
take little or no part in
campaign, communal,
or contacting activity.

11%   22%   4%   15%   7%   20%   21%

SOURCE: Adapted from Sidney Verba and Norman Nie, *Participation in America* (New York: Harper & Row, 1972), 79–80.

for office, and so on. In contrast, unconventional participation includes activities that are often dramatic, such as protesting, civil disobedience, and even violence.

The number of Americans for whom political activity is an important part of their everyday life is minuscule, numbering at most in the tens of thousands. In a classic study of American political participation conducted by Sidney Verba and Norman H. Nie, a sample of Americans was asked about their role in twelve kinds of political activities. Included were voting in presidential and local elections, contacting a government official, working in a campaign, and joining political groups. The majority of Americans participated in only one of the twelve activities—voting in presidential elections. Less than one-fifth had ever contacted a public official, given money to a candidate or party, or helped form a political group or organization.[28]

Participation in politics, like other tasks, reflects specialization and division of labor. Just as people in an organization have different specialities, so do citizens in a country. Voting is a common denominator among most political activists, but other kinds of participation attract different clusters of people. In Verba and Nie's classification of American political participants, 22 percent

Unconventional protest techniques are the trademark of ACT-UP, an AIDS protest group. Here, members of the group are lying down near the White House, defying police orders to disperse. Members of ACT-UP believe that such dramatic protests are necessary to keep the issue of AIDS in the public eye.

were inactive and 11 percent were complete activists. Between these groups were people who specialized as contacters, communalists, or campaigners. (For a discussion of these participant types, see Figure 5.2.)

Protest as Participation

Unconventional forms of political participation are missing from Verba and Nie's list of activities. From the Boston Tea Party to burning draft cards, Americans have engaged in countless political protests. **Protest** is a form of political participation designed to achieve policy change through dramatic and unconventional tactics. The media's willingness to cover the unusual can make protest worthwhile, drawing attention to a point of view that many Americans might never encounter. Indeed, protests today are often orchestrated to provide television cameras with vivid images. Demonstration coordinators steer participants to prearranged staging areas and provide facilities for press coverage.

Throughout American history, individuals and groups have sometimes used **civil disobedience**, that is, they have consciously broken a law that they thought was unjust. The Reverend Martin Luther King, Jr., won a Nobel Peace

Prize for his civil disobedience against segregationist law in the 1950s and 1960s. His "Letter from a Birmingham Jail" is a classic defense of civil disobedience.[29] Sometimes political participation can be violent. The history of violence in American politics is a long one—not surprising, perhaps, for a nation born in rebellion. The turbulent 1960s included many outbreaks of violence. African-American neighborhoods in American cities were torn by riots. College campuses were sometimes turned into battle zones as protestors against the Vietnam War fought police and national guard units. At Kent State, Jackson State, Cornell, Columbia, and elsewhere, peaceful demonstrations turned violent, and many were hurt (or, at Kent State and Jackson State, killed). Although supported by few people, throughout American history violence has been a means of pressuring the government to change its policies.

Class, Inequality, and Participation

Participation is unequal in American political life. Virtually every study of political participation ever conducted has come to the conclusion that "citizens of higher social economic status participate more in politics. This generalization . . . holds true whether one uses level of education, income, or occupation as the measure of social status."[30] Theorists who believe that America is ruled by a small, wealthy elite make much of this fact to support their point of view.

As one might expect from their generally poor education and income levels, minority groups like Hispanics and African Americans are also below average in terms of political participation. The differences are no longer enormous, however. For African Americans, the participation gap in 1992 was 10 percent below the national average; for Hispanic U.S. citizens it was 15 percent.[31] One reason for this smaller-than-expected participation gap is that minorities feel a group consciousness that gives them an extra incentive to vote. In fact, when blacks, Hispanics, and whites of equal incomes and educations are compared, it is the minorities that participate more in politics.[32] In other words, a poor Hispanic or African American is more likely to participate than a poor white. The reason the political participation rate of these minority groups is below average is because they are so much worse off in terms of socioeconomic status. People who believe in democracy should be concerned not only about inequalities in participation, but also about the low numbers of participants. Those who participate are easy to listen to; nonparticipants are easy to ignore. In a democracy, citizenship carries the promise—and the responsibility—of self-government.

DEMOCRACY, PUBLIC OPINION, AND POLITICAL ACTION

Throughout much of the communist world in 1989 people protested for democracy. Many said they wanted their political system to be just like America's, even though they had only a vague idea of how American democracy works. As this chapter has shown, there are many limits on the role Americans play in their political system. The average person, here and elsewhere, is not very well informed about political issues. Expecting the public to make decisions on intricate questions of public policy is clearly asking too much.

American democracy is representative rather than direct. As *The American Voter* stated many years ago, "The public's explicit task is to decide not what government shall do but rather who shall decide what government shall do."[33] When those under communist rule protested for democracy, what they wanted most was the right to have a say in choosing their leaders. Americans can—and often do—take for granted the opportunity to replace our leaders at the next election.

If the public's task in democracy is to choose who is to lead, it must still be asked whether it can do so wisely. If people know little about where the candidates stand on the issues, how can they make rational choices? Many people voted for Reagan even though they disagreed with his policies. In doing so, most were choosing performance criteria over policy criteria. As Morris Fiorina has written, citizens typically have one hard bit of data to go on: "They know what life has been like during the incumbent's administration. They need not know the precise economic or foreign policies of the incumbent administration in order to see or feel the results of those policies."[34] Thus, even if they are only voting according to the nature of the times, their voices are clearly being heard—holding presidents accountable for their actions.

SUMMARY

American society is ethnically varied. The ethnic makeup of America is changing to a minority majority, and Americans are moving towards warmer parts of the country and growing older as a society. All of these changes have policy consequences. One way of knowing the American people is through demography, the science of population changes. Demography, it is often said, is destiny.

Another way to understand the American people is through examination of public opinion in the United States. What Americans believe—and believe they know—is public opinion, the distribution of people's beliefs about politics and policy issues. Polling is one important way of studying public opinion; polls give us a fairly accurate gauge of public opinion on issues, products, and personalities. On the positive side for democracy, polls help keep political leaders in touch with the feelings of their constituents. On the negative side, though, they help politicians "play to the crowds" instead of providing leadership.

Polls have revealed again and again that the average American has a low level of political knowledge. Far more Americans know their astrological sign than know the names of their representatives in Congress. Ideological thinking is not widespread in the American public, nor are people necessarily consistent in their attitudes. Often they are conservative in principle but liberal in practice—that is, they are against big government but favor more spending on a wide variety of programs. Indeed, many people apparently voted for Reagan even though they disliked his policies.

Acting on one's opinions is political participation. Although Americans live in a participatory culture, their actual level of participation is unspectacular. In this country, participation is a class-biased activity, with certain groups participating more than others. Those who suffer the most inequality sometimes resort to protest as a form of participation. Perhaps the best indicator of how well socialized Americans are to democracy is that protest typically is aimed at getting the attention of the government, not overthrowing it.

FOR FURTHER READING

Asher, Herbert. *Polling and the Public: What Every Citizen Should Know.* Washington, DC: Congressional Quarterly Press, 1988. A highly readable introduction to the perils and possibilities of polling and surveys.

Campbell, Angus et al. *The American Voter.* New York: John Wiley, 1960. The classic study of the American voter, based upon data from the 1950s.

Conway, M. Margaret. *Political Participation,* 2nd ed. Washington, DC: Congressional Quarterly Press, 1990. An excellent text on political participation.

Jennings, M. Kent, and Richard G. Niemi. *Generations and Politics: A Panel Study of Young Adults and Their Parents.* Princeton, NJ: Princeton University Press, 1981. A highly influential study of the class of 1965, their parents, and how both generations changed over the course of eight years.

Neuman, W. Russell. *The Paradox of Mass Politics: Knowledge and Opinion in the American Electorate.* Cambridge, MA: Harvard University Press, 1986. Neuman addresses the question of how the system works as well as it does given the low level of public information about politics.

Niemi, Richard G., John Mueller, and Tom W. Smith. *Trends in Public Opinion: A Compendium of Survey Data.* New York: Greenwood Press, 1989. An excellent source of data over time on a wide range of public opinion questions.

Page, Benjamin I., and Robert Y. Shapiro. *The Rational Public: Fifty Years of Trends in Americans' Policy Preferences.* Chicago: University of Chicago Press, 1992. The authors argue that the public, as a collectivity, responds in a reasonable fashion to changing political circumstances and information.

Verba, Sidney, and Norman H. Nie. *Participation in America.* New York: Harper & Row, 1972. An important study of American political participation.

NOTES

1. See Margo Anderson, *The American Census: A Social History* (New Haven, CT: Yale University Press, 1988).
2. Harold W. Stanley and Richard G. Niemi, *Vital Statistics on American Politics*, 4th ed. (Washington, DC: Congressional Quarterly Press, 1994), 399.

3. Ronald T. Takaki, *Strangers From a Different Shore* (Boston: Little, Brown, 1989), chapter 11.

4. Judith Blake, *Family Size and Achievement* (Berkeley, CA: University of California Press, 1989).

5. Richard Dawson et al., *Political Socialization*, 2nd ed. (Boston: Little, Brown, 1977), 33.

6. See Kenneth P. Langton and M. Kent Jennings, "Political Socialization and the High School Civics Curriculum in the United States," *American Political Science Review* 62 (September 1968): 852–867. For African-American students, civics education is somewhat more significant.

7. See M. Kent Jennings and Richard G. Niemi, *Generations and Politics: A Panel Study of Young Adults and Their Parents* (Princeton, NJ: Princeton University Press, 1981).

8. "The Age of Indifference." Report of the Times Mirror Center for the People and the Press, June 28, 1990.

9. See Raymond E. Wolfinger and Steven J. Rosenstone, *Who Votes* (New Haven, CT: Yale University Press, 1980), chapter 3.

10. Philip E. Converse, *The Dynamics of Party Support* (Beverly Hills: Sage Publications, 1976), 12–13.

11. Jean M. Converse, *Survey Research in the United States: Roots and Emergence, 1890–1960* (Berkeley, CA: University of California Press, 1987), 116. Converse's work is the definitive study on the origins of public opinion sampling.

12. Herbert Asher, *Polling and the Public: What Every Citizen Should Know* (Washington, DC: Congressional Quarterly, 1988), 59.

13. Quoted in Norman M. Bradburn and Seymour Sudman, *Polls and Surveys: Understanding What They Tell Us* (San Francisco: Jossey-Bass, 1988), 39–40.

14. For a good summary of the evidence, see Seymour Sudman, "Do Exit Polls Influence Voting Behavior?" *Public Opinion Quarterly 50* (Fall 1986): 331–339.

15. David W. Moore, *The Superpollsters: How They Measure and Manipulate Public Opinion in America* (New York: Four Walls Eight Windows, 1992), 353–354.

16. W. Lance Bennett, *Public Opinion and American Politics* (New York: Harcourt Brace Jovanovich, 1980), 44.

17. W. Russell Neuman, *The Paradox of Mass Politics: Knowledge and Opinion in the American Electorate* (Cambridge, MA: Harvard University Press, 1986).

18. Angus Campbell et al., *The American Voter* (New York: John Wiley, 1960), chapter 10.

19. Norman H. Nie, Sidney Verba, and John R. Petrocik, *The Changing American Voter* (Cambridge, MA: Harvard University Press, 1976), chapter 7.

20. See, for example, John L. Sullivan, James E. Pierson, and George E. Marcus, "Ideological Constraint in the Mass Public: A Methodological Critique and Some New Findings," *American Journal of Political Science* 22 (May 1978): 233–249; and Eric R.A.N. Smith, *The Unchanging American Voter* (Berkeley, CA: University of California Press, 1989).

21. See the data presented in Richard G. Niemi, John Mueller, and Tom W. Smith, *Trends in Public Opinion: A Compendium of Survey Data* (New York: Greenwood Press, 1989), 77–91.

22. Martin P. Wattenberg, *The Rise of Candidate-Centered Politics: Presidential Elections of the 1980s* (Cambridge, MA: Harvard University Press, 1991).

23. Thomas Ferguson and Joel Rogers, *Right Turn* (New York: Hill and Wang, 1986), 28; for a long-term perspective on the movement of public opinion in a largely liberal direction, see Benjamin I. Page and Robert Y. Shapiro, *The Rational Public: Fifty Years of Trends in Americans' Policy Preferences* (Chicago: University of Chicago Press, 1992).

24. Wattenberg, *The Rise of Candidate-Centered Politics*.

25. This theory is carefully developed in Morris P. Fiorina, *Retrospective Voting in Presidential Elections* (New Haven, CT: Yale University Press, 1981).

26. This definition is a close paraphrase of one in Sidney Verba and Norman H. Nie, *Participation in America* (New York: Harper & Row, 1972), 2.

27. Russell J. Dalton, *Citizen Politics in Western Democracies* (Chatham, NJ: Chatham House, 1988), 237.

28. Verba and Nie, *Participation in America*, 31.

29. This letter can be found in Juan Williams, *Eyes on the Prize: America's Civil Rights Years, 1954–1965* (New York: Viking, 1987), 187–189.

30. Verba and Nie, *Participation in America*, 125.

31. "Voting and Registration in the Election of November 1992," Bureau of the Census, Series P-20, No. 466, April 1993.

32. On African Americans, see Verba and Nie, *Participation in America*, chapter 10; on Hispanics, see Wolfinger and Rosenstone, *Who Votes?*, 92.

33. Campbell et al., *The American Voter*, 541.

34. Fiorina, *Retrospective Voting*, 5.

CHAPTER 6 *Political Parties*

Despite the fact that the framers of the U.S. Constitution did not approve of political parties, parties have contributed greatly to American democracy. In one of the most frequently—and rightly—quoted observations about American politics, E. E. Schattschneider said that "political parties created democracy . . . and democracy is unthinkable save in terms of the parties."[1] Political scientists and politicians alike believe that a strong party system is desirable and bemoan the weakening of the parties in recent decades. As former President Bush once told a meeting of college interns in Washington, "as the strength of our parties erodes, so does the strength of our political system."[2]

The ups and downs of the two major parties are one of the most important elements in American politics. **Party competition** is the battle between Democrats and Republicans for the control of public offices. Without this competition there would be no choice, and without choice there would be no democracy. Americans have had a choice between two major political parties since the early 1800s, and this two-party system remains intact almost two centuries later.

THE MEANING OF PARTY

Almost all definitions of political parties have one thing in common: Parties try to win elections. This is their core function and the key to their definition. Interest groups do not nominate candidates for office, though they may try to influence elections. For example, no one has ever been elected to Congress as the nominee of the National Rifle Association, though many have received the NRA's endorsement. Thus, Anthony Downs defined a **political party** as a "team of men and women seeking to control the governing apparatus by gaining office in a duly constituted election."[3]

The word **team** is the slippery part of this definition. Party teams may not be so well disciplined and single-minded as teams fielded by fine football coaches. Party teams are often running every which way (sometimes toward the opposition's goal line) and are difficult to lead. In football, it is sometimes hard to tell the players without a scorecard; in American politics, it is sometimes hard to tell the players even with a scorecard. Party leaders often disagree about policy, and between elections the parties seem to all but disappear. So who are the members of these teams? A widely adopted way of thinking about parties in political science is as "three-headed political giants." The three heads are (1) the party-in-the-electorate, (2) the party as an organization, and (3) the party-in-government.[4]

By far the largest component of an American party is the **party-in-the-electorate**. Unlike many European political parties, American parties do not require dues or membership cards to distinguish members from nonmembers. Americans may register as Democrats, Republicans, or whatever, but registration is not legally binding and is easily changed. To be a member of a party, you need only claim to be a member. If you call yourself a Democrat, you are one—even if you never talk to a party official, never work in a campaign, and often vote for Republicans.

The **party as an organization** has a national office, a full-time staff, rules and bylaws, and budgets. In addition to a national office, each party maintains state and local headquarters. The party organization includes precinct leaders, county chairpersons, state chairpersons, state delegates to the national committee, and officials in the party's Washington office. These are the people who keep the party running between elections and make its rules.

The **party-in-government** consists of elected officials who label themselves as members of the party. Although presidents, members of Congress, governors, and lesser officeholders almost always run for election as Democrats or Republicans, they do not always agree on policy. Presidents and governors may have to wheedle and cajole their own party members into voting for their policies. In the United States, it is not uncommon to put personal principle—or ambition—above loyalty to the party's leaders. These leaders are the main spokespersons for the party, however; their words and actions personify the party to millions of Americans. If the party is to translate its promises into policy, the job must be done by the party-in-government.

Because parties are everywhere in American politics—present in the electorate's mind, as an organization, and in government offices—one of their major tasks is to link the people of the United States to their government and its policies.

Tasks of the Parties

The road from public opinion to public policy is long and winding. Masses of people cannot raise their voices to government and indicate their policy preferences in unison. If all 250 million Americans spoke at once, all that would be

The two major parties have different demographic bases of support. Of all social groups, African Americans tend to be the most solidly aligned with one party. Ever since the Civil Rights Act of 1964, they have voted overwhelmingly for Democratic candidates. In 1992, African-American voters cast 82 percent of their votes for Bill Clinton, 11 percent for George Bush, and 7 percent for Ross Perot.

heard is a roar of demands on government that could not possibly be dealt with. In a large democracy, **linkage institutions** translate inputs from the public into outputs from the policymakers.[5] Linkage institutions sift through all the issues, identify the most pressing concerns, and put these onto the governmental agenda. In other words, linkage institutions help ensure that public preferences are heard loud and clear. In the United States there are four main linkage institutions: parties, elections, interest groups, and the media.

Kay Lawson writes that "parties are seen, both by the members and by others, as agencies for forging links between citizens and policymakers."[6] Here is a checklist of the tasks parties perform, or should perform, if they are to serve as effective linkage institutions:

1. Parties pick policymakers. Rarely does someone get elected to a major federal or state office without winning a party's endorsement. A party's endorsement is called a *nomination*.

2. Parties run campaigns. Through their national, state, and local organizations, parties coordinate political campaigns. However, recent technology has made it easier for candidates to campaign on their own, without the help of the party organization.

3. Parties give cues to voters. Most voters have a **party image** of each party, that is, they know (or think they know) what the Republicans and Democrats stand for. Liberal, conservative, probusiness, antiminorities—these are some of the elements of each party's image. Even in the present era of weakened parties, many voters still rely on a party to give them cues for voting.

4. Parties articulate policies. Within the electorate and in the government, each political party advocates specific policy alternatives. The Democratic party has been a fervent backer of the Equal Rights Amendment; the Republican party has not. Republicans, on the other hand, are more likely than Democrats to favor increased military spending.

5. Parties coordinate policy-making. In America's fragmented government, parties are essential for coordination among the branches of government. Each president, cabinet official, and member of Congress is also a member of a party. When they need support to get something done, the first place they look is to their fellow partisans.

The importance of these tasks makes it easy to see why most political scientists accept Schattschneider's famous assertion that modern democracy is unthinkable without competition between political parties.

Parties, Voters, and Policy: The Downs Model

The parties compete (at least in theory) as in a marketplace. A party is in the market for voters; its products are its candidates and policies. Anthony Downs has provided a working model of the relationship among citizens, parties, and policy, employing a rational-choice perspective.[7] **Rational-choice theory** "seeks to explain political processes and outcomes as consequences of purposive behavior. Political actors are assumed to have goals and to pursue those goals sensibly and efficiently."[8] Downs argues that voters want to maximize the chance that policies they favor will be adopted by government, and that parties want to win office. Thus, in order to win office, the wise party selects policies that are widely favored. Parties and candidates may do all sorts of things to win—kiss babies, call opponents ugly names, even lie and cheat—but in a democracy they will primarily use their accomplishments and policy positions to attract votes. If Party A more accurately figures out what the voters want than Party B, then it should be more successful.

In the American electorate a few voters are extremely liberal, a few are extremely conservative, but the majority are in the middle (see Figure 6.1). If Downs is right, centrist parties will win, and extremist parties will be condemned to a footnote in the history books. Indeed, the long history of the

FIGURE 6.1 — The Downs Model: How Rational Parties Match Voters' Policy Preferences

In 1992, the National Opinion Research Center asked a sample of the American electorate to classify themselves on a scale from extremely liberal to extremely conservative. The graph shows how the people located themselves in terms of ideology, and how rational (and foolish) parties might reflect these identifications.

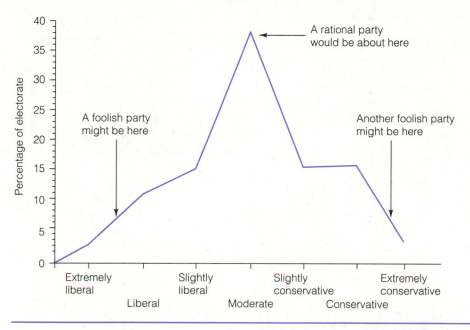

SOURCE: 1992 General Social Survey conducted by the University of Chicago's National Opinion Research Center

American party system has shown that successful parties rarely stray far from the midpoint of public opinion. Occasionally a party may misperceive voters' desires or take a risky stand on principle, hoping to persuade voters during the campaign, but in order to survive in a system where the majority opinion is middle-of-the-road, they must stay near the center.

We frequently hear criticism that there is not much difference between the Democrats and Republicans. Given the nature of the American political market, however, they have little choice. One would not expect two competing department stores to locate at opposite ends of town when most people live on Main Street. Downs also notes, though, that from a rational-choice perspective, one should expect the parties to differentiate themselves at least somewhat. Just as Chrysler tries to offer something different from and better than General Motors in order to build buyer loyalty, so Democrats and Republicans have to forge different identities to build voter loyalty. More than half of the population currently feels that important differences do exist between the parties. The result of these differences is that Republicans attract more conservatives whereas Democrats attract more liberals, as you can see in Figure 6.2.

PARTY REALIGNMENT AND DEALIGNMENT

While studying political parties, remember the following: *America's is a two-party system and always has been.* Of course, there are many minor parties around—Libertarians, Communists, Vegetarians—but they almost never have

FIGURE 6.2 — *Party Identification and Ideology: 1992*

Although there is a general tendency for the two parties to converge toward the center of the ideological spectrum, the parties need to differentiate themselves somewhat in order to give people incentive to identify with them. As you can see, there is a distinct difference in the ideology of the parties' members. Republicans are more than three times as likely to say they are conservatives than Democrats, and Democrats are nearly five times more likely to say they are liberals.

However, the terms liberal and conservative are not very meaningful for a large percentage of the American public. Notice that a very common response to the question of ideology is "haven't thought about it," especially among Independents and Democrats.

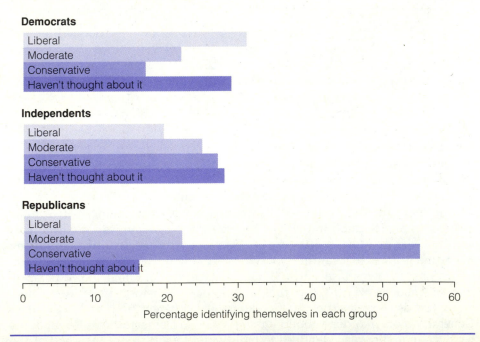

SOURCE: 1992 National Election Study conducted by the University of Michigan

a chance to win major office. In contrast, most democratic nations have more than two parties represented in their national legislature. Throughout American history, one party has been the dominant majority party for long periods of time. A majority of voters cling to the party in power, which thus tends to win a majority of the elections. Political scientists call these periods **party eras**. The majority party does not, of course, win every election; sometimes it suffers from intraparty squabbles (as the Republicans did in 1912) and loses power. Sometimes it nominates a weak candidate, and the opposition cashes in on the majority party's misfortune.

What punctuates these party eras is a **critical election**.[9] A critical election is an electoral earthquake: the ground shakes beneath the parties; fissures appear in each party's coalition and they begin to fracture; new issues appear, dividing the electorate. A new coalition is formed for each party—one that endures for years. A critical election period may require more than one election before change is apparent, but in the end, the party system will be transformed.

This process is called **party realignment**, a rare event in American political life akin to a political revolution. Realignments are typically associated with a major crisis or trauma in the nation's history. One of the major realignments, when the Republican party emerged, was connected to the Civil War. Another was linked to the Great Depression of the 1930s, when the majority Republicans were displaced by the Democrats. The following sections look more closely at the various party eras in American history.

1796–1824: The First Party System

In the *Federalist Papers*, Madison warned strongly against the dangers of "factions," or parties. Even though New York's Alexander Hamilton was one of the coauthors of the *Federalist Papers*, Hamilton did as much as anyone to inaugurate our party system. To garner congressional support for his pet policies (particularly a national bank), he needed votes. From this politicking and coalition building came the rudiments of the Federalist party, America's first political party. The Federalists, though, were also America's shortest-lived major party. After Federalist candidate John Adams was defeated in his reelection bid in 1800, the party faded quickly. The Federalists were poorly organized, and by 1820 they no longer even bothered to offer up a candidate for president. In this early period of American history, most party leaders did not regard themselves as professional politicians. Those who lost often withdrew completely from the political arena.

The party that crushed the Federalists was led by Virginians Jefferson, Madison, and Monroe—all of whom were elected president for two terms each in succession. They were known as the Democratic-Republicans, or sometimes as the Jeffersonians. Every political party depends upon a coalition, a set of individuals or groups supporting it. The Democratic-Republican party derived its coalition from agrarian interests rather than from the growing number of capitalists, who supported the Federalists. This made the party

*Aaron Burr dealt a near death-blow to the Federalist party when he killed its
leader, Alexander Hamilton, in this 1804 duel. Burr, then vice president, challenged
Hamilton to the duel after the former treasury secretary publicly called him a
traitor.*

particularly popular in the largely rural South. As the Federalists disappeared,
however, the old Jeffersonian coalition was torn apart by factionalism as it
tried to be all things to all people.

1828–1856: Jackson and the Democrats versus the Whigs

More than anyone else, it was General Andrew Jackson who founded the
modern American political party. In the election of 1828, he forged a new
coalition that included westerners as well as southerners, new immigrants as
well as settled Americans. Like most successful politicians of his day, Jackson
was initially a Democratic-Republican, but soon after his ascension to the presidency his party became known as simply the Democratic party, which continues to this day. The "Democratic" label was particularly appropriate for Jackson's supporters because their cause was to broaden political opportunity,
eliminating many vestiges of elitism and mobilizing the masses.

Whereas Jackson was the charismatic leader, the Democrats' behind-the-
scenes architect was Martin Van Buren, who succeeded Jackson as president.
Van Buren's one term in office was relatively undistinguished, but his view of
party competition left a lasting mark. A realist, Van Buren argued that a party

could not aspire to pleasing all the people all the time. He argued that a governing party needed a loyal opposition to represent parts of society that it could not. This opposition was provided by the Whigs. The Whig party included notables like Henry Clay and Daniel Webster, but was only able to win the presidency when it nominated aging but popular military heroes, such as William Henry Harrison (1840) and Zachary Taylor (1848). The Whigs had two distinct wings—northern industrialists and southern planters—who were brought together more by Democratic policies they opposed than by issues on which they agreed.

1860–1932: The Two Republican Eras

In the 1850s, the issue of slavery dominated American politics and split both the Whigs and the Democrats. Congress battled over the extension of slavery to the new states and territories. In *Dred Scott v. Sandford*, the Supreme Court of 1857 held that slaves could not be citizens and that former slaves could not be protected by the Constitution. This decision further sharpened the divisions in public opinion, making civil war increasingly likely.

The Republicans rose in the late 1850s as the antislavery party. Folding in the remnants of several minor parties, the Republicans in 1860 forged a coalition strong enough to elect former Illinois Congressman Abraham Lincoln and ignite the Civil War. The "War Between the States" was one of those political earthquakes that realigned the parties. Afterward, the Republican party was in ascendency for more than sixty years. The Democrats controlled the South, though, as the Republican label remained a dirty word in the old Confederacy.

A second Republican era was initiated with the watershed election of 1896, perhaps the most bitter battle in American electoral history. The Democrats nominated William Jennings Bryan, populist proponent of "free silver" (linking money with silver, which was more plentiful than gold, thus devaluing money to help debtors). The Republican party made clear its positions in favor of the gold standard, industrialization, the banks, high tariffs, and the industrial working classes against the "radical" western farmers and silverites. A staggeringly high turnout put William McKinley in the White House and brought the new working classes and moneyed interests into the Republican fold. Political scientists call the 1896 election a realigning one because it shifted the party coalitions and entrenched the Republicans for another generation.

For three decades more, until the stock market crash of 1929 and the ensuing Great Depression, the Republicans continued as the nation's majority party. The Depression brought about another fissure in the crust of the American party system.

1932–1968: The New Deal Coalition

President Herbert Hoover's handling of the Depression turned out to be disastrous for the Republicans. He solemnly pronounced that "economic depression cannot be cured by legislative action." Roosevelt handily defeated Hoover in 1932, promising a *New Deal*. In his first hundred days as president, Roosevelt prodded Congress into passing scores of anti-Depression measures. Party realignment began in earnest after the Roosevelt administration got the country moving again. First-time voters flocked into the electorate, pumping new blood into the Democratic ranks and providing much of the margin for Roosevelt's four presidential victories. Immigrant groups in the big cities had been initially attracted to the Democratic presidential candidacy of New York Governor Al Smith, a Catholic, in 1928. Roosevelt reinforced the partisanship of these groups, and the Democrats forged the **New Deal coalition**.

The basic elements of the New Deal coalition were as follows:

- *Urban dwellers.*   Big cities like Chicago and Philadelphia were staunchly Republican before the New Deal realignment; afterward, they were Democratic bastions.

- *Labor unions.*   FDR became the first president to enthusiastically support unions, and they returned the favor.

- *Catholics and Jews.*   During and after the Roosevelt period, Catholics and Jews were strongly Democratic.

- *The poor.*   Though the poor had low turnout rates, their votes went overwhelmingly to the party of Roosevelt and his successors.

- *Southerners.*   Ever since the pre–Civil War days, white southerners were Democratic loyalists. This continued unabated during the New Deal.

- *African Americans.*   The Republicans freed the slaves, but under FDR the Democrats attracted the majority of African Americans.

- *Intellectuals.*   Small in number, prominent intellectuals provided a wealth of new ideas that fueled the New Deal.

The New Deal coalition made the Democratic party the clear majority party for decades. Harry S Truman, who succeeded Roosevelt in 1945, promised a Fair Deal. World War II hero and Republican Dwight D. Eisenhower broke the Democrats' grip on power by being elected president twice during the 1950s, but the Democrats regained the presidency in 1960 with the election of John F. Kennedy. His New Frontier was in the New Deal tradition, with platforms and policies designed to help labor, the working classes, and minorities. Lyndon B. Johnson, picked as Kennedy's vice president because he could help win southern votes, became president upon Kennedy's assassination and was overwhelmingly elected to a term of his own in 1964. Johnson's Great Society programs included a major expansion of government programs to help the poor, the dispossessed, and minorities. His War on Poverty was reminiscent of Roosevelt's activism in dealing with the Depression. Johnson's Vietnam War policies, however, tore the Democratic party apart in 1968, leaving the door to the presidency wide open for Republican candidate Richard M. Nixon.

Political party conventions have changed dramatically as a result of technological progress. The Democratic Convention of 1932 (left) marked the first time that a nominee's acceptance speech was broadcast live across the nation via radio. Fifty years later, at the 1992 Democratic Convention, the entire proceedings were carefully orchestrated so as to present the best possible image of Bill Clinton on television.

1968–Present: The Era of Divided Government

Since 1968, the Republicans have won five out of seven presidential elections. At the same time, the 1994 elections marked the first time during this period that the Republicans had won a majority of seats in the House of Representitives, and they have usually been in the minority in the Senate as well. All told, both Houses of Congress and the presidency have been simultaneously controlled by the same party for just six of the twenty-eight years from 1969 to 1996.[10] The discrepancy between the patterns of presidential and congressional voting during this era of divided government is unprecedented in American history, as can be seen in Table 6.1

Because of the lack of correspondence between presidential and congressional election results in recent years, many political scientists believe that the party system has dealigned rather than realigned. Whereas realignment involves people changing from one party to another, **party dealignment** means that people are gradually moving away from both. When your car is realigned, it is adjusted in one direction or another to improve how it steers. Imagine if your mechanic were to remove the steering mechanism instead of adjusting it—your car would be useless and ineffective. This is what many scholars fear has been happening to the parties.

There is plenty of evidence that parties have fallen on hard times—the decline of party loyalty, for example, in the electorate. In the parties' heyday it was said that people would vote for a yellow dog if their party nominated one. Now, more than 90 percent of all Americans insist that "I always vote for the

TABLE 6.1 — *Democratic Party's Batting Average by Party Era*[a]

	President	House	Senate
Era of Divided Government			
1968–1994	.286	.929	.714
New Deal Era			
1932–1964	.714	.888	.888
McKinley Republicanism			
1896–1928	.223	.167	.167
Lincoln Republicanism			
1860–1892	.223	.445	.167
Jacksonian Era			
1824–1856	.666	.722	.833

[a]Table entries represent the percentage of elections in which the Democratic party won the presidency or gained majority control of the House or Senate. For the House and Senate, midterm elections are also included in the averages.

person whom I think is best, regardless of what party they belong to."[11] Rather than reflecting negative attitudes toward the parties, the recent dealignment has been characterized by a growing **party neutrality**.[12] For example, 38 percent of the 1990 National Election Study respondents and 29 percent of those interviewed in the 1992 study responded as follows to a set of four open-ended questions about the parties:

Q. Is there anything in particular that you like about the Democratic party?

A. No.

Q. Is there anything in particular that you don't like about the Democratic party?

A. No.

Q. Is there anything in particular that you like about the Republican party?

A. No.

Q. Is there anything in particular that you don't like about the Republican party?

A. No.

When these questions were first asked in the 1950s, only about 10 percent of respondents answered in this neutral way, generally indicating that they were not very politically knowledgeable. Now, many of those who say nothing about the parties are quite aware of the candidates. Lacking any party anchoring, though, they are easily swayed one way or the other. It is for this reason that they are often referred to as "the floating voters."

THE PARTIES TODAY: RENEWAL AND CHANGE

Even though party loyalty has lagged, party organizations have become more energetic and effective. For the Democrats, this has involved setting national standards for selection of delegates to the party convention; fund-raising and technological support for candidates have been the primary focus of activity at the Republicans' national headquarters. All told, the number of full-time staff members working at the Democratic and Republican National Committee headquarters rose from about 80 in 1972 to over 500 in 1992.[13] As Paul Herrnson documents, "The parties' national, congressional, and senatorial campaign committees are now wealthier, more stable, better organized, and better staffed than ever before."[14]

In sum, the past few years have seen the emergence of what has been called the **split-level party**—a party with a strong, vigorous organization but a weak following on the mass level.[15] Each party, though, has changed in distinctive ways. The following sections give a brief view of each.

The Democrats: Party of Representation

The most recent restructuring of the Democratic party began in 1968, the year of the rowdiest national convention ever. As the war in Southeast Asia raged, another war of sorts took place in the streets of Chicago, the Democratic convention city. Demonstrators against the war battled Mayor Richard Daley's Chicago police in what an official report later called a "police riot." Beaten up in the streets and defeated in the convention hall, the antiwar faction won one concession from the party regulars: a special committee to review the party's structure and delegate selection procedures, which they felt had discriminated against them. Minorities, women, youth, and other groups traditionally poorly represented in the party leadership also demanded a more open process of convention delegate selection. The result was a committee of inquiry, which was chaired first by Senator George McGovern and later by Representative Donald Fraser, who took over when McGovern left the committee to run for president.

The **McGovern-Fraser Commission** brought great changes in the Democratic party. The commission tried to make future conventions more representative; it adopted quotas requiring that state party organizations increase the representation and participation of minorities and women. No longer could party leaders handpick the convention delegates virtually in secret. All delegate selection procedures were required to be open, giving party leaders no more clout than college students or anyone else who wanted to participate. By 1972 these rules were in effect. Suddenly, the days of smoke-filled rooms were over; some of those who were protesting on the outside of the convention hall in 1968 were now on the inside. Most notably, Mayor Daley's 1972 Chicago delegation was unseated in favor of a more socially representative slate led by the young Jesse Jackson.

Since the McGovern-Fraser Commission, the party has replaced most of its quota requirements with affirmitive action guidelines, with the one exception being a firm rule that each delegation must be half male and half female. The Democrats have also tried to restore a role for its party leaders. Many thought the reforms went too far, cutting out state and national leaders whose support was needed to win elections. In 1982, another commission chaired by North Carolina's Governor Hunt recommended that a portion of the delegate slots be automatically set aside for party leaders and elected officials. These politicians who are awarded convention seats on the basis of their position are known as **superdelegates**. The idea of creating superdelegate slots at the convention was to restore an element of "peer review" to the process, ensuring participation of the people most familiar with the candidates. It was also thought that these party officials would be more likely than "amateur" issue enthusiasts to consider the long-term future of the party and would therefore support the most electable candidate.

Finding an electable candidate for the presidency has been a rather elusive task for the Democrats since they first started fiddling with the delegate selection process after 1968. In the six elections since the McGovern-Fraser reforms, the Democrats have won only two. Many believe that the divisiveness of the Democrats' new open procedures has hurt their ability to unite for the fall campaign against the Republicans.[16]

The Republicans: Putting Technology to Use

In 1968, as the Democratic party was coming apart at the seams, the Republicans were uniting around former Vice President Richard M. Nixon as their nominee. Six years later, in 1974, the Republicans faced a political catastrophe when Nixon, who had been resoundingly reelected in 1972, resigned the presidency in the wake of the Watergate scandal (see Chapter 11 for more on Watergate). As often happens when a party is beset by a crisis, friends of the party—in this case, the Republicans—feared for its survival, and the survival of the two-party system.

They need not have worried. The Republicans went through very few of the intraparty reforms that so absorbed the Democrats. There were few minorities and feminists in the Republican party to demand affirmative action and a fair share of the delegates. The Republicans had other work to do—mainly to regenerate their party. They were more concerned with winning elections than being balanced by race, sex, age, and ethnicity. One area where they quickly took the lead was in the use of computer technology to adapt the party to the modern age. Computerized lists of potential contributors—large and small—gave the Republican party a great advantage in fund-raising, which they still hold today. The Republicans could, for example, write a direct-mail letter to every voter over 45 who is registered in a California precinct that voted more than 60 percent for Reagan, and who lives in a house costing more than $100,000.[17] To help their candidates know what is and is not working, the Republicans have also made far more use of polling technology than have the Democrats. Democrats are trying to catch up with the Republicans' technological sophistication, but in the meantime the Republicans have the advantage in terms of organization.

Third Parties: Their Impact on American Politics

The story of American party struggle is primarily the story of two major parties, yet **third parties** pop up every year and occasionally attract the public's attention. American history is strewn with small and now-forgotten minor parties: the Free Soil party (a forerunner of the Republican party), the American party (called the "Know Nothings") in 1856, the Jobless party of 1932, the Poor Man's party of 1952, and many others.

Third parties come in three basic varieties. First are parties that promote certain causes—either a controversial single issue (prohibition of alcoholic beverages, for example) or an extreme ideological position such as socialism or libertarianism. Second are splinter parties, which are offshoots of a major

The Democratic National Committee meets to consider a new party symbol.

The Republican National Committee meets to consider a new party symbol.

party. Teddy Roosevelt's Progressives in 1912, Strom Thurmond's States' Righters in 1948, and George Wallace's American Independents in 1968 all claimed they did not get a fair hearing from Republicans or Democrats and thus formed their own new parties. Finally, some third parties are merely an extension of a popular individual with presidential aspirations. Both John Anderson in 1980 and Ross Perot in 1992 offered voters who were dissatisfied with the Democratic and Republican nominees another option.

Although third parties almost never win office in the United States, scholars believe they are often quite important.[18] They have brought new groups into the electorate and have served as "safety valves" for popular discontent. George Wallace, for example, told his supporters in 1968 that they had the chance to "send a message" to Washington—a message of support for tougher law-and-order measures, which is still being felt to this day. Ross Perot used his saturation of the TV airwaves in 1992 to ensure that the issue of the federal deficit was not ignored in the campaign.

Two Parties: So What?

Despite the regular appearance of third parties, the two-party system is firmly entrenched in American politics. Would it make a difference if America had a

Third party candidates for president are usually ignored during American presidential campaigns. In 1992, though, Ross Perot was invited to participate in three debates with George Bush and Bill Clinton. His witticisms and straight-talking style in the debates proved to be a major boost to his campaign.

multiparty system, as so many European countries have? The answer is clearly yes. The most obvious consequence of two-party governance is the moderation of political conflict. If America had many parties, each would have to make a special appeal in order to stand out from the crowd. With just two parties, both will cling to a centrist position in order to maximize their appeal to voters. The parties have often been criticized for this moderation. Their sternest critics think of them as a choice between "Tweedledum and Tweedledee." Third-party candidate George Wallace in 1968 used to say that "there's not a dime's worth of difference between the parties."

The result is often political ambiguity. Why should parties risk taking a strong stand on a controversial policy if doing so will only antagonize many voters? Ambiguity is a safe strategy, as extremist nominees Barry Goldwater in 1964 and George McGovern in 1972 found out the hard way. The two-party system thus throttles extreme or unconventional views.

It is not hard to imagine what a multiparty system might look like in the United States. Quite possibly, African-American groups would form their own party, pressing vigorously for more civil rights legislation. Environmentalists could constitute another party, vowing to clean up the rivers, oppose nuclear power, and save the wilderness. America could have religious parties, union-based parties, farmers' parties, and all sorts of others. As in some European countries, there could be half a dozen or so parties represented in Congress (see "America in Perspective: Multiparty Systems in Other Countries").

THE PARTY IN THE ELECTORATE

In most European nations, being a party member means formally joining a political party. You get a membership card to carry around in your wallet or purse, you pay dues, and you attend meetings to choose your local party lead-

AMERICA IN PERSPECTIVE

Multiparty Systems in Other Countries

One of the major reasons the United States has only two parties represented in government is structural. America has a **winner-take-all system**, in which whoever gets the most votes wins the election. There are no prizes awarded for second or third place. Suppose there are three parties: one receives 45 percent of the vote, another 40 percent, and the third 15 percent. Though it got less than a majority, the party that finished first is declared the winner. The others are out in the cold. In this way, the American system discourages small parties. Unless a party wins, there is no reward for the votes it gets. Thus, it makes more sense for a small party to form an alliance with one of the major parties than to struggle on its own with little hope. In the example used above, the second- and third-place parties might merge (if they can reach an agreement on policy) to challenge the governing party in the next election.

In a system that employs **proportional representation**, however, such a merger would not be necessary. Under this system, used in most European countries, legislative seats are allocated according to each party's percentage of the nationwide vote. If a party wins 15 percent of the vote, it then receives 15 percent of the seats. Even a small party can use its voice in Parliament to be a thorn in the side of the government, standing up strongly for its principles. Such is the role of the Greens in Germany, who are ardent environmentalists. In contrast,

Germany's other small party, the Free Democrats, typically uses its seats to combine with one of the larger parties to form a **coalition government** that together controls over half the seats. Coalition governments are common in Europe. Italy has regularly been ruled by a coalition since the end of World War II, for example.

Even with proportional representation, not every party gets represented in the legislature. To be awarded seats, a party must always achieve a certain percentage of votes, which varies from country to country. Israel has one of the lowest thresholds at 1 percent. This explains why there are so many parties represented in the Israeli Knesset—ten as of the 1992 election. The founders of Israel's system wanted to make sure that all points of view were represented, but in recent years this has turned into a nightmare, with small extremist parties often holding the balance of power.

Parties have to develop their own unique identities to appeal to voters in a multiparty system. This requires strong stands on the issues—yet, after the election, compromises must be made to form a coalition government. If an agreement cannot be reached on the major issues, the coalition is in trouble. Sometimes a new coalition can be formed; other times the result is the calling of a new election. In either case, one can see that proportional representation systems are more fluid than the two-party system in the United States.

ers. In America, being a party member takes far less work. There is no formal "membership" in the parties at all, and though some people make contributions, there are no dues required for participating in the selection of the party's candidates. Most states require registration as a Democrat or a Republican to be eligible to vote in party primaries, but that is all. Thus, the party-in-the-electorate consists largely of symbolic images and ideas. For most people, the party is a psychological label. They may never go to a party meeting, but they have images of the parties' stances on issues and of which groups the parties generally favor or oppose. Party images give citizens a picture of which party is probusiness or prolabor, which is the party of peace, or which is the better manager of the economy.

Party images help shape people's **party identification**, the self-proclaimed preference for one party or the other. Since 1952, the National Election Studies of the University of Michigan have asked a sample of citizens the question, "Generally speaking, do you usually think of yourself as a Republican, a Democrat, or an Independent?" Repeatedly asking this question permits political scientists to trace party identification over four decades of modern American politics (see Table 6.2). The clearest trend has been *the decline of both parties and resultant upsurge of independence* (mostly at the expense of the Democrats). In both 1988 and 1992, Independents outnumbered both Democrats and Republicans.

Virtually every major social group—Catholics, Jews, poor whites, southerners, and so on—has moved toward a position of increased independence.

TABLE 6.2 — *Party Identification in the United States, 1952–1992*[a]

Year	Democrats	Independents	Republicans
1952	48.6	23.3	28.1
1956	45.3	24.4	30.3
1960	46.4	23.4	30.2
1964	52.2	23.0	24.8
1968	46.0	29.5	24.5
1972	41.0	35.2	23.8
1976	40.2	36.8	23.0
1980	41.7	35.3	23.0
1984	37.7	34.8	27.6
1988	35.7	36.3	28.0
1992	35.8	38.7	25.5

[a]In percentage of people; the small percentage who identify with a minor party, or who cannot answer the question, are excluded.

SOURCE: 1952–1992 National Election Studies conducted by the University of Michigan.

The major exception has been African-American voters. A decade of Democratic civil rights policy in the 1960s moved African Americans even more solidly into the Democratic party. Only about 5 percent of blacks currently identify themselves as Republicans.

For many white Americans, though, the abandonment of either party for a nonpartisan stance is well advanced. This abandonment occurred at all age levels in the electorate, but it was most pronounced for younger voters, who have always had the weakest party ties to start with. Because of the baby boom and the lowering of the voting age to eighteen, these young voters swelled the tide of independence during the 1970s.

Not only are there more Independents now, but those who still identify with a party are no longer as loyal in the voting booth. For example, 42 percent of Democrats in 1972 voted for Richard Nixon rather than for their party's nominee, George McGovern. The Republicans' highest defection rate ever was in 1964, when 28 percent abandoned Barry Goldwater's candidacy for that of Lyndon Johnson. Yet party identification remains strongly linked to the voter's choice. The 1984 and 1988 elections showed a rebounding link between party identification and voting, at least on the presidential level. At the same time, **ticket-splitting**—voting with one party for one office and another for other offices—is near an all-time high.[19] Because voters prefer not to make a straight choice between one party or the other, divided government has become commonplace.

THE PARTY ORGANIZATIONS: FROM THE GRASS ROOTS TO WASHINGTON

An organization chart is usually shaped like a pyramid, with those who give orders at the top and those who carry them out at the bottom. In drawing an organization chart of an American political party, you could put the national committee and national convention of the party at the apex of your pyramid, the state party organizations in the middle, and the thousands of local party organizations at the bottom. When you finished with this chart, however, you would have a very incomplete picture of an American political party. The president of General Motors is at the top of GM in fact as well as on paper. By contrast, the chairperson of the Democratic or Republican national committee is on top on paper, but not in fact.

As organizations, American political parties are decentralized and fragmented. As Sorauf and Beck write, party organizations

> lack the hierarchical control and efficiency, the unified setting of priorities and strategy, and the central responsibility we associate with large contemporary organizations. . . . Instead of a continuity of relationships and of operations, the American party organizations feature only improvisatory, elusive, and sporadic structure and activities.[20]

It is no accident that a leading study of national party organizations is called *Politics Without Power*.[21] One can imagine a system in which the national office of a party resolves conflicts among its state and local branches, states the party's position on the issues, and then passes orders down through the hierarchy. One can even imagine a system in which the party leaders have the power to enforce their decisions by offering rewards—campaign funds, advice, appointments—to officeholders who follow the party line and punishing those who do not. Many European parties work just that way, but in America the formal party organizations have little such power. Candidates in the United States can get elected on their own. They do not need the help of the party most of the time, and hence the party organization is relegated to a relatively limited role.

It was not always this way. Once, the urban political party was the political party organization in America. From the late nineteenth century through the New Deal of the 1930s, scores of cities were dominated by **party machines**. A machine is a particular kind of party organization, different from the typical fragmented and disorganized political party in America. It can be defined as a "party organization that depends crucially on inducements that are both specific and material."[22] A specific inducement is one that can be given to someone and withheld from someone else; if you get a job as reward for your party work, for instance, someone else cannot have it. For it to be material, it must be monetary or convertible into money, such as a building contract.

Patronage is one of the key inducements used by machines. A patronage job is one that is given for political reasons rather than for merit or competence alone. Jobs are not the only form of patronage. In return for handsome campaign contributions, machines have been known to give out government contracts. Today, though, such activity has been greatly curtailed and the party machines are a relic of the past.

The Fifty State Party Systems

American national parties are a loose aggregation of state parties, which are themselves a fluid association of individuals, groups, and local organizations. There are fifty state party systems; no two are exactly alike. In a few states the parties are well organized, have sizable staffs, and spend a lot of money. Pennsylvania is one such state. In other states, however, parties are weak. It has been said of the California party system that to describe the parties' "function as minimal overstates the case. . . . The fact is that California has a political party system on paper, and that's about it."[23]

As recently as the 1960s, most state party organizations did not even maintain a permanent headquarters office; when the state party elected a new chairperson, the party organization simply shifted its office to his or her hometown.[24] In contrast, almost all state parties today have a physical headquarters, typically in the capital city or the largest city. State party budgets have also increased. In the early 1960s, more than half the parties had a budget of less than $50,000 (in 1967 constant dollars). By the start of the 1980s, the average state party had a budget ranging from $50,000 to $150,000.

Clearly, in terms of headquarters and budgets, state parties are better organized than they used to be—yet almost any national interest group in Washington will have a richer budget, plusher headquarters, and a bigger staff than even the best state party organization.

The National Party Organizations

The supreme power within each of the parties is its **national convention**. The convention meets every four years, and its main task is to write the party's platform and then nominate its candidates for president and vice president. (Chapter 7 will discuss conventions in detail.) Keeping the party operating between conventions is the job of the **national committee**, composed of representatives from the states and territories. Typically, each state will have a national committeeman and a national committeewoman as delegates to the party's national committee. (The Democratic committee also includes assorted governors, members of congress, and other party officials.)

Day-to-day activities of the national party are the responsibility of the **national chairperson** of the party. The national party chairperson hires the staff, raises the money, pays the bills, and attends to the daily duties of the party. This person is usually handpicked by the presidential nominee of the party. In the early 1970s, President Nixon asked George Bush to chair the Republican party, which he did for a year before moving back to government work.

THE PARTY IN GOVERNMENT: PROMISES AND POLICY

Government is a simple word used to describe a complex operation. American government includes the presidency, the Congress, the federal agencies, the governors and legislatures in the state capitals, and the courts. The winning party does not take over the entire government and get rid of government employees who support the opposition party (although Washington real estate agents do profit a bit when a new president is elected), but party control does matter because each party and the elected officials who represent it generally try to turn campaign promises into action. As a result, the party that has control will ultimately determine who gets what, where, when, and how.

Voters and coalitions of voters are attracted to different parties largely (though not entirely) by their performance and policies. What parties have done in office and what they promise to do greatly influences who will join their coalition. Sometimes voters suspect that political promises are made to be broken. To be sure, there are notable instances of politicians turning—sometimes 180 degrees—from their policy promises. Lyndon Johnson repeatedly promised in the 1964 presidential campaign that he would not "send American boys to do an Asian boy's job" and involve the United States in the Vietnam War, but he did. In the 1980 campaign, Ronald Reagan asserted that he would balance the budget by 1984, yet his administration quickly ran up the largest deficits in American history.

It is all too easy to forget how often parties and presidents do exactly what they say they will do. For every broken promise, many more are kept. Ronald Reagan promised to step up defense spending and cut back on social welfare expenditures, and within his first year in office he did just that. He promised a major tax cut and provided one. He promised less government regulation and quickly set about deregulating natural gas prices and occupational safety and environmental policies. Reagan knew that to go back on his campaign promises to lower taxes and reduce government regulation would not have been taken lightly. The impression that politicians and parties never produce policy out of promises is largely erroneous.

In fact, the parties have done a fairly good job over the years of translating their platform promises into public policy. Gerald Pomper has shown that party platforms are excellent predictors of a party's actual policy performance in office. He tabulated specific pledges in the major parties' platforms from 1944 to 1976. Over that period, the parties made exactly 3,194 specific policy pronouncements. Pomper then looked to see whether the winning party's policy promises were actually fulfilled. Nearly three-fourths of all promises resulted in policy actions. Others were tried but floundered for one reason or another. Only 10 percent were ignored altogether.[25]

If parties generally do what they say they will, then the party platforms adopted at the national conventions represent blueprints, however vague, for action. Consider what the two major parties promised the voters in 1992 (see Table 6.3). There is little doubt that the election of Clinton over Bush has directed the government in a different course than had the outcome been reversed.

UNDERSTANDING POLITICAL PARTIES

Political parties are considered essential elements of democratic government. Indeed, one of the first steps taken toward democracy in Eastern Europe has been the formation of competing political parties to contest elections. After years of one-party totalitarian rule, Eastern Europeans were ecstatic about the prospects of multiparty systems like those that had proved successful in the West. In contrast, the founding of the world's first party system in the United States was seen as a risky adventure in the then uncharted waters of democracy. Wary of having parties at all, the founders designed a system that has greatly restrained their political role to this day. Whether American parties should continue to be so loosely organized is at the heart of today's debate concerning their role in American democracy.

TABLE 6.3 — Party Platforms, 1992

Although few people actually read party platforms, they are one of the best written sources for what the parties believe in. A brief summary of some of the contrasting positions in the Democratic and Republican platforms in 1992 illustrates major differences in beliefs between the two parties.

Republicans	Democrats
THE LAST 12 YEARS Presidents Reagan and Bush turned our nation away from the path of overtaxation, hyper-regulation and megagovernment. Instead, we moved in a new direction. We cut taxes, reduced red tape, put people above bureaucracy.	The last 12 years have been a nightmare of Republican irresponsibility and neglect. Republican mismanagement has disarmed government as an instrument to make our economy work.
ABORTION We believe the unborn child has a fundamental individual right to life that cannot be infringed.	Democrats stand behind the right of every woman to choose, consistent with *Roe v. Wade.*
WELFARE Welfare is the enemy of opportunity and stable family life. Today's welfare system is anti-work and anti-marriage.	Welfare should be a second chance, not a way of life. No one is who is able to work can stay on welfare forever, and no one who works should live in poverty.
THE DEFICIT The only solution is for the voters to end divided government so that a Republican Congress can enact the balanced-budget amendment.	Addressing the deficit requires fair and shared sacrifice of all Americans for the common good.
HEALTH CARE Republicans believe government control of health care is irresponsible and ineffective.	All Americans should have universal access to quality, affordable health care—not as a privilege but as a right.
TAXES We will oppose any attempt to increase taxes.	We will relieve the tax burden on middle-class Americans by forcing the rich to pay their fair share.
DEFENSE SPENDING The greatest danger to America's security is here at home, among those who would leave the nation unprepared for the new realities of the post–Cold War World.	Our economy needs both the people and the funds released from defense at the Cold War's end.

(Continued)

TABLE 6.3 — Party Platforms, 1992 (continued)

Republicans	*Democrats*
ENERGY AND THE ENVIRONMENT	
Environmental progress must continue in tandem with economic growth. Crippling an industry is no solution at all. Bankrupt facilities only worsen environmental situations. Unemployment is a form of pollution too.	We reject the Republican myth that energy efficiency and environmental protection are enemies of economic growth. We will make our economy more efficient, using less energy, reducing our dependence on foreign oil, and producing less solid and toxic waste.

SOURCE: Excerpts from party platforms reprinted in *Congressional Quarterly Weekly Reports*, July 18, 1992 and August 22, 1992.

Democracy and Responsible Party Government

Ideally, in a democracy candidates should say what they mean to do if elected and be able to do what they promised once they are elected. Critics of the American party system lament that this is all too often not the case, and have called for a "more responsible two-party system."[26] Advocates of the **responsible party model** believe the parties should meet the following conditions:

1. Parties must present distinct, comprehensive programs for governing the nation.

2. Each party's candidates must be committed to its program and have the internal cohesion and discipline to carry out its program.

3. The majority party must implement its programs and the minority party must state what it would do if it were in power.

4. The majority party must accept responsibility for the performance of the government.

A two-party system operating under these conditions would make it easier to convert party promises into governmental policy. Because a party's officeholders would have control of the government, they would be collectively (rather than individually) responsible for their actions. Voters would therefore know whom to blame for what the government does and does not accomplish.

As this chapter has shown, American political parties fall far short of these conditions. They are too decentralized to take a single national position and then enforce it. Most candidates are self-selected, gaining their nomination by their own efforts rather than the party's. Because virtually anyone can vote in party primaries, parties do not have control over those who run under their labels. For example, in 1991 the former grand wizard of the Ku Klux Klan, David Duke, won the Republican nomination for Governor of Louisiana despite denunciations from President Bush, who ultimately said he preferred the Democratic nominee, Edwin Edwards.

In America's loosely organized party system, there simply is no mechanism for a party to discipline officeholders and thereby ensure cohesion in policy-making. As David Mayhew writes, "Unlike most politicians elsewhere, American ones at both legislative and executive levels have managed to navigate the last two centuries of history without becoming minions of party leaders."[27] Thus, it is rare to find congressional votes in which over 90 percent of Democrats vote in opposition to over 90 percent Republicans. Indeed, Mayhew's analysis of historic legislation from 1946 to 1990 failed to uncover a single case in which a major law was passed by such a clearly partisan vote.[28]

Not everyone thinks that American's decentralized parties are a problem, however. Critics of the responsible party model argue that the complexity and diversity of American society is too great to be captured by such a simple black and white model of party politics. Local differences need an outlet for expression, they say. One cannot expect Texas Democrats to always want to vote in line with New York Democrats. In the view of those opposed to the responsible party model, America's decentralized parties are appropriate for the type of limited government the founders sought to create and most Americans wish to maintain.[29]

American Political Parties and the Scope of Government

The lack of disciplined and cohesive European-style parties in America explains much of why the scope of governmental activity is less in the United States compared to other established democracies. The absence of a national health care system in America provides a perfect example. In Britain, the Labour Party had long proposed such a system, and after it won the 1945 election all of its members of Parliament voted to enact it into law. On the other side of the Atlantic, President Truman also proposed a national health care bill in the first election held after War World II. But even though he won the election and had majorities of his own party in both Houses of Congress, his proposal never got very far. The weak party structure in the United States allowed many congressional Democrats to oppose Truman's health care proposal. Over four decades later, President Clinton again proposed a system of universal health care and had a Democratic controlled Congress to work with. His experience in 1994 was much the same as Truman's; the Clinton health care bill never even came up for a vote in Congress due to the President's inability to get enough members of his own party to go along with him. Thus, substantially increasing the scope of government in America is not something that can be accomplished through the disciplined actions of one party's members, as is the case in other democracies.

Is the Party Over?

The key problem of the parties today is this: the parties are low-tech institutions in a high-tech political era. Political columnist David Broder once wrote that "a growing danger to the prospects for responsible party government is the technological revolution that has affected campaigning in the past decade."[30] The party, through its door-to-door canvassers, still makes house calls, yet more and more political communication is not face-to-face but rather through the mass media. The technology of campaigning—television, polls, computers, political consultants, media specialists, and the like—is available for hire to candidates who can afford it. Why should candidates rely on the parties for what they can buy for themselves?

No longer are parties the main source of political information, attention, and affection. The party of today has rivals that appeal to voters and politicians alike. The biggest rival is the media. With the advent of television, voters no longer need the party to find out what the candidates are like and what they stand for. The interest group is another party rival. As Chapter 8 will discuss, interest groups' power has grown enormously in recent years. They—not the parties—pioneered much of the technology of modern politics, including mass mailings and sophisticated fund-raising.

The parties have clearly been having a tough time of late, but there are indications that they are beginning to adapt to the high-tech age. Although the old city machines are largely extinct, state and national party organizations have become more visible and active than ever. More people are calling themselves Independents and splitting their tickets, but the majority still identify with a party.

For a time, some political scientists were concerned that parties were on the verge of disappearing from the political scene. A more realistic view is that parties will continue to play an important, but significantly diminished, role in American politics. Leon Epstein sees the situation as one in which the parties have become "frayed." He concludes that the parties will "survive and even moderately prosper in a society evidently unreceptive to strong parties and yet unready, and probably unable, to abandon parties altogether."[31]

SUMMARY

Even though political parties are one of Americans' least-beloved institutions, political scientists see them as a key linkage between policymakers and the people. Parties are ubiquitous; for each party there is a *party-in-the-electorate*, a *party organization*, and a *party-in-government*. Political parties affect policy through their platforms. Despite much cynicism about party platforms, they are taken seriously when their candidates are elected.

America's is a two-party system. This fact is of fundamental importance in understanding American politics. The ups and downs of the two parties constitute party competition. In the past, one party or the other has dominated the government for long periods of time. These periods were punctuated by critical elections, in which party coalitions underwent realignment. Since 1968, however, American government has experienced a unique period of party dealignment. Although parties are currently weaker at the mass level, they are stronger (and richer) than ever in terms of national and state organization. Some would have them be far more centralized and cohesive, following the responsible party model. American parties' loose structure allows politicians a great deal of individual freedom, but it also allows them to avoid collective responsibility for a party's performance in office. While the party system is certainly not about to disappear, it remains to be seen whether it can fully adapt itself to the high-tech age.

FOR FURTHER READING

Beck, Paul Allen, and Frank J. Sorauf. *Party Politics in America*, 7th ed. New York: HarperCollins, 1992. The standard textbook on political parties.

Black, Gordon S., and Benjamin D. Black. *The Politics of American Discontent: How a New Party Can Make Democracy Work Again.* New York: John Wiley, 1994. An indictment of the two-party system which calls for the formation of a third party.

Downs, Anthony. *An Economic Theory of Democracy.* New York: Harper & Row, 1957. An extremely influential theoretical work that applies rational-choice theory to party politics.

Epstein, Leon. *Political Parties in the American Mold.* Madison: University of Wisconsin Press, 1986. Epstein demonstrates the remarkable persistence of both parties during a century of profound social change.

Herrnson, Paul S. *Party Campaigning in the 1980s.* Cambridge, MA: Harvard University Press, 1988. An analysis of the role parties play in congressional elections, arguing that they are in the process of making a comeback.

Maisel, L. Sandy, ed. *The Parties Respond: Changes in American Parties and Campaigns,* 2nd ed. Boulder, CO: Westview Press, 1994. A good collection of readings on how parties have adapted to changes in the political system.

Sabato, Larry. *The Party's Just Begun: Shaping Political Parties for America's Future.* Glenview, IL: Scott, Foresman/Little, Brown, 1988. A spirited prescription for strengthening the parties.

Sundquist, James L. *Dynamics of the Party System,* rev. ed. Washington, DC: Brookings Institution, 1983. One of the best books ever on the major realignments in American history.

Wattenberg, Martin P. *The Decline of American Political Parties,* 1952–1992. Cambridge, MA: Harvard University Press, 1994. An account of the decline of parties in the electorate.

NOTES

1. E. E. Schattschneider, *Party Government* (New York: Farrar and Rinehart, 1942), 1.
2. James Gerstenzang, "Bush Campaign Reforms Seek Curbs on PACs," *Los Angeles Times,* June 30, 1989, 23.

3. Anthony Downs, *An Economic Theory of Democracy* (New York: Harper & Row, 1957).

4. Paul Allen Beck and Frank J. Sorauf, *Party Politics in America*, 7th ed. (New York: HarperCollins, 1992), 11.

5. The term *linkage* is introduced in V. O. Key's classic book, *Public Opinion and American Democracy* (New York: Knopf, 1963), chapter 16.

6. Kay Lawson, ed., *Political Parties and Linkage: A Comparative Perspective* (New Haven, CT: Yale University Press, 1980), 3.

7. Downs, *Economic Theory*.

8. Morris P. Fiorina, *Congress: Keystone of the Washington Establishment*, 2nd ed. (New Haven, CT: Yale University Press, 1989), 101.

9. The term is from V. O. Key. The standard source on critical elections is Walter Dean Burnham, *Critical Elections and the Mainsprings of American Politics* (New York: Norton, 1970).

10. For a good collection of readings on the causes and consequences of divided party government, see Gary W. Cox and Samuel Kernell, eds., *The Politics of Divided Government* (Boulder, CO: Westview Press, 1991).

11. Larry Sabato, *The Party's Just Begun: Shaping Political Parties for America's Future* (Glenview, IL: Scott, Foresman/Little, Brown, 1988), 133.

12. Martin P. Wattenberg, *The Decline of American Political Parties, 1952–1992* (Cambridge, MA: Harvard University Press, 1994).

13. Paul S. Herrnson, "American Political Parties After Three Decades of Growth and Change," in Gillian Peele et al., *Developments in American Politics 2* (New York: St. Martin's, 1994).

14. Paul S. Herrnson, *Party Campaigning in the 1980s* (Cambridge, MA: Harvard University Press, 1988), 121.

15. Denise Baer and David Bositis, *Elite Cadres and Party Coalitions: Representing the Public in Party Politics* (Westport, CT: Greenwood Press, 1988).

16. See Martin P. Wattenberg, *The Rise of Candidate-Centered Politics: Presidential Elections of the 1980s* (Cambridge, MA: Harvard University Press, 1991), chapter 3.

17. Xandra Kayden and Eddie Mahe, Jr., *The Party Goes On: The Persistence of the Two-Party System in the United States* (New York: Basic Books, 1985), 10.

18. Steven J. Rosenstone, Roy L. Behr, and Edward H. Lazarus, *Third Parties in America* (Princeton, NJ: Princeton University Press, 1984).

19. Wattenberg, *The Decline*, chapter 10.

20. Beck and Sorauf, *Party Politics in America*, 7th ed., 112.

21. Cornelius Cotter and Bernard C. Hennessey, *Politics Without Power* (New York: Atherton, 1964).

22. Edward C. Banfield and James Q. Wilson, *City Politics* (Cambridge, MA: Harvard University Press and MIT Press, 1963), 115.

23. Terry Christensen and Larry N. Gerston, *The California Connection* (Boston: Little, Brown, 1984), 37.

24. John Bibby et al., "Parties in State Politics," in Virginia Gray, Herbert Jacob, and Kenneth Vines, eds., *Politics in the American States*, 4th ed. (Boston: Little, Brown, 1984), 76–79.

25. Gerald M. Pomper, *Elections in America* (New York: Longman, 1980), 161. Another study of presidential promises from Kennedy through Reagan also reaches the conclusion that campaign pledges are taken seriously. See Jeff Fishel, *Presidents and Promises* (Washington, DC: Congressional Quarterly Press, 1985).

26. The classic statement on responsible parties can be found in "Toward a More Responsible Two-Party System: A report of the Committee on Political Parties, American Political Science Association," *American Political Science Review* 44 (1950): supplement, number 3, part 2.

27. David R. Mayhew, *Divided We Govern: Party Control, Lawmaking, and Investigations, 1946–1990* (New Haven, CT: Yale University Press, 1991), 199.

28. Mayhew, *Divided We Govern*, 126.

29. See Evron M. Kirkpatrick, "Toward a More Responsible Party System: Political Science, Policy Science, or Pseudo-Science?" *American Political Science Review* 65 (1971): 965–990.

30. David S. Broder, *The Party's Over* (New York: Harper & Row, 1972), 236.

31. Leon Epstein, *Political Parties in the American Mold* (Madison: University of Wisconsin Press, 1986), 346.

CHAPTER 7

Campaigns and Voting Behavior

lections serve many important functions in American society. They socialize and institutionalize political activity, making it possible for most political participation to be channeled through the electoral process rather than bubbling up through demonstrations, riots, or revolutions. Because elections provide regular access to political power, leaders can be replaced without being overthrown. This feature gives elections legitimacy in the eyes of people; that is, elections are accepted as a fair and free method of selecting political leaders.

With about half a million elected officials in this country, someone, somewhere, is always running for office. One of the campaigns is for the world's most powerful office—the presidency of the United States. This chapter will focus mainly on this election campaign, although it will explore some other campaigns as well. Chapter 10 will specifically discuss the congressional election process.

There are really two types of campaigns in American politics: campaigns for party nominations and campaigns between the two nominees. These are called nomination campaigns and election campaigns. The prize for the first is garnering a party's nod as its candidate; the prize for the second is winning an office.

THE NOMINATION GAME

A **nomination** is a party's official endorsement of a candidate for office. Anyone can play the nomination game, but few have any serious chance of victory. Generally, success in the nomination game requires money, media attention, and momentum. **Campaign strategy** is the way in which candidates attempt to manipulate each of these elements to achieve the nomination.

Most Americans feel that presidential campaigns are far too long—candidates often begin their quest for votes more than a year before the Iowa caucuses. Here, Richard Gephardt (currently House Minority leader) stumps for support in Iowa during one of the 144 days he spent in the state prior to its 1988 caucuses. Though Gephardt won in Iowa, many feel that by concentrating exclusively on the first contest his organization was not prepared to mount a strong campaign in later states.

A campaign, whether for a nomination or the election, is often unpredictable. Even with name recognition, money, and political savvy, a major blunder can change the political complexion virtually overnight, especially when the press pounces on it. In 1968, George Romney's promising campaign for the Republican nomination fell apart soon after he arrived back from a trip to Vietnam and said that he had been "brainwashed" about the war. After all, who would want a president who admitted to having been brainwashed? Four years later Edmund Muskie decided to attack a harsh newspaper report about his wife. When he broke down emotionally during his denunciation of the newspaper's publisher, his front-running campaign for the Democratic nomination soon collapsed.

Conscious choices and slips of the tongue help determine outcomes of the nomination and election games. One thing, though, is certain: a candidate must first win a nomination to get a chance at election.

Deciding to Run

Believe it or not, not every politician wants to run for president. One reason is that campaigns have become more taxing than ever. As former Speaker of the House Thomas Foley says, "I know of any number of people who I think would make good presidents, even great presidents, who are deterred from running by the torture candidates are obliged to put themselves through."[1] To run for president, a person needs what Walter Mondale once called a "fire in the belly." Remarking on his 1984 bid for the presidency, Mondale said, "For four years, that's all I did. I mean, all I did. That's all you think about. That's all you talk about ... That's your leisure. That's your luxury ... I told someone, 'The question is not whether I can get elected. The question is whether I can be elected and not be nuts when I get there.'"[2]

Strategies for the long campaign trail are often beneath the dignity of the office to which the candidate aspires. The *Washington Post* told the story of Democratic candidate (now House minority leader) Richard Gephardt as he campaigned in New Hampshire nearly a year before any primary votes were cast.[3] In a Nashua gift shop, Gephardt spotted a small statue of a German shepherd, bought it, and the next day took it to Cedar Rapids, Iowa, on a campaign swing through the nation's first caucus state. There Gephardt gave the statue to Connie Clark, a local Democratic activist who collected dog statues, and then spent four hours making pancakes for the breakfast assemblage at her house. By this point, Gephardt had seen Clark no less than six times, and she was not even planning to commit to a candidate for another few months. All told, Gephardt spent a whopping 144 days campaigning in Iowa.[4]

In Britain, campaigns are limited by law to five weeks. In contrast, American campaigns seem endless; a presidential candidacy needs to be either announced or an "open secret" at least a year before the election. It is often said that the presidency is the most difficult job in the world, but getting elected to it may well be tougher. It is arguable that the long campaign for the presidency puts candidates under more continuous stress than they could ever face in the White House. To give you an idea of the extraordinary demands placed upon a candidate, examine "In Focus: A Day in the Presidential Campaign of Bill Clinton."

Those who aspire to the presidency need an electoral base from which to begin. Rarely in American history has a major party's candidate sought the presidency without first holding a key political office; most of the exceptions have been famous generals, like Dwight Eisenhower in 1952. Three offices—U.S. senator, U.S. representative, and state governor—have provided the electoral base for about 80 percent of the major candidates since 1972.[5] All of the six Democratic candidates in 1992 could claim to have been successful in winning either their state's governorship or a U.S. Senate seat.

Having an electoral base is a first step, but the road to the convention is long and full of stumbling blocks. From the convention, held in the summer of election years, only one candidate will emerge as each party's standard-bearer.

IN FOCUS

A Day in the Presidential Campaign of Bill Clinton

The following is Bill Clinton's grueling five-state schedule for March 6, 1992:

- The campaigning begins in Houston, Texas, with a morning tour of a combined court, police station, and detention center.
- Around lunchtime the Governor's plane departs for Tampa, Florida, where he will spend four hours speaking to a crowd of senior citizens and taping an interview for the MacNeil-Lehrer Newshour.

- For dinner Clinton flies to Columbia, South Carolina, where he stays just long enough to give a quick stump speech.
- The next stop is Nashville, Tennessee, where he receives an endorsement from the state's Governor and then holds a news conference to respond to a new attack from one of his opponents.
- Finally, Clinton arrives late in the evening in Baton Rouge, Louisiana, where he can get a little sleep before he is to go out jogging in the morning with students from LSU.

SOURCE: "Campaign Calendar: 5 States in a Day." *New York Times*, March 9, 1992, A11.

Competing for Delegates

In some ways, the nomination game is tougher than the general election game; it whittles a very large number of players down to two. The goal of the nomination game is to win the majority of delegates' support at the **national party convention.**

There are fifty different roads to the national convention, one through each state. From February through June of the election year, the individual state parties busily choose their delegates to the national convention via either caucuses or primaries. Candidates hustle to try to ensure that delegates committed to them are chosen.

The Caucus Road. Before primaries existed, all state parties selected their delegates to the national convention in a meeting of state party leaders called a **caucus**. Sometimes one or two party "bosses" ran the caucus show—often the governor of the state or the mayor of its largest city. Such state party leaders could control who went to the convention and how the state's delegates voted once they got there. They were the kingmakers of presidential politics who met in smoke-filled rooms at the convention to cut deals and form coalitions.

Today's caucuses are different. In the dozen states which still have caususes, party rules mandate openness and strict adherence to complex rules of representation. The caucuses can sometimes be very important, as when Jesse Jackson leaped to the front of the Democratic pack with a surprise victory in the 1988 Michigan caucuses. Iowa traditionally holds the earliest caucus, and an obscure former Georgia governor named Jimmy Carter took his first big presidential step by winning there in 1976. George Bush also made his first big impact on the national scene with an upset victory in Iowa over Ronald Reagan in 1980.

Caucuses usually are organized like a pyramid. Small, neighborhood, precinct-level caucuses are held initially—often meeting in a church, an American Legion hall, or even someone's home. At this level, delegates are chosen (based on their preference for a certain candidate) to attend county caucuses and then congressional district caucuses where delegates are again chosen to go to a higher level—this time to a state convention. It is at the state convention (months after the precinct caucuses) that delegates are finally chosen to go to the national convention. Thus, the Iowa precinct caucuses are only the first step in a long process for selecting the state's delegates. Nevertheless, it is the first test of the candidates' vote-getting ability, and hence it often becomes a full-blown media extravaganza.[6] With Iowa Senator Tom Harkin being assured of an easy victory in 1992, the state's most recent caucuses did not get their usual spate of attention. However, come early 1996 it is likely that the candidates and the media will once again descend on Des Moines.

The Presidential Primary Road. Today, most of the delegates to the Democratic and Republican conventions are selected in **presidential primaries**, in which voters in a state go to the polls and vote for a candidate (or delegates pledged to one). The presidential primary was promoted around the turn of the century by reformers who wanted to take nominations out of the hands of the party bosses. Their idea was to let the people vote for the candidate of their choice and then bind the delegates to vote for that candidate at the convention. In 1992, 39 states held presidential primaries.

Few developments have transformed American politics as much as the proliferation of presidential primaries. Presidential election watcher Theodore White calls the primaries the "classic example of the triumph of goodwill over common sense." Says White:

> An entirely new breed of professionals has grown up, voyaging like Gauleiters from state to state, specializing in get-out-the-vote techniques, cross sectionings, media, ethnic breakdowns, and other specialties . . . Most of all, delegates, who were supposed to be free to vote their own common sense and conscience, have become for the most part anonymous faces, collected as background for the television cameras, sacks of potatoes packaged in primaries, divorced from party roots, and from the officials who rule states and nation.[7]

The primary season begins during the winter in New Hampshire, where license plates boldly state, "Live free or die." (One can only guess what the prison inmates of New Hampshire must think while making these plates.) Like the Iowa caucuses, the importance of New Hampshire is not the number of delegates or how representative the state is (if there is a representative American state, New Hampshire is certainly not it), but rather that it is always

Television enables many more people to see candidates for elected office than would ever be possible in person. In fact, people have become so accustomed to seeing politicians' faces when they speak that giant TV screens are now often used to enable those attending political events to see the speakers' facial expressions.

first. At this early stage the campaign is not for delegates, but for images—candidates want the rest of the country to immediately see them as frontrunners. The frenzy of political activity in this small state is given lavish attention in the national press. Because Iowa was not contested by the candidates in 1992, the attention given to New Hampshire was even greater than usual. In fact, 23 percent of TV coverage of the 1992 nomination races was devoted to the New Hampshire primary.[8]

Other state primaries follow New Hampshire's. The laws determining the way in which the primaries are set up and the delegates are allocated are made by state legislatures and state parties. Even the experts are often confused by the variety of different procedures used from state to state. One thing is certain, though—week after week the primaries serve as elimination contests. Politicians, press, and public all love a winner. Candidates who fail to win in the early primaries get labeled as losers and typically drop out of the race. Usually they have little choice, as losing quickly inhibits a candidate's ability to raise the money necessary to win in other states. In 1992, Senators Tsongas, Harkin, and Kerrey all withdrew from the race saying that their campaign was bankrupt.

In the 1980 delegate chase, a commonly used football term became established in the language of American politics. After George Bush scored a surprise victory over Ronald Reagan in the Iowa caucuses, he proudly claimed to possess "the big mo"—momentum. (Actually, Bush had only a little "mo," and quickly fell victim to a decisive Reagan victory in New Hampshire.) The term neatly describes what candidates for the nomination are after. Primaries and caucuses are more than an endurance contest, they are also proving grounds. Week after week, the challenge is to do better than expected. To get "mo" going, candidates have to beat people they were not expected to beat, collect margins above predictions, and never, above all else, lose to people they were expected to trounce. Momentum is good to have, but it is no guarantee of victory, as candidates with a strong base sometimes bounce back. Political scientist Larry Bartels found that "substantive political appeal may overwhelm the impact of momentum, as it did for Reagan against Bush and for Mondale against Hart."[9]

Evaluating the Primary and Caucus System.   The primaries and the caucuses are here to stay. That does not mean, however, that political scientists or commentators are particularly happy with the system. Criticisms of this marathon campaign are numerous; here are a few of the most important:

- *Disproportionate attention goes to the early caucuses and primaries.* Take a look at Figure 7.1, which shows how critics think America's media-dominated campaigns are distorted by early primaries and caucuses. Neither New Hampshire nor Iowa is particularly representative of the national electorate. Both are rural; both have only small minority populations; and neither is at the center of the political mainstream. Whereas Iowa is more liberal than the nation as a whole, New Hampshire is the reverse. Thus, although Iowa and New Hampshire are not always "make or break" contests, they play a key—and a disproportionate—role in building momentum, money, and media attention.

- *Money plays too big a role in the caucuses and primaries.* Momentum means money—getting more of it than your opponents. Many people think that money plays too large a role in American presidential elections. (This topic will be discussed in detail shortly.) Candidates who drop out early in the process often lament that their inability to raise money left them without a chance to really compete.

- *Participation in primaries and caucuses is low and unrepresentative.* Although about 50 percent of the population votes in the November presidential election, only about 25 percent cast ballots in presidential primaries. Participation in caucus states is much smaller, as a person must usually devote several hours to attending a caucus. Except for Iowa, where media attention usually boosts the turnout to about 20 percent, only about 5 percent of eligible voters typically show up for caucuses. Moreover, voters in primaries and caucuses are hardly representative of voters at large; they tend to be better educated and more affluent.

FIGURE 7.1 — *The Inflated Importance of Iowa and New Hampshire in the Presidential Nomination Process*

In 1984, 34 percent of all TV news stories about the nomination campaigns were focused on Iowa and New Hampshire, even though these two small states selected only about 2 percent of the convention delegates. Here are the fifty states drawn to scale according to the media attention their primaries and caucuses received in 1984, according to an analysis of coverage by the *New York Times*.

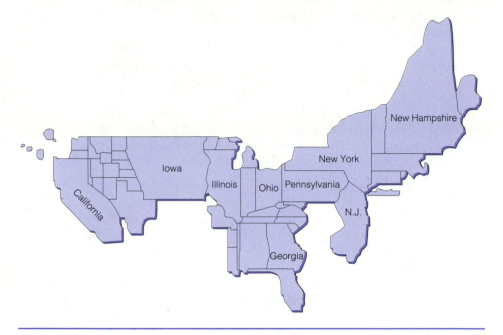

SOURCE: William C. Adams, "As New Hampshire Goes...," in Gary R. Orren and Nelson W. Polsby, eds, *Media and Momentum* (Chatham, NJ: Chatham House, 1987), 43.

- *Primaries and caucuses exaggerate regional factors in decision making.* In 1988, southern states, feeling that northern states like New Hampshire and Iowa had disproportionate influence in the choice of the Democratic nominee, created **Super Tuesday** by moving all their primaries to the same day in early March. No longer could conservative Democrats be ignored, said southern democratic leaders. Although the hope of southern Democrats did not materialize in 1988, in 1992 the Clinton campaign was given a big boost by resounding wins on Super Tuesday.
- *The system gives too much power to the media.* Critics contend that the media have replaced the party bosses as the new kingmakers. Deciding who has momentum at any given moment, the press readily labels candidates as winners and losers.

Is this, critics ask, the best way to pick a president? Critics answer their own question with a strong no, and have proposed either a **national presidential primary** or a series of **regional primaries.**

Nevertheless, the current system has powerful defenders—most notably the candidates themselves. For example, George Bush writes in his 1987 autobiography, *Looking Forward*, that

> our presidential selection process may be pressurized, chaotic, sometimes even unfair; but I disagree with critics who think that it needs a massive overhaul—especially those who argue that television, because it can reach millions, makes it unnecessary for a candidate to travel the country "retailing" his campaign message.
>
> For all its flaws, the virtue of the present system is that it brings presidential candidates—as well as Presidents—out of the insulated politics of television and electronic computers into contact with the flesh-and-blood world.[10]

Even candidates who finish well back in the pack usually support the process. Senator Paul Simon, who carried only his native Illinois, argues that it is best to start the race in small states where people can meet the candidates face-to-face and where a candidate lacking a big campaign war chest has a chance. He writes that the people of Iowa and New Hampshire, recognizing their important role in the process, "make their commitments with considerably more caution and care than do most citizens in other states."[11]   Former Arizona Governor Bruce Babbitt, who got great press coverage but few votes in 1988, defends the length of the nomination race. He argues that "it has to be long, to allow us to surface national leadership outside of a parliamentary system. Congress does not automatically produce national leadership."[12] It is important to enable new national leaders to emerge, says Babbitt, and the current American system facilitates this.

Obviously, some of the candidates would like to see some changes, but as long as most candidates and citizens support the process in general, major reform is unlikely. For the forseeable future, states will continue to select delegates in primaries and caucuses to attend the national conventions, where the nominees are formally chosen.

The Convention Send-off

Party conventions provided great drama in American politics for over a century. Great speeches were given, dark-horse candidates suddenly appeared, and ballot after ballot was held as candidates jockeyed to win the nomination. It took the Democrats 46 ballots in 1912, 44 in 1920, and a record 103 in 1924 to nominate their presidential standard-bearer. Multiballot conventions died out in 1952, however, with the advent of television.

Nevertheless, television did not immediately put an end to drama at the conventions. In fact, for a while it helped to create it. In 1964, NBC's John Chancellor was arrested for standing in the aisles while reporting from the floor of the Republican Convention. His producers promised him bail, and as he was escorted off the floor he signed off saying, "This is John Chancellor reporting under custody and now returning you to the anchor booth." Four years later, it was protestors in the streets of Chicago that were being arrested at the Democratic Convention. The networks shifted back and forth from scenes of violence in the streets to the bitter debate and occasional scuffles inside the convention hall. In 1972 the Democrats were at it again, this time extending their debates late into the night, causing nominee George McGovern to give his acceptance speech at three in the morning. Some delegates took pity on the overworked TV anchors, holding up signs like "Free Walter Cronkite" (who then anchored CBS's coverage).

Today, though, the drama has largely been drained from the conventions, as the winner is a foregone conclusion. No longer can a powerful governor shift a whole block of votes at the last minute. Delegates selected in primaries and open caucuses have known preferences. The last time there was any doubt as to who would win at the convention was in 1976, when Ford barely edged Reagan for the Republican nomination. The parties have also learned that it is not in their best interest to provide high drama. The raucous conventions held by the Republicans in 1964 and the Democrats in 1968 and 1972 captured the public's attention, but they also exposed such divisiveness that the parties were unable to unite for the fall campaign.

Without such drama, the networks have scaled back their coverage substantially and the Nielsen ratings have fallen to new lows.[13] When Bush and Quayle delivered their speeches at the 1992 Republican Convention, NBC and

ABC each got a rating of 7.0, and CBS trailed with a 5.7. By comparison, when CBS aired Murphy Brown's response to Quayle's criticism of her life-style choice, it got a rating of 29.3.

One can hardly blame people for tuning out the conventions, though, when little news is made at them. Today's conventions are carefully scripted to present the party in its best light. Delegates are no longer there to argue for their causes, but rather to merely support their candidate. The parties carefully orchestrate a massive send-off for the presidential and vice-presidential candidates. The party's leaders are there in force, as are many of its most important followers—people whose input will be key during the campaign. Thus, although conventions are no longer very interesting, they are a significant rallying point for the parties.

The conventions are also important in developing the party's policy positions and in promoting political representation. In the past, conventions were essentially an assembly of state- and local-party leaders, gathered together to bargain over the selection of the party's ticket. Almost all delegates were white, male, and over 40 years old. Lately, party reformers, especially among the Democrats, have worked hard to make the conventions far more demographically representative.

THE CAMPAIGN GAME

Once nominated, candidates concentrate on campaigning for the general election. These days, the word **campaign** is part of American political vocabulary, but it was not always so. The term was originally a military one: generals mounted campaigns, using their scarce resources to achieve strategic objectives. Political campaigns are like that, too—resources are scarce, expenditures in the presidential race are limited by federal law, and both have to be timed and targeted. A candidate's time and energy are also finite. Choices must be made concerning where to go and how long to spend at each stop.

More than organization and leadership are involved in campaigns. Artistry also enters the picture, for campaigns deal in images. The campaign is the canvas on which political strategists try to paint portraits of leadership, competence, caring, and other images Americans value in presidents. To project the right image to the voters, three ingredients are needed: a campaign organization, money, and media attention.

Organizing the Campaign

In every campaign, there is too much to do and too little time to do it. Every candidate must prepare for nightly banquets and endless handshaking. More importantly, to effectively organize their campaigns candidates must do the following:

- *Line up a campaign manager.*   Some candidates try to run their own campaign, but they usually end up regretting it. A professional campaign

In writing a party platform, disagreements between various factions of the party often become evident. In 1992, Ann Stone led a movement of Republican women in favor of a pro-choice plank on abortion. While Ann Stone drew a fair amount of media attention, she was unsuccessful in getting the Republican Convention to even consider changing its pro-life platform.

manager can keep the candidate from getting bogged down in organizational details.

- *Get a fund-raiser.*   Money, as this chapter will soon discuss in detail, is an important key to election victory.
- *Get a campaign counsel.*   With all the current federal regulation of campaign financing, legal assistance is essential to ensure compliance with the laws.
- *Hire media and campaign consultants.*   Candidates have more important things to do with their time than plan ad campaigns, contract for buttons and bumper stickers, and buy TV time and newspaper space. Professionals can get them the most exposure for their money.
- *Assemble a campaign staff.*   It is desirable to hire as many professionals as the campaign budget allows, but it is also important to get a coordinator of volunteers to ensure that envelopes are licked, doorbells rung, and other small but vital tasks are addressed.
- *Plan the logistics.*   A modern presidential campaign involves jetting around the country at an incredible pace. Good advance people handle

the complicated details of candidate scheduling and see to it that events are well publicized and attended.

- *Get a research staff and policy advisors.*   Candidates have little time to master the complex issues reporters will ask about. Policy advisors—often distinguished academics—feed them information they need to keep up with events.
- *Hire a pollster.*   There are dozens of professional polling firms that do opinion research to tell candidates how they are viewed by the voters and what is on the voters' minds.
- *Get a good press secretary.*   Candidates running for major office have reporters dogging them every step of the way. The reporters need news, and a good press secretary can help them make their deadlines with stories that the campaign would like to see reported.

Most of these tasks cost money. Campaigns are not cheap, and the role of money in campaigns is a controversial one.

Money and Campaigning

There is no doubt that campaigns are expensive and, in America's high-tech political arena, growing more so. As California Treasurer Jesse Unruh used to say, "Money is the mother's milk of politics." Candidates need money to build a campaign organization and to get their message out. Many people and groups who want certain things from the government are all too willing to give it—thus there is the common perception that money buys votes and influence. The following sections take a close look at the role of money in campaigns.

The Maze of Campaign Finance Reforms.   As the costs of campaigning skyrocketed with the growth of television, and as the Watergate scandal exposed large, illegal campaign contributions, momentum developed in the early 1970s for campaign financing reform. Several public interest lobbies (see Chapter 8), notably Common Cause and the National Committee for an Effective Congress, led the drive. In 1974, Congress passed the **Federal Election Campaign Act**. It had two main goals: tightening reporting requirements for contributions and limiting overall expenditures. In essence, here is what the act, with subsequent amendments did:

- *It created the* **Federal Election Commission (FEC)**.   A bipartisan body, the six-member FEC administers the campaign finance laws and enforces compliance with their requirements.
- *It provided public financing for presidential primaries and general elections.* Presidential candidates who raise five thousand dollars on their own in at least twenty states can get individual contributions of up to two hundred fifty dollars matched by the federal treasury. For the general election, the party nominees each get a fixed amount of money to cover all their campaign expenses.

- *It limited presidential campaign spending.* If presidential candidates accept federal support at any stage, they agree to limit their campaign expenditures to an amount prescribed by federal law.
- *It required disclosure.* Regardless of whether they accept any federal funding, all candidates must file periodic reports with the FEC, listing who contributed and how the money was spent.
- *It limited contributions.* Scandalized to find out that wealthy individuals like J. Willard Marriott had contributed $1 million to the 1972 Nixon campaign, Congress limited individual contributions to one thousand dollars.

Although the campaign reforms were generally welcomed by both parties, the constitutionality of the act was challenged in the 1976 case of *Buckley v. Valeo*. In this case, the Supreme Court struck down the portion of the act that had limited the amount individuals could contribute to their own campaigns as a violation of free speech. This aspect of the Court ruling made it possible for Ross Perot to spend over $50 million on his independent presidential candidacy in 1992.

Overall, there is little doubt that campaign spending reforms have made campaigns more open and honest. Small donors are encouraged and the rich are restricted. A campaign's financial records are now open for all to examine, and FEC auditors try to make sure that the regulations are enforced. As Frank Sorauf writes, the detailed FEC reports have "become a wonder of the democratic political world. Nowhere else do scholars and journalists find so much information about the funding of campaigns, and the openness of Americans about the flow of money stuns many other nationals accustomed to silence and secrecy about such traditionally private matters."[14]

The Proliferation of PACs. The campaign reforms also encouraged the spread of **Political Action Committees**, generally known as PACs. Before the 1974 reforms, corporations were technically forbidden from donating money to political campaigns, but many wrote big checks anyway. Unions could make indirect contributions, although limits were set on how they could aid candidates and political parties. The 1974 reforms created a new, more open, way for interest groups like business and labor to contribute to campaigns. Any interest group, large or small, can now get into the act by forming their own PAC to directly channel contributions of up to five thousand dollars per candidate. Because *Buckley v. Valeo* extended the right of free speech to PACs, they can spend unlimited amounts indirectly, that is, if such activities are not coordinated with the campaign.

PACs have proliferated in recent years. The FEC counted 4,195 PACs in 1992. These PACs contributed $178 million to congressional candidates for the 1992 campaign. Many believe that this has led to a system of open graft.[15] Few developments since the Watergate crisis have generated so much cynicism about government as the explosive growth of PACs over the last 15 years.

A PAC is formed when a business association, or some other interest group, decides to contribute to candidates they believe will be favorable toward their goals. The group registers as a PAC with the FEC, and then puts money into the PAC coffers. The PAC can collect money from stockholders, members, and other interested parties. It then donates the money to candidates, often after careful research on their issue stands and past voting records. One very important ground rule prevails: All expenditures must be meticulously accounted for to the FEC. If PACs are corrupting democracy, at least they are doing so openly.

Candidates need PACs because high-tech campaigning is expensive. Tightly contested races for the House of Representatives can sometimes cost $1 million; Senate races can easily cost $1 million for television alone. PACs play a major role in paying for expensive campaigns. Thus, there emerges a symbiotic relationship between the PACs and the candidates: candidates need money, which they insist can be used without compromising their integrity; PACs want access to officeholders, which they insist can be gained without buying votes. Justin Dart of Dart Industries, a close friend of former President Reagan, remarks of his PAC that "talking to politicians is fine, but with a little money, they hear you better."[16]

Critics of the PAC system worry that all this money leads to PAC control over what the winners do once in office. Archibald Cox and Fred Wertheimer of Common Cause write that the role of PACs in campaign finance "is robbing our nation of its democratic ideals and giving us a government of leaders beholden to the monied interests who make their election possible."[17] On some issues, it seems clear that PAC money has made a difference. The Federal Trade Commission, for example, once passed a regulation requiring that car dealers list known mechanical defects on the window sticker of used cars. The National Association of Automobile Dealers quickly became the fourth largest donor in the 1980 congressional elections, contributing just over $1 million to candidates of both parties. Soon afterwards, 216 representatives cosponsored a House resolution nullifying the FTC regulation. Of these, 186 had been aided by the auto dealers' PAC.[18]

It is questionable, however, whether such examples are the exception or the rule. Most PACs give money to candidates who agree with them in the first place. For instance, the antiabortion PACs will not waste their money supporting outspokenly pro-choice candidates. Frank Sorauf's careful review of the subject concludes that "there simply are no data in the systematic studies that would support the popular assertions about the 'buying' of the Congress or about any other massive influence of money on the legislative process."[19] (For more on the link between PACs and Congress, see "In Focus: Do PACs Buy Votes?" in Chapter 10.)

The impact of PAC money on presidents is even more doubtful. Presidential campaigns are, of course, partly subsidized by the public and so are less dependent upon PACs. Moreover, presidents have well-articulated positions on most important issues. A small contribution from any one PAC is not likely to turn a presidential candidate's head.

To summarize, money matters in campaigns. Because it matters during campaigns, it sometimes also matters during legislative votes. Although scare stories about the proliferation of PACs may be exaggerated, campaign finance is an old issue that is not likely to go away as long as campaigns continue to be so expensive.

Are Campaigns Too Expensive?   Every four years Americans spend over $2 billion on national, state, and local elections. This seems like a tremendous amount of money, yet compared with the amount of money Americans spend on items of far less importance, campaigns actually are relatively inexpensive. For example, each year a typical soap company will spend twice the cost of a presidential campaign to advertise its products.

What bothers politicians most about the rising costs of high-tech campaigning is that fund-raising has come to take up so much of their precious time. In 1988, former Florida Governor Reuben Askew pulled out of a Senate race he was favored to win for this very reason. "Something is seriously wrong with our system when many candidates for the Senate need to spend 75 percent of their time raising money," Askew said.[20] Many officeholders feel that the need for continuous fund-raising distracts them from their jobs as legislators.

Public financing of campaigns would take care of this problem. Some lawmakers support some sort of public financing reform; however, it will be very difficult to get Congress to consent to equal financing for the people who will challenge them for their seats. Incumbents will not readily give up the advantage they have in raising money.

Does Money Buy Victory?   Money is, of course, absolutely crucial to electoral victory; important offices are rarely won these days by candidates who spend virtually nothing. One of the last of this nonspending breed was Senator William Proxmire of Wisconsin, who recently retired. In 1988 he was succeeded by wealthy businessman Herbert Kohl, who funded his multimillion dollar campaign entirely out of his own pocket. (As Kohl said, he was so rich that no one had to worry about him being bought by special interests.) In this era of high-tech politics, pollsters, public relations people, direct-mail consultants, and many other specialists are crucial to a campaign, and they cost money.

Perhaps the most basic complaint about money and politics is that there may be a direct link between dollars spent and votes received. Few have done more to dispel this charge than political scientist Gary Jacobson. His research has shown that "the more incumbents spend, the worse they do."[21] This fact is not as odd as it at first sounds. It simply means that incumbents who face a tough opponent must raise more money to meet the challenge. When a challenger is not a serious threat (as they all too often are not), incumbents can afford to campaign cheaply.

More important than having "more" money is having "enough" money. Herbert Alexander calls this "the doctrine of sufficiency." As he writes,

Briefing the press every day about the candidate's activities is the job of the press secretary. During the 1992 Clinton campaign, this was the job of Dee Dee Myers. After the election, Ms. Myers continued to serve Clinton in this role through 1994, becoming the first woman to serve as a White House press secretary.

"Enough money must be spent to get a message across to compete effectively but outspending one's opponent is not always necessary—even an incumbent with a massive ratio of higher spending."[22] One case in point is that of Paul Wellstone, a previously obscure political science professor, who beat an incumbent senator in 1990 despite being outspent by eight to one.

The Media and the Campaign

Money matters, and so does media attention. Media coverage is determined by two factors: (1) how candidates use their advertising budget, and (2) the "free" attention they get as newsmakers. The first, obviously, is relatively easy to control; the second is harder, but not impossible. Almost every logistical decision in a campaign—where to eat breakfast, whom to include on the rostrum, when to announce a major policy proposal—is calculated according to its intended media impact. Years ago, the biggest item in a campaign budget might have been renting a railroad train. Today, the major item is unquestionably television advertising. About half the total budget for a presidential or senatorial campaign will be used for television advertising.

No major candidate these days can do without what political scientist Dan Nimmo calls "the political persuaders."[23] A new profession of political consultants has emerged, and for the right price, they can turn a disorganized campaign into a well-run, high-tech operation. They can do it all—polling or hiring the pollster, molding a candidate's image, advising a candidate on his or her spouse's role, handling campaign logistics, managing payrolls, and so forth. Incumbents as well as challengers turn to professional consultants for such help.

All this concern with public relations worries some observers of American politics. They fear a new era of politics in which the slick slogan and the image salesperson will dominate, an era when Madison Avenue will be more influential than Main Street. Most political scientists, however, are coming to the conclusion that such fears are overblown. Research has shown that campaign advertising can be a source of information about issues as well as about images. Thomas Patterson and Robert McClure examined the information contained in TV advertising and found it impressive. In fact, they concluded, viewers could learn more about candidates' stands on the issues from watching their ads than from watching the nightly news. Most news coverage stresses where the candidates went, how big their crowds were, and other campaign details. Only rarely do the networks delve into where the candidates stand on the issues. In contrast, political ads typically address issues.[24] Perhaps there is less conflict between issues and images than appears on the surface. The candidates' positions are a crucial part of their images. Getting those positions across to voters is as important as persuading them that a candidate is honest, competent, and a leader.

Candidates attempt to manipulate their images through advertising and image building, but they have less control over the other aspect of the media— coverage of the news. To be sure, most campaigns have press aides who feed "canned" news releases to reporters. Still, the media largely determine for themselves what is happening in a campaign. Campaign coverage seems to be a constant interplay between hard news about what candidates say and do and the human-interest angle, which most journalists think sells newspapers or interests television viewers.

Apparently, news organizations believe that policy issues are of less interest to voters than the campaign itself. The result is that news coverage is disproportionately devoted to campaign strategies, speculation about what will happen next, poll results, and other aspects of the campaign game. Patterson tabulated the amount of media attention to the campaign itself and the amount of attention to such substantive issues as the economy in the 1976 presidential race. Examining several newspapers and news magazines as well as television network news, he found that attention to the "game" far exceeded attention to substance.[25] Once a candidate has taken a policy position and it has been reported on, it becomes old news. The latest poll showing Smith ahead of Jones is thus more newsworthy in the eyes of the media. Bush's media consultant, Roger Ailes, calls this his "orchestra pit" theory of American politics: "If you have two guys on stage and one guy says, 'I have a solution to the Middle East problem,' and the other guy falls in the orchestra pit, who do you think is going to be on the evening news?"[26]

The Impact of Campaigns

Politicians are great believers in campaigns. Almost all of them figure that a good campaign is the key to victory. Many political scientists, however, question their importance. Reviewing the evidence, Dan Nimmo concluded, "Political campaigns are less crucial in elections than most politicians believe."[27] For years, researchers studying campaigns have stressed that campaigns have three effects on voters: **reinforcement, activation,** and **conversion**. Campaigns can reinforce voters' preferences for candidates; they can activate voters, getting them to contribute money or ring doorbells as opposed to merely voting; and they can convert, changing voters' minds.

Four decades of research on political campaigns lead to a single message: campaigns mostly reinforce and activate; only rarely do they convert. The evidence on the impact of campaigns points clearly to the conclusion that the best-laid plans of campaign managers change very few votes. Given the millions of dollars spent on political campaigns, it may be surprising to find that they do not have a great effect. Several factors tend to weaken campaigns' impact on voters:

- Most people pay relatively little attention to campaigns in the first place. People have a remarkable capacity for **selective perception**: paying most attention to things they already agree with and interpreting events according to their own predispositions.
- Factors such as party identification, though less important than they used to be, still influence voting behavior regardless of what happens in the campaign.
- Incumbents start with a substantial advantage in terms of name recognition and an established track record.

This does not mean, of course, that campaigns never change voters' minds, or that converting a small percentage is unimportant. In tight races, a good campaign can make the difference between winning and losing.

As the campaign nears its end, voters face two key choices: whether to vote and, if they chose to, how to vote. The following sections will investigate the ways that voters make these choices.

WHETHER TO VOTE: A CITIZEN'S FIRST CHOICE

The nearly two centuries of American electoral history have witnessed greatly expanded **suffrage**, the right to vote. Early in American history only property-owning white males over the age of twenty-one were typically allowed to vote. Now the right to vote is guaranteed to all over the age of eighteen—male or female, white or nonwhite, homeowner or homeless. (For these developments, particularly as they affect women and minorities, see Chapter 4.)

Interestingly, as the right to vote has been extended, proportionately fewer of those eligible have chosen to exercise that right. In the past hundred years, the 80 percent turnout in the 1896 election was the high point of electoral participation. In 1992, only 55 percent of the adult population voted in the presidential election (see Figure 7.2).

Who Votes and Who Stays Home?

When only half the population votes in a presidential election, the necessity of studying nonvoters takes on added importance. The most useful study of non-voting in American elections was done by Raymond Wolfinger and Steven Rosenstone.[28] Several conclusions are apparent from their research:

- *Voting is a class-biased activity.* People with higher-than-average educational and income levels vote more than people with lower educational and income levels. Among all factors affecting turnout, this one is the most important.

FIGURE 7.2 — *The Decline of Turnout: 1892–1992*

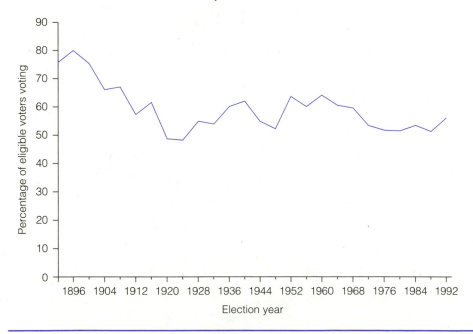

SOURCES: For data up to 1968, *Historical Statistics of the United States* (Washington DC: Government Printing Office, 1975), part 2, 1071. For 1972–1988, *Statistical Abstract of the United States*, 1990 (Washington, DC: Government Printing Office, 1990), 264. Data for 1992 comes from news reports.

- *Young people have the lowest turnout rate.*   As people age, their likelihood of voting increases, until the infirmities of old age make it difficult for them to get to the polls.

- *Whites vote with greater frequency than members of minority groups.* African Americans, Puerto Ricans, and Chicanos are all underrepresented among the ranks of voters, but this can be explained by their generally low level of education and income. Blacks and other minority groups with high levels of income and education vote more than whites with comparable socioeconomic status.

- *Southerners do less voting than northerners.*   Although the 1965 Voting Rights Act forced the South to make it easier for its citizens (particularly African Americans) to vote, the historical legacy of low participation remains.

- *Voting is not very strongly related to gender.*   In an earlier period many women were discouraged from voting, but today women vote just about as frequently as men do.

These differences in turnout rates are often cumulative. Possessing several of these traits (say, being well educated, middle-aged, and a northerner) adds significantly to one's likelihood of voting. Conversely, being young, poorly educated, and southern is likely to add up to a very low probability of voting.

As Wolfinger and Rosenstone point out, the best predictor of whether a person will vote is whether that person is registered. America's unique registration system is in part to blame for why Americans are significantly less likely to go to the polls than citizens of other democratic nations (see "America In Perspective: Why Turnout in the United States Is So Low Compared to Other Countries").

The Registration System

A century ago politicians used to say, "Vote early and often." Cases such as West Virginia's 159,000 votes being cast by 147,000 eligible voters in 1888 were not unusual. Largely to prevent corruption associated with stuffing ballot boxes, states adopted **voter registration** around the turn of the century. By requiring citizens to register in advance of election day, elections were made much more ethical.

Registration procedures differ greatly from state to state. Presently, states in the upper Great Plains and the Northwest make it easiest to register: voters can sign up at many everyday locations such as supermarkets, and no elaborate procedures are used. In sparsely populated North Dakota there is no registration at all, and in Minnesota, Wisconsin, and Maine voters can register just prior to voting on election day. It is probably no coincidence that these four states consistently rank near the top in voting turnout. By contrast, states in the South have long had the most difficult hurdles to clear when it comes to registering to vote, leading them to have the nation's lowest turnout rates.

AMERICA IN PERSPECTIVE

Why Turnout in the United States Is So Low Compared to Other Countries

Despite living in a culture that encourages participation, Americans have a woefully low turnout rate compared to other democracies. Here are some figures on voting rates in the United States and other industrial nations:

Australia, 1993	93%
Bulgaria, 1990	88%
Luxembourg, 1990	87%
Nicaragua, 1990	86%
Iceland, 1991	86%
Belgium, 1991	85%
Sweden, 1991	85%
New Zealand, 1993	85%
Czech Republic, 1992	84%
Austria, 1992	84%
Italy, 1992	83%
Denmark, 1990	82%
Greece, 1993	82%
Finland, 1994	82%
Great Britain, 1992	78%
Germany, 1990	78%
Costa Rica, 1990	77%
Spain, 1993	77%
Israel, 1992	77%
Norway, 1993	75%
South Korea, 1992	72%
Canada, 1993	71%
Ireland, 1992	69%
Portugal, 1991	68%
Estonia, 1992	68%
Japan, 1993	67%
Nepal, 1991	65%
Russia, 1993	55%
United States, 1992	**55%**
Switzerland, 1991	46%

There are several reasons given for Americans' abysmally low turnout rate. Probably the most often cited reason is the unique American requirement of voter registration. The governments of other democracies take the responsibility of seeing to it that all of their eligible citizens are on the voting lists. In America the responsibility for registration lies solely with the individual.

A second difference between the United States and other countries is that the American government asks citizens to vote far more often. While the typical European voter may be called upon to cast two or three ballots in a four-year period, many Americans are faced with a dozen or more separate elections in the space of four years. Furthermore, Americans are expected to vote for a much wider range of political offices. With 1 elected official for every 442 citizens and elections held somewhere virtually every week, it is no wonder that it is so difficult to get Americans to the polls. It is probably no coincidence that the one European country that has a comparable turnout rate—Switzerland—has also overwhelmed its citizens with voting opportunities, typically asking people to vote three times every year.

Finally, the stimulus to vote is not as high in the United States because the choice offered Americans is not as great as in other countries. This is because the United States stands virtually alone in the democratic world in lacking a major left-wing socialist party. When European voters go the polls they are deciding on whether or not their country will be run by parties with socialist goals or alternatively by conservative, and in some cases religious, parties. The consequences of their vote for redistribution of income and the scope of government are far greater than the ordinary American voter can conceive of.

SOURCE: For turnout figures around the world see the various election reports in recent issues of *Electoral Studies.*

In every state other than North Dakota, eligible voters must first register in order to be able to vote. The bureaucratic hassle involved in registering is often blamed for the low turnout rates of minority groups in the United States.

This will change when the 1993 **Motor Voter Act** goes into effect in 1996. The act requires states to permit people to register at the same time citizens apply for driver's licenses. Whereas less than 70 percent of all eligible voters are currently registered, nearly 90 percent of this group have driver's licenses. The Motor Voter Act will make voter registration much easier by allowing eligible voters to simply check a box on their driver's license application or renewal form. No one knows for sure how much of an impact this reform will have, but Ruy Teixeria estimates that it "might raise turnout as much as 4.2 percentage points."[29]

Yet Teixeria also notes that turnout has steadily declined in the United States since 1960, even though registration procedures have actually been made easier. For example, many states have enacted postal registration and permitted deputy registrars to go out and register people rather than have the people come to them. Thus, in recent decades those who have been registered have shown less propensity to actually vote. Teixeria traces the drop in turnout to a decline in Americans' social and political connectedness. A younger, single, and less church-going electorate has resulted in voters being less socially tied to their political communities. Furthermore, political withdrawal has resulted from declines in partisanship, political interest, and the belief that government is responsive, according to Teixeira's research.[30]

A Policy Approach to Deciding Whether to Vote

Realistically, when 100 million people vote in a presidential election the chance of one vote affecting the outcome is very, very slight. Once in a while, of course, an election is decided by a handful of votes. In 1948, Lyndon Johnson won a race for the U.S. Senate by a total of 87—very suspicious—votes, earning him the nickname "Landslide Lyndon."[31] In 1960, John Kennedy carried the state of Hawaii by a mere 115 votes. It is more likely, however, that you will be struck by lightning during your lifetime than participate in an election decided by a single vote.

Not only does your vote probably not make much difference to the outcome, but voting is somewhat costly. You have to spend some of your valuable time becoming informed, making up your mind, and getting to the polls. If you carefully calculate your time and energy, you might rationally decide that the costs of voting outweigh the benefits.

Economist Anthony Downs, in his model of democracy, tries to explain why a rational person would ever bother to vote. He argues that rational people vote if they believe that the policies of one party will bring more benefits than the policies of the other party.[32] Thus, people who see **policy differences** between the parties are more likely to join the ranks of voters. If you are an environmentalist and you expect the Democrats to pass more environmental legislation than the Republicans, then you have an additional incentive to go to the polls. On the other hand, if you are truly indifferent—that is, if you see no difference whatsoever between the two parties—you may rationally decide to abstain. You may also abstain if you believe that the Democrats' pro-environmental platform is balanced by Republican policies, such as those to control inflation. Even if you are indifferent about the outcome, you may decide to vote anyway, simply to support democratic government. In this case, you are impelled to vote by a sense of **civic duty.**

Why, then, is there so much inequality in voting, with the rich and the well-educated participating more than the poor and the less-educated? First, in nearly every election, on nearly every issue, the upper classes are more likely to recognize and understand policy differences than the lower classes. In particular, higher education trains a person to see the impact of policy decisions and the nuances of party platforms. Second, upper-class people score higher on **political efficacy,** the belief that ordinary people can influence the government. In other words, people low in socioeconomic status turn out less because they are more likely to think their votes do not really matter. Third, the poor and less educated find the bureaucratic hurdles of the registration process especially difficult. It might not seem much of a chore for you to register to vote after having gone through course registration at your school, but for those not fortunate enough to go to college it does not seem so easy.

Until some of the various factors that inhibit voting change dramatically, it is likely that American elections will continue to be decided by only about half the eligible voters. How these voters make their decisions will be discussed in the following sections.

HOW AMERICANS VOTE: EXPLAINING CITIZENS' DECISIONS

Here is a common explanation of how Americans vote, one favored by journalists and politicians: Americans vote because they agree more with the policy views of Candidate A than of Candidate B. Of course, Candidate A has gone to a lot of time and trouble to get those views implanted in the public mind. Because citizens vote for the candidate whose policy promises they favor, say many journalists and politicians, the election winner has a mandate from the people to carry out the promised policies. This idea is sometimes called the **mandate theory of elections.**

Politicians, of course, are attracted to the mandate theory. It lets them justify what they want to do by claiming public support for their policies. As President Clinton said during the final presidential debate in 1992: "That's why I am trying to be so specific in this campaign—to have a mandate, if elected, so the Congress will know what the American people have voted for."

Political scientists, however, think very little of the mandate theory of elections.[33] Whereas victorious politicians are eager to proclaim "the people have spoken," political scientists know that the people rarely vote a certain way for the same reasons. Instead, political scientists focus on three major elements of voters' decisions: (1) voters' party identification; (2) voters' evaluation of the candidates; and (3) the match between voters' policy positions and those of the candidates and parties—a factor termed policy voting.

Party Identification

Party identifications are crucial for many voters in that they provide a regular perspective through which they can view the political world. "Presumably," say Niemi and Weisberg, "people choose to identify with a party with which they generally agree. . . . As a result they need not concern themselves with every issue that comes along, but can generally rely on their party identification to guide them."[34] Parties tend to rely on groups that lean heavily in their favor to form their basic coalition. Even before an election campaign begins, Republicans usually assume they will not receive much support from African Americans, Jews, Mexican Americans, and most intellectuals. Democrats have an uphill struggle attracting groups that are staunchly Republican in their leanings, such as conservative evangelical Christians or upper-income voters.

With the emergence of television and candidate-centered politics, the hold of the party on the voter eroded substantially during the 1960s and 1970s, and then stabilized at a new and lower level.[35] In the 1950s, scholars singled out party affiliation as the best single predictor of a voter's decision. "My party— right or wrong" was the motto that typified strong party identifiers. Voting along party lines is still quite common, but considerably less so than it was several decades ago. Many voters have come to feel that they no longer need the parties to guide their choices, given that modern technology makes it possible for them to evaluate the candidates and make their own decisions.

Candidate Evaluations: How Americans See the Candidates

All candidates try to present a favorable personal image. Using laboratory experiments, political psychologists Shawn Rosenberg and Patrick McCafferty show that it is possible to manipulate a candidate's appearance in a way that affects voters' choices. Holding a candidate's issue stands and party identification constant, they find that when good pictures are substituted for bad ones, a candidate's vote-getting ability is significantly increased. Although a laboratory setting may not be representative of the real world, Rosenberg and McCafferty conclude that "with appropriate pretesting and adequate control over a candidate's public appearance, a campaign consultant should be able to significantly manipulate the image projected to the voting public."[36]

To do so, a consultant would need to know what sort of candidate images voters are most attuned to. Research by Miller, Wattenberg, and Malanchuk shows that the three most important dimensions of candidate image are integrity, reliability, and competence.[37] In 1976, Jimmy Carter told Americans, "I will never lie to you." Even going down to defeat in 1980, Carter was still seen as a man with great integrity. Therefore it obviously takes more than honesty to win. A candidate must also be seen as being dependable, strong, and decisive—traits that Miller, Wattenberg, and Malanchuk label as "reliability." When George Bush broke his "no new taxes" pledge prior to the 1992 campaign, his image of reliability clearly suffered. The personal traits most often mentioned by voters, though, involve competence. In 1988 Michael Dukakis proudly proclaimed that the major election issue was not ideology but competence. Ironically, the majority of voters were more impressed with Bush's wide experience in office than with Dukakis's lawyer-like precision.

Such evaluations of candidate personality are sometimes seen as superficial and irrational judgments. Miller and his colleagues disagree with this interpretation, arguing that "candidate assessments actually concentrate on instrumental concerns about the manner in which a candidate would conduct governmental affairs."[38] If a candidate is too incompetent to carry out policy promises, or too dishonest for those promises to be trusted, it makes perfect sense for a voter to pay more attention to personality than policies. Interestingly, Miller and his colleagues find that college-educated voters are actually the most likely to view the candidates in terms of their personal attributes.

Policy Voting

Policy voting occurs when people base their choices in an election on their own issue preferences. True policy voting can only take place when several conditions are met. First, voters must have a clear view of their own policy positions. Second, voters must know where the candidates stand on policy issues. Third, they must actually cast a vote for the candidate whose policy positions coincide with their own.

Given these conditions, policy voting is not always easy—even for the educated voter. One recurrent problem is that candidates often decide that the best way to handle an issue is to cloud their positions in rhetoric. For example, in 1968 both major party candidates—Nixon and Humphrey—were deliberately ambiguous about what they would do to end the Vietnam War. This made it extremely difficult for voters to cast their ballots according to how they felt about the war. The media may not be of much help, either, as they typically focus more on the "horse race" aspects of the campaign than on the policy stands of the candidates. Voters thus often have to work very hard to engage in policy voting.

In the early days of voting research, the evidence seemed clear—voters rarely voted on policies, preferring to rely on party identification or candidate evaluations to make up their minds. In the 1950s, the authors of *The American Voter* stressed that only a small percentage of the American electorate relied on issues to decide their votes.[39] *The Changing American Voter* challenged this claim, however, arguing that voters in more recent years had become more sophisticated about issues and better able to use policy positions to gauge candidates.[40]

Although it is questionable whether voters are really much more sophisticated now about issues (see Chapter 5), policy voting has become somewhat easier than in the past; today's candidates are regularly forced to take some clear stands in order to appeal to their own party's primary voters. As late as 1968 it was still possible to win a nomination by dealing with the party bosses: now it is the issue-oriented activists in the primaries that candidates must appeal to first. No longer can a candidate get a party's nomination without taking stands on the major issues of the day, as both Humphrey and Nixon did concerning the Vietnam War in 1968. Thus, what has changed is not the voters, but the electoral process which once discouraged policy voting by greatly blurring differences between the candidates.

The 1992 Presidential Election

The issues that dominated the 1992 presidential election were the economy and the national debt. With the end of the Cold War, voter concern was more focused on domestic problems than at any time since World War II. Given the conditions of economic stagnation and a record budget deficit, this focus led many voters to express anger at the political system. Polls asking whether the country was on the right or wrong track routinely found 80 percent responding negatively.

The belief that it was "time for a change" was thus overwhelming. Even President Bush argued that a change was needed, though he naturally focused on reshaping the Congress more in line with his conservative views of less government spending, lower taxes, and fewer regulations. Democratic nominee Bill Clinton, on the other hand, argued that: (1) government spending for social needs like education and health care should be increased; (2) taxes should be raised on people making over $200,000 a year; and (3) military spending should be cut more sharply than proposed by the Bush Administration. At the heart of Clinton's plan was the call for a new government strategy to increase economic growth and to put people back to work in high-wage, high-skill jobs. President Bush's basic response was that government was already too big and spending too much. Thus, once again the debate focused on the scope of government—one of the continuing themes of this book.

One fact about the scope of government that both Clinton and Bush agreed on was that the deficit was too large. This became the focal point for Ross Perot's independent bid for the presidency. Whereas the two major party candidates tried to avoid specifics about the deficit, Perot spent millions of his own money to buy TV time to outline his plan of "fair shared sacrifices," involving both substantial tax increases and cuts in entitlements like Medicare. Perot's witticisms and forthright talk led political pundits to declare him the winner in two of the three presidential debates.

The Perot candidacy had the twin effects of changing the way candidates appeared on television and energizing the American electorate. Perot pioneered the use of talk shows to communicate with the voters. Soon the candidates were everywhere on the dial. All three became regular guests on programs such as "Larry King Live" and "Good Morning America," where they took questions from the host as well as voters who called in. In particular, Bill Clinton made himself available to virtually every TV forum. He answered questions from young people on MTV, was a guest on the "Arsenio Hall Show" to talk politics and play the saxaphone, and appeared on the Nashville Network—where, among other things, he demonstrated the "pig-sooey" chant of the Arkansas Razorbacks. Some in the press criticized these forums as unpresidential and unsuited for serious discussion of the issues. However, voters seemed to like the idea of candidates cutting through the journalistic filters and talking directly to them on programs they regulary watched. Polls recorded a much higher level of interest in the 1992 campaign than in recent elections, and on November third turnout was 5 percentage points higher than in 1988.

With three major candidates in the race, the popular vote in 1992 was unusually split. Ross Perot's 19 percent of the vote was the best showing for a third party candidate in eighty years, despite the fact that he failed to carry a single state. On the other side of the coin, the figure of 38 percent for George Bush was the lowest for any incumbent president in eighty years. But it was Bill Clinton's 43 percent of the vote that carried the day. This translated into victories in 32 states and the District of Columbia, totalling 370 of the 538 electoral college votes (see Figure 7.3).

The results of the 1992 election show how important it is to understand how the electoral college works. In presidential elections, once voters make their decision it is not just a simple matter of counting the ballots to see who has won the most support nationwide. Rather, the complicated process of determining electoral college votes begins.

THE LAST BATTLE: THE ELECTORAL COLLEGE

It is the **electoral college**, not the popular vote, that actually determines the president of the United States. The electoral college is a unique American institution, created by the Constitution. The American Bar Association once called

FIGURE 7.3 — The Electoral College Results For 1992

The following map shows the number of delegates each state has in the electoral college and which states were carried by Bill Clinton (shaded) and George Bush (white) in 1992.

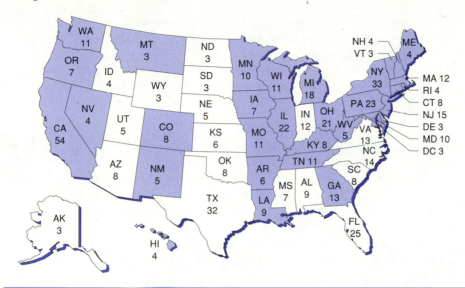

it "archaic, undemocratic, complex, ambiguous, indirect, and dangerous."[41] Many (but certainly not all) political scientists oppose its continued use, as do most voters.

Because the founders wanted the president to be selected by the nation's elite, not directly by the people, they created the electoral college, a body of electors who are charged solely with the task of voting for the president and vice president. Fortunately, political practice since 1828 has made the vote of members of the electoral college responsive to popular majorities. Today, the electors almost always vote for the candidate who won their state's popular vote. Occasionally, though, electors will exercise the right to vote their conscience, as did one West Virginia elector in 1988 who voted for Bentsen for president and Dukakis for vice president.

The following list outlines the way in which the electoral college system works today:

- Each state, according to the Constitution, has as many electoral votes as it has U.S. senators and representatives.[42] The state parties select slates of electors, positions they use as a reward for faithful service to the party.
- Aside from Maine and Nebraska, each state has a winner-take-all system.[43] Electors vote as a bloc for the winner, whether the winner got 35 percent or 95 percent of the popular vote.

- Electors meet in their states in December, following the November election, and then mail their votes to the vice president (who is also president of the Senate). The vote is counted when the new congressional session opens in January, and is reported by the vice president. Thus, Dan Quayle had the duty of announcing Bill Clinton's election in early 1993.
- If no candidate receives an electoral college majority, then the election is thrown into the House of Representatives, which must choose from among the top three electoral vote winners. An interesting quirk in the House voting is that each state delegation has one vote, thus giving the one representative from Wyoming an equal say with the fifty-two representatives from California.

The electoral college is important to the presidential election for two reasons. First, it introduces a bias into the campaign and electoral process. Providing the election is not thrown into the House, it gives extra clout to big states. The winner-take-all rule means that winning big states like California, New York, Texas, and Ohio is more important than piling up big leads in small states (see Figure 7.3). Politicians would rather get New York's thirty-three votes than North Dakota's three. Furthermore, big states are likely to have big cities (New York has New York City, Texas has Houston, California has Los Angeles, Illinois has Chicago, and so on). Thus, the big-state bias produces an urban bias in the electoral college.

The electoral college attracts special attention when the prospect looms that either the election will be thrown into the House or that the electoral college result may not reflect the popular vote. Only twice has the election been decided by the House—in 1800 and in 1824. Not since 1888 has the popular-vote winner lost in the electoral college. In almost every close election, however, a few changes here and there have the potential to produce an incompatible result. In 1976, a shift of just 6,000 votes in Ohio and 4,000 votes in Hawaii would have given Ford the election even though Carter would still have led by a substantial margin in the popular vote. Until either a popular-vote winner is denied election or a decision is again thrown into the House, reform of the electoral college is unlikely. On this issue, most politicians abide by the old adage, "If it ain't broke, don't fix it." Whether the American electoral system as a whole is compatible with democratic theory is a broader question to which this chapter now turns.

UNDERSTANDING CAMPAIGNS AND VOTING BEHAVIOR

Throughout the history of American politics, election campaigns have become longer and longer as the system has become increasingly open to public participation. Reformers in both the nineteenth and twentieth centuries held that the solution to democratic problems was more democracy—or, as John Lennon sang, "Power to the people." In principle, more democracy always sounds better than less, but it is not such a simple issue in practice.

Are Nominations and Campaigns Too Democratic?

If one judges American campaigns solely by how open they are, then certainly the American system must be viewed favorably. In other countries, the process of leadership nomination occurs within a relatively small circle of party elites. Thus, politicians must work their way up through an apprenticeship system. In contrast, America has an entrepreneurial system in which the people play a crucial role at every stage, from nomination to election. As a result, party outsiders can get elected in a way virtually unknown outside the United States. By appealing directly to the people, a candidate can emerge from nowhere to win the White House, as did Jimmy Carter. In this sense, the chance to win high office is open to almost everyone.

There is a price to be paid for all this openness, however. The process of selecting American leaders is a convoluted one, which has little downtime before it revs up all over again. Some have even called the American electoral process "the permanent campaign."[44] Many analysts wonder if people would pay more attention to politics if it did not ask so much of them. Given so much democratic opportunity, many citizens are simply overwhelmed by the process and stay on the sidelines. Similarly, the burdens of the modern campaign can discourage good candidates from throwing their hats into the ring. One of the most worrisome burdens candidates must face is amassing a sufficient campaign war chest. The system may be open, but it requires a lot of fund-raising to be able to take one's case to the people.

Do Elections Affect Public Policy?

Whether elections in fact make the government pay attention to what the people think is at the center of debate concerning how well democracy works in America. In the hypothetical world of rational choice theory and the Downs model (see Chapter 6), elections do in fact guide public policy; however, over a generation of social-science research on this question has produced mixed findings. It is more accurate to describe the connection between elections and public policy as a two-way street: elections, to some degree, affect public policy, and public-policy decisions partly affect electoral outcomes. There will probably never be a definitive answer to the question of how much elections affect public policy, for it is a somewhat subjective matter. The broad contours of the answer, however, seem reasonably clear: *the greater the policy differences between the candidates, the more likely voters will be able to steer government policies by their choices.*

Of course, the candidates do not always do their best to clarify the issues. One result is that the policy stands are often shaped by what Benjamin Page

Drawing by Martin; © 1988 The New Yorker Magazine, Inc.

"And here with us this evening, to skirt the issues, are Senator Tom Kirkland and Congressman Alan Sullivan."

once called "the art of ambiguity," in which "presidential candidates are skilled at appearing to say much while actually saying little."[45] Learning how to sidestep controversial questions and hedge answers is indeed part of becoming a professional politician, as you can observe at most every presidential press conference. So long as politicians can take refuge in ambiguity (and the skimpy coverage of issues in the media does little to make them clarify their policy stands), the possibility of democratic control of policy is lessened.

When individual candidates do offer a plain choice to the voters (what 1964 Republican nominee Barry Goldwater once called "a choice, not an echo"), voters are more able to guide the government's policy direction. The voter's clear preferences for Lyndon Johnson's policies over Goldwater in that election led to the enactment of many liberal-supported measures such as Medicare, Medicaid, federal aid to education, and the Voting Rights Act. A change of course followed in the 1980s, when Ronald Reagan made clear his intention to cut the growth of domestic spending, reduce taxes, and build up American military capability. Once elected, he proceeded to do just what he said he would.

Do Campaigns Lead to Increases in the Scope of Government?

Today's long and vigorous campaigns involve much more communication between candidates and voters than America's founders ever could have imagined. In their view, the presidency was to be an office responsible for seeing to the public interest as a whole. They wished to avoid "a contest in which the candidates would have to pose as 'friends' of the people or make specific policy commitments."[46] Thus, the founders would probably be horrified by the modern practice of political candidates making numerous promises during nomination and election campaigns.

Because states are the key battlegrounds of presidential campaigns, candidates must tailor their appeals to the particular interests of each major state. In Iowa, for instance, promises are typically made to keep agricultural subsidies high; federal programs to help big cities are usually announced in New York; and in Texas, oil industry tax breaks are promised. To secure votes from each region of the country, candidates end up supporting a variety of local interests. Promises mount as the campaign goes on, and these promises usually add up to new government programs and money. The way modern campaigns are conducted is thus one of many reasons why politicians often find it easier to expand the scope of American government than to limit it.

Elections also help to increase generalized support for government and its powers. Because voters know that the government can be replaced at the next election, they are much more likely to feel that it will be responsive to their needs. Thus, when people have the power to dole out electoral reward and punishment, they are more likely to see government as their servant instead of their master. As Benjamin Ginsberg writes, "Democratic elections help to persuade citizens that expansion of the state's powers represents an increase in the state's capacity to serve them."[47]

Therefore, rather than wishing to be protected from the state, citizens in a democracy often seek to benefit from it. It is no coincidence that "individuals who believe they can influence the government's actions are also more likely to believe, in turn, that the government should have more power."[48] Voters like to feel that they are sending a message to the government to accomplish something. It should be no surprise that as democracy has spread, government has come to do more and more, and its scope has grown.

SUMMARY

In this age of high-tech politics, campaigns have become more media-oriented and far more expensive. There are really two campaigns of importance in presidential (and other) contests: the campaign for nomination and the campaign for election.

There are two ways by which delegates are selected to the national party conventions—state caucuses and primaries. The first caucus is traditionally held in Iowa, the first primary in New Hampshire. These two small atypical American states have disproportionate power in determining who will be nominated and thus become president. This influence stems from the massive media attention devoted to these early contests and the momentum generated by winning them.

Money matters in political campaigns. As the costs of campaigning have increased, it has become all the more essential to raise large campaign war chests. Although federal campaign finance reform in the 1970s lessened the impact of big contributors, it also allowed the proliferation of PACs. Some believe that PACs have created a system of legal graft in campaigning; others feel that the evidence for this view is relatively weak.

In general, politicians tend to overestimate the impact of campaigns; political scientists have found that campaigning serves primarily to reinforce citizens' views as opposed to converting them. Voters make two basic decisions at election time. The first is whether to vote. Americans' right to vote is well established, but in order to do so citizens must go through the registration process. America's unique registration system is one major reason why turnout in American elections is much lower than in most other democracies. The 1992 election between George Bush and Bill Clinton was another in a long string of low-turnout elections. Second, those who choose to vote must decide for whom to cast their ballots. Over a generation of research on voting behavior has helped political scientists to understand the dominant role played by three factors in voter's choices: party identification, candidate evaluations, and policy positions.

Elections are the centerpiece of democracy. Few questions are more important in understanding American government than this: Do elections matter? Under the right conditions, elections can influence public policy, and policy outcomes can influence elections. Elections also legitimize the power of the state, thereby making it easier to expand the scope of the government. For better or worse, American election campaigns are clearly the most open and democratic in the world.

FOR FURTHER READING

Asher, Herbert B. *Presidential Elections and American Politics*, 5th ed. Pacific Grove, CA: Brooks/Cole, 1992. A standard text on the electoral process.

Bartels, Larry M. *Presidential Primaries and the Dynamics of Public Choice.* Princeton, NJ: Princeton University Press, 1988. The best recent book on voters' choices in the nominating season.

Campbell, Angus, et al. *The American Voter.* New York: John Wiley, 1960. The classic study of the American electorate in the 1950s, which has shaped scholarly approaches to the subject ever since.

Nie, Norman H., Sidney Verba, and John R. Petrocik. *The Changing American Voter.* Cambridge, MA: Harvard University Press, 1976. Challenges some of the assumptions of Campbell et al.'s *The American Voter.*

Niemi, Richard G. and Herbert F. Weisberg. *Classics in Voting Behavior.* Washington, DC: Congressional Quarterly Press, 1993. An excellent set of readings on voting that have stood the test of time.

Orren, Gary R., and Nelson W. Polsby, eds. *Media and Momentum.* Chatham, NJ: Chatham House, 1987. The story of the exaggerated impact of New Hampshire on our presidential selection process.

Shafer, Byron E. *Bifurcated Politics: Evolution and Reform in the National Party Convention.* Cambridge, MA: Harvard University Press, 1988. The story of how conventions have been transformed from important decision-making bodies to TV sideshows.

Sorauf, Frank J. *Inside Campaign Finance: Myths and Realities.* New Haven, CT: Yale University Press, 1992. A definitive work on the impact of money on elections, an impact that Sorauf thinks is often exaggerated.

Teixeira, Ruy A. *The Disappearing American Voter.* Washington, DC: Brookings Institution, 1992. A good review of the reasons for declining voter turnout, as well as what can be done about it.

Wolfinger, Raymond E., and Steven J. Rosenstone. *Who Votes?* New Haven, CT: Yale University Press, 1980. The best quantitative study of who turns out and why.

NOTES

1. R. W. Apple, Jr., "Foley Assesses Presidential Elections and Tells Why He Wouldn't Run," *New York Times*, November 4, 1988, A12.

2. Paul Taylor, "Is This Any Way to Pick a President?" *Washington Post National Weekly Edition*, April 13, 1987, 6.

3. Ibid.

4. *USA Today*, February 9, 1988, 4a.

5. Paul R. Abramson, John H. Aldrich, and David W. Rohde, *Change and Continuity in the 1992 Elections* (Washington, DC: Congressional Quarterly Press, 1994), 20.

6. See Hugh Winebrenner, *The Iowa Precinct Caucuses: The Making of a Media Event* (Ames: Iowa State University Press, 1987).

7. Theodore White, *America in Search of Itself: The Making of the President 1956–1980* (New York: Harper & Row, 1982), 285.

8. Harold W. Stanley and Richard G. Niemi, *Vital Statistics on American Politics*, 4th ed. (Washington, DC: Congressional Quarterly Press, 1994), 61. The same research also showed that New Hampshire received just 1 percent of the TV coverage during the general election—a figure roughly proportionate to its population size.

9. Larry M. Bartels, *Presidential Primaries and the Dynamics of Public Choice* (Princeton, NJ: Princeton University Press, 1988), 269.

10. George Bush, *Looking Forward* (New York: Doubleday, 1987).

11. Paul Simon, *Winners and Losers: The 1988 Race for the Presidency—One Candidate's Perspective* (New York: Continuum, 1989), 112.

12. Bruce Babbitt, "Bruce Babbitt's View from the Wayside," *Washington Post National Weekly Edition*, February 29, 1988, 24.

13. See Martin P. Wattenberg, "When You Can't Beat Them, Join Them: Shaping the Presidential Nominating Process to the Television Age." *Polity* 21 (Spring 1989): 587–597.

14. Frank J. Sorauf, *Inside Campaign Finance: Myths and Realities* (New Haven, CT: Yale University Press, 1992), 229.

15. See, for example, Brooks Jackson, *Honest Graft: Big Money and the American Political Process* (New York: Knopf, 1988).

16. Quoted in Jeffrey Berry, *The Interest Group Society* (Boston: Little, Brown, 1984), 162.

17. Archibald Cox and Fred Wertheimer, "The Choice Is Clear: It's People vs. the PACs," In Peter Woll, ed., *Debating American Government*, 2nd ed. (Glenview, IL: Scott, Foresman, 1988), 125.
18. This is discussed in Berry, *The Interest Group Society*, 172.
19. Frank J. Sorauf, *Money in American Elections* (Glenview, IL: Scott, Foresman, 1988), 312.
20. Dexter Filkins, "The Only Issue Is Money," *Washington Post National Weekly Edition*, June 13, 1988, 28.
21. Gary C. Jacobson, "The Effects of Campaign Spending in Congressional Elections," *American Political Science Review* 72 (June 1978): 469. For an updated analysis of this argument, see Gary C. Jacobson, "The Effects of Campaign Spending in House Elections: New Evidence for Old Arguments," *American Journal of Political Science* 34 (May 1990): 334–362.
22. Herbert E. Alexander, *Financing Politics: Money, Elections, and Political Reform*, 4th ed. (Washington, DC: Congressional Quarterly Press, 1992), 96.
23. Dan Nimmo, *The Political Persuaders: The Techniques of Modern Campaigning* (Englewood Cliffs, NJ: Prentice Hall, 1970).
24. Thomas E. Patterson and Robert D. McClure, *The Unseeing Eye* (New York: Putnam, 1976).
25. Thomas E. Patterson, *The Mass Media Election* (New York: Praeger, 1980). Also see Thomas E. Patterson, *Out of Order* (New York: Knopf, 1993).
26. David R. Runkel, ed., *Campaign for President: The Managers Look at '88* (Dover, MA: Auburn, 1989), 136.
27. Nimmo, *The Political Persuaders*, 5.
28. Raymond E. Wolfinger and Steven J. Rosenstone, *Who Votes?* (New Haven, CT: Yale University Press, 1980).
29. Ruy Teixeira, *The Disappearing American Voter* (Washington, DC: Brookings Institution, 1992), 131.
30. Ibid., chapter 2.
31. For a gripping account of Johnson's manipulations to win this election, see Robert A. Caro, *The Years of Lyndon Johnson: Means of Ascent* (New York: Knopf, 1990).
32. Anthony Downs, *An Economic Theory of Democracy* (New York: Harper & Row, 1957), chapter 14.
33. See George C. Edwards III, *At the Margins* (New Haven, CT: Yale University Press, 1989), chapter 8.
34. Richard G. Niemi and Herbert F. Weisberg, eds., *Controversies in Voting Behavior*, 2nd ed. (Washington, DC: Congressional Quarterly Press, 1984), 164–165.
35. See Martin P. Wattenberg, *The Decline of American Political Parties, 1952–1992* (Cambridge, MA: Harvard University Press, 1994).
36. Shawn W. Rosenberg with Patrick McCafferty, "Image and Voter Preference," *Public Opinion Quarterly* 51 (Spring 1987): 44.
37. Arthur H. Miller, Martin P. Wattenberg, and Oksana Malanchuk, "Schematic Assessments of Presidential Candidates," *American Political Science Review* 80 (1986): 521–540.
38. Ibid., 536.
39. Angus Campbell et al., *The American Voter* (New York: John Wiley, 1960), chapter 6.
40. Norman H. Nie, Sidney Verba, and John R. Petrocik, *The Changing American Voter* (Cambridge, MA: Harvard University Press, 1976).
41. American Bar Association, *Electing the President* (Chicago: ABA, 1967), 3.

42. The Twenty-third Amendment (1961) permits the District of Columbia to have three electors, even though it has no representatives in Congress.

43. In Maine and Nebraska, an elector is allocated for every congressional district won, and whoever wins the state as a whole wins the two electors alloted to the state for its senators.

44. Sidney Blumenthal, *The Permanent Campaign* (New York: Simon & Schuster, 1982).

45. Benjamin Page, *Choices and Echoes in American Presidential Elections* (Chicago: University of Chicago Press, 1978), 153.

46. James W. Caeser, *Presidential Selection: Theory and Development* (Princeton, NJ: Princeton University Press, 1979), 83.

47. Benjamin Ginsberg, *Consequences of Consent* (Reading, MA: Addison-Wesley, 1982), 194.

48. Ibid., 198.

Our nation's capital has become a hub of interest group activity. On any given day it is possible to observe pressure groups in action in many forums. In the morning you could attend congressional hearings in which you are sure to see interest groups testifying for and against proposed legislation. At the Supreme Court you might stop in to watch a public interest lawyer arguing for strict enforcement of environmental regulations. Take a break for lunch at a nice Washington restaurant and you may see a lobbyist entertaining a member of Congress. The afternoon could be spent in any department of the executive branch (such as commerce, defense, or the interior), where you might catch bureaucrats working out rules and regulations with friendly—or sometimes unfriendly—representatives of the interests they are charged with overseeing. You could stroll past the impressive headquarters of the National Rifle Association, the AFL-CIO, or the National Association of Manufacturers to get a sense of the size of some of the major lobbying organizations. To see some lobbying done on college students' behalf, you might drop by One Dupont Circle, where all the higher-education groups have their offices. These groups lobby for student loans and scholarships, as well as aid to educational institutions. At dinner time, if you were able to wangle an invitation to a Georgetown cocktail party, you may see lobbyists trying to get the ear of government officials—both elected and unelected.

All of this lobbying activity poses an interesting paradox: Although turnout in elections has declined since 1960, participation in interest groups has mushroomed. As Kay Schlozman and John Tierney write, "Recent decades have witnessed an expansion of astonishing proportions in the involvement of private organizations in Washington politics."[1] This chapter will explore the multifaceted array of interest groups, how these groups enter the policy-making process, and what they get out of it.

DEFINING INTEREST GROUPS

The term interest group seems simple enough to define. Interest refers to a policy goal; a group is a combination of people. An **interest group,** therefore, is an organization of people with similar policy goals who enter the political process to try to achieve those aims. Whatever their goals—outlawing abortion or ensuring the right to one, regulating tax loopholes or creating new ones—interest groups pursue them in many arenas. Every branch of government is fair game; every level of government, local to federal, is a possible target. A policy battle lost in Congress may be turned around when it comes to bureaucratic implementation or the judicial process.

This multiplicity of policy arenas helps distinguish interest groups from political parties. Parties fight their battles through the electoral process—they run candidates for public office. Interest groups may support candidates for office, but American interest groups do not run their own slate of candidates, as in some other countries. In other words, no one is ever listed on the ballot as a candidate of the National Rifle Association or Common Cause. It may be well known that a candidate is actively supported by a particular group, but that candidate faces the voters as a Democrat or a Republican.

Another key difference between parties and interest groups is that *interest groups are often policy specialists, whereas parties are policy generalists.* Most interest groups have a handful of key policies to push: a farm group cares little about the status of urban transit; an environmental group has its hands full bringing polluters into court without worrying about the minimum wage. Unlike political parties, these groups do not face the constraint imposed by trying to appeal to everyone.

THEORIES OF INTEREST GROUP POLITICS

All Americans have some interests they want represented. Organizing to promote these interests is an essential part of democracy. The right to organize groups is protected by the Constitution, which guarantees people the right "peaceably to assemble, and to petition the Government for a redress of grievances." This important First Amendment right has been carefully defended by the Supreme Court. The freedom to organize is as fundamental to democratic government as freedom of speech.

Despite their importance to democratic government, interest groups have been viewed as at best a "necessary evil" by many political theorists. James Madison's derogatory term *faction* was general enough to include both parties and groups. Today, on a slow news day editorial cartoonists can always depict lobbyists skulking around in the congressional hallways, their pockets stuffed with money, just waiting to funnel it to a legislator's wallet.

Understanding the debate over whether interest groups play primarily positive or negative roles in American political life requires an in-depth examination of three important theories, which were briefly introduced in Chapter 1.

All candidates for public office seek to obtain the votes of various interest groups. Here, Clinton and Gore pose as construction workers to show their support for blue-collar workers.

Pluralist theory argues that interest group activity brings representation to all. According to pluralists, groups compete and counterbalance one another in the political marketplace. In contrast, **elite theory** argues that just a few groups, primarily the wealthy, have most of the power. Finally, **hyperpluralist theory** asserts that too many groups are getting too much of what they want, resulting in a government policy that is often contradictory and lacking in direction. The following sections will examine each of these three theories more closely.

Pluralism and Group Theory

Pluralist theory rests its case on the many centers of power in the American political system. The extensive organization of competing groups is seen as evidence that influence is widely dispersed among them. Pluralists believe that groups win some and lose some, but no group wins or loses all the time. A considerable body of writings by pluralist theorists offers a *group theory of politics,*[2] which contains several essential arguments.

- *Groups provide a key linkage between people and government.* All legitimate interests in the political system can get a hearing from government once they are organized.

- *Groups compete.*   Labor, business, farmers, consumers, environmentalists, and other interests constantly make claims on one another.
- *No one group is likely to become too dominant.*   When one group throws its weight around too much, its opponents are likely to intensify their organization and thus restore balance to the system. For every action, there is a reaction.
- *Groups usually play by the "rules of the game."*   In the United States, group politics is a fair fight, with few groups lying, cheating, stealing, or engaging in violence to get their way.
- *Groups weak in one resource can use another.*   Big business may have money on its side, but labor has numbers. All legitimate groups are able to affect public policy by one means or another.

Pluralists would never deny that some groups are stronger than others, or that competing interests do not always get an equal hearing. Still, they can point to many cases in which a potential group organized itself and once organized, affected policy decisions. African Americans, women, and consumers are all groups who were long ignored by government officials, but once organized, redirected the course of public policy. In sum, pluralists argue that lobbying is open to all and is therefore not to be regarded as a problem.

Elites and the Denial of Pluralism

Whereas pluralists are impressed by the vast number of organized interests, elitists are impressed by how insignificant most of them are. *Real* power, elitists say, is held by relatively few people, key groups, and institutions. They maintain that the government is run by a few big interests looking out for themselves—a view that the majority of the public has agreed with for the last two decades (see Figure 8.1).

Elitists critique pluralist theory by pointing to the concentration of power in a few hands. Where pluralists find dispersion of power, elitists find interlocking and concentrated power centers. About one-third of top institutional positions—corporate boards, foundation boards, university trusteeships, and so on—are occupied by people who hold more than one such position.[3] Elitists see the rise of mighty multinational corporations as further tightening the control of corporate elites. A prime example is America's giant oil companies.[4] When confronted with the power of these multinational corporations, consumer interests are readily pushed aside, according to elitists.

In sum, the elitist view of the interest group system makes the following points:

- The fact that there are numerous groups proves nothing, because groups are extremely unequal in power.
- Awesome power is controlled by the largest corporations.
- The power of a few is fortified by an extensive system of interlocking directorates.

FIGURE 8.1 — Perceptions of the Dominance of Big Interests

Would you say the government is pretty much run by a few big interests looking out for themselves or that it is run for the benefit of all the people?

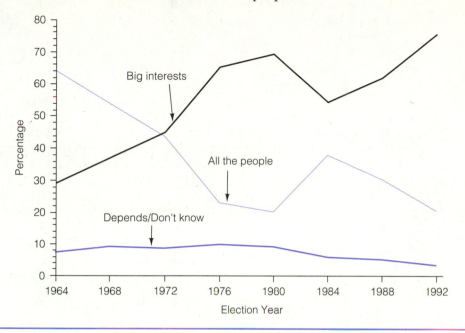

SOURCE: The question as worded is taken directly from National Election Studies conducted by the University of Michigan.

- Other groups may win many minor policy battles, but the corporate elites prevail when it comes to the big decisions.

Thus, interest group lobbying is a problem, say elite theorists, because it benefits the few at the expense of the many.

Hyperpluralism and Interest Group Liberalism

Hyperpluralism, also critical of pluralism, argues that the pluralist system is out of control. Theodore Lowi coined the phrase *interest group liberalism* to refer to the government's excessive deference to groups. Interest group liberalism holds that virtually all pressure group demands are legitimate and that the job of the government is to advance them all.[5]

In an effort to please and appease every interest, agencies proliferate, conflicting regulations expand, programs multiply, and, of course, the budget skyrockets. If environmentalists want clean air, government imposes clean-air rules; if businesses complain that cleaning up pollution is expensive, government gives them a tax write-off for pollution-control equipment. If the direct-mail industry wants cheap rates, government gives it to them; if people complain about junk mail, the Postal Service gives them a way to take their name off mailing lists. If cancer researchers convince the government to launch an antismoking campaign, tobacco sales may drop; if they do, government will subsidize tobacco farmers to ease their loss.

Interest group liberalism is promoted by the network of **subgovernments** in the American political system. These subgovernments (which are also known as iron triangles, and will be discussed in greater detail in Chapter 12) are composed of key interest group leaders interested in policy X, the government agency in charge of administering policy X, and the members of congressional committees and subcommittees handling policy X.

All the elements composing subgovernments have a similar goal: protecting their self-interest. The network of subgovernments in the agricultural policy area of tobacco is an excellent example. Tobacco interest groups include the Tobacco Institute, the Retail Tobacco Distributors of America, and the tobacco growers. Various agencies in the Department of Agriculture administer tobacco programs, and they depend on the tobacco industry's clout in Congress to help keep their agency budgets safe from cuts. Finally, most of the members of the House Tobacco Subcommittee are from tobacco growing regions. All of these elements thus have a common desire in protecting the interests of tobacco farmers. Similar subgovernments of group-agency-committee ties exist in scores of other policy areas.

Hyperpluralists' major criticism of the interest group system is that relations between groups and the government become too cozy. Hard choices about national policy rarely get made. Instead of making choices between X or Y, the government pretends there is no need at all to choose and tries to favor them both. It is a perfect script for policy paralysis. In short, the hyperpluralist position on group politics is that

- Groups have become too powerful in the political process as government tries to aid every conceivable interest.
- Interest group liberalism is aggravated by numerous subgovernments—comfortable relationships among a government agency, the interest group it deals with, and congressional subcommittees.
- Trying to please every group results in contradictory and confusing policy.

Ironically, the recent interest group explosion is seen by some as weakening the power of subgovernments. As Morris Fiorina writes, "A world of active public interest groups, jealous business competitors, and packs of budding investigative reporters is less hospitable to subgovernment politics than a world lacking in them."[6] With so many more interest groups to satisfy, and with many of them competing against one another, a cozy relationship between groups and the government is plainly more difficult to sustain.

Hyperpluralist theorists often point to the government's contradictory tobacco-related policies as an example of interest group liberalism. The government has responded to the demands of tobacco farmers with subsidies to keep them in business while at the same time running health ads warning of the dangers of the product.

HOW GROUPS TRY TO SHAPE POLICY

No interest group has enough staff, money, or time to do everything possible to achieve their policy goals. Interest groups must therefore choose from a variety of tactics. The three traditional strategies are lobbying, electioneering, and litigation. In addition, groups have lately developed a variety of sophisticated techniques to appeal to the public for widespread support. These four general strategies are the topic of the next four sections.

Lobbying

The term **lobbying** comes from the place where petitioners used to collar legislators. In the early years of politics in Washington, members of Congress had no offices and typically stayed in boarding houses or hotels while Congress was in session. A person could not call them up on the phone or make an appointment with their secretary; the only sure way of getting in touch with them was to wait in the lobby where they were staying, so as to catch them either coming in or going out. Because these people spent so much of their time waiting in lobbies they were dubbed "lobbyists."

Of course, merely loitering in a lobby does not make one a lobbyist—there must be a particular reason for such action. Lester Milbrath has offered a more precise definition of the practice. He writes that lobbying is a "communication, by someone other than a citizen acting on his or her own behalf, directed to a governmental decision-maker with the hope of influencing his or her decision."[7] Lobbyists, in other words, are political persuaders who represent organized groups. They normally work in Washington, handling groups' legislative business.

Although lobbyists are primarily out to influence members of Congress, it is important to remember that they can be of help to them as well. Ornstein and Elder list five ways lobbyists can help a member of Congress.

- They are an important source of information. Members of Congress have to concern themselves with many policy areas; lobbyists can confine themselves to only one area, and thus can provide specialized expertise.

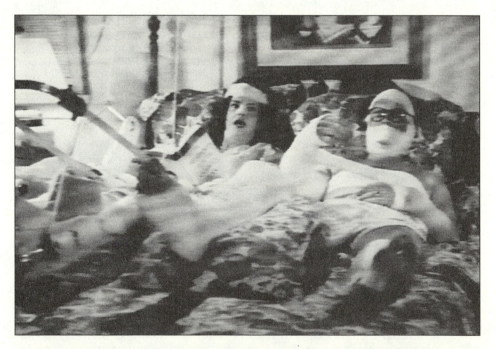

Interest groups spent over $50 million appealing to public opinion during the debate over health care in 1994. The health insurance industry's "Harry and Louise" ads opposing national health care even drew a counter ad from the Democratic National Committee. Here, Harry and Louise are shown after Harry has lost his job. The couple is bemoaning the financial toll of their illnesses now that they are uninsured.

- They can help a member with political strategy. Lobbyists are politically savvy people, and they are free consultants.
- They can help formulate campaign strategy and get the group's members behind a politician's reelection campaign.
- They are a source of ideas and innovations. Lobbyists cannot introduce bills, but they can peddle their ideas to politicians eager to attach their name to an idea that will bring them political credit.
- They provide friendship. It is a rare member of Congress who could not say, "Some of my best friends are lobbyists."[8]

Like anything else, lobbying can be done crudely or gracefully. Lobbyists can sometimes be heavy-handed. They can threaten or cajole a legislator, implying that electoral defeat is a certain result of not "going along." They can even make it clear that money flows to the reelection coffers of those who cooperate. It is often difficult to tell the difference between lobbying as a shady business and as a strictly professional representation of legitimate interests.

Political scientists disagree about the effectiveness of lobbying. Much evidence suggests that lobbyists' power over policy is often exaggerated. A classic 1950s study of the influence of groups on foreign-trade policy started with the hypothesis that when major business lobbies spoke, Congress listened—and acted accordingly.[9] Instead, the study found groups involved in trade policy to be ineffective, understaffed, and underfinanced. Usually the lobbyists were too disorganized to be effective. Members of Congress often had to pressure the interest groups to actively support legislation which would be in their own interest. Similarly, Milbrath concluded his own analysis of lobbying by arguing that "there is relatively little influence or power in lobbying per se."[10] Lobbyists are most effective, he claims, as information sources and are relatively ineffectual in winning over legislators.

There is plenty of contrary evidence to suggest that sometimes lobbying can persuade legislators to support a certain policy. The National Rifle Association, which for years kept major gun control policies off the congressional agenda, has proved to be a largely successful lobby. In a more specific example, intensive lobbying by the nation's most wealthy senior citizens—enraged by the tax burden imposed upon them by the 1988 Catastrophic Health Care Act—led Congress to repeal the act only a year after it was passed.

Nailing down the specific effects of lobbying is difficult, partly because it is hard to isolate its effects from other influences. Lobbying clearly works best on people already committed to the lobbyist's policy position. Thus, like campaigning, lobbying is directed primarily toward activating and reinforcing one's supporters. For example, antiabortion lobbyists would not think of approaching Colorado's Patricia Schroeder to attempt to convert her to their position, since Schroeder clearly supports the pro-choice movement. If Congresswoman Schroeder is lobbied by anyone on the abortion issue, it will be by the pro-choice faction—urging her not to compromise with the opposition.

Electioneering

Because lobbying works best with those already on the same side, getting the right people into office or keeping them there is also a key strategy of interest groups. Many groups therefore get involved in **electioneering,** aiding candidates financially and getting group members out to support them.

In recent years, **Political Action Committees** (PACs) have provided a means for groups to participate in electioneering more than ever before. The number of PACs has exploded from 608 in 1974 to 4,195 in 1992.[11] (See Figure 8.2.) No major interest group seeking to exert influence on the electoral process these days can pass up the opportunity to honestly and openly funnel money into the campaign coffers of their supporters. As campaign costs have risen in recent years, PACs have come along to help pay the bill. PACs now finance nearly half the costs of congressional elections. They have also tilted the scales even further in the direction of incumbents. PACs gave a whopping $99 million to House incumbents during the 1991–1992 election cycle, compared to a mere $12 million to the challengers.[12]

Why does the PAC money go so overwhelmingly to incumbents? The answer is that PAC contributions are basically investments for the future, and incumbents are the most likely to be able to return the investment. Sometimes

---

FIGURE 8.2 — The PAC Explosion: 1974–1992

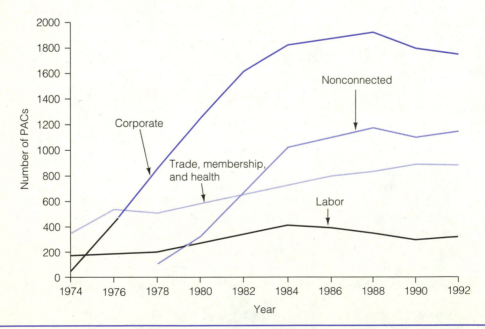

SOURCE: Federal Election Commission, 1993.

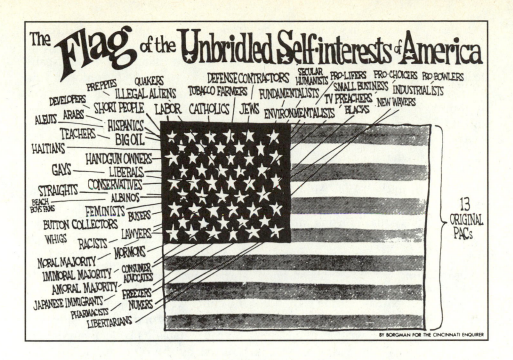

PACs like to play it safe, however; an examination of seven hotly contested Senate races in 1988 showed that 274 PACs guaranteed that their investments were risk free by contributing to both the Democratic and Republican candidates for the same seat.[13]

Only a handful of candidates have resisted the lure of PAC money in recent years. One candidate described his experiences trying to get on the PAC bandwagon. When Democrat Steve Sovern ran for the House from Iowa's Second District in 1980, he made the now common pilgrimage to Washington to meet with potential contributors. "I found myself in line with candidates from all over," he reported. Each PAC had eager candidates fill out a multiple-choice questionnaire on issues important to the PAC. Candidates who shared the same concerns and views and who looked like winners got the money. Sovern later reported that "the process made me sick." After his defeat, he organized his own PAC called LASTPAC (for Let the American System Triumph), which urged candidates to shun PAC campaign contributions.[14] The grandfather of public interest lobbies, Common Cause, is also waging a public campaign against PACs.

Litigation

If interest groups fail in Congress or get only a vague piece of legislation, the next step is to go to court in the hope of getting specific rulings. Karen Orren has linked much of the success of environmental interest groups to their use of lawsuits. "Frustrated in Congress," she wrote, "they have made an end run to the courts, where they have skillfully exploited and magnified limited legislative gains."[15]   Environmental legislation, such as the Clean Air Act, typically includes written provisions allowing ordinary citizens to sue for enforcement. As a result, every federal agency involved in environmental regulation now has hundreds of suits pending against it at any given time. These suits may not halt environmentally troublesome practices, but the constant threat of a lawsuit increases the likelihood that businesses will consider the environmental impact of what they do.

Perhaps the most famous interest group victories in court were by civil rights groups in the 1950s. Although civil rights bills remained stalled in Congress, these groups won major victories in court cases concerning school desegregation, equal housing, and labor market equality. More recently, consumer groups have used suits against businesses and federal agencies as a means of enforcing consumer regulations. As long as law schools keep producing lawyers, groups will fight for their interests in court.

One tactic that groups employ to make their views heard by the judiciary is the filing of **amicus curiae** ("friend of the court") **briefs.** *Amicus* briefs consist of written arguments submitted to the courts in support of one side of a case. Through these written depositions, a group states its collective position as well as how its own welfare will be affected by the outcome of the case. Numerous groups may file friend of the court briefs in highly publicized and emotionally charged cases. For example, in the case of *Regents of the University of California v. Bakke*, which challenged affirmative action programs as reverse discrimination, over a hundred different groups filed *amicus* briefs. A study of *amici* briefs by Caldeira and Wright found that the Supreme Court has been accessible to a wide array of organized interests, both in terms of deciding which cases to hear as well as on how to rule.[16]

A more direct judicial strategy employed by interest groups is the filing of **class action lawsuits,** which enables a group of similarly situated plaintiffs to combine similar grievances into a single suit. For instance, flight attendants won a class action suit against the airline industry's regulation that all stewardesses had to be unmarried. As one lawyer who specializes in such cases states, "The class action is the greatest, most effective legal engine to remedy mass wrongs."[17]

Going Public

Groups are also interested in the opinions of the public. Because public opinion ultimately makes its way to policymakers, interest groups carefully cultivate their public image. Interest groups market not only their stand on issues, but their reputations as well. Business interests want people to see them as what made America great (not as wealthy Americans trying to ensure large profits). The Teamsters Union likes to be known as a united organization of hard-working men and women (not as an organization often influenced by organized crime). Farmers cultivate the image of a sturdy family working to put bread on the table (not the huge agribusinesses that have largely replaced family farms). In this way, many groups try to create a reservoir of goodwill with the public.

The practice of interest groups appealing to the public for support has a long tradition in American politics. In 1908, AT&T launched a major magazine advertising campaign to convince people of the need for a telephone monopoly. Similarly, after President Truman proposed a system of national health insurance in 1948, the American Medical Association spent millions of dollars on ads attacking "socialized medicine." In 1994, the Health Insurance Association of America ran nationally televised ads criticizing President Clinton's health care package, which many analysts felt lessened public support for the reform bill. Mobil Oil currently runs the most regularly visible corporate public relations effort to influence public opinion (and in turn, public policy) with its op-ed style ads in the *New York Times* and other major publications every week. These ads typically address issues affecting the oil industry and big business in general. One time it even ran an ad entitled "Why Do We Buy This Space?" which answered "that business needs voices in the media, the same way labor unions, consumers, and other groups in our society do."[18] No one knows just how effective these image-molding efforts are, but many groups seem to firmly believe that advertising pays off.

TYPES OF INTEREST GROUPS

Whether they are lobbying, electioneering, litigating, or appealing to the public, interest groups are omnipresent in the American political system. As with other aspects of American politics and policy-making, political scientists loosely categorize interest groups into clusters. Some deal mainly with economic issues, others with issues of energy and the environment, and still others with equality issues.

Economic Interests

All economic interests are ultimately concerned with wages, prices, and profits. In the American economy, government does not determine these directly. Only on rare occasions has the government imposed wage and price controls. This has usually been during wartime, although the Nixon administration briefly used wage and price controls to combat inflation. More commonly, public policy in America has economic effects through regulations, tax advantages, subsidies and contracts, and international trade policy.

Business, labor, and farmers all fret over the impact of government regulations. Even a minor change in government regulatory policy can cost industries a great deal or bring increased profits. Tax policies also affect the livelihood of individuals and firms. How the tax code is written determines whether people and producers pay a lot or a little of their incomes to the government. Because government often provides subsidies (to farmers, small businesses, railroads, minority businesses, and others), every economic group wants to get its share of direct aid and government contracts. In this era of economic global interdependence, all groups worry about import quotas, tariffs (fees placed on imports), and the soundness of the American dollar. In short, business executives, factory workers, and farmers seek to influence government because regulations, taxes, subsidies, and international economic policy all affect their economic livelihoods. The following sections discuss the impact of some of the major organized interests in the economic policy arena.

Labor.   Numerically, labor has more affiliated members than any other interest group. Fourteen million workers are members of unions belonging to the AFL-CIO, itself a union of unions. Several million others are members of non-AFL-CIO unions, such as the National Education Association, which represents schoolteachers.

Like labor unions everywhere, American unions press for policies to ensure better working conditions and higher wages. Recognizing that many workers would like to enjoy union benefits without actually joining a union and paying dues, unions have fought hard to establish the **union shop,** which requires new employees to join the union representing them. In contrast, business groups have supported **right-to-work laws,** which outlaw union membership as a condition of employment. They argue that such laws deny basic freedoms—namely the right not to belong to a group. In 1947 the biggest blow ever to the American labor movement occurred when Congress passed the Taft-Hartley Act, permitting states to adopt right-to-work laws (known as "slave labor laws" within the AFL-CIO). Most of the states that have right-to-work laws are in the South, which traditionally has had the lowest percentage of unionized workers.

The American labor movement reached its peak in 1956, when 33 percent of the non-agricultural work force belonged to a union; since then the percentage has declined to about 16 percent. One factor behind this decline is that low wages in other countries have diminished the American job market in a number of key manufacturing areas. Steel, once made by American workers, is now made more cheaply in Korea and imported to the United States. The United Auto Workers have found their clout greatly reduced as Detroit has faced heavy competition from Japanese automakers. Some political scientists, however, see labor's problems resulting from more than the decline of blue collar industries. Paul Johnson argues that the most important reason for the decline in union membership is the problems unions have had in getting today's workers to believe they will benefit from unionization. In particular, Johnson argues that this task has become more difficult in recent years due to the efforts of employers to make nonunion jobs satisfying.[19]

Agriculture.   Once the occupation of the majority of Americans, only 3 percent now make their living as farmers. The family farm has given way to massive agribusinesses, often heavily involved with exports. To the vast majority who have never lived on a farm, the tangled policies of acreage controls, price supports, and import quotas are mysterious and confusing. To agribusinesses and the few family farmers still around, however, government policies are often more important than the whims of nature.

There are several broad-based agricultural groups (the American Farm Bureau Federation, the National Farmers' Organization), but equally important are the commodity associations formed of peanut farmers, potato growers, dairy farmers, and other producers. The U.S. Department of Agriculture and the agricultural subcommittees in Congress are organized along commodity lines. As mentioned earlier in this chapter, this organizational system leads to very cordial relations between the policymakers, the bureaucrats, and the interest groups—promoting classic examples of what hyperpluralists call subgovernments.

Business.   If the elite theorists are correct, however, and there is an American power elite, certainly it would be dominated by leaders of the biggest banks, insurance companies, and multinational corporations. Elitists' views may or may not be exaggerated, but business is certainly well organized for political action. Business PACs have increased more dramatically than any other category of PACs, as shown in Figure 8.2. Most large firms, such as AT&T and Ford, now have offices in Washington that monitor legislative activity. Two umbrella organizations, the National Association of Manufacturers (NAM) and the Chamber of Commerce, include most corporations and businesses and speak for them when general business interests are at stake.

Different business interests compete on many specific issues, however. Trucking and construction companies want more highways, but railroads do not. An increase in international trade will help some businesses expand their markets, but others may be hurt by foreign competition. Business interests are generally unified when it comes to promoting greater profits, but are often fragmented when policy choices have to be made.

The hundreds of trade and product associations are far less visible than the NAM and the Chamber of Commerce, but they are at least as important in pursuing policy goals for their members. These associations fight regulations that would reduce their profits and seek preferential tax treatment as well as government subsidies and contracts. America's complex schedule of tariffs are monuments to the activities of the trade associations. Although they are the least visible of Washington lobbies, their successes are measured in amendments won, regulations rewritten, and exceptions made. It is not only American trade associations that are concerned with these policies, but foreign corporations and governments as well. The practice of foreign economic interests hiring influential former governmental officials to lobby on their behalf has recently led to a number of reform proposals (see "In Focus: Restricting Lobbying for Foreign Interests").

Consumers and Public Interest Lobbies.   Pluralist theory holds that for virtually every interest in society there is an organized group, but what about the

---

IN FOCUS

Restricting Lobbying for Foreign Interests

In the 1992 campaign, H. Ross Perot frequently called for restrictions on government officials leaving public service to lobby on behalf of foreign corporations and governments. Perhaps the most influential study of this practice has been produced by Pat Choate, who authored a best-selling book entitled *Agents of Influence*. Choate details how a revolving door exists by which American trade negotiators switch sides after a short period of government service to become lobbyists for foreign concerns. In particular, Choate maintains that the Japanese have acquired great influence over U.S. trade policy by building a network of high-priced lobbyists. These former government officials turned lobbyists are extremely valuable to foreign interests given their contacts in high places, their knowledge of the American political process, and (in some cases) their inside information regarding the American trade negotiating position.

Choate believes that foreign lobbying clearly poses a threat to America's ability to compete in a global economy. He suggests several steps be taken to restrict and more carefully monitor lobbying by foreign interests. First, he recommends that officials such as the Cabinet Secretaries, members of Congress, and those in charge of U.S. trade negotiations be banned for life from working as foreign lobbyists. Second, he proposes that the current "cooling-off" period (which restricts federal officials from lobbying or advising on trade matters for one year) be extended to at least five years. Third,

he advocates closing the loopholes in the Foreign Agents Registration Act of 1938 so that all those who represent foreign clients will be required to provide full disclosure to the Justice Department. And finally, he argues that a flat prohibition should be placed on foreign contributions to American political campaigns.

After the attention drawn by Perot to the matter of foreign lobbying, in 1993 Congress began serious deliberation regarding this issue. Many members felt that something had to be done, but a number of objections were raised on constitutional and policy grounds. Here are a few reservations you should take into account as you decide what should be done.

- Would such restrictions be an infringement on the right to petition the government, as guaranteed by the U.S. Constitution?
- Do foreigners operating in the United States not have the same constitutional rights as American citizens?
- Will these reforms lead to retaliation by foreign governments against U.S. companies operating abroad?
- Could these restrictions be so strict that they would prevent former government officials from providing assistance to foreigners that would further American interests? For example, might they prevent former officials from advising the first post-Castro Cuban government about reestablishing trade ties with the United States?

SOURCE: Pat Choate, *Agents of Influence: How Japan Manipulates America's Political and Economic System* (New York: Simon and Schuster, 1990).

---

interests of all of us—the buying public? Today over two thousand organized groups are championing various causes or ideas "in the public interest."[20] These **public interest lobbies** can be defined as organizations that seek "a collective good, the achievement of which will not selectively and materially benefit the membership or activists of the organization."[21] If products are made safer by the lobbying of consumer protection groups, it is not the members of such groups alone that will benefit. Rather, everyone should be better off, regardless of whether they joined in the lobbying.

Consumer groups have won many legislative victories in recent years. In 1973, Congress responded to consumer advocacy by creating the Consumer Product Safety Commission. Congress authorized it to regulate all consumer products and even gave it the power to ban particularly dangerous ones— bearing in mind that household products are responsible for thirty thousand deaths annually. Among the products the commission has investigated are children's sleepwear (some of which contained a carcinogen), hot tubs, and lawn mowers.

Consumer groups are not the only ones claiming to be public interest groups. Groups speaking for those who cannot speak for themselves seek to protect children, animals, and the mentally ill; good-government groups such as Common Cause push for openness and fairness in government; religious groups like the now-disbanded Moral Majority crusade for the protection of ethical and moral standards in American society; and environmental groups seek to preserve ecological balance.

Energy and Environmental Interests

Among the newest political interest groups are the environmentalists. A handful, like the Sierra Club and the Audubon Society, have been around since the nineteenth century, but many others trace their origins to the first Earth Day, April 22, 1970. On that day, ecology-minded people marched on Washington and other places to symbolize their support for environmental protection. The twentieth anniversary of Earth Day was celebrated in 1990 with another round of rallies calling for continued attention to the state of the environment.

Environmental groups have promoted pollution-control policies, wilderness protection, and population control. Perhaps more significant, however, is what they have opposed. Their hit list has included strip-mining, supersonic aircraft, the Alaskan oil pipeline, offshore oil drilling, and nuclear power plants. On these and other issues environmentalists have exerted a great deal of influence on Congress and state legislatures.

The concerns of environmentalists often come into direct conflict with energy goals. Environmentalists insist that, in the long run, energy supplies can be ensured without harming the environment or risking radiation exposure from nuclear power plants. On the issue of nuclear power plants, their arguments have had a profound impact on public policy. No new nuclear power plants have been approved since 1977, and many that had been in the works were canceled.[22] Short-term energy needs, however, have won out over environmental concerns in many other cases. Energy producers argue that environmentalists oppose nearly every new energy project. Given that there is no sign of a major drop in energy demands, they argue that some limited risks have to be taken. What is worse, they ask—an occasional oil spill off the shore of Alaska or long lines every day at the gas pumps? Thus, despite environmentalist's opposition, Congress subsidized the massive trans-Alaskan pipeline, which a consortium of companies use to transport oil from Alaska's North Slope. Similarly, the strip-mining of coal continues despite the constant objections from environmentalists. Group politics intensifies when two public interests clash, such as environmental protection and an ensured supply of energy.

Equality Interests

The Fourteenth Amendment guarantees equal protection under the law. American history, though, shows that this is easier said than done. Two sets of interest groups, representing women and minorities, have made equal rights their main policy goal. Chapter 4 reviewed the long history of the civil rights movement; this section is concerned with its policy goals and organizational base.

Equality at the polls, in housing, on the job, in education, and in all other facets of American life has long been the dominant goal of African-American groups. The oldest and largest of these groups is the National Association for the Advancement of Colored People (NAACP). It argued and won the monumental *Brown v. Board of Education* case in 1954. In that decision the Supreme Court held that segregated schools were unconstitutional. The NAACP and other civil rights groups have also lobbied and pressed court cases to forbid discrimination in voting, employment, and housing. Although they have won many victories in principle, equality in practice has been much slower in coming. Today, civil rights groups continue to push for more effective affirmative action programs to ensure that minority groups are given educational and employment opportunities. The NAACP's main vehicle in recent years has been the Fair Share program, which negotiates agreements with national and regional businesses to increase minority hiring and the use of minority contractors. Affirmative action is not as emotionally charged an issue as desegregation, but it too has been controversial.

When the NAACP was just starting up, suffragists were in the streets and legislative lobbies demanding women's right to vote. The Nineteenth Amendment, ratified in 1920, guaranteed women the vote, but other guarantees of equal protection remained absent from the Constitution. More recently, women's rights groups, such as the National Organization for Women (NOW), have lobbied for an end to sexual discrimination. Their primary goal has been the passage of the Equal Rights Amendment (ERA), which states that "equality of rights under the law shall not be abridged on account of sex." Though the ERA seems dead for the moment, NOW remains committed to enacting the protection the amendment would have constitutionally guaranteed by advocating the enactment of many individual statutes. As is often the case with

The National Organization for Women (NOW) is a relatively new interest group, founded in 1966, but has quickly become one of the best known in the country, with over a quarter of a million members. NOW can be expected to play a prominent role in issues concerning women's rights.

interest group politics, issues are rarely settled once and for all; rather, they shift to different policy arenas.

WHAT MAKES AN INTEREST GROUP SUCCESSFUL?

There are many factors that affect the success of an interest group. Among these factors are the size of the group (the smaller the better), its intensity, and its financial resources. It is somewhat counterintuitive to learn that small groups are actually more likely to get their way than large groups. Thus, considerable space will be devoted here to explaining this surprising finding. The discussion will then turn to some of the other, less surprising factors.

The Surprising Ineffectiveness of Large Groups

In one of the most oft-quoted statements concerning interest groups, E. E. Schattschneider wrote that "pressure politics is essentially the politics of small groups. . . . Pressure tactics are not remarkably successful in mobilizing general interests."[23] There are perfectly good reasons why consumer groups are less effective than producer groups, patients are less effective than doctors, and energy conservationists are less effective than oil companies—small groups have organizational advantages over large groups.

To shed light on this point, it is important to distinguish between a potential and an actual group. A **potential group** is composed of all people who might be group members because they share some common interest.[24] In contrast, an **actual group** is composed of those in the potential group who choose to join. The examples in Table 8.1 show that groups vary enormously in the degree to which they enroll their potential membership. Consumer organizations are minuscule when compared with the total number of consumers, which is almost every American. Some organizations, however, do very well in organizing virtually all of their potential members. For example, the U.S. Savings and Loan League, the Tobacco Institute, and the Air Transport Association include a good portion of their potential members. Compared with consumers, these groups are tightly organized.

Economist Mancur Olson explains this phenomenon in his book, *The Logic of Collective Action.*[25] Olson points out that all groups, as opposed to individuals, are in the business of providing collective goods. A **collective good** is something of value, such as clean air, that cannot be withheld from a potential group member. When the AFL-CIO wins a higher minimum wage, all low-paid workers benefit, regardless of whether they are a member of the union. In other words, members of the potential group share in benefits that members of the actual group work to secure. If this is the case, an obvious and difficult problem results: why should potential members work for something if they can get it for free? Why join the group, pay dues, and work hard for a goal when a person can benefit from the group's activity without doing anything at all? A perfectly rational response is thus to sit back and let other people do the work. This is commonly known as the **free-rider problem.**

The bigger the group, the more serious the free-rider problem. That is the gist of **Olson's law of large groups**: "The larger the group, the further it will fall short of providing an optimal amount of a collective good."[26] Small groups thus have an organizational advantage over large ones. In a small group, members' shares of the collective good may be great enough that they will try to secure it. The old saying that "everyone can make a difference" is much more credible in the case of a small group. In the largest groups, however, each member can only expect to get a tiny share of the policy gains. Weighing the costs of participation against the relatively small benefits, the temptation is always to "let George do it." Therefore, as Olson argues, the larger the potential group, the less likely potential members are to contribute.

In sum, Olson's law helps explain why small interest groups are generally more effective. The power of business in the American political system is thus due to more than just money, as proponents of elite theory would have us

TABLE 8.1 — Potential versus Actual Groups

Some groups organize most of their potential membership. Others suffer an enormous shortfall between their actual membership and the groups they claim to speak for. Obviously, estimating the true potential membership of a group is difficult, but if you will tolerate some very rough approximations, we can compare groups' actual to potential membership. In the following table, the first four groups have a tiny fraction of their potential membership; the last four have a very high proportion of their potential members.

Group	Organization	Membership
Consumers	National Consumers League, a Washington-based consumer action group	Potential: 250,000,000 (Every American) Actual: 8,000
African Americans	National Association for the Advancement of Colored People, the largest civil rights organization	Potential: 30,500,000 (Every African American)[a] Actual: 400,000
Women	National Organization for Women, a leading women's rights organization	Potential: 130,000,000 (Every woman)[a] Actual: 250,000
Taxpayers	National Taxpayers Union, a "taxpayers' rights" group advocating tax and government spending cuts	Potential: 180,000,000 (Every adult 18 and over) Actual: 200,000
Physicians	American Medical Association, a professional organization of medical doctors	Potential: 620,000 (All M.D.s) Actual: 271,000
Savings and Loan Associations	U.S. League of Savings Institutions, an organization of local savings and loan associations	Potential: 3,785 (All S&Ls) Actual: 2,500
Tobacco	Tobacco Institute, the organization of tobacco manufacturers	Potential: 11 (All cigarette manufacturers) Actual: 11
Airlines	Air Transport Association of America, the organization of U.S. airlines	Potential: 60 (All U.S. air carriers) Actual: 22

[a]The membership of these organizations is open to all, but practically speaking their potential membership is mostly determined by the name of the group.

SOURCES: For data on actual organizational memberships, see Denise Akey, ed. *Encyclopedia of Associations, 1993* (Detroit: Gale Research Company, 1992); for data on potential organizational memberships, see U.S. Bureau of the Census, *Statistical Abstract of the United States: 1992* (Washington DC: Government Printing Office, 1992).

believe. Besides their financial strength, large corporations also enjoy an inherent size advantage. Small potential groups like business have an easier time organizing themselves for political action than large potential groups, such as consumers. Once well organized, large groups may be quite effective, but it is much harder for them to get together in the first place.

Many public interest groups claim to speak for those who cannot speak for themselves. Animal rights groups, for example, protest against what they see as cruel practices used by fur trappers and try to discourage people from buying furs.

Intensity

One way a large potential group may be mobilized is through an issue that people feel intensely about, such as abortion. Intensity is a psychological advantage that can be enjoyed by small and large groups alike. When a group shows that it cares deeply about an issue, politicians are more likely to listen—many votes may be won or lost on a single issue. Because of this, the rise of single-issue groups has been one of the most dramatic political developments in recent years.

A **single-issue group** can be defined as a group that has a narrow interest, dislikes compromise, and single-mindedly pursues its goal. Anti–Vietnam War activists may have formed the first modern single-issue groups. Opponents of nuclear power plants, gun control, and abortion are some of the many such groups that exist today. All these groups deal with issues that evoke the strong emotions characteristic of single-interest groups.

Perhaps the most emotional issue of all has been that of abortion. The 1973 Supreme Court ruling in *Roe v. Wade,* upholding the right of a woman to secure an abortion during the first trimester of pregnancy, spurred a wave of group formation. Opponents quickly labeled this court decision as legalized murder and formed such organizations as the National Right to Life Committee. In recent elections they adamantly supported the campaigns of Presidents

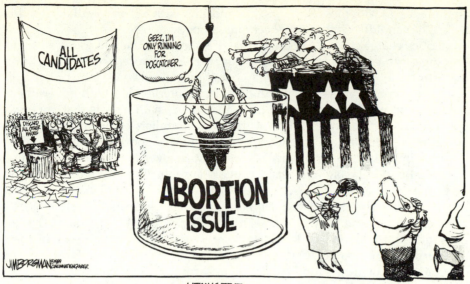

LITMUS TEST

Reagan and Bush and hounded pro-choice candidates like Geraldine Ferraro and Bill Clinton. Befitting the intensity of the issue, their activities have not been limited to electioneering and lobbying. Protesting—often in the form of blocking entrances to abortion clinics—has now become a common practice for antiabortion activists.

Pro-choice activists have organized as well, forming groups like the National Abortion Rights Action League. Since the 1989 *Webster v. Reproductive Health Services* case allowed states greater freedom to restrict abortions, the pro-choice side has become better mobilized than ever before. When the law was on their side, pro-choice advocates could not match the antiabortionists in terms of intensity. Now that the legal tide has turned against them, their intensity level has risen. Like the antiabortionists, their position is clear, not subject to compromise, and influences their vote. Regardless of which side candidates for political office are on, they will be taking heat on the abortion issue for years to come.

Financial Resources

One of the major indictments of the American interest group system is that it is biased toward the wealthy. There is no doubt that money talks in the American political system, and those who have it get heard. A big campaign contribution may ensure a phone call, a meeting, or even a direct *quid pro quo*. When Lincoln Savings and Loan Chairman Charles Keating was asked whether the $1.3 million he had funnelled into the campaigns of five U.S. Senators had anything to do with these Senators later meeting with federal regulators on his behalf, he candidly responded, "I certainly hope so."

Critics charge that PACs, the source of so much money in today's expensive high-tech campaigns, distort the governmental process in favor of those that can raise the most money. A PAC may only want to be remembered on one or two crucial votes or with an occasional intervention with government agencies, but multiply this by the thousands of special interests that are organized today and the worst fears of the hyperpluralists could be realized—a government that constantly yields to every organized special interest.

It is important to emphasize, however, that even on some of the most important issues the big interests do not always win. The best recent example of this is the Tax Reform Act of 1986. In *Showdown at Gucci Gulch*, two reporters from the *Wall Street Journal* chronicle the improbable victory of sweeping tax reform.[27] In this case, a large group of well-organized, highly paid (and thus Gucci-clad) lobbyists were unable to preserve many of their most prized tax loopholes. One of the heroes of the book, Senator Packwood of Oregon, was Congress's top PAC recipient during the tax reform struggle. As Chair of the Senate Finance Committee, however, Packwood ultimately turned against the hordes of lobbyists trying to get his ear on behalf of various loopholes. The only way to deal with the tax loophole problem, he concluded, was to go virtually cold turkey by eliminating all but a very few. "There is special interest after special interest that is hit in this bill," Packwood gloated, pointing out that many of them contributed to his campaign. In the end, passage of the reform bill offered "encouraging proof that moneyed interests could not always buy their way to success in Congress."[28]

UNDERSTANDING INTEREST GROUPS

The problem of interest groups in America today remains much the same as Madison defined it over 200 years ago. A free society must allow for the representation of all groups that seek to influence political decision making; yet because groups are usually more concerned with their own self-interest rather than with the needs of society as a whole, for democracy to work well it is important that they not be allowed to assume a dominant position.

Interest Groups and Democracy

James Madison's solution to the problems posed by interest groups was to create a wide-open system in which many groups would be able to participate. By extending the sphere of influence, according to Madison, groups with opposing interests would counterbalance one another. Pluralist theorists believe that a rough approximation of the public interest emerges from this competition.

With the tremendous growth of interest group politics in recent years, some observers feel that Madison may at last have gotten his wish. For every group with an interest there now seems to be a competing group to watch over them—not to mention public interest lobbies to keep a watch over them all. Robert Salisbury argues that "the growth in the number, variety, and sophistication of interest groups represented in Washington" has transformed policy-making such that it "is not dominated so often by a relatively small number of powerful interest groups as it may once have been."[29] Paradoxically, Salisbury concludes that the increase in lobbying activity has resulted in less clout overall for interest groups—and better democracy.

Elite theorists clearly disagree with this conclusion and point to the proliferation of business PACs as evidence that the interest group system is corrupting American politics more than ever. A democratic process requires a free and open exchange of ideas in which candidates and voters should be able to hear one another out, but PACs, the source of so much money in elections, distort the process. Elite theorists particularly note that wealthier interests are greatly advantaged by the PAC system. Business PACs have become the dominant force in the fund-raising game. Furthermore, out of approximately 2,000 corporate PACs, the top 135 accounted for half of the campaign contributions from such groups in 1988.

Interest Groups and the Scope of Government

The power of special interest groups through PACs and other means also has implications for the scope of government. Two recent presidents each remarked at the end of their time in office that their attempts to cut federal spending had been frustrated by interest groups. In his farewell address, Carter "suggested that the reason he had so much difficulty in dealing with Congress was the fragmentation of power and decision making that was exploited by interest groups."[30] Similarly, Reagan remarked in December 1988 that "special interest groups, bolstered by campaign contributions, pressure lawmakers into creating and defending spending programs."[31] Above all, most special interest groups strive to maintain established programs that benefit them—and thus frustrate any attempts to reduce the scope of government.

However, one can also argue that the growth in the scope of government in recent decades accounts for a good portion of the proliferation of interest groups. The more areas the federal government has become involved in, the more interest groups have arisen to attempt to influence policy. As William Lunch notes, "a great part of the increase was occasioned by the new government responsibility for civil rights, environmental protection, and greater public health and safety."[32] For example, once the government got seriously into the business of protecting the environment, many groups sprung up to lobby for strong standards and enforcement. Given the tremendous effects of environmental regulations on many industries, it should come as no surprise that they also organized to ensure that their interests were taken into account. As Salisbury writes, many groups have "come to Washington out of need and dependence rather than because they have influence."[33]

SUMMARY

This chapter's discussion of group politics has familiarized you with the vast array of interest groups in American politics, all vying for policies they prefer. Pluralists see groups as the most important way people can have their policy preferences represented in government. Hyperpluralists, though, fear that too many groups are getting too much of what they want, skillfully working the many subgovernments in the American system. Elitists believe that a few wealthy individuals and multinational corporations exert control over the major decisions regarding distribution of goods and services.

Interest groups can choose from among four basic strategies to maximize their effectiveness. Lobbying is one well-known group strategy. Although the evidence on its influence is mixed, it is clear that lobbyists are most effective with those legislators already sympathetic to their side. Thus electioneering becomes critical because it helps put supportive people in office. Often today, groups operate in the judicial as well as the legislative process, using litigation when lobbying fails or is not enough. Many also find it important to shape a good image, employing public relations techniques to present themselves in the most favorable light.

This chapter also examined some of the major kinds of interest groups, particularly those concerned with economic, equality, and energy and environmental policy. Public interest lobbies claim to look after the general good. Recently there has been a rapid growth of single-interest groups, which focus narrowly on one issue and are not inclined to compromise.

A number of factors influence a group's success in achieving its policy goals. Most surprising is that small groups have an organizational advantage over large groups. Large groups often fall victim to the free-rider problem (Olson's law of large groups). Both large and small groups can benefit from intensity. Money always helps lubricate the wheels of power, though it is hardly a sure-fire guarantee of success.

The problem of controlling interest groups remains as crucial to democracy today as it was in Madison's time. Some believe that the growth of interest groups has worked to divide political influence just as Madison hoped it would. Others point to the PAC system as the new way in which special interests corrupt American democracy.

FOR FURTHER READING

Berry, Jeffrey M. *The Interest Group Society*, 2nd ed. Glenview, IL: Scott, Foresman, 1989. One of the best contemporary textbooks on interest groups.

Birnbaum, Jeffrey H., and Alan S. Murray. *Showdown at Gucci Gulch: Lawmakers, Lobbyists, and the Unlikely Triumph of Tax Reform.* New York: Vintage, 1987. A fascinating account of how the 1986 tax reform bill passed over the objections of the Gucci-clad lobbyists.

Cigler, Allan J., and Burdett A. Loomis, eds. *Interest Group Politics*, 4th ed. Washington, DC: Congressional Quarterly Press, 1995. An excellent collection of original articles on the modern interest group system.

Dye, Thomas R. *Who's Running America? The Bush Era*, 5th ed. Englewood Cliffs, NJ: Prentice Hall, 1990. A good summary of the elitist view of interest groups.

Lowi, Theodore J. *The End of Liberalism*, 2nd ed. New York: Norton, 1979. A critique of the role of subgovernments and the excessive deference to interest groups in the American political system.

Olson, Mancur. *The Logic of Collective Action*. Cambridge, MA: Harvard University Press, 1965. Develops an economic theory of groups, showing how the cards are stacked against larger groups.

Schlozman, Kay L., and John T. Tierney. *Organized Interests and American Democracy*. New York: Harper & Row, 1986. Survey results from a sample of Washington lobbyists are used to draw a portrait of the interest group system.

Walker, Jack L. *Mobilizing Interest Groups in America: Patrons, Professions and Social Movements*. Ann Arbor: University of Michigan Press, 1991. An important collection of essays on the formation and activities of interest groups.

NOTES

1. Kay L. Schlozman and John T. Tierney, *Organized Interests and American Democracy* (New York: Harper & Row, 1986), 1.
2. The classic work is David B. Truman, *The Governmental Process*, 2nd ed. (New York: Knopf, 1971).
3. Thomas R. Dye, *Who's Running America? The Bush Era*, 5th ed. (Englewood Cliffs, NJ: Prentice Hall, 1990), 170.
4. Robert Engler, *The Brotherhood of Oil* (Chicago: University of Chicago Press, 1977).
5. Theodore J. Lowi, *The End of Liberalism*, 2nd ed. (New York: Norton, 1979).
6. Morris P. Fiorina, *Congress: Keystone of the Washington Establishment*, 2nd ed. (New Haven, CT: Yale University Press, 1989), 122.
7. Lester W. Milbrath, *The Washington Lobbyists* (Chicago: Rand McNally, 1963), 8.
8. Norman Ornstein and Shirley Elder, *Interest Groups, Lobbying, and Policymaking* (Washington, DC: Congressional Quarterly Press, 1978), 59–60.
9. Raymond A. Bauer, Ithiel de Sola Pool, and Lewis A. Dexter, *American Business and Public Policy* (New York: Atherton, 1963).
10. Milbrath, *The Washington Lobbyists*, 354.
11. Harold W. Stanley and Richard G. Niemi, *Vital Statistics on American Politics*, 4th ed. (Washington, DC: Congressional Quarterly Press, 1994), 175.
12. Ibid., 183.
13. "No Risk Investments," *Common Cause News*, May 9, 1989.
14. The Sovern story is told in "Taking an Ax to PACs," *Time*, August 20, 1984, 27.
15. Karen Orren, "Standing to Sue: Interest Group Conflict in Federal Courts," *American Political Science Review* 70 (September 1976): 724.
16. Gregory A. Caldeira and John R. Wright, "*Amici Curiae* Before the Supreme Court: Who Participates, When, and How Much?" *Journal of Politics* 52 (August 1990): 782–804.
17. Ronald J. Hrebenar and Ruth K. Scott, *Interest Group Politics in America*, 2nd ed. (Englewood Cliffs, NJ: Prentice Hall, 1990), 201.
18. Quoted in Jeffrey M. Berry, *The Interest Group Society*, 2nd ed. (Glenview, IL: Scott, Foresman, 1989), 103.
19. Paul Edward Johnson, "Organized Labor in an Era of Blue-Collar Decline," in Allan J. Cigler and Burdett A. Loomis, eds., *Interest Group Politics*, 3rd ed. (Washington, DC: Congressional Quarterly Press, 1991), 33–62.

20. H. R. Mahood, *Interest Group Politics in America: A New Intensity* (Englewood Cliffs, NJ: Prentice Hall, 1990), 162.
21. Jeffrey M. Berry, *Lobbying for the People* (Princeton, NJ: Princeton University Press, 1977), 7.
22. For an interesting analysis of how changes in the regulatory environment, congressional oversight, and public opinion altered the debate on nuclear power, see Frank R. Baumgartner and Byran D. Jones, *Agendas and Instability in American Politics* (Chicago: University of Chicago Press, 1993).
23. E. E. Schattschneider, *The Semisovereign People* (New York: Holt, Rinehart & Winston, 1960), 35.
24. Truman, *The Governmental Process*, 2nd ed., 511.
25. Mancur Olson, *The Logic of Collective Action* (Cambridge, MA: Harvard University Press, 1965), especially 9–36.
26. Ibid., 35.
27. Jeffrey H. Birnbaum and Alan S. Murray, *Showdown at Gucci Gulch: Lawmakers, Lobbyists, and the Unlikely Triumph of Tax Reform* (New York: Vintage, 1987).
28. Ibid., 235.
29. Robert H. Salisbury, "The Paradox of Interest Groups in Washington—More Groups, Less Clout" in Anthony King, ed., *The New American Political System,* 2nd version (Washington, DC: American Enterprise Institute, 1990), 204.
30. Hrebenar and Scott, *Interest Group Politics in America*, 2nd ed., 234.
31. Steven V. Roberts, "Angered President Blames Others for the Huge Deficit," *New York Times*, December 14, 1988, A16.
32. William M. Lunch, *The Nationalization of American Politics* (Berkeley: University of California Press, 1987), 206.
33. Salisbury, "The Paradox of Interest Groups," 229.

CHAPTER 9 *The Mass Media*

In today's technological world, the media—like computers, atomic power, aircraft, and automobiles—are everywhere. The American political system has entered a new period of **high-tech politics**, a politics in which the behavior of citizens and policymakers, as well as the political agenda itself, is increasingly shaped by technology. The **mass media** are a key part of this technology. Television, radio, newspapers, magazines, and other means of popular communication are called mass media because they reach and profoundly influence not only the elites but the masses. This chapter examines media politics, focusing on the following topics:

- The rise of the media in America's advanced technological society
- How news gets made and presented through the media
- The biases in the news
- The impact of the media on policymakers and the public

This chapter also reintroduces the concept of the policy agenda, in which the media play an important role.

THE MASS MEDIA TODAY

These days, the news media often make the news as well as report it. Television news anchors are paid Hollywood-style salaries and sometimes behave in Hollywood style (as Dan Rather did when he stalked off the set of the evening news one night, and as Diane Sawyer did when she modeled for *Vanity Fair*). At the 1992 political party conventions, Tom Brokaw not only reported the news but also appeared on the "Tonight Show," trading jokes with Jay Leno.

When Americans came ashore in Somalia later in the year, Brokaw, Ted Koppel, and Dan Rather had been reporting from Mogadishu for two days in anticipation of their arrival. Secure in their jobs as long as their ratings remain high, TV anchors have taken their place beside presidents, senators, and others who shape public opinion and policy.

An effective media strategy is thus crucial to any presidential campaign. Candidates have learned that the secret to controlling the media's focus is limiting what they can report on to carefully scripted events. These are known as media events. A **media event** is staged primarily for the purpose of being covered. If the media are not there, the event would probably not happen or would have no significance. For example, on the eve of the 1992 New Hampshire primary, Bill and Hillary Clinton went door-to-door in a middle-class neighborhood with TV crews in tow. The few dozen people the Clintons met could scarcely have made a difference, but they were not really there to win votes by personal contact. Rather, the point was to get pictures on TV of the Clintons reaching out to ordinary people.

Getting the right image on TV news for just 30 seconds can easily have a greater payoff than a whole day's worth of handshaking. Whereas once a candidate's G.O.T.V. program stood for "Get Out the Vote," today it is more likely to mean "Get on TV." Indeed, the 1992 Clinton organization had two or three staff members in each state whose sole job was to work at getting plentiful andfavorable TV coverage for the campaign.[1]

In addition, a large part of today's so-called 30-second presidency is the slickly produced TV commercial. In recent years, negative commercials have come to dominate many campaigns.[2] Many people are worried that the tirade of accusations, innuendos, and countercharges in political commercials is poisoning the American political process. Some would even use the government's regulatory power over television to curb negative advertising.

Yet image making doesn't stop with the campaign—it is also a critical element in day-to-day governing. Politicians' images in the press are seen as good indicators of their clout. This is especially true of presidents, who in recent years have devoted major attention to maintaining a well-honed public image. As President Nixon wrote in an internal White House memo in 1969:

> When I think of the millions of dollars that go into one lousy 30-second television spot advertising a deodorant, it seems to me unbelievable that we don't do a better job in seeing that Presidential appearances always have the very best professional advice whenever they are to be covered on TV. . . . The President should never be without the very best professional advice for making a television appearance.[3]

Few, if any, administrations devoted so much concern and energy to the president's media appearances than did Ronald Reagan's. It has often been said that Reagan played to the media as he had played to the cameras in Hollywood. According to Mark Hertsgaard, news management in the Reagan White House operated on the following seven principles: (1) plan ahead, (2) stay on the offensive, (3) control the flow of information, (4) limit reporters' access to the president, (5) talk about the issues you want to talk about, (6) speak in one voice, and (7) repeat the same message many times.[4] To Ronald Reagan, the presidency was often a performance, and his aides worked hard to carefully choreograph his every public appearance. Perhaps there will never again be a president so concerned with public relations as Reagan, but for a president to ignore the power of image and the media would be perilous. In today's high-tech age, presidents can hardly lead the country if they cannot effectively communicate with it.

The media have helped create what Elinor Fuchs calls the "theatricalization of American politics."[5] Colonel Oliver North outscored the soap operas in his televised Iran-Contra testimony. The trials and tribulations of Gary Hart were a political soap opera. The villains (the Ayatollah, Noriega, Saddam Hussein), the victims (the Iranian hostages, the starving African children, the AIDS sufferers), the heroes (Lech Walesa, American soldiers in the Persian Gulf), the scripts (Watergate, the Iran-Contra hearings, the Anita Hill-Clarence Thomas hearings)—all these combine to make politics theater. With the media, as Shakespeare said, "All the world's a stage, and all the men and women merely players."

THE DEVELOPMENT OF THE MASS MEDIA

We clearly live in a mass media age today, but it was not always this way. There was virtually no daily press when the First Amendment was written during Washington's presidency. The daily newspaper is largely a product of the late nineteenth century; radio and television have been around only since the first half of the twentieth. As recently as the presidency of Herbert Hoover (1929–1933), reporters submitted their questions to the president in writing, and he responded in writing—if at all. As Hoover put it, "The President of the United States will not stand and be questioned like a chicken thief by men whose names he does not even know."[6]

Hoover's successor, Franklin D. Roosevelt (1933–1945), practically invented media politics. To Roosevelt, the media were a potential ally. Power radiated from Washington under him—and so did news. Roosevelt promised reporters **two press conferences**—presidential meetings with reporters—a week, and he delivered them. He held 337 press conferences in his first term, 374 in his second, and 279 in his third. Roosevelt was *the* newsmaker. Stories and leads flowed from the White House like a flood; the United Press news syndicate carried four times as much Washington news under FDR as it had under Hoover.[7] FDR was also the first president to use radio, broadcasting a series of reassuring "fireside chats" to the Depression-ridden nation. Roosevelt's crafty use of radio helped him win four presidential elections. Theodore White tells the story of the time in 1944 when FDR found out that his opponent, Thomas E. Dewey, had purchased 15 minutes of air time on NBC immediately following his own address. Roosevelt spoke for 14 minutes and then left one minute silent. Thinking that the network had experienced technical difficulties, many changed their dials before Dewey came on the air.[8]

Another Roosevelt talent was knowing how to feed the right story to the right reporter. He used presidential wrath to warn reporters off material he did not want covered, and chastised news reports he deemed inaccurate. His wrath was rarely invoked, however, and the press revered him, never even reporting to the American public that the President was confined to a wheelchair. The idea that a political leader's private life might be public business was alien to journalists in FDR's day.

This relatively cozy relationship betwen politicians and the press lasted through the early 1960s. As ABC's Sam Donaldson writes, when he first came to Washington in 1961, "many reporters saw themselves as an extension of the government, accepting, with very little skepticism, what government officials told them."[9] The events of the Vietnam War and the Watergate scandal, though, soured the press on government. Today's newspeople work in an environment of cynicism. To them, politicians rarely tell the whole story; the press sees ferreting out the truth as their job. No one epitomized this attitude in the 1980s better than Donaldson, who earned a hard-nosed reputation by regularly shouting unwanted questions at President Reagan. In his book, *Hold On, Mr. President!*, Donaldson says,

Franklin D. Roosevelt was the first president to use the media effectively. A favorite of reporters, FDR held over 1000 press conferences during more than twelve years in office. He was also the first president to use radio as a political tool, giving "fireside chats" to reassure the nation during the Great Depression.

> If you send me to cover a pie-baking contest on Mother's Day, I'm going to ask dear old Mom whether she used artificial sweetener in violations of the rules, and while she's at it, could I see the receipt for the apples to prove she didn't steal them. I maintain that if Mom has nothing to hide, no harm will have been done. But the questions should be asked.[10]

Critics of aggressive reporters like Donaldson believe that the media undermine public confidence in government, as well as discourage people from public service due to the microscopic attention they can expect to receive.[11]

Scholars distinguish between two kinds of media: the **print media**, which include newspapers and magazines, and the **broadcast media**, which consist of television and radio. Each has reshaped political communication at different points in American history. The following sections look at their development and role in the political system.

The Print Media

The first American daily newspaper was printed in Philadelphia in 1783, but such papers did not proliferate until the technological advances of the mid-nineteenth century. Rapid printing and cheap paper made possible the "penny press," which could be bought for a penny and read at home. In 1841 Horace Greeley's *New York Tribune* was founded, and in 1851 the *New York Times* started up. By the 1840s the telegraph permitted a primitive "wire service," which relayed news stories from city to city faster than ever before. The Associated Press, founded in 1849, depended heavily on this new technology.

Two newspaper magnates, Joseph Pulitzer and William Randolph Hearst, enlivened journalism around the turn of the century. Between them—Pulitzer operating in New York and Hearst in burgeoning San Francisco—they published many stories about hijinks in high places. This was the era of yellow journalism, wherein violence, corruption, wars, and gossip were the main topics. On a visit to the United States at that time, young Winston Churchill said that "the essence of American journalism is vulgarity divested of truth."[12]

Newspapers consolidated into **chains** during the early part of the twentieth century. Today's massive media conglomerates (Gannett, Knight-Ridder, and Newhouse are the largest) control newspapers with 78 percent of the nation's daily circulation.[13] Thus, three of four Americans now read a newspaper owned not by a fearless local editor but by a corporation headquartered elsewhere. Often these chains control television and radio stations as well.

Magazines—the other component of the print media—are read avidly by Americans, although the political content of leading magazines is slim. The so-called newsweeklies—mainly *Time*, *Newsweek*, and *U.S. News and World Report*—rank well behind such popular favorites as the *Reader's Digest*, *TV Guide*, and *Family Circle*. Although *Time*'s circulation is a bit better than that of the *National Enquirer* (for "people with enquiring minds," its ads tell us), the *Star* and *Playboy* edge out *Newsweek* in sales competition. Serious magazines of political news and opinion are basically reserved for the educated elite in America; magazines such as the *New Republic*, the *National Review*, and *Commentary* are greatly outsold by such American favorites as *Hot Rod*, *Weightwatchers Magazine*, and *Organic Gardening*.

The Broadcast Media

Gradually, the broadcast media have displaced the print media as Americans' principal source of news and information. The radio was invented in 1903, the same year as the Wright brothers' famous flight. The first modern commercial radio station was Pittsburgh's KDKA, whose maiden broadcast was of the 1920 Harding-Cox presidential election returns. By the middle of the 1930s, radio ownership had become almost universal in America, and during World War II radio went into the news business in earnest.

The 1950s and early 1960s were the adolescent years for American television. During those years the political career of Richard Nixon was made and unmade by television. In 1952, while running as Dwight Eisenhower's vice-presidential candidate, Nixon made a famous speech denying that he took under-the-table gifts and payments. Claiming that his wife, Pat, wore only a

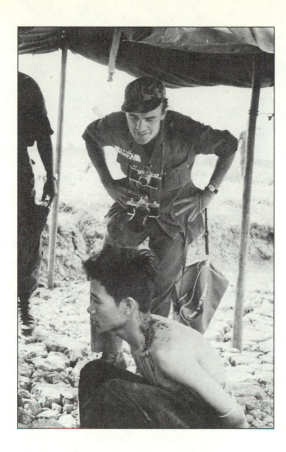

Vietnam was the major conflict in which the horrors of war were reported extensively to the public. Here, war correspondent Peter Arnett is shown watching an interrogation of a North Vietnamese prisoner.

"Republican cloth coat," he did admit that one gift he had accepted was his dog Checkers. Noting that his daughters loved the dog, Nixon said that regardless of his political future they would keep it. His homey appeal brought a flood of sympathetic telegrams to the Republican National Committee, and party leaders had little choice but to leave him on the ticket.

In 1960 Nixon was again on television's center stage, this time in the first televised **presidential debate** against Senator John F. Kennedy. Nixon blamed his poor appearance in the first of the four debates for his narrow defeat in the election. Haggard from a week in the hospital and with his five o'clock shadow and perspiration clearly visible, Nixon looked awful compared to the crisp, clean, attractive Kennedy. The poll results from this debate illustrate the visual power of television in American politics; whereas people listening on the radio gave the edge to Nixon, those who saw it on television thought Kennedy won. Russell Baker, who covered the event for the *New York Times*, writes in his memoirs that "television replaced newspapers as the most important communications medium in American politics" that very night.[14]

Just as radio had taken the nation to the war in Europe and the Pacific during the 1940s, television took the nation to the war in Vietnam during the

1960s. TV exposed governmental naivete (some said it was outright lying) about the progress of the war. Napoleon once said that "four hostile newspapers are more to be feared than a thousand bayonets." Lyndon Johnson learned the hard way that three television networks could be even more consequential. Every night, in living color, Americans watched the horrors of war through television. President Johnson soon had two wars on his hands, one in faraway Vietnam and the other at home with antiwar protesters, both covered in detail by the media. In 1968, CBS anchorman Walter Cronkite journeyed to Vietnam for a firsthand look at the state of the war. In an extraordinary TV special, Cronkite reported that the war was not being won, nor was it likely to be. Watching from the White House, Johnson sadly remarked that if he had lost Cronkite, he had lost the support of the American people.

With the growth of cable TV, particularly the Cable News Network (CNN), television has recently entered a new era of bringing the news to people—and political leaders—as it happens. President Bush and his aides regularly watched CNN during the Gulf War, as did the Iraqi leadership. Marlin Fitzwater, Bush's press secretary, states that "CNN has opened up a whole new communications system between governments in terms of immediacy and directness. In many cases it's the first communication we have."[15]

Television has become so important in world politics that the leaders of the abortive 1991 Soviet coup felt compelled to hold a press conference on the day they seized power. With their hands visibly shaking, they tried in vain to convince the world that Mikhail Gorbachev had suddenly been taken ill. Pummeled by hostile questions from the press, their lies were clear for all to see. And on the same day, Boris Yeltsin stood on a tank to give a defiant speech condemning the attempted coup. His brave appeal was heard in person by relatively few people (he did not even have a microphone), but the televised pictures of it had an enormous impact throughout Russia and the world. With such images broadcast to them, Russians could choose which side to support based on a reasonable knowledge of the alternatives—an option that Americans all too often take for granted.

Since 1963, surveys have consistently shown that more people rely on TV for the news than any other medium (see Figure 9.1). Furthermore, by a regular two to one margin, people think television reports are more believable than newspaper stories. (Consider the old sayings "Don't believe everything you read" and "I'll believe it when I see it.") People are predisposed to be skeptical about what they read in a newspaper; with television, seeing is believing.

REPORTING THE NEWS

Regardless of the medium, it cannot be emphasized enough that news reporting is a business in America. Striving for the bottom line—profits—shapes how journalists define the news, where they get the news, and how they present it. Because some news stories attract more viewers or readers than others, there are certain inherent biases in what the American public sees and reads.

FIGURE 9.1 — *Where Citizens Get Their News and What They Trust]*

Where do you usually get most of your news about what's going on in the world today—from the newspapers or radio or television or magazines or talking to people? (More than one answer permitted.)

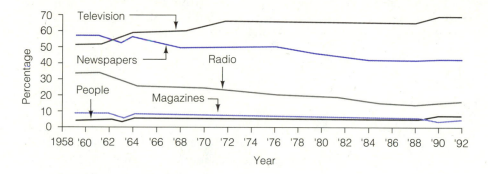

If you got conflicting or different reports of the same news story from radio, television, the magazines, and the newspapers, which of the four versions would you be most inclined to believe?

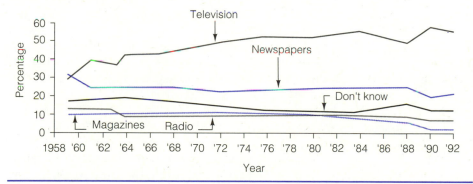

SOURCE: The questions as worded are taken directly from Harold W. Stanley and Richard G. Niemi, *Vital Statistics on American Politics*, 4th ed. (Washington DC: Congressional Quarterly Press, 1994), 74.

Defining News

As every journalism student will quickly tell you, news is what is timely and different. It is when a man bites a dog as opposed to when a dog bites a man. An oft-repeated speech on foreign policy or a well-worn statement on fighting drug abuse is less newsworthy than an odd episode. The public rarely hears about the routine ceremonies at state dinners, but when President Bush threw up all over the Japanese Prime Minister, the world's media jumped on the story. In its search for the unusual, the news media can give its audience a very peculiar view of events and policymakers.

Millions of new and different events happen every day; journalists must decide which of them are newsworthy. No one has taken a more careful look at the definition and production of news than Edward J. Epstein, who, given a unique opportunity to observe NBC's news department for a year, wrote *News from Nowhere*, an inside account of the TV news business.[16] Epstein found that some important characteristics of the TV news business result from the nature of the viewing audience. In their pursuit of high ratings, news shows are tailored to a fairly low level of audience sophistication. To a large extent, TV networks define news as what is entertaining to the average viewer.

Finding the News

Epstein called his book *News from Nowhere* to make the point that the organizational process shapes the news. Of course, news does come from somewhere. Americans' popular image of correspondents or reporters somehow uncovering the news is accurate in some cases, yet a surprising amount of news comes from well-established sources. Most news organizations assign their best reporters to particular **beats**—specific locations where news frequently emanates from, such as Congress. For example, during the Persian Gulf War more than 50 percent of the lead stories on the TV newscasts came from the White House, Pentagon, and State Department beats.[17] Numerous studies of both the electronic and print media have found that journalists rely almost exclusively on such established sources to get their information. Reporters and their official sources have a symbiotic relationship. Those who make the news depend on the media to spread certain information and ideas to the general public. Sometimes they feed stories to reporters in the form of **trial balloons**, information leaked to the media to see what the political reaction will be.

When reporters feel that their access to information is being impeded, complaints of censorship become widespread. During the Gulf War, reporters' freedom of movement and observation was severely restricted. After the fighting was over, 15 influential news organizations sent a letter to the Secretary of Defense complaining that the rules for reporting the war were designed more to control the news than to facilitate it.[18] While the signers of the letter vowed not to let this happen again, there is probably little they can do about it. Official sources who have the information usually have the upper hand over those who merely report it.

Despite this reliance on familiar sources, an enterprising reporter occasionally has an opportunity to live up to the image of the crusading truth-seeker. Local reporters Carl Bernstein and Bob Woodward of the *Washington Post* uncovered important evidence in the Watergate case. Columnists like Jack Anderson regularly expose the uglier side of government corruption and inefficiency.

Such reporting is highly valued among the media. Pulitzer prizes typically go to reporters who get exclusive stories through painstaking legwork.

Presenting the News

Once the news has been "found," it has to be neatly compressed into a 30-second news segment or fit in among the advertisements in a newspaper. If you had to pick a single word to describe news coverage by the print and broadcast media, it would be *superficial*. "The name of the game," says former White House press secretary Jody Powell, "is skimming off the cream, seizing on the most interesting, controversial, and unusual aspects of an issue."[19] TV news, in particular, is little more than a headline service. Except for the little-watched but highly regarded "MacNeil-Lehrer Newshour" on PBS and ABC's late-night "Nightline," analysis of news events rarely lasts more than a minute. Patterson's careful study of campaign coverage (see Chapter 7) found only skimpy attention given to the issues during a presidential campaign. Clearly, if coverage of political events during the height of an election campaign is thin, coverage of day-to-day policy questions is even thinner. Issues such as nuclear power, money supply, and pollution control are complex, and complex issues are difficult to treat in a short news clip.

Strangely enough, as technology has enabled the media to pass along information with greater speed, news coverage has become less complete.[20] Newspapers once routinely reprinted the entire text of important political speeches; now the *New York Times* is virtually the only paper that does this—and even they have cut back sharply on this practice. In place of speeches, Americans now hear **sound bites** of 15 seconds or less on TV. As you can see in Figure 9.2, the average length of time that a presidential candidate has been given to talk uninterrupted on the TV news steadily declined from 1968 to 1988. Responding to criticism of sound-bite journalism, in 1992 CBS News briefly vowed it would let a candidate speak for at least 30 seconds at a time. However, CBS found this to be unworkable, and soon dropped the threshold to 20 seconds, and said that even this was flexible.[21]

Even successful politicians often feel frustrated by this process. A year after his 1976 election victory Jimmy Carter told a reporter that

> it's a strange thing that you can go through your campaign for president, and you have a basic theme that you express in a 15- or 20-minute standard speech, . . . but the traveling press—sometimes exceeding 100 people—will never report that speech to the public. The peripheral aspects become the headlines, but the basic essence of what you stand for and what you hope to accomplish is never reported.[22]

Rather than presenting their audience with the whole chicken, the media typically gives just a McNugget. Why then should politicians work to build a carefully crafted case for their point of view when a catchy line will do just as well? Indeed, one major reason that CBS's 1992 plan to provide longer sound

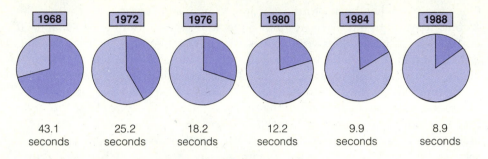

FIGURE 9.2 — *The Incredible Shrinking Sound Bite*

Following is the average length of time a presidential candidate was shown speaking uninterrupted on the evening network news from 1968 to 1988:

1968	1972	1976	1980	1984	1988
43.1 seconds	25.2 seconds	18.2 seconds	12.2 seconds	9.9 seconds	8.9 seconds

SOURCE: Daniel Hallin, "Sound Bite News: Television Coverage of Elections," *Journal of Communications*, Spring 1992.

bites failed was that the candidates rarely said anything that lent itself to lengthy coverage.

Bias in the News

Many people believe that the news is biased in favor of one point of view. During the 1992 presidential campaign, George Bush often charged that the press was against him. "Annoy the Media—Reelect Bush" became one of his favorite lines. The charge that the media have a liberal bias has become a familiar one in American politics, and there is some limited evidence to support it. A lengthy study by the *Los Angeles Times* in the mid-1980s found that reporters were twice as likely to call themselves liberal as the general public.[23] And a 1992 survey of 1400 journalists found that 44 percent identified themselves as Democrats, compared to just 16 percent who said they were Republicans.[24]

However, there is little reason to believe that journalists' personal attitudes sway their reporting of the news. The vast majority of social science studies have found that reporting is not systematically biased toward a particular ideology or party.[25] Most stories are presented in a "point/counterpoint" format in which two opposing views (such as liberal and conservative) are presented, and the audience is left to draw its own conclusions. A number of factors help to explain why the news is typically characterized by political neutrality. Most reporters strongly believe in journalistic objectivity, and those who practice it best are usually rewarded by their editors. In addition, media outlets have a direct financial stake in attracting viewers and subscribers and do not want to lose their audience by appearing biased—especially when there are multiple

versions of the same story readily available. It seems paradoxical to say that competition produces uniformity, but this often happens in the news business.

However, to conclude that the news contains little explicit partisan or ideological bias is not to argue that it does not distort reality in its coverage. Ideally the news should mirror reality; in practice there are far too many possible stories for this to be the case. Journalists must select which stories to cover and to what degree. Because news reporting is a business, the overriding bias is toward stories which will draw the largest audience. Surveys show that people are most fascinated by stories with conflict, violence, disaster, or scandal (see Table 9.1). Good news is unexciting; bad news has the drama that brings in big audiences.

Television is particularly biased toward stories that generate good pictures. Seeing a **talking head** (a shot of a person's face talking directly to the camera) is boring; viewers will switch channels in search of more interesting visual stimulation. For example, during the nine-minute heated interview of George Bush by Dan Rather in 1987, CBS's ratings actually went down as people tired of watching two talking heads argue for an extended period of time.[26] A shot of ambassadors squaring off in a fistfight at the United Nations, on the other hand, will up the ratings. Such a scene was shown three times in one day on CBS in 1973. Not once, though, was the cause of the fight discussed.[27] Network practices like these have led observers such as Lance Bennett to write that "the public is exposed to a world driven into chaos by seemingly arbitrary and mysterious forces."[28]

TABLE 9.1 — Stories Citizens Have Tuned In and Out

Since 1986, the monthly survey of the Times-Mirror Center for the People and the Press has asked Americans how closely they have followed major news stories. As one would expect, stories involving disaster or human drama have drawn more attention than complicated issues of public policy. A representative selection of their findings is presented below. The percentage in each case is the proportion who reported the story "very closely."

The explosion of the space shuttle *Challenger*	80%
San Francisco earthquake	73%
Los Angeles riots	70%
Rescue of baby Jessica McClure from a well	69%
Iraq's invasion of Kuwait	66%
Hurricane Andrew	66%
Oil spill in Alaska	52%
Supreme Court decision on flag burning	51%
Opening of the Berlin Wall	50%
Murder of Lt. Col. Higgins in Lebanon	49%
Introduction of President Clinton's economic program	49%
Arrest of O. J. Simpson	48%
Nuclear accident at Chernobyl	46%
Attack on Nancy Kerrigan	45%
Iran-Contra hearings	33%
Passage of the 1994 Crime Bill	30%
Congressional Debate over NAFTA	21%
Congressional repeal of catastrophic health insurance	19%
Nomination of Robert Bork to the Supreme Court	17%
Education summit held by Bush and the nation's governors	15%
1991 Civil Rights Bill debate	11%

SOURCE: "Public Interest and Awareness of the News" (Report issued by the Times-Mirror Center for the People and the Press, September 1994).

THE NEWS AND PUBLIC OPINION

How does the threatening, hostile, and corrupt world often depicted by the news media shape what people believe about the American political system? For many years students of the subject tended to doubt that the media had more than a marginal effect on public opinion. The "minimal effects hypothesis" stemmed from the fact that early scholars were looking for direct impacts—for example, whether the media affected how people voted.[29] When the focus turned to how the media affect **what Americans think about**, more positive results were uncovered. In a series of controlled laboratory experiments, Shanto Iyengar and Donald Kinder subtly manipulated the stories participants saw on TV news.[30] They found they could significantly affect the

Conservative Republicans often criticize the media for being biased against them. Studies have indeed shown that TV and newspaper reporters are more likely to be liberals than conservatives. However, there is little evidence that the personal views of reporters influence their coverage.

importance people attached to a given problem by splicing a few stories about it into the news over the course of a week. Iyengar and Kinder do not maintain that the networks can make something out of nothing or conceal problems that actually exist. They conclude that "what television news does, instead, is alter the priorities Americans attach to a circumscribed set of problems, all of which are plausible contenders for public concern."[31] This effect has far-reaching consequences. By increasing public attention to specific problems, television news can influence the criteria by which the public evaluates political leaders. When unemployment goes up but inflation goes down, does public support for the president increase or decrease? The answer could depend in large part on which story is emphasized in the media.

In another study, Page, Shapiro, and Dempsey examined changes in public attitudes about issues over time. They examined public opinion polls on the same issues at two points in time, carefully coding the news coverage of these issues on the networks and in print during the interim. People's opinions did indeed shift with the tone of the news coverage. Of all the influences on opinion change these researchers examined, the impact of news commentators, such as John Chancellor and David Brinkley, was the strongest. If Page and his colleagues are correct, the news media today are some of the most potent engines of public opinion change in America.[32]

The media's decision to cover—or ignore—certain issues can affect public opinion. Here, Bosnians demonstrate outside the United Nations headquarters in New York to try and draw public attention to the War in the former Yugoslavia and claims of mass killings of Bosnians.

Much remains unknown about the effects of the media and the news on American political behavior. Enough is known, however, to conclude that the media are a key political institution. The media controls much of the technology that in turn controls much of what Americans believe about politics and government. For this reason, it is important to look at the American policy agenda and the media's role in shaping it.

THE POLICY AGENDA AND THE SPECIAL ROLE OF THE MEDIA

When someone asks you, "What's your agenda?" he or she wants to know something about your priorities. As discussed in Chapter 1, governments also have agendas. John Kingdon defines **policy agenda** as "the list of subjects or problems to which government officials, and people outside of government closely associated with those officials, are paying some serious attention at any given time."[33] Interest groups, political parties, individual politicians, public relations firms, bureaucratic agencies—and, of course, the president and Congress—are all pushing for their priorities to take precedence over others.

Health care, education, inflation, welfare reform—these and scores of other issues compete for attention from the government.

Political activists depend heavily upon the media to get their ideas placed high on the governmental agenda. Political activists are often called **policy entrepreneurs**—people who invest their political "capital" in an issue (as an economic entrepreneur invests capital into an idea for making money). Kingdon says that policy entrepreneurs can "be in or out of government, in elected or appointed positions, in interest groups or research organizations."[34] Policy entrepreneurs' arsenal of weapons includes press releases, press conferences, and letter writing; buttonholing reporters and columnists; trading on personal contacts; and in cases of desperation, resorting to the dramatic. In addition, people in power can use a **leak**, a carefully placed bit of inside information given to a friendly reporter. Leaks benefit both the leaker and the recipient: leakers win points with the press for sharing "secret" information, and reporters can print or broadcast exclusive information.

Because so much of politics is theater, the staging of political events to attract media attention is a political art form. Dictators, revolutionaries, prime ministers, and presidents alike all play to the cameras. When Henry Kissinger, Nixon's top foreign policy advisor, arranged Nixon's famous trip to China, he was reminded that domestic appearances were as important as foreign policy gains. Meeting with Kissinger and Nixon, White House Chief of Staff Bob Haldeman "saw no sense in making history if television were not there to broadcast it."[35] The three men then had a lengthy discussion regarding how to obtain plentiful, favorable media coverage. Orchestrated minute by minute, Nixon's 1972 trip to China was perhaps the biggest media event of all time. In the end, Nixon's trip to China was presented to the American public as a TV miniseries. Befitting the art form that it was, years later the trip became the subject of a successful opera production.

The media are not always monopolized by political elites; the poor and downtrodden can use it, too. Civil rights groups in the 1960s relied heavily on the media to tell their stories of unjust treatment. Many believe that the introduction of television helped to accelerate the movement by showing Americans—in the North and South alike—just what the situation was.[36] Protest groups have learned that if they can stage an interesting event that attracts the media's attention, at least their point of view will be heard. Radical activist Saul Alinsky once dramatized the plight of one neighborhood by having its residents collect rats and dump them on the mayor's front lawn. The story was one local reporters could hardly resist.

More important, though, than a few dramatic events is conveying a long-term, positive image via the media. Policy entrepreneurs—individuals or groups, in or out of government—depend on good will and good images. Sometimes it helps to hire a public relations firm, one that specializes in getting a specific message across. Groups, individuals, and even countries have hired public relations firms to improve their image and their ability to peddle their issue positions.

UNDERSTANDING THE MASS MEDIA

The media are so crucial in today's society that they are often referred to as the "fourth branch of government." The media act as a key linkage institution between the people and the policymakers, having a profound impact on the political policy agenda. Bernard Cohen goes so far as to state that "no major act of the American Congress, no foreign adventure, no act of diplomacy, no great social reform can succeed unless the press prepares the public mind."[37]   If Cohen is right, the growth in the scope of government in America would have been impossible without the need for it being established through the media. The following sections will consider the extent to which the media have paved the way for a more active government, and will also look at how the media have helped, as well as hindered, democracy.

The Media and the Scope of Government

The watchdog function of the media helps to constrict politicians. Many observers feel that the press is biased against whoever holds office at the moment and that reporters want to expose officeholders in the media. Reporters, they argue, hold disparaging views of most public officials, believing that they are self-serving, hypocritical, lacking in integrity, and preoccupied with reelection. Thus, it is not surprising that journalists see a need to debunk public officials and their policy proposals. With every new proposal being met with such skepticism, regular constraints are placed on the scope of what government can do. The watchdog orientation of the press can be characterized as neither liberal nor conservative, but reformist. Reporters often see their job as crusading against foul play and unfairness in government and society. It is when they focus on injustice in society that they inevitably encourage enlarging the scope of government. Once the media identifies a problem in society—such as poverty, inadequate medical care for the aged, or poor education for certain children—reporters usually begin to ask what the government is doing about the problem. Could it be acting more effectively to solve the problem? What do people in the White House and the Congress have to say about it? In this way, the media portrays government as responsible for handling almost every major problem. Though skeptical of what politicians say and do, the media report on America's social problems in a manner that encourages government to take on more and more tasks.

Democracy and the Mass Media

As Ronald Berkman and Laura Kitch remark, "Information is the fuel of democracy."[38]   Widespread access to information could be the greatest boon to democracy since the secret ballot, yet most observers think it has fallen far short of this potential. Noting the vast increase in information available through the news media, Berkman and Kitch state that "if the sheer quantity of news produced greater competency in the citizenry, then we would have a society of political masters. Yet, just the opposite is happening."[39] The rise of the "information society" has not brought about the rise of the "informed society." For one thing, thorny issues like the economy, nuclear power, and biotechnology are not well covered in the media. The media does a much better job of covering the "horse race" aspects of politics than they do covering substantive issues.

Whenever the media are criticized for being superficial, its defense is to say that this is what people want. Network executives remark that if people suddenly started to watch shows such as the "MacNeil-Lehrer Newshour," then they would gladly imitate them. If the American people want serious coverage of the issues, they will be happy to give it to them. Network executives claim that they are in business to make a profit, and to do so they have to appeal to the maximum number of people. It is not their fault if the resulting news coverage is superficial, they argue; blame capitalism, or blame the people—most of whom like news to be more entertaining than educational. Thus, if people are not more informed in the high-tech age, it is largely because they do not care to hear about complex political issues. In this sense one can say that the people really do rule through the media.

SUMMARY

Plenty of evidence points to the power of the media in American politics. The media are ubiquitous. There is evidence that the news and its presentation are an important—perhaps the most important—shaper of public opinion on political issues. The media are an important ingredient in shaping the policy agenda, and political entrepreneurs carefully use the media for this purpose.

The media can be categorized as the print and the broadcast media. Gradually, the broadcast media has replaced the print media as the principal source of news. The media largely define "news" as people and events out of the ordinary. Due to economic pressures, the media are biased in favor of stories with high drama that will attract people's interest, instead of extended analyses of complex issues. With the media's superficial treatment of important policy issues, it should be no surprise that the incredible amount of information available to Americans today has not visibly increased their political awareness or participation.

FOR FURTHER READING

Bennett, W. Lance. *News: The Politics of Illusion,* 2nd ed. New York: Longman, 1988. A critical look at how the media distorts our view of the world.

Epstein, Edward J. *News from Nowhere: Television and the News.* New York: Random House, 1973. Although somewhat dated, this account still provides an excellent view of network news.

Graber, Doris A. *Mass Media and American Politics,* 4th ed. Washington, DC: Congressional Quarterly Press, 1993. The standard textbook on the subject.

Halberstam, David. *The Powers That Be.* New York: Dell Books, 1979. A massive inquiry into the origins and influence of the *Washington Post*, *Los Angeles Times*, CBS, and *Time.*

Hertsgaard, Mark. *On Bended Knee: The Press and the Reagan Presidency.* New York: Farrar, Straus & Giroux, 1988. An in-depth look at how the press treated Reagan, and vice versa.

Iyengar, Shanto, and Donald R. Kinder. *News That Matters.* Chicago: University of Chicago Press, 1987. Two political psychologists show how the media can affect the public agenda.

Jamieson, Kathleen Hall. *Eloquence in an Electronic Age.* New York: Oxford University Press, 1988. A noted communications scholar takes a look at how television has altered political discourse.

Kingdon, John W. *Agendas, Alternatives, and Public Policy.* Boston: Little, Brown, 1984. The best overall study of the formation of the policy agenda.

Patterson, Thomas E. *Out of Order.* New York: Knopf, 1993. A highly critical and well-documented examination of how the media covers election campaigns.

West, Darrell M. *Air Wars: Television Advertising in Election Campaigns, 1952–1992.* Washington, DC: Congressional Quarterly Press, 1993. An analysis of how TV campaign ads have changed over the last four decades and what impact they have had on elections.

NOTES

1. Michael Kelly, "Those Chicken Georges and What They Mean," *New York Times*, September 30, 1992, A11.
2. See Darrell M. West, *Air Wars: Television Advertising in Election Campaigns, 1952–1992* (Washington, DC: Congressional Quarterly Press, 1993), 46–52.
3. December 1, 1969 memo from Nixon to H. R. Haldeman in Bruce Oudes, ed., *From: The President—Richard Nixon's Secret Files* (New York: Harper & Row, 1988), 76–77.
4. Mark Hertsgaard, *On Bended Knee: The Press and the Reagan Presidency* (New York: Farrar, Straus & Giroux, 1988), 34.
5. Elinor Fuchs, "Theatricalization of American Politics," *American Theatre*, January 1987, 18.
6. Quoted in David Brinkley, *Washington Goes to War* (New York: Knopf, 1988), 171.
7. David Halberstam, *The Powers That Be* (New York: Dell Books, 1979), 15–16.
8. Theodore H. White, *The Making of the President, 1972* (New York: Atheneum, 1973), 250.
9. Sam Donaldson, *Hold On, Mr. President!* (New York: Random House, 1987), 54.
10. Ibid., 20.
11. See Thomas E. Patterson, *Out of Order* (New York: Knopf, 1993).
12. William Manchester, *The Last Lion: Winston Churchill, Visions of Glory, 1874–1932* (Boston: Little, Brown, 1984), 225.
13. Doris A. Graber, *Mass Media and American Politics*, 4th ed. (Washington, DC: Congressional Quarterly Press, 1993), 44.
14. Russell Baker, *The Good Times* (New York: William Morrow, 1989), 326.

15. Maureen Dowd, "Where Bush Turns for the Latest," *New York Times*, August 11, 1989, A11.

16. Edward J. Epstein, *News from Nowhere: Television and the News* (New York: Random House, 1973). Many of this text's observations on TV news come from Epstein.

17. Steven Ansolabehere, Roy Behr, and Shanto Iyengar, *The Media Game: American Politics in the Television Age* (New York: Macmillan, 1993), 53.

18. This letter can be found in Hedrik Smith, ed., *The Media and the Gulf War: The Press and Democracy in Wartime* (Washington, DC: Seven Locks Press, 1992), 378–380. Smith's book contains an excellent set of readings concerning media coverage of the war.

19. Jody Powell, "White House Flackery," in Peter Woll, ed., *Debating American Government*, 2nd ed. (Glenview, IL: Scott, Foresman, 1988), 180.

20. This point is well-argued in Kathleen Hall Jamieson, *Eloquence in an Electronic Age* (New York: Oxford University Press, 1988).

21. "Food for Thought on Sound Bites," *New York Times*, September 15, 1992, A10.

22. Quoted in Austin Ranney, *Channels of Power* (New York: Basic Books, 1983), 116.

23. William Schneider and I. A. Lewis, "Views on the News," *Public Opinion* 8 (August-September 1985), 6–11.

24. William Glaberson, "More Reporters Leaning Democratic, Study Says," *New York Times*, November 18, 1992, A13.

25. See Michael J. Robinson and Margaret A. Sheehan, *Over the Wire and On TV: CBS and UPI in Campaign '80* (New York: Russell Sage Foundation, 1983); and C. Richard Hofstetter, *Bias in the News: Network Television Coverage of the 1972 Election Campaign* (Columbus, OH: Ohio State University Press, 1976).

26. Michael J. Robinson and Margaret Petrella, "Who Won the George Bush-Dan Rather Debate?" *Public Opinion* 10 (March-April 1988): 43.

27. Michael J. Robinson, "Public Affairs Television and the Growth of Political Malaise: The Case of 'The Selling of the Pentagon'," *American Political Science Review* 70 (June 1976): 409–432.

28. W. Lance Bennett, *News: The Politics of Illusion*, 2nd ed. (New York: Longman, 1988), 46.

29. See Paul F. Lazarsfeld et al., *The People's Choice* (New York: Columbia University Press, 1944).

30. Shanto Iyengar and Donald R. Kinder, *News That Matters* (Chicago: University of Chicago Press, 1987).

31. Ibid., 118–119.

32. See their report in "What Moves Public Opinion?" *American Political Science Review* 81 (March 1987): 23–44.

33. John W. Kingdon, *Agendas, Alternatives, and Public Policies* (Boston: Little, Brown, 1984), 3.

34. Ibid., 129.

35. Henry A. Kissinger, *White House Years* (Boston: Little, Brown, 1979), 757.

36. See the interview with Richard Valeriani in Juan Williams, *Eyes on the Prize* (New York: Viking, 1987), 270–271.

37. Bernard Cohen, *The Press and Foreign Policy* (Princeton, NJ: Princeton University Press, 1963), 13.

38. Ronald W. Berkman and Laura W. Kitch, *Politics in the Media Age* (New York: McGraw-Hill, 1986), 311.

39. Ibid., 313.

The framers of the Constitution conceived of Congress as the center of policy-making in America. The great disputes over public policy were to be resolved there—not in the White House or the Supreme Court. Although the prominence of Congress has ebbed and flowed over the course of American history, in recent years Congress has been the true center of power in Washington.

Congress's tasks become more difficult each year. The rush of legislation through the congressional labyrinth has never been more complicated. On any day a representative or senator can be required to make a sensible judgment about nuclear missiles, nuclear waste dumps, abortion, trade competition with Japan, the enormous federal deficit, the soaring costs of Social Security and Medicare, and countless other issues. The following sections will introduce you to the people who make these decisions.

THE REPRESENTATIVES AND SENATORS

Being a member of Congress is a difficult and unusual job. A person must be willing to spend considerable time, trouble, and money to obtain a crowded office on Capitol Hill.

The Job

Hard work is perhaps the most prominent characteristic of a congressperson's job. Representatives and senators deeply resent popular beliefs that they are overpaid, underworked, corrupt, and ineffective. Members have even commissioned their own time-and-motion studies of their efficiency to demonstrate that they do work hard (see Table 10.1). For example, the typical representative is a member of about six committees and subcommittees; a senator is

As woman have become more active in politics, they have begun to assume more leadership roles. Here, Diane Feinstein and Barbara Boxer celebrate their 1992 victories in the U.S. Senate races in California, marking the first time a state has been represented in the Senate by two female senators.

a member of about ten. Contrary to the laws of physics, members are often scheduled to be in two places at the same time.

There are attractions to the job, however. First and foremost is power. Members of Congress make key decisions about important matters of public policy. In addition, the salary and the perks that go with it make the job tolerable. Members of Congress receive a salary of $134,000; free office space in Washington and in their constituency, usually cramped with staffers who practically sit on top of one another; a substantial congressional staff who serve individual members, committees, and party leaders; handsome travel allowances to visit their constituents each year, plus opportunities to travel at low fares or even free to foreign nations on congressional inquiries (what critics call "junkets"); virtually unlimited franking privileges—the free use of the mail system to communicate with constituents; generous retirement benefits; and plenty of small privileges such as free flowers from the National Botanical

TABLE 10.1 — A Representative's "Average Day"

Activity	Average Time
In the House chamber	TOTAL 2:53 HOURS
In committee/subcommittee work	
Hearings	26 minutes
Business	9 minutes
Markups	42 minutes
Other	7 minutes
	TOTAL 1:24 HOURS
In his or her office	
With constituents	17 minutes
With organized groups	9 minutes
With others	20 minutes
With staff aides	53 minutes
With other representatives	5 minutes
Answering mail	46 minutes
Preparing legislation, speeches	12 minutes
Reading	11 minutes
On the telephone	26 minutes
	TOTAL 3:19 HOURS
In other Washington locations	
With constituents at the Capitol	9 minutes
At events	33 minutes
With leadership	3 minutes
With other representatives	11 minutes
With informal groups	8 minutes
In party meetings	5 minutes
Personal time	28 minutes
Other	25 minutes
	TOTAL 2:02 HOURS
Other	TOTAL 1:40 HOURS
TOTAL AVERAGE REPRESENTATIVE'S DAY	11:18 HOURS

SOURCE: U.S. House of Representatives, Commission on Administrative Review, *Administrative Reorganization and Legislative Management* (95th Congress, 1st session, 1977, H. Doc. 95–232): 18–19.

Gardens, research services from the Library of Congress, and exercise rooms and pools.

The People

There are 535 members of Congress. An even hundred, two from each state, are members of the Senate. The other 435 are members of the House of Representatives. The Constitution specifies only that members of the House must be at least 25 years old and must have been American citizens for seven years; senators must be at least 30 years old and have been American citizens for nine years. In addition, all members of Congress must be residents of the states from which they are elected.

Members of Congress are not typical or average Americans, however. They come mostly from occupations with high status and usually have substantial incomes. If one looks at a collective portrait of the Congress, as in Table 10.2, one quickly discovers what an atypical collection of Americans it is. Law is the dominant occupation, with other elite occupations—business and academia—also well represented.

Nine percent (or 38 voting members) of the House are African American (compared with about 12 percent of the total population), and almost all of these representatives have been elected from overwhelmingly black constituencies. No state is predominantly black, and there is only one African American in the Senate. There are seventeen Hispanics in the House. In terms of numbers, though, women are the most underrepresented group; half the population is female, but only eight senators and forty-eight voting representatives are female (the representative from Washington D.C. does not vote).

How important are the personal characteristics of members of Congress? Because power in Congress is highly decentralized, the backgrounds of representatives and senators could be important if they influence how officials vote on issues. Can a group of predominantly white, upper-middle-class, middle-aged Protestant males adequately represent a much more diverse population? On the other hand, would a group of average citizens be more effective in making major policy decisions?

Obviously, members of Congress cannot claim *descriptive* representation, that is, representing constituents through mirroring their personal, politically relevant characteristics. They may, however, engage in *substantive* representation, representing the interests of groups. For example, members of Congress with a background of wealth and privilege, such as Senator Edward Kennedy, can be champions of the interests of the poor.[1] Moreover, most members of Congress have lived for many years in the constituencies they represent and share the beliefs and attitudes of at least a large proportion of their constituents. If they do not share such perspectives, they may find it difficult to keep their seats. The next sections will examine just how members of Congress obtain their positions in the first place.

TABLE 10.2 — A Portrait of the 104th Congress: Some Statistics

Characteristic	House (435 total)	Senate (100 total)
PARTY		
Democrat	204	47
Republican	230	53
Independent	1	–
SEX		
Men	387	92
Women	48	8
RACE		
Asian	4	2
Black	38	1
Hispanic	17	0
White and other	376	97
AVERAGE AGE	51 years	58 years
RELIGION		
Protestant	278	65
Roman Catholic	125	20
Jewish	24	9
Other and unspecified	8	6
PRIOR OCCUPATION[a]		
Law	170	54
Business and banking	163	24
Education	76	10
Public service/politics	102	12
Agriculture	19	9
Journalism	15	8

[a]Some members specify more than one occupation.
SOURCE: *Congressional Quarterly Weekly Report*, November 12, 1994 (Supplement).

CONGRESSIONAL ELECTIONS

Congressional elections are wearing, expensive,[2] and, as you will see, generally foregone conclusions—yet the role of politician is the most universal one in Congress. Men and women may run for Congress to forge new policy initiatives, but they also run because they are politicians, because they enjoy politics, and because a position in Congress is near the top of their chosen profession. Even if they dislike politics, without reelection they will not be around long enough to shape policy.

Who Wins?

Everyone in Congress is a politician, and politicians continually have their eyes on the next election. The players in the congressional election game are the incumbents and the challengers.

Incumbents are individuals who already hold office. Sometime during each term, the incumbent has to decide whether to run again or to retire voluntarily. Most will decide to run for reelection, enter their party's primary, almost always emerge victorious (four incumbents lost in 1994), and will typically win in the November general election, too. Indeed, the most important fact about congressional elections is this: *Incumbents usually win* (see Figure 10.1).

Not only do at least 90 percent of the incumbents seeking reelection win (89 percent of House incumbents won in 1994—a year of political upheaval), but they tend to win with big electoral margins. In 1994, most of the House in-

'You mean, like, wow, we can actually get rid of, you know, incumbents with this whatcha-ma-callit?!'

FIGURE 10.1 — *The Incumbency Factor in Congressional Elections*

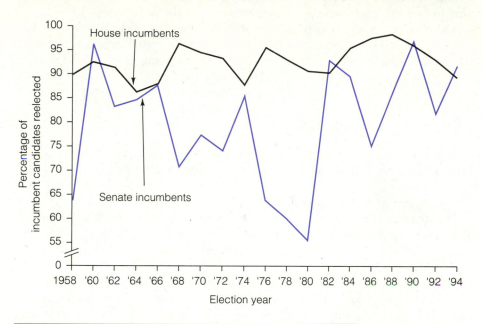

SOURCE: Norman J. Ornstein, Thomas E. Mann, and Michael J. Malbin, *Vital Statistics on Congress, 1993–1994* (Washington DC: American Enterprise Institute, 1994). Data for 1994 compiled by authors. Figures reflect incumbents running in both primary and general elections.

cumbents in contested elections won with at least 60 percent of the vote. Perhaps most astonishing of all is the fact that even when challengers' positions on the issues are closer to the voters' positions, incumbents still tend to win.[3]

The picture for the Senate is a little different. Even though senators still have a better-than-even chance of beating back a challenge, the odds are hardly as handsome as for House incumbents (although there are exceptions—in 1994 only two of twenty-six incumbents seeking reelection lost), and senators typically win by narrower margins (only 38 percent of the incumbent senators seeking reelection in 1994 won with 60 percent or more of the vote).

One reason for the greater competition in the Senate is that an entire state is almost always more diverse than a congressional district and thus provides more of a base for opposition to an incumbent. At the same time, senators have less personal contact with their constituencies, which on average are nearly ten times larger than those of members of the House of Representatives. Senators also receive more coverage in the media than representatives do and are more likely to be held accountable on controversial issues. Moreover, senators tend to draw more visible challengers, such as governors or members of the House, who are already known to voters and who have substantial financial backing—a factor that lessens the advantages of incumbency. Many of these challengers, as one might expect, know that the Senate is a stepping-stone to national prominence and sometimes even the presidency.

Despite their success at reelection, incumbents often feel quite vulnerable. Thus, they have been raising and spending more campaign funds, sending more mail to their constituents, traveling more to their states and districts, and staffing more local offices than ever before.[4] They realize that with the decline of partisan loyalty in the electorate, they bear more of the burden of obtaining votes.

The Advantages of Incumbents

Members of Congress engage in three primary activities that increase the probability of their reelections: advertising, credit claiming, and position taking.[5]

Advertising.   For members of Congress, *advertising* means much more than placing ads in the newspapers and on television. Most congressional advertising takes place between elections in the form of contact with constituents. The goal is *visibility*.

Members of Congress work hard to get themselves known in their constituencies, and they usually succeed. Not surprisingly, members concentrate on staying visible. Trips home are frequent. The average member will make about thirty-five trips back to their home district every year.[6] The franking privilege provides free mailings of self-serving letters and newsletters to constituents.

Credit Claiming.   Congresspersons also engage in *credit claiming*, which involves personal and district service. One member told Richard Fenno about the image he tried to cultivate in his constituency:

> [I have] a very high recognition factor. And of all the things said about me, none of them said, "He's a conservative or a liberal," or "He votes this way on such and such an issue." None of that at all. There were two things said. One, "He works hard." Two, "He works for us." Nothing more than that. So we made it our theme, "O'Connor gets things done"; and we emphasized the dams, the highways, the buildings, the casework.[7]

One thing always wins friends and almost never makes enemies: *servicing the constituency*. There are two ways members of Congress can service their constituencies: through casework and through the pork barrel. **Casework** is helping constituents as individuals—cutting through some bureaucratic red tape to get people what they think they have a right to get. The **pork barrel** is the mighty list of federal projects, grants, and contracts available to cities, businesses, colleges, and institutions. Getting things done for the folks back home often gets an incumbent the chance to serve them again.

As a result of the advantages of incumbency in advertising and credit claiming, incumbents, especially in the House, are usually much better known

Representative Silvio Conte used a pig nose and ears to protest pork barrel spending—until he wanted multimillion dollar federal grants for his Massachusetts district. Because credit claiming is so important to reelection, members of Congress rarely pass up the opportunity to increase federal spending in their state or district.

and have a more favorable public image than their opponents.[8] Shrewd use of the resources available to incumbents may give them an advantage, but congressional elections are not determined solely by casework and pork barrel.[9] Other factors play a role as well.

Position Taking. Members of Congress must also engage in *position taking* on matters of public policy when they vote on issues and when they respond to constituents' questions about where they stand on issues. You have seen that in establishing their public images, members of Congress emphasize their personal qualities as experienced, hardworking, trustworthy representatives who have served their constituencies—an image often devoid of partisan or programmatic content. Nevertheless, all members must take policy stands, and the positions they take may affect the outcome of an election, especially if the issues are salient to voters and the candidates' stands differ from those of a majority of their constituents. This is especially the case in elections for the Senate, in which issues are likely to play a greater role than in House elections.

Weak Opponents.   Another advantage for incumbents is that they are likely to face weak opponents. Faced with the advantages of incumbency, potentially effective opponents are often unlikely to risk challenging members of the House.[10] Those individuals who do run are usually not well known or well qualified and lack experience as well as organizational and financial backing.[11] The lack of adequate campaign funds is a special burden, because challengers need money to become as well known to voters as incumbents are from their advertising and credit claiming.[12]

The Role of Party Identification

At the base of every electoral coalition are the members of the candidate's *party* in the constituency. Although party loyalty at the voting booth is not as strong as it was a generation ago, it is still a good predictor of voting behavior. In the 1994 congressional elections, for example, about 90 percent of the voters who identified with a party voted for House candidates of their party. Most members of Congress represent constituencies in which their party is in the majority.

Defeating Incumbents

In light of the advantages of incumbents, it is reasonable to ask why anyone challenges them at all. Sometimes challengers get some unexpected help: incumbents almost have to beat themselves, and some do. An incumbent tarnished by scandal or corruption becomes instantly vulnerable. Clearly, voters *do* take out their anger at the polls. For example, in 1992 representatives who bounced large numbers of checks at the House bank were much more likely to lose their seats than their more fiscally responsible colleagues. In a close election, negative publicity can turn easy victory into defeat.[13]

Incumbents may also be redistricted out of their familiar turfs. After each federal census, Congress reapportions its membership. States that have gained in population will be given more seats; states that have lost population will lose one or more of their seats. The state legislatures then have to redraw their states' district lines; one incumbent may be moved into another's district, where the two must battle for one seat. A state party majority is more likely to move two of the opposition party's representatives into the same district than two of its own.

Money in Congressional Elections

When an incumbent is not running for reelection and the seat is open, there is a greater likelihood of competition. If the party balance in a constituency is such that either party has a chance of winning, there may be strong candidates running for each side—each with enough money to establish name recognition among the voters. Most of the turnover in the membership of Congress results from vacated seats, particularly in the House.

"Listen, pal! I didn't spend seven million bucks to get here so I could yield the floor to you."

It costs a great deal more money to elect a Congress than to elect a president. In 1992 George Bush, Bill Clinton, and Ross Perot spent about $200 million on their presidential campaigns. The 1992 general election Senate races alone cost that much, and House candidates spent another $300 million. Thus, the cost of congressional elections in the 1991–1992 election cycle—for those who made it to the general election—was more than half a billion dollars! In the 1992 Senate elections, the average winner spent over $3.5 million. In the 1992 House elections, the average winning candidate spent about $550,000.

Aside from the fact that candidates spend enormous sums on campaigns for Congress, it is important to ask where this money comes from and what it buys. Although most of the money spent in congressional elections comes from individuals, a fourth of the funds raised by major party candidates in the general elections for Congress comes from the more than 4,000 Political Action Committees (PACs) (see Chapter 8). Critics of PACs offer plenty of complaints about the present system of campaign finance. Why, they ask, is money spent to pay the campaign costs of a candidate already heavily favored to win? In 1992, incumbents in both houses got $121 million from PACs, challengers received $18 million, and the rest went to candidates for open seats. Even more interesting is that PACs often make contributions *after* the election. The House freshmen elected in 1992, for example, received $1.2 million from PACs in the two months following the election. Much of this money came from groups that had supported the winners' opponents during the election.[14]

What PACs are seeking is *access* to policymakers. Thus, they give most of their money to incumbents, who are likely to win anyway, and when they support someone who loses, they quickly make amends and contribute to the winner. PACs want to keep the lines of communication open and create a receptive atmosphere in which to be heard. Since each PAC is limited to an expenditure of $5,000 per candidate (most give less), a single PAC can at most account for only a small percentage of a winner's total spending. If one PAC does not contribute to a candidate, there are plenty of other PACs from which to seek funds.

Some organized interests circumvent the limitations on contributions, however, and create or contribute to several PACs. This may increase their leverage with those to whom they contribute. In the late 1980s one tycoon, Charles Keating, managed to contribute *$1.3 million* to the campaigns of five senators. These senators then interceded with the Federal Home Loan Bank Board to avoid (for awhile, at least) enforcement of banking regulations on Keating's savings and loan. Many people saw a connection between the campaign contributions and the senators' actions (see "In Focus: Do PACs Buy Votes?").

Aside from the question of money buying influence, what does it buy the candidates who spend it? In 1994 Californian Michael Huffington spent about $30 million—most of it his own money—about three times the expenditures of his rival, Senator Diane Feinstein, and still lost. Oliver North spent about $20 million in the much smaller state of Virginia, and he lost as well. Obviously, spending a lot of money in a campaign is no guarantee of success.

Money is important, however, for challengers. The more they spend, the more votes they receive. Money buys them name recognition and a chance to be heard. Incumbents, by contrast, already have high levels of recognition among their constituents and benefit less from campaign spending; what matters most is how much their opponents spend. Challengers have to raise a lot of money if they hope to succeed in defeating an incumbent, but they usually are substantially outspent by incumbents.[15] In open seats, the candidate who spends the most usually wins.

Stability and Change

As a result of incumbents usually winning reelection, there is some stability in the membership of Congress. This provides the opportunity for representatives and senators to gain some expertise in dealing with complex questions of public policy. At the same time, it also insulates them from the winds of political change. Safe seats make it more difficult for citizens to "send a message to Washington" with their votes. Particularly in the House, it takes a large shift in votes to affect the outcomes of most elections.

IN FOCUS

Do PACs Buy Votes?

The effect of PAC campaign contributions is one of the hottest ethical issues on Capitol Hill today. Critics of PACs, including Common Cause, are convinced that PACs are not trying to elect but to influence. Critics are fond of suggesting links between donations and congressional votes. For example, in November 1983 the 250 House members who voted to retain dairy price supports had recieved $1.7 million—about $6,800 each—from a dairy PAC. Most critics fear the worst; Gregg Easterbrook summarizes his argument this way: "Money can . . . buy individual congressmen's votes on a bill, or distort congressmen's thinking on an issue—normally all an interest group needs to achieve its ends."

Connection is not causation, however. Most senators and representatives are firm in their conviction that their decisions are not affected by PAC contributions. Political scientists are also skeptical of the influence of PACs. There is little systematic evidence that contributions affect outcomes on voting in Congress.

PACs usually contribute to those who already agree with them or to those who are likely to win (or who have already won). In addition, because national organizations are dependent on local units for raising money, Washington lobbyists must be repsonsive to the desires of local contributors. Thus, funds often go to candidates that the lobbyists feel are undeserving, which weakens their bargaining power. Moreover, PACs are not "outside" interests—they usually contribute to or lobby members of Congress from districts or states to which they have geographic ties.

Of course, PACs may influence voting in Congress by reinforcing members in their views and activating some to work on behalf of the interest PACs represent, rather than by converting ("buying") those opposed to the interests' goals. Such influence is less dramatic than conversion, but it can be crucial to legislative success.

President Bush called for banning business, labor, and trade association PACs—the source of most of the millions PACs give congressional candidates. Less concerned about selling their votes than losing their seats, members of Congress did not support the president.

Whatever *your* conclusion about PACs, keep Bo Pilgrim in mind. In July 1989, Lonnie (Bo) Pilgrim, a millionaire chicken farmer with interests in legislation, visited the chamber of the Texas state Senate and handed several senators checks for ten thousands dollars—with a blank for them to fill in their names.

SOURCES: Easterbrook's quote is from his "What's Wrong with Congress?" *Atlantic Monthly*, December 1984, 70. Other information is from John R. Wright, "PACs, Contributions, and Roll Calls," *American Political Science Review* 79 (June 1985): 400–414; Janet M. Grenzke, "PACs and the Congressional Supermarket: The Currency Is Complex," *American Journal of Political Science 33* (February 1989): 1–24, John R. Wright, "PAC Contributions, Lobbying, and Presentation," *Journal of Politics 51* (August 1989): 713–729; Richard L. Holland and Frank W. Wayman, "Buying Time: Moneyed Interests and the Mobilization of Bias in Congressional Committees," *American Political Science Review 84* (September 1990): 797–820; and John R. Wright, "Contributions, Lobbying, and Committee Voting in the U.S. House of Representatives," *American Political Science Review 84* (June 1990): 417–438.

To increase turnover in the membership of Congress, some reformers have proposed *term limitations* for representatives and senators.[16] Most such proposals would restrict members of Congress to six or twelve years in office. Twenty-two states have enacted term limitations for members of Congress, and in the 1994 congressional elections, Republicans promised to vote on a constitutional amendment on term limitations if they won a majority in Congress (which they did).

Opponents question the constitutionality of states setting the terms of national officials. They also object to the loss of experienced legislators and of the American people's ability to vote for whomever they please. In addition, they add, there is plenty of new blood in the legislature: at the beginning of the 104th Congress, one-fourth of the Senate and almost half of the House had less than three years experience in Congress. In the meantime, most people seem comfortable with their *own* representatives and senators and appear content to reelect them again and again.

HOW CONGRESS IS ORGANIZED TO MAKE POLICY

Of all the senators' and representatives' roles, making policy is the toughest. Congress is a collection of generalists trying to make policy on specialized topics. Members are short of time, and of expertise as well. Amateurs in almost every subject, they are surrounded by people who know (or claim to know) more than they do—lobbyists, agency administrators, even their own staffs. Even if they had time to study all the issues thoroughly, making wise national policy would be difficult. If economists disagree about policies to fight unemployment, how are legislators to know which ones may work better than others?

So when ringing bells announce a roll-call vote, representatives or senators rush into the chamber from their offices or from a hearing, often unsure of what is being voted on. Frequently, "uncertain of their position, members of Congress will seek out one or two people who serve on the committee which considered and reported the bill, in whose judgment they have confidence."[17] Congress's constitutional organization gave it just a hint of specialization, when it was split into the House and the Senate. The complexity of today's issues requires much more specialization. Congress tries to cope with these demands through its elaborate committee system, which will be discussed in the following sections.

American Bicameralism

A **bicameral legislature** is a legislature divided into two houses. The U.S. Congress is bicameral, as is every American state legislature except Nebraska's, which has one house (unicameral). As discussed in Chapter 2, the Connecticut Compromise at the Constitutional Convention created a bicameral Congress. Each state is guaranteed two senators, and its number of representatives is determined by the population of the state (California has fifty-two representatives; Alaska, Delaware, Montana, North Dakota, South Dakota, Vermont, and Wyoming have just one each). By creating a bicameral Congress, the Constitution set up yet another check and balance. No bill can be passed unless both House and Senate agree on it; each body can thus veto the policies of the other. Some of the basic differences between the two houses are shown in Table 10.3.

TABLE 10.3 — House versus Senate: Some Key Differences

Characteristic	House of Representatives	Senate
Constitutional powers	Must initiate all revenue bills; must pass all articles of impeachment	Must give "advice and consent" to many presidential nominations; must approve treaties; tries impeached officials
Membership	435 members	100 members
Term of office	2 years	6 years
Centralization of power	More centralized; stronger leadership	Less centralized; weaker leadership
Political prestige	Less prestige	More prestige
Role in policy	More influential on budget; more specialized	More influential on foreign affairs; less specialized
Turnover	Small	Moderate
Role of seniority	More important in determining power	Less important in determining power

The House.   More than four times larger than the Senate, the House is also more institutionalized; that is, more centralized, more hierarchical, and less anarchic.[18] Party loyalty to leadership and party-line voting are more common in the House than in the Senate. Partly because there are more members, leaders in the House do more leading than leaders in the Senate. First-term House members, however, are still more likely to be seen and not heard, and have less power than senior representatives.[19]

Both the House and the Senate set their own agendas. Both use committees, which will be examined shortly, to winnow down the thousands of bills introduced. One institution unique to the House, though, plays a key role in agenda setting: the **House Rules Committee**. This committee reviews most bills coming from a House committee before they go to the full House. Performing a traffic-cop function, the committee gives each bill a "rule," which schedules the bill on the calendar, allots time for debate, and sometimes even specifies what kind of amendments may be offered. The Rules Committee is generally responsive to the House leadership, in part because the Speaker of the House appoints its members.

The Senate.   The Constitution's framers thought the Senate would protect elite interests against the tendencies of the House to protect the masses. Thus to the House they gave the power of initiating all revenue bills and of impeaching officials; to the Senate they gave responsibility for ratifying all treaties, for confirming important presidential nominations (including nominations to the Supreme Court), and for trying impeached officials. Experience has shown that when the same party controls each chamber, the Senate is just as liberal as (some say more liberal than) the House. The real differences between the bodies lie in the Senate's organization and decentralized power.

Smaller than the House, the Senate is also less disciplined and less centralized. Today's senators are more equal in power than representatives are. Even very new senators get top committee assignments; some even become chairs of key subcommittees.

Committees and the party leadership are important in determining the Senate's legislative agenda, just as they are in the House. Party leaders do for Senate scheduling what the Rules Committee does in the House. One institution unique to the Senate is the *filibuster.* In the House, debate can be ended by a simple majority vote. Priding itself on freedom of discussion, the Senate in the past permitted unlimited debate on a bill. But if debate is unlimited, opponents of a bill may try to talk it to death; Strom Thurmond of South Carolina once held forth for a full twenty-four hours. Yielding at times to a fresh voice, filibusterers can tie up the legislative agenda until proponents decide to give up their battle. Filibusters were a favorite device of southern senators to prevent civil rights legislation. In 1959, 1975, and again in 1979, the Senate adopted rules to make it easier to close off debate. Today sixty members present and voting can halt a filibuster by voting for *cloture* on debate.

Congressional Leadership

Leading 100 senators or 435 representatives in Congress, each jealous of his or her own power and responsible to no higher power than the constituency, is no easy task. Chapter 6 discussed the party-in-government. Much of the leadership in Congress is really party leadership. There are a few formal posts, whose occupants are chosen by nonparty procedures, but those who have the real power in the congressional hierarchy are those whose party put them there.

The House. Chief among leadership positions in the House of Representatives is the **Speaker of the House.** This is the only legislative office mandated by the Constitution. In practice, the majority party does the choosing. Typically, the Speaker is a senior member of the party. Newt Gingrich of Georgia was elected Speaker in 1995. The Speaker is also two heartbeats away from the presidency, being second in line (after the vice president) to succeed a president who resigns or dies in office.

The Speaker of the House has some important formal powers. The Speaker

- presides over the House when it is in session.
- plays a major role in making committee assignments, which are coveted by all members to ensure their electoral advantage.

- appoints or plays a key role in appointing the party's legislative leaders and the party leadership staff.
- exercises substantial control over which bills get assigned to which committees.

In addition, the Speaker has a great deal of informal clout inside and outside Congress. When the Speaker's party differs from the president's party, the Speaker is often a national spokesperson for the party. A good Speaker also knows the members well—including their past improprieties, the ambitions they harbor, and the pressures they are under.

Leadership in the House, though, is not a one-person show. The Speaker's principal partisan ally is the **majority leader**—a job that has been the main stepping-stone to the Speaker's role. The majority leader is responsible for scheduling bills in the House. More importantly, the majority leader is responsible for rounding up votes in behalf of the party's position on legislation. Working with the majority leader are the party's **whips**, who carry the word to party troops, counting votes beforehand and leaning on waverers whose votes are crucial to a bill. Party whips also report the views and complaints of the party rank-and-file back to the leadership.

The minority party is also organized, poised to take over the Speakership and other key posts if it should win a majority in the House. The Republicans had been the minority party in the House for forty years before 1995, although they had a president to look to for leadership for much of that period. Now the Democrats are experiencing minority status, led by **minority leader** Richard Gephardt of Missouri.

The Senate.   The Constitution makes the vice president of the United States the president of the Senate; this is the vice president's only constitutional job. But even the mighty Lyndon Johnson, who had been the Senate majority leader before becoming vice president, found himself an outsider when he returned as the Senate's president. Vice presidents usually slight their senatorial chores, except in the rare case when their vote can break a tie (they leave the chore of presiding over the Senate to the *president pro tempore*—the senior member of the majority party). Real power in the Senate is in the hands of the party leaders.

Thus the Senate majority leader—aided by the majority whips—is a party's wheelhorse, corralling votes, scheduling the floor action, and influencing committee assignments. The majority leader has other responsibilities as well. This individual must possess a polished style in public speaking to represent the party to the public, especially on television. This skill is important in today's political climate, because power is no longer in the hands of a few key members of Congress who are insulated from the public. Instead, power is widely dispersed, requiring leaders to appeal broadly for support.

Congressional Leadership in Perspective.   Despite their stature and power, congressional leaders are not in strong positions to move their troops. Both houses of Congress are highly decentralized and rarely show an inclination for major changes in the way they operate. Leaders are elected by their fellow party members and must remain responsive to them. Except in the most egregious cases (which rarely arise), leaders cannot punish those who do not support the party's stand, and no one expects members to vote against their constituents' interests. Senator Robert Dole nicely summed up the leader's situation when he once dubbed himself the "Majority Pleader."

Nevertheless, party leadership, at least in the House, has been more effective in recent years. As the House Democratic contingent has become more homogeneous and more liberal, there has been more policy agreement within the party and thus more party unity in voting on the floor. Increased agreement has made it easier for the Speaker to exercise his prerogatives regarding the assignment of bills and members to committees, the rules by which legislation is brought to the floor, and the use of an expanded whip system, permitting the Democrats to advance an agenda that reflects party preferences.[20] Following the Republican takeover in 1995, Speaker Newt Gingrich began centralizing power and exercising vigorous legislative leadership.

The Committees and Subcommittees

Will Rogers, the famous Oklahoma humorist, once remarked that "outside of traffic, there is nothing that has held this country back as much as committees." Members of the Senate and the House would apparently disagree. Most of the real work of Congress goes on in committees, which dominate congressional policy-making in all its stages.

Committees regularly hold hearings to investigate problems and possible wrongdoings and to oversee the executive branch. Most of all, *they control the congressional agenda and guide legislation* from its introduction to its send-off for the president's signature. Committees can be grouped into four types, of which the first is by far the most important.

1. **Standing committees** are formed to handle bills in different policy areas (see Table 10.4). Each house of Congress has its own standing committees; members do not belong to a committee in the other house. In the 104th Congress, the typical representative served on 2 committees and 4 subcommittees, while the smaller number of senators averaged 3 committees and 7 subcommittees each.

2. **Joint committees** exist in a few policy areas; their membership is drawn from both the Senate and the House.

3. **Conference committees** are formed when the Senate and the House pass a particular bill in different forms. Appointed by the party leadership, a conference committee consists of members of each house chosen to iron out Senate and House differences and report back a compromise bill.

4. **Select committees** are appointed for a specific purpose. The Senate select committee that looked into Watergate is a well-known example.

Most of Congress's work takes place—and most of its members' power is wielded—in the standing committees and their numerous subcommittees. Here a subcommittee of the House committee on Banking, Finance and Urban Affairs holds a hearing on housing policy.

The Committees at Work: Legislation and Oversight.   With more than 11,000 bills submitted by members every two years, some winnowing is essential. Every bill goes to a committee, which then has virtually the power of life and death over it. Usually only bills getting a favorable committee report are considered by the whole House or Senate.

New bills sent to a committee typically go directly to a subcommittee, which can hold hearings on the bill. Sizable committee and subcommittee staffs conduct research, line up witnesses for hearings, and write and rewrite bills. Committees and their subcommittees report on proposed legislation; these reports are typically bound in beige or green covers and are available from the Government Printing Office. A committee's most important output, though, is the "marked up" (rewritten) bill itself, submitted to the full House or Senate for debate and voting.

The work of committees does not stop when the bill leaves the committee room. Members of the committee will usually serve as "floor managers" of the bill, helping party leaders hustle votes for it. They will also be the cue-givers to whom other members turn for advice. When the Senate and House pass different versions of the same bill, some committee members will be on the conference committee.

TABLE 10.4 — Standing Committees in the Senate and in the House

Senate Committees	House Committees
Agriculture, Nutrition, and Forestry	Agriculture
Appropriations	Appropriations
Armed Services	Banking and Financial Services
Banking, Housing, and Urban Affairs	Budget
Budget	Commerce
Commerce, Science, and Transportation	Economic and Educational Opportunities
Energy and Natural Resources	Government Reform and Oversight
Environment and Public Works	House Oversight
Finance	International Relations
Foreign Relations	Judiciary
Governmental Affairs	National Security
Judiciary	Natural Resources
Labor and Human Resources	Rules
Rules and Administration	Science
Small Business	Small Business
Veterans' Affairs	Standards of Official Conduct
	Technology and Competitiveness
	Transportation and Infrastructure
	Veterans' Affairs
	Ways and Means

The committees and subcommittees do not leave the scene even after legislation is passed. They stay busy in legislative **oversight**—the process of monitoring the bureaucracy and its administration of policy. Oversight is handled mainly through hearings. When an agency wants a bigger budget, the use of its present budget is reviewed. Even if no budgetary issues are involved, members of committees constantly monitor how a law is being implemented. Agency heads and even cabinet secretaries testify, bringing graphs, charts, and data on the progress they have made and the problems they face. Committee staffs and committee members grill agency heads about particular problems. For example, a member may ask a Small Business Administration official why constituents who are applying for loans get a runaround. On another committee, officials charged with listing endangered species may defend the grey wolf against a member of Congress whose sheep-ranching constituents are not fond of wolves. Oversight, one of the checks Congress can exercise on the executive branch, gives Congress the power to pressure agencies and, in the extreme, to cut their budgets in order to secure compliance with congressional wishes, even congressional whims.[21]

Congress keeps tabs on more routine activities of the executive branch through its committee staff members. These members have expertise in the specialized fields of the agencies that their committees oversee and maintain an extensive network of formal and informal contacts with the bureaucracy. Through reading the voluminous reports Congress requires of the executive branch and receiving information from agency sources, complaining citizens, members of Congress and their personal staff, state and local officials, interest groups, and professional organizations—staff members can keep track of the implementation of public policy.[22]

Members of Congress have many competing responsibilities, and there are few political payoffs for carefully watching a government agency if it is implementing policy properly. It is difficult to go to voters and say, "Vote for me. I oversaw the routine handling of road building." Because of this lack of incentives, problems may be overlooked until it is too late to do much about them. A major scandal involving the Department of Housing and Urban Development's administration of housing programs during the Reagan presidency was not uncovered until 1989, after Reagan had left office. Taxpayers could have saved well over $100 billion if Congress had insisted that the agencies regulating the savings and loan industry enforce their regulations more rigorously.

Nevertheless, Congress *did* substantially increase its oversight activities in the 1970s and 1980s. As the size and complexity of the national government grew in the 1960s, and after numerous charges that the executive branch had become too powerful (especially in response to the widespread belief that Presidents Johnson and Nixon had abused their power), Congress responded with more oversight. The tight budgets of recent years have provided additional incentives for oversight as members of Congress have sought to protect programs they favor from budget cuts and to get more value for the tax dollars spent on them. As the publicity value of receiving credit for controlling governmental spending has increased, so has the number of representatives and senators interested in oversight.[23]

Getting on a Committee.   Every committee includes members from both parties, but a majority of each committee's members as well as its chair come from the majority party. Party leaders almost always play a key role in picking committee members. Members seek committees that will help them achieve three goals: reelection, influence in Congress, and the opportunity to make policy in areas they think are important.[24]   The parties try to grant member's requests for committee assignments whenever possible. They want their members to please their constituents (being on the right committee should help them play their role of constituency representative more effectively) and develop expertise in an area of policy. The parties also try to apportion among the state delegations the influence that comes with committee membership, in order to accord representation to diverse components of the party.[25]

Getting Ahead on the Committee: Chairs and the Seniority System.   If committees are the most important influencers of the congressional agenda, **committee chairs** are the most important influencers of the committee agenda.

They play dominant—though no longer monopolistic—roles in scheduling hearings, hiring staff, appointing subcommittees, and managing committee bills when they are brought before the full House.

Until the 1970s, there was a simple rule for picking committee chairs—the **seniority system.** If committee members had served on their committee longest and their party controlled the chamber, they got to be chairs—whatever their party loyalty, mental state, or competence.

This system gave a decisive edge to members from "safe" districts. They were least likely to be challenged for reelection and most likely to achieve seniority. In the Democratic party, most safe districts were in the South; as a result, southern politicians exercised power beyond their numbers. But in the 1970s, Congress faced a revolt of its younger members. Both parties in both branches permitted members to vote on committee chairs; in 1975 the House Democrats dumped four chairs with 154 years of seniority among them.

Today seniority remains the *general rule* for selecting chairs, but there are exceptions. For example, ailing Jamie Whitten of Mississippi was stripped of his Appropriations Committee gavel in 1992. When his successor, William Natcher of Kentucky, died in 1994, David Obey of Wisconsin became chair, although he was not the most senior Democrat on the committee. The Republicans skipped over several senior representatives when they gained the House committee chairs in 1995. These and other reforms have somewhat reduced the clout of the chairs.

The Mushrooming Caucuses: The Informal Organization of Congress

Although the formal organization of Congress consists of its party leadership and its committee structures, equally important is the informal organization of the House and Senate. The informal networks of trust and mutual interest can spring from numerous sources. Friendship, ideology, and geography are long-standing sources of informal organization.

Lately these traditional informal groupings have been dominated by a growing number of caucuses. A **caucus** is a grouping of members of Congress who share some interest or characteristic. In the 104th Congress there are more than 140 of these caucuses, most of them containing members from both parties and some from both the House and the Senate. The goal of all caucuses is to promote the interests around which they are formed. Within Congress, caucuses press for committees to hold hearings, they push particular legislation, and they pull together votes on bills they favor. They are rather like interest groups, but with a difference: their members are members of Congress, not petitioners to Congress on the outside looking in. Thus caucuses—interest groups within Congress—are nicely situated to pack more punch than interest groups outside Congress.

Some, such as the Black Caucus, the Congresswomen's Caucus, and the Hispanic Caucus, are based on characteristics of the members. Others, such as the Sunbelt Caucus and the Northeast-Midwest Congressional Coalition, are

The proliferation of congressional caucuses gives members of Congress an informal, yet powerful, means of shaping the policy agenda. Composed of legislative insiders who share similar concerns, the caucuses—like the Hispanic Caucus pictured here— exert a much greater influence on policy-making than most citizen-based interest groups.

based on regional groupings. Still others, such as the Moderate/Conservative Democrats, are ideological groupings. And still others, such as the Steel, Travel and Tourism, Coal, and Mushroom caucuses, are based on some economic interest important to a set of constituencies.

As with other interest groups, the caucuses must proceed within the legislative process—following a bill from its introduction to its approval. The following sections will discuss this process, which is often termed "labyrinthine," in that getting a bill through Congress is very much like completing a difficult, intricate maze.

THE CONGRESSIONAL PROCESS

Congress's agenda is, of course, a crowded one: about fifty-five hundred bills are introduced annually. A **bill** is a proposed law, drafted in precise, legal language. Anyone—even you or I—can draft a bill. The White House and interest groups are common sources of polished bills. However, only members of the House or the Senate can formally submit a bill for consideration. What happens to a bill as it works its way through the legislative labyrinth is depicted in Figure 10.2. Most bills are quietly killed off early in the process. Some are introduced mostly as a favor to a group or a constituent; others are private bills, granting citizenship to a constituent or paying a settlement to a person whose car was demolished by a Postal Service truck; still other bills may alter the course of the nation.

Basically, Congress is a reactive and cumbersome decision-making body. Rules are piled upon rules and procedures upon procedures.[26288]

FIGURE 10.2 — How a Bill Becomes Law

Many bills travel, in effect, full circle, coming first from the White House as part of the presidential agenda, then returning to the president at the end of the process. In the interim, there are two parallel processes in the Senate and House, starting with committee action. If a committee gives a bill a favorable report, the whole chamber considers it. When it is passed in different versions by the two chambers, a conference committee drafts a single compromise bill.

Bill introduction

HOUSE
The bill is put into the legislative "hopper" by a member and assigned to a committee.

SENATE
The bill is put into the legislative "hopper" by a member and assigned to a committee.

Committee action

The bill is usually referred by a committee to a sub-committee for study, hearings, revisions, and approval.

The bill goes back to the full committee, which may amend or rewrite the bill.

The committee decides whether to send the bill to the House floor, recommending its approval, or to kill it.

The bill is usually referred by a committee to a sub-committee for study, hearings, revisions, and approval.

The bill goes back to the full committee, which may amend or rewrite the bill.

The committee decides whether to send the bill to the Senate floor, recommending its approval, or to kill it.

Floor action

Usually the bill goes to the Rules Committee to grant a rule governing debate. The leadership schedules the bill.

The bill is debated, amendments are offered, and a vote is taken.

The leadership of the Senate schedules the bill.

The bill is debated, amendments are offered, and a vote is taken.

Conference action

If the bill is passed in different versions by the Senate and the House, a conference committee composed of members of each house irons out differences.

The conference committee bill is returned to each house.

Presidential decision

The president signs or vetoes the bill.

Some congressional strategists are masters of the art of the *rider*, an amendment, typically unrelated to the bill itself, intended to be carried along on the back of another bill. Legislators often use riders to pass a bill that does not have enough support to pass on its own. A bill must pass one procedure after another to get through the system.

There are, of course, countless influences on this legislative process. Presidents, parties, constituents, groups, the congressional and committee leadership structure—these influences and more offer members cues for their decision making.

Presidents and Congress: Partners and Protagonists

Presidents are partners with Congress in the legislative process, but all presidents are also Congress's antagonists, struggling with Congress to control legislative outcomes. It seems a wonder that presidents—even with all their power and influence—can push and wheedle anything through the complex congressional process. The president must usually win at least ten times to hope for final passage: (1) in one House subcommittee, (2) in the full House committee, (3) in the House Rules Committee to move to the floor, (4) on the House floor, (5) in one Senate subcommittee, (6) in the full Senate committee, (7) on the Senate floor, (8) in the House-Senate conference committee to work out the differences between the two bills, (9) back to the House floor for final passage, and (10) back to the Senate floor for final passage.

Presidents have their own legislative agenda, based in part on their party's platform and their electoral coalition. Their task is to persuade Congress that their agenda should also be Congress's agenda. Political scientists sometimes call the president the *chief legislator*, a phrase that might have appalled the Constitution writers, with their insistence on separation of powers. Presidents do, however, help create the congressional agenda. They are also their own best lobbyists.

Presidents have many resources with which to influence Congress. (Presidential leadership will be studied in the next chapter.) They may try to influence members directly—calling up wavering members and telling them that the country's future hinges on this one vote, for example—but not often. If presidents picked just one key bill and spent ten minutes on the telephone with each of the 535 members of Congress, they would spend eighty-nine hours chatting with them. Instead, presidents wisely leave most White House lobbying to the congressional liaison office and work mainly through regular meetings with the party's leaders in the House and Senate.

As one scholar puts it, presidential leadership of Congress is *at the margins*.[27] In general, successful presidential leadership of Congress has not been the result of the dominant chief executive of political folklore who reshapes the contours of the political landscape to pave the way for change. Rather than creating the conditions for important shifts in public policy, the effective American leader is the less heroic *facilitator* who works at the margins of coalition building to recognize and exploit opportunities presented by a favorable configuration of political forces.

Presidents are only one of many claimants for the attention of Congress, especially on domestic policy. As the next chapter will show, popular presidents or presidents with a large majority of their party in each house of Congress have a good chance of getting their way. Yet presidents often lose. Ronald Reagan was considered a strong chief executive, and budgeting was one of his principal tools for affecting public policy. Yet the budgets he proposed to Congress were typically pronounced DOA, dead on arrival. Congress truly constitutes an independent branch.

Party, Constituency, and Ideology

Presidents come and go; the parties linger on. Presidents do not determine a congressional member's electoral fortunes; constituents do. Where presidents are less influential, on domestic policies especially, party and constituency are more important.

Party Influence.   On some issues, members of the parties stick together like a marching band. They are most cohesive when Congress is electing its official leaders. A vote for Speaker of the House is a straight party-line vote, with every Democrat on one side and every Republican on the other. On other issues, however, the party coalition may come unglued. Votes on civil rights policies, for example, have shown deep divisions within each party.

Differences between the parties are sharpest on questions of social welfare and economic policy.[28] When voting on labor issues, Democrats traditionally cling together, leaning toward the side of the unions, whereas Republicans almost always vote with business. On social welfare issues—poverty, unemployment aid, help to the cities—Democrats are more generous than Republicans. This split between parties should not be too surprising if you recall the party coalitions described in Chapter 6. Once in office, party members favor their electoral coalitions.

Party leaders in Congress help "whip" their members into line. Their power to do so is limited, of course. They cannot drum a recalcitrant member out of the party. Leaders have plenty of influence, however, including some say about committee posts, the power to boost a member's pet projects, and the subtle but significant influence of information to which a member is not privy.

Recently the parties, especially the Republicans, have been a growing source of money for congressional campaigns. The congressional campaign committees have energized both parties, helping to recruit candidates, running seminars in campaign skills, and conducting polls. Equally important, the congressional campaign committees today have money to hand out to promising candidates. The parties can thus make an impact on the kinds of people who sit in Congress on either side of the aisle.

Constituency versus Ideology. Members of Congress are representatives; their constituents expect them to represent their interests in Washington. In 1714, Anthony Henry, a member of the British Parliament, received a letter from some of his constituents asking him to vote against an excise tax. He is reputed to have replied in part:

> Gentlemen: I have received your letter about the excise, and I am surprised at your insolence in writing to me at all. . . .
> . . . may God's curse light upon you all, and may it make your homes as open and as free to the excise officers as your wives and daughters have always been to me while I have represented your rascally constituency.[29]

Needless to say, notions of representation have changed since Henry's time.

Sometimes representation requires a balancing act, however. If some representatives favor more defense spending, but suspect that their constituents do not, what are they to do? The English politician and philosopher Edmund Burke favored the concept of legislators as *trustees*, using their best judgment to make policy in the interests of the people. Others prefer the concept of representatives as *instructed delegates*, mirroring the preferences of their constituents. Actually, members of Congress are *politicos,* adopting both the trustee and instructed delegate roles as they strive to be both representatives and policymakers.[30] The best way constituents can influence congressional voting is simple: elect a representative or senator who agrees with their views. Congressional candidates tend to take policy positions different from each other's. Moreover, the winners generally vote as they said they would.[31] If voters use their good sense to elect candidates who share their policy positions, then constituents *can* influence congressional policy.

If voters miss their chance and elect someone out of step with their thinking, it may be difficult to influence that person's votes. It is difficult even for well-intentioned legislators to know what people want. Some pay careful attention to their mail, but the mail is a notoriously unreliable indicator of people's thinking; individuals with extreme opinions on an issue are more likely to write than those with moderate views. Some members send questionnaires to constituents, but the answers they receive are unreliable because few people respond. Some try public opinion polling, but it is expensive if professionally done and unreliable if not.

Defeating an incumbent is no easy task. Even legislators whose votes conflict with the views of their constituents tend to be reelected. Most citizens have trouble recalling the names of their congressional representatives, let alone keeping up with their representatives' voting records. According to one expert, "Probably less than a third of all constituents can recognize who their representatives are and what policy positions they have generally taken—and even that third tends not to evaluate incumbents on the basis of policy."[32] A National Election Study found that only 11 percent of the people even claimed to remember a particular vote of their representative. On some controversial issues, however, legislators ignore constituent opinion at great peril. For years, southern members of Congress would not have dared to vote for a civil rights law. Lately representatives and senators have been concerned about the many new "single-issue groups." Such groups care little about a member's overall record; to them, a vote on one issue—gun control, abortion, the ERA, or what-ever—is all that counts. Ready to pounce on one wrong vote and pour money into an opponent's campaign, these new forces in constituency politics make every legislator nervous.

Nevertheless, most issues remain obscure. On such issues legislators can safely ignore constituency opinion. On a typical issue the prime determinant of a congressional member's vote is personal ideology. On issues where ideological divisions are sharp and constituency preferences and knowledge are likely to be weak, such as defense and foreign policy, ideology is virtually the only determinant of voting.[33] As ideological divisions weaken and constituency preferences strengthen, members are more likely to deviate from their own position and adopt those of their constituencies. Thus, when they have differences of opinion with their constituencies, members of Congress consider constituency preferences but are not controlled by them.[34]

Lobbyists and Interest Groups

The nation's capital is crawling with lawyers, lobbyists, registered foreign agents, public relations consultants, and others—more than 14,000 individuals representing nearly 12,000 organizations at last count—all seeking to influence Congress. Forty groups alone are concerned with the single issue of protecting Alaska's environment; the bigger the issue, the more lobbyists are involved in it. Any group interested in influencing national policy-making, and that includes almost everyone, either hires Washington lobbyists or sends it own. Washington lobbyists can be a formidable group.

Lobbyists have a dismal image, one worsened by periodic scandals in which someone seeking to influence Congress presents huge amounts of cash to senators and representatives. No one knows how much lobbyists spend to influence legislation, but it undoubtedly runs into the billions—recall the $1.3 million Charles Keating alone gave to five senators to encourage them to intercede with the Federal Home Loan Bank Board. Such stories give lobbyists a bad name, no doubt often deserved. But lobbyists have a job to do, namely, to represent the interests of their organization. Lobbyists, some of them former members of Congress, can provide legislators with crucial information and often with assurances of financial aid in the next campaign.

Lobbyists do not hold all the high cards in their dealings with Congress; congressional representatives hold some trump cards of their own. The easiest way to frustrate lobbyists is to ignore them. Lobbyists usually make little headway with their opponents anyway: the lobbyist for General Motors arguing against automobile pollution controls would not have much influence with a legislator concerned about air pollution. Members of Congress can

Lobbyists have never been held in high esteem by the public, and they have come under especially harsh criticism in recent years. Nevertheless, lobbyists play an important role in the legislative process. Here, they crowd a Capitol hallway popularly know as "Gucci Gulch," as the House Ways and Means Committee works on a tax bill.

make life uncomfortable for lobbyists, too. They can embarrass them, expose heavy-handed tactics, and spread the word among an organization's members that it is being poorly represented in Washington. Last but not least, Congress *can* regulate lobbyists, although it has never done so very strictly.

There are many forces that affect senators and representatives as they decide how to vote on a bill. After his exhaustive study of influences on congressional decision making, John Kingdon concluded that no single influence was important enough to determine congresspeople's votes.[35] The process is as complex for individual legislators as it is for those who want to influence their votes.

UNDERSTANDING CONGRESS

Congress is a complex institution. Its members want to make sound national policy, but they also want to return to Washington after the next election. How do these sometimes conflicting desires affect American democracy and the scope of American government?

Congress and Democracy

In a large nation, the success of democratic government depends on the quality of representation. In a tiny decision-making body, people can cast their own votes, but Americans could hardly hold a national referendum on every policy issue on the government agenda. Instead, Americans delegate decision-making power to representatives. If Congress is a successful democratic institution, it will have to be a successful representative institution.

Certainly some aspects of Congress make it very *un*representative. Its members are an American elite. Its leadership is chosen by its own members, not by any vote of the American people. Voters have little direct influence over the individuals who chair key committees or lead congressional parties. Voters in just a single constituency control the fate of committee chairs and party leaders; voters in the other 434 House districts and the other 49 states have no real say, for example, about who chairs a committee considering new forms of energy, a committee considering defense buildups, or a committee making economic policy.

Nevertheless, Congress does try to listen to the American people. Who voters elect makes a difference in congressional votes; which party is in power affects policies. Linkage institutions *do* link voters to policymakers. Perhaps Congress could do a better job at representation than it does, but there are many obstacles to improved representation. Legislators find it hard to know what constituents want. Groups may keep important issues off the legislative agenda. Members may spend so much time servicing their constituencies that they have little time left to represent those constituencies in the policy-making process.

Members of Congress are responsive to the people, if the people make it clear what they want. In response to popular demands, Congress established a program in 1988 to shield the elderly against the catastrophic costs associated with acute illness. In 1989, in response to complaints from the elderly about higher Medicare premiums, Congress abolished most of what it had created the previous year.

Reforming Congress

Reformers have tried to promote a more open, democratic Congress. To a large degree, they have succeeded. Looking at Congress in the 1950s, one could say that it was like a stepladder. The members advanced one rung at a time toward the heights of power with each reelection. At the top was real power in Congress. Committee chairs were automatically selected by seniority. Their power on the committee was unquestioned. Bills disappeared forever into chairs' "vest pockets" if they did not like them. They alone created subcommittees, picked their members, and routed bills to them. If committees controlled bills from the cradle to the grave, the chairs were both midwives and undertakers. At the bottom of the ladder, the norm of apprenticeship—"be seen and not heard"—prevailed. The system was democratic—one person, one vote—when the roll call came, but it was not democratic when the bill itself was shaped, shelved, or sunk.

Democratization.   The waves of congressional reform in the 1960s and especially the 1970s changed this political atmosphere. Lyndon Johnson had started the reform ball rolling during his majority leadership with the "Johnson rule," which gave each senator a seat on at least one key committee. This reform allowed junior members more room at the top.

By the 1970s, the reform movement, bent on democratizing Congress, picked up speed.[36] Reformers tried to create more democracy by spreading power around. First to go was the automatic and often autocratic dominance of the most senior members as committee chairs. Instead, chairs were elected by the majority party, and some of the most objectionable chairs were dropped. The chairs' power was also reduced by the proliferation of subcommittees, which widened the distribution of authority, visibility, and resources in both chambers.

Subcommittees became the new centers of power in Congress. First-term senators and representatives came to chair major subcommittees. In the House five separate subcommittees focused on consumer legislation, a dozen on welfare policy, and six on energy. Legislative hurdles became harder to overcome because of the proliferation of subcommittees.

Seniority reform and the subcommittee explosion, as well as the burgeoning caucuses, have fragmented the power of Congress. Richard Fenno, a veteran congressional observer, has remarked that the "performance of Congress as an institution is very largely the performance of its committees" but that the committee system is the "epitome of fragmentation and decentralization."[37] Interest groups grow on committees and subcommittees like barnacles on a boat. After a while, these groups develop intimacy and influence with "their" committee. Committee decisions usually carry the day on the roll-call vote. Thus, the committee system may link congressional policy-making to a multiplicity of interest rather than to a majority's preferences.

Representativeness versus Effectiveness.   The central legislative dilemma for Congress is combining the faithful representation of constituents with the making of effective public policy. Supporters see Congress as a forum in which many interests compete for a spot on the policy agenda and over the form of a particular policy—just as the founders intended it to be.

Critics charge that Congress is responsive to so many interests that policy is as uncoordinated, fragmented, and decentralized as Congress itself. The agricultural committees busily tend to the interests of tobacco farmers, while committees on health and welfare spend millions for lung cancer research. One committee wrestles with domestic unemployment while another makes tax policy that encourages businesses to open new plants outside the country.

In addition, some observers feel Congress is too representative—so much so that it is incapable of taking decisive action to deal with difficult problems.

One reason government cannot balance the budget, they say, is that Congress is protecting the interests of too many people. With each interest trying to preserve the status quo, bold reforms cannot be enacted. On the other hand, defenders of Congress point out that, being decentralized, there is no oligarchy in control to prevent the legislature from taking comprehensive action. In fact, Congress has enacted the huge tax cut of 1981, the comprehensive (and complicated) tax reform of 1986, and various bills structuring the budgetary process designed to balance the budget.[38] There is no simple solution to Congress's dilemma. It tries to be both a representative and an objective policy-making institution. As long as this is true, it is unlikely to please all its critics.

Congress and the Scope of Government

If Congress is responsive to a multitude of interests and those interests desire government policies to aid them in some way, does the nature of Congress predispose it to continually increase the scope of the public sector?

In addition, do the benefits of servicing constituents provide an incentive for members of Congress to tolerate, even to expand, an already big government? The more policies there are, the more potential ways members can help their constituencies. The more bureaucracies there are, the more red tape members can help cut. Big government helps members of Congress get reelected and even gives them good reason to support making it bigger.

Members of Congress vigorously protect the interests of their constituents. At the same time, there are many members who agree with Ronald Reagan that government is not the answer to problems but *is* the problem. They make careers out of fighting against government programs (although these same senators and representatives typically support programs aimed at their constituents).

Americans have contradictory preferences regarding public policy. As discussed in previous chapters, they want to balance the budget and pay low taxes, but they also support most government programs. Congress does not impose programs upon a reluctant public; instead, it responds to the public's demands for them.

SUMMARY

According to the Constitution, members of Congress are the government's policymakers, but legislative policymaker is only one of the roles of a member of Congress. They are also politicians, and politicians always have their eye on the next election. Success in congressional elections may be determined as much by constituency service—casework and the pork barrel—as by policymaking. Senators and representatives have become so skilled at constituency service that incumbents have a big edge over challengers. Not only do incumbents tend to win, but they tend to win by big margins.

The structure of Congress is so complex that it seems remarkable that legislation gets passed at all. Its bicameral division means that bills have two sets of committee hurdles to clear. Recent reforms have decentralized power, and so the job of leading Congress is more difficult than ever.

Presidents try hard to influence Congress, and parties and elections can also shape legislators' choices. The impact of these factors clearly differs from one policy area to another. Party impacts are clearest on issues for which the party's coalitions are clearest—social welfare and economic issues, in particular. Constituencies influence policy mostly by the initial choice of a representative. Members of Congress do pay attention to voters, especially on visible issues, but most issues do not interest voters. On these less visible issues, other factors, such as lobbyists and members' individual ideologies, influence policy decisions.

Congress clearly has some undemocratic and unrepresentative features. Its members are hardly average Americans. Even so, they pay attention to popular preferences, when they can figure out what they are. People inside and outside the institution, however, think that Congress is ineffective. Its objective policy-making decisions and representative functions sometimes conflict, yet from time to time Congress does show that it can deal with major issues in a comprehensive fashion. Many members of Congress have incentives to increase the scope of the federal government, but these incentives are provided by the people who put them in office.

FOR FURTHER READING

Aberbach, Joel D. *Keeping A Watchful Eye.* Washington, DC: Brookings Institution, 1990.
    A thorough study of congressional oversight of the executive branch.
Bernstein, Robert A. *Elections, Representation, and Congressional Voting Behavior.*
    Englewood Cliffs, NJ: Prentice Hall, 1989. Examines the issue of constituency
    control over members of Congress.
Dodd, Lawrence C., and Bruce I. Oppenheimer, eds. *Congress Reconsidered,* 5th ed.
    Washington, DC: Congressional Quarterly Press, 1993. Excellent essays on many
    aspects of Congress.
Fenno, Richard F. Jr., *Home Style.* Boston: Little, Brown, 1978. How members of
    Congress mend fences and stay in political touch with the folks back home.
Fiorina, Morris P. *Congress: Keystone of the Washington Establishment,* 2nd ed. New
    Haven, CT: Yale University Press, 1989. Argues that members of Congress are self-
    serving in serving their constituents, ensuring their reelection but harming the
    national interest.
Jacobson, Gary C. *The Politics of Congressional Elections,* 3rd ed. New York:
    HarperCollins, 1992. An excellent review of congressional elections.
Kingdon, John W. *Congressmen's Voting Decisions,* 3rd ed. Ann Arbor: University of
    Michigan Press, 1989. A thorough and insightful study of voting decisions.
Loomis, Burdett. *The New American Politician.* New York: Basic Books, 1988. Focuses on
    how a new generation of political entrepreneurs has come to dominate Congress.

Mayhew, David R. *Congress: The Electoral Connection.* New Haven, CT: Yale University Press, 1974. An analysis of Congress based on the premise that the principal motivation of congressional behavior is reelection.

Sinclair, Barbara. *Majority Leadership in the U.S. House.* Baltimore: Johns Hopkins University Press, 1983. Examines how leaders go about building coalitions.

Smith, Steven S., and Christopher J. Deering. *Committees in Congress.* Washington, DC: Congressional Quarterly Press, 1984. A thorough overview of the complex committee structure in the House and Senate.

Sorauf, Frank J. *Money in American Elections.* Boston: Little, Brown, 1988. A clear, careful overview of campaign finance.

NOTES

1. On various views of representation, see Hanna Pitkin, *The Concept of Representation* (Berkeley, CA: University of California Press, 1967).
2. An excellent review of the costs of congressional campaigns and the uses to which money is put in them is Edie N. Goldenberg and Michael W. Traugott, *Campaigning for Congress* (Washington, DC: Congressional Quarterly Press, 1984).
3. John L. Sullivan and Eric Uslaner, "Congressional Behavior and Electoral Marginality," *American Journal of Political Science* 22 (August 1978): 536–553.
4. Glen R. Parker, *Homeward Bound* (Pittsburgh: University of Pittsburgh Press, 1986); and John R. Johannes, *To Serve the People* (Lincoln, NE: University of Nebraska Press, 1984).
5. David R. Mayhew, *Congress: The Electoral Connection* (New Haven, CT: Yale University Press, 1974).
6. Richard F. Fenno, Jr., *Home Style* (Boston: Little, Brown, 1978), 32.
7. Ibid., 106–107.
8. Gary C. Jacobson, *The Politics of Congressional Elections*, 3rd ed. (New York: HarperCollins), 114–130.
9. See, for example, Paul Feldman and James Jondrow, "Congressional Elections and Local Federal Spending," *American Journal of Political Science* 28 (February 1984): 147–163; Glenn R. Parker and Suzanne L. Parker, "The Correlates and Effects of Attention to District by U.S. House Members," *Legislative Studies Quarterly* 10 (May 1985): 223–242; and John C. McAdams and John R. Johannes, "Congressmen, Perquisites, and Elections," *Journal of Politics* 50 (May 1988): 412–439.
10. On strategies of challengers, see Gary C. Jacobson and Samuel Kernell, *Strategy and Choice in Congressional Elections*, 2nd ed. (New Haven, CT: Yale University Press, 1983); and Gary C. Jacobson, "Strategic Politicians and the Dynamics of U.S. House Elections, 1946–1986," *American Political Science Review* 83 (September 1989): 773–794.
11. See Gary C. Jacobson, *Money in Congressional Elections* (New Haven, CT: Yale University Press, 1980).
12. On the importance of challenger quality and financing, see Alan I. Abramowitz, "Explaining Senate Election Outcomes," *American Political Science Review* 82 (June 1988): 385–403; Donald Philip Green and Jonathan S. Krasno, "Salvation for the Spendthrift Incumbent," *American Journal of Political Science* 32 (November 1988): 884–907.

13. John G. Peters and Susan Welch, "The Effects of Corruption on Voting Behavior in Congressional Elections," *American Political Science Review* 74 (September 1980): 697–708.

14. Federal Election Commission, 1993.

15. Jacobson, *The Politics of Congressional Elections,* 50–60, 130–132. See also Gary C. Jacobson, "The Effects of Campaign Spending in House Elections: New Evidence for Old Arguments," *American Journal of Political Science* 34 (May 1990): 334–362.

16. On term limits, see Gerald Benjamin and Michael J. Malbin, eds., *Limiting Legislative Terms* (Washington, D.C.: Congressional Quarterly Press, 1992).

17. So says former House Speaker Jim Wright, in *You and Your Congressman* (New York: Putnam, 1976), 190. See also Donald R. Matthews and James Stimson, *Yeas and Nays: Normal Decision-Making in the House of Representatives* (New York: John Wiley, 1975); and John L. Sullivan et al., "The Dimensions of Cue-Taking in the House of Representatives: Variations by Issue Area," *Journal of Politics* 55 (November 1993): 975–997.

18. Nelson W. Polsby et al., "Institutionalization of the House of Representatives," *American Political Science Review* 62 (1968): 144–168.

19. John R. Hibbing, "Contours of the Modern Congressional Career," *American Political Science Review* 85 (June 1991): 405–428.

20. On the increasing importance of party leadership in the House, see David W. Rohde, *Parties and Leaders in the Postreform House* (Chicago: University of Chicago Press, 1991); Barbara Sinclair, "The Emergence of Strong Leadership in the 1980s House of Representatives," *Journal of Politics* 54 (August 1992): 657–684.

21. For more on congressional oversight, see Christopher H. Foreman, Jr., *Signals From the Hill* (New Haven, CT: Yale University Press, 1988).

22. Joel D. Aberbach, *Keeping a Watchful Eye: The Politics of Congressional Oversight* (Washington, DC: Brookings Institution, 1990).

23. Aberbach, *Keeping a Watchful Eye.*

24. Richard F. Fenno, Jr., *Congressmen in Committees* (Boston: Little, Brown, 1973).

25. A good study of committee assignments is Kenneth Shepsle, *The Giant Jigsaw Puzzle* (Chicago: University of Chicago Press, 1978).

26. For a thorough discussion of recent rule changes and the impact of procedures, see Steven S. Smith, *Call to Order: Floor Politics in the House and Senate* (Washington, DC: Brookings Institution, 1989).

27. George C. Edwards III, *At the Margins: Presidential Leadership of Congress* (New Haven, CT: Yale University Press, 1989).

28. Aage Clausen, *How Congressmen Decide: A Policy Focus* (New York: St. Martin's, 1973).

29. Quoted in Peter G. Richards, *Honourable Members* (London: Faber and Faber, 1959), 157.

30. See Roger H. Davidson, *The Role of the Congressman* (New York: Pegasus, 1969); and Thomas E. Cavanaugh, "Role Orientations of House Members: The Process of Representation" (Paper delivered at the annual meeting of the American Political Science Association, Washington, DC, August 1979).

31. John L. Sullivan and Robert E. O'Connor, "Electoral Choice and Popular Control of Public Policy: The Case of the 1966 House Elections," *American Political Science Review* 66 (December 1972): 1256–1268.

32. Robert A. Bernstein, *Elections, Representation, and Congressional Voting Behavior* (Englewood Cliffs, NJ: Prentice Hall, 1989), 99.

33. Larry M. Bartels found that members of Congress were responsive to constituency opinion in supporting the Reagan defense buildup. See "Constituency Opinion and Congressional Policy Making: The Reagan Defense Buildup," *American Political Science Review* 85 (June 1991): 457–474.

34. On the importance of ideology, see Bernstein, *Elections, Representation, and Congressional Voting Behavior.*

35. John W. Kingdon, *Congressmen's Voting Decisions*, 3rd ed. (Ann Arbor: University of Michigan Press, 1989), 242.

36. For more on congressional reform, see Leroy N. Rieselbach, *Congressional Reform* (Washington, DC: Congressional Quarterly Press, 1986).

37. Richard F. Fenno, Jr., "If, as Ralph Nader Says, Congress Is the 'Broken Branch,' How Come We Love Our Congressmen So Much?" in *Congress in Change*, ed. Norman Ornstein (New York: Praeger, 1975), 282.

38. See M. Darrell West, *Congress and Economic Policymaking* (Pittsburgh: University of Pittsburgh Press, 1987).

Powerful, strong, leader of the free world, commander in chief—these are common images of the American president. In this presidency-as-powerhouse myth, presidents are the government's command center. Problems are brought to their desk; they decide the right courses of action, issue orders, and an army of aides and bureaucrats carry out their commands. Nothing could be further from the truth, as presidents themselves soon discover. As one presidential aide put it, "Every time you turn around people resist you."[1]

The main reason presidents have trouble getting things done is that other policymakers with whom they deal have their own agendas, their own interests, and their own sources of power. Congress is beholden not to the president but to the individual constituencies of its members. Cabinet members often push their departmental interests and their constituencies (the Department of Agriculture has farmers as its constituency, the Department of Labor has unions, and so on). Presidents operate in an environment filled with checks and balances and competing centers of power. As Richard Neustadt has argued, presidential power is the power to *persuade*, not to command.[2] Since not everyone bends easily to even the most persuasive president, the president must also be a *leader*. This chapter will examine presidential leadership, but first, you will meet some of the presidents themselves.

THE PRESIDENTS

The presidency is an institution composed of the roles presidents must play, the powers at their disposal, and the large bureaucracy at their command. It is also a highly personal office. The personality of the individual serving as president makes a difference.

Who They Are

When Warren G. Harding, one of the least illustrious American presidents, was in office, Clarence Darrow remarked, "When I was a boy, I was told that anybody could become president. Now I'm beginning to believe it." The Constitution simply states that the president must be a natural-born citizen at least 35 years old and have resided in the United States for at least fourteen years. In fact, all American presidents have been white, male, and, except for John Kennedy, Protestant. In other ways, however, the recent collection of presidents suggests considerable variety. Since World War II, there has been a Missouri haberdasher; a war hero; a Boston Irish politician; a small-town Texas boy who grew up to become the biggest wheeler-dealer in the Senate; a California lawyer described by his enemies as "Tricky Dick" and by his friends as a misunderstood master of national leadership; a former Rose Bowl player who had spent his entire political career in the House; a former governor who had been a Georgia peanut wholesaler; an actor who was also a former governor of California; a former CIA chief and ambassador who was the son of a U.S. senator; and an ambitious young governor from a small state.

In this potpourri of personalities, James David Barber has looked for some patterns in order to understand how presidents perform. He suggests that presidents can be examined by looking at their *presidential character*.[3] Presidents like Lyndon Johnson and Richard Nixon, he argues, are prone to tragedy. When such presidents experience certain kinds of stress, he says, their psychological needs will cause them to persist in failed policies.

Not all presidential scholars agree with Barber's typology of presidential character. Garry Wills describes Barber's analysis as an example of the "games academics play."[4] There are many opinions, but no single answer to the question of what makes a successful president.

How They Got There

No one is born to be the future president of the United States in the way that someone is born to be the future king or queen of England. Regardless of their background or character, all presidents must come to the job through one of two basic routes.

Elections: The Normal Road to the White House.   Most presidents take a familiar journey to 1600 Pennsylvania Avenue: they run for president through the electoral process, which is described in Chapter 7. Once in office, presidents are guaranteed a four-year term by the Constitution, but the **Twenty-second Amendment**, passed in 1951, limits them to two terms.

Only eleven of the forty-one presidents before Bill Clinton have actually served two or more full terms in the White House: Washington, Jefferson, Madison, Monroe, Jackson, Grant, Cleveland (whose terms were not consecutive), Wilson, Franklin Roosevelt, Eisenhower, and Reagan. A few decided against a second term ("Silent Cal" Coolidge said simply, "I do not choose to

Each president has shaped the office in his own image. Lyndon Johnson's presidency was characterized by a willingness to attack a broad range of issues, from communism in Vietnam to poverty in America—and by exhaustion from grappling with so many complex problems.

run"). Four other presidents (Polk, Pierce, Buchanan, and Hayes) also threw in the towel at the end of one full term. Seven others (both of the Adamses, Van Buren, Taft, Hoover, Carter, and Bush) thought the voters owed them a second term but the voters disagreed.

The Vice Presidency: Another Road to the White House.   For more than 10 percent of American history, the presidency has actually been occupied by an individual not elected to the office. About one in five presidents got the job not through the normal road of elections, but because they were vice president when the incumbent president either died or (in Nixon's case) resigned (see Table 11.1). In the twentieth century almost one-third (five of sixteen) of those who occupied the office were "accidental presidents." The most accidental of all was Gerald Ford, who did not run for either the vice presidency or the presidency before taking office. Ford was nominated vice president by President Nixon when Vice President Spiro Agnew resigned; he then assumed the presidency when Nixon himself resigned.

Neither politicians nor political scientists have paid much attention to the vice presidency. Once the choice of a party's "second team" was an afterthought; now it is often an effort to placate some important symbolic

TABLE 11.1 — Incomplete Presidential Terms

President	Term	Succeeded By
William Henry Harrison	March 4, 1841–April 4, 1841	John Tyler
Zachary Taylor	March 5, 1849–July 9, 1850	Millard Fillmore
Abraham Lincoln	March 4, 1865–April 15, 1865[a]	Andrew Johnson
James A. Garfield	March 4, 1881–September 19, 1881	Chester A. Arthur
William McKinley	March 4, 1901–September 14, 1901[a]	Theodore Roosevelt
Warren G. Harding	March 4, 1921–August 2, 1923	Calvin Coolidge
Franklin D. Roosevelt	January 20, 1945–April 12, 1945[b]	Harry S Truman
John F. Kennedy	January 20, 1961–November 22, 1963	Lyndon B. Johnson
Richard M. Nixon	January 20, 1969–August 9, 1974[a]	Gerald R. Ford

[a]Second term.
[b]Fourth term.

constituency. Southerner Jimmy Carter selected a well-known liberal, Walter Mondale, as his running mate, and Ronald Reagan chose his chief rival, George Bush, in part to please Republican moderates

The occupants have rarely enjoyed the job. John Nance Garner of Texas, one of Franklin Roosevelt's vice presidents, said the job was "not worth a warm bucket of spit." Some have performed so poorly as to have been an embarrassment to the president. After Woodrow Wilson's debilitating stroke, almost everyone agreed that Vice President Thomas Marshall—a man who shirked all responsibility, including cabinet meetings—would be a disaster as acting president. Spiro Agnew, Richard Nixon's first vice president, had to resign and was convicted of evading taxes (on bribes he had accepted).

Once in office, vice presidents find that their main job is waiting. Constitutionally, they are assigned the minor task of presiding over the Senate and voting in case of a tie. As George Bush said when he was vice president, "The buck *doesn't* stop here." Recent presidents, though, have taken their vice presidents more seriously, involving them in policy discussions and important diplomacy.[5] Jimmy Carter and Ronald Reagan, both Washington outsiders, chose vice presidents who had substantial Washington experience: Walter Mondale and George Bush. To become intimates of the president, both had to be completely loyal, losing their political independence in the process. Vice President Bush, for example, was accused of knowing more about the Iran-Contra affair than he admitted, but he steadfastly refused to reveal his discussions with President Reagan on the matter. When his turn came to choose a vice president, Bush selected Senator Dan Quayle of Indiana, considered by many a political lightweight. Bill Clinton chose another senator, highly regarded Albert Gore of Tennessee, who has played a prominent role in the administration.

Richard Nixon was the only American president ever to resign his office. Nixon decided to resign rather than face impeachment for his role in the Watergate scandal, a series of illegal wiretaps, break-ins, and cover-ups.

Impeachment and Succession. Getting rid of a discredited president before the end of a term is not easy. The Constitution prescribes the process through **impeachment**, which is roughly the political equivalent of an indictment in criminal law. The House of Representatives may, by majority vote, impeach the president for "Treason, Bribery, or other high Crimes and Misdemeanors." Once the House votes for impeachment, the case goes to the Senate, which tries the accused president, with the chief justice of the Supreme Court presiding. By a two-thirds vote, the Senate may convict and remove the president from office.

Only once has a president been impeached: Andrew Johnson, Lincoln's successor, was impeached by the House in 1868 on charges stemming from his disagreement with radical Republicans. He narrowly escaped conviction. Richard Nixon came as close to impeachment as any president since. On July 31, 1974, the House Judiciary Committee voted to recommend his impeachment to the full House as a result of the **Watergate** scandal. Nixon escaped a certain vote for impeachment by resigning (see "In Focus: Watergate").

Constitutional amendments cover one other important problem concerning the presidential term: presidential disability and succession. Several times a president has become disabled, incapable of carrying out the job for weeks or even months at a time. After Woodrow Wilson suffered a stroke, his wife became virtual acting president. The **Twenty-fifth Amendment** (1967) clarified

IN FOCUS

Watergate

If a novelist had invented Watergate, it would have made a fascinating but not very believable story. As reality, it forced the resignation of Richard M. Nixon, the president who was elected by what was then the largest popular majority in American history.

Dozens of events and decisions produced the Watergate affair. Many centered on Nixon's 1972 reelection campaign. His campaign manager, former Attorney General John Mitchell, hired a man named G. Gordon Liddy as counsel to the Committee to Reelect the President (CREEP). Liddy did little lawyering at CREEP, but he did develop an expensive "counterintelligence" program.

On January 2, 1972, Liddy presented his multimillion-dollar plan to Mitchell, who later described the plan as including "mugging squads, kidnapping teams, prostitutes to compromise the opposition, and electronic surveillance." He ordered Liddy to scale down the program.

One offshoot of Liddy's plan was the planting of a wiretap at the headquarters of the Democratic National Committee (DNC) in Washington's Watergate complex. On June 17, 1972, five men were caught inside the DNC headquarters with burglary tools, bugging devices, and a stack of $100 bills. Their links to CREEP soon became known, and Liddy himself was arrested. Nixon's press secretary, Ron Ziegler, dismissed the incident as a "third-rate burglary," and Nixon assured the press that the White House had no involvement whatsoever in the bungled break-in.

To this day, no one has demonstrated that Nixon had prior knowledge of the break-in. But within hours after the arrests, paper shredders at the White House and CREEP were destroying documents that might link the burglars to the White House. CREEP and White House officials pressured Nixon's personal lawyer, Herbert Kalmbach, to collect funds quietly to "support the families" of the accused. Anthony Ulasewicz, a former New York policeman working for the White House, later regaled the Watergate Committee

with stories of leaving money in paper bags to be picked up and delivered to the accused burglars. *Washington Post* reporters Robert Woodward and Carl Bernstein began an investigation that eventually tracked the Watergate break-in and its cover-up to the very door of the Oval Office.

As the trail got closer, Nixon's aides resigned one by one. Chief of Staff Bob Haldeman, domestic-policy adviser John Ehrlichman, and others were writing their resignations and ringing up their lawyers simultaneously. On May 17, 1973, hearings of the Senate Select Committee on Campaign Activities opened, chaired by Senator Sam Ervin (D-N.C.). Nixon's former White House counsel, John Dean, claimed that Nixon had known more than he was admitting and had played fast and loose with the truth about White House involvement. Haldeman and Ehrlichman defended the president.

One White House functionary, Alexander Butterfield, broke the news that Nixon had a secret taping system that recorded every conversation in the Oval Office. The battle for control of the tapes began. The Ervin committee demanded access to the tapes. Courts trying the Watergate defendants subpoenaed them. Nixon asserted that executive privilege permitted him to refuse to disclose them. Finally, the Supreme Court, in *United States v. Nixon* (1974), ruled that Nixon had to hand over the tapes to courts trying the Watergate burglars. The tapes confirmed that Nixon *had* been involved in the cover-up (a felony) and had been lying to the American people.

As the Watergate cover-up unraveled, more became known about what John Mitchell called "the White House horrors." Nixon's White House aides and CREEP officials had sponsored the burglary of the office of a psychiatrist treating Daniel Ellsberg, an opponent of the Vietnam War who had leaked classified documents to the press; they had had the administration's opponents' income tax records audited, had tapped phones illegally, had collected

Continued

IN FOCUS — **Watergate** *(continued)*

campaign contributions (preferably cash) in return for specific favors, and had manipulated Nixon's own tax returns

The House launched impeachment hearings in 1974. On July 31, 1974, the Judiciary Committee recommended Nixon's impeachment. Facing almost certain impeachment by the House and probable conviction by the Senate, Nixon resigned ten days later. Shortly after assuming the presidency, Gerald Ford pardoned Nixon, arguing that years of trials and appeals would aggravate bitterness over Watergate. Most of Nixon's aides were not so lucky—many were convicted and served prison sentences.

Nevertheless, to this day there are some, perhaps many, who believe that Richard Nixon was unfairly hounded from office. They claim he and his aides really did nothing that was uncommon in American politics. His only problem, they contend, is that he got caught. Should Nixon have lost his presidency? What do *you* think?

---

some of the Constitution's vagueness about disability. The amendment permits the vice president to become acting president if the vice president and the president's cabinet determine that the president is disabled, and it outlines how a recuperated president can reclaim the Oval Office. Other laws specify the order of presidential succession—from the vice president, to the Speaker of the House, to the president *pro tempore* of the Senate, and down through the cabinet.

The Twenty-fifth Amendment also created a means for selecting a new vice president when the office becomes vacant—a frequent occurrence. The president nominates a new vice president, who assumes the office when both houses of Congress approve the nomination.

PRESIDENTIAL POWERS

The contemporary presidency hardly resembles the one the Constitution framers designed in 1787. The executive office they conceived had more limited authority, fewer responsibilities, and much less organizational structure than today's presidency. The founders feared both anarchy and monarchy. They wanted an independent executive but disagreed both on the form the office should take and the powers it should exercise. In the end, they created an executive unlike any the world had ever seen.

Constitutional Powers

The Constitution says remarkably little about presidential power. The discussion of the presidency begins with these general words: "The executive power shall be vested in a president of the United States of America." It goes on to list just a few powers (see Table 11.2). The framers' invention fit nicely within the Madisonian system of shared power and checks and balances. There is little that presidents can do on their own, and they share executive, legislative, and judicial power with the other branches of government.

TABLE 11.2 — *Constitutional Powers of the President*

NATIONAL SECURITY POWERS

Commander in chief of the armed forces

Make treaties with other nations, subject to the agreement of two-thirds of the Senate

Nominate ambassadors, with the agreement of a majority of the Senate

Receive ambassadors of other nations, thereby conferring diplomatic recognition on other governments

LEGISLATIVE POWERS

Present information on the state of the union to Congress

Recommend legislation to Congress

Convene both houses of Congress on extraordinary occasions

Adjourn Congress if the House and Senate cannot agree on adjournment

Veto legislation (Congress may overrule with two-thirds vote of each house)

ADMINISTRATIVE POWERS

"Take care that the laws be faithfully executed"

Appoint officials as provided for by Congress and with the agreement of a majority of the Senate

Request written opinions of administrative officials

Fill administrative vacancies during congressional recesses

JUDICIAL POWERS

Grant reprieves and pardons for federal offenses (except impeachment)

Appoint federal judges, with the agreement of a majority of the Senate

Institutional balance was essential to the convention delegates, who had in mind the abuses of past executives combined with the excesses of state legislatures (discussed in Chapter 2). The problem was how to preserve the balance without jeopardizing the independence of the separate branches or impeding the lawful exercise of their authority. The framers resolved this problem by checking those powers that they believed to be most dangerous, the ones that historically had been subject to the greatest abuse (for example, they gave Congress the power to declare war and approve treaties and presidential appointments), while protecting the general spheres of authority from encroachment (the executive, for instance, was given a qualified veto).

Presidential responsibility was also encouraged by provisions for reelection and a short term of office. For those executives who flagrantly abused their authority, impeachment was the ultimate recourse.

The Expansion of Power

Today there is more to presidential power than the Constitution alone suggests, and that power is derived from many sources. Chapter 2 showed that the role of the president has changed as America increased in prominence on the world stage and that technology has also reshaped the presidency. George Washington's ragtag militias (mostly disbanded by the time the first commander in chief took command) are of a different order than the mighty nuclear arsenal that today's president commands.

Presidents themselves have taken the lead in developing new roles for the office. In fact, many presidents enlarged the power of the presidency by expanding the president's responsibilities and political resources. Thomas Jefferson was the first leader of a mass political party. Andrew Jackson presented himself as the direct representative of the people. Lincoln mobilized the country to war, while Theodore Roosevelt mobilized the public behind his policies. He and Woodrow Wilson set precedents for presidents serving as world leaders, and Wilson and Franklin D. Roosevelt developed the role of the president as manager of the economy. The following sections will explore the relationship between the president's responsibilities and resources by examining how contemporary presidents try to lead the nation.

RUNNING THE GOVERNMENT: THE CHIEF EXECUTIVE

Although the president is often called the "chief executive," it is easy to forget that one of the president's most important roles is presiding over the administration of government. This role does not receive as much publicity as appealing to the public for support for policy initiatives, dealing with Congress, or negotiating with foreign powers, but it is of great importance nevertheless.

We saw in Table 11.2 that the Constitution tells the president to "take care that the laws be faithfully executed." In the early days of the republic, this clerical-sounding function was fairly easy. Today, the sprawling federal bureaucracy spends more than $1.5 trillion a year and numbers nearly five million civilian and military employees. Running such a large organization would be a full-time job for even the most talented of executives, yet it is only one of the president's many jobs.

One of the resources for controlling this bureaucracy is the presidential power to appoint top-level administrators. New presidents have about three hundred of these high-level positions available for appointment—cabinet and subcabinet jobs, agency heads, and other noncivil service posts—plus 2,000 lesser jobs. Since passage of the Budgeting and Accounting Act of 1921, presidents have had one other important executive tool—the power to recommend agency budgets to Congress.

The vastness of the executive branch, the complexity of public policy, and the desire to accomplish policy goals have led presidents in recent years to pay even closer attention to appointing officials who will be responsive to the president's policies. Presidents have also taken more interest in the regulations issued by agencies. This trend toward centralizing decision making in the White House pleases those who feel the bureaucracy should be more responsive to elected officials. On the other hand, it dismays those who believe that increased politicization of policy-making will undermine the "neutral competence" of professional bureaucrats and may encourage them to follow the policy preferences of the president rather than the intent of laws as passed by Congress.

Chapter 12 explores the president's role as chief executive more fully. This chapter will focus on how presidents go about organizing and using the part of the executive branch most under their control: the cabinet, the Executive Office of the President, and the White House staff.

The Cabinet

Although the Constitution does not mention the group of presidential advisors known as the **cabinet**, every president has had one. The cabinet is too large, too diverse, and its members too concerned with representing the interests of their departments for it to serve as a collective board of directors, however. The major decisions remain in the president's hands. Legend has it that Abraham Lincoln asked his cabinet to vote on an issue, and the result was unanimity in opposition to his view. He announced the decision as "seven nays and one aye, the ayes have it."

George Washington's cabinet was small, consisting of just three secretaries (state, treasury, and war) and the attorney general. Presidents since Washington have increased the size of the cabinet by requesting that new executive departments be established. These requests must be approved by Congress, which creates the department. Today thirteen secretaries and the attorney general head executive departments and constitute the cabinet. In addition, presidents may designate other officials as cabinet members (the ambassador to the United Nations is a common choice).

Even in his "official family," the president is subject to the constitutional system of checks and balances. President Bush met resistance when he nominated John Tower, a former senator, to be secretary of defense. After a bitter debate, Tower was rejected by the Senate, handing the president a serious defeat. President Clinton's first nominee to serve as attorney general, Zoe Baird, had to withdraw from consideration after she came under fire from senators of both parties for hiring an illegal alien as her baby-sitter and failing to pay social security taxes for her employee.

The Executive Office

Next to the White House sits an ornate building called the EOB, or Executive Office Building. It houses a collection of offices and organizations loosely grouped into the Executive Office of the President. Some of these offices (such as the Council of Economic Advisors) are created by legislation, and some are organized essentially by the president. Starting small in 1939, when it was established by President Roosevelt, the Executive Office has grown with the rest

Members of the president's cabinet are important for both the power they exercise and the status they symbolize. President Clinton promised to form a cabinet that was representative of America's diversity. Pictured here is the Secretary of Energy, Hazel O'Leary, an African American.

of government. In the Executive Office are housed three major policy-making bodies—the National Security Council, the Council of Economic Advisors, and the Office of Management and Budget—plus several other units serving the president.

The **National Security Council (NSC)** is the committee that links the president's key foreign and military policy advisors. Its members include the president, vice president, and secretaries of state and defense, but its informal membership is broader. The president's special assistant for national security affairs plays a major role in the NSC. The occupant of this post has responsibility for running the council's staff. This assistant and the staff provide the president with information and policy recommendations on national security, aid the president in national security crisis management, coordinate agency and departmental activities bearing on national security, and monitor the implementation of national security policy.

The **Council of Economic Advisors (CEA)** has three members, each appointed by the president, who advise him on economic policy. They prepare the *Annual Report of the Council of Economic Advisors* and help the president make policy on inflation, unemployment, and other economic matters.

The **Office of Management and Budget (OMB)** grew out of the Bureau of the Budget (BOB) created in 1921. The OMB is composed of a handful of political appointees and more than six hundred career officials, many of whom are highly skilled professionals. Its major responsibility is to prepare the president's budget. President Nixon revamped the BOB in 1970 in an attempt to make it a managerial as well as a budgetary agency, changing its name in the process to stress its managerial functions.

Because each presidential appointee and department have their own agenda, presidents need a clearinghouse—the OMB. Presidents use the OMB to review legislative proposals from the cabinet and other executive agencies to determine whether they want an agency to present the proposal to Congress. The OMB assesses the proposals' budgetary implications and advises presidents on the proposals' consistency with their overall program. It also plays an important role in reviewing regulations proposed by departments and agencies.

Though presidents find that the Executive Office is smaller and less unwieldy than the cabinet departments, it is still filled with people performing jobs required by law. There is, however, one part of the presidential system that presidents can truly call their own—the White House staff.

The White House Staff

The White House staff consists of the key aides the president sees daily—the chief of staff, congressional liaison people, press secretary, national security advisor, and a few other administrative and political assistants. Actually, there are about six hundred people at work on the White House staff—many of whom the president rarely sees—providing the chief executive with a wide variety of services ranging from advance travel preparations to answering the thousands of letters received each year (see Figure 11.1).

Presidents rely heavily on their staffs for information, policy options, and analysis. Different presidents have different relationships with their staffs. They each organize the White House to serve their own political and policy needs and their own decision-making style. Most presidents end up choosing some form of *hierarchical* organization with a chief of staff at the top, whose job it is to see that everyone else is doing his or her job and that the president's time and interests are protected. A few presidents, such as John Kennedy, have employed a *wheel-and-spokes* system of White House management in which many aides have equal status and are balanced against one another in the process of decision making. In all systems, White House aides are central in the policy-making process, fashioning options, negotiating agreements, writing presidential statements, controlling paperwork, molding legislative details, and generally giving the president their opinions on most matters.

FIGURE 11.1 — Principal Offices in the White House

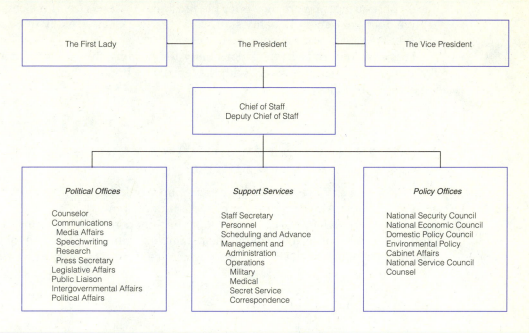

SOURCE: Adapted from George C. Edwards III and Stephan J. Wayne, *Presidential Leadership*, 3rd ed (New York: St. Martin's, 1994), 186.

No presidential management styles contrasted more sharply than those of Presidents Carter and Reagan. Carter was a detail man, pouring endlessly over memoranda and facts. President Reagan was the consummate delegator. So adept at dispersing authority was Reagan that his advisors—the news media often called them "his handlers"—felt it periodically necessary to have the president insist that "I am the boss" in media interviews.

George Bush's operating style fell between the extremes of his two immediate predecessors. He consulted widely both within and outside of government, and he insisted on letting others' views reach him unfiltered by his staff. He was considerably more accessible than Reagan and devoted more energy to decision making. At the same time, he liked to delegate responsibility to his subordinates and had respect for the expertise of others.

President Clinton, like Carter, immerses himself in the details of policy. He has run an open White House, dealing directly with a large number of aides and reading countless policy memoranda. His emphasis on deliberation and his fluid staffing system have generated criticism that his White House is "indecisive" and "chaotic."

Despite presidents' reliance on their staffs, it is the president who sets the tone for the White House. Although it is common to blame presidential advisors for mistakes made in the White House, it is the president's responsibility to demand that staff members analyze a full range of options and their likely consequences before they offer the president their advice. If the chief executive does not demand quality staff work, the work is less likely to be done and disaster or embarrassment may follow.

Presidents not only have responsibility for running the executive branch. They must also deal intensively with the legislative branch; these dealings are the topic of the following sections.

PRESIDENTIAL LEADERSHIP OF CONGRESS: THE POLITICS OF SHARED POWERS

Near the top of any presidential job description would be "working with Congress." Since the American system of separation of powers is actually one of *shared* powers, presidents can rarely operate independently of Congress. If presidents are to succeed in leaving their stamp on public policy, much of their time in office must be devoted to leading the legislature to support presidential initiatives.

Chief Legislator

Nowhere does the Constitution use the phrase *chief legislator*; it is strictly a phrase invented by textbook writers to emphasize the executive's importance in the legislative process. The Constitution does require that the president give a State of the Union address to Congress and instructs the president to bring other matters to Congress's attention "from time to time." In fact, as Chapter 10 discussed, the president plays a major role in shaping congressional agenda.

The Constitution also gives the president power to **veto** congressional legislation. Once Congress passes a bill, the president may (1) sign it, making it law; (2) veto it, sending it back to Congress with the reasons for rejecting it; or (3) let it become law after ten working days by not doing anything. Congress can pass a vetoed law, however, if two-thirds of each house vote to override the president. At one point in the lawmaking process the president has the last word, however: if Congress adjourns within ten days after submitting a bill, the president can simply let it die by neither signing nor vetoing it. This process is called a **pocket veto**. Table 11.3 shows how frequently recent presidents have used the veto.

The presidential veto is usually effective; only about 4 percent of all vetoed bills have been overridden by Congress since the nation's founding. Thus, even the threat of a presidential veto can be an effective tool for persuading Congress to give more weight to presidents' views. On the other hand, the veto is a blunt instrument. Presidents must accept or reject bills in their entirety; they cannot veto only the parts they do not like (most governors have a *line item veto* that allows them to veto particular portions of a bill). As a

TABLE 11.3 — Presidential Vetoes

President	Regular Vetoes	Vetoes Overridden	Percentage of Vetoes Overridden	Pocket Vetoes	Total Vetoes
Eisenhower	73	2	3	108	181
Kennedy	12	0	0	9	21
Johnson	16	0	0	14	30
Nixon	26	7	27	17	43
Ford	48	12	25	18	66
Carter	13	2	15	18	31
Reagan	39	9	23	39	78
Bush	31	1	3	15	46
Clinton[a]	0	0	0	0	0

[a]As of January 1995.

result, the White House often must accept provisions of a bill it opposes in order to obtain provisions that it desires. For example, in 1987, Congress passed the entire discretionary budget of the federal government in one omnibus bill. President Reagan had to accept the whole package or lose appropriations for the entire government.

The presidential veto is an inherently negative resource. It is most useful for preventing legislation. Much of the time, however, presidents are more interested in passing their own legislation. To do so, they must marshall their political resources to obtain positive support for their programs. Presidents' three most useful resources are their party leadership, public support, and their own legislative skills.

Party Leadership

No matter what other resources presidents may have at their disposal, they remain highly dependent upon their party to move their legislative programs. Representatives and senators of the president's party almost always form the nucleus of coalitions supporting presidential proposals and provide considerably more support than do members of the opposition party. Thus, party leadership in Congress is every president's principal task when seeking to counter the natural tendencies toward conflict between the executive and legislative branches inherent in the American government's system of checks and balances.[6]

If presidents could rely on their fellow party members to vote for whatever the White House sent up to Capitol Hill, presidential leadership of Congress would be rather easy. All presidents would have to do is make sure members

Since the 1994 election of a Republican majority in Congress, President Clinton must now maintain the support of a Democratic minority while establishing working relations with a new Republican majority. All presidents must work hard to receive such support, especially by courting the favors of the party's congressional leaders. Here, President Clinton meets with House Speaker Newt Gingrich, Majority Leader Bob Dole, and Vice President Al Gore.

of their party showed up to vote. If their party had the majority, presidents would always win. If their party was in the minority, presidents would only have to concentrate on converting a few members of the other party.

Things are not so simple, however. Despite the pull of party ties, all presidents experience substantial slippage in the support of their party in Congress. Presidents can count on their own party members for support only about two-thirds of the time, even on key votes. Presidents are thus forced to be active in party leadership and to devote their efforts to conversion as much as to mobilization of members of their party.

The primary obstacle to party unity is the lack of consensus among party members on policies, especially in the Democratic party. Jimmy Carter, the last Democratic president, remarked, "I learned the hard way that there was no party loyalty or discipline when a complicated or controversial issue was at stake—none."[7]   This diversity of views often reflects the diversity of constituencies represented by party members. When constituency opinion and the president's proposals conflict, members of Congress are more likely to vote with their constituents, whom they rely on for reelection.

The president's relationship with congressional party leaders is a delicate one. Although the leaders are predisposed to support presidential policies and typically work closely with the White House, they are free to oppose the president or lend only symbolic support; some party leaders may be ineffective themselves. Moreover, party leaders are not in a position to reward or discipline members of Congress on the basis of presidential support.

To create goodwill with congressional party members, the White House provides them with many amenities, ranging from photographs with the president to rides on Air Force One. Although this arrangement is to the president's advantage and may earn the benefit of the doubt on some policy initiatives, party members consider it their right to receive benefits from the White House and are unlikely to be especially responsive to the president as a result.

Just as the president can offer a carrot, so, too, can the president wield a stick in the form of withholding favors, although this is rarely done. Despite the resources available to the president, if party members wish to oppose the White House, there is little the president can do to stop them. The parties are highly decentralized, as you have seen in Chapter 6. National party leaders do not control those aspects of politics that are of vital concern to members of Congress: nominations and elections. Members of Congress are largely self-recruited, gain their party's nomination by their own efforts and not the party's, and provide most of the money and organizational support needed for their elections. The president can do little to influence the results of these activities.

One way for the president to improve the chances of obtaining support in Congress is to increase the number of fellow party members in the legislature. The term **presidential coattails** refers to voters casting their ballots for congressional candidates of the president's party because those candidates support the president. Most recent studies show a diminishing connection between presidential and congressional voting, however, and few races are determined by presidential coattails.[8] The change in party balance that usually occurs when the electoral dust has settled is strikingly small. In the eleven presidential elections between 1952 and 1992, the party of the winning presidential candidate gained an average of eight seats (out of 435) per election in the House. In the Senate, the opposition party actually gained seats in five of the elections (1956, 1960, 1972, 1984, and 1988), and there was no change in 1976 and 1992. The net gain for the president's party in the Senate averaged only one seat per election (see Table 11.4).

The picture is even more bleak for midterm elections, those held between presidential elections. The president's party typically *loses* seats in these elections (see Table 11.5). In 1986, the Republicans lost eight seats in the Senate, depriving President Reagan of a majority. In 1994, the Democrats not only lost 53 seats in the House and 8 in the Senate, but also majority status in each chamber.

TABLE 11.4 — Congressional Gains or Losses for the President's Party in Presidential Election Years

Presidents cannot rely on their coattails to carry into office senators and representatives of their party to help pass presidential legislative programs. The president's party typically gains, few, if any, seats when the president wins an election. For instance, the Democrats lost seats in the House and gained none in the Senate when President Clinton was elected in 1992.

Year	President	House	Senate
1952	Eisenhower	+22	+1
1956	Eisenhower	–2	–1
1960	Kennedy	–22	–2
1964	Johnson	+37	+1
1968	Nixon	+5	+6
1972	Nixon	+12	–2
1976	Carter	+1	0
1980	Reagan	+34	+12
1984	Reagan	+14	–2
1988	Bush	–3	–1
1992	Clinton	–10	0

To add to these party leadership burdens, the president's party often lacks a majority in one or both houses of Congress. Between 1953 and 1992, there were twenty-six years in which Republican presidents faced a Democratic House of Representatives and twenty years in which they encountered a Democratic Senate. Since 1995 President Clinton has faced both a House and a Senate with Republican majorities.

As a result of election returns and the lack of dependable party support, the president usually has to solicit help from the opposition party. The opposition is generally not fertile ground for seeking support. Nevertheless, even a few votes may be enough to give the president the required majority.

Public Support

One of the president's most important resources for leading Congress is public support. Presidents with the backing of the public have an easier time influencing Congress. Said one top aide to Ronald Reagan, "Everything here is built on the idea that the president's success depends on grassroots support."[9] Presidents with low approval ratings in the polls find it difficult to influence Congress. Members of Congress and others in Washington closely watch two indicators of public support for the president: approval in the polls and mandates in presidential elections.

TABLE 11.5 — *Congressional Gains or Losses for the President's Party in Midterm Election Years*

The president's party typically *loses* seats in midterm elections. Thus, presidents cannot rely on helping elect members of their party once in office.

Year	President	House	Senate
1954	Eisenhower	−18	−1
1958	Eisenhower	− 47	−13
1962	Kennedy	−4	+3
1966	Johnson	− 47	− 4
1970	Nixon	−12	+2
1974	Ford	− 47	−5
1978	Carter	−15	−3
1982	Reagan	−26	0
1986	Reagan	−5	−8
1990	Bush	−9	−1
1994	Clinton	−53	−8

Public Approval.   Members of Congress anticipate the public's reactions to their support for or opposition to presidents and their policies. They may choose to be close to or independent from the White House—depending on the president's standing with the public—to increase their chances for reelection. Representatives and senators may also use the president's standing in the polls as an indicator of the ability to mobilize public opinion against presidential opponents.

Public approval also makes other leadership resources more efficacious. If the president is high in the public's esteem, the president's party is more likely to be responsive, the public is more easily moved, and legislative skills become more effective. Thus, public approval is the political resource that has the most potential to turn a situation of stalemate between the president and Congress into one supportive of the president's legislative proposals.

Public approval operates mostly in the background and sets the limits of what Congress will do for or to the president. Widespread support gives the president leeway and weakens resistance to presidential policies. It provides a cover for members of Congress to cast votes to which their constituents might otherwise object. They can defend their votes as support for the president rather than support for a certain policy alone.

Lack of public support strengthens the resolve of those inclined to oppose the president and narrows the range in which presidential policies receive the benefit of the doubt. In addition, low ratings in the polls may create incentives to attack the president, further eroding an already weakened position. For example, after the arms sales to Iran and the diversion of funds to the contras became a *cause célèbre* in late 1986, it became more acceptable in Congress and in the press to raise questions about Ronald Reagan's capacities as president. Disillusionment is a difficult force for the White House to combat.

The impact of public approval or disapproval on the support the president receives in Congress is important, but it occurs at the margins of the effort to build coalitions behind proposed policies. No matter how low presidential standing dips, the president still receives support from a substantial number of senators and representatives. Similarly, no matter how high approval levels climb, a significant portion of Congress will still oppose certain presidential policies. Members of Congress are unlikely to vote against the clear interests of their constituencies or the firm tenets of their ideology out of deference to a widely supported chief executive. Public approval gives the president leverage, not control.[10]

In addition, presidents cannot depend on having the approval of the public, and it is not a resource over which they have much control, as you will see later. Once again, it is clear that presidents' leadership resources do not allow them to dominate Congress.

Mandates.   The results of presidential elections are another indicator of public opinion regarding presidents. An electoral mandate, the perception that the voters strongly support the president's character *and* policies, can be a powerful symbol in American politics. It accords added legitimacy and credibility to the newly elected president's proposals. Moreover, concerns for both representation and political survival encourage members of Congress to support new presidents if they feel the people have spoken.

More importantly, mandates change the premises of decision. In 1981, Ronald Reagan's victory placed a stigma on big government and exalted the unregulated marketplace and large defense efforts. Reagan had won a major victory even before the first congressional vote.

Although presidential elections can structure choices for Congress, merely winning an election does not provide presidents with a mandate. Every election produces a winner, but mandates are much less common. Even large electoral victories, such as Richard Nixon's in 1972 and Ronald Reagan's in 1984, carry no guarantee that Congress will interpret the results as mandates from the people to support the president's programs, especially if the voters also elect majorities in Congress from the other party (of course, the winner may claim a mandate anyway).[11]

Legislative Skills

Presidential legislative skills come in a variety of forms. Of these skills, bargaining receives perhaps the most attention from commentators on the presidency. There is no question that many bargains occur and that they occur in numerous forms. Reagan's Budget Director, David Stockman, recalled that

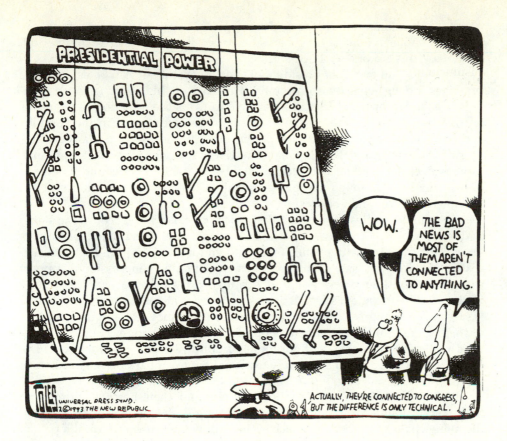

"the last 10 or 20 percent of the votes needed for a majority of both houses on the 1981 tax cut had to be bought, period." "The hogs were really feeding."[12]

Nevertheless, bargaining in the form of trading support on two or more policies or providing specific benefits for representatives and senators, occurs less often and plays a less critical role in the creation of presidential coalitions in Congress than one might think. For obvious reasons, the White House does not want to encourage the type of bargaining Stockman describes, and there is a scarcity of resources with which to bargain, especially in an era of large budget deficits. Moreover, the president does not have to bargain with every member of Congress to receive support. On controversial issues on which bargaining may be useful, the president almost always starts with a sizable core of party supporters and may add to this group those of the opposition party who provide support on ideological or policy grounds. Others may support the president because of relevant constituency interests or strong public approval. The president needs to bargain only if this coalition does not provide a majority (two-thirds on treaties and one-third on veto overrides).

Presidents may improve their chances of success in Congress by making certain strategic moves. It is wise, for example, for a new president to be ready to send legislation to the Hill early during the first year in office in order to exploit the "honeymoon" atmosphere that typically characterizes this period. Obviously, this is a one-shot opportunity.

An important aspect of presidential legislative strategy can be establishing priorities among legislative proposals. The goal of this effort is to set Congress's agenda, for if presidents are unable to focus the attention of Congress on their priority programs, these programs may become lost in the complex and overloaded legislative process. Setting priorities is also important because presidents and their staffs can lobby effectively for only a few bills at a time. Moreover, each president's political capital is inevitably limited, and it is sensible to focus it on a limited range of personally important issues; otherwise this precious resource might be wasted.

Systematic studies have found that, once one takes into account the status of their party in Congress and their standing with the public, presidents known for their legislative skills (such as Lyndon Johnson) are no more successful in winning votes, even close ones, or obtaining congressional support than those considered less adept at dealing with Congress (such as Jimmy Carter).[13] The president's legislative skills are not at the core of presidential leadership of Congress. Even skilled presidents cannot reshape the contours of the political landscape and *create* opportunities for change. They can, however, recognize favorable configurations of political forces, such as existed in 1933, 1965, and 1981, and effectively exploit them to embark on major shifts in public policy.

Perhaps presidents' most important role, and their heaviest burden, is their responsibility for national security. Dealing with Congress is only one of the many challenges presidents face in the realm of defense and foreign policy.

THE PRESIDENT AND NATIONAL SECURITY POLICY

Constitutionally, the president has the leading role in American defense and foreign policy (often termed *national security* policy). Such matters are of obvious importance to the country—involving issues ranging from foreign trade to war and peace—and occupy much of the president's time. There are several dimensions to the president's national security responsibilities, including negotiating with other nations, commanding the armed forces, waging war, and obtaining the necessary support in Congress.

Chief Diplomat

The Constitution allocates certain powers in the realm of national security exclusively to the executive. The president alone extends diplomatic recognition to foreign governments, as Jimmy Carter did on December 14, 1978, when he announced the exchange of ambassadors with the People's Republic of China and the downgrading of the U.S. Embassy of Taiwan. The president also can terminate relations with other nations, as Carter did with Iran after Americans were taken hostage in Tehran.

The president also has the sole power to negotiate treaties with other nations, although the Constitution requires the Senate to approve them by a two-thirds vote. Sometimes presidents win and sometimes they lose when presenting a treaty to the Senate. After extensive lobbying, Jimmy Carter persuaded the Senate to approve a treaty returning the Panama Canal to Panama (over objections such as those of one senator who declared, "We stole it fair and square"). Carter was not so lucky when he presented the SALT II treaty on arms control; it never even made it to a vote on the Senate floor.

In addition to treaties, presidents also negotiate *executive agreements* with the heads of foreign governments. The difference between treaties and executive agreements is that executive agreements do not require Senate ratification (although they are supposed to be reported to Congress). While most executive agreements are routine and deal with noncontroversial subjects such as food deliveries or customs enforcement, some implement important and controversial policies, such as the SALT I agreement limiting offensive nuclear weapons and the Vietnam peace agreement.

Occasionally presidential diplomacy involves more than negotiating on behalf of the United States. Theodore Roosevelt won the Nobel Peace Prize for his role in settling the war between Japan and Russia. One of Jimmy Carter's greatest achievements was forging a peace treaty between Egypt and Israel. For thirteen days he mediated negotiations between the leaders of both countries at his presidential retreat, Camp David.

As the leader of the Western world, the president must try to lead America's allies on matters of both economics and defense. This is not an easy task, given the natural independence of sovereign nations; the reduced status of the United States as an economic power relative to other countries, such as Japan and Germany; and the many competing influences on policy-making in other nations. As in domestic policy-making, the president must rely principally on persuasion to lead.

Commander in Chief

Because the Constitution's framers wanted civilian control of the military, they made the president the commander in chief of the armed forces. President George Washington actually led troops to crush the Whiskey Rebellion in 1794. Today, presidents do not take the task quite so literally, but their military decisions have changed the course of history. George Bush ordered the invasion of Panama in 1989 and moved half a million troops to Saudi Arabia to liberate Kuwait following its invasion by Iraq in 1990.

When the Constitution was written, the United States did not have—nor did anyone expect it to have—a large standing or permanent army. Today the president is commander in chief of more than 1.5 million uniformed men and women. In his farewell address, George Washington warned against "entangling alliances," but today America has commitments to defend nations across the globe. Even more importantly, the president commands a vast nuclear arsenal. Never more than a few steps from the president is "the football," a macabre briefcase with the codes needed to unleash nuclear war. The Constitution, of course, states that only Congress has the power to declare war, but it is unreasonable to believe that Congress can convene, debate, and vote on a declaration of war in the case of a nuclear attack. The House and Senate chambers would be gone—*literally* gone—before the conclusion of a debate.

War Powers

Perhaps no issue of executive-legislative relations generates more controversy than the continuing dispute over war powers. Though charged by the Constitution with declaring war and voting on the military budget, Congress long ago became accustomed to presidents making short-term military commitments of troops or naval vessels. In recent decades, though, presidents have paid even less attention to constitutional details; for example, Congress never declared war during the conflicts in either Korea or Vietnam.

The Constitution makes the president commander in chief of the armed forces. Some presidents have involved themselves more deeply in war-making than others. President Bush made the important decisions regarding the 1991 war in the Persian Gulf but left the details to his military commanders.

In 1973, Congress passed (over President Nixon's veto) the **War Powers Resolution**. A reaction to disillusionment about American fighting in Vietnam and Cambodia, the law was intended to give Congress a greater voice in the introduction of American troops into hostilities. It required presidents to consult with Congress, whenever possible, prior to using military force, and it mandated the withdrawal of forces after sixty days unless Congress declared war or granted an extension. Congress could at any time pass a concurrent resolution (which could not be vetoed) ending American participation in hostilities.

The War Powers Resolution cannot be regarded as a success for Congress, however. All presidents serving since 1973 have deemed the law an unconstitutional infringement on their powers, and there is reason to believe the Supreme Court would consider the law's use of the **legislative veto** to end American involvement in fighting a violation of the doctrine of separation of powers. As in the case of the 1989 invasion of Panama, presidents have largely ignored the spirit of the law and sent troops into hostilities, sometimes with heavy loss of life, without effectually consulting with Congress. The legislature has found it difficult to challenge the president, especially when American troops were endangered, and the courts have been reluctant to hear a congressional challenge on what would be construed as a political, rather than legal, issue.[14]

Matters came to a head in January 1991. President Bush had given President Saddam Hussein of Iraq until January 15 to pull out of Kuwait. At that point, President Bush threatened to move the Iraqis out by force. Debate raged over the president's power to act unilaterally to engage in war. A constitutional crisis was averted when Congress passed (on a divided vote) a resolution on January 12 authorizing the president to use force against Iraq.

Questions continue to be raised about the relevance of American's 200-year-old constitutional mechanisms for engaging in war. Some observers are concerned that modern technology allows the president to engage in conflicts so quickly that opposing points of view do not receive proper consideration, thereby undermining the separation of powers. Others stress the importance of the commander in chief having the flexibility to meet America's global responsibilities and combat international terrorism without the hindrance of congressional checks and balances. All agree that the change in the nature of warfare brought about by nuclear weapons inevitably delegates to the president the ultimate decision to use them.

Working with Congress

As America begins its third century under the Constitution, presidents might wish the framers had been less concerned with checks and balances in the area of national security. In recent years, Congress has challenged presidents on all fronts, including foreign aid; arms sales; the development, procurement, and deployment of weapon systems; the negotiation and interpretation of treaties; the selection of diplomats; and the continuation of nuclear testing.

Congress has a central constitutional role in making national security policy, although this role is often misunderstood. The allocation of responsibilities for such matters is based upon the founders' apprehensions about the concentration and subsequent potential for abuse of power. They divided the powers of supply and command, for example, in order to thwart adventurism in national security affairs. Congress can thus refuse to provide the necessary authorizations and appropriations for presidential actions, whereas the chief executive can refuse to act (for example, by not sending troops into battle at the behest of the legislature).

Despite the constitutional role of Congress, the president is the driving force behind national security policy, providing energy and direction. Although Congress is well organized to openly deliberate on the discrete components of policy, it is not well designed to take the lead on national security matters. Its role has typically been oversight of the executive rather than initiation of policy. Congress frequently originates proposals for domestic policy, but is less involved in national security policy. The president has a more prominent role as the country's sole representative in dealing with other nations and as commander in chief of the armed forces (functions that effectively preclude a wide range of congressional diplomatic and military initiatives). In addition, the nature of national security issues may make the failure to integrate the elements of policy more costly than in domestic policy. Thus, members of Congress typically prefer to encourage, criticize, or support the president rather than initiate their own national security policy. If leadership occurs, it will usually be centered in the White House.[15]

Presidents need resources to persuade others to support their policies. As noted earlier, an important presidential asset can be the support of the American people. The following sections will take a closer look at how the White House tries to increase and use public support.

POWER FROM THE PEOPLE: THE PUBLIC PRESIDENCY

"Public sentiment is everything. With public sentiment nothing can fail; without it nothing can succeed." These words, spoken by Abraham Lincoln, pose what is perhaps the greatest challenge to any president: to obtain and maintain the public's support. Because presidents are rarely in a position to command others to comply with their wishes, they must rely on persuasion. *Public support is perhaps the greatest source of influence a president has*, for it is difficult for other power holders in a democracy to deny the legitimate demands of a president who has popular backing.

Going Public

Presidents are not passive followers of public opinion. The White House is a virtual whirlwind of public relations activity.[16] John Kennedy, the first "televi-

John Kennedy was the first president to regularly use public appearances to seek popular backing for his policies. Despite his popularity and skills as a communicator, Kennedy was often frustrated in his attempts to win widespread support for his administration's "New Frontier" policies.

sion president," considerably increased the rate of public appearances held by his predecessors. Kennedy's successors, with the notable exception of Richard Nixon, have been even more active in making public appearances. Indeed, they have averaged more than one appearance every weekday of the year. Bill Clinton is a tireless campaigner who invests enormous time and energy in attempting to sell his programs to the public.

Often the president's appearances are staged purely to obtain the public's attention. When George Bush introduced his clean-air bill, he flew to Idaho to use the eye-catching Grand Tetons as a backdrop. He announced his support for a constitutional amendment to prohibit flag burning in front of the Iwo Jima Memorial in Arlington National Cemetery. In cases such as these the president could have simply made an announcement, but the necessity of public support drives the White House to employ public relations techniques similar to those used to publicize commercial products.

In many democracies, the jobs of head of state and head of government are occupied by different people. For example, the queen is head of state in England, but she holds little power in government and politics. In America, these roles are fused. As head of state, the president is America's ceremonial leader and symbol of government. Trivial but time-consuming activities—

tossing out the first baseball of the season, lighting the White House Christmas tree, meeting some extraordinary Boy Scout—are part of the ceremonial function of the presidency. Meeting foreign heads of state, receiving ambassadors' credentials, and making global goodwill tours represent the international side of this role. Presidents rarely shirk these duties, even when they are not inherently important. Ceremonial activities give them an important symbolic aura and a great deal of favorable press coverage, contributing to their efforts to build public support.

Presidential Approval

Much of the energy the White House devotes to public relations is aimed at increasing the president's public approval. The reason is simple: the higher the president stands in the polls, the easier it is to persuade others to support presidential initiatives.

Because of the connection between public support and presidential influence, the president's standing in the polls is monitored closely by the press, members of Congress, and others in the Washington political community. "President watching" is a favorite American pastime. For years, the Gallup Poll (and now many others) has asked Americans this question: "Do you approve or disapprove of the way John Kennedy, George Bush, or whoever, is handling his job as president?" You can see the results in Figure 11.2.

Presidents frequently do not have widespread public support, often failing to win even majority approval. Presidents Nixon, Ford, and Carter did not even receive approval from 50 percent of the public on the average. Ronald Reagan, a "popular" president, had only a 52 percent approval level. For three years, George Bush enjoyed much higher levels of approval on the average than his predecessors. In his fourth year, however, his ratings in the polls fell below the 40 percent mark. President Clinton has struggled to rise above 50 percent approval.

Presidential approval is the product of many factors.[17]   At the base of presidential evaluations is the predisposition of many people to support the president. Political party identification provides the basic underpinning of approval or disapproval and mediates the impact of other factors. On average, those who identify with the president's party give nearly 40 percentage points higher approval than those who identify with the opposition party. In other words, Democrats love Democratic presidents and Republicans are equally fond of GOP chief executives. Moreover, partisans are not prone to approving presidents of the other party. Presidents also usually benefit from a "honeymoon" with the American people after taking office. Predispositions provide the foundations of presidential approval and furnish it with a basic stability.

Changes in approval levels appear to be due primarily to the public's evaluation of how the president is handling policy areas such as the economy, war, energy, and foreign affairs. Different policies are salient to the public at different times. For example, if communism is collapsing, then foreign policy is likely to

FIGURE 11.2 — *Average Yearly Presidential Approval*

For years, the Gallup Poll has asked Americans, "Do you approve or disapprove of the way _____ is handling his job as president?" This figure allows you to track presidential approval from Eisenhower to Clinton. Notice that all presidents seem to be most popular when they first enter office; later on, their popularity often erodes.

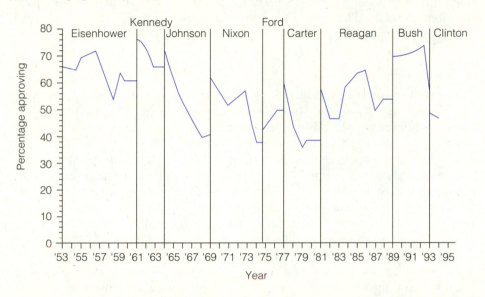

SOURCE: George C. Edwards III, *Presidential Approval* (Baltimore: Johns Hopkins University Press, 1990); updated by authors.

dominate the news and be on the minds of Americans. If the economy turns sour, then people are going to be concerned about unemployment.

Contrary to conventional wisdom, citizens seem to focus on the president's efforts and stands on issues rather than on personality ("popularity") or simply how presidential policies affect them (the "pocketbook"). Job-related personal characteristics of the president, such as integrity and leadership skills, also play an important role in influencing presidential approval.

Sometimes public approval of the president takes sudden jumps. One popular explanation for these surges of support are "rally events," which John Mueller defined as events that relate to international relations, directly involve the United States and particularly the president, and are specific, dramatic, and sharply focused.[18] A classic example is the 18 percentage point rise in President Bush's approval ratings immediately after the fighting began in the Gulf War in 1991. Such occurrences are unusual and isolated events, however; they have little enduring impact on a president's public approval. President Bush, for example, dropped precipitously in the polls and lost his bid for reelection in 1992.

The criteria on which the public evaluates presidents—such as the way they are handling the economy, where they stand on complex issues, and whether they are "strong" leaders—are open to many interpretations. The modern White House makes extraordinary efforts to control the context in which presidents appear in public and the way they are portrayed by the press, in order to try to influence how the public views them. The fact that presidents are frequently low in the polls anyway is persuasive testimony to the limits of presidential leadership of the public. As one student of the public presidency put it, "The supply of popular support rests on opinion dynamics over which the president may exert little direct control."[19]

Policy Support

Commentators on the presidency often refer to it as a "bully pulpit," implying that presidents can persuade or even mobilize the public to support their policies if only they are skilled-enough communicators. Certainly presidents frequently do attempt to obtain public support for their policies with speeches over television or radio or to large groups.[20] All presidents since Truman have had media advice from experts on lighting, makeup, stage settings, camera angles, clothing, pacing of delivery, and other facets of making speeches.

Despite this aid and despite the experience that politicians have in speaking, presidential speeches aimed at directly leading public opinion have typically been rather unimpressive. In the modern era only Franklin D. Roosevelt, John Kennedy, Ronald Reagan, and Bill Clinton could be considered effective speakers. The rest were not, and usually did not look good under the glare of hot lights and the unflattering gaze of television cameras. Partly because of his limitations as a public speaker, President Bush waited until he had been in office for over seven months before making his first nationally televised address.

Moreover, the public is not always receptive to the president's message. Policy-making is a very complex enterprise, and, as we saw in Chapter 5, most voters do not have the time, expertise, or inclination to think extensively about most issues, especially those as distant from their everyday experiences as federal regulations, nuclear weapons, and bureaucratic organization. An issue even closer to home, after two decades of political controversy, nearly half of Americans do not realize that we must import oil.[21]

The public may misperceive or ignore even the most basic facts regarding presidential policy. For example, at the end of October 1994, 59 percent of the public thought the economy was still in recession (although it was growing so fast that the Federal Reserve Board was taking strong action to cool it off), only 34 percent knew the deficit had decreased since Clinton became president (it had decreased substantially), and 65 percent thought taxes on the middle class had increased during that period (income taxes had been raised for less than two percent of the public). The president was frustrated repeatedly in his efforts to obtain public support for his policy initiatives.[22]

Citizens also have predispositions about public policy (however ill-informed) that act as screens for presidential messages. In the absence of national crises, most people are unreceptive to political appeals[23]; thus, they often fail. Ronald Reagan, sometimes called the "Great Communicator," was certainly interested in policy change and went to unprecedented lengths to influence public opinion on behalf of such policies as deregulation, decreases in spending on domestic policy, and increases in the defense budget. Nevertheless, public opinion on these issues moved in the *opposite* direction during Reagan's tenure.[24]

Mobilizing the Public

Sometimes merely changing public opinion is not sufficient, and the president wants the public to communicate its views directly to Congress. Mobilization of the public may be the ultimate weapon in the president's arsenal of resources with which to influence Congress. When the people speak, especially when they speak clearly, Congress listens attentively.

Mobilizing the public involves overcoming formidable barriers and accepting substantial risks. It entails the double burden of obtaining both opinion *support* and political *action* from a generally inattentive and apathetic public. If the president tries to mobilize the public and fails, the lack of response speaks clearly to members of Congress.

Perhaps the most notable recent example of the president mobilizing public opinion to pressure Congress is Ronald Reagan's effort to obtain passage of his tax-cut bill in 1981. Shortly before the crucial vote in the House, the president made a televised plea for support of his tax-cut proposals and asked the people to let their representatives in Congress know how they felt. Evidently Reagan's plea worked, as thousands of phone calls, letters, and telegrams poured into congressional offices. On the morning of the vote, Speaker Tip O'Neill declared, "We are experiencing a telephone blitz like this nation has never seen. It's had a devastating effect."[25] The president easily carried the day.

The Reagan administration's effort at mobilizing the public on behalf of the 1981 tax cut is significant not only because of the success of presidential leadership, but also because it appears to be an anomaly. In the remainder of Reagan's tenure, the president went repeatedly to the people regarding a wide range of policies. Despite high levels of approval for much of that time, Reagan was never again able to arouse many in his audience to communicate their support of his policies to Congress. Most issues hold less appeal to the public than substantial tax cuts.

THE PRESIDENT AND THE PRESS

Despite all their efforts to lead public opinion, presidents do not directly reach the American people on a day-to-day basis. It is the mass media that provide people with most of what they know about chief executives and their policies. The media also interpret and analyze presidential activities, even the president's direct appeals to the public. The press is thus the principal intermediary between the president and the public, and relations with the press are an important aspect of the president's efforts to lead public opinion.

No matter who is in the White House or who reports on presidential activities, presidents and the press tend to be in conflict. Thomas Jefferson once declared that "nothing in a newspaper is to be believed." Presidents are inherently policy advocates. They want to control the amount and timing of information about their administration, whereas the press want all the information that exists without delay. As long as their goals are different, presidents and the media are likely to be adversaries.

Because of the importance of the press to the president, the White House monitors the media closely. Some presidents have installed special televisions so they can watch the news on all the networks at once; Lyndon Johnson even had news tickers from AP, UPI, and Reuters in the Oval Office. The White House also goes to great lengths to encourage the media to project a positive image of the president's activities and policies. About one-third of the high-level White House staff members are directly involved in media relations and policy of one type or another, and most staff members are involved at some time in trying to influence the media's portrayal of the president.

The person who most often deals directly with the press is the president's *press secretary*, who serves as a conduit of information from the White House to the press. Press secretaries conduct daily press briefings, giving prepared announcements and answering questions. They and their staff also arrange private interviews with White House officials (often done on a background basis, in which the reporter may not attribute remarks to the person being interviewed), photo opportunities, and travel arrangements for reporters when the president leaves Washington.

The best-known direct interaction between the president and the press is the presidential press conference. Presidents since Eisenhower have typically met with the press about twice a month (the exceptions were Nixon and Reagan, who averaged a press conference only about every two months). George Bush often met with the press in informal sessions, but rarely held a prime-time, televised press conference. Bill Clinton took office with an antagonistic attitude to the national media and planned to bypass it rather than use it as part of his political strategy. He waited two months before holding his first formal news conference and five months before he held one in prime time viewing hours in the evening. After a rocky start in his press relations, the president made himself somewhat more accessible to the national press.

Despite their visibility, press conferences are not very useful means of eliciting information. Presidents and their staffs can anticipate most of the questions that will be asked and prepare answers to them ahead of time, reducing the spontaneity of the sessions. Moreover, the large size and public nature of press conferences reduce the candor with which the president can respond to questions.

Most of the news coverage of the White House comes under the heading "body watch." In other words, reporters focus on the most visible layer of presidents' personal and official activities and provide the public with step-by-step accounts. They are interested in what presidents are going to do, how their actions will affect others, how they view policies and individuals, and how they present themselves, rather than in the substance of policies or the fundamental processes operating in the executive branch. Former ABC White House correspondent Sam Donaldson tells the story of covering a meeting of Western leaders on the island of Guadeloupe. It was a slow news day, so Donaldson did a story on the roasting of the pig the leaders would be eating that night, including "an exclusive look at the oven in which the pig would be roasted."[26] Since there are daily deadlines to meet and television reporters must squeeze their stories into sound bites measured in seconds, not minutes, there is little time for reflection, analysis, or comprehensive coverage.

Bias is the most politically charged issue in relations between the president and the press. A large number of studies have concluded that the news media, including the television networks and major newspapers, are not biased *systematically* toward a particular person, party, or ideology, as measured in the amount of favorability of coverage. The bias found in such studies is inconsistent; the news is typically characterized by careful neutrality.[27]

Some observers believe that news coverage of the presidency often tends to emphasize the negative (although the negative stories are typically presented in a neutral manner). Stories on brewing scandals involving presidential appointees are one example. Another example is reflected in an excerpt from President Carter's diary, regarding a visit to an army base in Panama in 1978:

> I told the Army troops that I was in the Navy for 11 years, and they booed. I told them that we depended on the Army to keep the Canal open, and they cheered. Later, the news reports said that there were boos and cheers during my speech.[28]

Reporters' vision of politics as a strategic game and the narratives they use to tell this story often set a negative tone for their interpretations of presidential politics, and journalists are increasingly likely to provide most of the tone of stories as opposed to the partisan sources they interview.[29]

On the other hand, one could argue that the press is inherently biased *toward* the White House. Coverage of the White House presents the president in a dignified context, and he is typically treated with deference.[30] According to Sam Donaldson, generally considered an aggressive White House reporter, "For every truly tough question I've put to officials, I've asked a dozen that were about as tough as Grandma's apple dumplings."[31] Remember that the White House can largely control the environment in which the president meets the press—even going so far as to have the Marine helicopters revved as Ronald Reagan approached them so that he could not hear reporters' questions and give unrehearsed responses.

UNDERSTANDING THE AMERICAN PRESIDENCY

Because the presidency is the single most important office in American politics, there has always been concern about whether the president is a threat to democracy. The importance of the president has raised similar concerns for the scope of government in America.

The Presidency and Democracy

From the time the Constitution was written, there has been a fear that the presidency would degenerate into a monarchy or a dictatorship. Even America's greatest presidents have heightened these fears at times. Despite George Washington's well-deserved reputation for peacefully relinquishing power, he also had certain regal tendencies that fanned the suspicions of the Jeffersonians. Abraham Lincoln, for all his humility, exercised extraordinary powers at the outbreak of the Civil War.

In recent years, however, concerns have been different. Many critics saw Gerald Ford and Jimmy Carter as weak leaders and failures. Ford himself spoke out in 1980, claiming that Carter's weakness had created an "imperiled" presidency. In the 1980s, Ronald Reagan experienced short periods of great influence and longer ones of frustration as the American political system settled back into its characteristic mode of stalemate and incremental policy-making. Both of Reagan's successors, George Bush and Bill Clinton, found it difficult to get things done.

Concerns over presidential power are generally closely related to policy views. Those who oppose the president's policies are the most likely to be concerned about too much presidential power. As you have seen, however, aside from acting outside the law and the Constitution, there is little prospect of the presidency being a threat to democracy. The Madisonian system of checks and balances remains intact.

This is especially evident in an era characterized by divided government, one in which the president is often a Republican and the majority in each house of Congress is Democratic. Some observers are concerned that there is too much checking and balancing and too little capacity to act on pressing national challenges. However, the best evidence indicates that major policy change is *not* hindered by divided government—that change is just as likely to occur when the parties share control as when one party holds both the presidency and a majority in each house of Congress.[32]

The Presidency and the Scope of Government

The president is the central leader in American politics, and some of the most noteworthy presidents in the twentieth century (including Theodore Roosevelt, Woodrow Wilson, and Franklin Roosevelt) have successfully advocated substantial increases in the role of the national government. Supporting an increased role for government is not inherent in the presidency, however; leadership can move in many directions.

All six of the presidents since Lyndon Johnson have championed constraints on government and limits on spending, especially in domestic policy. It is often said that the American people are ideologically conservative and operationally liberal. In the past generation it has been their will to choose presidents who reflected their ideology and a Congress that represented their appetite for public service. It has been the president more often than Congress who has said "no" to government growth.

SUMMARY

This chapter has focused on the president and the presidency. Americans expect a lot from presidents—perhaps too much. The myth of the president as powerhouse clouds America's image of presidential reality. Presidents mainly have the power to persuade, not to impose their will.

Presidents do not work alone. Gone are the days when the presidency meant the president plus a few aides and advisors; the cabinet, the Executive Office of the President, and the White House staff all assist today's presidents. These services come at a price, however, and presidents must organize their subordinates effectively for decision making and policy execution.

Although presidential leadership of Congress is central to all administrations, it often proves frustrating. Presidents rely on their party, the public, and their own legislative skills to persuade Congress to support their policies, but most of the time their efforts are at the margins of coalition building. Rarely are presidents in a position to create—through their own leadership—opportunities for major changes in public policy. They may, however, use their skills to exploit favorable political conditions to bring about policy change.

Some of the president's most important responsibilities fall in the area of national security. As chief diplomat and commander in chief of the armed forces, the president is the country's crisis manager. Still, disputes with Congress over war powers and presidential discretion in foreign affairs demonstrate that even in regard to national security the president operates within the Madisonian system of checks and balances.

Since presidents are dependent on others to accomplish their goals, their greatest challenge is to obtain support. Public opinion can be an important resource for presidential persuasion, and the White House works hard to influence the public. Public approval of presidents and their policies is often elusive, however; the public does not reliably respond to presidential leadership.

FOR FURTHER READING

Barber, James David. *The Presidential Character*, 4th ed. Englewood Cliffs, NJ: Prentice Hall, 1992. Provocative work predicting performance in the White House.

Burke, John P., and Fred I. Greenstein. *How Presidents Test Reality*. New York: Russell Sage Foundation, 1989. Excellent work on presidential decision making.

Burke, John P. *The Institutional Presidency*. Baltimore: Johns Hopkins University Press, 1992. Examines White House organization and presidential advising.

Edwards, George C., III. *At the Margins: Presidential Leadership of Congress.* New Haven, CT: Yale University Press, 1989. Examines the president's efforts to lead Congress and explains the limitations of these efforts.

Edwards, George C., III. *Presidential Approval.* Baltimore: Johns Hopkins University Press, 1990. The relationship between the president and public opinion in the White House's pursuit of popular support.

Fisher, Louis. *Constitutional Conflicts Between Congress and the President,* 3rd ed., revised. Lawrence, KS: University Press of Kansas, 1991. Presents the constitutional dimensions of the separation of powers.

Grossman, Michael Baruch, and Martha Joynt Kumar. *Portraying the President: The White House and the News Media.* Baltimore: Johns Hopkins University Press, 1981. A comprehensive study of presidential relations with the press.

Nathan, Richard P. *The Administrative Presidency.* New York: John Wiley, 1983. The president's role in managing the bureaucracy.

Neustadt, Richard E. *Presidential Power and the Modern Presidents.* New York: Free Press, 1990. The most influential book on the American presidency; argues that presidential power is the power to persuade.

Pfiffner, James P. *The Strategic Presidency.* Chicago: Dorsey, 1988. Organizing the presidency.

NOTES

1. Quoted in Thomas E. Cronin, *The State of the Presidency,* 2nd ed. (Boston: Little, Brown, 1980), 223.
2. Richard E. Neustadt, *Presidential Power and the Modern Presidents* (New York: Free Press, 1990).
3. James David Barber, *The Presidential Character,* 4th ed. (Englewood Cliffs, NJ: Prentice Hall, 1992).
4. Garry Wills, *The Kennedy Imprisonment* (Boston: Atlantic-Little, Brown, 1982), 186. See also Alexander George, "Assessing Presidential Character," *World Politics 26* (January 1974): 10–30.
5. See Paul C. Light, *Vice Presidential Power* (Baltimore: Johns Hopkins University Press, 1984).
6. For a discussion of presidential party leadership in Congress, see George C. Edwards III, *At the Margins: Presidential Leadership of Congress* (New Haven, CT: Yale University Press, 1989), chapters 3–5.
7. Jimmy Carter, *Keeping Faith* (New York: Bantam, 1982), 80.
8. For a review of these studies and an analysis showing the limited impact of presidential coattails on congressional election outcomes, see George C. Edwards III, *The Public Presidency* (New York: St. Martin's, 1983), 83–93.
9. Quoted in Sidney Blumenthal, "Marketing the President," *New York Times Magazine,* September 13, 1981, 110.
10. Edwards, *At the Margins,* chapters 6–7.
11. For an analysis of the factors that affect perceptions of mandates, see Edwards, *At the Margins,* chapter 8.
12. David Stockman, *The Triumph of Politics* (New York: Harper & Row, 1986), 251, 253, 260–261, 264–265; and William Greider, "The Education of David Stockman," *Atlantic,* December 1981, 51.

13. Edwards, *At the Margins*, chapters 9–10; and Jon R. Bond and Richard Fleisher, *The President in the Legislative Arena* (Chicago: University of Chicago Press, 1990), chapter 8.

14. For an analysis of war powers and other issues related to separation of powers, see Louis Fisher, *Constitutional Conflicts Between Congress and the President*, 3rd ed., revised (Lawrence, KS: University Press of Kansas, 1991).

15. For more on the role of Congress in foreign policy, see Barbara Hinckley, *Less than Meets the Eye* (Chicago: University of Chicago Press, 1994).

16. See William W. Lammers, "Presidential Attention-Focusing Activities," in *The President and the Public*, ed. Doris A. Graber (Philadelphia: ISHI, 1982), 145–171; and Samuel Kernell, *Going Public*, 2nd ed. (Washington, DC: Congressional Quarterly Press, 1992), chapter 4.

17. Edwards, The *Public Presidency*, chapter 6, and George C. Edwards III, *Presidential Approval* (Baltimore: Johns Hopkins University Press, 1990).

18. Mueller also included the inaugural period of a president's term as a rally event. John E. Mueller, *War, Presidents and Public Opinion* (New York: John Wiley, 1973), 208–213.

19. Kernell, *Going Public*, 148.

20. See Jeffrey K. Tulis, *The Rhetorical Presidency* (Princeton, NJ: Princeton University Press, 1987), on presidents' efforts to build policy support.

21. "U.S. Dependence on Foreign Oil," *Gallup Poll Monthly*, February 1991, 35.

22. George C. Edwards III, "Frustration and Folly: Bill Clinton and the Public Presidency," in Colin Campbell and Bert A. Rockman, eds., *The Clinton Presidency: First Appraisals* (Chatham, NJ: Chatham House, 1995).

23. For a recent discussion of the social flow of information, see Robert Huckfeldt and John Sprague, "Networks in Context: The Social Flow of Political Information," *American Political Science Review* 81 (December 1987): 1197–1216.

24. See Edwards, *At the Margins*, chapter 7, fns. 48–51; Benjamin I. Page and Robert Y. Shapiro, *The Rational Public* (Chicago: University of Chicago Press, 1992); James A. Stimson, *Public Opinion in America: Moods, Cycles, and Swings* (Boulder, CO: Westview, 1991); and William G. Mayer, *The Changing American Mind* (Ann Arbor, MI: University of Michigan Press, 1992).

25. Quoted in "Tax Cut Passed by Solid Margin in House, Senate," *Congressional Quarterly Weekly Report*, August 1, 1981, 1,374.

26. Sam Donaldson, *Hold On, Mr. President!* (New York: Random House, 1987), 196–197.

27. Two of the leading studies are Michael J. Robinson and Margaret A. Sheehan, *Over the Wire and on TV* (New York: Russell Sage Foundation, 1983); and Daniel C. Hallin, "The Media, the War in Vietnam, and Political Support," *Journal of Politics* 46 (February 1984): 2–24.

28. Carter, *Keeping Faith*, 179–180.

29. See Thomas E. Patterson, *Out of Order* (New York: Knopf, 1993).

30. Michael Baruch Grossman and Martha Joynt Kumar, *Portraying the President: The White House and the News Media* (Baltimore: Johns Hopkins University Press, 1981), chapters 10–11.

31. Donaldson, *Hold On, Mr. President!*, 237–238.

32. David R. Mayhew, *Divided We Govern* (New Haven, CT: Yale University Press, 1991).

Nothing better illustrates the complexity of modern government than its massive bureaucracies. The *Federal Register* lists all the government regulations issued annually by Washington bureaucracies; each year this list exceeds 50,000 pages. Americans are required to submit more than two billion forms and documents (mostly about taxes) to the government each year. One plant with seventy-five employees kept two people working half-time writing reports required by the federal government.

Bureaucratic power extends to every corner of American economic and social life, yet bureaucracies are scarcely hinted at in the Constitution. Each bureaucratic agency is created by Congress, which sets its budget and writes the policies it administers. Most agencies are responsible to the president, whose constitutional responsibility to "take care that the laws shall be faithfully executed" sheds only a dim light on the problems of managing so large a government. How to manage and control bureaucracies is, in this bureaucratic age, a central problem of democratic government.

The classic conception of bureaucracy was advanced by the German sociologist Max Weber, who stressed that the bureaucracy was a "rational" way for a modern society to conduct its business.[1] According to Weber, a **bureaucracy** depends upon certain elements: it has a *hierarchical authority structure*, in which power flows from the top down and responsibility from the bottom up; it uses *task specialization*, so that experts instead of amateurs perform technical jobs; and it develops extensive *rules*, which may seem nit-picking at times, but which allow similar cases to be handled similarly instead of capriciously. Bureaucracies also operate on the *merit principle*, in which entrance and promotion are awarded on the basis of demonstrated abilities rather than on "who you know." Bureaucracies behave with *impersonality* so that all of their clients are treated impartially. Weber's classic prototype of bureaucratic organization depicts the bureaucracy as a well-organized machine. In this chapter we will see how closely Weber's conception of bureaucracy corresponds to how bureaucracies actually work.

THE BUREAUCRATS

Bureaucrats are typically much less visible than the president or members of Congress. As a result, Americans usually know little about them. This section will examine some myths about bureaucrats and explain who they are, how they got their jobs, and what they do.

Some Bureaucratic Myths and Realities

Bureaucrat-baiting is a popular American pastime. Any object of such unpopularity will spawn plenty of myths. The following are some of the most prevalent myths about bureaucracy:

- *Americans dislike bureaucrats.* Despite the rhetoric about bureaucracies, Americans are generally satisfied with bureaucrats and the treatment they get from them. Americans may dislike bureaucracies, but they like bureaucrats. One major study found a "relative high degree of satisfaction" with bureaucratic encounters.[2] Some 57 percent thought that the bureaucrats they dealt with did the "right amount" to help them; an additional 16 percent thought the bureaucrats did "more than they had to."

Bureaucrats are the scapegoats of American politics. Paperwork and red tape represent the image of bureaucracy to many Americans. Yet no society can operate without bureaucracy, and most people are satisfied with their encounters with bureaucrats.

- *Most federal bureaucrats work in Washington, DC.* Only about 16 percent of 3 million federal civilian employees work in Washington. California leads the nation in federal employees, with 325,000. New York and Texas have more than 150,000 each, and an additional 120,000 federal employees work in foreign countries and American territories. You can see where federal bureaucrats work by looking in your local phone book under "U.S. Government." You will probably find, among many others, listings for the local offices of the Postal Service, the Social Security Administration, the FBI, the Department of Agriculture's county agents, recruiters for the armed services, air traffic controllers, and, of course, the Internal Revenue Service.

- *Bureaucracies are growing bigger each year.* This myth is half true and half false. The number of government employees has been expanding, but the number of *federal* employees has not. Almost all the growth in the number of public employees has occurred in state and local governments. The 14 million state and local public employees far outnumber the 3 million civilian federal government employees (see Figure 12.1). As a percentage of America's total work force, federal government employment has been shrinking, not growing; it now accounts for about 3 percent of all civilian jobs. Of course, many state and local employees work on programs that are federally funded, and the federal government hires many private contractors to provide goods and services ranging from hot meals to weapons systems.

- *Bureaucracies are ineffective, inefficient, and always mired in red tape.* No words describing bureaucratic behavior are better known than "red tape." Bureaucracy, however, is simply a way of organizing people to perform work. General Motors, a college or university, the U.S. army, the Department of Health and Human Services, and the Roman Catholic Church are all bureaucracies. Bureaucracies are a little like referees: when they work well, no one gives them much credit, but when they work poorly, everyone calls them unfair or incompetent or inefficient. Bureaucracies may be inefficient at times, but no one has found a substitute for them; and no one has yet demonstrated that government bureaucracies are more or less inefficient, ineffective, or mired in red tape than private bureaucracies.[3]

Anyone who looks with disdain on American bureaucracies should contemplate life without them. Despite all the carping about bureaucracies, the vast majority of tasks carried out by governments at all levels are noncontroversial. Bureaucrats deliver mail, test milk, clean streets, issue Social Security and student loan checks, run national parks, and perform other perfectly acceptable governmental tasks. Most of the people who work for cities, states, and the national government are typical Americans, the sort who are likely to be your neighbors.

FIGURE 12.1 — *Growth in Government Employees*

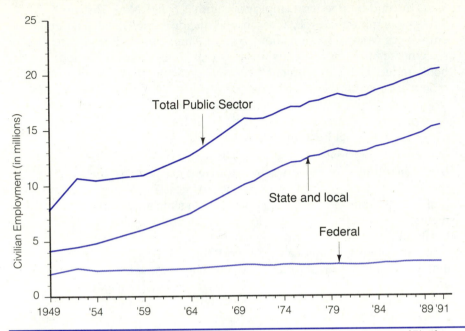

SOURCE: Advisory Commission on Intergovernment Relations, *Significant Features of Fiscal Federalism*, 1992 Edition, vol. 2 (Washington, DC: Government Printing Office, 1993), 15.

A plurality of all federal civilian employees work for just a few agencies (see Table 12.1). The Department of Defense employs nearly one-third of federal *civilian* workers in addition to the 1.6 million men and women in uniform. Altogether, the DOD (Washington's abbreviation for the Department of Defense) makes up more than half of the federal bureaucracy. Clearly, most federal bureaucrats serve in one way or another in the area of national defense.

The Postal Service accounts for an additional 25 percent of federal civilian employees, and the various health professions constitute nearly 10 percent (one in three doctors, for example, works for the government). The Department of Veterans Affairs, clearly related to national defense, has more than 230,000 employees. All other functions of government are handled by the remaining 5 percent of federal employees.

Who They Are and How They Got There

Because there are 3 million civilian bureaucrats (17 million if we include state and local public employees), it is hard to imagine a statistically typical bureau-

Table 12.1 — Federal Civilian Employment

Executive Departments	Number of Employees[a]
Agriculture	113,400
Commerce	36,100
Defense—Military functions	931,800
Education	4,900
Energy	20,300
Health and Human Services	129,000
Housing and Urban Development	13,300
Interior	76,700
Justice	95,400
Labor	19,600
State	25,600
Transportation	69,900
Treasury	161,100
Veterans Affairs	234,400
Larger Independent Agencies	
Environmental Protection Agency	18,300
General Services Administration	20,200
National Aeronautics and Space Administration	25,700
Tennessee Valley Authority	19,100
U.S. Information Agency	8,700
U.S. Postal Service	753,799

[a]Figures are for 1993.

SOURCE: *Budget of the United States Government, Fiscal Year 1995: Analytical Perspectives* (Washington, DC: Government Printing Office, 1994), 178–180.

crat. Bureaucrats are male and female, black and white, well paid and not so well paid. Like other institutions, the federal government has been under pressure to expand its hiring of women and minorities. Congress has ordered federal agencies to make special efforts to recruit and promote previously disadvantaged groups, but women and nonwhites still cluster at the lower ranks. As a whole, the permanent bureaucracy is more broadly representative of the American people than legislators, judges, or presidential appointees in the executive branch (see Figure 12.2).[4]

The diversity of bureaucratic jobs mirrors the diversity of private sector jobs, including occupations literally ranging from A to Z. Working for government are accountants, bankers, census analysts, defense procurement specialists, electricians, foreign service officers, guards in federal prisons, home economists, Indian Affairs agents, judges, kitchen workers, lawyers, missile technologists, narcotics

FIGURE 12.2 — Characteristics of Federal Civilian Employees[a]

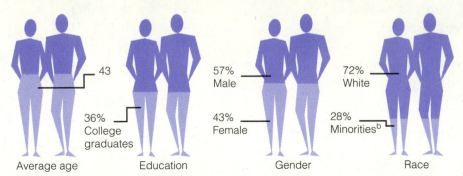

43

36% College graduates

Average age   Education

57% Male

43% Female

Gender

72% White

28% Minorities[b]

Race

[a]Does not include postal workers.
[b]Includes African Americans, Orientals, Native Americans, and Hispanics.

SOURCE: U. S. Office of Personnel Management, *Federal Civilian Workforce Statistics, Employment and Trends, November 1992* (Washington, DC: Government Printing Office, 1993).

agents, ophthalmologists, postal carriers, quarantine specialists, radiologists, stenographers, truck drivers, underwater demolition experts, virologists, wardens, X-ray technicians, youth counselors, and zoologists (see Table 12.2).

Civil Service: From Patronage to Protection. Until roughly one hundred years ago, a person got a job with the government through the patronage system. **Patronage** is a hiring and promotion system based on knowing the right people. Working in a congressional campaign, making large donations, and having the right connections helped secure jobs with the government. Nineteenth-century presidents staffed the government with their friends and allies. Scores of office seekers would swarm over the White House after Inauguration Day. It is said that during a bout with malaria, Lincoln told an aide to "send in the office seekers" because he finally had something to give them all.

It was a disappointed office seeker named Charles Guiteau who helped end this "spoils system"("to the victor belongs the spoils") of federal appointments in 1881. Frustrated because President James A. Garfield would not give him a job, Guiteau shot and killed Garfield. The so-called Prince of Patronage himself, Vice President Chester A. Arthur, then became president. Arthur, who had been collector of the customs for New York—a patronage-rich post—surprised his critics by encouraging passage of the **Pendleton Civil Service Act** (1883), which created the federal Civil Service. Today, most federal agencies are covered by some sort of civil service system.

All **civil service** systems are based on the idea of merit and the desire to create a nonpartisan government service. The **merit principle**—using entrance

TABLE 12.2 — *Full-Time Civilian White-Collar Employees of the Federal Government (by Selected Occupational Categories)*

Employment Categories	Number of Employees
General Administrative, Clerical, and Office Services	466,114
Engineering and Architecture	172,472
Accounting and Budget	153,566
Medical, Dental, and Public Health	149,250
Business and Industry	105,631
Legal and Kindred	81,878
Investigation	75,488
Biological Sciences	64,680
Social Science, Psychology, and Welfare	60,406
Personnel Management and Industrial Relations	53,545
Supply	50,571
Transportation	44,981
Physical Sciences	44,166
Education	34,371
Information and the Arts	21,894
Equipment, Facilities, and Service	17,851
Quality Assurance	17,729
Mathematics and Statistics	15,768
Library and Archives	9,842
Copyright, Patent and Trademark	2,532
Veterinary Medical Science	2,492

SOURCE: U.S. Office of Personnel Management, *Occupations of Federal White-Collar and Blue-Collar Workers, Federal Civilian Workforce Statistics, as of September 1991* (Washington DC: Government Printing Office, 1991), 7.

exams and promotion ratings to reward qualified individuals—is intended to produce an administration of people with talent and skill. Creating a nonpartisan civil service means insulating government workers from the risk of being fired because a new party comes to power. At the same time, the **Hatch Act,** originally passed in 1939 and amended most recently in 1993, prohibits civil service employees from active participation in partisan politics while on duty. (While off duty they may engage in political activities, but they cannot run for partisan elective offices or solicit contributions from the public. Employees with sensitive positions—such as those in the national security area—may not engage in political activities even while off duty.)

The Other Route to Federal Jobs: Recruiting from the Plum Book.   As an incoming administration celebrates its victory and prepares to take control of the government, Congress publishes the *plum book*, which lists top federal jobs (that is, "plums") available for direct presidential appointment, often with Senate confirmation. Hugh Heclo has estimated that there are about 300 of these top policy-making posts, mostly cabinet secretaries, undersecretaries, assistant secretaries, and bureau chiefs, and a few thousand lesser positions.[5]

Every incoming president launches a nationwide talent search for qualified personnel. He seeks individuals who combine executive talent, political skills, and sympathy for similar policy positions. Often, the president tries to include men and women, blacks and whites, people from different regions, and party members representing different interests. Some positions, especially ambassadorships, go to large campaign contributors. A few of these top appointees will be civil servants, temporarily elevated to a "supergrade" status; most, though, will be political appointees, "in-and-outers" who stay for a while and then leave.

Once in office, these administrative policymakers constitute what Heclo has called a "government of strangers." Their most important trait is their transience. The average assistant secretary or undersecretary lasts about 22 months.[6] Few top officials stay long enough to know their own subordinates well, much less people in other agencies. Administrative routines, budget cycles, and legal complexities are often new to them. To these new political executives, the possibilities of power may seem endless. Yet although plum-book appointees may have the outward signs of power, many of them find it challenging to exercise real control over much of what their subordinates do and have difficulty leaving their mark on policy. They soon learn that they are dependent on senior civil servants, who know more, have been there longer, and will outlast them.

HOW BUREAUCRACIES ARE ORGANIZED

A complete organizational chart of the American federal government would be big enough to occupy a large wall. You could pore over this chart, trace the lines of responsibility and authority, and see how government is organized—at least on paper. You can see a very simplified organizational chart of the executive branch in Figure 12.3. A much easier way to look at how the federal executive branch is organized is to group agencies into four basic types: cabinet departments, regulatory agencies, government corporations, and independent agencies.

The Cabinet Departments

Each of the fourteen cabinet departments is headed by a secretary (with the exception of the Department of Justice, headed by the attorney general) chosen by the

FIGURE 12.3 — *Organization of the Executive Branch*

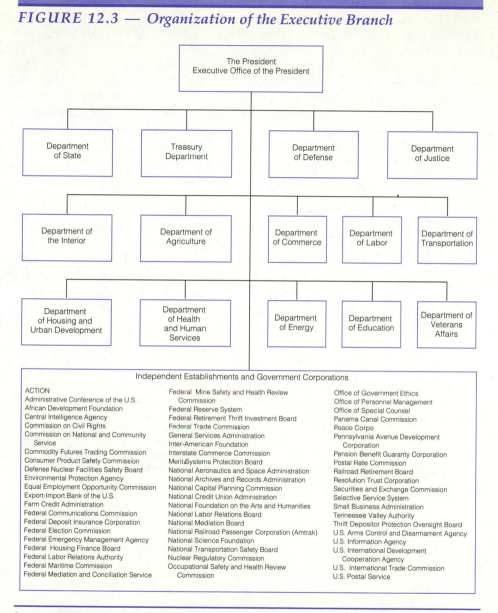

The President
Executive Office of the President

| Department of State | Treasury Department | Department of Defense | Department of Justice |

| Department of the Interior | Department of Agriculture | Department of Commerce | Department of Labor | Department of Transportation |

| Department of Housing and Urban Development | Department of Health and Human Services | Department of Energy | Department of Education | Department of Veterans Affairs |

Independent Establishments and Government Corporations

ACTION
Administrative Conference of the U.S.
African Development Foundation
Central Intelligence Agency
Commission on Civil Rights
Commission on National and Community
 Service
Commodity Futures Trading Commission
Consumer Product Safety Commission
Defense Nuclear Facilities Safety Board
Environmental Protection Agency
Equal Employment Opportunity Commission
Export-Import Bank of the U.S.
Farm Credit Administration
Federal Communications Commission
Federal Deposit Insurance Corporation
Federal Election Commission
Federal Emergency Management Agency
Federal Housing Finance Board
Federal Labor Relations Authority
Federal Maritime Commission
Federal Mediation and Conciliation Service

Federal Mine Safety and Health Review
 Commission
Federal Reserve System
Federal Retirement Thrift Investment Board
Federal Trade Commission
General Services Administration
Inter-American Foundation
Interstate Commerce Commission
Merit Systems Protection Board
National Aeronautics and Space Administration
National Archives and Records Administration
National Capital Planning Commission
National Credit Union Administration
National Foundation on the Arts and Humanities
National Labor Relations Board
National Mediation Board
National Railroad Passenger Corporation (Amtrak)
National Science Foundation
National Transportation Safety Board
Nuclear Regulatory Commission
Occupational Safety and Health Review
 Commission

Office of Government Ethics
Office of Personnel Management
Office of Special Counsel
Panama Canal Commission
Peace Corps
Pennsylvania Avenue Development
 Corporation
Pension Benefit Guaranty Corporation
Postal Rate Commission
Railroad Retirement Board
Resolution Trust Corporation
Securities and Exchange Commission
Selective Service System
Small Business Administration
Tennessee Valley Authority
Thrift Depositor Protection Oversight Board
U.S. Arms Control and Disarmament Agency
U.S. Information Agency
U.S. International Development
 Cooperation Agency
U.S. International Trade Commission
U.S. Postal Service

SOURCE: Office of the Federal Register, *United States Government Manual 1993–1994* (Washington, DC: Government Printing Office, 1993), 21.

president and approved by the Senate. Reporting to the secretary are undersecretaries, deputy undersecretaries, and assistant secretaries. Each department manages some specific policy areas, and each has its own budget and its own staff.

Each department has a unique mission and is organized somewhat differently. The real work of a department is done in the bureaus (sometimes called a *service, office, administration,* or some other name), which divide the work into more specialized areas.

Until the 1970s the largest cabinet department was the Department of Defense. Until 1995 the Department of Health and Human Services (HHS) was the largest federal department in dollars spent (although the Department of Defense still had more employees). That year the Social Security Administration became an independent agency, spending one-third of the federal budget on the massive programs of Social Security and Medicare.

The Regulatory Agencies

Each **independent regulatory agency** has responsibility for some sector of the economy, making and enforcing rules designed to protect the public interest. These agencies also judge disputes over these rules. Their powers are so far-reaching that they are sometimes called "the fourth branch of government." They are also sometimes called the alphabet soup of American government, because most such agencies are known in Washington by their initials. Here are some of these independent regulatory agencies:

- *ICC (the Interstate Commerce Commission),* the oldest of the regulatory agencies, founded in 1887 to regulate railroads and, later, other interstate commerce, specifically trucking
- *FRB (the Federal Reserve Board),* charged with governing banks and, even more importantly, regulating the supply of money
- *NLRB (the National Labor Relations Board),* created to regulate labor-management relations
- *FCC (the Federal Communications Commission),* charged with licensing radio and TV stations and regulating their programming in the public interest, as well as with regulating interstate long-distance telephone rates and cable television
- *FTC (the Federal Trade Commission),* intended to regulate business practices and control monopolistic behavior, and now involved in policing the accuracy of advertising
- *SEC (the Securities and Exchange Commission),* created to police the stock market

Each of these independent regulatory agencies is governed by a small commission, usually with five to ten members appointed by the president and confirmed by the Senate for fixed terms. Unlike cabinet officers or members of the president's staff, regulatory commission members cannot be fired by the president. The Supreme Court made this decision after President Franklin Roosevelt fired a man named Humphrey from the Federal Trade Commission. Humphrey died shortly afterward, but his angry executors sued for back pay, and the Court held that presidents could not fire members of regulatory agencies without just cause (*Humphrey's Executor v. United States*, 1935).

Interest groups consider the rule making by independent regulatory agencies—and, of course, their membership—to be very important. The FCC can deny a multimillion-dollar TV station a license renewal, a power that certainly sparks the interest of the National Association of Broadcasters. The FTC regulates business practices, a power prompting both business and consumers to pay careful attention to its activities and membership.

Interest groups are so concerned with these regulatory bodies that critics often point to the "capture" of the regulators by the regulatees.[7] It is common for members of commissions to be drawn from the ranks of the regulated. Sometimes, too, members of commissions or staffs of these agencies move on to jobs in the very industries they were regulating. Some lawyers among them can use contacts and information gleaned at the agency later, when they represent clients before their former employers at the agency. The bureaucracy's relationship with interest groups will be discussed in more detail later in this chapter.

The Government Corporations

The federal government also has a handful of *government corporations*. These are not exactly like private corporations in which you can buy stock and collect dividends, but they are like private corporations—and different from other parts of the government—in two ways. First, they provide a service that *could be* handled by the private sector. Second, they typically charge for their services, though often at cheaper rates than the consumer would pay a private sector producer.

The granddaddy of the government corporations is the Tennessee Valley Authority (TVA), which, at least until recently, provided inexpensive electricity to millions of Americans in Tennessee, Kentucky, Alabama, and neighboring states. Comsat is a modern-day government corporation that sells time-sharing on NASA satellites; through it you can rent time on a space satellite for radio communications. Even the post office, one of the original cabinet departments (first headed by Benjamin Franklin), has become a government corporation: the U.S. Postal Service. Occasionally, the government has taken over a "sick industry" and turned it into a government corporation. Amtrak, the railroad passenger service, is one example.

The Independent Executive Agencies

The **independent executive agencies** are essentially all the rest of the government—not cabinet departments, not regulatory commissions, and not government corporations. Their administrators are typically appointed by the president and serve at his will. To list and describe these scores of bureaus would be tedious, but they are listed in the current issue of the *United*

States Government Manual. The following are a few of the biggest independent executive agencies (in size of budget):

- *General Services Administration (GSA)*, the government's landlord, which handles buildings, supplies, and purchasing
- *National Science Foundation (NSF)*, which supports scientific research
- *National Aeronautics and Space Administration (NASA)*, the agency that takes Americans to the moon and points beyond

BUREAUCRACIES AS IMPLEMENTORS

In modern government, bureaucracies are essentially implementors of policy. They take congressional, presidential, and sometimes even judicial pronouncements and develop procedures and rules for implementing policy goals. They also manage the routines of government, from delivering mail to collecting taxes to training troops. The following sections will focus more closely on this crucial function of governing.

What Implementation Means

Public policies are rarely self-executing. One of the few policies that administers itself is the president's decision to "recognize" a foreign government. It is entirely the chief executive's prerogative to do so, and once it is done, diplomatic relations with the country are thereby established.

Most policies, though, are not self-executing. Congress typically announces the goals of a policy in broad terms, sets up an administrative apparatus, and leaves to the bureaucracy the task of working out the details of the policy—in other words, the bureaucracy is left to implement the program. Policy **implementation** is the stage of policy-making between the establishment of a policy (such as the passage of a legislative act, the issuing of an executive order, the handing down of a judicial decision, or the promulgation of a regulatory rule) and the consequences of the policy for the people whom it affects.[8] To loosely paraphrase a famous line about war from German General Karl von Clausewitz: "Implementation is the continuation of policymaking by other means."[9]

At a minimum, implementation includes three elements:

- Creation of a new agency or assignment of responsibility to an old agency
- Translation of policy goals into operational rules; development of guidelines for the program or policy
- Coordination of resources and personnel to achieve the intended goals[10]

Why the Best-Laid Plans Sometimes Flunk the Implementation Test

There is a famous line from the Scottish poet Robert Burns: "The best laid schemes o' mice and men/Gang aft a-gley often go awry." So, too, with the best intended public policies. Policies that people expect to work often fail. Martha Derthick told the sad tale of a "new towns in-town" program in which the government was to sell surplus property to groups that were helping to expand urban housing. In fact, little property was sold and few houses were built.[11] High expectations followed by dashed hopes is the all-too-common fate of well-intentioned public policies.

Program Design.   Implementation can break down for several reasons. One is faulty program design. "It is impossible," said Eugene Bardach, "to implement well a policy or program that is defective in its basic theoretical conception." Consider, he suggested, the following hypothetical example:

> If Congress were to establish an agency charged with squaring the circle with compass and straight edge—a task mathematicians have long ago shown is impossible—we could envision an agency coming into being, hiring a vast number of consultants, commissioning studies, reporting that progress was being made, while at the same time urging in their appropriations request for the coming year that the Congress augment the agency's budget.[12]

And the circle would remain round.

Lack of Clarity.   Congress is fond of stating a broad policy goal in legislation and then leaving implementation up to the bureaucracies. Members of Congress can thus escape messy details, and blame for the implementation decisions can be placed elsewhere.

One such policy was the controversial Title IX of the Education Amendments of 1972,[13] which said: "No person in the United States shall, on the basis of sex, be excluded from participation in, be denied the benefits of, or be subjected to discrimination under any education program or activity receiving federal financial assistance." Because almost every college and university receives some federal financial assistance, almost all were thereby forbidden to discriminate by sex. Interest groups supporting women's athletics had convinced Congress to include a provision about college athletics as well. So Section 844 reads:

> The Secretary [of HEW then, today of Education] shall prepare and publish . . . proposed regulations implementing the provisions of Title IX . . . relating to prohibition of sex discrimination in Federally assisted education programs *which shall include with respect to intercollegiate athletic activities reasonable provisions considering the nature of the particular sports* [italics added].

Just what did this section mean? Supporters of women's athletics thought it meant that discrimination against women's sports was also prohibited.

Bureaucracies are often asked to implement unclear laws. When Congress decided to prohibit sexual discrimination in college athletics, for example, it left to bureaucrats the task of creating guidelines that would end discrimination while addressing the diverse needs of different sports. It took years—and several lawsuits—to establish the law's meaning.

Some, with good reason, looked forward to seeing women's sports on an equal footing with men's. One member of the House-Senate Conference Committee had proposed language specifically exempting "revenue-producing athletics" (meaning men's football and basketball) from the prohibition. The committee rejected this suggestion, but to colleges and universities with sizeable athletic programs, and to some alumni, the vague Section 844 called for equality in golf and swimming, not men's football and basketball programs, which could continue to have the lion's share of athletic budgets.

Joseph Califano, President Carter's secretary of HEW, was the man in the middle on this tricky problem. His staff developed a "policy interpretation" of the legislation, which he announced in December 1978. HEW's interpretation of the hundred or so words of Section 844 of Title IX numbered thirty pages. The interpretation recognized that football was "unique" among college sports. If football was unique, the interpretation implied (but did not directly say) that male-dominated football programs could continue to outspend women's athletic programs.

Supporters of equal budgets for male and female athletics were outraged. Charlotte West of the Association for Intercollegiate Athletics for Women called it "a multitude of imprecise and confusing explanations, exceptions, and caveats." Even the football-oriented National Collegiate Athletic Association was wary of the interpretation. One of its lawyers allowed, "They are trying to be fair. The question is how successful they are." A 100-word section in a congressional statute, which prompted a thirty-page interpretation by the bureaucracy, in turn prompted scores of court suits. The courts have had to rule on such matters as whether Title IX requires that exactly equivalent dollar amounts be spent on women's and men's athletics.

The complex case of implementing Title IX for intercollegiate athletics contains an important lesson: policy problems that Congress cannot resolve are not likely to be resolved easily by bureaucracies.

Bureaucrats receive not only unclear orders but also contradictory ones. James Q. Wilson points out that the Immigration and Naturalization Service is supposed to keep out illegal immigrants but let in necessary agricultural workers, carefully screen foreigners seeking to enter the country but facilitate the entry of foreign tourists; and find and expel illegal aliens but not break up families, impose hardships, violate civil rights, or deprive employers of low-paid workers. No organization can accomplish all of these goals well, especially when advocates of each have the power to mount newspaper and congressional investigations of the agency's failures."[14]

Lack of Resources. As noted earlier, bureaucracies are often perceived as bloated. The important issue, however, is not the size of the bureaucracy in the abstract but whether it is the appropriate size to do the job it has been assigned to do. Often, as big as a bureaucracy may seem in the aggregate, it frequently lacks the staff, along with the necessary training, funding, supplies, and equipment, to carry out the tasks it has been assigned. Recently, for example, the news has been filled with complaints such as:

- A shortage of staff caused delays in the testing of new drugs to combat AIDS.
- Because of lack of funding, the popular Head Start program serves less than half the children who are theoretically eligible to participate in the program.
- The Department of Education's lack of sufficient auditors prevented it from detecting fraud in the federal government's student-aid programs.
- In their inspections of facilities handling and storing hazardous wastes, inadequately trained inspectors for the Environmental Protection Agency were found to be overlooking more than half of the serious violations.

- Some observers fear that the lack of financing to maintain the national parks will lead to permanent deterioration of such treasured American vacation spots as Yosemite and Yellowstone.
- Drug runners had more and faster ships and planes for smuggling drugs into the country than government agents who were trying to catch them.

Agencies may also lack the authority necessary to meet their responsibilities. For example, many observers feel that the Food and Drug Administration (FDA) lacks adequate powers to protect the public from dangerous drugs and devices such as silicon breast implants, the sleeping pill Halcion, and the sedative Versed. The FDA does no testing of its own and must rely entirely on the test results submitted by manufacturers. Yet it lacks the subpoena power to obtain documents from drug companies when its suspicions are aroused regarding the withholding of data about adverse drug reactions or fraudulent representation of test results. It also often lacks access to potentially damaging company documents that have been involved in private product liability cases.

Administrative Routine.   For most bureaucrats, most of the time, administration is a routine matter. They follow **standard operating procedures**, better known as SOPs, to help them make numerous everyday decisions. Such rules save time. If a Social Security caseworker had to invent a new rule for every potential client and have it cleared at higher levels, few clients would be served. Thus, detailed manuals are written to cover as many particular situations as officials can anticipate. The regulations elaborating the Internal Revenue Code compose the bible of an IRS agent; similarly, a customs agent has binders filled with rules and regulations about what can and cannot be brought into the United States free of duty.

SOPs also bring uniformity to complex organizations, and justice is better served if rules are applied uniformly, as in the implementation of welfare policies that distribute benefits to the needy or in the levying of fines for underpayment of taxes. Uniformity also makes personnel interchangeable. Soldiers, for example, can be transferred to any spot in the world and still know how to do their job by referring to the appropriate manual.

Routines, then, are essential to bureaucracy. They become frustrating to citizens, who term them "red tape" when they do not appear to appropriately address a situation. SOPs then become obstacles to action. Presidents have had many plans thwarted by SOPs. In an October 1983 terrorist attack on their barracks outside Beirut, Lebanon, 241 Marines were killed while they slept. A presidential commission appointed to examine the causes of the tragedy concluded that, among other factors contributing to the disaster, the Marines in the peacekeeping force were "not trained, organized, staffed or supported to deal effectively with the terrorist threat."[15]   In other words, they had not altered their SOPs regarding security, basic to any military unit, to meet the unique challenges of a terrorist attack.

Bureaucrats typically apply thousands of pages of rules in the performance of routine tasks, but many of them—especially street-level bureaucrats—must exercise administrative discretion as well. This border patrol officer, for example, must judge who he will search carefully and who he will let by with a quick check.

Administrators' Dispositions. Paradoxically, bureaucrats operate not only within the confines of routines, but often with considerable discretion to behave independently. **Administrative discretion** is the authority of administrative actors to select among various responses to a given problem. Discretion is greatest when rules do not fit a particular case, and this often occurs, even in agencies with elaborate rules and regulations. Although the income tax code is massive, the IRS wields vast discretion because of the complexity of the U.S. economy and the multitude of tax situations it produces.

Some administrators exercise more discretion than others. Michael Lipsky coined the phrase **street-level bureaucrats** to refer to those bureaucrats who are in constant contact with the public (often a hostile one) and have considerable discretion; they include police officers, welfare workers, and lower court judges.[16] No amount of rules, not even the thousands of pages of IRS rules, will eliminate the need for bureaucratic discretion on some policies. Since bureaucrats will inevitably exercise discretion, it is important to understand how they use it. Ultimately, how they use discretion depends on their dispositions about the policies and rules they administer. Although some bureaucrats may be indifferent to the implementation of many policies, others will be in conflict with their policy views or personal or organizational interests. When people are asked to execute orders with which they do not agree, slippage is likely to occur between policy decisions and performance. A great deal of mischief may occur as well.

On one occasion, President Nixon ordered Secretary of Defense Melvin Laird to bomb a hideaway of the Palestine Liberation Organization, a move Laird opposed. According to the secretary, "We had bad weather for forty-eight hours. The Secretary of Defense can always find a reason not to do something."[17] Thus, the president's order was stalled for days and eventually rescinded.

Controlling the exercise of discretion is a difficult task. It is not easy to fire bureaucrats in the Civil Service, and removing appointed officials may be politically embarrassing to the president, especially if those officials have strong support in Congress and among interest groups. In the private sector, leaders of organizations provide incentives such as pay raises to encourage employees to perform their tasks in a certain way. In the public sector, however, special bonuses are rare, and pay raises tend to be small and across-the-board. Moreover, there is not necessarily room at the top for qualified bureaucrats. Unlike a typical private business, a government agency cannot expand just because it is performing a service effectively and efficiently.

In the absence of positive and negative incentives, the government relies heavily on rules to limit the discretion of implementors. As Vice President Al Gore put it in a report issued by the National Performance Review:

> Because we don't want politicians' families, friends, and supporters placed in "no-show" jobs, we have more than 100,000 pages of personnel rules and regulations defining in exquisite detail how to hire, promote, or fire federal employees. Because we don't want employees or private companies profiteering from federal contracts, we create procurement processes that require endless signatures and long months to buy almost anything. Because we don't want agencies using tax dollars for any unapproved purpose, we dictate precisely how much they can spend on everything from telephones to travel.[18]

Often these rules end up creating new obstacles to effective and efficient governing, however. As U.S. forces were streaming toward the Persian Gulf in the fall of 1990 to liberate Kuwait from Iraq, the Air Force placed an emergency order for 6,000 Motorola commercial radio receivers. But Motorola refused to do business with the Air Force because of a government requirement that the company set up separate accounting and cost-control systems to fill the order. The only way the Air Force could acquire the much-needed receivers was for Japan to buy them and donate them to the United States.

Fragmentation.   Sometimes responsibility for a policy area is dispersed among several units within the bureaucracy. The federal government has more than 150 training and employment programs spread across fourteen departments, agencies, and commissions. In the field of welfare, more than one hundred federal human services programs are administered by ten different departments and agencies. The Department of Health and Human Services has responsibility for the Aid to Families with Dependent Children program; the Department of Housing and Urban Development provides housing assistance; the Department of Agriculture runs the Food Stamp program; and the Department of Labor administers manpower-training programs and provides assistance in obtaining employment.

This diffusion of responsibility makes the coordination of policies both time-consuming and difficult. For years, efforts to control the flow of illicit drugs into the country have been hindered by lack of cooperation among the Drug Enforcement Administration in the Department of Justice, the Customs Service in the Treasury Department, the State Department, and other relevant agencies.

Sometimes those who are supposed to comply with a law receive contradictory signals from different agencies. The regulation of hazardous wastes, such as the radioactive waste produced by the nuclear power industry, is one of the major concerns of the Environmental Protection Agency and a matter of paramount concern to the public. The Department of Energy, however, has routinely paid all the fines its contractors have received for violating laws designed to protect the environment, and it has even paid the legal fees the contractors incurred while defending themselves against the fines. The Energy Department has also given generous bonuses to its contractors even while they were being fined by the EPA. Such contradictory policies obviously undermine efforts to limit pollution of the environment.

If fragmentation is a problem, why not reorganize the government? Congressional committees recognize that they would lose jurisdiction over agencies if they were merged with others. Interest groups (such as the nuclear power industry) do not want to give up the close relationships they have developed with "their" agencies. Agencies themselves do not want to be submerged within a broader bureaucratic unit. All these forces fight reorganization, and, usually, they win.

BUREAUCRACIES AS REGULATORS

Government **regulation** is the use of governmental authority to control or change some practice in the private sector. All sorts of activities are subject to government regulation. Regulations by government pervade Americans' everyday lives and the lives of businesses, universities, hospitals, and other institutions. Regulation is the most controversial role of the bureaucracies, yet Congress gives them broad mandates to regulate activities as diverse as interest rates, the location of nuclear power plants, and food additives.

Regulation in the Economy and in Everyday Life

The notion that the American economy is largely a "free enterprise" system, unfettered by government intervention, is about as up-to-date as a shiny new Model T Ford. You can begin to understand the sweeping scope of governmental regulation by examining how the automobile industry is regulated. Buying and selling stock in an automobile corporation are regulated by the Securities and Exchange Commission; relations between the workers and managers of the

Most government regulation is clearly in the public interest. For example, the U.S. Department of Agriculture is charged with regulating the quality of meat products, a task it was given after Upton Sinclair exposed the meat-packaging industry's unsanitary conditions in his 1906 novel **The Jungle.**

company come under the scrutiny of the National Labor Relations Board; because automakers are major government contractors, affirmative action in hiring workers is mandated and administered by the Department of Labor and the Equal Employment Opportunity Commission; pollution-control, energy-saving, and safety devices are required by the Environmental Protection Agency, the National Highway Traffic Safety Administration, and the Department of Transportation; and unfair advertising and deceptive consumer practices in marketing cars come under the watchful eye of the Federal Trade Commission.

Everyday life itself is the subject of bureaucratic regulation (see "In Focus: A Full Day of Regulation"). Almost all bureaucratic agencies—not merely the ones called independent regulatory agencies—are in the regulatory business.

Regulation: How It Grew, How It Works

From the beginnings of the American republic until 1887, the federal government made almost no regulatory policies; the little regulation produced was handled by state and local authorities. Even the minimum regulatory powers

IN FOCUS

A Full Day of Regulation

Factory worker John Glasswich (not his real name) works in the city of Chicago and lives with his wife and three young children in suburban Mount Prospect, Illinois. Both at work and at home, federal regulations impact his life. He is awakened at 5:30 A.M.. by his clock radio, set to a country music station licensed to operate by the Federal Communications Commission. For breakfast he has cereal, which has passed inspection by the Food and Drug Administration, as has the lunch his wife packs for him. The processed meat in his sandwich is packed under the careful supervision of the Food Safety and Quality Service of the U.S. Department of Agriculture.

John takes the train to work, buying a quick cup of coffee before the journey. The caffeine in his coffee, the FDA has warned, has caused birth defects in laboratory animals, and there is discussion in Washington about regulating it. Paying his fare (regulated by the government), he hops aboard and shortly arrives at work, a small firm making refrigeration equipment for the food industry.

At home, Mrs. Glasswich is preparing breakfast for the children. The price of the milk she serves is affected by the dairy price supports regulated by the Agricultural Stabilization and Conservation Service. As the children play, she takes note of the toys they use, wanting to avoid any that could be dangerous. A Washington agency, the Consumer Product Safety Commission, also takes note of children's toys, regulating their manufacture and sale. The lawn mower, the appliances, the microwave oven, and numerous other items around the Glasswich house are also regulated by the Consumer Product Safety Commission.

Setting out for the grocery store and the bank, Mrs. Glasswich encounters even more government regulations. The car has seat belts mandated by the National Highway Traffic Safety Administration and gets gas mileage certified by the Department of Transportation. It happens that the car's pollution control devices are now in need of service, because they do not meet the requirements of the Environmental Protection Agency. The bank at which Mrs. Glasswich deposits money and writes a check is among the most heavily regulated institutions she encounters in her daily life. Her passbook savings rate is regulated by the Depository Institutions Deregulation Committee.

Meanwhile, John Glasswich is at work assembling food-processing machinery. He and his fellow workers are members of the International Association of Machinists. Their negotiations with the firm are held under rules laid down by the National Labor Relations Board. Not long ago, the firm was visited by inspectors from the Occupational Safety and Health Administration, a federal agency charged with ensuring worker safety. OSHA inspectors noted several violations and forwarded a letter recommending safety changes to the head of the firm. Arriving home, Glasswich has a beer before dinner. It was made in a brewery carefully supervised by the Bureau of Alcohol, Tobacco, and Firearms, and when it was sold, federal taxes and state taxes were collected.

After dinner (almost all the food served has been transported by the heavily regulated trucking industry), the children are sent to bed. An hour or so of television, broadcast on regulated airwaves, is followed by bedtime for the Glasswiches. A switch will turn off the electric lights, whose rates are regulated by the Illinois Commerce Commission and the Federal Regulatory Commission.

SOURCE: Based on a more elaborate account by James Worsham, "A Typical Day Is Full of Rules," *Chicago Tribune*, July 12, 1981 1ff.

of state and local governments were much disputed. In 1877, the Supreme Court upheld the right of government to regulate the business operations of a firm. The case, *Munn v. Illinois*, involved the right of the state of Illinois to regulate the charges and services of a Chicago warehouse. During this time, farmers were seething about alleged overcharging by railroads, grain elevator companies, and other business firms. In 1887—a decade after *Munn*—Congress created the first regulatory agency, the Interstate Commerce Commission (ICC), and charged it with regulating the railroads, their prices, and their services to farmers; the ICC thus set the precedent for regulatory policy-making.

As regulators, bureaucratic agencies typically operate with a large grant of power from Congress, which may detail goals to be achieved but permits the agencies to sketch out the regulatory means. In 1935, for example, Congress created the National Labor Relations Board to control "unfair labor practices," but the NLRB had to play a major role in defining "fair" and "unfair." Most agencies charged with regulation first have to develop a set of rules, often called guidelines. The appropriate agency may specify how much food coloring it will permit in a wiener, how many contaminants it will permit an industry to dump into a stream, how much radiation from a nuclear reactor is too much, and so forth. Guidelines are developed in consultation with, and sometimes with the agreement of, the people or industries being regulated.

Next, the agency must apply and enforce its rules and guidelines, either in court or through its own administrative procedures. Sometimes it waits for complaints to come to it, as the Equal Employment Opportunity Commission does; sometimes it sends inspectors into the field, as the Occupational Safety and Health Administration does; and sometimes it requires applicants for a permit or license to demonstrate performance consistent with congressional goals and agency rules, as the Federal Communications Commission does. Often government agencies take violators to court, hoping to secure a judgment and fine against an offender. Whatever strategy Congress permits a regulating agency to use, all regulation contains these elements: (1) *a grant of power and set of directions* from Congress; (2) *a set of rules and guidelines* by the regulatory agency itself; and (3) *some means of enforcing compliance* with congressional goals and agency regulations.

Government regulation of the American economy and society has, of course, grown in recent decades. The budgets of regulatory agencies, their level of employment, and the number of rules they issue are all increasing—and did so even during the Reagan administration. As "In Focus: A Full Day of Regulation" shows, there are few niches of American society not affected by regulation. Not surprisingly, this situation has led to charges that government is overdoing it.

Toward Deregulation.   These days, **deregulation** is currently a fashionable term in Washington and elsewhere. The idea behind deregulation is that the number and complexity of regulatory policies have made regulation too complex and burdensome. To critics, the problem with regulation is that it raises prices, distorts market forces, and—worst of all—does not work. Specifically, here are some of the accusations against the regulatory system:

- *It raises prices.* If the producer is faced with expensive regulations, the cost will inevitably be borne by the consumer in the form of higher prices.
- *It hurts America's competitive position abroad.* Other nations may have fewer regulations on pollution, worker safety, and other business practices than the United States. Thus American products may cost more in the international marketplace, hurting sales in other countries.
- *It does not always work well.* Tales of failed regulatory policies are numerous. Regulations may be difficult or cumbersome to enforce. Critics charge that regulations sometimes do not achieve the results that Congress intended, and that they simply create massive regulatory bureaucracies.

President Reagan's conservative political philosophy was opposed to much government regulation, but even before the Reagan administration, sentiment toward deregulation was building in the Washington community. Even liberals sometimes joined the antiregulation chorus; for example, Senator Edward Kennedy of Massachusetts pushed for airline deregulation. Indeed, the airline industry pressed for deregulation too, and in 1978 the Civil Aeronautics Board (CAB) began to deregulate airline prices and airline routes. Today, competitive airline fares, including inexpensive "no frills" flights, are the result of Congress's and the bureaucracy's decisions to dismantle the regulation of airlines. In 1984, the CAB formally disbanded, even bringing in a military bugler to play taps at its last meeting.

Not everyone, though, believes that deregulation is in the nation's best interest. For example, critics point to severe environmental damage resulting from lax enforcement of environmental protection standards during the Reagan administration. Similarly, many observers attribute at least a substantial portion of the blame for the enormously expensive bailout of the savings and loan industry to deregulation in the 1980s. Many people now argue for *more* regulation of savings and loan institutions. Equally important, defenders of regulation argue that we suffer fewer traffic fatalities and workplace injuries, our air is more breathable, and our water is more drinkable—all because of regulation.

UNDERSTANDING BUREAUCRACIES

You have looked at bureaucracies as implementors and regulators. In performing each of these functions, bureaucracies are making public policy—not just administering someone else's decisions. The fact that bureaucrats, who are not elected, compose most of the government raises fundamental issues regarding who controls governing and what the bureaucracy's role should be.

Bureaucracy and Democracy

Bureaucracies constitute one of America's two unelected policy-making institutions (courts being the other). In democratic theory, popular control of government depends on elections, but we could not possibly elect the nearly five million federal civilian and military employees, or even the few thousand top men and women, though they spend more than $1.5 trillion of the American GDP. Nevertheless, the fact that voters do not elect civil servants does not mean that bureaucracies cannot respond to and represent the public's interests. (Figure 12.2 showed that bureaucrats are actually more representative of the public than presidents or members of Congress.) Much depends on whether bureaucracies are effectively controlled by the policymakers that citizens do elect—the president and Congress.

Presidents Try to Control the Bureaucracy.   Chapter 11 looked at some of the frustrations presidents endure in trying to control the government they are elected to run. Presidents try hard—not always with success—to impose their policy preferences on agencies. The following are some of their methods for doing this:

- *Appoint the right people to head the agency.* Normally, presidents control the appointments of agency heads and subheads. Putting their people in charge is one good way for presidents to influence agency policy, yet even this has its problems. President Reagan's efforts to whittle the powers of the Environmental Protection Agency led to his appointment of controversial Anne Gorsuch to head the agency. Gorsuch had previously supported policies contrary to the goals of the EPA. When Gorsuch attempted to implement her policies, legal squabbles with Congress and political controversy ensued, which ultimately led to her resignation. To patch up the damage Gorsuch had done to his reputation, Reagan named a moderate and seasoned administrator, William Ruckelshaus, to run the agency. Ironically, Ruckelshaus demanded, and got, more freedom from the White House than Gorsuch had sought.

- *Issue orders.* Presidents can issue **executive orders** to agencies. More typically, presidential aides pass the word that "the President was wondering if . . . " These messages usually suffice, although agency heads are reluctant to run afoul of Congress or the press on the basis of a broad presidential hint.

- *Tinker with an agency's budget.* The Office of Management and Budget is the president's own final authority on any agency's budget. The OMB's threats to cut here or add there will usually get an agency's attention. Each agency, however, has its constituents within and outside of Congress, and Congress, not the president, does the appropriating.

- *Reorganize an agency.* Although President Reagan promised, proposed, and pressured to abolish the Department of Energy and the Department of Education, he never succeeded, largely because each was in the hands of an entrenched bureaucracy, backed by elements in Congress and strong constituent groups. Reorganizing an agency is hard to do if it is a large and strong one, and often not worth the trouble if it is a small and weak one.

Congress Tries to Control the Bureaucracy.   Congress exhibits a paradoxical relationship with the bureaucracies. On the one hand, members of Congress often find a big bureaucracy congenial. Big government provides services to constituents. Moreover, when Congress lacks the answers to policy problems, it hopes the bureaucracies will find them. Unable itself, for example, to resolve the touchy issue of equality in intercollegiate athletics, Congress passed the ball to HEW. Unable to decide how to make workplaces safer, Congress produced OSHA. As you saw in Chapter 10, Congress is increasingly the problem-identifying branch of government, setting the bureaucratic agenda but letting the agencies decide how to implement the goals it sets.

On the other hand, Congress has found it hard to control the government it helped create. There are several measures Congress can take to oversee the bureaucracy:

- *Influence the appointment of agency heads.* Even when senatorial approval of a presidential appointment is not required, members of Congress are not shy in offering their ideas about who should and should not be running the agencies. When congressional approval is required, members are doubly influential. Committee hearings on proposed appointments are almost guaranteed to produce lively debates if some members find the nominee's likely orientations unpalatable.

- *Tinker with an agency's budget.* With the congressional power of the purse comes a mighty weapon for controlling bureaucratic behavior. At the same time, Congress knows that agencies perform services that its constituents demand. Too much budget cutting may make an agency more responsive, at the price of losing an interest group's support for a reelection campaign.

- *Hold hearings.* Committees and subcommittees can hold periodic hearings as part of their oversight job. Flagrant agency abuses of congressional intent can be paraded in front of the press, but responsibility for oversight typically goes to the very committee that created a program; the committee thus has some stake in showing the agency in a favorable light.

- *Rewrite the legislation or make it more detailed.* Every statute is filled with instructions to its administrators. To limit bureaucratic discretion and make its instructions clearer, Congress can write new or more detailed legislation. Still, even voluminous detail, as you have seen, can never eliminate discretion.

Through these and other devices, Congress tries to keep bureaucracies under its control. Never entirely successful, Congress faces a constant battle to limit and channel the vast powers that it delegated to the bureaucracy in the first place.

Sometimes these efforts are detrimental to bureaucratic performance. The explosion of legislative subcommittees has greatly increased Congress's oversight activities. Numerous subcommittees may review the actions of a single agency. A half-dozen or more subcommittees may review the activities of the Department of Energy, the Department of Agriculture, or the Department of Commerce. Different committees may send different signals to the same agency. One may press for stricter enforcement, another for more exemptions. As the oversight process has become more vigorous, it has also become more fragmented, thus limiting the effectiveness of the bureaucracies.

Iron Triangles and Issue Networks. There is one other crucial explanation for the difficulty presidents and Congress face in controlling bureaucracies: agencies have strong ties to interest groups on the one hand and to congressional committees and subcommittees on the other. You learned in Chapter 8 that bureaucracies often enjoy cozy relationships with interest groups and with committees or subcommittees of Congress. When agencies, groups, and committees all depend on one another and are in close, frequent contact, they form what are sometimes called *iron triangles* or *subgovernments*. These triads have advantages on all sides (see Figure 12.4).

There are plenty of examples of subgovernments at work. A subcommittee on aging, senior citizens' interest groups, and the Social Security Administration are likely to agree on the need for more Social Security benefits. Richard Rettig has recounted how an alliance slowly jelled around the issue of fighting cancer. It rested on three pillars: cancer researchers, agencies within the National Institutes of Health, and members of congressional health subcommittees.[19] When these iron triangles shape policies for senior citizens or cancer or tobacco or any other interest, each policy is made independently of the others, sometimes even in contradiction to other policies. Moreover, their decisions tend to bind larger institutions, like Congress and the White House. Congress willingly lets its committees and subcommittees make decisions. The White House may be too busy wrestling with global concerns to fret over agricultural issues, older Americans, or cancer. If so, these subgovernments add a strong decentralizing and fragmenting element to the policy-making process.

Hugh Heclo points out that the system of subgovernments is now overlaid with an amorphous system of *issue networks*. There is now more widespread participation in bureaucratic policy-making, and many of the participants have technical policy expertise and are interested in issues because of intellectual or emotional commitments rather than material interests. Those interested in environmental protection, for example, have challenged formerly closed subgovernments on numerous fronts. This opening of the policy-making process complicates the calculations and decreases the predictability of those involved in the stable and relatively narrow relationships of subgovernments.[20]

FIGURE 12.4 — Iron Triangles: One Example

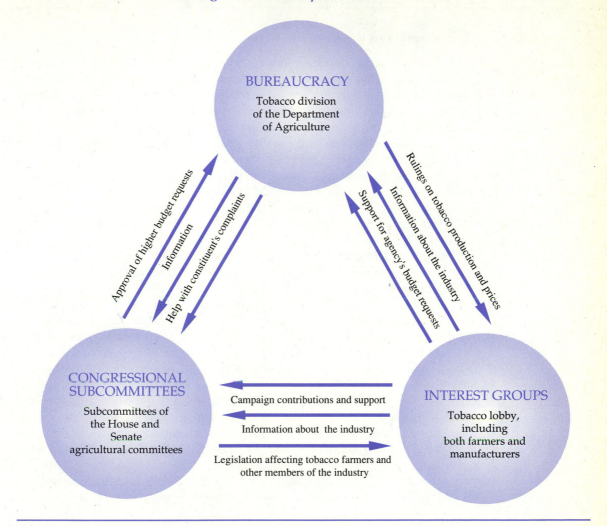

Although subgovernments are often able to dominate policy-making for decades, they are not indestructible.[21] For example, the subgovernment pictured in Figure 12.4 long dominated smoking and tobacco policy, focusing on crop subsidies to tobacco farmers. But increasingly, these policies have come under fire from health authorities, who were not involved in tobacco policy-making in earlier years. Similarly, pesticide policy, once dominated by chemical companies and agricultural interests, is no longer considered separately from environmental and health concerns. An especially vivid example of the death of an iron triangle is the case of nuclear power, swept away by the wave of environmental concerns that developed in the late-1960s.

Bureaucracy and the Scope of Government

To many, the huge American bureaucracy is the prime example of a federal government growing out of control. As mentioned earlier in this chapter, some observers view the bureaucracy as acquisitive, constantly seeking to expand its size, budgets, and authority. Much of the political rhetoric against "big government" also adopts this line of argument, along with complaints about red tape, senseless regulations, and the like. It is easy to take pot shots at a faceless bureaucracy that usually cannot answer back.

One should keep in mind, however, that the federal bureaucracy, as Figure 12.1 illustrates, has not grown over the past two generations. Indeed, considering the fact that the population of the country has grown significantly over this period, the federal bureaucracy has actually *shrunk* in size relative to the population it serves.

Originally, the federal bureaucracy had a modest role in promoting the economy, defending the country, managing foreign affairs, providing justice, and delivering the mail. Its role gradually expanded to providing services to farmers, businesses, and workers. The discussion of federalism in Chapter 3 showed that as the economy and the society of the United States changed, additional demands were made on government. Government—and the bureaucracy—is now expected to play an active role in dealing with social and economic problems. Thus, as stated earlier in this chapter, a good case can be made that the bureaucracy is actually too *small* for many of the tasks currently assigned to it, tasks ranging from the control of illicit drugs to the protection of the environment.

In addition, it is important to remember that when the president and Congress chose to deregulate certain areas of the economy or cut taxes, the bureaucracy could not and did not prevent them from doing so. The question of what and how much the federal government should do—and thus how big the bureaucracy should be—is answered primarily at the polls and in Congress, the White House, and the courts—not by "faceless bureaucrats."

SUMMARY

Bureaucrats shape policy as administrators, as implementors, and as regulators. In this chapter you examined who bureaucrats are, how they got their positions, and what they do. Today, most bureaucrats working for the federal government got their jobs through the Civil Service system, although a few at the very top are appointed by the president.

In general, there are four types of bureaucracies: the cabinet departments, the regulatory agencies, the government corporations, and the independent executive agencies.

As policymakers, bureaucrats play three key roles. First, they are policy implementors, translating legislative policy goals into programs. Policy implementation does not always work well, and when it does not, bureaucrats usually take the blame, whether they deserve it or not. Second, bureaucrats administer public policy. Much of administration involves a routine, but almost all bureaucrats still have some discretion. Third, bureaucrats are regulators. Congress increasingly delegates large amounts of power to bureaucratic agencies and expects them to develop rules and regulations. Scarcely a nook or cranny of American society or the American economy escapes the long reach of bureaucratic regulation.

Although bureaucrats are not elected, bureaucracies are not necessarily undemocratic. It is essential that bureaucracies be controlled by elected decision makers, but presidential or congressional control over bureaucracies is difficult. Bureaus have strong support from interest groups—a factor that contributes to pluralism because interest groups try to forge common links with the bureaucracies and congressional committees. These iron triangles tend to decentralize policy-making, thereby contributing to hyperpluralism.

FOR FURTHER READING

Arnold, Peri E. *Making the Managerial Presidency*. Princeton, NJ: Princeton University Press, 1986. A careful examination of efforts to reorganize the federal bureaucracy.

Derthick, Martha, and Paul J. Quirk. *The Politics of Deregulation*. Washington, DC: Brookings Institution, 1985. Explains why advocates of deregulation prevailed over the special interests that benefited from regulation.

Edwards, George C., III. *Implementing Public Policy*. Washington, DC: Congressional Quarterly Press, 1980. A good review of the issues involved in implementation.

Goodsell, Charles T. *The Case for Bureaucracy*, 3rd ed. Chatham, NJ: Chatham House, 1993. A strong case on behalf of the effectiveness of bureaucracy.

Gormley, William T., Jr. *Taming the Bureaucracy*. Princeton, NJ: Princeton University Press, 1989. Examines methods for controlling bureaucracies.

Heclo, Hugh M. *Government of Strangers: Executive Powers in Washington*. Washington, DC: Brookings Institution, 1977. A study of the top executives of the federal government, who constitute (says the author) a "government of strangers."

Peterson, Paul, Barry G. Rabe, and Kenneth K. Wong. *When Federalism Works*. Washington, DC: Brookings Institution, 1986. Examines federal grant-in-aid programs and explains why they are implemented better in some areas than in others.

Pressman, Jeffrey, and Aaron Wildavsky. *Implementation*, 3rd ed. Berkeley, CA: University of California Press, 1984. The classic—and often witty—case study of implementation.

Rourke, Francis E. *Bureaucratic Power in National Policymaking*, 4th ed. Boston: Little, Brown, 1986. Classic work on bureaucratic politics.

Rourke, Francis E. *Bureaucracy, Politics, and Public Policy*, 3rd ed. Boston: Little, Brown, 1984. An excellent introduction to the role of bureaucracy in policy-making.

Savas, E. S. *Privatization: The Key to Better Government.* Chatham, NJ: Chatham House, 1987. A conservative economist's argument that many public services performed by bureaucracies would be better handled by the private sector.

Wilson, James Q. *Bureaucracy.* New York: Basic Books, 1989. Presents a "bottom up" approach to understanding how bureaucrats, managers, and executives decide what to do.

NOTES

1. H. H. Gerth and C. Wright Mills, *From Max Weber: Essays in Sociology* (New York: Oxford University Press, 1958), chapter 8.
2. Daniel Katz et al., *Bureaucratic Encounters: A Pilot Study in the Evaluation of Government Services* (Ann Arbor: Survey Research Center, University of Michigan, 1975), 184. See also Charles T. Goodsell, *The Case for Bureaucracy*, 3rd ed. (Chatham, NJ: Chatham House, 1993), chapter 2.
3. See Goodsell, *The Case for Bureaucracy*, 61–69.
4. Ibid., chapter 5.
5. Hugh M. Heclo, *A Government of Strangers: Executive Politics in Washington* (Washington, DC: Brookings Institution, 1977), 94.
6. Ibid., 103.
7. Marver Bernstein, *Regulating Business by Independent Commissions* (Princeton, NJ: Princeton University Press, 1955), 90. For a partial test of the capture theory that finds the theory not altogether accurate, see John P. Plumlee and Kenneth J. Meier, "Capture and Rigidity in Regulatory Administration," in *The Policy Cycle*, ed. Judith May and Aaron Wildavsky (Beverly Hills, CA: Russell Sage Foundation, 1978). Another critique of the capture theory is Paul J. Quirk's *Industry Influence in Federal Regulatory Agencies* (Princeton, NJ: Princeton University Press, 1981).
8. George C. Edwards III, *Implementing Public Policy* (Washington, DC: Congressional Quarterly Press, 1980), 1.
9. Eugene Bardach, *The Implementation Game* (Cambridge, MA: The MIT Press, 1977), 85; and Robert L. Lineberry, *American Public Policy: What Government Does and What Difference It Makes* (New York: Harper & Row, 1977), 71. Clausewitz called war "the continuation of politics by other means."
10. Lineberry, *American Public Policy*, 70–71.
11. Martha Derthick, *New Towns In-Town* (Washington, DC: The Urban Institute Press, 1972).
12. Bardach, *The Implementation Game*, 250–251.
13. The implementation of the athletics policy is well documented in two articles by Cheryl M. Fields in the *Chronicle of Higher Education*, December 11 and 18, 1978, on which this account relies.
14. James Q. Wilson, *Bureaucracy* (New York: Basic Books, 1989), 158.
15. *Report of the DOD Commission on Beirut International Airport Terrorist Act, October 23, 1983*, December 20, 1983, 133.
16. Michael Lipsky, *Street-Level Bureaucracy* (New York: Russell Sage Foundation, 1980).
17. Quoted in Seymour Hersh, *The Price of Power: Kissinger in the Nixon White House* (New York: Summit, 1983), 235–236.

18. Albert Gore, *From Red Tape to Results: Creating a Government that Works Better and Costs Less* (New York: Times Books, 1993), 11.

19. Richard A. Rettig, *Cancer Crusade* (Princeton, NJ: Princeton University Press, 1977).

20. Hugh M. Heclo, "Issue Networks and the Executive Establishment," in *The New American Political System*, ed. Anthony King (Washington, DC: American Enterprise Institute, 1978), 87–124.

21. Frank R. Baumgartner and Bryan D. Jones, *Agendas and Instability in American Politics* (Chicago: University of Chicago Press, 1993).

If you happen to visit the Supreme Court, you will first be impressed by the marble Supreme Court building, with the motto "Equal Justice under Law" engraved over its imposing columns. The Court's surroundings and procedures suggest the nineteenth century. The justices, clothed in black robes, take their seats at the bench in front of a red velvet curtain. Behind the bench there are still spittoons, one for each justice. (Today the spittoons are used as wastebaskets.) The few cases the Court selects for oral arguments are scheduled for about an hour each. Lawyers arguing before the Court often wear frock coats and striped trousers. They find a goose quill pen on their desk, bought by the Court from a Virginia supplier. (They may take it with them as a memento of their day in court.) Each side is normally allotted 30 minutes to present its case. The justices may, and do, interrupt the lawyers with questions. When the time is up, a discreet red light goes on at the lawyer's lectern.

However impressive the Supreme Court may be, only the tiniest fraction of American judicial policy is made there. To be sure, the Court decides a handful of key issues each year. Some will shape people's lives, perhaps even decide issues of life and death. In recent years the Court has authorized abortion, upheld busing to end school segregation, vacillated about capital punishment, upheld some forms of affirmative action programs while rejecting others, and ordered President Nixon to release secret White House tapes during the Watergate affair. In addition to the Supreme Court, there are twelve federal courts of appeal, ninety-four federal district courts, and thousands of state and local courts. It is in these less-noticed courts that the majority of American legal business is transacted.

This chapter will discuss all sorts of courts, both state and federal, as well as all sorts of judges—the men and women in black robes who are important judicial policymakers.

THE NATURE OF THE JUDICIAL SYSTEM

The judicial system in the United States is, at least in principle, an adversarial one in which the courts provide an arena for two parties to bring their conflict before an impartial arbiter (a judge). The system is based on the theory that justice will emerge out of the struggle between two contending points of view. In reality, most cases never reach trial because they are settled by agreements reached out of court.

Federal judges are restricted by the Constitution to deciding "cases or controversies," that is, actual disputes rather than hypothetical ones. They do not issue advisory opinions on what they think, in the abstract, may be the meaning or constitutionality of a law. Two parties must bring a case to the court. This arrangement also illustrates that the judiciary is essentially passive, dependent on others to take the initiative.

Another constraint on the courts is that they may decide only **justiciable disputes**. Conflicts must not only arise from actual cases, but must also be capable of being settled by legal methods. Thus, one would not go to court to determine whether Congress should fund the Strategic Defense Initiative (SDI), for the matter could not be resolved through legal methods or knowledge.

The Courts at Work

The task of the judges is to apply and interpret the law in a particular case. Every case is a dispute between a *plaintiff* and a *defendant*—the former bringing some charge against the latter. Sometimes the plaintiff is the government itself, which may bring a charge against an individual or a corporation. The government may charge the defendant with the brutal murder of Jones, or the XYZ Corporation with illegal trade practices. All cases are identified with the name of the plaintiff first and of the defendant second, for example, *State v. Smith* or *Anderson v. Baker*. The task of the judge or judges is to apply the law to the case, determining whether the plaintiff or the defendant is legally correct. In many (but not all) cases, a *jury*, a group of citizens (usually twelve), is responsible for determining the success of a lawsuit.

There are two basic kinds of cases: *criminal law* and *civil law*. In **criminal law** cases an individual is charged by the government with violating a specific law. The offense may be harmful to an individual or to society as a whole, but in either case it warrants punishment, such as imprisonment or a fine. **Civil law** involves no charge of criminality, no charge that a law has been violated. It concerns a dispute between two parties (one of whom, of course, may be the government itself) and defines relationships between them. It consists of both statutes and common law (the accumulation of judicial decisions).

Just as it is important not to confuse criminal and civil law, it is important not to confuse state and federal courts. The vast majority of all criminal and civil cases involve state law and are tried in state courts. Criminal cases such as burglary and civil cases such as divorce normally begin and end in the state, not the federal, courts.

The American court system is complex. The serenity and majesty of the U.S. Supreme Court is a far cry from the grimy urban court where strings of defendants are bused from the local jail for their day—often only a few minutes—in court. One important distinction among American courts comes in the matter of jurisdiction. Courts with **original jurisdiction** are those in which a case is heard first, usually in a trial. These are the courts that determine the facts about a case. The great majority of judicial business is transacted in courts of original jurisdiction—the county or municipal courts first hear a traffic charge, a divorce case, or a criminal charge. Most judicial business also ends in these courts. More than 90 percent of court cases begin and end in the court of original jurisdiction.

Lawyers can sometimes appeal an adverse decision to a higher court for another decision. Courts with **appellate jurisdiction** hear cases brought to them on appeal from a lower court. Appellate courts do not review the factual record, only the legal issues involved. At the state level, the appellate process normally ends with the state's highest court of appeal, usually called the state supreme court. Appeals from a state high court can be taken only to the U.S. Supreme Court.

Participants in the Judicial System

Although judges are the policymakers of the American judicial system, they are not the only participants. In judicial policy-making, only a small part of the action takes place in the courtroom, and only a few persons participate: the judge; the *litigants* (the plaintiff and the defendant), nervously watching a process they do not always understand; the ever-present lawyers; and sometimes a jury, paying close attention to the proceedings.

Litigants end up in court for a variety of reasons. Some are reluctant participants—the defendant in a criminal case, for example. Others are eager for their day in court. For some, the courts can be a potent weapon in the search for a preferred policy. For example, atheist Madelyn Murray O'Hair was an enthusiastic litigant, always ready to take the government to court for (as she saw it) promoting religion.

Not everyone can challenge a law, however. Litigants must have what is called **standing to sue**. Essentially this means that litigants must have serious interest in a case, which is typically determined by whether they have sustained or are in immediate danger of sustaining a direct and substantial injury from another party or an action of government. Except in cases pertaining to governmental support for religion, merely being a taxpayer and being opposed to a law do not provide the standing necessary to challenge that law in court. Nevertheless, Congress and the Supreme Court have liberalized the rules for standing, making it somewhat easier for citizens to challenge governmental or corporate actions in court.

In recent years there has been some broadening of the concept of standing to sue. **Class action** suits permit a small number of people to sue on behalf of

Sometimes people find themselves involved in extraordinary court decisions. Linda Brown was a plaintiff in **Brown v. Board of Education,** *a key civil rights case in which the Supreme Court overturned its earlier* **Plessy v. Ferguson** *ruling that had legalized segregation.*

all other people similarly situated. These suits may be useful in cases as varied as civil rights, in which a few persons seek an end to discriminatory practices on behalf of all who might be discriminated against, and environmental protection, in which a few persons may sue a polluting industry on behalf of all who are affected by the air or water the industry pollutes. Following an explosion of such cases, the Supreme Court in 1974 began making it more difficult to file class action suits.

Because they recognize the courts' ability to shape policy, interest groups often seek out litigants whose cases seem particularly strong. Few groups have been more successful in finding good cases and good litigants than the National Association for the Advancement of Colored People, which selected the school board of Topeka, Kansas, and a young schoolgirl named Linda Brown as the litigants in *Brown v. Board of Education.* NAACP legal counsel Thurgood Marshall (later a Supreme Court justice) believed that Topeka presented a stronger case than other school districts in the United States. The American Civil Liberties Union, an ardent defender of individual liberties, is another interest group that is always seeking good cases and good litigants. (For an example, see Chapter 4 about the case of the Nazis who tried to march in Skokie, Illinois.)

Lawyers have become another indispensable actor in the judicial system. Law is the nation's fastest growing profession. The United States counted about one hundred thousand lawyers in 1960 but about seven hundred thousand in 1990, one for every thirty-six Americans. Lawyers busily translate policies into legal language and then enforce them or challenge them.

Once lawyers were generally available only for the rich. Today, public interest law firms can sometimes handle legal problems of the poor and middle classes. The federally funded Legal Service Corporation employs lawyers to serve the legal needs of the poor, though the Reagan administration made drastic cuts in legal aid. Some employers and unions now provide legal insurance, which works like medical insurance. Members with legal needs—for a divorce, a consumer complaint, or whatever—can secure legal aid through prepaid plans. As a result, more people than ever before can take their problems to the courts.

The audience for this judicial drama is a large and attentive one that includes interest groups, the press (a close observer of the judicial process, especially of its more sensational aspects), and the public, who often have very strong opinions about how the process works. All these participants—plaintiffs, defendants, lawyers, interest groups, and others—play a role in the judicial drama, even though many of their activities take place outside the courtroom. How they arrive in the courtroom and which court they go to reflect the structure of the court system.

The central participants in the judicial system are, of course, the judges. Once on the bench they must draw upon their backgrounds and beliefs to guide their decision making. Some, for example, will be more supportive of abortion or of prayer in the public schools than others will. Because presidents and others involved in the appointment process know perfectly well that judges are not neutral automatons who methodically and literally interpret the law, they work diligently to place candidates of their choice on the bench. Who, then, are the men and women who serve as federal judges and justices (only members of the Supreme Court are called justices; all others are called judges), and how did they obtain their positions?

THE POLITICS OF JUDICIAL SELECTION

Appointing a federal judge or a Supreme Court justice is a president's chance to leave an enduring mark on the American legal system. Guaranteed by the Constitution the right to serve "during good behavior," federal judges and justices enjoy, for all practical purposes, lifetime positions. They may be removed only by conviction of impeachment, which has occurred only seven times in the two centuries under the Constitution. No Supreme Court justice has ever been removed from office, although one, Samuel Chase, was tried but not convicted by the Senate in 1805. Nor can members of the federal judiciary have their salaries reduced, a stipulation that further insulates them from political pressures.

Although the president nominates persons to fill judicial slots, the Senate must confirm each nomination by majority vote. Because the judiciary is a co-equal branch, the upper house of the legislature sees no reason to be especially deferential to the executive's recommendations. Thus, the president's discretion, because of the Senate's role, is actually less important than it appears.

The Lower Courts

The customary manner in which the Senate disposes of state-level federal judicial nominations is through **senatorial courtesy**. Under this unwritten tradition (which began under George Washington in 1789), nominations for lower court positions are not confirmed when opposed by a senator of the president's party from the state in which the nominee is to serve (all states have at least one federal district court). In the case of judges for courts of appeal, nominees are not confirmed if opposed by a senator of the president's party from the state of the nominee's residence.

To invoke the right of senatorial courtesy, the relevant senator usually simply states a general reason for opposition. Other senators then honor their colleague's views and oppose the nomination, regardless of their personal evaluations or the candidate's merits.

Because of the strength of this informal practice, presidents usually check carefully with the relevant senator or senators ahead of time so that they will avoid making a nomination that will fail to be confirmed. In many instances this is tantamount to giving the power of nomination to these senators. Typically, when there is a vacancy for a federal district judgeship, the one or two senators of the president's party from the state where the judge will serve suggest one or more names to the attorney general and the president. If neither senator is of the president's party, the party's state congresspersons or other state party leaders may make suggestions.

The Department of Justice and the Federal Bureau of Investigation then conduct competency and background checks on these persons, and the president usually selects a nominee from those who survive the screening process. It is difficult for the president to reject the recommendation of the party's senator in favor of someone else if the person recommended clears the hurdles of professional standing and integrity. Thus, in the typical case the Constitution is turned on its head, and the Senate ends up making nominations, which the president then approves.

Others have input in judicial selection as well. The Department of Justice may ask sitting judges, usually federal judges, to evaluate prospective nominees. Sitting judges may also initiate recommendations to advance or retard someone's chances of being nominated. In addition, candidates for the nomination are often active on their own behalf. They have to alert the relevant parties that they desire the position and may orchestrate a campaign of support. As one appellate judge observed, "People don't just get judgeships without seeking them. Anybody who thinks judicial office seeks the man is mistaken. There's not a man on the court who didn't do what he thought needed to be done."[1]

The president usually has more influence in the selection of judges to the federal courts of appeal than to federal district courts. Because the decisions of appellate courts are generally more significant than those of lower courts, the president naturally takes a greater interest in appointing people to these courts. At the same time, individual senators are in a weaker position to determine who the nominee will be because the jurisdiction of an appeals court encompasses several states. Although custom and pragmatic politics require that these judgeships be apportioned among the states in a circuit, the president has some discretion in doing this and therefore has a greater role in recruiting appellate judges than district court judges. Even here, however, senators from the state in which the candidate resides may be able to veto a nomination.

The Supreme Court

The president is vitally interested in the Supreme Court because of the importance of its work and will generally be intimately involved in recruiting potential justices. Nominations to the Court may be a president's most important legacy to the nation.

A president cannot have much impact on the Court unless there are vacancies to fill. Although on the average there has been an opening on the Supreme Court every two years, there is a substantial variance around this mean. Franklin D. Roosevelt had to wait five years before he could nominate a justice; in the meantime he was faced with a Court that found much of his New Deal legislation unconstitutional. In more recent years, Jimmy Carter was never able to nominate a justice. Indeed, between 1972 and 1984 there were only two vacancies on the Court. Nevertheless, Richard Nixon was able to nominate four justices in his first three years in office, and Ronald Reagan had the opportunity to add three new members to the Court.

When the chief justice's position is vacant, the president may nominate either someone already on the Court or someone from outside it to fill the position. Usually presidents choose the latter course to widen their range of options, but if they decide to elevate a sitting associate justice—as President Reagan did with William Rehnquist in 1986—the nominee must go through a new confirmation hearing before the Senate Judiciary Committee.

The president operates under fewer constraints in nominating members to the Supreme Court than to the lower courts. Although many of the same actors are present in the case of Supreme Court nominations, their influence is typically quite different. The president usually relies on the attorney general and the Department of Justice to identify and screen candidates for the Court.

Sitting justices often try to influence the nominations of their future colleagues, but presidents feel no obligation to follow their advice.

Senators play a lesser role in the recruitment of Supreme Court justices than in the selection of lower court judges. No senator can claim that the jurisdiction of the Court falls within the realm of his or her special expertise, interest, or sphere of influence. Thus, presidents typically consult with senators from the state of residence of a nominee after they have decided whom to select. At this point senators are unlikely to oppose a nomination, because they like having their state receive the honor and are well aware that the president can simply select someone from another state.

Candidates for nomination usually keep a low profile. Little can be accomplished through aggressive politicking, and because of the Court's standing, actively pursuing the position might offend those who play important roles in selecting nominees. The American Bar Association's (ABA) Standing Committee on the Federal Judiciary has played a varied but typically modest role at the Supreme Court level. Presidents have not generally been willing to allow the committee to prescreen candidates before their nominations are announced.

Through 1994, 108 persons have served on the Supreme Court. Of the 148 nominees, 4 were nominated and confirmed twice, 8 were confirmed but never served, and 28 failed to secure Senate confirmation. Presidents, then, have failed 20 percent of the time to appoint the nominees of their choice to the Court—a percentage much higher than that for any other federal position.

Thus, although home-state senators do not play prominent roles in the selection process for the Court, the Senate as a whole does. Through its Judiciary Committee it may probe a nominee's judicial philosophy in great detail.

Seven nominees have failed to receive Senate confirmation in this century (see Table 13.1). The last two of these occurred in 1987. President Reagan nom-

TABLE 13.1 — Twentieth-Century Senate Rejections of Supreme Court Nominees

Nominee	Year	President
John J. Parker	1930	Hoover
Abe Fortas[a]	1968	Johnson
Homer Thornberry[b]	1968	Johnson
Clement F. Haynsworth, Jr.	1969	Nixon
G. Harrold Carswell	1970	Nixon
Robert H. Bork	1987	Reagan
Douglas H. Ginsburg[a]	1987	Reagan

[a]Nominations withdrawn. Fortas was serving on the Court as an associate justice and was nominated to be chief justice.
[b]The Senate took no action on Thornberry's nomination.

inated Robert H. Bork to fill the vacancy created by the resignation of Justice Lewis Powell. Bork testified before the Senate Judiciary Committee for twenty-three hours. A wide range of interest groups entered the fray, mostly in opposition to the nominee, and in the end, following a bitter floor debate, the Senate rejected the president's nomination by a vote of forty-two to fifty-eight.

Six days after the Senate vote on Bork, the president nominated Judge Douglas H. Ginsburg to the high court. Just nine days later, however, Ginsburg withdrew his nomination after disclosures that he had used marijuana while he was a law professor at Harvard.

In June 1991, at the end of the Supreme Court's term, Associate Justice Thurgood Marshall announced his retirement from the Court. Shortly thereafter, President Bush announced his nomination of another African American, federal appeals judge Clarence Thomas, to replace Marshall on the Court. Because Thomas was a conservative, this decision was consistent with the Bush administration's emphasis on placing conservative judges on the federal bench.

The president claimed that he was not employing quotas when he chose another African American to replace the only African American ever to sit on the Supreme Court. Not everyone believed him, but liberals were placed in a dilemma. On the one hand, they favored a minority group member serving on the nation's highest court. On the other hand, Thomas was unlikely to vote the same way as Thurgood Marshall had voted. Instead, Thomas presented the prospect of strengthening the conservative trend in the Court's decisions. In the end, this ambivalence inhibited spirited opposition to Thomas, who was circumspect about his judicial philosophy in his appearances before the Senate Judiciary Committee. The committee sent his nomination to the Senate floor on a split vote.

Just as the Senate was about to vote on the nomination, however, charges of sexual harassment leveled against Thomas by University of Oklahoma law professor Anita Hill were made public. Hearings were reopened on the charges in response to criticism that the Senate was sexist for not seriously considering them in the first place. For several days, citizens sat transfixed before their television sets as Professor Hill calmly and graphically described her recollections of Thomas' behavior. Thomas then emphatically denied any such behavior and charged the Senate with racism for raising the issue. Ultimately, public opinion polls showed that most people believed Thomas, and he was confirmed in a 52–48 vote, the closest vote on a Supreme Court nomination in more than a century.

Nominations are most likely to run into trouble under certain conditions. Presidents whose parties are in the minority in the Senate or who make a nomination at the end of their terms face a greatly increased probability of substantial opposition. Equally important, opponents of a nomination usually must be able to question a nominee's competence or ethics in order to defeat a nomination. Opposition based on a nominee's ideology is generally not considered a valid reason to vote against confirmation, as the case of Chief Justice William Rehnquist, who was strongly opposed by liberals, illustrates. Questions of the legal competence and ethics of nominees must usually be raised by their opponents in order to attract moderate senators to their side and to make ideological protests seem less partisan.

THE BACKGROUNDS OF JUDGES AND JUSTICES

What is the result of this complex process of judicial recruitment? What kind of people are selected? The Constitution sets no special requirements for judges, but most observers agree that the federal judiciary is composed of a distinguished group of men and women. Competence and ethical behavior are important to presidents for reasons beyond merely obtaining Senate confirmation of their judicial nominees. Skilled and honorable judges and justices reflect well on the president and are likely to do so for many years. Moreover, these individuals are more effective representatives of the president's views.

Although the criteria of competence and character screen out some possible candidates, there is still a wide field from which to choose. Other characteristics then play prominent roles.

The judges serving on the federal district and circuit courts are not a representative sample of American people. They are all lawyers (although this is not a constitutional requirement), and they are overwhelmingly white males. Jimmy Carter appointed forty women, thirty-seven African Americans, and sixteen Hispanics to the federal bench, more than all previous presidents combined. Ronald Reagan did not continue this trend, although he was the first to appoint a woman to the Supreme Court. His administration placed a higher priority on screening candidates on the basis of ideology than on screening them in terms of ascriptive characteristics. George Bush continued to place conservatives on the bench, but was much more likely to appoint women and minorities than was Reagan.[2] Bill Clinton's nominees have been more liberal than those of Reagan and Bush, and more likely to be women and minorities.

Federal judges have typically held office as a judge or prosecutor, and often they have been involved in partisan politics. This involvement is generally what brings them to the attention of senators and the Department of Justice when they seek nominees for judgeships. As former U.S. Attorney General and Circuit Court Judge Griffin Bell once remarked, "For me, becoming a federal judge wasn't very difficult. I managed John F. Kennedy's presidential campaign in Georgia. Two of my oldest and closest friends were senators from Georgia. And I was campaign manager and special unpaid counsel for the governor."[3]

Like their colleagues on the lower federal courts, Supreme Court justices share characteristics that are quite unlike those of the typical American and that qualify them as an elite group. All have been lawyers, and all but four (Thurgood Marshall, nominated in 1967; Sandra Day O'Connor, nominated in 1981; Clarence Thomas, nominated in 1991; and Ruth Bader Ginsburg, nominated in 1993) have been white males. Most have been in their fifties and sixties when they took office, from the upper-middle to upper class, and Protestants.[4]

Race and sex have become more salient criteria in recent years. In the 1980 presidential campaign, Ronald Reagan even promised to appoint a woman to the first vacancy on the Court if he were elected. President Bush chose to replace the first African-American justice, Thurgood Marshall, with another African American, Clarence Thomas. Women and minorities may serve on all federal courts more frequently in the future because of increased opportunity for legal education and decreased prejudice against their judicial activity, as well as because of their increasing political clout.

Geography was once a prominent criterion for selection to the Court, but it is no longer very important. Presidents do like to spread the slots around, however, as was the case when Richard Nixon decided that he wanted to nominate a Southerner. At various times there have been what some have termed a "Jewish seat" and a "Catholic seat" on the Court, but these guidelines are not binding on the president.

Typically justices have held high administrative or judicial positions before moving to the Supreme Court (see Table 13.2). Most have had some experience as a judge, often at the appellate level, and many have worked for the Department of Justice. Some have held elective office, and a few have had no government service but have been distinguished attorneys. The fact that many justices, including some of the most distinguished ones, have not had previous judicial experience may seem surprising, but the unique work of the Court renders this background much less important than it might be for other appellate courts.

Partisanship is another important influence on the selection of judges and justices. Only 13 of 108 members of the Supreme Court have been nominated by presidents of a different party. Moreover, many of the thirteen exceptions were actually close to the president in ideology, as was the case in Richard

TABLE 13.2 — Supreme Court Justices, 1995

Name	Year of Birth	Previous Position	Nominating President	Year of Appointment
William H. Rehnquist[a]	1924	Assistant U.S. Attorney General	Nixon	1971
John Paul Stevens	1920	U.S. Court of Appeals	Ford	1975
Sandra Day O'Connor	1930	State Court of Appeals	Reagan	1981
Antonin Scalia	1936	U.S. Court of Appeals	Reagan	1986
Anthony M. Kennedy	1936	U.S. Court of Appeals	Reagan	1988
David H. Souter	1939	U.S. Court of Appeals	Bush	1990
Clarence Thomas	1948	U.S. Court of Appeals	Bush	1991
Ruth Bader Ginsburg	1933	U.S. Court of Appeals	Clinton	1993
Stephen G. Breyer	1938	U.S. Court of Appeals	Clinton	1994

[a]William Rehnquist was promoted from associate justice to chief justice by President Reagan in 1986.

Nixon's appointment of Lewis Powell. Herbert Hoover's nomination of Benjamin Cardozo seems to be one of the few cases in which partisanship was completely dominated by merit as a criterion for selection. Usually more than 90 percent of presidents' judicial nominations are of members of their own parties.

The role of partisanship is really not surprising. Most of a president's acquaintances are made through the party, and there is usually a certain congruity between party and political views. Most judges and justices have at one time been active partisans, an experience that gave them visibility and helped them obtain the positions from which they moved to the courts.

Judgeships are also considered very prestigious patronage plums. Indeed, the decisions of Congress to create new judgeships, and thus new positions for party members, are closely related to whether the majority party in Congress is the same as the party of the president. Members of the majority party in the legislature want to avoid providing an opposition party president with new positions to fill with their opponents.

Ideology is equally important in the selection of judges and justices. Presidents want to appoint to the federal bench people who share their views. In effect, all presidents try to "pack" the courts. They want more than "justice"; they want policies with which they agree. Presidential aides survey candidates' decisions (if they have served on a lower court), speeches, political stands, writings, and other expressions of opinion. They also turn to people who know the candidates well for information. Although it is considered improper to question judicial candidates about upcoming court cases, it is appropriate to discuss broader questions of political and judicial philosophy. The Reagan administration was especially concerned about such matters and had each potential nominee fill out a lengthy questionnaire and be interviewed by a special committee in the Department of Justice. The Bush administration was also attentive to appointing conservative judges.

Members of the federal bench also play the game of politics, of course, and may try to time their retirements so that a president with compatible views will choose their successors. This is one reason justices remain on the Supreme Court for so long, even when they are clearly infirm. William Howard Taft, a rigid conservative, even feared a successor being named by Herbert Hoover, a more moderate conservative.

Presidents are typically pleased with their nominees to the Supreme Court and through them have slowed or reversed trends in the Court's decisions. Franklin D. Roosevelt's nominees substantially liberalized the Court, whereas Richard Nixon's turned it in a conservative direction.

Nevertheless, it is not always easy to predict the policy inclinations of candidates, and presidents have been disappointed in their nominees about one fourth of the time. President Eisenhower, for example, was displeased with the liberal decisions of both Earl Warren and William Brennan. Once when asked whether he had made any mistakes as president, he replied, "Yes, two, and they are both sitting on the Supreme Court."[5] Richard Nixon was certainly disappointed when Warren Burger, whom he had nominated as chief justice, wrote the Court's decision calling for immediate desegregation of the nation's schools shortly after his confirmation. This turn of events did little for the president's "southern strategy." Burger also wrote the Court's opinion in *United States v. Nixon*, which forced the president to release the Watergate tapes. Nixon's resignation soon followed.

Thus, presidents influence policy through the values of their judicial nominations, but this impact is limited by numerous legal and extra-legal factors beyond the chief executive's control. As Harry Truman put it, "Packing the Supreme Court simply can't be done... I've tried it and it won't work.... Whenever you put a man on the Supreme Court, he ceases to be your friend. I'm sure of that."[6] There is no doubt that various women's, racial, ethnic, and religious groups desire to have as many of their members as possible appointed to the federal bench. At the very least, judgeships have symbolic importance for them. Thus presidents face many of the same pressures for representativeness in selecting judges that they experience in naming their cabinet.

What is less clear is what policy differences result when presidents nominate persons with different backgrounds to the bench. The number of female and minority group judges is too few and their service too recent to serve as a sound basis for generalizations about their decisions. Many members of each party have been appointed, of course, and it appears that Republican judges in general are somewhat more conservative than Democratic judges. Former prosecutors serving on the Supreme Court have tended to be less sympathetic toward defendants' rights than other justices have. It seems that background does make some difference,[7] yet for reasons you will examine in the following sections, on many issues, party affiliation and other characteristics bring no more predictability to the courts than they do to Congress.

THE STRUCTURE OF THE FEDERAL JUDICIAL SYSTEM

The Constitution is vague about the federal court system. Aside from specifying that there will be a Supreme Court, the Constitution left it to Congress's discretion to establish lower federal courts of general jurisdiction. In the Judiciary Act of 1789, Congress created these *constitutional courts*, and although the system has been altered over the years, America has never been without them. The current organization of the federal court system is displayed in Figure 13.1.

Congress has also established *legislative courts* for specialized purposes. These courts include the Court of Military Appeals, the Court of Claims, the Court of International Trade, and the Tax Court. They are staffed by judges who have fixed terms of office and who lack the protections of judges on constitutional courts against removal or salary reductions. The following sections, however, will focus on the courts of general jurisdiction.

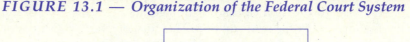

FIGURE 13.1 — Organization of the Federal Court System

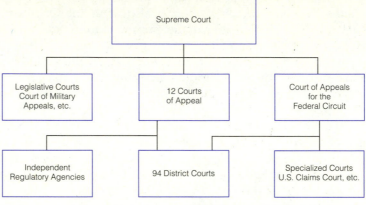

District Courts

The entry point for most litigation in the federal courts is one of the ninety-four **district courts**, at least one of which is located in each state, plus one in Washington, DC, and one in Puerto Rico (there are also three somewhat different territorial courts for Guam, the Virgin Islands, and the Northern Mariana Islands). The district courts are courts of original jurisdiction; they hear no appeals. They are the only federal courts in which trials are held and in which juries may be empaneled. The 576 district court judges usually preside over cases alone, but certain rare cases require that three judges constitute the court. Each district court has between two and twenty-seven judges, depending on the amount of judicial work within its territory.

The jurisdiction of the district courts extends to the following:

- Federal crimes
- Civil suits under federal law
- Civil suits between citizens of different states where the amount exceeds $50,000
- Supervision of bankruptcy proceedings
- Review of the actions of some federal administrative agencies
- Admiralty and maritime law cases
- Supervision of the naturalization of aliens

It is important to remember that about 98 percent of all the criminal cases in the United States are heard in state and local court systems, not in the federal courts. Moreover, only a small percentage of the persons convicted of federal crimes in the federal district courts actually have a trial. Most enter guilty pleas as part of a bargain to receive lighter punishment.

Most civil suits in the United States are also handled in state and local courts. The vast majority of civil cases commenced in the federal courts are settled out of court. Only about 5 percent of the more than 200,000 civil cases resolved each year are decided by trial.

Diversity of citizenship cases involve civil suits between citizens of different states (such as a citizen of California suing a citizen of Texas) or suits in which one of the parties is a citizen of a foreign nation and the matter in question exceeds $50,000. Congress established this jurisdiction to protect against the possible bias of a state court in favor of a citizen from that state. In these cases, federal judges are to apply the appropriate state laws.

District judges are assisted by an elaborate supporting cast. In addition to clerks, bailiffs, law clerks, stenographers, court reporters, and probation officers, they have U.S. marshalls assigned to each district to protect the judicial process and to serve the writs they issue. Federal magistrates, appointed to eight-year terms, issue warrants for arrest, determine whether to hold arrested persons for action by a grand jury, and set bail. They also hear motions subject to review by their district judge and, with the consent of both parties in civil cases and defendants in petty criminal cases, preside over some trials. Federal magistrates are becoming essential components of the federal judicial system.

Another important player at the district court level is the U.S. attorney. Each district has a U.S. attorney who is nominated by the president and confirmed by the Senate, and he or she serves at the will of the president (U.S. attorneys do not have lifetime appointments). These attorneys and their staffs prosecute violations of federal law and represent the U.S. government in civil cases.

Most of the cases handled in the district courts are routine, and few result in policy innovations. Usually district court judges do not even publish their decisions. Although most federal litigation ends at this level, a large percentage of those cases that district court judges actually decide (as opposed to those settled out of court or by guilty pleas in criminal matters) are appealed by the losers. A distinguishing feature of the American legal system is the relative ease with which appeals can be made; as a result, it may take a long time to reach final resolution on an issue.

Courts of Appeal

The U.S. **courts of appeal** are appellate courts empowered to review all final decisions of district courts, except in the rare instances in which the law provides for direct review by the Supreme Court (injunctive orders of special three-judge district courts and certain decisions holding acts of Congress unconstitutional). Courts of appeal also have authority to review and enforce orders of many federal regulatory agencies, such as the Securities and Exchange Commission and the National Labor Relations Board. About 90 percent of the more than 40,000 cases heard in the courts of appeal come from the district courts.

The United States is divided into twelve judicial circuits, including one for the District of Columbia (see Figure 13.2). Each circuit includes at least two states and has between six and twenty-eight permanent circuit judgeships (179 in all), depending on the amount of judicial work in the circuit. Each court of appeals normally hears cases in panels consisting of three judges, but each may sit *en banc* (with all judges present) in particularly important cases. Decisions in either arrangement are made by majority vote of the participating judges.

There is also a special appeals court called the U.S. Court of Appeals for the Federal Circuit. Composed of twelve judges, it was established by Congress in 1982 to hear appeals in specialized cases, such as those regarding patents, claims against the United States, and international trade.

The courts of appeal focus on correcting errors of procedure and law that occurred in the original proceedings of legal cases. These courts hold no trials and hear no testimony. Their decisions set precedent for all the courts and agencies within their jurisdictions.

The Supreme Court

Sitting at the pinnacle of the American judicial system is the U.S. **Supreme Court**. The Court does much more for the American political system than decide discrete cases. Among its most important functions are resolving conflicts

FIGURE 13.2 — *The Federal Judicial Circuits*

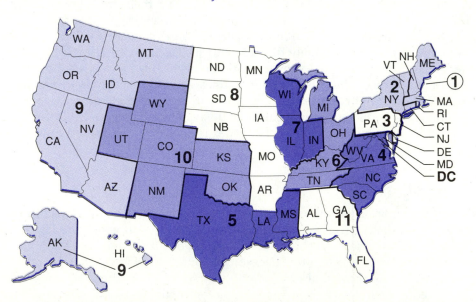

Not shown are Puerto Rico (First Circuit), Virgin Islands (Third Circuit), and Guam and the Northern Mariana Islands (Ninth Circuit).

among the states and maintaining national supremacy in the law. It also plays an important role in ensuring uniformity in the interpretation of national laws. For example, in 1984 Congress created a federal sentencing commission to write guidelines aimed at reducing the wide disparities that existed in punishment for similar crimes tried in federal courts. By 1989, more than 150 federal district judges had declared the law unconstitutional, while another 115 had ruled it was valid. Only the Supreme Court could resolve this inconsistency in the administration of justice, which it did when it upheld the law.

There are nine justices on the Supreme Court: eight associates and one chief justice. The Constitution does not require that number, however, and there have been as few as 6 justices and as many as 10. The size of the Supreme Court was altered many times between 1801 and 1869. In 1866, Congress reduced the size of the Court from ten to eight members so that President Andrew Johnson could not nominate new justices to fill two vacancies. When Ulysses S. Grant took office, Congress increased the number of justices to nine, since it had confidence he would nominate members to its liking. Since then, the number of justices has remained stable.

All nine justices sit together to hear cases and make decisions. They must first decide which cases to hear. A familiar battle cry for losers in litigation in lower courts is "I'll appeal this all the way to the Supreme Court!" In reality, this is highly unlikely. Unlike other federal courts, the Supreme Court controls its own agenda (it decides what cases it will hear).

You can see in Figure 13.3 that the court does have an original jurisdiction, yet very few cases arise under it, as Table 13.3 illustrates. Almost all the business of the Court comes from the appellate process, and cases may be appealed from both federal and state courts. In the latter instance, however, a "substantial federal question" must be involved. In deference to the states, cases from state courts involving federal law are heard only in the Supreme Court and then only after the petitioner has exhausted all the potential remedies in the state court system.

The Court will not try to settle matters of state law or determine guilt or innocence in state criminal proceedings. To obtain a hearing in the Supreme Court, a defendant convicted in a state court might demonstrate, for example, that the trial was not fair as required by the Bill of Rights, which was extended to cover state court proceedings by the due process clause of the Fourteenth Amendment. The great majority of cases heard by the Supreme Court come from the lower federal courts.

THE COURTS AS POLICYMAKERS

"Judicial decision making," a former Supreme Court law clerk wrote in the *Harvard Law Review*, "involves, at bottom, a choice between competing values by fallible, pragmatic, and at times nonrational men and women in a highly complex process in a very human setting."[8] This is an apt description of

FIGURE 13.3 — The Organization and Jurisdiction of the Courts

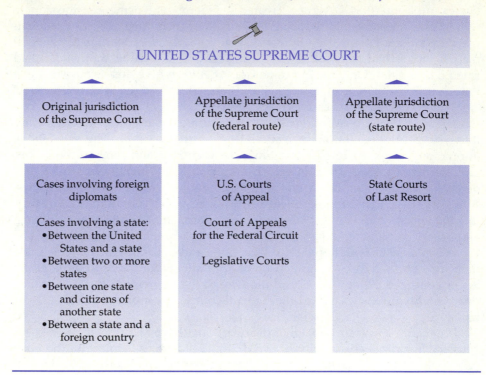

UNITED STATES SUPREME COURT

| Original jurisdiction of the Supreme Court | Appellate jurisdiction of the Supreme Court (federal route) | Appellate jurisdiction of the Supreme Court (state route) |

Cases involving foreign diplomats

Cases involving a state:
• Between the United States and a state
• Between two or more states
• Between one state and citizens of another state
• Between a state and a foreign country

U.S. Courts of Appeal

Court of Appeals for the Federal Circuit

Legislative Courts

State Courts of Last Resort

TABLE 13.3 — Full Opinions in the Supreme Court's 1992 Term

Type of Case	Number of Cases
Original jurisdiction	3
Civil actions from lower federal courts	77
Federal criminal and habeas corpus cases	21
Civil actions from state courts	4
State criminal cases	9
TOTAL	114

SOURCE: "The Supreme Court, 1992 Term: The Statistics," *Harvard Law Review* 107 (November 1993): 377–379.

policy-making on the Supreme Court and on other courts, too. The next sections will look at how courts make policy, paying particular attention to the role of the U.S. Supreme Court; although it is not the only court involved in policy-making and policy interpretation, its decisions have the widest implications for public policy.

Accepting Cases

Deciding what to decide about is the first step in all policy-making. Courts of original jurisdiction cannot very easily refuse to consider a case; appeals courts, including the U.S. Supreme Court, have much more control over their agendas. The approximately 5,000 cases submitted annually to the U.S. Supreme Court must be read, culled, and sifted. Every Wednesday afternoon and every Friday morning the nine justices meet in conference. With them in the conference room sit some twenty-five carts, each wheeled in from the office of one of the nine justices, and each filled with petitions, briefs, memoranda, and every item the justices are likely to need during their discussions. These meetings operate under the strictest secrecy; only the justices themselves attend.

Twice each week the Supreme Court justices meet in this conference room to choose, discuss, or dismiss cases. The Court rules on only about 5 percent of the cases on its docket each year, and it issues written opinions on an even smaller percentage of them.

At these weekly conferences two important matters are hammered out. First is an agenda: the justices consider the chief justice's "discuss list" and decide which cases they want to discuss. Since few of the justices can take the time to read materials on every case submitted to the Court, most rely heavily on their law clerks (each justice now has up to four) to screen each case. If four justices agree to take on a case, it can be scheduled for oral argument or decided on the basis of the written record already on file with the Court.

The most common way for the Court to put a case on its docket is by issuing to a lower federal or state court a *writ of certiorari*, a formal document that calls up a case. Until 1988, some cases—principally those in which federal laws have been found unconstitutional, in which federal courts have concluded that state laws violate the federal Constitution, or in which state laws have been upheld in state courts despite claims that they violate federal law or the Constitution—were technically supposed to be heard by the Court "on appeal." In reality, though, the Court always exercised broad discretion over hearing these cases.

Cases that involve major issues—especially civil liberties, conflict between different lower courts on the interpretation of federal law, or disagreement between a majority of the Supreme Court and lower court decisions—are likely to be selected by the Court.[9]

Since getting into the Supreme Court is half the battle, it is important to remember this chapter's earlier discussion of standing to sue, a criterion the Court often uses to decide whether to hear a case. In addition, the Court has used other means to avoid deciding cases that are too politically "hot" to handle or that divide the Court too sharply.[10]

Another important influence on the Supreme Court is the **solicitor general**. As a presidential appointee and the third-ranking official in the Department of Justice, the solicitor general is in charge of the appellate court litigation of the federal government. The solicitor general and a staff of about two dozen experienced attorneys (1) decide whether to appeal cases the government has lost in the lower courts, (2) review and modify the briefs presented in government appeals, (3) represent the government before the Supreme Court, and (4) submit a brief on behalf of a litigant in a case in which the government is not directly involved. Unlike attorneys for private parties, the solicitors general are careful to seek Court review only of important cases. By avoiding frivolous appeals and displaying a high degree of competence, they typically have the confidence of the Court, which in turn grants review of a large percentage of the cases for which they seek it.

Ultimately, the Supreme Court decides very few cases. In recent years the Court has issued fewer than 120 formal written opinions that could serve as precedent and thus as the basis of guidance for lower courts. In a few dozen additional cases the Court reaches a *per curiam decision*—that is, a decision without explanation. Such decisions resolve the immediate case but have no value as precedent because the Court does not offer reasoning that would guide lower courts in future decisions.[11]

Making decisions

The second task of the justices' weekly conferences is to discuss cases actually accepted and argued before the Court. Beginning the first Monday in October and lasting until June, the Court hears oral arguments in two-week cycles— two weeks of courtroom arguments followed by two weeks of reflecting on cases and writing opinions about them.

Before the justices enter the courtroom to hear the lawyers for each side present their arguments, they have received elaborately prepared written briefs from each party to the case. They have also probably received several other briefs from parties (often groups) who are interested in the outcome of the case but are not formal litigants. These **amicus curiae** ("friend of the court") **briefs** may, in an attempt to influence the Court's decision, raise additional points of view and present information not contained in the briefs of the attorneys for the official parties to the case. In controversial cases there may be many such briefs submitted to the Court; fifty-eight were presented in the landmark *Bakke* case on affirmative action (discussed in Chapter 4).

Amicus curiae briefs have another important role: the government, under the direction of the solicitor general, may submit them in cases in which it has an interest. For instance, a case between two parties may involve the question of the constitutionality of a federal law. The federal government naturally wants to have its voice heard on such matters, even if it is not formally a party to the case. These briefs are also a means, frequently used by the Reagan administration, to urge the Court to change established doctrine, such as the law dealing with defendants' rights.

In most instances, the attorneys for each side have only a half-hour to address the Court. During this time they summarize their briefs, emphasizing their most compelling points. The justices may listen attentively, interrupt with penetrating or helpful questions, request information, talk to one another, read (presumably briefs), or simply gaze at the ceiling. After 25 minutes a white light comes on at the lectern from which the lawyer is speaking, and five minutes later a red light signals the end of that lawyer's presentation, even if he or she is in midsentence. Oral argument is over.

Back in the conference room, the chief justice, who presides, raises a particular case and invites discussion, turning first to the senior associate justice. Discussion can range from perfunctory to profound and from brotherly to bitter. If the votes are not clear from the individual discussions, the chief justice may ask each justice to vote. Once a tentative vote has been reached, it is necessary to write an **opinion**, a statement of the legal reasoning behind the decision.

Opinion writing is no mere formality. In fact, the content of an opinion may be as important as the decision itself. Broad and bold opinions have far-reaching implications for future cases; narrowly drawn opinions may have little impact beyond the case being decided. Tradition in the Supreme Court requires that the chief justice, if in the majority, either write the opinion or assign it to some other justice in the majority. If the chief justice is part of the minority, the opinion is assigned by the senior associate justice in the majority. Drafts are then circulated among the majority, suggestions are made, and negotiations take place among the justices. Votes can be gained or lost by the content of the opinion. An opinion that proves unacceptable to a clear majority is reworked and redrafted.

Justices are free to write their own opinions, to join in other opinions, or to associate themselves with part of one opinion and part of another. *Dissenting opinions* are those written by justices opposed to all or part of the majority's decision. *Concurring opinions* are those written not only to support a majority decision but also to stress a different constitutional or legal basis for the judgment. When the opinions are written and the final vote taken, the decision is announced. At least six justices must participate in a case, and decisions are made by majority vote. If there is a tie (because of a vacancy on the Court or because a justice chooses not to participate), the decision of the lower court from which the case came is sustained. Five votes in agreement on the reasoning underlying an opinion are necessary for the logic to serve as precedent for judges of lower courts.

The vast majority of cases reaching the courts are settled on the principle of **stare decisis** ("let the decision stand"), meaning that an earlier decision should hold for the case being considered. All courts rely heavily upon **precedent**—the way similar cases were handled in the past—as a guide to current decisions. Lower courts, of course, are expected to follow the precedents of higher courts in their decision making. If the Supreme Court, for example, rules in favor of the right to abortion under certain conditions, it has established a precedent that lower courts are expected to follow.

The Supreme Court is in a position to overrule its own precedents, and it has done so dozens of times.[12] One of the most famous such instances occurred with *Brown v. Board of Education* (1954) (see Chapter 4), in which the court overruled *Plessy v. Ferguson* (1896) and found that segregation in the public schools violated the Constitution.

What happens when precedents are unclear? This is especially a problem for the Supreme Court, which is more likely than other courts to handle cases at the forefront of the law. Precedent is typically less firmly established on these matters. Moreover, the justices are often asked to apply the vague phrases of the Constitution ("due process of law," "equal protection," "unreasonable searches and seizures") or vague statutes passed by Congress to concrete situations. This ambiguity provides leeway for the justices to disagree (only about one-fourth of the cases in which full opinions are handed down are decided unanimously) and for their values to influence their judgment.

As a result, it is often easy to identify consistent patterns in the decisions of justices. For example, if there is division on the Court (indicating that precedent is not clear) and you can identify a conservative side to the issue at hand, there is a high probability that Chief Justice William Rehnquist will be on that side. Justice Ruth Bader Ginsburg may very well be voting on the other side of the issue. Liberalism and conservatism have several dimensions, including freedom, equality, and economic regulation. The point is that policy preferences do matter in judicial decision making, especially on the nation's highest court (see "You Are The Policymaker: The Debate over Original Intentions").[13]

Once announced, copies of a decision are conveyed to the press as it is being formally announced in open court. Media coverage of the court remains primitive—short and shallow. Doris Graber explains that "much court reporting, even at the Supreme Court level, is imprecise and sometimes even wrong."[14] More importantly in the legal community, the decisions are bound weekly and made available to every law library and lawyer in the United States. There is, of course, an air of finality to the public announcement of a decision, but, in fact, even Supreme Court decisions are not self-implementing; they are actually "remands" to lower courts, instructing them to act in accordance with the Court's decisions.

Implementing Court Decisions

Reacting bitterly to Chief Justice Marshall's decision in *Worcester v. Georgia* (1832), President Jackson is said to have grumbled: "John Marshall has made his decision; now let him enforce it." Court decisions carry legal, even moral, authority, but courts do not possess a staff of police officers to enforce their decisions. They must rely upon other units of government to carry out their enforcement. **Judicial implementation** refers to how and whether court decisions are translated into actual policy, affecting the behavior of others.

You should think of any judicial decision as the end of one process—the litigation process—and the beginning of another process—the process of judicial implementation. Sometimes delay and foot-dragging follow upon even decisive court decisions. There is, for example, the story of the tortured efforts of a young African-American man named Virgil Hawkins to get himself admitted to the University of Florida Law School.[15] Hawkins's efforts began in 1949, when he first applied for admission, and ended unsuccessfully in 1958, after a decade of court decisions. Despite a 1956 order from the U.S. Supreme Court to admit Hawkins, continued legal skirmishing produced a 1958 decision by the U.S. District Court in Florida ordering the admission of nonwhites, but upholding the denial of admission to Hawkins himself. Other courts and other institutions of government can be roadblocks in the way of judicial implementation.

Charles Johnson and Bradley Canon suggest that implementation of court decisions involves several elements.[16] First, there is an *interpreting population*, heavily composed of judges and other lawyers. They must correctly sense the intent of the original decision in their subsequent actions. Second, there is an *implementing population*. Suppose the Supreme Court held (as it did) that prayers in the public schools are unconstitutional. The implementing population (school boards and school administrators) must then actually abandon prayers. Police departments, hospitals, corporations, government agencies—all may be part of the implementing population. Judicial decisions are more likely to be smoothly implemented if implementation is concentrated in the hands of a few highly visible officials, such as the president or state legislators.

YOU ARE THE POLICYMAKER

The Debate over Original Intentions

The most contentious issue involving the courts is the role of judicial discretion. According to Christopher Wolfe, the difficulty is this: "The Constitution itself nowhere specifies a particular set of rules by which it is to be interpreted. Where does one go, then, in order to discover the proper way to interpret the Constitution?"

Some have argued for a jurisprudence of **original intent** (sometimes referred to as *strict constructionism*). This view holds that judges and justices should determine the intent of the framers of the Constitution regarding a particular matter and decide cases in line with that intent. Such a view is popular with conservatives, such as Ronald Reagan's close adviser and attorney general, Edwin Meese. Advocates of strict constructionism view it as a means of constraining the exercise of judicial discretion, which they see as the foundation of the liberal decisions of the past four decades, especially on matters of civil liberties, civil rights, and defendants' rights (discussed in Chapter 4).

They also see following original intent as the only basis of interpretation consistent with democracy. Judges, they argue, should not dress up constitutional interpretations with *their* views on "contemporary needs," "today's conditions," or "what is right." It is the job of legislators, not judges, to make such judgments.

Other jurists, such as former Justice William Brennan, disagree. They maintain that what appears to be deference to the intentions of the framers is simply cover for making conservative decisions. They assert that the Constitution is subject to multiple meanings by thoughtful people in different ages. Judges will differ in time and place about what they think the Constitution means. Thus, basing decisions on original intent is not likely to have much affect on judicial discretion.

In addition, Brennan and his supporters contend that the Constitution is not like a paint-by-numbers kit. Trying to reconstruct or guess the framers' intentions is very difficult. Recent key cases before the Supreme Court have concerned issues, such as school busing, abortions, and wire tapping, that the framers could not have imagined; there were no public schools or buses, no contraceptives or modern abortion techniques, and certainly no electronic surveillance equipment or telephones in 1787. Not long ago the Supreme Court was asked to rule on the case of a female tourist from Colombia whose stomach, filled with more than eighty small balloons of cocaine, had been pumped by the authorities. She claimed it was an "unreasonable search and seizure," but was it a violation of the intent of the framers, who never heard of "coke" and could not imagine a stomach pump?

As you have seen, the founders embraced general principles, not specific solutions, when they wrote the Constitution. They frequently lacked discrete, discoverable intent. Moreover, there is often no record of their intentions, nor is it clear whose intentions should count—those of the writers of the Constitution, those of the more than sixteen hundred members who attended the ratifying conventions, or those of the voters who sent them there. This problem grows more complex when you consider the amendments to the Constitution, which involve thousands of additional "framers."

Others point out that it is not even clear that the framers expected that their "original intent" should guide others' interpretations of their document. Historian Jack N. Rakove points out that there is little historical evidence that the framers believed their intentions should guide later interpretations of the Constitution. In fact, there is some evidence for believing that Madison—the key delegate—left the Constitutional Convention bitterly disappointed with the results, and wrote as much to his friend Jefferson. What if Madison had one set of intentions

Continued

YOU ARE THE POLICYMAKER— **The Debate over Original Intentions,** *continued*

but—like anyone working in a committee—got a different set of results?

Thus, the lines are drawn. On one side is the argument that any deviation from following the original intentions of the Constitution framers is a deviation from principle, leaving unelected judges to impose their views on the American people. If judges do not follow original intentions, then on what do they base their decisions?

On the other side are those who believe that it is often impossible to discern the views of the framers and that there is no good reason to be constrained by the views of the eighteenth century, which reflect a more limited conception of constitutional rights. In order to cope with current needs, they argue, it is necessary to adapt the principles in the Constitution to the demands of each era.

The choice here is at the very heart of the judicial process. If you were a justice sitting on the Supreme Court and were asked to interpret the meaning of the Constitution, what would *you* do?

SOURCES: Christopher Wolfe, *The Rise of Modern Judicial Review* (New York: Basic Books, 1986), 17. Wolfe is a strong critic of the rise of judicial activism and the lack of adherence to the original intent criteria of judicial review. For further arguments in favor of original intent see Raoul Berger, *Government by Judiciary: The Transformation of the Fourteenth Amendment* (Cambridge, MA: Harvard University Press, 1977). For views in favor of judicial activism see Traciel V. Reid, "A Critique of Interpretivism and Its Claimed Influence upon Judicial Decision Making," *American Politics Quarterly 16* (July 1988): 329–356, and Jack N. Rakove, "Mr. Meese, Meet Mr. Madison." *Atlantic Monthly*, December 1986, 79.

Third, every decision involves a *consumer population*. The potential "consumers" of an abortion decision are those who want abortions (and those who oppose them); the consumers of the *Miranda* decision (see Chapter 4) are criminal defendants and their attorneys. The consumer population must be aware of its newfound rights and stand up for them.

Congress and presidents can also help or hinder judicial implementation. In 1954, the Supreme Court held that segregated schools were "inherently unconstitutional" and ordered public schools desegregated with "all deliberate speed." President Eisenhower refused to state clearly that Americans should comply with this famous decision in *Brown v. Board of Education*. Congress was not much more helpful; only a decade later did it pass legislation denying federal aid to segregated schools. Different presidents have different commitments to a particular judicial policy. After years of court and presidential decisions supporting busing to end racial segregation, the Reagan administration in December 1984 went before the Supreme Court and argued against a school-busing case in Norfolk, Virginia.

UNDERSTANDING THE COURTS

Powerful courts are unusual; few nations have them. The power of American judges raises questions about the compatibility of unelected courts with a democracy and about the appropriate role for the judiciary in policy-making.

Interest groups often use the judicial system to pursue their policy goals by forcing the courts to rule on important social issues. Some Hispanic parents, for example, have successfully sued local school districts to compel bilingual education.

The Courts and Democracy

Announcing his retirement in 1981, Justice Potter Stewart made a few remarks to the handful of reporters present. Embedded in his brief statement was this observation: "It seems to me that there's nothing more antithetical to the idea of what a good judge should be than to think it has something to do with representative democracy." He meant that judges should not be subject to the whims of popular majorities. In a nation that insists so strongly that it is democratic, where do the courts fit in?

In some ways, the courts are not a very democratic institution. Federal judges are not elected and are almost impossible to remove. Indeed, their social backgrounds probably make the courts the most elite-dominated policy-making institution. If democracy requires that key policymakers always be elected or be continually responsible to those who are, then the courts diverge sharply from the requirements of democratic government. As you saw in Chapter 2, the Constitution's framers wanted it that way. Chief Justice Rehnquist, a judicial conservative, put the case as follows: "A mere change in public opinion since the adoption of the Constitution, unaccompanied by a constitutional amendment, should not change the meaning of the Constitution. A merely temporary majoritarian groundswell should not abrogate some individual liberty protected by the Constitution."[17]

The courts are not entirely independent of popular preferences, however. Turn-of-the-century Chicago humorist Finley Peter Dunne had his Irish saloonkeeper character "Mr. Dooley" quip that "th' Supreme Court follows th' iliction returns." Many years later, political scientist Richard Funston analyzed the Supreme Court decisions in critical election periods. He found that "the Court is normally in line with popular majorities."[18] Even when the Court seems out of step with other policymakers, it eventually swings around to join the policy consensus, as it did in the New Deal. A study of the period from 1937 to 1980 found that only on the issue of prayers in the public schools was the Court clearly out of line with public opinion.[19]

Despite the fact that the Supreme Court sits in a "marble palace," it is not as insulated from the normal forms of politics as one might think. The two sides in the abortion debate flooded the Court with mail, encompassed it in advertisements and protests, and bombarded it with seventy-eight amicus curiae briefs in the *Webster v. Reproductive Health Services* case. It is unlikely that members of the Supreme Court cave in to interest group pressures, but they are aware of the public's concern about issues and this awareness becomes part of their consciousness as they decide cases. Political scientists have found that the Court is more likely to hear the cases for which interest groups have filed amicus curiae briefs.[20]

Courts can also promote pluralism. When groups go to court, they use litigation to achieve their policy objectives.[21] Both civil rights groups and environmentalists, for example, have blazed a path to show how interest groups can effectively use the courts to achieve their policy goals. The legal wizard of the NAACP's litigation strategy, Thurgood Marshall, not only won most of his cases, but also won for himself a seat on the Supreme Court. Almost every major policy decision these days ends up in court. Chances are good that some judge can be found who will rule in an interest group's favor. On the other hand, agencies and businesses commonly find themselves ordered by different courts to do opposite things. The habit of always turning to the courts as a last resort can add to policy delay, deadlock, and inconsistency.

"Call it 'legislating from the bench,' if you will, but on this occasion I should like to repeal the First Amendment."

Drawing by Handelsman; © 1992 The New Yorker Magazine, Inc.

What Courts Should Do: The Issue of Judicial Power

The courts, Alexander Hamilton wrote in the *Federalist #78*, "will be least in capacity to annoy or injure" the people and their liberties. Throughout American history, critics of judicial power have disagreed. They see the courts as too powerful for their own—or the nation's—good. Courts make policy on both large and small issues. In recent years, courts have made policies on major issues involving school busing, abortion, affirmative action, nuclear power, and other key issues. In other cases around the country, courts have done the following:

- Ordered the city of Mobile, Alabama, to change its form of government because it allegedly discriminated against minorities (the Supreme Court overturned this decision)
- Closed some prisons and ordered other states to expand their prison size
- Eliminated high school diplomas as a requirement for a fire fighter's job
- Decided that Mexican-American children have a constitutional right to a bilingual education[22]

There are strong disagreements concerning the appropriateness of allowing the courts to have a policy-making role. Many scholars and judges favor a policy of **judicial restraint**, in which judges adhere closely to precedent and play minimal policy-making roles, leaving policy decisions strictly to the legislatures. These observers stress that the federal courts, composed of unelected judges, are the least democratic branch of government and they therefore question the qualifications of judges for making policy decisions and balancing interests. Advocates of judicial restraint believe that decisions such as those on abortion and school prayer go well beyond the "referee" role they feel is appropriate for courts in a democracy.

On the other side are proponents of **judicial activism**, in which judges make bolder policy decisions, even charting new constitutional ground with a particular decision. Advocates of judicial activism emphasize that the courts may alleviate pressing needs—especially of those who are politically or economically weak—left unmet by the majoritarian political process.

It is important not to confuse judicial activism or restraint with liberalism or conservatism. In Table 13.4 you can see the varying levels of the Supreme Court's use of judicial review to void laws passed by Congress in different eras. The table shows that in the early years of the New Deal, judicial activists were conservatives. During the tenure of Earl Warren as chief justice (1953–69), activists made liberal decisions. It is interesting to note that the tenure of the conservative Chief Justice Warren Burger (1969–86) and several conservative nominees of Republican presidents marked the most active use of judicial review in the nation's history.

The problem remains of reconciling the American democratic heritage with an active policy-making role for the judiciary. The federal courts have developed a doctrine of **political questions** as a means to avoid deciding some cases, principally those regarding conflicts between the president and Congress. The courts have shown no willingness, for example, to settle disputes regarding the War Powers Resolution (see Chapter 11).

Similarly, judges typically attempt, whenever possible, to avoid deciding a case on the basis of the Constitution, preferring less contentious "technical" grounds. They also employ issues of jurisdiction, mootness (whether a case presents an issue of contention), standing, ripeness (whether the issues of a case are clear enough and evolved enough to serve as the basis of a decision), and other conditions to avoid adjudication of some politically charged cases. The Supreme Court refused to decide, for example, whether it was legal to carry out the war in Vietnam without an explicit declaration of war from Congress.

Thus, as we saw in the discussion of *Marbury v. Madison* in Chapter 2, from the earliest days of the Republic federal judges have been politically astute in their efforts to maintain the legitimacy of the judiciary and to husband their resources. (Remember, judges are typically recruited from political backgrounds.) They have tried not to take on too many politically controversial issues at one time. They have also been much more likely to find state laws (more than 1000) rather than federal laws (approximately 142, as shown in Table 13.4) unconstitutional.

Another factor that increases the acceptability of activist courts is the ability to overturn their decisions. First, the president and the Senate determine who sits on the federal bench. Second, Congress, with or without the president's

TABLE 13.4 — *Supreme Court Rulings in which Federal Statutes Have Been Found Unconstitutional*

Period	Statutes Voided[a]
1798–1864	2
1864–1910	33 (34)[b]
1910–1930	24
1930–1936	14
1936–1953	3
1953–1969	25
1969–1986	34
1986–present	7
TOTAL	142

[a]In whole or in part.
[b]An 1883 decision in the *Civil Rights Cases* consolidated five different cases into one opinion declaring one act of Congress void. In 1895, *Pollock v. Farmers Loan and Trust Co.* was heard twice, with the same result each time.

SOURCE: Adapted from Henry J. Abraham, *The Judicial Process*, 6th ed. (New York: Oxford University Press, 1993), 272; Lawrence Baum, *The Supreme Court*, 4th ed. (Washington, DC: Congressional Quarterly Press, 1992), 188.

Today's Supreme Court is headed by Chief Justice William Rehnquist. Front row, from left: Antonin Scalia, John Paul Stevens, Chief Justice Rehnquist, Sandra Day O'Connor, Anthony M. Kennedy. Back row, from left: Ruth Bader Ginsburg, David H. Souter, Clarence Thomas, and Stephen G. Breyer.

urging, can begin the process of amending the Constitution to overcome a constitutional decision of the Supreme Court. Although this process does not occur rapidly, it is a safety valve. The Sixteenth Amendment, providing for a federal income tax, was passed in response to a decision of the Supreme Court nullifying the existing income tax. When the Supreme Court voided state laws prohibiting flag burning, President Bush immediately proposed a constitutional amendment that would permit such laws.

Even more drastic options are available as well. In 1801, the Federalists, just before leaving office, created a tier of circuit courts and populated them with Federalist judges; the Jeffersonian Democrats took over the reins of power and promptly abolished the entire level of courts. In 1869 the Radical Republicans in Congress altered the appellate jurisdiction of the Supreme Court to prevent it from hearing a case (*Ex parte McCardle*) that concerned the Reconstruction Acts. This kind of alteration has never recurred, although Congress did threaten to employ the method in the 1950s regarding some matters of civil liberties.

Finally, if the issue is one of **statutory construction,** in which a court interprets an act of Congress, the legislature routinely passes legislation that clarifies existing laws and, in effect, overturns the courts.[23] In 1984, for example, the Supreme Court ruled in *Grove City College v. Bell* that when an institution receives federal aid, only the program or activity that actually gets the aid, not the entire institution, is covered by four federal civil rights laws. In 1988, Congress passed a new law specifying that the entire institution is affected. Thus, the description of the judiciary as the "ultimate arbiter of the Constitution" is hyperbolic; all the branches of government help define and shape the Constitution.

SUMMARY

The American judicial system is complex. Sitting at the pinnacle of the judicial system is the Supreme Court, but its importance is often exaggerated. Most judicial policy-making and norm enforcement take place in the state courts and the lower federal courts.

Throughout American political history, courts have shaped public policy about the economy, liberty, equality, and, most recently, ecology. In the economic arena, until the time of Franklin D. Roosevelt, courts traditionally favored corporations, especially when government tried to regulate them. Since the New Deal, though, the courts have been more tolerant of government regulation of business, shifting much of their policy-making attention to issues of liberty and equality. From *Dred Scott* to *Plessy* to *Brown*, the Court has moved from a role of reinforcing discriminatory policy toward racial minorities to a role of shaping new policies for protecting civil rights. Most recently, environmental groups have used the courts to achieve their policy goals.

A critical view of the courts claims that they are too powerful for the nation's own good and are rather ineffective policymakers besides. Throughout American history, however, judges have been important agenda-setters in the political system. Many of the most important political questions make their way into the courts at one time or another. The judiciary is an alternative point of access for those seeking to obtain public policy decisions to their liking, especially those who are not advantaged in the majoritarian political process.

Once in court, litigants face judges whose discretion in decision making is typically limited by precedent. Nevertheless, on questions that raise novel issues, as do many of the most important questions that reach the Supreme Court, the law is less firmly established. Here there is more leeway and judges become more purely political players, balancing different interests and linked to the rest of the political system by their own policy preferences and the politics of their selection.

FOR FURTHER READING

Abraham, Henry J. *Justices and Presidents: A Political History of Appointments to the Supreme Court*, 3rd ed. New York: Oxford University Press, 1992. A readable history of the relationships between presidents and the justices they appointed.

Baum, Lawrence. *The Supreme Court*, 4th ed. Washington, DC: Congressional Quarterly Press, 1992. An excellent work on the operations and impact of the Court.

Carp, Robert A., and C. K. Rowland. *Policymaking and Politics in the Federal District Courts.* Knoxville: University of Tennessee Press, 1983. The best work on the operations of the lower federal courts.

Ely, John Hart. *Democracy and Distrust.* Cambridge, MA: Harvard University Press, 1980. An appraisal of judicial review and an effort to create a balanced justification for the role of the courts in policy-making.

Gates, John B., and Charles A. Johnson, eds. *The American Courts: A Critical Assessment. Washington*, DC: Congressional Quarterly Press, 1991. Useful essays covering many aspects of judicial politics.

Horowitz, Donald. *The Courts and Social Policy.* Washington, DC: Brookings Institution, 1977. A critical assessment of the courts' role in social issues.

Howard, J. Woodford, Jr. *Courts of Appeals in the Federal Judicial System.* Princeton, NJ: Princeton University Press, 1981. A leading work on the federal courts of appeal.

Jacob, Herbert. *Law and Politics in the United States.* 2nd ed. Boston: Little, Brown, 1995. An introduction to the American legal system with an emphasis on linkages to the political arena.

Johnson, Charles A., and Bradley C. Canon. *Judicial Policies: Implementation and Impact.* Washington, DC: Congressional Quarterly Press, 1984. One of the best overviews of judicial policy implementation.

O'Brien, David M. *Storm Center*, 3rd ed. New York: Norton, 1993. An overview of the Supreme Court's role in American politics.

Woodward, Bob, and Scott Armstrong. *The Brethren.* New York: Simon & Schuster, 1979. A gossipy "insider's" portrayal of the Supreme Court.

NOTES

1. Quoted in J. Woodford Howard, Jr., *Courts of Appeals in the Federal Judicial System: A Study of the Second, Fifth, and District of Columbia Circuits* (Princeton, NJ: Princeton University Press, 1981), 101.

2. Sheldon Goldman, "Bush's Judicial Legacy," *Judicature* 76 (April-May 1993): 282–297.

3. Quoted in Nina Totenberg, "Will Judges Be Chosen Rationally?" *Judicature* 60 (August-September 1976): 93.

4. See John Schmidhauser, *Judges and Justices: The Federal Appellate Judiciary* (Boston: Little, Brown, 1978).

5. Quoted in Henry J. Abraham, *Justices and Presidents: A Political History of Appointments to the Supreme Court*, 3rd ed. (New York: Oxford University Press, 1992), 266.

6. Ibid., 70.

7. On the impact of the background of members of the judiciary, see Robert A. Carp and C. K. Rowland, *Policymaking and Politics in the Federal District Courts* (Knoxville: University of Tennessee Press, 1983); Thomas G. Walker and Deborah J. Barrow, "The Diversification of the Federal Bench: Policy and Process Ramifications," *Journal of Politics* 47 (May 1985): 596–617; and C. Neal Tate and Roger Handberg, "Time Binding and Theory Building in Personal Attribute

Models of Supreme Court Voting Behavior, 1916–1988," American *Journal of Political Science* 35 (May 1981): 460–480.

8. Quoted in Nina Totenberg, "Behind the Marble, Beneath the Robes," *The New York Times Magazine*, March 16, 1975, 37.

9. Doris Marie Provine, *Case Selection in the United States Supreme Court* (Chicago: University of Chicago Press, 1980); and Stuart H. Teger and Douglas Kosinski, "The Cue Theory of Supreme Court Certiorari Jurisdiction: A Reconsideration," *Journal of Politics* 42 (August 1980): 834–846.

10. Sidney Ulmer, "The Supreme Court's Certiorari Decisions: Conflict as a Predictive Variable," *American Political Science Review* 78 (December 1984): 901–911.

11. Data on Supreme Court decisions can be found in the November issue of the *Harvard Law Review*.

12. A. P. Blaustein and A. H. Field, "Overruling Opinions in the Supreme Court," *Michigan Law Review* 57, No. 2 (1957): 151.

13. See, for example, David W. Rohde and Harold J. Spaeth, *Supreme Court Decision Making* (San Francisco: W. H. Freeman, 1976); and Jeffrey A. Segal and Albert O. Cover, "Ideological Values and the Votes of U.S. Supreme Court Justices," *American Political Science Review* 83 (June 1989): 557–566; and Tracey E. George and Lee Epstein, "On the Nature of Supreme Court Decision Making," *American Political Science Review* 86 (June 1992): 323–337.

14. Doris Graber, *Mass Media and American Politics*, 4th ed. (Washington, DC: Congressional Quarterly Press, 1993), 329.

15. Lawrence Baum, *The Supreme Court*, 4th ed. (Washington, DC: Congressional Quarterly Press, 1992), 181–182.

16. Charles A. Johnson and Bradley C. Canon, *Judicial Policies: Implementation and Impact* (Washington, DC: Congressional Quarterly Press, 1984), chapter 1.

17. William Rehnquist, "The Notion of a Living Constitution," in *Views from the Bench*, ed. Mark W. Cannon and David M. O'Brien (Chatham, NJ: Chatham House, 1985), 129.

18. Richard Funston, "The Supreme Court and Critical Elections," *American Political Science Review* 69 (1975): 810.

19. David G. Barnum, "The Supreme Court and Public Opinion: Judicial Decision Making in the Post–New Deal Period," *Journal of Politics* 47 (May 1985): 652–662. See also John B. Gates, "Partisan Realignment, Unconstitutional State Policies, and the U.S. Supreme Court, 1837–1964," *American Journal of Political Science* 31 (May 1987): 259–280; Thomas R. Marshall, "Public Opinion, Representation, and the Modern Supreme Court," *American Politics Quarterly* 16 (July 1988): 296–316; and William Mishler and Reginald S. Sheehan, "The Supreme Court as a Countermajoritarian Institution? The Impact of Public Opinion on Supreme Court Decisions," *American Political Science Review* 87 (March 1993): 87–101.

20. Gregory A. Caldeira and John R. Wright, "Organized Interests and Agenda Setting in the U.S. Supreme Court," *American Political Science Review* 82 (December 1988): 1109–1128.

21. On group use of the litigation process, see Karen Orren, "Standing to Sue: Interest Group Conflict in the Federal Courts," *American Political Science Review* 70 (September 1976): 723–742; Karen O'Connor and Lee Epstein, "The Rise of Conservative Interest Group Litigation," *Journal of Politics* 45 (May 1983): 479–489; and Lee Epstein and C. K. Rowland, "Debunking the Myth of Interest Group

Invincibility in the Courts," *American Political Science Review* 85 (March 1991): 205–217.

22. These and other examples of judicial activism are reported in a critical assessment of judicial intervention by Donald Horowitz, *The Courts and Social Policy* (Washington, DC: The Brookings Institution, 1977).

23. William N. Eskridge, "Overriding Supreme Court Statutory Interpretation Decisions," *Yale Law Journal* 101 (1991): 331–455; Joseph Ignagni and James Meernik, "Explaining Congressional Attempts to Reverse Supreme Court Decisions," *Political Research Quarterly* 10 (June 1994): 353–372.

Two questions are central to politics: Who should bear the burden of paying for government? Who should receive the benefits? Most of the political struggles you read about in the newspapers result from policy questions concerning revenues and expenditures.

Everyone has some understanding of budgeting. Public budgets are superficially like personal budgets. Aaron Wildavsky has remarked that a budget is a document that "contains words and figures that propose expenditures for certain objects and purposes." There is more to public budgets than bookkeeping, however, because a public **budget** is a policy document allocating burdens (taxes) and benefits (expenditures). Thus, "budgeting is concerned with translating financial resources into human purposes. A budget therefore may also be characterized as a series of goals with price tags attached."[1]

For years, the dominant issue at the national level has not been whether it is good for the government to spend money to feed the poor, provide health care for the elderly, or clean up the environment. Most people support such policies. Instead, the dominant political issue has been how to pay for these policies. Financial resources have always been scarce, and during the 1980s and the 1990s the national government incurred a large budget deficit. A budget **deficit** occurs when **expenditures** exceed **revenues** in a fiscal year. In other words, the national government spends more money than it receives in taxes. As a result, the total national debt rose sharply during the 1980s, increasing from less than $1 trillion to about $4.5 trillion by 1994. About 14 percent of all current budget expenditures go to paying just the *interest* on this debt.

With the national government awash in red ink, the president and Congress have been caught in a budgetary squeeze: Americans want them to balance the budget, maintain or increase the level of government spending on

FIGURE 14.1 — *The Federal Government Dollar (Fiscal Year 1994 Estimate)*

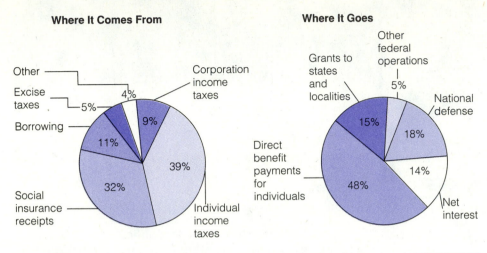

Where It Comes From

Other — 4%
Excise taxes — 5%
Corporation income taxes — 9%
Borrowing — 11%
Social insurance receipts — 32%
Individual income taxes — 39%

Where It Goes

Grants to states and localities — 15%
Other federal operations — 5%
National defense — 18%
Direct benefit payments for individuals — 48%
Net interest — 14%

SOURCE: *Budget of the United States Government, Fiscal Year 1995* (Washington, DC: Government Printing Office, 1994), 12.

most policies, and keep taxes low. As a result, the president and Congress are preoccupied with budgeting, trying to cope with these contradictory demands.

Budgets are also central to the policy-making process, because they reflect the values of decision makers regarding public policy. Indeed, for many programs, budgeting *is* policy. The amount of money spent on a program determines how many people are served, how well they are served, or how much of something (weapons, vaccines, and so on) the government can purchase.

Figure 14.1 gives a quick overview of the federal budget. It offers a simplified picture of the two sides of the budgetary coin—revenues and expenditures. The distribution of the government's budget results from a very complex budgetary process. Nestled inside the tax and expenditures figures are thousands of policy choices, each prompting plenty of politics.

This chapter will provide you with a brief overview of how the American government raises money and where that money is spent. In short, you will look at how government manages its money—really, of course, *your* money. The following section will begin this investigation by asking the logical first question: Where does the government get its money?

THE GOVERNMENT'S SOURCE OF REVENUES

"Taxes," said the late Supreme Court Justice Oliver Wendell Holmes, Jr., "are what we pay for civilization." Despite his assertion that "I like to pay taxes," most taxpayers throughout history would not agree. The art of taxation, said

Jean-Baptiste Colbert, Louis XIV's finance minister, is in "so plucking the goose as to procure the largest quantity of feathers with the least possible amount of squealing."[2] You can see in Figure 14.2 where the federal government has been getting its feathers. Only a small share come from excise taxes (for example, those on gasoline) and other sources; the three major sources of federal revenues are the personal and corporate income tax, social insurance taxes, and borrowing.

Income Tax: The Government's Golden Egg?

Bleary-eyed, millions of American taxpayers struggle to the post office before midnight every April 15 to mail their income tax forms. Individuals are required to pay the government a portion of the money they earn; this portion is an **income tax**. Although the government briefly adopted an income tax during the Civil War, the first peacetime income tax was enacted in 1894. Even though the tax was only 2 percent of income earned beyond the then-magnificent sum of $4,000, a lawyer opposing it called the tax the first step of a "communist march."

FIGURE 14.2 — Federal Revenues

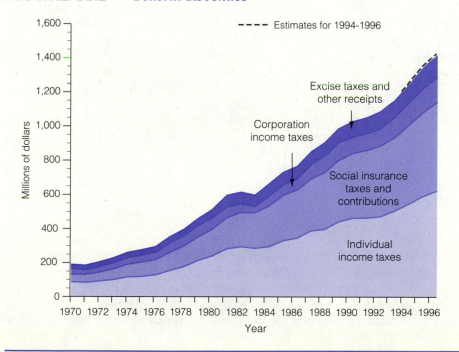

SOURCE: *Budget of the United States Government, Fiscal Year 1995, Historical Tables* (Washington DC: U.S. Government Printing Office, 1994), 23–24.

"You know, the idea of taxation with representation doesn't appeal to me very much either."
Drawing by Handelsman: © 1970 The New Yorker Magazine, Inc.

The Supreme Court wasted little time in declaring the tax unconstitutional in *Pollock v. Farmer's Loan and Trust Co.* (1895).

In 1913, the **Sixteenth Amendment** was added to the Constitution, explicitly permitting Congress to levy an income tax. Congress was already receiving income tax revenue before the amendment was ratified, however, and the **Internal Revenue Service** was established to collect it. Today the IRS receives about 145 million tax returns each year. Each return is scrutized by people or computers. In addition, the IRS audits in greater detail more than 1.5 million tax returns, investigates thousands of suspected criminal violations of the tax laws, and annually prosecutes and secures the conviction of thousands of errant taxpayers or nonpayers.[3] Corporations, like individuals, pay income taxes. Although corporate taxes once yielded more revenues than individual income taxes, this is no longer true. Today corporate taxes yield about eight cents of every federal revenue dollar, compared to forty-five cents coming from individual income taxes.

Social Insurance Taxes

Social Security taxes come from both employers and employees. Money is deducted from employees' paychecks and matched by their employers. Unlike other taxes, these payments do not go into the government's general money fund but are earmarked for a specific purpose—the Social Security Trust Fund that pays benefits to the elderly, the disabled, the widowed, and the unemployed.

Social Security taxes have grown faster than any other source of federal revenue, and they will surely grow even more. In 1957, these taxes made up a mere 12 percent of federal revenues; today they account for about one-third. In 1995, employees and employers each paid a Social Security tax equal to 6.2 percent of the first $57,800 of earnings, and for Medicare they paid another 1.45 percent on the first $135,000 of all earnings.

Borrowing

Like families and firms, the federal government may borrow money to make ends meet. When families and firms need money, they go to their neighborhood bank, savings and loan association, or moneylender. When the federal government wants to borrow money, the Treasury Department sells bonds, guaranteeing to pay interest to the bondholder. Citizens, corporations, mutual funds, and other financial institutions can all purchase these bonds; there is always a lively market for government bonds.

Today the **federal debt**—all of the money borrowed over the years that is still outstanding—exceeds $4.5 trillion (see Figure 14.3). Fourteen percent of all federal expenditures go to paying interest on this debt rather than being allocated for current policies. Yesterday's consumption of public policies is at the expense of tomorrow's taxpayers, because borrowing money shifts the burden of repayment to future taxpayers who will have to service the debt and pay the principal.

Government borrowing also crowds out private borrowers, both individuals and businesses, from the loan marketplace. (For instance, your local bank may know that you are a low-risk borrower, but it thinks the federal government is an even lower risk.) The bulk of all the net private savings in the country goes to the federal government. The American government is also dependent on foreign investors, including other governments, to fund its debt—not a favorable position for a superpower. Most economists believe that this competition to borrow money increases interest rates and makes it more difficult for businesses to invest in capital expenditures (such as new plants and equipment) that produce economic growth.

Aside from its impact on private borrowing, the federal debt raises additional concerns. Every dollar that the government borrows today will cost taxpayers many more dollars in interest over the next 30 years. Government is borrowing not so much for its capital needs (as individuals and firms do when they buy a house or build a factory) as for its day-to-day expenses. Most families wisely do not borrow money for their food and clothing, yet the government is largely borrowing money for its farm subsidies, its military pensions, and its aid to states and cities.

Most observers are concerned about the national debt.[4] The perceived perils of gigantic deficits have led to calls for a **balanced budget amendment**. The proposed amendment to the Constitution would require Congress to balance

FIGURE 14.3 — Total Federal Debt, 1970–1995

The national debt mushroomed in the 1980s. One principal cause of this huge increase in debt was the loss of revenue resulting from the huge tax cut proposed by President Reagan in 1981. The large increase in defense expenditures in the early years of the Reagan administration was another contributing factor.

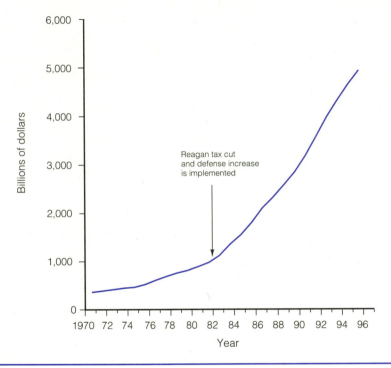

SOURCE: *Budget of the United States Government, Fiscal Year 1995, Historical Tables* (Washington,DC: Government Printing Office, 1994), 8990.

peacetime federal budgets. Only a supermajority (larger than a simple majority) vote in both houses of Congress could authorize a specific expenditure beyond the government's expected revenues. Opponents argue that it is difficult to estimate both expenditures and revenues more than a year ahead (if the economy performs worse than expected, for example, revenues go down and expenditures go up). And both Congress and the president could circumvent the intent of the amendment by adjusting economic assumptions or even changing the dates of the fiscal year.

Despite its borrowing habits, most of the government's income still comes from taxes. Few government policies provoke more heated discussion than taxation.

Taxes and Public Policy

No government policy affects as many Americans as tax policy. In addition to raising revenues to finance its services, the government can use taxes to make citizens' incomes more or less equal, to encourage or discourage growth in the economy, and to promote specific interests. The following sections will focus on how tax policies can promote the interests of particular groups or encourage specific activities.

Tax Loopholes. No discussion of taxes goes very far before the subject of tax loopholes comes up. Difficult to define, a tax loophole is presumably tax break or tax benefit. The IRS Code, which specifies what income is subject to taxation, is riddled with exemptions, deductions, and special cases. Jimmy Carter, campaigning for the presidency, called the American tax system a "national disgrace" because of its special treatment of favored taxpayers. Some taxpayers, he stressed, get advantages from the tax code that are not available to everyone. Businesspeople can deduct half of the cost of "three-martini lunches" as business expenses while ordinary workers, carrying a sandwich and coffee in a thermos to work, cannot write off their lunch expenses.

In 1975, Texas computer magnate and 1992 presidential candidate H. Ross Perot hired a former Internal Revenue Service commissioner to aid him in changing the tax code. The proposed changes would have saved Perot $15 million. The amendment passed through the House Ways and Means Committee (billionaire Perot was reported to be a generous contributor to the campaign chests of several members), but was killed on the House floor when the press reported that only Perot would benefit from this provision.

Tax loopholes may offend Americans' sense of fair play, but they cost the federal government very little. Loopholes are actually only one type of tax expenditure.

Tax Expenditures. What *does* cost the federal budget a substantial sum is the system of **tax expenditures**, defined by the 1974 Budget Act as "revenue losses attributable to provisions of the federal tax laws which allow a special exemption, exclusion, or deduction." These expenditures represent the difference between what the government actually collects in taxes and what it would have collected without special exemptions. Tax expenditures thus amount to subsidies for different activities. For example:

- The government *could* send checks for billions of dollars to charities. Instead, it permits some taxpayers to deduct their contributions to charities from their income, thus encouraging charitable contributions.
- The government *could* give cash to families with the desire and financial means to buy a home. Instead, it permits homeowners to deduct from their income the billions of dollars they collectively pay each year in mortgage interest.
- The government *could* write a check to all those businesses that invest in new plants and equipment. It does not do so, but it does allow such businesses to deduct these expenses from their taxes at a more rapid rate than they deduct other expenses. In effect, the owners of these businesses, including stockholders, get a subsidy unavailable to owners of other businesses.

Tax expenditures are among the most obscure aspects of a generally obscure budgetary process, partly because they receive no regular review by Congress—a great advantage for those who benefit from a tax expenditure. On the whole, tax expenditures benefit middle- and upper-income taxpayers and corporations. Poorer people, who tend not to own homes, can take little advantage of provisions that permit homeowners to deduct mortgage interest payments. Likewise, poorer people in general can take less advantage of a deduction for charitable expenses.

To some, tax expenditures like business-related deductions, tuition tax credits, and capital gains tax rates are loopholes. To others, they are public policy choices supporting a social activity worth subsidizing. Either way they amount to the same thing—revenues that the government loses because certain items are exempted from normal taxation or are taxed at lower rates. The Office of Management and Budget (OMB) estimates that the total tax expenditures in 1995 equaled about one-third of the total federal receipts.

Tax Reduction.   The annual rite of spring—the preparation of individual tax returns—is invariably accompanied by calls for tax reform and, frequently, tax reduction. Early in his administration, President Reagan proposed a massive tax-cut bill. Standing in the way of tax cuts is never easy, and in July 1981 Congress passed Reagan's tax-cutting proposal. Over a three-year period, Americans would have their federal tax bills reduced 25 percent, corporate income taxes were also reduced, new tax incentives were provided for personal savings and corporate investment, and taxes were *indexed* to the cost of living. This meant that, beginning in 1985, government no longer received a larger share of income when inflation pushed incomes into higher brackets while the tax rates stayed the same. (This is important because people with high incomes also pay a higher *percentage* of their incomes in taxes.)

Families with high incomes saved thousands of dollars on taxes, but those at the lower end of the income ladder saw little change in their tax burden because social insurance and excise taxes (which fall disproportionately on these

"Sir, we've come to the conclusion that it's absolutely impossible to assemble a tax plan that <u>doesn't</u> benefit the rich."

people) rose during the same period. Many blamed the massive deficits of the 1980s and 1990s at least partially on the 1981 tax cuts, as government continued to spend but reduced its revenues. The appropriate level of taxation remains one of the most vexing problems in American politics (see "America in Perspective: How Much Is Too Much?").

Tax Reform. Gripes about taxes are at least as old in America as the Boston Tea Party. When President Reagan first revealed his massive tax simplification plan in 1985, with its proposals to eliminate many tax deductions and tax expenditures, it was met with howls of protest. The insurance industry, for example, launched a $6 million advertising campaign to save the tax deductions for fringe benefits (much of which are in the form of life and health insurance) that employers set aside for employees. A pitched battle was waging between tax reformers and interest groups determined to hold on to their tax benefits.

For once, however, a tax reform plan was not derailed. For one thing, Democrats, including the powerful chairman of the House Ways and Means Committee, Dan Rostenkowski, were enthusiastic about tax reform. They also did not want the Republicans to get all the credit for reform. In fact, the president actually had more problems obtaining the support of those in his own

AMERICA IN PERSPECTIVE

How Much Is Too Much?

No one likes to pay taxes, and it is common for Americans—and citizens all over the world—to complain that taxes are too high. The figures in the accompanying graph show that the national, state, and local governments in the United States taxed a smaller percentage of the country's resources than do those in almost all other democracies with developed economies.

The Scandinavian countries of Sweden, Norway, and Denmark take half of the wealth of the country in taxes each year.

Comparatively, citizens in the United States have a rather light tax burden. Naturally, tax levels are related to the level of public services that governments provide. The big taxers are also the big spenders.

Country	Tax revenues as percentage of GDP
United States	30
Japan	31
Australia	31
Switzerland	32
Spain	34
Portugal	35
Canada	37
Italy	37
Greece	37
United Kingdom	37

Tax revenues as percentage of GDP

Country	Tax revenues as percentage of GDP
Finland	38
Germany	38
New Zealand	38
Austria	42
France	44
Belgium	45
Netherlands	45
Norway	46
Denmark	49
Sweden	57

Tax revenues as percentage of GDP

aGross Domestic Product is Gross National Product minus the value of goods and services produced outside the country.
SOURCE: U.S. Department of Commerce. Statistical Abstract of the United States 1993, (Washington, DC: Government Printing Office, 1993), 857.

party and had to make an unusual trip to Capitol Hill to plead with House Republicans to support the tax bill after its initial defeat when it came to the floor.

The Senate posed an even bigger problem, as the bill was loaded with special tax treatments for a wide variety of groups. While the president was on a trip abroad, the Finance Committee met behind closed doors and emerged with a bill similar in spirit to the bill supported by the president and the House. The Tax Reform Act of 1986 was one of the most sweeping alterations in federal tax policy history. It eliminated or reduced the value of many tax deductions, removed several million low-income individuals from the tax rolls, and reduced the fifteen separate tax brackets to just two generally lower rates (28 percent and 15 percent). In 1990, a third bracket of 31 percent was added for those with higher incomes.

In 1993, Congress agreed to President Clinton's proposal to raise the income tax rate to 36 percent for families with incomes over $140,000 and add an additional surcharge of 3.6 percent to those families with incomes over $250,000. Congress also increased the top corporate income tax and an energy tax paid by all but those with low incomes.

FEDERAL EXPENDITURES: WHERE REVENUES GO

In 1932, when President Franklin D. Roosevelt took office in the midst of the Great Depression, the federal government was spending just over $3 billion a year. Today that sum would get the federal government through less than a day. Program costs once measured in the millions are now measured in billions. Comparisons over time are, of course, a little misleading, because they do not account for changes in the value of the dollar. You can see in Figure 14.4 how the federal budget has grown in actual dollars.

Figure 14.4 makes two interesting points. First, the policies and programs the government spends money on change over time. Second, expenditures

FIGURE 14.4 — Federal Expenditures

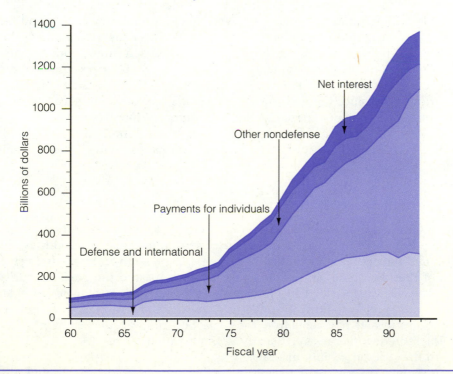

SOURCE: *Budget of the United States Government, Fiscal Year 1995, Historical Tables* (Washington, DC: Government Printing Office, 1994), 240.

keep rising. Thus, the following sections explore two important questions: Where does the money go? Why is it difficult to control federal expenditures?

The Rise and Decline of the National Security State

A generation ago, the most expensive part of the federal budget was not its social services but its military budget. Before World War II, the United States customarily disbanded a large part of its military forces at the end of a war. After World War II, however, the "cold war" with the Soviet Union resulted in a permanent military establishment and expensive military technology. Fueling the military machine greatly increased the cost of government.

Things soon changed, however. Over a decade and a half, from the mid-1960s to the early 1980s, defense expenditures crept downward in real dollars while social welfare expenditures more than doubled. Although President Reagan proposed scrapping scores of domestic programs in his annual budget requests, he also urged Congress to substantially increase the defense budget. Throughout his entire second term Congress balked, however, and in the 1990s, defense expenditures have decreased in response to the lessening tensions in Europe. The budget of the Department of Defense, once the driving force in the expansion of the federal budget, now constitutes only about one-sixth of all federal expenditures.

Payrolls and pensions for the 2.7 million Pentagon employees, the million reservists, the 1.7 million people who receive military retirement pay, and the more than one million veterans who receive pensions constitute a large component of the defense budget. So do the research, development, and *procurement* (purchasing) of military hardware. The costs of procurement are high, even though total military expenditures have declined as a percentage of American GDP since the end of World War II. The cost of advanced technology makes any weapon, fighter plane, or component more expensive than its predecessors. Moreover, cost overruns are common. The American fleet of Stealth bombers will cost almost twice the original estimate—over one-half *billion* dollars each.

The Social Service State

The biggest slice of the budget pie now belongs to *income security* expenditures, a bundle of policies extending direct and indirect aid to the elderly, the poor, and the needy. In 1935, during the Great Depression and the administration of President Franklin D. Roosevelt, Congress passed the **Social Security Act**. The act was intended to provide a minimal level of sustenance to older Americans, saving them from poverty. These days, more than forty million Americans receive payments from the Social Security system each month. The typical retired worker received nearly $700 a month in 1995.

In the 1950s, disability insurance was included in the Social Security program; thus, workers who had not retired but who were disabled could also

Since the Great Dedpression, the federal government's funding of social services has increased dramatically. One of the most controversial, but by no means the most expensive, of these programs is welfare. Most federal money for welfare goes to children under a program that also recieves state funding. Here, an applicant peruses a form in a country welfare office.

collect benefits. In 1965, **Medicare**, which provides both hospital and physician coverage to the elderly, was added to the system. Although most Social Security checks go to retired workers, many also go to the disabled, to Medicare patients, and to nonelderly spouses of workers who have died.

Social Security is less an insurance program than a kind of intergenerational contract. Essentially, money is taken from the working members of the population and spent on the retired members. As the 1980s began, the Social Security program was going broke fast. More money was going out in benefits than was coming in.[5] And that was only the short-term problem. The aging population added more people to the Social Security rolls annually; as life expectancy has increased, the Social Security problem has become even more critical.

Social Security is the largest social policy of the federal government (Social Security and Medicare account for almost one-third of the federal budget). In health, education, job training, and scores of other areas, the rise of the social service state has also contributed to America's growing budget. No brief list could do justice to the range of government social programs, which provide funds for the aged, businesses run by minority entrepreneurs, consumer education, drug rehabilitation, environmental education, food subsidies for the poor, guaranteed loans to college students, housing allowances for the poor, inspections of hospitals, and so on. Liberals often favor these programs to assist individuals and groups in society; conservatives see them as a drain on the federal treasury. In any event, they cost money—a lot of it.

Together, these programs add to the already burgeoning budget for social expenditures. Why is it so difficult to bring this increasing federal budget under control?

Incrementalism

Sometimes political scientists use the term *incrementalism* to describe the spending and appropriations process. **Incrementalism** means simply that the best predictor of this year's budget is last year's budget plus a little bit more (an increment). According to Aaron Wildavsky, "The largest determining factor of the size and content of this year's budget is last year's. Most of each budget is a product of previous decisions."[6] Incremental budgeting has several features:

- Very little attention is focused on the budgetary base—the amounts agencies have had over the previous years.
- Usually, agencies can safely assume they will get at least the budget they had the previous year. Most of the debate and attention of the budgeting process are focused on the proposed increment.
- The budget for any given agency tends to grow a little bit every year.

This picture of the federal budget is one of constant, slow growth. Expenditures mandated by an existing law or obligation (such as Social Security) are particularly likely to follow a neat pattern of increase. There are exceptions, however. Paul Schulman observed that budgets for the National Aeronautics and Space Administration (NASA) were hardly incremental; initially, they rose as fast as a NASA rocket but later plummeted to a fraction of their former size.[7] Incrementalism may be a general tendency of the budget, but it does not fully describe all budgetary politics.

Because so much of the budgetary process looks incremental, there is a never-ending call for budgetary reform. The idea is always to make it easier to compare programs so that the "most deserving" ones can be supported and the "wasteful" ones cut. Lyndon Johnson tried to impose *Program Planning Budgeting Systems* (PPBS) on the whole government. Under this system, agencies must budget programs and demonstrate that the program's goals are being achieved. Jimmy Carter brought *zero-based budgeting (ZBB)* to Washington—an idea he had used as the governor of Georgia. ZBB requires agencies making budget requests to assume that their base is zero and then justify any additional funding needs above zero, a very difficult task. Each of these reforms has been instituted with high hopes, but in the end the budget has proven to be too big and too complex for thorough, "rational" analysis.[8]

The budgetary process, like all aspects of government, is affected by relevant interests. It is these interests that make it difficult to pare the budget. In addition, the budget is too big to review from scratch each year, even for the most systematic and conscientious members of Congress. There is another reason federal spending is hard to control—more and more of it has become "uncontrollable."

"Uncontrollable" Expenditures

At first glance, it is hard to see how one could call the federal budget uncontrollable. After all, Congress has the constitutional authority to budget to add or subtract money from an agency. Indeed, Presidents Reagan, Bush, and Clinton proposed and Congress adopted some proposals to cut the growth of government spending. How, then, can one speak of an uncontrollable budget?

Consider for a moment what we might call the "allowance theory" of the budget. In this theory, a government budget works rather like an allowance. Mom and Dad hand over to Mary Jean and Tommy a monthly allowance, say $10 each, with the stern admonition, "Make that last till the end of the month because that's all we're giving you until then." In the allowance model of the budget, Congress plays this parental role; the agencies play the roles of Mary Jean and Tommy. Congress thus allocates a lump sum—say, $5.2 billion—and instructs agencies to meet their payrolls and other expenses throughout the fiscal year. When most Americans think of the government's budget, they envision the budget as something of an allowance to the agencies.

About two-thirds of the government's budget, however, does not work this way at all. Vast expenditures are determined not by how much Congress appropriates to an agency, but by *how many eligible beneficiaries* there are for some particular program. **Uncontrollable expenditures** result from policies that make some group automatically eligible for some benefit. Thus, an expenditure is classified as uncontrollable if it is mandated under current law or by a previous obligation. Congress writes the eligibility rules; the number of people eligible and their level of guaranteed benefits determine how much Congress must spend. The Social Security Administration, for example, does not merely provide benefits on a first come, first served basis until the money runs out. Many expenditures are uncontrollable because Congress has in effect obligated itself to pay X level of benefits to Y number of recipients. Such policies are called **entitlements**. Each year, Congress's bill is a straightforward function of the X level of benefits times the Y beneficiaries.

The biggest uncontrollable expenditure of all is, of course, the Social Security system, including Medicare, costing nearly $500 billion per year. Eligible individuals automatically receive Social Security payments. Of course, Congress can, if it desires, cut the benefits or tighten eligibility restrictions. Doing so, however, would provoke a monumental outcry from millions of elderly voters. Other items—veterans aid, agricultural subsidies, military pensions, civil service workers' retirement benefits, interest on the national debt—are uncontrollable expenditures also. Government cannot decide this year, for example, that it will not pay the interest on the federal debt, or that is will chop the pensions earned by former military personnel in half.

Altogether, the federal budget document itself estimates that *fully two-thirds of the federal budget is uncontrollable*—meaning that Congress *can* control such expenditures, but only by changing a law or altering existing benefit levels. To control the uncontrollables, Congress can either cut benefits or cut down on beneficiaries. You can see why neither would be a popular strategy for an elected Congress (see "You Are the Policymaker: Balancing the Budget").

UNDERSTANDING BUDGETING

Citizens and politicians alike fret about whether government is too big. President Bush was elected by claiming that government has too many hands in Americans' pockets. He promised not to raise taxes to pay for more government spending. Of course, not everyone agrees that the national government is too large (even Bush had backtracked on his "no new taxes" pledge by 1990 and was defeated by the more activist Bill Clinton in 1992). There is agreement

YOU ARE THE POLICYMAKER

Balancing the Budget

You have seen that the national government is running budget deficits of unprecedented size and that the national debt has ballooned. Moreover, public-opinion polls indicate that Americans believe the deficit is a serious problem.

You have also seen that two-thirds of the federal budget is "uncontrollable," primarily going to groups automatically eligible for certain benefits. Most of these expenditures have widespread public support, such as payments to individuals under Social Security.

Thus, here is the situation you would face as a budget decision maker: According to the OMB, in fiscal year 1995 the national government will have revenues (including Social Security taxes) of about $1.338 trillion—and this is *after* the tax increase passed in 1993. Mandatory expenditures for domestic policy (entitlements and other prior obligations) total about $764 billion. Nondiscretionary payments on the national debt will cost another $214 billion.

Even with cuts, national defense programs will cost an additional $271 billion. This leaves you with just $89 billion to spend and still balance the budget. Continuing discretionary domestic policy programs will take $271 billion, however. If you spend this amount you will run a deficit of $182 billion—and you have not even had a chance to fund any significant new programs.

What would *you* do? Would you drastically reduce defense expenditures futher? Or would you leave them alone and close down the entire rest of the government, including programs for space and science, transportation and public works, economic subsidies and development, education and social services, health research and servcies, and law enforcement and other core funcitons of governmnet—programs that also have broad public support? Perhaps you would show great political courage and seek a tax increase to pay for these programs. What *would* you do?

on the centrality of budgeting to modern government and politics, however. Exploring the themes of democracy and the scope of government will help you to better understand the federal budgeting process.

Democracy and Budgeting

Almost all democracies have seen a substantial growth in government in the twentieth century. One explanation for this growth is that politicians spend money to "buy" votes. They do not buy votes in the sense that a corrupt political machine pays off voters to vote for its candidates; rather, policymakers spend public money on things voters will like and will remember on election day. As you saw in Chapter 10, members of Congress have incentives to make government grow; they use both constituency services and pork barrel policies to deliver benefits to the folks back home, and government grows as a result.

Economists Allen Meltzer and Scott Richard have argued that government grows in a democracy because of the equality of suffrage. They maintain that in the private sector people's incomes are unequal, whereas in the political arena power is much more equally distributed. Each voter has one vote. Parties must appeal to a majority of the voters. Hence, claim Meltzer and Richard, poorer voters will always use their votes to support public policies that redistribute benefits from the rich to the poor. Even if such voters cannot win in the marketplace, they can use the electoral process to their advantage. As Meltzer and Richard summarize, "Government continues to grow because there is a decisive difference between the political process and the market process. The market process produces a distribution of income that is less equal than the distribution of votes. Consequently, those with the lowest income use the political process to increase their income."[9] Many politicians willingly cooperate with the desire of the working class voters to expand their benefits, because voters return the favor at election time. Not surprising, the most rapidly growing expenditures are items like Social Security, Medicaid, Medicare, and social welfare programs, which benefit the poor more than the rich.

Often one thinks of elites, particularly corporate elites, as opposing big government. Recently, however, Lockheed and Chrysler Corporation have appealed to the government for large bailouts when times got rough. Corporations support a big government that offers them contracts, subsidies, and other benefits. A huge procurement budget at the Department of Defense benefits defense contractors, their workers, and their shareholders.

Low-income and wealthy voters alike have voted for parties and politicians who promised them benefits. When the air is foul, Americans expect government to help clean it up. When Americans get old, they expect a Social Security check. In a democracy, what people want affects what government does. Citizens are not helpless victims of big government and its big taxes; they are at least co-conspirators.

Government also grows by responding to groups and their demands. The parade of PACs is one example of groups asking government for assistance.

From agricultural lobbies supporting loans to zoologists pressing for aid from the National Science Foundation, groups seek to expand their favorite part of the budget. They are aided by committees and government agencies that work to fund projects favored by supportive groups.

You have also seen, however, that some politicians compete for votes by promising *not* to spend money. After all, Ronald Reagan did not win election to the presidency twice by promising to raise taxes and provide more services. No country has a more open political system than the United States, but Americans have chosen to tax less and spend less on public services than almost all other democracies with developed economies. The size of government budgets varies widely among democratic nations. Thus, democracy may encourage government spending, but it does not compel it.

One of the most common criticisms of government is the failure to balance the budget. Public officials are often criticized for lacking the will to deal with the problem, yet it is not lack of resolve that prevents a solution to enormous budget deficits. Instead, it is a lack of consensus on policy. Americans want to spend but not pay taxes, and, being a democracy, this is exactly what the government does. The inevitable result is red ink.

The Budget and the Scope of Government

One of this text's themes, the scope of government, has pervaded this chapter. The reason is obvious—in many ways the budget *is* the scope of government. The bigger the budget, the bigger the government.

The budgetary process can also limit government. One could accurately characterize policy-making in the American government since 1980 as the "politics of scarcity"—scarcity of funds, that is. Thus, the budget can be a force for reining in the government as well as for expanding its role.[10] President Clinton came into office hoping to make new investments in education,worker training, and the country's physical infrastructure, like roads and bridges. He soon found, however, that there was no money to fund new programs. The president was reduced to speaking loudly and carrying a small budgetary stick in other policy areas as well. There was not enough money in the budget to pay for health care reform, so he had to accept a reduced benefits package and advocate the politically difficult option of forcing employers to pay for their employees. Welfare reform faces a similar obstacle. America's large budget deficit is as much a constraint on government as it is evidence of a burgeoning public sector.

SUMMARY

When the federal government's budget consumes one-fifth of America's gross domestic product, it demands close attention. The government's biggest revenue source remains the income tax, but the Social Security tax is becoming increasingly important. Lately, more and more of the government's budget has been financed through borrowing. Annual deficits of $200–$300 billion have boosted the federal debt to over $4.5 trillion.

Government spending has also experienced significant change. Dominated by defense spending during the 1950s, social services spending has dominated the 1990s. President Reagan, for one, wanted to reverse this balance by increasing military expenditures and cutting domestic ones. Nonetheless, much of the American budget consists of "uncontrollable" expenditures that are extremely difficult to pare. Many of these expenditures are associated with Social Security payments and with grants-in-aid.

Some believe that democracy turns politics into a bidding war for votes, increasing the size of the budget in the process. In the United States, however, many candidates campaign on not spending money or increasing taxes. Although larger budgets mean larger government, the budget, at least in times of substantial deficits such as those the United States has experienced in the past decade, can also serve as a constraint on further government growth.

FOR FURTHER READING

Bennett, Linda L. M., and Stephen Earl Bennett. *Living with Leviathan*. Lawrence, KS: University Press of Kansas, 1990. Examines Americans coming to terms with big government and their expectations of government largesse.

Berry, William D., and David Lowery. *Understanding United States Government Growth*. New York: Praeger, 1987. An empirical analysis of the causes of the growth of government in the period since World War II.

Light, Paul. *Artful Work: The Politics of Social Security Reform*. New York: Random House, 1985. A case study of the perennial crisis of Social Security and what has been done about it.

Pechman, Joseph A. *Federal Tax Policy*, 5th ed. Washington, DC: Brookings Institution, 1987. The standard work on the substance of federal tax policy.

Schuman, Howard E. *Politics and the Budget*, 3rd ed. Englewood Cliffs, NJ: PrenticeHall, 1992. An excellent primer on the entire budgetary process.

Wildavsky, Aaron. *The New Politics of the Budgetary Process*, 2nd ed. New York: HarperCollins, 1992. The standard work on the budgetary process.

NOTES

1. Aaron Wildavsky, *The New Politics of the Budgetary Process*, 2nd ed. (New York: HarperCollins, 1992), 2.
2. Quoted in Gerald Carson, *The Golden Egg: The Personal Income Tax, Where It Came From, How It Grew* (Boston: Houghton Mifflin, 1977), 12.
3. Statistics on the number of returns and audits come from the U.S. Department of Commerce, *Statistical Abstract of the United States*, 1993 (Washington, DC: U.S. Government Printing Office, 1993), 338.

4. An exception is Robert Eisner, who argues that if the government counted its debt as families and business firms do, that is, by balancing assets against liabilities, the government would be in pretty good shape. See *How Real Is the Federal Deficit?* (New York: Free Press, 1986).

5. See Paul Light, *Artful Work: The Politics of Social Security Reform* (New York: Random House, 1985).

6. Wildavsky, *The New Politics of the Budgetary Process*, 82.

7. Paul R. Schulman, "Nonincremental Policymaking: Notes Toward an Alternative Paradigm," *American Political Science Review* 69 (December 1975): 1354-1370.

8. See, for example, Wildavsky, *The New Politics of the Budgetary Process*, 2nd ed., 436-440.

9. Allen Meltzer and Scott F. Richard, "Why the Government Grows (and Grows) in a Democracy," *The Public Interest* 52 (Summer 1978): 117.

10. See James D. Savage, *Balanced Budgets and American Politics* (Ithaca, NY: Cornell University Press, 1988) for a study of the influence the principle of budget balancing has had on politics and public policy from the earliest days of our history.

THE DECLARATION OF INDEPENDENCE*

IN CONGRESS, JULY 4, 1776

The unanimous Declaration of the thirteen united States of America

When in the Course of human events it becomes necessary for one people to dissolve the political bonds which have connected them with another, and to assume among the powers of the earth, the separate and equal station to which the Laws of Nature and of Nature's God entitle them, a decent respect to the opinions of mankind requires that they should declare the causes which impel them to the separation.

We hold these truths to be self-evident, that all men are created equal, that they are endowed by their Creator with certain unalienable Rights, that among these are Life, Liberty and the pursuit of Happiness.

That to secure these rights, Governments are instituted among Men, deriving their just powers from the consent of the governed.

That whenever any Form of Government becomes destructive of these ends, it is the Right of the People to alter or to abolish it, and to institute new Government, laying its foundation on such principles and organizing its powers in such form, as to them shall seem most likely to effect their Safety and Happiness. Prudence, indeed, will dictate that Governments long established should not be changed for light and transient causes; and accordingly all experience hath shewn that mankind are more disposed to suffer, while evils are sufferable, than to right themselves by abolishing the forms to which they are accustomed. But when a long train of abuses and usurpations, pursuing

* This text retains the spelling, capitalization, and punctuation of the original.

invariably the same Object evinces a design to reduce them under absolute Despotism, it is their right, it is their duty, to throw off such Government, and to provide new Guards for their future security.

Such has been the patient sufferance of these Colonies; and such is now the necessity which constrains them to alter their former Systems of Government. The history of the present King of Great Britain is a history of repeated injuries and usurpations, all having in direct object the establishment of an absolute Tyranny over these States. To prove this, let Facts be submitted to a candid world.

He has refused his Assent to Laws, the most wholesome and necessary for the public good.

He has forbidden his Governors to pass Laws of immediate and pressing importance, unless suspended in their operation till his Assent should be obtained; and when so suspended, he has utterly neglected to attend to them.

He has refused to pass other Laws for the accommodation of large districts of people, unless those people would relinquish the right of Representation in the Legislature, a right inestimable to them and formidable to tyrants only.

He has called together legislative bodies at places unusual, uncomfortable, and distant from the depository of their Public Records, for the sole purpose of fatiguing them into compliance with his measures.

He has dissolved Representative Houses repeatedly, for opposing with manly firmness his invasions on the rights of the people.

He has refused for a long time, after such dissolutions, to cause others to be elected; whereby the Legislative Powers, incapable of Annihilation, have returned to the People at large for their exercise; the State remaining in the mean time exposed to all the dangers of invasion from without, and convulsions within.

He has endeavored to prevent the population of these States; for that purpose obstructing the Laws for Naturalization of Foreigners; refusing to pass others to encourage their migration hither, and raising the conditions of new Appropriations of Lands.

He has obstructed the Administration of Justice, by refusing his Assent to Laws for establishing Judiciary powers.

He has made Judges dependent on his Will alone, for the tenure of their offices, and the amount and payment of their salaries.

He has erected a multitude of New Offices, and sent hither swarms of Officers to harass our people, and eat out their substance.

He has kept among us, in times of peace, Standing Armies without the Consent of our legislatures.

He has affected to render the Military independent of and superior to the Civil power.

He has combined with others to subject us to a jurisdiction foreign to our constitution, and unacknowledged by our laws; giving his Assent to their Acts of pretended Legislation:

For quartering large bodies of armed troops among us:

For protecting them, by a mock Trial, from punishment for any Murders which they should commit on the Inhabitants of these States:

For cutting off our Trade with all parts of the world:

For imposing Taxes on us without our Consent:

For depriving us in many cases, of the benefits of Trial by Jury:

For transporting us beyond Seas to be tried for pretended offences:

For abolishing the free System of English Laws in a neighboring Province, establishing therein an Arbitrary government, and enlarging its Boundaries so as to render it at once an example and fit instrument for introducing the same absolute rule into these Colonies:

For taking away our Charters, abolishing our most valuable Laws, and altering fundamentally the Forms of our Governments:

For suspending our own Legislatures, and declaring themselves invested with power to legislate for us in all cases whatsoever.

He has abdicated Government here, by declaring us out of his Protection and waging War against us.

He has plundered our seas, ravaged our Coasts, burnt our towns, and destroyed the lives of our people.

He is at this time transporting large Armies of foreign Mercenaries to compleat the works of death, desolation and tyranny, already begun with circumstances of Cruelty & perfidy scarcely paralleled in the most barbarous ages, and totally unworthy the Head of a civilized nation.

He has constrained our fellow Citizens taken Captive on the high Seas to bear Arms against their Country, to become the executioners of their friends and Brethren, or to fall themselves by their Hands.

He has excited domestic insurrections amongst us, and has endeavored to bring on the inhabitants of our frontiers, the merciless Indian Savages, whose known rule of warfare, is an undistinguished destruction of all ages, sexes and conditions.

In every stage of these Oppressions We have Petitioned for Redress in the most humble terms: Our repeated Petitions have been answered only by repeated injury. A Prince, whose character is thus marked by every act which may define a Tyrant, is unfit to be the ruler of a free people.

Nor have We been wanting in attention to our British brethren. We have warned them from time to time of attempts by their legislature to extend an unwarrantable jurisdiction over us. We have reminded them of the circumstances of our emigration and settlement here. We have appealed to their native justice and magnanimity, and we have conjured them by the ties of our common kindred to disavow these usurpations, which would inevitably interrupt our connections and correspondence. They too have been deaf to the voice of justice and consanguinity. We must, therefore, acquiesce in the necessity, which denounces our Separation, and hold them, as we hold the rest of mankind, Enemies in War, in Peace Friends.

We, therefore, the Representatives of the united States of America, in General Congress, Assembled, appealing to the Supreme Judge of the world for the rectitude of our intentions, do, in the Name, and by Authority of the good

People of these Colonies, solemnly publish and declare, That these United Colonies are, and of Right ought to be Free and Independent States; that they are Absolved from all Allegiance to the British Crown, and that all political connection between them and the State of Great Britain, is and ought to be totally dissolved; and that as Free and Independent States, they have full Power to levy War, conclude Peace, contract Alliances, establish Commerce, and to do all other Acts and Things which Independent States may of right do.

And for the support of this Declaration, with a firm reliance on the protection of divine Providence, we mutually pledge to each other our Lives, our Fortunes and our sacred Honor.

JOHN HANCOCK

NEW HAMPSHIRE
Josiah Bartlett,
Wm. Whipple,
Matthew Thornton.

MASSACHUSETTS BAY
Saml. Adams,
John Adams,
Robt. Treat Paine,
Elbridge Gerry.

RHODE ISLAND
Step. Hopkins,
William Ellery.

CONNECTICUT
Roger Sherman,
Samuel Huntington,
Wm. Williams,
Oliver Wolcott.

NEW YORK
Wm. Floyd,
Phil. Livingston,
Frans. Lewis,
Lewis Morris.

NEW JERSEY
Richd. Stockton,
Jno. Witherspoon,
Fras. Hopkinson,
John Hart,
Abra. Clark.

PENNSYLVANIA
Robt. Morris,
Benjamin Rush,
Benjamin Franklin,
John Morton,
Geo. Clymer,
Jas. Smith,
Geo. Taylor,
James Wilson,
Geo. Ross.

DELAWARE
Caesar Rodney,
Geo. Read,
Tho. M'kean.

MARYLAND
Samuel Chase,
Wm. Paca,
Thos. Stone,
Charles Caroll of
Carrollton.

VIRGINIA
George Wythe,
Richard Henry Lee,
Th. Jefferson,
Benjamin Harrison,
Thos. Nelson, jr.,
Francis Lightfoot Lee,
Carter Braxton.

NORTH CAROLINA
Wm. Hooper,
Joseph Hewes,
John Penn.

SOUTH CAROLINA
Edward Rutledge,
Thos. Heyward, Junr.,
Thomas Lynch, jnr.,
Arthur Middleton.

GEORGIA
Button Gwinnett,
Lyman Hall,
Geo. Walton.

JAMES MADISON
November 22, 1787

TO THE PEOPLE OF THE STATE OF NEW YORK

Among the numerous advantages promised by a well constructed Union, none deserves to be more accurately developed than its tendency to break and control the violence of faction. The friend of popular governments, never finds himself so much alarmed for their character and fate, as when he contemplates their propensity to this dangerous vice. He will not fail therefore to set a due value on any plan which, without violating the principles to which he is attached, provides a proper cure for it. The instability, injustice and confusion introduced into the public councils, have in truth been the mortal diseases under which popular governments have every where perished; as they continue to be the favorite and fruitful topics from which the adversaries to liberty derive their most specious declamations. The valuable improvements made by the American Constitutions on the popular models, both ancient and modern, cannot certainly be too much admired; but it would be an unwarrantable partiality, to contend that they have as effectually obviated the danger on this side as was wished and expected. Complaints are every where heard from our most considerate and virtuous citizens, equally the friends of public and private faith, and of public and personal liberty; that our governments are too unstable; that the public good is disregarded in the conflicts of rival parties; and that measures are too often decided, not according to the rules of justice, and the rights of the minor party; but by the superior force of an interested and over-bearing majority. However anxiously we may wish that these complaints had no foundation, the evidence of known facts will not permit us to deny that they are in some degree true. It will be found indeed, on a candid review of our situation, that some of the distresses under which we labor, have been erroneously charged on the operation of our governments; but it will be found, at the same time, that other causes will not alone account for many of our heaviest misfortunes; and particularly, for that prevailing and increasing distrust of public engagements, and alarm for private rights, which are echoed from one end of the continent to the other. These must be chiefly, if not wholly, effects of the unsteadiness and injustice, with which a factious spirit has tainted our public administrations.

By a faction I understand a number of citizens, whether amounting to a majority or minority of the whole, who are united and actuated by some common impulse of passion, or of interest, adverse to the rights of other citizens, or to the permanent and aggregate interests of the community.

There are two methods of curing the mischiefs of faction: the one, by removing its causes; the other, by controlling its effects.

There are again two methods of removing the causes of faction: the one by destroying the liberty which is essential to its existence; the other, by giving to every citizen the same opinions, the same passions, and the same interests.

It could never be more truly said than of the first remedy, that it is worse than the disease. Liberty is to faction, what air is to fire, an aliment without which it instantly expires. But it could not be a less folly to abolish liberty, which is essential to political life, because it nourishes faction, than it would be to wish the annihilation of air, which is essential to animal life, because it imparts to fire its destructive agency.

The second expedient is as impracticable as the first would be unwise. As long as the reason of man continues fallible, and he is at liberty to exercise it, different opinions will be formed. As long as the connection subsists between his reason and his self-love, his opinions and his passions will have a reciprocal influence on each other; and the former will be objects to which the latter will attach themselves. The diversity in the faculties of men from which the rights of property originate, is not less an insuperable obstacle to a uniformity of interests. The protection of these faculties is the first object of Government. From the protection of different and unequal faculties of acquiring property, the possession of different degrees and kinds of property immediately results: and from the influence of these on the sentiments and views of the respective proprietors, ensues a division of the society into different interests and parties.

The latent causes of faction are thus sown in the nature of man; and we see them every where brought into different degrees of activity, according to the different circumstances of civil society. A zeal for different opinions concerning religion, concerning Government and many other points, as well of speculation as of practice; an attachment to different leaders ambitiously contending for preeminence and power; or to persons of other descriptions whose fortunes have been interesting to the human passions, have in turn divided mankind into parties, inflamed them with mutual animosity, and rendered them much more disposed to vex and oppress each other, than to co-operate for their common good. So strong is this propensity of mankind to fall into mutual animosities, that where no substantial occasion presents itself, the most frivolous and fanciful distinctions have been sufficient to kindle their unfriendly passions, and excite their most violent conflicts. But the most common and durable source of factions, has been the various and unequal distribution of property. Those who hold, and those who are without property, have ever formed distinct interests in society. Those who are creditors, and those who are debtors, fall under a like discrimination. A landed interest, a manufacturing interest, a mercantile interest, a monied interest, with many lesser interests, grow up of necessity in civilized nations, and divide them into different classes, actuated by different sentiments and views. The regulation of these various and interfering interests forms the principal task of modern Legislation, and involves the spirit of party and faction in the necessary and ordinary operations of Government.

No man is allowed to be a judge in his own cause; because his interest would certainly bias his judgment, and, not improbably, corrupt his integrity. With equal, nay with greater reason, a body of men, are unfit to be both judges and parties, at the same time; yet, what are many of the most important acts of legislation, but so many judicial determinations, not indeed concerning the rights of single persons, but concerning the rights of large bodies of citizens, and what are the different classes of legislators, but advocates and parties to the causes which they determine? Is a law proposed concerning private debts? It is a question to which the creditors are parties on one side, and the debtors on the other. Justice ought to hold the balance between them. Yet the parties are and must be themselves the judges; and the most numerous party, or, in other words, the most powerful faction must be expected to prevail. Shall domestic manufactures be encouraged, and in what degree, by restrictions on foreign manufactures? Are questions which would be differently decided by the landed and the manufacturing classes; and probably by neither, with a sole regard to justice and the public good. The apportionment of taxes on the various descriptions of property, is an act which seems to require the most exact impartiality; yet, there is perhaps no legislative act in which greater opportunity and temptation are given to a predominant party, to trample on the rules of justice. Every shilling with which they over-burden the inferior number, is a shilling saved to their own pockets.

It is in vain to say, that enlightened statesmen will be able to adjust these clashing interests, and render them all subservient to the public good. Enlightened statesmen will not always be at the helm: Nor, in many cases, can such an adjustment be made at all, without taking into view indirect and remote considerations, which will rarely prevail over the immediate interest which one party may find in disregarding the rights of another, or the good of the whole.

The inference to which we are brought, is, that the causes of faction cannot be removed; and that relief is only to be sought in the means of controlling its effects.

If a faction consists of less than a majority, relief is supplied by the republican principle, which enables the majority to defeat its sinister views by regular vote: It may clog the administration, it may convulse the society; but it will be unable to execute and mask its violence under the forms of the Constitution.

When a majority is included in a faction, the form of popular government on the other hand enables it to sacrifice to its ruling passion or interest, both the public good and the rights of other citizens. To secure the public good, and private rights, against the danger of such a faction, and at the same time to preserve the spirit and the form of popular government, is then the great object to which our enquiries are directed: Let me add that it is the great desideratum, by which alone this form of government can be rescued from the opprobrium under which it has so long labored, and be recommended to the esteem and adoption of mankind.

By what means is this object attainable? Evidently by one of two only. Either the existence of the same passion or interest in a majority at the same time, must be prevented; or the majority, having such co-existent passion or interest, must be rendered, by their number and local situation, unable to concert and carry into effect schemes of oppression. If the impulse and the opportunity be suffered to coincide, we well know that neither moral nor religious motives can be relied on as an adequate control. They are not found to be such on the injustice and violence of individuals, and lose their efficacy in proportion to the number combined together; that is, in proportion as their efficacy becomes needful.

From this view of the subject, it may be concluded, that a pure Democracy, by which I mean, a Society, consisting of a small number of citizens, who assemble and administer the Government in person, can admit of no cure for the mischiefs of faction. A common passion or interest will, in almost every case, be felt by a majority of the whole; a communication and concert results from the form of Government itself; and there is nothing to check the inducements to sacrifice the weaker party, or an obnoxious individual. Hence it is, that such Democracies have ever been spectacles of turbulence and contention; have ever been found incompatible with personal security, or the rights of property; and have in general been as short in their lives, as they have been violent in their deaths. Theoretic politicians, who have patronized this species of Government, have erroneously supposed, that by reducing mankind to a perfect equality in their political rights, they would, at the same time, be perfectly equalized and assimilated in their possessions, their opinions, and their passions.

A republic, by which I mean a government in which the scheme of representation takes place, opens a different prospect, and promises the cure for which we are seeking. Let us examine the points in which it varies from pure democracy, and we shall comprehend both the nature of the cure and the efficacy which it must derive from the union.

The two great points of difference, between a democracy and a republic, are, first, the delegation of the government, in the latter, to a small number of citizens, elected by the rest; secondly, the greater number of citizens, and greater sphere of country, over which the latter may be extended.

The effect of the first difference is, on the one hand, to refine and enlarge the public views, by passing them through the medium of a chosen body of citizens, whose wisdom may best discern the true interest of their country, and whose patriotism and love of justice, will be least likely to sacrifice it to temporary or partial considerations. Under such a regulation, it may well happen, that the public voice, pronounced by the representatives of the people, will be more consonant to the public good, than if pronounced by the people themselves, convened for the purpose. On the other hand the effect may be inverted. Men of factious tempers, of local prejudices, or of sinister designs, may by intrigue, by corruption, or by other means, first obtain the suffrages, and then betray the interest of the people. The question resulting is, whether small or extensive republics are most favorable to the election of proper guardians of the public weal, and it is clearly decided in favor of the latter by two obvious considerations.

In the first place, it is to be remarked that, however small the republic may be, the representatives must be raised to a certain number, in order to guard against the cabals of a few; and that however large it may be, they must be limited to a certain number, in order to guard against the confusion of a multitude. Hence, the number of representatives in the two cases not being in proportion to that of the constituents, and being proportionally greatest in the small republic, it follows, that if the proportion of fit characters be not less in the large than in the small republic, the former will present a greater option, and consequently a greater probability of a fit choice.

In the next place, as each Representative will be chosen by a greater number of citizens in the large than in the small Republic, it will be more difficult for unworthy candidates to practise with success the vicious arts, by which elections are too often carried; and the suffrages of the people being more free, will be more likely to center on men who possess the most attractive merit, and the most diffusive and established characters.

It must be confessed, that in this, as in most other cases, there is a mean, on both sides of which inconveniences will be found to lie. By enlarging too much the number of electors, you render the representative too little acquainted with all their local circumstances and lesser interests; as by reducing it too much, you render him unduly attached to these, and too little fit to comprehend and pursue great and national objects. The Federal Constitution forms a happy combination in this respect; the great and aggregate interests being referred to the national, the local and particular, to the state legislatures.

The other point of difference is, the greater number of citizens and extent of territory which may be brought within the compass of Republican, than of Democratic Government; and it is this circumstance principally which renders factious combinations less to be dreaded in the former, than in the latter. The smaller the society, the fewer probably will be the distinct parties and interests composing it; the fewer the distinct parties and interests, the more frequently will a majority be found of the same party; and the smaller the number of individuals composing a majority, and the smaller the compass within which they are placed, the more easily will they concert and execute their plans of oppression. Extend the sphere, and you take in a greater variety of parties and interests; you make it less probable that a majority of the whole will have a common motive to invade the rights of other citizens; or if such a common motive exists, it will be more difficult for all who feel it to discover their own strength, and to act in unison with each other. Besides other impediments, it may be remarked, that where there is a consciousness of unjust or dishonorable purposes, communication is always checked by distrust, in proportion to the number whose concurrence is necessary.

Hence it clearly appears, that the same advantage, which a Republic has over a Democracy, in controlling the effects of faction, is enjoyed by a large over a small Republic — is enjoyed by the Union over the States composing it. Does this advantage consist in the substitution of Representatives, whose enlightened views and virtuous sentiments render them superior to local prejudices, and to schemes of injustice? It will not be denied, that the Representation of the Union will be most likely to possess these requisite endowments. Does it consist in the greater security afforded by a greater variety of parties, against the event of any one party being able to outnumber and oppress the rest? In an equal degree does the increased variety of parties, comprised within the Union, increase this security? Does it, in fine, consist in the greater obstacles opposed to the concert and accomplishment of the secret wishes of an unjust and interested majority? Here, again, the extent of the Union gives it the most palpable advantage.

The influence of factious leaders may kindle a flame within their particular States, but will be unable to spread a general conflagration through the other States: a religious sect may degenerate into a political faction in a part of the Confederacy but the variety of sects dispersed over the entire face of it, must secure the national Councils against any danger from that source: a rage for paper money, for an abolition of debts, for an equal division of property, or for any other improper or wicked project, will be less apt to pervade the whole body of the Union, than a particular member of it; in the same proportion as such a malady is more likely to taint a particular county or district, than an entire State.

In the extent and proper structure of the Union, therefore, we behold a Republican remedy for the diseases most incident to Republican Government. And according to the degree of pleasure and pride, we feel in being Republicans, ought to be our zeal in cherishing the spirit, and supporting the character of Federalists.

— PUBLIUS

JAMES MADISON
February 6, 1788

TO THE PEOPLE OF THE STATE OF NEW YORK

To what expedient then shall we finally resort for maintaining in practice the necessary partition of power among the several departments, as laid down in the constitution? The only answer that can be given is, that as all these exterior provisions are found to be inadequate, the defect must be supplied, by so contriving the interior structure of the government, as that its several constituent parts may, by their mutual relations, be the means of keeping each other in their proper places. Without presuming to undertake a full development of this important idea, I will hazard a few general observations, which may perhaps place it in a clearer light, and enable us to form a more correct judgment of the principles and structure of the government planned by the convention.

In order to lay a due foundation for that separate and distinct exercise of the different powers of government, which to a certain extent, is admitted on all hands to be essential to the preservation of liberty, it is evident that each department should have a will of its own; and consequently should be so constituted, that the members of each should have as little agency as possible in the appointment of the members of the others. Were this principle rigorously adhered to, it would require that all the appointments for the supreme executive, legislative, and judiciary magistracies, should be drawn from the same fountain of authority, the people, through channels, having no communication whatever with one another. Perhaps such a plan of constructing the several departments would be less difficult in practice than it may in contemplation appear. Some difficulties however, and some additional expense, would attend the execution of it. Some deviations therefore from the principle must be admitted. In the constitution of the judiciary department in particular, it might be inexpedient to insist rigorously on the principle; first, because peculiar qualifications being essential in the members, the primary consideration ought to be to select that mode of choice, which best secures these qualifications; secondly, because the permanent tenure by which the appointments are held in that department, must soon destroy all sense of dependence on the authority conferring them.

It is equally evident that the members of each department should be as little dependent as possible on those of the others, for the emoluments annexed to their offices. Were the executive magistrate, or the judges, not independent of the legislature in this particular, their independence in every other would be merely nominal.

But the great security against a gradual concentration of the several powers in the same department, consists in giving to those who administer each department, the necessary constitutional means, and personal motives, to resist encroachments of the others. The provision for defense must in this, as in all other cases, be made commensurate to the danger of attack. Ambition must be made to counteract ambition. The interest of the man must be connected with the constitutional right of the place. It may be a reflection on human nature, that such devices should be necessary to control the abuses of government. But what is government itself but the greatest of all reflections on human nature? If men were angels, no government would be necessary. If angels were to govern men, neither external nor internal controls on government would be necessary. In framing a government which is to be administered by men over men, the great difficulty lies in this: You must first enable the government to control the governed; and in the next place, oblige it to control itself. A dependence on the people is no doubt the primary control on the government; but experience has taught mankind the necessity of auxiliary precautions.

This policy of supplying by opposite and rival interests, the defect of better motives, might be traced through the whole system of human affairs, private as well as public. We see it particularly displayed in all the subordinate distributions of power; where the constant aim is to divide and arrange the several offices in such a manner as that each may be a check on the other; that the private interest of every individual, may be a sentinel over the public rights. These inventions of prudence cannot be less requisite in the distribution of the supreme powers of the state.

But it is not possible to give to each department an equal power of self defense. In republican government the legislative authority, necessarily, predominates. The remedy for this inconveniency is, to divide the legislature into different branches; and to render them by different modes of election, and different principles of action, as little connected with each other, as the nature of their common functions, and their common dependence on the society, will admit. It may even be necessary to guard against dangerous encroachments by still further precautions. As the weight of the legislative authority requires that it should be thus divided, the weakness of the executive may require, on the other hand, that it should be fortified. An absolute negative, on the legislature, appears at first view to be the natural defense with which the executive magistrate should be armed. But perhaps it would be neither altogether safe, nor alone sufficient. On ordinary occasions, it might not be exerted with the requisite firmness; and on extraordinary occasions, it might be prefidiously abused. May not this defect of an absolute negative be supplied, by some qualified connection between this weaker department, and the weaker branch of the stronger department, by which the latter may be led to support the constitutional rights of the former, without being too much detached from the rights of its own department?

If the principles on which these observations are founded be just, as I persuade myself they are, and they be applied as a criterion, to the several state constitutions, and to the federal constitution, it will be found, that if the latter does not perfectly correspond with them, the former are infinitely less able to bear such a test.

There are moreover two considerations particularly applicable to the federal system of America, which place that system in a very interesting point of view.

First. In a single republic, all the power surrendered by the people, is submitted to the administration of a single government; and usurpations are guarded against by a division of the government into distinct and separate departments. In the compound republic of America, the power surrendered by the people, is first divided between two distinct governments, and then the portion allotted to each, subdivided among distinct and separate departments. Hence a double security arises to the rights of the people. The different governments will control each other; at the same time that each will be controlled by itself.

Second. It is of great importance in a republic, not only to guard the society against the oppression of its rulers; but to guard one part of the society against the injustice of the other part. Different interests necessarily exist in different classes of citizens. If a majority be united by a common interest, the rights of the minority will be insecure. There are but two methods of providing against this evil: The one by creating a will in the community independent of the majority, that is, of the society itself, the other by comprehending in the society so many separate descriptions of citizens, as will render an unjust combination of a majority of the whole, very improbable, if not impracticable. The first method prevails in all governments possessing an hereditary or self appointed authority. This at best is but a precarious security; because a power independent of the society may as well espouse the unjust views of the major, as the rightful interests, of the minor party, and may possibly be turned against both parties. The second method will be exemplified in the federal republic of the United States. While all authority in it will be derived from and dependent on the society, the society itself will be broken into so many parts, interests and classes of citizens, that the rights of individuals or of the minority, will be in little danger from interested combinations of the majority. In a free government, the security for civil rights must be the same as for religious rights. It consists in the one case in the multiplicity of interests, and in the other, in the multiplicity of sects. The degree of security in both cases will depend on the number of interests and sects; and this may be presumed to depend on the extent of country and number of people comprehended under the same government. This view of the subject must particularly recommend a proper federal system to all the sincere and considerate friends of republican government: Since it shows that in exact proportion as the territory of the union may be formed into more circumscribed confederacies or states, oppressive combinations of a majority will be facilitated, the best security under the republican form, for the rights of every class of citizens, will be diminished; and consequently, the stability and independence of some member of the government, the only other security, must be proportionally increased. Justice is the end of government. It is the end of civil society. It ever has been, and ever will be pursued, until it be obtained, or until liberty be lost in the pursuit. In a society under the forms of which the stronger faction can readily unite and oppress the weaker, anarchy may as truly be said to reign, as in a state of nature where the weaker individual is not secured against the violence of the stronger: And as in the latter state even the stronger individuals are prompted by the uncertainty of their condition, to submit to a government which may protect the weak as well as themselves: So in the former state, will the more powerful factions or parties be gradually induced by a like motive, to wish for a government which will protect all parties, the weaker as well as the more powerful. It can be little doubted, that if the state of Rhode Island was separated from the confederacy, and left to itself, the insecurity of rights under the popular form of government within such narrow limits, would be displayed by such reiterated oppressions of factious majorities, that some power altogether independent of the people would soon be called for by the voice of the very factions whose misrule had proved the necessity of it. In the extended republic of the United States, and among the great variety of interests, parties and sects which it embraces, a coalition of a majority of the whole society could seldom take place on any other principles than those of justice and the general good; and there being thus less danger to a minor from the will of the major party, there must be less pretext also, to provide for the security of the former, by introducing into the government a will not dependent on the latter; or in other words, a will independent of the society itself. It is no less certain than it is important, notwithstanding the contrary opinions which have been entertained, that the larger the society, provided it lie within a practicable sphere, the more duly capable it will be of self government. And happily for the *republican cause*, the practicable sphere may be carried to a very great extent, by a judicious modification and mixture of the *federal principle*.

— PUBLIUS

THE CONSTITUTION OF THE UNITED STATES OF AMERICA*

(Preamble)

We the People of the United States, in Order to form a more perfect Union, establish Justice, insure domestic Tranquility, provide for the common defence, promote the general Welfare, and secure the Blessings of Liberty to ourselves and our Posterity, do ordain and establish this Constitution for the United States of America.

ARTICLE I.

(The Legislature)

Section 1. All legislative Powers herein granted shall be vested in a Congress of the United States, which shall consist of a Senate and House of Representatives.

Section 2. The House of Representatives shall be composed of Members chosen every second Year by the People of the several States, and the Electors in each State shall have the Qualifications requisite for Electors of the most numerous Branch of the State Legislature.

No person shall be a Representative who shall not have attained to the Age of twenty five Years, and been seven Years a Citizen of the United States, and who shall not, when elected, be an Inhabitant of that State in which he shall be chosen.

*This text retains the spelling, capitalization, and punctuation of the original. Brackets indicate passages that have been altered by amendments.

Representatives and direct [Taxes][1] shall be apportioned among the several States which may be included within this Union, according to their respective Numbers [which shall be determined by adding to the whole Number of free Persons, including those bound to Service for a Term of Years, and excluding Indians not taxed, three fifths of all other Persons].[2] The actual Enumeration shall be made within three Years after the first Meeting of the Congress of the United States, and within every subsequent Term of ten Years, in such Manner as they shall by Law direct. The Number of Representatives shall not exceed one for every thirty Thousand, but each State shall have at Least one Representative; and until such enumeration shall be made, the State of New Hampshire shall be entitled to chuse three, Massachusetts eight, Rhode-Island and Providence Plantations one, Connecticut five, New-York six, New Jersey four, Pennsylvania eight, Delaware one, Maryland six, Virginia ten, North Carolina five, South Carolina five, and Georgia three.

When vacancies happen in the Representation from any State, the Executive Authority thereof shall issue Writs of Election to fill such Vacancies.

The House of Representatives shall chuse their speaker and other Officers; and shall have the sole Power of Impeachment.

Section 3. The Senate of the United States shall be composed of two Senators from each State [chosen by the Legislature thereof],[3] for six Years; and each Senator shall have one Vote.

Immediately after they shall be assembled in Consequence of the first Election, they shall be divided as equally as may be into three Classes. The Seats of the Senators of the first Class shall be vacated at the Expiration of the second year, of the second Class at the Expiration of the fourth Year, and of the third Class at the Expiration of the sixth Year, so that one third may be chosen every second Year [and if Vacancies happen by Resignation, or otherwise, during the Recess of the Legislature of any State, the Executive thereof may make temporary Appointments until the next Meeting of the Legislature, which shall then fill such Vacancies].[4]

No Person shall be a Senator who shall not have attained to the Age of thirty Years, and been nine Years a Citizen of the United States, and who shall not, when elected, be an Inhabitant of that State for which he shall be chosen.

The Vice President of the United States shall be President of the Senate, but shall have no Vote, unless they be equally divided.

The Senate shall chuse their other Officers, and also a President pro tempore, in the Absence of the Vice President, or when he shall exercise the Office of President of the United States.

The Senate shall have the sole Power to try all Impeachments. When sitting for that Purpose, they shall be on Oath or Affirmation. When the Presi-

[1] See Amendment XVI.

[2] See Amendment XIV.

[3] See Amendment XVII.

[4] See Amendment XVII.

dent of the United States is tried, the Chief Justice shall preside: And no Person shall be convicted without the Concurrence of two thirds of the Members present.

Judgment in Cases of Impeachment shall not extend further than to removal from Office, and disqualification to hold and enjoy any Office of honor, Trust or Profit under the United States; but the Party convicted shall nevertheless be liable and subject to Indictment, Trial, Judgment and Punishment, according to Law.

Section 4. The Times, Places and Manner of holding Elections for Senators and Representatives, shall be prescribed in each State by the Legislature thereof; but the Congress may at any time by Law make or alter such Regulations, except as to the Places of chusing Senators.

[The Congress shall assemble at least once in every Year, and such Meeting shall be on the first Monday in December, unless they shall by Law appoint a different Day.][5]

Section 5. Each House shall be the Judge of the Elections, Returns and Qualifications of its own Members, and a Majority of each shall constitute a Quorum to do Business; but a smaller Number may adjourn from day to day, and may be authorized to compel the Attendance of absent Members, in such Manner, and under such Penalties as each House may provide.

Each House may determine the Rules of its Proceedings, punish its Members for disorderly Behaviour, and, with the Concurrence of two thirds, expel a Member.

Each House shall keep a Journal of its Proceedings, and from time to time publish the same, excepting such Parts as may in their judgment require Secrecy; and the Yeas and Nays of the Members of either House on any question shall, at the Desire of one fifth of those present, be entered on the Journal.

Neither House, during the Session of Congress, shall, without the Consent of the other, adjourn for more than three days, nor to any other Place than that in which the two Houses shall be sitting.

Section 6. The Senators and Representatives shall receive a Compensation for their Services, to be ascertained by Law, and paid out of the Treasury of the United States. They shall in all Cases, except Treason, Felony and Breach of the Peace, be privileged from Arrest during their Attendance at the Session of their respective Houses, and in going to and returning from the same; and for any Speech or Debate in either House, they shall not be questioned in any other Place.

No Senator or Representative shall, during the Time for which he was elected, be appointed to any civil Office under the Authority of the United States, which shall have been created, or the Emoluments whereof shall have been encreased during such time; and no Person holding any Office under the United States, shall be a Member of either House during his Continuance in Office.

[5] See Amendment XX.

Section 7. All Bills for raising Revenue shall originate in the House of Representatives; but the Senate may propose or concur with Amendments as on other Bills.

Every Bill which shall have passed the House of Representatives and the Senate, shall, before it becomes a Law, be presented to the President of the United States; If he approves he shall sign it, but if not he shall return it, with his Objections to that House in which it shall have originated, who shall enter the Objections at large on their Journal, and proceed to reconsider it. If after such Reconsideration two thirds of that House shall agree to pass the Bill, it shall be sent, together with the Objections, to the other House, by which it shall likewise be reconsidered, and if approved by two thirds of that House, it shall become a Law. But in all such Cases the Votes of both Houses shall be determined by yeas and Nays, and the Names of the Persons voting for and against the Bill shall be entered on the Journal of each House respectively. If any Bill shall not be returned by the President within ten Days (Sundays excepted) after it shall have been presented to him, the Same shall be a Law, in like Manner as if he had signed it, unless the Congress by their Adjournment prevent its Return, in which Case it shall not be a Law.

Every Order, Resolution, or Vote to which the Concurrence of the Senate and House of Representatives may be necessary (except on a question of Adjournment) shall be presented to the President of the United States; and before the Same shall take Effect, shall be approved by him, or being disapproved by him, shall be repassed by two thirds of the Senate and House of Representatives, according to the Rules and Limitations prescribed in the Case of a Bill.

Section 8. The Congress shall have Power To lay and collect Taxes, Duties, Imposts and Excises, to pay the Debts and provide for the common Defence and general Welfare of the United States; but all Duties, Imposts and Excises shall be uniform throughout the United States;

To borrow Money on the credit of the United States;

To regulate Commerce with foreign Nations, and among the several States, and with the Indian Tribes;

To establish a uniform Rule of Naturalization, and uniform Laws on the subject of Bankruptcies throughout the United States;

To coin Money, regulate the Value thereof, and of foreign Coin, and fix the Standard of Weights and Measures;

To provide for the Punishment of counterfeiting the Securities and current Coin of the United States;

To establish Post Offices and post Roads;

To promote the Progress of Science and useful Arts, by securing for limited Times to Authors and Inventors the exclusive Right to their respective Writings and Discoveries;

To constitute Tribunals inferior to the supreme Court;

To define and punish Piracies and Felonies committed on the high Seas, and Offences against the Law of Nations;

To declare War, grant Letters of Marque and Reprisal, and make Rules concerning Captures on Land and Water;

To raise and support Armies, but no Appropriation of Money to that Use shall be for a longer Term than two Years;

To provide and maintain a Navy;

To make Rules for the Government and Regulation of the land and naval Forces;

To provide for calling forth the Militia to execute the Laws of the Union, suppress Insurrections and repel Invasions;

To provide for organizing, arming, and disciplining, the Militia, and for governing such Part of them as may be employed in the Service of the United States, reserving to the States respectively, the Appointment of the Officers, and the Authority of training the Militia according to the discipline prescribed by Congress;

To exercise exclusive Legislation in all Cases whatsoever, over such District (not exceeding ten Miles square) as may, by Cession of particular States, and the Acceptance of Congress, become the Seat of the Government of the United States, and to exercise like Authority over all Places purchased by the Consent of the Legislature of the State in which the Same shall be, for the Erection of Forts, Magazines, Arsenals, dock-Yards, and other needful Buildings; — And

To make all Laws which shall be necessary and proper for carrying into Execution the foregoing Powers, and all other Powers vested by this Constitution in the Government of the United States, or in any Department or Officer thereof.

Section 9. The Migration or Importation of such Persons as any of the States now existing shall think proper to admit, shall not be prohibited by the Congress prior to the Year one thousand eight hundred and eight, but a Tax or duty may be imposed on such Importation, not exceeding ten dollars for each Person.

The Privilege of the Writ of Habeas Corpus shall not be suspended, unless when in Cases of Rebellion or Invasion the public Safety may require it.

No Bill of Attainder or ex post facto Law shall be passed.

[No Capitation, or other direct, Tax shall be laid, unless in Proportion to the Census or Enumeration herein before directed to be taken.][6]

No Tax or Duty shall be laid on Articles exported from any State.

No Preference shall be given by any Regulation of Commerce or Revenue to the Ports of one State over those of another; nor shall Vessels bound to, or from, one State, be obliged to enter, clear, or pay Duties in another.

No Money shall be drawn from the Treasury, but in Consequence of Appropriations made by Law; and a regular Statement and Account of the Receipts and Expenditures of all public Money shall be published from time to time.

No Title of Nobility shall be granted by the United States: And no Person holding any Office of Profit or Trust under them, shall, without the Consent of

[6] See Amendment XVI.

the Congress, accept of any present, Emolument, Office, or Title, of any kind whatever, from any King, Prince, or foreign State.

Section 10. No State shall enter into any Treaty, Alliance, or Confederation; grant Letters of Marque and Reprisal; coin Money; emit Bills of Credit; make any Thing but gold and silver Coin a Tender in Payment of Debts; pass any Bill of Attainder, ex post facto Law, or Law impairing the Obligation of Contracts, or grant any Title of Nobility.

No State shall, without the Consent of the Congress, lay any Imposts or Duties on Imports or Exports, except what may be absolutely necessary for executing its inspection Laws: and the net Produce of all Duties and Imposts, laid by any State on Imports or Exports, shall be for the Use of the Treasury of the United States; and all such Laws shall be subject to the Revision and Control of the Congress.

No State shall, without the Consent of Congress, lay any Duty of Tonnage, keep Troops, or Ships of War in time of Peace, enter into any Agreement or Compact with another State, or with a foreign Power, or engage in War, unless actually invaded, or in such imminent Danger as will not admit of delay.

ARTICLE II.
(The Executive)

Section 1. The executive Power shall be vested in a President of the United States of America. He shall hold his Office during the Term of four Years, and, together with the Vice President, chosen for the same Term, be elected, as follows.

Each State shall appoint, in such Manner as the Legislature thereof may direct, a Number of Electors, equal to the whole Number of Senators and Representatives to which the State may be entitled in the Congress; but no Senator or Representative, or Person holding an Office of Trust or Profit under the United States, shall be appointed an Elector.

[The Electors shall meet in their respective States, and vote by Ballot for two Persons, of whom one at least shall not be an Inhabitant of the same State with themselves. And they shall make a List of all the Persons voted for, and of the Number of Votes for each; which List they shall sign and certify, and transmit sealed to the Seat of the Government of the United States, directed to the President of the Senate. The President of the Senate shall, in the Presence of the Senate and House of Representatives, open all the Certificates, and the Votes shall then be counted. The Person having the greatest Number of Votes shall be the President, if such Number be a Majority of the whole Number of Electors appointed; and if there be more than one who have such Majority, and have an equal Number of Votes, then the House of Representatives shall immediately chuse by Ballot one of them for President; and if no Person have a Majority, then from the five highest on the List the said House shall in like Manner chuse the President. But in chusing the President, the Votes shall be taken by States, the Representation from each State having one Vote; A quorum for this Purpose shall consist of a Member or Members from two thirds of the States, and a Majority of all the States shall be necessary to a Choice. In every Case, after the Choice of the President, the Person having the greatest Number of Votes of the Electors shall be the Vice President. But if there should remain two or more who have equal Votes, the Senate shall chuse from them by Ballot the Vice President.][7]

The Congress may determine the Time of chusing the Electors, and the Day on which they shall give their Votes; which Day shall be the same throughout the United States.

No Person except a natural born Citizen, or a Citizen of the United States, at the time of the Adoption of this Constitution, shall be eligible to the Office of President; neither shall any Person be eligible to that Office who shall not have attained to the Age of thirty five Years, and been fourteen Years a Resident within the United States.

[In Case of the Removal of the President from Office, or of his Death, Resignation, or Inability to discharge the Powers and Duties of the said Office, the Same shall devolve on the Vice President, and the Congress may by Law provide for the Case of Removal, Death, Resignation or Inability, both of the President and Vice President, declaring what Officer shall then act as President, and such Officer shall act accordingly, until the Disability be removed, or a President shall be elected.][8]

The President shall, at stated Times, receive for his Services, a Compensation, which shall neither be encreased nor diminished during the Period for which he shall have been elected, and he shall not receive within that Period any other Emolument from the United States, or any of them.

Before he enter on the Execution of his Office, he shall take the following Oath or Affirmation:—"I do solemnly swear (or affirm) that I will faithfully execute the Office of President of the United States, and will to the best of my Ability, preserve, protect and defend the Constitution of the United States."

Section 2. The President shall be Commander in Chief of the Army and Navy of the United States, and of the Militia of the several States, when called into the actual Service of the United States; he may require the Opinion, in writing, of the principal Officer in each of the executive Departments, upon any Subject relating to the Duties of their respective Offices, and he shall have Power to grant Reprieves and Pardons for Offences against the United States, except in Cases of Impeachment.

He shall have Power, by and with the Advice and Consent of the Senate, to make Treaties, provided two thirds of the Senators present concur; and he shall nominate, and by and with the Advice and Consent of the Senate, shall appoint Ambassadors, other public Ministers and Consuls, Judges of the supreme Court, and all other Officers of the United States, whose Appointments are not herein otherwise provided for, and which shall be established by

[7] See Amendment XII.

[8] See Amendment XXV.

Law: but the Congress may by Law vest the Appointment of such inferior Officers, as they think proper, in the President alone, in the Courts of Law, or in the Heads of Departments.

The President shall have Power to fill up all Vacancies that may happen during the Recess of the Senate, by granting Commissions which shall expire at the end of their next Session.

Section 3. He shall from time to time give to the Congress Information of the State of the Union, and recommend to their Consideration such Measures as he shall judge necessary and expedient; he may, on extraordinary Occasions, convene both Houses, or either of them, and in Case of Disagreement between them, with Respect to the Time of Adjournment, he may adjourn them to such Time as he shall think proper; he shall receive Ambassadors and other public Ministers; he shall take Care that the Laws be faithfully executed, and shall Commission all the Officers of the United States.

Section 4. The President, Vice President and all civil Officers of the United States, shall be removed from Office on Impeachment for, and Conviction of, Treason, Bribery, or other high Crimes and Misdemeanors.

ARTICLE III.
(The Judiciary)

Section 1. The judicial Power of the United States, shall be vested in one supreme Court, and in such inferior Courts as the Congress may from time to time ordain and establish. The Judges, both of the supreme and inferior Courts, shall hold their Offices during good Behaviour, and shall, at stated Times, receive for their Services, a Compensation, which shall not be diminished during their Continuance in Office.

Section 2. The judicial Power shall extend to all Cases, in Law and Equity, arising under this Constitution, the Laws of the United States, and Treaties made, or which shall be made, under their Authority;—to all Cases affecting Ambassadors, other public Ministers and Consuls;—to all Cases of admiralty and maritime Jurisdiction;—to Controversies to which the United States shall be a Party;—to Controversies between two or more States; [—between a State and Citizens of another State;—][9] between Citizens of different States,—between Citizens of the same State claiming Lands under Grants of different States, [and between a State, or the Citizens thereof, and foreign States, Citizens or Subjects.][10]

In all Cases affecting Ambassadors, other public Ministers and Consuls, and those in which a State shall be Party, the supreme Court shall have original Jurisdiction. In all the other Cases before mentioned, the supreme Court shall have appellate Jurisdiction, both as to Law and Fact, with such Exceptions, and under such Regulations as the Congress shall make.

The Trial of all Crimes, except in Cases of Impeachment, shall be by Jury; and such Trial shall be held in the State where the said Crimes shall have been

[9] See Amendment XI.

[10] See Amendment XI.

committed; but when not committed within any State, the Trial shall be at such Place or Places as the Congress may by Law have directed.

Section 3. Treason against the United States, shall consist only in levying War against them, or in adhering to their Enemies, giving them Aid and Comfort. No Person shall be convicted of Treason unless on the Testimony of two Witnesses to the same overt Act, or on Confession in open Court.

The Congress shall have Power to declare the Punishment of Treason, but no Attainder of Treason shall work Corruption of Blood, or Forfeiture except during the Life of the Person attainted.

ARTICLE IV.
(Interstate Relations)

Section 1. Full Faith and Credit shall be given in each State to the public Acts, Records, and judicial Proceedings of every other State. And the Congress may by general Laws prescribe the Manner in which such Acts, Records and Proceedings shall be proved, and the Effect thereof.

Section 2. The Citizens of each State shall be entitled to all Privileges and Immunities of Citizens in the several States.

A Person charged in any State with Treason, Felony, or other Crime, who shall flee from Justice, and be found in another State, shall on Demand of the executive Authority of the State from which he fled, be delivered up, to be removed to the State having Jurisdiction of the Crime.

[No Person held to Service or Labour in one State under the Laws thereof, escaping into another, shall, in Consequence of any Law or Regulation therein, be discharged from such Service or Labour, but shall be delivered up on Claim of the Party to whom such Service or Labour may be due.][11]

Section 3. New States may be admitted by the Congress into this Union; but no new State shall be formed or erected within the Jurisdiction of any other State; nor any State be formed by the Junction of two or more States, or Parts of States, without the Consent of the Legislatures of the States concerned as well as of the Congress.

The Congress shall have Power to dispose of and make all needful Rules and Regulations respecting the Territory or other Property belonging to the United States; and nothing in this Constitution shall be so construed as to Prejudice any Claims of the United States, or of any particular State.

Section 4. The United States shall guarantee to every State in this Union a Republican Form of Government, and shall protect each of them against Invasion, and on Application of the Legislature, or of the Executive (when the Legislature cannot be convened) against domestic Violence.

ARTICLE V.
(Amending the Constitution)

The Congress, whenever two thirds of both Houses shall deem it necessary, shall propose Amendments to this Constitution, or, on the Application of

[11] See Amendment XIII.

the Legislatures of two thirds of the several States, shall call a Convention for proposing Amendments, which, in either Case, shall be valid to all Intents and Purposes, as Part of this Constitution, when ratified by the Legislatures of three fourths of the several States, or by Conventions in three fourths thereof, as the one or the other Mode of Ratification may be proposed by the Congress; Provided that no Amendment which may be made prior to the Year One thousand eight hundred and eight shall in any Manner affect the first and fourth Clauses in the Ninth Section of the first Article; and that no State, without its Consent, shall be deprived of its equal Suffrage in the Senate.

ARTICLE VI.
(Debts, Supremacy, Oaths)

All Debts contracted and Engagements entered into, before the Adoption of this Constitution, shall be as valid against the United States under this Constitution, as under the Confederation.

This Constitution, and the laws of the United States which shall be made in Pursuance thereof; and all Treaties made, or which shall be made, under the Authority of the United States, shall be the supreme Law of the Land; and the Judges in every State shall be bound thereby, any Thing in the Constitution or Laws of any State to the Contrary notwithstanding.

The Senators and Representatives before mentioned, and the Members of the several State Legislatures, and all executive and judicial Officers, both of the United States and of the several States, shall be bound by Oath or Affirmation, to support this Constitution; but no religious Test shall ever be required as a Qualification to any Office or public Trust under the United States.

ARTICLE VII.
(Ratifying the Constitution)

The Ratification of the Conventions of nine States, shall be sufficient for the Establishment of this Constitution between the States so ratifying the Same.

Done in Convention by the Unanimous Consent of the States present the Seventeenth Day of September in the Year of our Lord one thousand seven hundred and Eighty seven and of the Independence of the United States of America the Twelfth. IN WITNESS whereof we have hereunto subscribed our Names.

Go. WASHINGTON
Presid't. and deputy from Virginia

Attest
WILLIAM JACKSON
Secretary

DELAWARE
Geo. Read
Gunning Bedford jun
John Dickinson
Richard Basset
Jaco. Broom

MASSACHUSETTS
Nathaniel Gorbam
Rufus King

CONNECTICUT
Wm. Saml. Johnson
Roger Sherman

NEW YORK
Alexander Hamilton

NEW JERSEY
Wh. Livingston
David Brearley
Wm. Paterson
Jona. Dayton

PENNSYLVANIA
B. Franklin
Thomas Mifflin
Robt. Morris
Geo. Clymer
Thos. FitzSimons
Jared Ingersoll
James Wilson
Gouv. Morris

NEW HAMPSHIRE
John Langdon
Nicholas Gilman

MARYLAND
James McHenry
Dan of St. Thos. Jenifer
Danl. Carroll

VIRGINIA
John Blair
James Madison Jr.

NORTH CAROLINA
Wm. Blount
Richd. Dobbs Spaight
Hu. Williamson

SOUTH CAROLINA
J. Rutledge
Charles Cotesworth Pinckney
Charles Pinckney
Pierce Butler

GEORGIA
William Few
Abr. Baldwin

Articles in addition to, and amendment of the Constitution of the United States of America, proposed by Congress and ratified by the Legislatures of the several states, pursuant to the Fifth Article of the original Constitution.

(The first ten amendments were passed by Congress on September 25, 1789, and were ratified on December 15, 1791.)

AMENDMENT I
Religion, Speech, Assembly, Petition
Congress shall make no law respecting an establishment of religion, or prohibiting the free exercise thereof; or abridging the freedom of speech, or of the press; or the right of the people peaceably to assemble, and to petition the Government for a redress of grievances.

AMENDMENT II
Right to Bear Arms
A well regulated Militia, being necessary to the security of a free State, the right of the people to keep and bear Arms, shall not be infringed.

AMENDMENT III
Quartering of Soldiers
No Soldier shall, in time of peace be quartered in any house, without the consent of the Owner, nor in time of war, but in a manner to be prescribed by law.

AMENDMENT IV
Searches and Seizures

The right of the people to be secure in their persons, houses, papers, and effects, against unreasonable searches and seizures, shall not be violated, and no warrants shall issue, but upon probable cause, supported by Oath or affirmation, and particularly describing the place to be searched, and the persons or things to be seized.

AMENDMENT V
Grand Juries, Double Jeopardy, Self-incrimination, Due Process, Eminent Domain

No person shall be held to answer for a capital, or otherwise infamous crime, unless on a presentment or indictment of a Grand Jury, except in cases arising in the land or naval forces, or in the Militia, when in actual service in time of War or public danger; nor shall any person be subject for the same offence to be twice put in jeopardy of life or limb; nor shall be compelled in any criminal case to be a witness against himself, nor be deprived of life, liberty, or property, without due process of law; nor shall private property be taken for public use, without just compensation.

AMENDMENT VI
Criminal Court Procedures

In all criminal prosecutions, the accused shall enjoy the right to a speedy and public trial, by an impartial jury of the State and district wherein the crime shall have been committed, which district shall have been previously ascertained by law, and to be informed of the nature and cause of the accusation; to be confronted with the witnesses against him; to have compulsory process for obtaining witnesses in his favor, and to have the assistance of counsel for his defence.

AMENDMENT VII
Trial by Jury in Common-law Cases

In Suits at common law, where the value in controversy shall exceed twenty dollars, the right of trial by jury shall be preserved, and no fact tried by a jury, shall be otherwise re-examined in any Court of the United States, than according to the rules of the common law.

AMENDMENT VIII
Bails, Fines, and Punishment

Excessive bail shall not be required, nor excessive fines imposed, nor cruel and unusual punishments inflicted.

AMENDMENT IX
Rights Retained by the People

The enumeration in the Constitution, of certain rights, shall not be construed to deny or disparage others retained by the people.

AMENDMENT X
Rights Reserved to the States

The powers not delegated to the United States by the Constitution, nor prohibited by it to the States, are reserved to the States respectively, or to the people.

AMENDMENT XI
Suits against the States (Ratified February 7, 1795)

The Judicial power of the United States shall not be construed to extend to any suit in law or equity, commenced or prosecuted against one of the United States by Citizens of another State, or by Citizens or Subjects of any Foreign State.

AMENDMENT XII
Election of the President and Vice President (Ratified June 15, 1804)

The Electors shall meet in their respective states, and vote by ballot for President and Vice-President, one of whom, at least, shall not be an inhabitant of the same state with themselves; they shall name in their ballots the person voted for as President, and in distinct ballots the person voted for as Vice-President, and they shall make distinct lists of all persons voted for as President, and of all persons voted for as Vice-President, and of the number of votes for each, which lists they shall sign and certify, and transmit sealed to the seat of the government of the United States, directed to the President of the Senate; — The President of the Senate shall, in the presence of the Senate and House of Representatives, open all the certificates and the votes shall then be counted; — The person having the greatest number of votes for President, shall be the President, if such number be a majority of the whole number of Electors appointed; and if no person have such majority, then from the persons having the highest numbers not exceeding three on the list of those voted for as President, the House of Representatives shall choose immediately, by ballot, the President. But in choosing the President, the votes shall be taken by states, the representation from each state having one vote; a quorum for this purpose shall consist of a member or members from two-thirds of the states, and a majority of all the states shall be necessary to a choice. [And if the House of Representatives shall not choose a President whenever the right of choice shall devolve upon them, before the fourth day of March next following, then the Vice-President shall act as President, as in the case of the death or other constitutional disability of the President.][12] — The person having the greatest number of votes as Vice-President, shall be the Vice-President, if such number be a majority of the whole number of Electors appointed, and if no person have a majority, then from the two highest numbers on the list, the Senate shall choose the Vice-President; a quorum for the purpose shall consist of two-thirds of the whole number of Senators, and a majority of the whole number shall be necessary to a choice. But no person

---

[12] See Amendment XX.

constitutionally ineligible to the office of President shall be eligible to that of Vice President of the United States.

AMENDMENT XIII

Slavery (Ratified on December 6, 1865)

Section 1. Neither slavery nor involuntary servitude, except as a punishment for crime whereof the party shall have been duly convicted, shall exist within the United States, or any place subject to their jurisdiction.

Section 2. Congress shall have power to enforce this article by appropriate legislation.

AMENDMENT XIV

Citizenship, Due Process, and Equal Protection of the Laws (Ratified on July 9, 1868)

Section 1. All persons born or naturalized in the United States, and subject to the jurisdiction thereof, are citizens of the United States and of the State wherein they reside. No State shall make or enforce any law which shall abridge the privileges or immunities of citizens of the United States; nor shall any State deprive any person of life, liberty, or property, without due process of law; nor deny to any person within its jurisdiction the equal protection of the laws.

Section 2. Representatives shall be apportioned among the several States according to their respective numbers, counting the whole number of persons in each State, excluding Indians not taxed. But when the right to vote at any election for the choice of electors for President and Vice President of the United States, Representatives in Congress, the Executive and Judicial officers of a State, or the members of the Legislature thereof, is denied to any of the male inhabitants of such State, being twenty-one years of age, and citizens of the United States, or in any way abridged, except for participation in rebellion, or other crime, the basis of representation therein shall be reduced in the proportion which the number of such male citizens shall bear to the whole number of male citizens twenty-one years of age in such State.

Section 3. No person shall be a Senator or Representative in Congress, or elector of President and Vice President, or hold any office, civil or military, under the United States, or under any State, who, having previously taken an oath, as a member of Congress, or as an officer of the United States, or as a member of any State legislature, or as an executive or judicial officer of any State, to support the Constitution of the United States, shall have engaged in insurrection or rebellion against the same, or given aid or comfort to the enemies thereof. But Congress may by a vote of two-thirds of each House, remove such disability.

Section 4. The validity of the public debt of the United States, authorized by law, including debts incurred for payment of pensions and bounties for services in suppressing insurrection or rebellion, shall not be questioned. But neither the United States nor any State shall assume or pay any debt or obligation incurred in aid of insurrection or rebellion against the United States, or any claim for the loss or emancipation of any slave, but all such debts, obligations and claims shall be held illegal and void.

Section 5. The Congress shall have power to enforce, by appropriate legislation, the provisions of this article.

AMENDMENT XV
The Right to Vote (Ratified on February 3, 1870)

Section 1. The right of citizens of the United States to vote shall not be denied or abridged by the United States or by any State on account of race, color, or previous condition of servitude.

Section 2. The Congress shall have power to enforce this article by appropriate legislation.

AMENDMENT XVI
Income Taxes (Ratified on February 3, 1913)

The Congress shall have power to lay and collect taxes on incomes, from whatever source derived, without apportionment among the several States, and without regard to any census or enumeration.

AMENDMENT XVII
Election of Senators (Ratified on April 8, 1913)

The Senate of the United States shall be composed of two Senators from each State, elected by the people thereof, for six years; and each Senator shall have one vote. The electors in each State shall have the qualifications requisite for electors of the most numerous branch of the State legislatures.

When vacancies happen in the representation of any State in the Senate, the executive authority of such State shall issue writs of election to fill such vacancies: *Provided,* That the legislature of any State may empower the executive thereof to make temporary appointments until the people fill the vacancies by election as the legislature may direct.

This amendment shall not be so construed as to affect the election or term of any Senator chosen before it becomes valid as part of the Constitution.

AMENDMENT XVIII
Prohibition (Ratified on January 16, 1919)

Section 1. After one year from the ratification of this article the manufacture, sale, or transportation of intoxicating liquors within, the importation thereof into, or the exportation thereof from the United States and all territory subject to the jurisdiction thereof for beverage purposes is hereby prohibited.

Section 2. The Congress and the several States shall have concurrent power to enforce this article by appropriate legislation.

Section 3. This article shall be inoperative unless it shall have been ratified as an amendment to the Constitution by the legislatures of the several States, as provided in the Constitution, within seven years from the date of the submission hereof to the States by the Congress.[13]

---

[13] See Amendment XXI.

AMENDMENT XIX
Women's Right to Vote (Ratified on August 18, 1920)

The right of citizens of the United States to vote shall not be denied or abridged by the United States or by any State on account of sex.

Congress shall have power to enforce this article by appropriate legislation.

AMENDMENT XX
Terms of Office, Convening of Congress, and Succession (Ratified February 6, 1933)

Section 1. The terms of the President and Vice President shall end at noon on the 20th day of January, and the terms of Senators and Representatives at noon on the 3d day of January, of the years in which such terms would have ended if this article had not been ratified; and the terms of their successors shall then begin.

Section 2. The Congress shall assemble at least once in every year, and such meeting shall begin at noon on the 3d day of January, unless they shall by law appoint a different day.

Section 3. If, at the time fixed for the beginning of the term of the President, the President elect shall have died, the Vice President elect shall become President. If a President shall not have been chosen before the time fixed for the beginning of his term, or if the President elect shall have failed to qualify, then the Vice President elect shall act as President until a President shall have qualified; and the Congress may by law provide for the case wherein neither a President elect nor a Vice President elect shall have qualified, declaring who shall then act as President, or the manner in which one who is to act shall be selected, and such person shall act accordingly until a President or Vice President shall have qualified.

Section 4. The Congress may by law provide for the case of the death of any of the persons from whom the House of Representatives may choose a President whenever the rights of choice shall have devolved upon them, and for the case of the death of any of the persons from whom the Senate may choose a Vice President whenever the right of choice shall have devolved upon them.

Section 5. Sections 1 and 2 shall take effect on the 15th day of October following the ratification of this article.

Section 6. This article shall be inoperative unless it shall have been ratified as an amendment to the Constitution by the legislatures of three-fourths of the several States within seven years from the date of its submission.

AMENDMENT XXI
Repeal of Prohibition (Ratified on December 5, 1933)

Section 1. The eighteenth article of amendment to the Constitution of the United States is hereby repealed.

Section 2. The transportation or importation into any State, Territory, or possession of the United States for delivery or use therein of intoxicating liquors, in violation of the laws thereof, is hereby prohibited.

Section 3. This article shall be inoperative unless it shall have been ratified as an amendment to the Constitution by conventions in the several States, as provided in the Constitution, within seven years from the date of the submission hereof to the States by the Congress.

AMENDMENT XXII
Number of Presidential Terms (Ratified on February 27, 1951)

No person shall be elected to the office of the President more than twice, and no person who has held the office of President, or acted as President, for more than two years of a term to which some other person was elected President shall be elected to the office of the President more than once. But this Article shall not apply to any person holding the office of President when this Article was proposed by the Congress, and shall not prevent any person who may be holding the office of President, or acting as President, during the term within which this Article becomes operative from holding the office of President or acting as President during the remainder of such term.

AMENDMENT XXIII
Presidential Electors for the District of Columbia (Ratified on March 29, 1961)

Section 1. The District constituting the seat of Government of the United States shall appoint in such manner as the Congress may direct:

A number of electors of President and Vice President equal to the whole number of Senators and Representatives in Congress to which the District would be entitled if it were a State, but in no event more than the least populous State; they shall be in addition to those appointed by the States, but they shall be considered, for the purposes of the election of President and Vice President, to be electors appointed by a State; and they shall meet in the District and perform such duties as provided by the twelfth article of amendment.

Section 2. The Congress shall have power to enforce this article by appropriate legislation.

AMENDMENT XXIV
Poll Tax (Ratified on January 23, 1964)

Section 1. The right of citizens of the United States to vote in any primary or other election for President or Vice President, for electors for President or Vice President, or for Senator or Representative in Congress, shall not be denied or abridged by the United States or any State by reason of failure to pay any poll tax or other tax.

Section 2. The Congress shall have power to enforce this article by appropriate legislation.

AMENDMENT XXV
Presidential Disability and Vice Presidential Vacancies (Ratified on February 10, 1967)

Section 1. In case of the removal of the President from office or of his death or resignation, the Vice President shall become President.

Section 2. Whenever there is a vacancy in the office of the Vice President, the President shall nominate a Vice President who shall take office upon confirmation by a majority vote of both Houses of Congress.

Section 3. Whenever the President transmits to the President pro tempore of the Senate and the Speaker of the House of Representatives his written declaration that he is unable to discharge the powers and duties of his office, and until he transmits to them a written declaration to the contrary, such powers and duties shall be discharged by the Vice President as Acting President.

Section 4. Whenever the Vice President and a majority of either the principal officers of the executive departments or of such other body as Congress may by law provide, transmit to the President pro tempore of the Senate and the Speaker of the House of Representatives their written declaration that the President is unable to discharge the powers and duties of his office, the Vice President shall immediately assume the powers and duties of the office as Acting President.

Thereafter, when the President transmits to the President pro tempore of the Senate and the Speaker of the House of Representatives his written declaration that no inability exists, he shall resume the powers and duties of his office unless the Vice President and a majority of either the principal officers of the executive department or of such other body as Congress may by law provide, transmit within four days to the President pro tempore of the Senate and the Speaker of the House of Representatives their written declaration that the President is unable to discharge the powers and duties of his office. Thereupon Congress shall decide the issue, assembling within forty-eight hours for that purpose if not in session. If the Congress, within twenty-one days after receipt of the latter written declaration, or, if Congress is not in session, within twenty-one days after Congress is required to assemble, determines by two-thirds vote of both Houses that the President is unable to discharge the powers and duties of his office, the Vice President shall continue to discharge the same as Acting President; otherwise, the President shall resume the powers and duties of his office.

AMENDMENT XXVI
Eighteen-year-old Vote (Ratified on July 1, 1971)

Section 1. The right of citizens of the United States, who are eighteen years of age or older, to vote shall not be denied or abridged by the United States or by any State on account of age.

Section 2. The Congress shall have power to enforce this article by appropriate legislation.

AMENDMENT XXVII
Congressional salaries (Ratified on May 18, 1992)

Section 1. No law varying the compensation for the services of the Senators and Representatives, shall take effect, until an election of Representatives shall have intervened.

PRESIDENTS OF THE UNITED STATES

YEAR	PRESIDENTIAL CANDIDATES	POLITICAL PARTY	ELECTORAL VOTE	POPULAR VOTE (%)
1789	**George Washington**	—	69	—
	John Adams		34	
	Others		35	
1792	**George Washington**	—	132	—
	John Adams		77	
	Others		55	
1796	**John Adams**	Federalist	71	—
	Thomas Jefferson	Democratic-Republican	68	
	Thomas Pinckney	Federalist	59	
	Aaron Burr	Anti-Federalist	30	
	Others		48	
1800	**Thomas Jefferson**	Democratic-Republican	73	—
	Aaron Burr	Democratic-Republican	73	
	John Adams	Federalist	65	
	C. C. Pinckney	Federalist	64	
	John Jay	Federalist	1	
1804	**Thomas Jefferson**	Democratic-Republican	162	—
	C. C. Pinckney	Federalist	14	
1808	**James Madison**	Democratic-Republican	122	—
	C. C. Pinckney	Federalist	47	
	George Clinton	Independent-Republican	6	

Note: Presidents are shown in boldface.
*Died in office, succeeding vice president shown in parentheses.
†Resigned
‡Appointed vice president
**Horace Greeley died between the popular vote and the meeting of the presidential electors.

YEAR	PRESIDENTIAL CANDIDATES	POLITICAL PARTY	ELECTORAL VOTE	POPULAR VOTE (%)
1812	**James Madison**	Democratic-Republican	128	—
	De Witt Clinton	Fusion	89	
1816	**James Monroe**	Democratic-Republican	183	—
	Rufus King	Federalist	34	
1820	**James Monroe**	Democratic-Republican	231	—
	John Q. Adams	Independent-Republican	1	
1824	**John Q. Adams**	National Republican	84	30.5
	Andrew Jackson	Democratic	99	
	Henry Clay	Democratic-Republican	37	
	W. H. Crawford	Democratic-Republican	41	
1828	**Andrew Jackson**	Democratic	178	56.0
	John Q. Adams	National Republican	83	
1832	**Andrew Jackson**	Democratic	219	55.0
	Henry Clay	National Republican	49	
	William Wirt	Anti-Masonic	7	
	John Floyd	Nullifiers	11	
1836	**Martin Van Buren**	Democratic	170	50.9
	William H. Harrison	Whig	73	
	Hugh L. White	Whig	26	
	Daniel Webster	Whig	14	
1840	**William H. Harrison***	Whig	234	53.0
	Martin Van Buren	Democratic	60	
	(**John Tyler**, 1841)			
1844	**James K. Polk**	Democratic	170	49.6
	Henry Clay	Whig	105	
1848	**Zachary Taylor***	Whig	163	47.4
	Lewis Cass	Democratic	127	
	(**Millard Fillmore**, 1850)			
1852	**Franklin Pierce**	Democratic	254	50.9
	Winfield Scott	Whig	42	
1856	**James Buchanan**	Democratic	174	45.4
	John C. Fremont	Republican	114	
	Millard Fillmore	American	8	
1860	**Abraham Lincoln**	Republican	180	39.8
	J. C. Breckinridge	Democratic	72	
	Stephen A. Douglas	Democratic	12	
	John Bell	Constitutional Union	39	
1864	**Abraham Lincoln***	Republican	212	55.0
	George B. McClellan	Democratic	21	
	(**Andrew Johnson**, 1865)			
1868	**Ulysses S. Grant**	Republican	214	52.7
	Horatio Seymour	Democratic	80	

YEAR	PRESIDENTIAL CANDIDATES	POLITICAL PARTY	ELECTORAL VOTE	POPULAR VOTE (%)
1872	**Ulysses S. Grant**	Republican	286	55.6
	Horace Greeley	Democratic	**	
1876	**Rutherford B. Hayes**	Republican	185	47.9
	Samuel J. Tilden	Democratic	184	
1880	**James A. Garfield***	Republican	214	48.3
	Winfield S. Hancock	Democratic	155	
	(**Chester A. Arthur**, 1881)			
1884	**Grover Cleveland**	Democratic	219	48.5
	James G. Blaine	Republican	182	
1888	**Benjamin Harrison**	Republican	233	47.8
	Grover Cleveland	Democratic	168	
1892	**Grover Cleveland**	Democratic	277	46.0
	Benjamin Harrison	Republican	145	
	James B. Weaver	People's	22	
1896	**William McKinley**	Republican	271	51.0
	William J. Bryan	Democratic	176	
1900	**William McKinley***	Republican	292	51.7
	William J. Bryan	Democratic	155	
	(**Theodore Roosevelt**, 1901)			
1904	**Theodore Roosevelt**	Republican	336	56.4
	Alton B. Parker	Democratic	140	
1908	**William H.Taft**	Republican	321	51.6
	William J. Bryan	Democratic	162	
1912	**Woodrow Wilson**	Democratic	435	41.8
	Theodore Roosevelt	Progressive	88	
	William H. Taft	Republican	8	
1916	**Woodrow Wilson**	Democratic	277	49.2
	Charles E. Hughes	Republican	254	
1920	**Warren G. Harding***	Republican	404	60.3
	James M. Cox	Democratic	127	
	(**Calvin Coolidge**, 1923)			
1924	**Calvin Coolidge**	Republican	382	54.1
	John W. Davis	Democratic	136	
	Robert M. LaFollette	Progressive	13	
1928	**Herbert C. Hoover**	Republican	444	58.2
	Alfred E. Smith	Democratic	87	
1932	**Franklin D. Roosevelt**	Democratic	472	57.4
	Herbert C. Hoover	Republican	59	
1936	**Franklin D. Roosevelt**	Democratic	523	60.8
	Alfred M. Landon	Republican	8	
1940	**Franklin D. Roosevelt**	Democratic	449	54.7
	Wendell L. Wilkie	Republican	82	

YEAR	PRESIDENTIAL CANDIDATES	POLITICAL PARTY	ELECTORAL VOTE	POPULAR VOTE (%)
1944	**Franklin D. Roosevelt***	Democratic	432	53.4
	Thomas E. Dewey	Republican	99	
	(**Harry S. Truman**, 1945)			
1948	**Harry S. Truman**	Democratic	303	49.5
	Thomas E. Dewey	Republican	189	
	J. Strom Thurmond	States' Rights	39	
1952	**Dwight D. Eisenhower**	Republican	442	55.1
	Adlai E. Stevenson	Democratic	89	
1956	**Dwight D. Eisenhower**	Republican	457	57.4
	Adlai E. Stevenson	Democratic	73	
1960	**John F. Kennedy***	Democratic	303	49.7
	Richard M. Nixon	Republican	219	
	(**Lyndon B. Johnson**, 1963)			
1964	**Lyndon B. Johnson**	Democratic	486	61.0
	Barry M. Goldwater	Republican	52	
1968	**Richard M. Nixon**	Republican	301	43.4
	Hubert H. Humphrey	Democratic	191	
	George C. Wallace	American Independent	46	
1972	**Richard M. Nixon**†	Republican	520	60.7
	George S. McGovern	Democratic	17	
	(**Gerald R. Ford**, 1974)‡			
1976	**Jimmy Carter**	Democratic	297	50.1
	Gerald R. Ford	Republican	240	
1980	**Ronald Reagan**	Republican	489	50.7
	Jimmy Carter	Democratic	49	
	John Anderson	Independent	—	
1984	**Ronald Reagan**	Republican	525	58.8
	Walter Mondale	Democratic	13	
1988	**George Bush**	Republican	426	53.4
	Michael Dukakis	Democratic	112	
1992	**Bill Clinton**	Democratic	370	43.0
	George Bush	Republican	168	
	H. Ross Perot	Independent	—	

activation One of three key consequences of electoral campaigns for voters, meaning that the voter is activated to contribute money or ring doorbells instead of just voting. See also **reinforcement** and **conversion.**

actual group That part of the **potential group** consisting of members who actually join. See also **interest group.**

administrative discretion The authority of administrative actors to select among various responses to a given problem. Discretion is greatest when routines, or **standard operating procedures**, do not fit a case.

affirmative action A policy designed to give special attention to or compensatory treatment of members of some previously disadvantaged group.

amicus curiae briefs Legal briefs submitted by a "friend of the court" for the purpose of raising additional points of view and presenting information not contained in the briefs of the formal parties. These briefs attempt to influence a court's decision.

Anti-Federalists Opponents of the **American Constitution** at the time when the states were contemplating its adoption. They argued that the Constitution was a class-based document, that it would erode fundamental liberties, and that it would weaken the power of the states. See also **Federalists**.

appellate jurisdiction The jurisdiction of courts that hear cases brought to them on appeal from lower courts. These courts do not review the factual record, only the legal issues involved. Compare **original jurisdiction**.

Articles of Confederation The first constitution of the United States, adopted by Congress in 1777 and enacted in 1781. The Articles established a national legislature, but gave most authority to the state legislatures.

balanced budget amendment A proposed amendment to the Constitution that would instruct Congress to hold a national convention to propose to the states a requirement that peacetime federal budgets be balanced. The amendment has been passed in varied forms by the legislatures of nearly two-thirds of the states.

bicameral legislature A legislature divided into two houses. The U.S. Congress and every American state legislature except Nebraska's are bicameral.

bill A proposed law, drafted in precise, legal language. Anyone can draft a bill, but only a member of the House of Representatives or the Senate can formally submit a bill for consideration.

Bill of Rights The first ten amendments to the **U.S. Constitution**, drafted in response to some of the **Anti-Federalist** concerns. These amendments define such basic liberties as freedom of religion, speech, and press, and offer protections against arbitrary searches by the police and being held without talking to a lawyer.

block grants Federal grants given more or less automatically to states or communities to support broad programs in areas like community development and social services. Compare **categorical grants**.

broadcast media Television and radio, as compared with **print media**.

Brown v. Board of Education The 1954 Supreme Court decision holding that school segregation in Topeka, Kansas, was inherently unconstitutional because it violated the **Fourteenth Amendment's** guarantee of **equal protection**. This case marked the end of legal segregation in the United States. See also *Plessy v. Ferguson*.

budget A policy document allocating burdens (taxes) and benefits (expenditures). See also **balanced budget amendment**.

bureaucracy According to Max Weber, a hierarchical authority structure that uses task specialization, operates on the merit principle, and behaves with impersonality. Bureaucracies govern modern states.

cabinet A group of presidential advisors not mentioned in the Constitution, although every president has appointed individuals to these positions. Today the cabinet is composed of thirteen secretaries and the attorney general.

campaign strategy Candidates' master game plans that guide their electoral campaigns.

casework Helping constituents as individuals; cutting through bureaucratic red tape to get people what they think they have a right to get. See also **pork barrel**.

categorical grants Federal grants that can be used only for specific purposes, or "categories," of state and local spending. They come with strings attached, such as nondiscrimination provisions. Compare **block grants**.

caucus (congressional) A grouping of members of Congress sharing some interest or characteristic. Most are composed of members from both parties and some from both houses.

caucus (state party) A meeting of all state party leaders where delegates to the **national party convention** are selected. Caucuses are usually organized as a pyramid.

census A valuable tool for understanding demographic changes. The Constitution requires that the government conduct an "actual enumeration" of the population every ten years. See also **demography**.

chains See **newspaper chains**.

checks and balances An important part of the Madisonian model designed to limit government's power by requiring that power be balanced among the different governmental institutions. These institutions continually check one another's activities. This system reflects Madison's goal of setting power against power. See also **separation of powers**.

civic duty The belief that, in order to support democratic government, a citizen should always vote.

civil disobedience A form of **political participation** that reflects a conscious decision to break a law believed to be immoral and to suffer the consequences. See also **protest**.

civil law The body of law involving cases without a charge of criminality. It concerns disputes between two parties and consists of both statutes and **common law**. Compare **criminal law**.

civil liberties The legal constitutional protections against government. Although our civil liberties are formally set down in the **Bill of Rights**, the courts, police, and legislatures define their meaning.

civil rights The policies extending basic rights to minority groups or other groups historically subject to discrimination. Many groups, especially African Americans and more recently women, have raised constitutional questions about slavery, segregation, equal pay, and other issues. See also **Civil Rights Act of 1964**.

Civil Rights Act of 1964 The law that made racial discrimination against any group in hotels, motels, and restaurants illegal and forbade many forms of job discrimination. See also **civil rights movement** and **civil rights policies**.

civil service A system of hiring and promoting based on the **merit principle** and the desire to create a nonpartisan government service. Compare **patronage**.

class action lawsuits Lawsuits permitting a small number of people to sue on behalf of all other people similarly situated.

coalition government When two or more parties join together to form a majority in a national legislature. This form of government is quite common in the multiparty systems of Europe.

collective good Something of value (money, a tax write-off, prestige, clean air, and so on) that cannot be withheld from a group member.

committee chairs The most important influencers of the congressional agenda. They play dominant roles in scheduling hearings, hiring staff, appointing subcommittees, and managing committee bills when they are brought before the full House.

conference committees Congressional committees formed when the Senate and the House pass a particular bill in different forms. Party leadership appoints members from each house who iron out the differences and report back a single bill. See also **standing committees**, **joint committees**, and **select committees**.

Connecticut Compromise The compromise reached at the Constitutional Convention that established two houses of Congress: the House of Representatives, in which **representation** is based on a state's share of the U.S. population, and the Senate, in which each state has two representatives. Compare **New Jersey Plan** and **Virginia Plan**.

consent of the governed According to John Locke, the required basis for government. The **Declaration of Independence** reflects Locke's view that governments derive their authority from the consent of the governed.

constitution A nation's basic law. It creates political institutions, assigns or divides powers in government, and often provides certain guarantees to citizens. Constitutions can be both written and unwritten. See also **U.S. Constitution**.

conversion One of three key consequences of electoral campaigns for voters, meaning that the voter's mind is actually changed. See also **reinforcement** and **activation**.

cooperative federalism A system of government in which powers and policy assignments are shared between states and the national government. They may also share costs, administration, and even blame for programs that work poorly. Compare **dual federalism**.

Council of Economic Advisors (CEA) A three-member body appointed by the president to advise the president on economic policy.

courts of appeal Appellate courts empowered to review all final decisions of district courts, except in rare cases. In addition, they also hear appeals to orders of many federal regulatory agencies. Compare **district courts**.

criminal law The body of law involving a case in which an individual is charged with violating a specific law. The offense may be harmful to an individual or society and in either case warrants punishment, such as imprisonment or a fine. Compare **civil law**.

critical election An electoral "earthquake" whereby new issues emerge, new coalitions replace old, and the majority party is often displaced by the minority party. Critical election periods are sometimes marked by a national crisis and may require more than one election to bring about a new **party era**. See also **party realignment**.

cruel and unusual punishment Court sentences prohibited by the **Eighth Amendment**. Although the Supreme Court has ruled that mandatory death sentences for certain offenses are unconstitutional, it has not held that the death penalty itself constitutes cruel and unusual punishment. See also *Furman v. Georgia*, *Gregg v. Georgia*, and *McClesky v. Kemp*.

Declaration of Independence The document approved by representatives of the American colonies in 1776 stating their grievances against the British monarch and declaring their independence.

deficit An excess of federal **expenditures** over federal **revenues**. See also **budget**.

demography The science of population changes. See also **census**.

deregulation The lifting of restrictions on business, industry, and other professional activities for which government rules had been established and bureaucracies had been created to administer.

district courts The ninety-four federal courts of original jurisdiction. They are the only federal courts in which trials are held and in which juries may be empaneled. Compare **courts of appeal**.

dual federalism A system of government in which states and the national government each remain supreme within their own spheres, each responsible for some policies. Compare **cooperative federalism**.

elastic clause The final paragraph of Article I, Section 8, of the Constitution, which authorizes Congress to pass all laws "necessary and proper" to carry out the **enumerated powers**. See also **implied powers**.

electioneering Direct group involvement in the electoral process. Groups can help fund campaigns, provide testimony, and get members to work for candidates, and some form **Political Action Committees (PACs)**.

electoral college A unique American institution, created by the Constitution, providing for the selection of the president by electors chosen by the state parties. Although the electoral college vote usually reflects a popular majority, the winner-take-all rule gives clout to big states.

elite theory A theory of government and politics contending that societies are divided along class lines and that an upper class **elite** will rule, regardless of the formal niceties of governmental organization. Compare **hyperpluralism, pluralist theory,** and **traditional democratic theory**.

Engel v. Vitale The 1962 Supreme Court decision holding that state officials violated the **First Amendment** when they wrote a prayer to be recited by New York's schoolchildren. Compare **School District of Abington Township,** *Pennsylvania v. Schempp*.

entitlements Policies for which expenditures are uncontrollable because Congress has obligated itself to pay X level of benefits to Y number of recipients. Each year, Congress's bill is a straightforward function of the X level of benefits times the Y beneficiaries. Social Security benefits are an example.

enumerated powers Powers of the federal government that are specifically addressed in the Constitution; for Congress, these powers are listed in Article I, Section 8, and include the power to coin money, regulate its value, and impose taxes. Compare **implied powers**.

equal protection of the laws Part of the **Fourteenth Amendment** emphasizing that the laws must provide equivalent "protection" to all people. As one member of Congress said during debate on the amendment, it should provide "equal protection of life, liberty, and property" to all a state's citizens.

Equal Rights Amendment A constitutional amendment passed by Congress in 1978 and sent to the state legislatures for ratification, stating that "equality of rights under the law shall not be denied or abridged by the United States or by any state on account of sex." Despite substantial public support and an extended deadline, the amendment failed to acquire the necessary support of three-fourths of the state legislatures.

establishment clause Part of the **First Amendment** stating that "Congress shall make no law respecting an establishment of religion."

exclusionary rule The rule that evidence, no matter how incriminating, cannot be introduced into a trial if it was not constitutionally obtained. The rule prohibits use of evidence obtained through **unreasonable search and seizure**.

executive orders Regulations originating from the executive branch. Executive orders are one method presidents can use to control the bureaucracy; more often, though, presidents pass along their wishes through their aides.

exit polls **Public opinion** surveys used by major media pollsters to predict electoral winners with speed and precision.

expenditures Federal spending of **revenues**. Major areas receiving such spending are social services and the military.

extradition A legal process whereby an alleged criminal offender is surrendered by the officials of one state to officials of the state in which the crime is alleged to have been committed.

factions Interest groups arising from the unequal distribution of property or wealth that James Madison attacked in the **Federalist Papers** No. 10. Today's parties or interest groups are what Madison had in mind when he warned of the instability in government caused by factions.

federal debt All the money borrowed by the federal government over the years and still outstanding. Today the federal debt is about $4.5 trillion.

Federal Election Campaign Act A law passed in 1974 for reforming campaign finances. It created the **Federal Election Commission (FEC)**, provided public financing for presidential primaries and general elections, limited presidential campaign spending, required disclosure, and attempted to limit contributions.

Federal Election Commission (FEC) A six-member bipartisan agency created by the **Federal Election Campaign Act** of 1974. The FEC administers the campaign finance laws and enforces compliance with their requirements.

federalism Organizing a nation so that two levels of government have formal authority over the same land and people. It is a system of shared power between units of government. Compare **unitary government**.

Federalist Papers A collection of eighty-five articles written by Alexander Hamilton, John Jay, and James Madison under the name "Publius" to defend the Constitution. Collectively, these papers are second only to the **U.S. Constitution** in characterizing the framers' intents.

Federalists Supporters of the **U.S. Constitution** at the time the states were contemplating its adoption. See also **Anti-Federalists** and **Federalist Papers**.

Fifth Amendment The constitutional amendment designed to protect the rights of persons accused of crimes, including protection against double jeopardy, **self-incrimination**, and punishment without due process of law.

filibuster A strategy unique to the Senate whereby opponents of a piece of legislation try to talk it to death, based on the tradition of unlimited debate. Today, sixty members present and voting can halt a filibuster.

First Amendment The constitutional amendment that establishes the four great liberties: freedom of the press, speech, religion, and assembly.

fiscal federalism The patterns of spending, taxing, and awarding grants between governmental units in a federal system.

formula grants Federal **categorical grants** distributed according to a formula specified in legislation or in administrative regulations.

Fourteenth Amendment The constitutional amendment adopted after the Civil War that states, "No State shall make or enforce any law which shall abridge the privileges or immunities of citizens of the United States; nor shall any state deprive any person of life, liberty, or property, without due process of law; nor deny to any person within its jurisdiction the **equal protection of the laws**." See also **due process clause**.

Free Exercise clause A **First Amendment** provision that prohibits government from interfering with the practice of religion.

free-rider problem The problem faced by unions and other groups when people do not join because they can benefit from the group's activities without officially joining. The bigger the group, the more serious the free-rider problem. See also **interest group**.

full faith and credit clause A clause in Article IV, Section 1, of the Constitution requiring each state to recognize the official documents and civil judgments rendered by the courts of the other states.

Gibbons v. Ogden A landmark case decided in 1824 in which the Supreme Court interpreted very broadly the clause in Article I, Section 8, of the Constitution giving Congress the power to regulate interstate commerce, encompassing virtually every form of commercial activity. The commerce clause has been the constitutional basis for much of Congress's regulation of the economy.

Gideon v. Wainwright The 1963 Supreme Court decision holding that anyone accused of a felony, where imprisonment may be imposed, has a right to a lawyer, however poor he or she might be. See also **Sixth Amendment.**

Gitlow v. New York The 1925 Supreme Court decision holding that freedoms of press and speech are "fundamental personal rights and liberties protected by the **due process clause** of the **Fourteenth Amendment** from impairment by the states" as well as the federal government. Compare *Barron v. Baltimore*.

government corporation A government organization that, like business corporations, provides a service that could be provided by the private sector and typically charges for its services. The U.S. Postal Service is one example. Compare **independent regulatory agency** and **independent executive agency.**

Hatch Act A federal law prohibiting government employees from active participation in partisan politics.

high-tech politics A politics in which the behavior of citizens and policymakers and the political agenda itself are increasingly shaped by technology.

House Rules Committee An institution unique to the House of Representatives that reviews all bills (except revenue, budget, and appropriations bills) coming from a House committee before they go to the full House.

hyperpluralism A theory of government and politics contending that groups are so strong that government is weakened. Hyperpluralism is an extreme, exaggerated, or perverted form of pluralism. Compare **elite and class theory**, **pluralist theory**, and **traditional democratic theory.**

impeachment The political equivalent of an indictment in criminal law, prescribed by the Constitution. The House of Representatives may impeach the president by a majority vote for "Treason, Bribery, or other high Crimes and Misdemeanors."

implementation The stage of policy-making between the establishment of a policy and the consequences of the policy for the people whom it affects. Implementation involves translating the goals and objectives of a policy into an operating, ongoing program. See also **judicial implementation.**

implied powers Powers of the federal government that go beyond those enumerated in the Constitution. The Constitution states that Congress has the power to "make all laws necessary and proper for carrying into execution" the powers enumerated in Article I. Many federal policies are justified on the basis of implied powers. See also *McCulloch v. Maryland*, **elastic clause**, and **enumerated powers.**

incentive system According to Charles Shultze, a more effective and efficient policy than **command-and-control**; in the incentive system, marketlike strategies are used to manage public policy.

income taxes Shares of individual wages and corporate revenues collected by the government. The first income tax was declared unconstitutional by the Supreme Court in 1895, but the **Sixteenth Amendment** explicitly authorized Congress to levy a tax on income. See also **Internal Revenue Service.**

incrementalism The belief that the best predictor of this year's budget is last year's **budget**, plus a little bit more (an increment). According to Aaron Wildavsky, "Most of the budget is a product of previous decisions."

incumbents Those already holding office. The most important fact about congressional elections is that incumbents usually win.

independent executive agency The government not accounted for by **cabinet** departments, **independent regulatory agencies**, and **government corporations**. Its administrators are typically appointed by the president and serve at his will. NASA is one example.

independent regulatory agency A government agency with responsibility for some sector of the economy, making and enforcing rules to protect the public interest. It also judges disputes over these rules. The Interstate Commerce Commission is one example. Compare **government corporation** and **independent executive agency**.

interest group An organization of people with shared policy goals entering the policy process at several points to try to achieve those goals. Interest groups pursue their goals in many arenas.

intergovernmental relations The workings of the federal system, by which is meant the entire set of interactions among national, state, and local governments.

Internal Revenue Service The office established to collect federal **income taxes**, investigate violations of the tax laws, and prosecute tax criminals.

joint committees Congressional committees on a few subject-matter areas with membership drawn from both houses. See also **standing committees**, **conference committees**, and **select committees**.

judicial activism A judicial philosophy in which judges make bold policy decisions, even charting new constitutional ground. Advocates of this approach emphasize that the courts can correct pressing needs, especially those unmet by the majoritarian political process. Compare **judicial restraint**.

judicial implementation How and whether court decisions are translated into actual policy, affecting the behavior of others. The courts rely on other units of government to enforce their decisions.

judicial restraint A judicial philosophy in which judges play minimal policy-making roles, leaving policy decisions strictly to the legislatures. Compare **judicial activism**.

judicial review The power of the courts to determine whether acts of Congress, and by implication the executive, are in accord with the **U.S. Constitution**. Judicial review was established by John Marshall and

his associates in *Marbury v. Madison*. See also **judicial interpretation**.

justiciable disputes A constraint on the courts, meaning that a case must be capable of being settled by legal methods.

leak See **news leak**.

legislative veto The ability of Congress to override a presidential decision. Although the **War Powers Resolution** asserts this authority, there is reason to believe that, if challenged, the Supreme Court would find the legislative veto in violation of the doctrine of separation of powers.

libel The publication of knowingly false or malicious statements that damage someone's reputation.

limited government The idea that certain things are out of bounds for government because of the **natural rights** of citizens. Limited government was central to John Locke's philosophy in the seventeenth century, which contrasted sharply with the prevailing view of the divine rights of monarchs.

linkage institutions The channels or access points through which issues and people's policy preferences get on the government's **policy agenda**. In the United States, elections, **political parties, mass media**, and **interest groups** are the three main linkage institutions.

lobbying According to Lester Milbrath, a "communication, by someone other than a citizen acting on his own behalf, directed to a governmental decisionmaker with the hope of influencing a decision."

McCulloch v. Maryland An 1819 Supreme Court decision that established the supremacy of the national government over state governments. In deciding this case, Chief Justice John Marshall and his colleagues held that Congress had certain **implied powers** in addition to the **enumerated powers** found in the Constitution.

McGovern-Fraser Commission A commission formed at the 1968 Democratic convention in response to demands for reform by minority groups and others who sought better representation.

majority leader The principle partisan ally of the Speaker of the House or the party's wheelhorse in the Senate. The majority leader is responsible for scheduling bills, influencing committee assignments, and rounding up votes in behalf of the party's legislative positions.

mandate theory of elections The idea that winning candidates have a mandate from the people to carry out their platforms and policies. Politicians like the theory better than political scientists do.

Mapp v. Ohio The 1961 Supreme Court decision ruling that the Fourth Amendment's protection against **unreasonable searches and seizures** must be extended to the states as well as the federal government. See also **exclusionary rule.**

Marbury v. Madison The 1803 case in which Chief Justice John Marshall and his associates first asserted the right of the **Supreme Court** to determine the meaning of the **American Constitution.** The decision established the Court's power of **judicial review** over acts of Congress, in this case the Judiciary Act of 1789.

mass media Television, radio, newspapers, magazines, and other influential means of popular communication. They are a key part of **high-tech politics.** See also **broadcast media** and **print media.**

media events Purposely staged events in front of the media that nonetheless look spontaneous. In keeping with politics as theater, media events can be staged by individuals, groups, and government officials, especially presidents.

Medicare A program added to the Social Security system in 1965 that provides hospitalization insurance for the elderly and permits older Americans to purchase inexpensive coverage for doctor fees and other expenses. Compare **Medicaid.**

melting pot The mixing of cultures, ideas, and peoples that have changed the American nation. The United States, with its history of immigration, has often been called a melting pot.

merit principle The idea that hiring should use entrance exams and promotion ratings to produce administration by people with talent and skill. See also **civil service** and compare **patronage.**

Miller v. California A 1973 Supreme Court decision that avoided defining obscenity by holding that community standards be used to determine whether material is obscene in terms of appealing to a "prurient interest."

minority leader The principal leader of the minority party in the House of Representatives or in the Senate.

minority majority The emergence of a non-Caucasian majority, as compared with a white, generally Anglo-Saxon majority. It is predicted that, by about the middle of the next century, Hispanic Americans, African Americans, and Asian Americans will outnumber white Americans.

Miranda v. Arizona The 1966 Supreme Court decision that sets guidelines for police questioning of accused persons to protect them against **self-incrimination** and to protect their right to counsel.

national chairperson One of the institutions that keeps the party operating between conventions. The national chairperson is responsible for the day-to-day activities of the party and is usually handpicked by the presidential nominee. See also **national committee.**

national committee One of the institutions that keeps the party operating between conventions. The national committee is composed of representatives from the states and territories. See also **national chairperson.**

national convention The meeting of party delegates every four years to choose a presidential ticket and write the party's platform.

national party convention The supreme power within each of the parties. It meets every four years to nominate the presidential and vice-presidential candidates of the party and to write the party's platform.

national primary A proposal by critics of the **caucuses** and **presidential primaries** system that would replace these electoral methods with a nationwide primary held early in the election year.

National Security Council An office created in 1947 to coordinate the president's foreign and military policy advisors. Its formal members are the president, **secretary of state,** and **secretary of defense,** and it is managed by the president's national security advisor.

natural rights Rights held to be inherent in human beings, not dependent on governments. John Locke asserted that natural law, which is superior to human law, specifies certain rights of "life, liberty, and property," a sentiment reflected in the **Declaration of Independence.**

New Deal Coalition A **coalition** forged by Franklin Roosevelt and the Democrats who dominated American politics from the 1930s to the 1960s. Its basic elements were the urban working class, ethnic groups, Catholics and Jews, the poor, southerners, African Americans, and Democratic intellectuals.

New Jersey Plan The proposal at the Constitutional Convention that called for equal **representation** of each state in Congress regardless of the state's population. Compare **Virginia Plan** and **Connecticut Compromise.**

New York Times v. Sullivan Decided in 1964, this case established the guidelines for determining whether public officials and public figures could win damage suits for libel. To do so, said the Court, they must prove that the defamatory statements made about them were made with "actual malice" and reckless disregard for the truth.

news leak A carefully placed bit of inside information given to a friendly reporter. Leaks can benefit both the leaker and the leakee.

nomination The official endorsement of a candidate for office by a **political party.** Generally, success in the nomination game requires momentum, money, and media attention.

Office of Management and Budget (OMB) An office that grew out of the Bureau of the Budget, created in 1921, consisting of a handful of political appointees and hundreds of skilled professionals. The OMB performs both managerial and budgetary functions, and although the president is its boss, the director and staff have considerable independence in the budgetary process. See also **Congressional Budget Office.**

Olson's law of large groups Advanced by Mancur Olson, a principle stating that "the larger the group, the further it will fall short of providing an optimal amount of a collective good." See also **interest group.**

opinion A statement of legal reasoning behind a judicial decision. The content of an opinion may be as important as the decision itself.

original intent A view that the Constitution should be interpreted according to the original intent of the framers. Many **conservatives** support this view.

original jurisdiction The jurisdiction of courts that hear a case first, usually in a trial. These are the courts that determine the facts about a case. Compare **appellate jurisdiction.**

oversight The process of monitoring the bureaucracy and its administration of policy, mainly through congressional hearings.

PACs See **Political Action Committees (PACs).**

party competition The battle of the parties for control of public offices. Ups and downs of the two major parties are one of the most important elements in American politics.

party dealignment The gradual disengagement of people and politicians from the parties, as seen in part by shrinking **party identification.**

party eras Historical periods in which a majority of voters cling to the party in power, which tends to win a majority of the election. See also **critical election** and **party realignment.**

party identification A citizen's self-proclaimed preference for one party or the other.

party image The voter's perception of what the Republicans or Democrats stand for, such as **conservatism** or **liberalism.**

party machines A type of political party organization that relies heavily on material inducements such as patronage to win votes and govern.

party neutrality A term used to describe the fact that many Americans are indifferent toward the two major political parties. See also **party dealignment.**

party realignment The displacement of the majority party by the minority party occurring during a **critical election period.** See also **party era.**

patronage One of the key inducements used by **party machines.** A patronage job, promotion, or contract is one that is given for political reasons rather than for merit or competence alone. Compare **civil service** and the **merit principle**.

Pendleton Civil Service Act Passed in 1883, an act that created a federal **civil service** so that hiring and promotion would be based on merit rather than **patronage**.

per curiam decision A court decision without explanation—in other words, without an **opinion**.

plea bargain An actual bargain struck between the defendant's lawyer and the prosecutor to the effect that the defendant will plead guilty to a lesser crime in exchange for the state's promise not to prosecute the defendant for the more serious one.

Plessy v. Ferguson An 1896 Supreme Court decision that provided a constitutional justification for segregation by ruling that a Louisiana law requiring "equal but separate accommodations for the white and colored races" was not unconstitutional.

pluralist theory A theory of government and politics emphasizing that politics is mainly a competition among groups, each one pressing for its own preferred policies. Compare **elite** and **class theory**, **hyperpluralism**, and **traditional democratic theory**.

pocket veto A veto taking place when Congress adjourns within ten days of having submitted a **bill** to the president, who simply lets the bill die by neither signing nor vetoing it. See also **veto**.

policy agenda According to John Kingdon, "the list of subjects or problems to which government officials, and people outside of government closely associated with those officials, are paying some serious attention at any given time."

policy differences The perception of a clear choice between the parties. Those who see such choices are more likely to vote.

policy entrepreneurs People who invest their political "capital" in an issue. According to John Kingdon, a policy entrepreneur "could be in or out of government, in elected or appointed positions, in interest groups or research organizations."

policy voting Voting that occurs when electoral choices are made on the basis of the voters' policy preferences and on where the candidates stand on policy issues. For the voter, policy voting is hard work.

Political Action Committees (PACs) Funding vehicles created by the 1974 campaign finance reforms. A corporation, union, or some other interest group can create a PAC and register it with the **Federal Election Commission (FEC),** which will meticulously monitor the PAC's expenditures.

political efficacy The belief that one's **political participation** really matters, that one's vote can actually make a difference.

political ideology A coherent set of beliefs about politics, public policy, and public purpose. It helps give meaning to political events, personalities, and policies. See also **liberalism** and **conservatism**.

political participation All the activities used by citizens to influence the selection of political leaders or the policies they pursue. The most common, but not the only, means of political participation in a **democracy** is voting. Other means include **protest** and **civil disobedience**.

political party According to Anthony Downs, a "team of men [and women] seeking to control the governing apparatus by gaining office in a duly constituted election."

political questions A doctrine developed by the federal courts and used as a means to avoid deciding some cases, principally those involving conflicts between the president and Congress.

political socialization According to Richard Dawson, "the process through which an individual acquires his [or her] particular political orientations—his [or her] knowledge, feelings, and evaluations regarding his [or her] political world." See also **agents of socialization**.

pork barrel The mighty list of federal projects, grants, and contracts available to cities, businesses, colleges, and institutions in the district of a member of Congress.

potential group All the people who might be **interest group** members because they share some common interest. A potential group is almost always larger than an **actual group**.

precedents How a similar case has been decided in the past.

presidential coattails The situation occurring when voters cast their ballots for congressional candidates of the president's party because they support the president. Recent studies show that few races are won this way.

presidential debate A debate between presidential candidates. The first televised debate was between Richard Nixon and John Kennedy during the 1960 campaign.

presidential primaries Elections in which voters in a state vote for a candidate (or delegates pledged to a certain candidate). Most delegates to the **national party conventions** are chosen this way.

press conference Meetings of public officials with reporters. President Franklin D. Roosevelt promised and delivered two press conferences each week.

primaries Elections that select candidates. In addition to **presidential primaries**, there are **direct primaries** for selecting party nominees for congressional and state offices and proposals for **regional primaries**.

print media Newspapers and magazines, as compared with **broadcast media**.

prior restraint A government's preventing material from being published. This is a common method of limiting the press in some nations, but it is unconstitutional in the United States, according to the **First Amendment** and as confirmed in the 1931 Supreme Court case of *Near v. Minnesota*.

privileges and immunities clause A clause in Article IV, Section 2, of the Constitution according citizens of each state some of the privileges of citizens of other states.

project grants Federal grants given for specific purposes and awarded on the basis of the merits of applications. A type of the **categorical grants** available to states and localities.

proportional representation An electoral system used throughout most of Europe that awards legislative seats to political parties in proportion to the number of votes won in an election. Compare **winner-take-all system**.

protest A form of **political participation** designed to achieve policy change through dramatic and unconventional tactics. See also **civil disobedience**.

public interest lobbies According to Jeffrey Berry, organizations that seek "a collective good, the achievement of which will not selectively and materially benefit the membership or activities of the organization." See also **lobbying** and **public interest**.

public opinion The distribution of the population's beliefs about politics and policy issues.

random digit dialing A technique used to place telephone calls randomly to both listed and unlisted numbers when conducting a survey. See also **random sample**.

random sample The key technique employed by sophisticated survey researchers, which operates on the principle that everyone should have an equal probability of being selected for the sample. See also **sample**.

rational-choice theory A popular theory in political science to explain the actions of voters as well as politicians. It assumes that individuals act in their best interest, carefully weighing the costs and benefits of possible alternatives.

reapportionment The process of reallocating seats in the House of Representatives every ten years based on the results of the census.

Reed v. Reed The landmark case in 1971 in which the Supreme Court for the first time upheld a claim of sexual discrimination.

regional primaries A proposal by critics of the **caucuses** and **presidential primaries** to replace these electoral methods with regional primaries held early in the election year.

regulation The use of governmental authority to control or change some practice in the private sector. Regulations pervade the daily lives of people and institutions.

reinforcement One of three key consequences of electoral campaigns for voters, meaning that the voter's candidate preference is reinforced. See also **activation** and **conversion**.

republic A form of government that derives its power, directly or indirectly, from the people. Those chosen to govern are accountable to those whom they govern. In a republic, the people select representatives who make the laws, as opposed to a direct democracy, in which people make laws themselves.

responsible party model A view favored by some political scientists about how parties should work. According to the model, parties should offer clear choices to the voters, who can then use these choices as cues to their candidate preference. Once in office, parties would carry out their campaign promises.

revenues The financial resources of the federal government. The individual income tax and Social Security tax are two major sources of revenue. Compare **expenditures.**

right to privacy According to Paul Bender, "the right to keep the details of [one's] life confidential; the free and untrammeled use and enjoyment of one's intellect, body, and private property . . . the right, in sum, to a private personal life free from the intrusion of government or the dictates of society." The right to privacy is implicitly protected by the **Bill of Rights.** See also **Privacy Act.**

right-to-work law A state law forbidding requirements that workers must join a union to hold their jobs. State right-to-work laws were specifically permitted by the Taft-Hartley Act of 1947.

Roe v. Wade The 1973 Supreme Court decision holding that a state ban on all abortions was unconstitutional. The decision forbade state control over abortions during the first trimester of pregnancy, permitted states to limit abortions to protect the mother's health in the second trimester, and permitted states to protect the fetus during the third trimester.

sample A relatively small proportion of people who are chosen in a survey so as to be representative of the whole.

sampling error The level of confidence in the findings of a public opinion poll. The more people interviewed, the more confident one can be of the results.

School District of Abington Township, Pennsylvania v. Schempp A 1963 Supreme Court decision holding that a Pennsylvania law requiring Bible reading in schools violated the **establishment clause** of the **First Amendment.** Compare *Engel v. Vitale.*

select committees Congressional committees appointed for a specific purpose, such as the Watergate investigation. See also **joint committees, standing committees,** and **conference committees.**

selective perception The phenomenon that people often pay the most attention to things they already agree with, and interpret them according to their own predispositions.

senatorial courtesy An unwritten tradition whereby nominations for state-level federal judicial posts are not confirmed if they are opposed by the senator from the state in which the nominee will serve. The tradition also applies to courts of appeal when there is opposition from the nominee's state senator, if the senator belongs to the president's party.

seniority system A simple method of selecting **committee chairs,** in effect until the 1970s. The member who had served on the committee the longest and whose party controlled Congress became chair, regardless of party loyalty, mental state, or competence.

separation of powers An important part of the **Madisonian model** that required each of the three branches of government—executive, legislative, and judicial—to be relatively independent of one another so that one branch could not control the others. Power is shared among these three institutions. See also **checks and balances.**

Shays' Rebellion A series of attacks on courthouses by a small band of farmers led by revolutionary war Captain Daniel Shays to block foreclosure proceedings.

Simpson-Mazzolli Act An immigration law, named after its legislative sponsors, that as of June 1, 1987, requires employers to document the citizenship of their employees. Civil and criminal penalties can be assessed against employers who knowingly employ illegal immigrants.

single-issue groups Groups that have a narrow interest, tend to dislike compromise, and often draw membership from people new to politics. These features distinguish them from traditional **interest groups.**

Sixteenth Amendment The constitutional amendment adopted in 1915 that explicitly permitted Congress to levy an **income tax.**

Social Security Act A 1935 law passed during the Great Depression that was intended to provide a minimal level of sustenance to older Americans and thus save them from poverty.

solicitor general A presidential appointee and the third-ranking office in the Department of Justice. The solicitor general is in charge of the appellate court litigation of the federal government.

sound bites Short video clips of approximately 15 seconds, which are typically all that is shown from a politician's speech or activities on the nightly television news.

Speaker of the House An office mandated by the Constitution. The Speaker is chosen in practice by the majority party, has both formal and informal powers, and is second in line to succeed a deceased president.

split-level party A party with a strong, vigorous organization, but a weak following on the mass level.

standard operating procedures Better known as SOPs, these procedures are used by bureaucrats to bring uniformity to complex organizations. Uniformity improves fairness and makes personnel interchangeable. See also **administrative discretion.**

standing committees Separate subject-matter committees in each house of Congress that handle **bills** in different policy areas. See also **joint committees, conference committees,** and **select committees.**

standing to sue The requirement that **plaintiffs** have a serious interest in a **case,** which depends on whether they have sustained or are likely to sustain a direct and substantial injury from a party or an action of government.

stare decisis A Latin phrase meaning "let the decision stand." The vast majority of cases reaching the courts are settled on this principle.

statutory construction The judicial interpretation of an act of Congress. In some cases where statutory construction is an issue, Congress passes new legislation to clarify existing laws.

street-level bureaucrats A phrase coined by Michael Lipsky, referring to those bureaucrats who are in constant contact with the public and have considerable **administrative discretion.**

subgovernments Also known as "iron triangles," subgovernments are composed of key interest group leaders interested in a policy, the government agency responsible for the policy's administration, and the members of the congressional committees and subcommittees handling the policy.

suffrage The legal right to vote, extended to African Americans by the **Fifteenth Amendment,** to women by the **Nineteenth Amendment,** and to people over the age of 18 by the **Twenty-sixth Amendment.**

Super Tuesday Created by a group of southern states when they held their **presidential primaries** in early March 1988, the states hoped to promote a regional advantage as well as a more conservative candidate.

superdelegates National party leaders who automatically get a delegate slot at the Democratic **national party convention.**

supremacy clause Article VI of the Constitution, which makes the Constitution, national laws, and treaties supreme over state laws when the national government is acting within its constitutional limits.

Supreme Court The pinnacle of the American judicial system. The Court ensures uniformity in interpreting national laws, resolves conflicts among states, and maintains national supremacy in law. It has both **original jurisdiction** and **appellate jurisdiction**. Unlike other federal courts, the Supreme Court controls its own agenda.

talking head A shot of a person's face talking directly to the camera. Because this is visually unappealing, the major commercial networks rarely show a politician talking one-on-one for very long. See also **sound bites.**

tax expenditures Defined by the 1974 Budget Act as "revenue losses attributable to provisions of the federal tax laws which allow a special exemption, exclusion, or deduction." Tax expenditures represent the difference between what the government actually collects in taxes and what it would have collected without special exemptions.

Tenth Amendment The constitutional amendment stating that "The powers not delegated to the United States by the Constitution, nor prohibited by it to the states, are reserved to the states respectively, or to the people."

third parties Electoral contenders other than the two major parties. American third parties are not unusual.

three-fifths compromise The compromise at the Constitutional Convention establishing representation and taxation for slave states would be based upon the number of free people plus three-fifths of the number of "all other people," meaning each slave counted as three-fifths of one free person.

ticket splitting Voting with one party for one office and another party for other offices. It has become the norm in American voting behavior.

trial balloons An intentional **news leak** for the purpose of assessing the political reaction.

Twenty-fifth Amendment Passed in 1951, the amendment that permits the vice president to become acting president if both the vice president and the president's cabinet determine that the president is disabled. The amendment also outlines how a recuperated president can reclaim the job.

Twenty-second Amendment Passed in 1951, the amendment that limits presidents to two terms of office.

uncontrollable expenditures Expenditures that are determined by how many eligible beneficiaries there are for a particular program. According to Lance LeLoup, an expenditure is classified as uncontrollable "if it is mandated under current law or by a previous obligation." Two-thirds of the federal **budget** is uncontrollable. Congress can change uncontrollable expenditures only by changing a law or existing benefit levels.

union shop A provision found in some collective bargaining agreements requiring all employees of a business to join the union within a short period,

usually thirty days, and remain members as a condition of employment.

unitary government A way of organizing a nation so that all power resides in the central government. Most governments today, including those of Britain and Japan, are unitary governments. Compare **federalism.**

unreasonable searches and seizures Obtaining evidence in a haphazard or random manner, a practice prohibited by the Fourth Amendment. Both **probable cause** and a **search warrant** are required for a legal and proper search for and seizure of incriminating evidence.

U.S. Constitution The document written in 1787 and ratified in 1788 that sets forth the institutional structure of U.S. government and the tasks these institutions perform. It replaced the Articles of Confederation.

veto The constitutional power of the president to send a **bill** back to Congress with reasons for rejecting it. A two-thirds vote in each house can override a veto. See also **pocket veto** and **legislative veto.**

Virginia Plan The proposal at the Constitutional Convention that called for representation of each state in Congress in proportion to each state's share of the U.S. population. Compare **New Jersey Plan** and **Connecticut Compromise.**

voter registration A system adopted by the states that requires voters to sign up well in advance of election day. Although some states permit virtually instant registration for presidential elections, registration dampens voter turnout.

Voting Rights Act of 1965 A law designed to help put an end to formal and informal barriers to African-American **suffrage.** Under the law, federal registrars were sent to southern states and counties that had long histories of discrimination; as a result, hundreds of thousands of African Americans were registered and the number of African-American elected officials increased dramatically.

War Powers Resolution A law, passed in 1973 in reaction to American fighting in Vietnam and Cambodia, requiring presidents to consult with Congress whenever possible prior to using military force and to withdraw forces after sixty days unless Congress declares war or grants an extension. Presidents view the resolution as unconstitutional. See also **legislative veto.**

Watergate The events and scandal surrounding a break-in at the Democratic National Committee headquarters in 1972 and the subsequent cover-up of White House involvement, leading to the eventual resignation of President Nixon under the threat of **impeachment.**

whips Party leaders who work with the **majority leader** to count votes beforehand and lean on waverers whose votes are crucial to a **bill** favored by the party.

winner-take-all system An electoral system in which legislative seats are awarded only to the candidates who come in first in their constituencies. In American presidential elections, the system in which the winner of the popular vote in a state receives all the electoral votes of that state. Compare **proportional representation.**

writ of certiorari A formal document issued by the **Supreme Court** to a lower federal or state court that calls up a case.

writ of habeas corpus A court order requiring jailers to explain to a judge why they are holding a prisoner in custody.

ACKNOWLEDGMENTS

PAGE COVER: F.Sieb/H. Armstrong Roberts. *PAGE 4:* Michael Newman/Photo Edit. *PAGE 5:* Permission granted by the Detroit News. *PAGE 6:* Reuters/Bettmann. *PAGE 9:* AP/Wide World. *PAGE 13:* Natsuko Utsumi/Gamma-Liaison. *PAGE 30:* Library of Congress. *PAGE 31:* Doonesbury by Garry Trudeau/Universal Press Syndicate Reprinted with permission. All Rights Reserved. *PAGE 38:* Virginia Museum, Gift of Colonel and Mrs. Edgar W. Garbisch. *PAGE 43:* Library of Congress. *PAGE 48:* Mike Luckovich, Courtesy Times-Picayune, New Orleans. *PAGE 55:* U.S. Dept. of Transportation. *PAGE 61:* UPI/Bettmann. *PAGE 64:* AP/Wide World. *PAGE 68:* Paul Conklin/Uniphoto. *PAGE 90:* AP/Wide World. *PAGE 92:* Drawing by Mankoff; ©1992/The New Yorker Magazine, Inc. *PAGE 94:* Reuters/Bettmann. *PAGE 96:* Drawing by Richter; © 1991/The New Yorker Magazine, Inc. *PAGE 104:* Reuters/Bettmann. *PAGE 107:* Bettmann Archive. *PAGE 120:* Paul Hosefros/NYT Pictures. *PAGE 121:* Bart Bartholomew/NYT Pictures. *PAGE 123:* Drawing by Handelsman; ©1992/The New Yorker Magazine, Inc. *PAGE 127:* Hella Hamid/Photo Researchers. *PAGE 132:* Drawing by Saxon; ©1984/The New Yorker Magazine, Inc. *PAGE 136:* AP/Wide World.

PAGE 141: Jeffrey Markowitz/Sygma. *PAGE 149:* Les Stone/Sygma. *PAGE 154:* Bettmann Archive. *PAGE 157:* UPI/AP/Wide World. *PAGE 157:* JVS/Stock Boston. *PAGE 162:* From THE PARTY GOES ON, by Xandra Kayden and Eddie Mahe, Jr. ©1985, Reprinted by permission of Basic Books, Inc., New York. *PAGE 163:* Reuters/Bettmann. *PAGE 178:* Steve Liss/Gamma-Liaison. *PAGE 182:* Reuters/Bettmann. *PAGE 185:* Don Wright. *PAGE 188:* Howell/Gamma-Liaison. *PAGE 193:* Mark Reinstein/Uniphoto. *PAGE 199:* Reuters/ Bettmann. *PAGE 208:* Drawing by Martin; ©1988/The New Yorker Magazine, Inc. *PAGE 217:* Les Stone/Sygma. *PAGE 221:* Gamma-Liaison. *PAGE 222:* AP/Wide World. *PAGE 225:* By Borgman for the Cincinnati Enquirer, Reprinted with special permission of King Features Syndicate. *PAGE 233:* AP/Wide World. *PAGE 236:* Tannenbaum/Sygma. *PAGE 237:* By Jim Borgman for the Cincinnati Enquirer/ Reprinted with special permission of King Features Syndicate. *PAGE 244:* Waggerman/ The Boston Globe/Los Angeles Times Syndicate. *PAGE 247:* The Franklin D. Roosevelt Library. *PAGE 249:* AP/Wide World. *PAGE 255:* Ohman for The Oregonian/Reprinted by permission: Tribune Media Services. *PAGE 257:* Reuters/Bettmann. *PAGE 258:*

AP/Wide World. *PAGE 266:* Reuters/UPI/Bettmann. *PAGE 273:* AP/Wide World. *PAGE 275:* Drawing by Dana Fradon; ©1987/The New Yorker Magazine, Inc. *PAGE 283:* Bettmann. *PAGE 287:* Courtesy of the Hispanic caucus. *PAGE 293:* Jose R. Lopez/NYT Pictures. *PAGE 303:* Photo: Jack Kightlinger/Courtesy Lyndon Baines Johnson Library, Austin, TX. *PAGE 305:* Keiko Morris/Magnum Photos. *PAGE 311:* Bill Pugliano/Gamma-Liaison. *PAGE 316:* AP/Wide World. *PAGE 321:* Toles/The New Republic 1993/Universal Press Syndicate. Reprinted with permission. All Rights Reserved. *PAGE 324:* AP/Wide World. *PAGE 327:* UPI/Bettmann. PAGE 340: David Powers/Stock Boston. *PAGE 352:* Courtesy University of Iowa. *PAGE 355:* Bob Daemmrich/Stock Boston. *PAGE 358:* Jim Pickerell/Stock Boston. *PAGE 374:* Carl Iwasaki/Life Magazine/Time Warner Inc. *PAGE 389:* Supreme Court Historical Society. *PAGE 396:* Bob Daemmrich/Stock Boston. *PAGE 397:* Drawing by Handelsman; ©1992/The New Yorker Magazine, Inc. *PAGE 400:* AP/Wide World. *PAGE 408:* Drawing by Handelsman; ©1970/The New Yorker Magazine, Inc. *PAGE 413:* Drawing by Dana Fradon; ©1985/The New Yorker Magazine, Inc. *PAGE 417:* Spencer Grant/Stock Boston.

meaning of, 1
presidents and, 334
public opinion and political action in,
142–143
and responsible party government,
171–172
rise of worldwide, 9–10
role of polls in, 131–132
traditional theory of, 10–11
and the U.S. Constitution, 48–49
Democratic National Committee, 168, 306
Democratic party
delegate selection process, 160
1968 convention, 160, 186
1992 platform, 170–171
origins of, 154–155
restructuring of, 160
Democratic-Republican party, 153–154
Demography, 119
Dennis v. United States, 94–95
Deregulation, 360–361
Derthick, Martha, 351, 367, 368*n*.11
Descriptive representation, 268
Desegregation, 55, 75, 108, 232, 383, 392, 393
de Tocqueville, Alexis, 11, 20*n*.9
Dewey, Thomas E., 246
Dexter, Lewis A., 241*n*.9
Dinkins, David, 122
Disabled Americans, 81, 113
Discrimination, 374
age, 81, 112
against AIDS victims, 81, 113, 245
and awarding of federal grants, 66–67,
112, 395
disability, 81, 113
racial, 44, 49, 60, 73, 80–81, 106–110, 232
reverse, 114–115, 226
sexual, 81, 111–112, 232–233, 351–353
sexual preference, 81
wage, 111–112
Dissenting opinions, 392
District courts, 384–385
District of Columbia, 45, 49, 54, 268, 341,
384, 385
Diversity of citizenship court cases, 385
Divided government, 158, 317–318, 334
Divine rights, 23
Dodd, Lawrence C., 297
Dole, Elizabeth, 55, 56
Dole, Robert, 282, 316
Dollar, value of, 228
Donaldson, Sam, 246–247, 262*n*.9, 262*n*.10,
333, 337*n*.26, 337*n*.31
Doolittle, Fred C., 77, 77*n*.2
Dowd, Maureen, 263*n*.15
Downs, Anthony, 147, 150, 174, 175*n*.3,
175*n*.7, 200, 212*n*.32

Downs Model, 150–152, 200, 207
Draft, resistance to, 94, 142
Dred Scott v. Sandford, 106, 155
Drinking age, 55, 56, 58
Drug Enforcement Administration, 357
Drugs, 100, 354, 357, 394
Dual federalism, 63–65
Dukakis, Michael, 202, 205
Duke, David, 172
Dunne, Finley Peter, 397
Dye, Thomas R., 241, 241*n*.3

Earth Day, 231
Eastern Europe, 9–10, 139, 169
East Germany, 9
Easton, David, 20*n*.5
Economic inequality, 27, 28–29
Education, 3, 70
bilingual, 398
funding for, 15, 64–65
national government role in, 64–65
in religious schools, 85–87
spending on, by state, 72
Education, U.S. Department of, 353,
362–363
Education Act of 1972, Title IX, 111, 351–353
Edwards, Edwin, 172
Edwards, George C., III, 212*n*.33, 299*n*.27,
313, 329, 336, 336*n*.6, 336*n*.8, 336*n*.10,
336*n*.11, 337*n*.13, 337*n*.17, 337*n*.22,
337*n*.24, 367, 368*n*.8
Edwards v. Aguillard, 87
Ehrlichman, John, 306
Eighteenth Amendment, 41
Eighth Amendment, 101
Eisenhower, Dwight D., 109, 137, 156, 179,
248, 302, 332, 382, 395
Eisner, Robert, 424*n*.4
Elastic clause, 60
Elazar, Daniel J., 77, 77*n*.4
Elder, Shirley, 222, 241*n*.8
Election campaign(s), 187–195
advertising, 194, 204, 245
attention to issues in, 194, 203–204, 253
cost of, 191, 192–193, 207
effects of, on voters, 195
impact of, 195
mass media in, 193–194, 204, 244–245, 253
money and, 189–193, 224
organizing, 187–189
proliferation of PACs in, 190–192,
224–225, 239
Electioneering, 224–225
Elections, 7
ambiguity in, 208
candidate evaluations and, 202
Congressional, 269–278